Detroit Monographs in Musicology/Studies in Music, No. 29

Editor
J. Bunker Clark
University of Kansas

The Varieties of Musicology

ESSAYS IN HONOR OF
Murray Lefkowitz

Edited by

JOHN DAVERIO

and

JOHN OGASAPIAN

HARMONIE PARK PRESS
WARREN, MICHIGAN
2000

Copyright 2000 by Harmonie Park Press

Printed and bound in the United States of America
Published by
Harmonie Park Press
23630 Pinewood
Warren, Michigan 48091

Production Manager, Elaine J. Gorzelski
Editor, J. Bunker Clark
Book Design and Typographer, Colleen McRorie
Music Typographer, Don Harris

Library of Congress Cataloging-in-Publication Data

The varieties of musicology : essays in honor of Murray Lefkowitz / edited by John
Daverio and John Ogasapian.
    p. cm. – (Detroit monographs in musicology/Studies in music ; no. 29)
  Includes bibliographical references and index.
  ISBN 0-89990-093-3
  1. Music–History and criticism. I. Lefkowitz, Murray. II. Daverio, John. III.
Ogasapian, John. IV. Series.

ML55.L265 2000
780–dc21   00-039666

Contents

Illustrations

Music Examples

EXAMPLES

Tables

Preface

Murray Lefkowitz was born 20 April 1924 in Mineola, Long Island. After service in the U.S. Army, he studied violin at the University of Southern California, where he earned the Mus.B. in 1950 and the Mus.M. in musicology a year later. From 1954 to 1964, he taught music in the public schools of Los Angeles and Hollywood. During those years he also pursued doctoral studies in musicology at the University of Southern California, and was awarded the Ph.D. in 1963. His dissertation on William Lawes, the product of research undertaken on a Fulbright grant to England, was published by Routledge and Kegan Paul in 1960. In 1964, he joined the faculty at San Fernando State College.

In 1967, he moved from California to Massachusetts to take over the chair of musicology at Boston University previously held by Karl Geiringer. Over the next nineteen years, he set an example of scholarly quality and discipline in his own area of seventeenth-century English music for the many graduate students he trained and advised. He helped them define their particular fields of research interest, encouraging each one's work while at the same time demanding the same rigorous attention to detail and graceful writing style that he imposed on his own scholarship.

During his many years as director of the university's Collegium in Early Music, he emphasized the complementarity of research and performance. Indeed, some of us had the opportunity to absorb the results of his research first hand, as members of the William Lawes Consort of Viols.

One by one, his students have gone their separate ways to work in areas ranging from mediæval chant to Stravinsky, from American church music to Romantic æsthetics. Now, a decade after Murray's retirement and on the occasion of his seventieth birthday, several of his former students and colleagues have come together to prepare this collection of essays.

The volume and its title reflect the diversity and freedom he allowed us to develop in varied directions (many of which must surely have surprised him over the years): the meaning behind an Obrecht mass title, a hitherto unknown mediæval manuscript, an unexpected source for a well-known Stravinsky movement, a reinterpretation of evidence on Bach's religion and vocation. Each of these essays is a contribution to the literature in its own area of specialization and an offering of tribute and gratitude to an exemplary scholar, inspiring and exacting mentor, and warm friend.

We express our gratitude for the warm assistance and numerous kindnesses rendered us by Harmonie Park Press. J. Bunker Clark and Elaine Gorzelski took an immediate interest in the project when we first approached them. Having as our editor a scholar like Bunker was good fortune indeed, and his expertise and eagle eye kept many a lapse from getting through. Elaine guided us through the process, from beginning to end, with grace and tact. Colleen McRorie encouraged us, gently prodded us as necessary, and helped us in ways to numerous to recount. Editing a book can be trying, as we learned; but Bunker, Elaine, and Colleen made it at least as much a joy for us, and we shall always be grateful.

JOHN DAVERIO
JOHN OGASAPIAN

The Varieties of Musicology

Essays in Honor of

Murray Lefkowitz

CHAPTER 1

A Royal French Breviary
from the Reign of Saint Louis

Rebecca A. Baltzer

According to the testimony of his contemporaries, King Louis IX of France numbered among his personal books a breviary of Paris use, since it was his devout custom to follow the services of the divine office every day. Louis's breviary, which he already owned when he left on his first crusade in the late 1240s, remained in possession of his descendants through the fourteenth century and into the fifteenth, when it then disappeared. As recounted by Pope Boniface VIII when he canonized Saint Louis, the king's breviary acquired miraculous properties even before its saintly owner's death.[1]

Louis IX was apparently the first French monarch to have felt the need for this type of liturgical book for his personal use, in addition to the more typical illuminated psalters his royal ancestors had had made for themselves. The breviary, as a book containing all the texts for the Canonical Hours—Matins, Lauds, Prime, Terce, Sext, None, Vespers, and Compline—for all the days of the church year, was in the mid thirteenth century a necessary book only for those whose vows required the performance of the Canonical Hours, namely monks and nuns, the clerics of secular churches and cathedrals, and members of the mendicant orders.[2] To say that Louis's breviary was of Paris use means that it followed the liturgy of the cathedral of Paris, a liturgy distinct from that of surrounding locales and also from the liturgies of the various monasteries and mendicant orders within the city. The Paris use was distinct in the fact of which saints' feasts were celebrated and at what rank, but also in the fact that the major feasts had nine lessons and responsories at Matins rather than the twelve of monastic use. In following the Paris use, although the royal household and the Sainte-Chapelle made a few changes appropriate to their own liturgical situation, their liturgical books were nonetheless copied from books which originated at Notre-Dame.

While a Paris breviary owned by the Library of Congress in Washington cannot claim to be the king's miraculous book, it is one that dates from the 1260s, and it may well have belonged to one of

---

[1] Léopold Delisle, *Notice de douze livres royaux du XIIIe et du XIVe siècle* (Paris: Imprimerie Nationale, 1902), 53-56.

[2] On the function and contents of breviaries see the introductory discussion in Victor Leroquais, *Les Bréviarires manuscrits des bibliothèques publiques de France*, 5 vols. and atlas of plates (Paris: Protat Frères, 1934), and Andrew Hughes, *Medieval Manuscripts for Mass and Office: A Guide to Their Organization and Terminology* (Toronto: University of Toronto Press, 1982). Brief overviews are given in *The New Grove Dictionary of Music and Musicians* (1980), s.v. "Breviary," by Michel Huglo, and in David Hiley, *Western Plainchant: A Handbook* (Oxford: Clarendon Press, 1993), 320-21.

Louis's sons. Thus this book has its own very good claims to significance, for if, as I hope to show, it is a royal manuscript, then it is the earliest extant royal French breviary, antedating by a generation Ms. Latin 1023 in the Bibliothèque Nationale, the breviary long associated with Louis's grandson Philip the Fair.[3] In addition, though not a luxury book itself, the Washington breviary can be shown to have originated in the same large Parisian workshop responsible for two of the most magnificent manuscripts produced in the thirteenth century, the Saint Louis Psalter in the Bibliothèque Nationale (lat. 10525) and the Isabelle Psalter and Hours (Ms. 300) in the Fitzwilliam Museum in Cambridge, and it bears a particularly close relationship to the latter.

The breviary in question is Library of Congress Ms. 15, acquired in 1916 from the collection of the Reverend Edwin A. Dalrymple, D.D., of Baltimore.[4] Its significance went unnoticed until 1979 because the only published description of it prior to 1989, by Seymour DeRicci, is inaccurate in several respects, most notably regarding the date. DeRicci described L.C. 15 as an early fifteenth-century breviary of Paris use, and he apparently confused the binding with that of another manuscript in the library's collection, saying that it was bound in the original wooden boards and red velvet, when in actuality it has a nineteenth-century brown morocco cover. He also gave no indication that the manuscript contained any illuminated initials, and described it as "imperfect," without any further particulars as to what might be missing.[5] In view of this less than enticing description, it is not surprising that this breviary attracted no notice for so many years.[6]

Of importance to historians of liturgy, music, and art, L.C. 15 is a manuscript of 563 folios, each measuring ca. 188 x 123 mm. The main body of text is regularly disposed in two columns with a writing space of approximately 122 x 80 mm.; musical notation is not included. Gatherings are most often of sixteen leaves, with some catchwords still evident, but this structure is not consistent and cannot always be determined now because of the tight binding. The manuscript is lacking only four leaves from the psalter and the last eight months of the calendar, which would also have required four leaves. Two leaves apparently intended for the calendar succeed it directly as folios 4-5; they were pricked for the calendar but were left blank. They are followed by a ten-folio insertion containing the Parisian *ordo officii* for Advent, probably in a later hand (ff. 6-15v), and two more blank folios (17-18) pricked for the same kind of text.[7]

---

[3] Ellen Kosmer has demonstrated that while Ms. lat. 1023 was certainly made for a royal owner, there is no documentary evidence to support Delisle's idea that it was illuminated by the artist Honoré for Philip the Fair in 1296. Kosmer does not argue against the manuscript being made for Philip the Fair, but she points out that there are no documents which confirm this—see her "Master Honoré: A Reconsideration of the Documents," *Gesta* 14 (1975): 63-68, and n. 16 below.

[4] See Svato Schutzner, *Medieval and Renaissance Manuscript Books in the Library of Congress: A Descriptive Catalog*, vol. 1: *Bibles, Liturgy, Books of Hours* (Washington: Library of Congress, 1989), 106-12, and color plate 8, showing initials on ff. 380v and 381r. At the Library of Congress, William Matheson, then Chief, and Thomas D. Burney of the Rare Book and Special Collections Division provided information and extended numerous courtesies during my work on this manuscript, which began in April 1979. I am also indebted to the Bibliothèque Nationale de France, the Bibliothèque de l'Arsenal, and the Fitzwilliam Museum for their courtesies, and to Eleanor Simmons Greenhill, Christopher Hohler, and Harvey Stahl, who read earlier versions of this paper and offered useful suggestions.

[5] DeRicci, *Census of Medieval and Renaissance Manuscripts in the United States and Canada*, 3 vols. (New York: H. W. Wilson, 1935-40), 1:229, no. 103.

[6] In particular, had the late Robert Branner seen the manuscript, he would have recognized at once that L.C. 15 belonged in his monumental study of Parisian illuminated manuscripts in the reign of Saint Louis, but DeRicci's description surely gave him no cause to examine the book. Branner, *Manuscript Painting in Paris during the Reign of Saint Louis: A Study of Styles* (Berkeley: University of California Press, 1977).

[7] I am grateful to Svato Schutzner of the Special Materials Cataloging Divison of the Library of Congress, who began compiling a detailed catalog description of L.C. 15 in the spring of 1982, for information on the pricking of the blank folios.

After the calendar and *ordo officii* are a ferial psalter, as is characteristic of many breviaries, plus the three essential sections of any such liturgical book: services for the feasts of the Temporale, the Common of Saints, and the Sanctorale (see table 1.1). It is worth noting that even though the manuscript was produced in the 1260s, the Sanctorale contains no feast instituted after 1200. Like a number of other royal liturgical books of the thirteenth century, it seems to have been copied from a very old exemplar.[8] To remedy this lack, a later hand of ca. 1300 has added material for more than thirty feasts that were either newly instituted or elevated in rank in the Church of Paris in the thirteenth century (see the list in table 1.2).[9]

Table 1.1

Contents of Library of Congress, Ms. 15–Paris Breviary

f.1	A free end-leaf.
ff. 2-3v	Paris calendar for royal use; January-April only.
ff. 4-5v	Two blank folios apparently intended for more of the calendar.
ff. 6-15v	Ordo officii for Advent; 10 folios of rubrics. Very small script, probably a later hand.
ff. 16-17v	Two blank folios.
ff. 18-87v	Ferial psalter, canticles, Athanasian creed, and litanies. Half of f. 87 and all of 87v are ruled but blank.
ff. 88-305v	Temporale for the whole church year, beginning with the first Sunday of Advent.
ff. 306-27v	Common of the Saints.
ff. 328-506v	Sanctorale, beginning with Andrew (November 30) and extending through late November. Includes the feast of the Reception of the Relics at Notre-Dame (December 4). F. 506 is blank and unruled.
ff. 507-58v	Written in a later hand; additional feasts for the Sanctorale that were either instituted or elevated in rank during the thirteenth century. In calendar order (December through November) except for the three last and latest feasts, including Saint Louis.
ff. 559-63v	Later additions: miscellaneous prayers and benedictions; 3 lessons for Saint Paula (January 29).

As table 1.2 makes clear, these added feasts are all in liturgical order, going from early December through November, except for the last three: Rigobert (January 8), Nicaise (December 14), and Saint Louis (August 25). Along with Theobald on July 9, they are the most recent feasts included in the manuscript. This distinction is signalled by the fact that only these four begin with the words "Incipit

Schutzner also believes that the four missing leaves of the calendar were once there between ff. 3v and 4r, for the blank f. 4 reveals the iimpression of a calendar page once opposite it that he identifies as December. This suggests an original gathering of eight leaves for the calendar, including the two blank folios pricked in the same fashion. See Schutzner, 1:107 and n. 8.

[8] Other thirteenth-century royal books copied from old exemplars include four evangeliaries that belonged to the Sainte-Chapelle, Bibliothèque Nationale, Mss. lat. 8892, lat. 9455, lat. 17326, and British Library, Add. Ms. 17341 (see Robert Branner, "Le Premier Évangéliaire de la Sainte-Chapelle," *Revue de l'Art* 3 [1969]: 37-48)—plus the breviary of Philip the Fair, Bibliothèque Nationale, Ms. lat. 1023. The latter includes a supplement of some two dozen feasts added by the main scribe to update the Sanctorale (plus four more feasts added later in the fourteenth century); see n. 15 below. Still another royal book based on an old exemplar is the Bari Gradual mentioned in n. 11 below.

[9] What prompted the royal house still to rely on exemplars from ca. 1200 for liturgical books copied decades later? If the royal liturgical books were indeed part of Philip Augustus's treasure lost at Fréteval in 1194, new exemplars from Notre-Dame would have been required soon thereafter—books that must have continued to serve as royal exemplars for the next hundred years. It was no doubt easier to assemble a small amount of supplementary material to add to these exemplars than to replace the exemplars themselves. Thus, supplements of more recent feasts were sometimes added at the end of a manuscript, as in L.C. 15 and Bibliothèque Nationale, Ms. lat. 1023, and sometimes preserved as a separate manuscript, as in Brussels, Bibliothèque Royale Albert Ier, Ms. IV.72 (from the mid thirteenth century), but both types of additions prolonged the usefulness of older royal books. For more on the loss at Fréteval, see Marie-Madeleine Gauthier, "Un Patronage énigmatique: Les Orfèvres-émailleurs à Paris au temps de Philippe Auguste," in *La France de Philippe Auguste: Le Temps de mutation*, ed. Robert-Henri Bautier, Colloques Internationaux du Centre national de la Recherche Scientifique, 602 (Paris: Éditions du CNRS, 1982), 983.

Table 1.2
List of Added Feasts in Library of Congress, Ms. 15

In susceptione reliquiarum [December 4]*
In festo conceptionis beate marie virginis [December 8]
De sancto g(uillermo bituriensis) [January 10]
De sancto sulpicio [January 17]
De sancto juliano [January 27]
In festo beate marie egyptiace [April 2]
De sancto petro martyre [April 29]
De sancto quiriaco [May 4]
In translacione sancti nicholai [May 9]
In vigilia sancti basilii (et in die) [June 13-14]
(Sanctorum iohannis et pauli) [June 26]
In dominica infra octabam sancti iohannis (baptiste) et per oct. et in die oct. [June 24-July 1]
Translacio sancte thome martyris [July 7]
Incipit vita beati theobaldi confessoris et heremite [July 9]
De sancta anna [July 28]
De susceptione sancte crucis domini [August 11]
De sancto bernardo abbate [August 25]
Georgii et amelii (sic; aureliani) [August 27]
De sancto lupo ep. et conf. [September 3]
De sancto audomaro [September 17]
De sancto francisco [October 3]
De sancto potentiano et seviniano [October 19]
Undecim millium virginum [October 21]
De sancto mellono episcopo et conf. [October 25]
In die mortuorum [November 2]
De sancto claro episcopo et martyre [November 5]
De sancto martino pape et verano episcopo [November 10]
De sancta elizabeth [November 19]
Incipit vita sancti rigoberti episcopi et confessoris [January 8]
Incipit vita sancti nichasii episcopi et martiris [December 14]
Incipit vita et officium sancti ludovici regis et confessoris [August 25]

* The December 4 feast for the Reception of the Relics at Notre-Dame appears both in this group of additions
and in the original Sanctorale of the manuscript. Also, the feast of Basilius has three lessons in the original
Sanctorale but is elevated to semiduplex rank, with nine lessons, in the additions.

vita . . ." rather than the usual "De sancto. . . ." That for Saint Louis goes one step further ("Incipit vita
et officium"), since it includes not only the complete Office but the Mass as well. This was an unusual
step for a breviary and one that gives evidence of the importance of Saint Louis to the owner of the
manuscript around 1300. (See Appendix 2 for a discussion of this liturgy for Saint Louis.) All four of
these feasts were added to the Paris calendar during the tenure of Bishop Simon Mattifas de Bucy (1289-
1304). Theobald was added ca. 1290; Bishop Simon himself instituted feasts for Nicaise and Rigobert
in 1296; and Saint Louis was canonized by Boniface VIII in August 1297, with the first observance
of his feast taking place at the abbey church of Saint-Denis outside Paris on 25 August 1298.[10]

---

[10] The feast of Theobald, confessor, was instituted by the chapter of Notre-Dame at the request of Theobald of Corbeil,
canon and succentor, who left the chapter a bequest of 60 pounds for this purpose. His obit is on July 9 in the Notre-Dame
obituary; see Benjamin E. C. Guérard, ed., *Cartulaire de l'église Notre-Dame de Paris*, 4 vols., Collection des cartulaires de

It is the surviving four months of the calendar, January through April (transcribed as Appendix 1), that betray this breviary as a royal book. Here it is important to observe that from at least the founding of the Sainte-Chapelle through the Renaissance, royal calendars were based upon Paris cathedral calendars, and royal books were copied from cathedral books, since, as we have noted, the royal liturgical use was but a slight modification of the Paris cathedral use.[11] If a scribe making a calendar for royal use worked directly from a cathedral exemplar, usually he was informed enough about the task to make at least some of the alterations and additions peculiar to the royal use, though he sometimes missed a few of the less obvious ones. Thus it is the deviations from the normal cathedral calendar that require our scrutiny.

In the calendar of L.C. 15, the first sign of royal connections is an obit in gold letters on the 8th of February (see fig. 1.1): *obitus Roberti comitis attrenbatensis* (*sic*; on the spelling of this last word, see below). This is the notice for Robert, Count of Artois (d. 1250), the brother of Saint Louis, an obit which also appears in the Saint Louis and Isabelle Psalters. Both of the latter manuscripts contain Paris calendars, and both Lépold Delisle and Sydney Cockerell have pointed out the overall closeness and the small variants of detail between the two.[12] When the calendar of L.C. 15 is compared with them, in every case of variant readings between the two royal psalters the breviary sides with the Isabelle Psalter, which it resembles very closely in design and script. Unlike the calendar of the Saint Louis Psalter, written primarily in black and red, the calendars in the Isabelle Psalter and the L.C. breviary are both written in blue and gold, in usually the same alternation of colors; only the large KL initials are handled differently (compare figs. 1.1 and 1.2).[13]

The obit for Robert of Artois on February 8 gives an example of the similarities among all three manuscripts, for the Latin "Attrebatensis" is misspelled "Attrenbatensis" in each. And on February 17 for the indication of the zodiac, all three calendars have "Sol in piscis" instead of "Sol in pisces." On February 22 after the feast of St. Peter's Chair, the Saint Louis Psalter correctly reads "initium veris," but the Isabelle Psalter and L.C. 15 both have "initium neris." In January on the 17th, all three calendars misspell the unusual saints' names of Speusippus and Meleusippus; only the middle

---

France, 4-7 (Paris: Imprimerie de Crapelet, 1850), 4:108. Bishop Simon de Bucy's obit mentions his institution of the feasts of Nicaise and Rigobert, but this portion of the text is ellipsed in Guérard's edition. It is found in the manuscript of the obituary, Paris, Bibliothèque Nationale, Ms. lat. 5185cc, f. 224-224v, and in Gérard Dubois, *Historiae ecclesiae parisiensis*, 2 vols. (Paris: F. Mugruet, 1690-1710), 1:531. For more on the establishment of the feast of Saint Louis, see Appendix 2.

[11] Among royal books of the missal, gradual, or breviary type, the only exception to this practice known to me is the Bari Gradual, which has too many variants from cathedral use to have been copied from a cathedral exemplar. (For example, in the Mass propers, on more than two dozen major saints' feasts either the Gradual or the Alleluia or both differ from those prescribed in cathedral books.) Unfortunately, the manuscript lacks a calendar. On this gradual see Robert Branner, "Two Parisian *Capella* Books in Bari," *Gesta* 7 (1969): 14-19, and Branner, *Manuscript Painting*, 102-07 and 229.

[12] Delisle, 105-11, printed a combined transcription of both calendars. Cockerell printed a transcription of the calendar of the Isabelle Psalter, including notes on the variants, in his *Psalter and Hours of Isabelle of France* (London: Chiswick Press, 1905), 11-18. Cockerell's eye for discrepancies was a bit sharper than Delisle's. Three other royal obits, for Philip Augustus (July 14), Louis VIII (November 8) and Blanche of Castille (November 27) are included in the Saint Louis and Isabelle calendars (see Cockerell, 13); these months are missing from L.C. 15. Two important studies that deal with the late medieval Paris calendar (fifteenth century) are Victor Leroquais, *Le Bréviaire de Philippe le Bon: Bréviaire parisien du XVe siècle* (Paris: Maurice Rousseau, 1929), and Paul Perdrizet, *Le Calendrier parisien à la fin du moyen âge*, Publications de la Faculté des Lettres de l'Université de Strasbourg, fasicule 63 (Paris: Les Belles Lettres, 1933). More recently, Jean Vezin has discussed a slightly earlier period in "L'Evolution du culte des saints à Paris aux XIIIe et XIVe siècles," in *Rituels: Mélanges offerts à Pierre-Marie Gy, O.P.*, ed. Paul de Clerck and Eric Palazzo (Paris: Éditions du Cerf, 1990), 473-79.

[13] Water damage is heavy and very evident in much of the Isabelle Psalter, which spent several days submerged in the London house of its absent owner during a flood in the 1850s; the gold lettering in the calendar is particularly difficult to read in photographs.

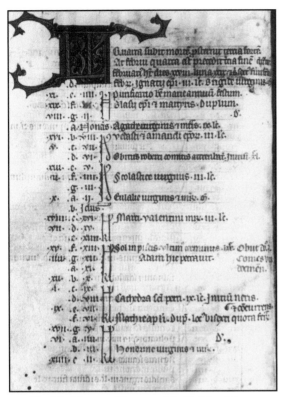

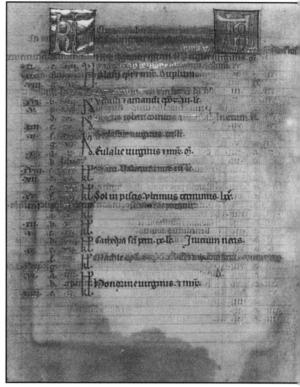

Fig. 1.1. Library of Congress, Ms. 15, f. 2v: February

Photo by author

**Fig. 1.2. Cambridge, Fitzwilliam Museum, Ms. 300
(Isabelle Psalter/Hours), f. vii b: February**

Photo by Fitzwilliam Museum

one, Eleusippus, is written correctly.[14] Occasionally L.C. 15 has its own variant, as on January 8. What should be "Maximiniani" in all three calendars reads "Maxiani" in Saint Louis and Isabelle, but "Maximiani" in L.C. 15. And the breviary stands alone in error on March 12, where "Gregorii pape" (Pope Gregory the Great) is written "Georgii pape" instead.

The month of April (see Appendix 1) is important for the dating of all three calendars, and by implication, of the manuscripts themselves. On April 29 appears the most recent feast included in these calendars, that of the Dominican saint Peter Martyr, canonized in 1253. Ten years later, in 1263, the bishop and chapter of Notre-Dame of Paris instituted the feast of the Egyptian Mary at semiduplex rank on April 2. That feast is not present in these three calendars, nor are several other changes in the Paris calendar that occurred between ca. 1255 and the early 1260s.[15] While the absence of these additions and elevations cannot be taken to mean that the three royal calendars were copied before 1263, it does indicate that the *content* of the calendars represents a liturgical state prior to that date, one of ca. 1255. As a rule in thirteenth-century Parisian liturgical books, the calendar is the most up-to-date section of the book and was probably the last part to be produced; it has been my

---

[14] "Speusippi" is written "Pseusippi," and "Meleusippi" is written "Meseulippi." See Cockerell, 13.

[15] Regarding the institution of the feast of the Egyptian Mary, see Guérard, 2:254. To cite two other examples of an alteration in the calendar, about 1260 both the feast of the Translation of St. Éloi (June 25) and that of Cosmas and Damian (September 27) were raised from nine lessons to semiduplex rank in the church of Paris, a change not reflected in the two psalter calendars. Evidence for the change in rank of these two feasts comes from the obit of Hugh de Viriaco; see Guérard, 4:160.

experience that the manuscripts were usually copied within five to fifteen years after the liturgical state represented in the calendar.[16] I am not prepared to comment on whether the Saint Louis Psalter was produced before or after the Isabelle Psalter, but in terms of their calendars, my conclusion is that those in the Isabelle Psalter and the Library of Congress breviary were completed in the 1260s. The editor/scribe of L.C. 15, knowing that he needed an up-to-date calendar to begin his breviary, may well have directly copied the source used for the calendar of the Isabelle Psalter, faithfully reproducing most of the errors of his model and occasionally making mistakes of his own.[17]

Besides the royal obit for Robert of Artois, there are three other hallmarks of royal use evident in the first four months of all three calendars. Each instance points up the sometimes slight but none-theless telling differences that existed between royal practice and cathedral practice in the thirteenth century. The most obvious royal hallmark occurs on April 26, namely the feast for the Dedication of the Sainte-Chapelle, which event took place on 26 April 1248; this feast appears only in royal books. Secondly, in these three calendars on February 3 the feast of St. Blaise, bishop and martyr, has duplex rank; in the cathedral use, he has a rank of only nine lessons. He is given more importance in the royal books because the Sainte-Chapelle possessed his head as one of its major relics.[18]

And lastly, on February 24 St. Matthias the Apostle is also ranked *duplum*, though he too has only nine lessons at Notre-Dame. The reason for this difference is not immediately apparent. During the lifetime of Louis IX, the Sainte-Chapelle had no relics of Matthias or any other apostle except James the Less, and there is no indication that Saint Louis himself was moved by unusual devotion to the twelve apostles. Yet in the second half of the thirteenth century, it is an unequivocal sign of royal use to find all the feasts of apostles elevated to duplex rank in a Paris calendar. This distinction, interestingly, seems to have been prompted by the iconography of the Sainte-Chapelle itself. In the upper chapel, where the priceless relics of the Crown of Thorns, the True Cross, and the rest were kept, there were large polychromed statues of the twelve apostles, visible witnesses to the passion of Christ represented by the relics of his crucifixion enshrined in the apse. The presence of the apostles at the liturgical ceremonies in the upper chapel was constant and unforgettable; they were an inextricable part of what was being commemorated in this building-become-reliquary, namely the redemptive passion

---

[16] A special and complicated exception to this rule is the calendar in Bibliothèque Nationale, Ms. lat. 1023, the breviary of Philip the Fair. Though the manuscript dates from the end of the thirteenth century, the calendar was copied from an old exemplar representing a liturgical state of the early thirteenth century. The original scribe himself updated his source to a state of ca. 1260, adding royal occasions as well, but later changes were also very skillfully made by other hands. Many of the alterations are virtually undetectable as such in photographs. A description of this manuscript is in Leroquais, *Les Bréviaires manuscrits*, 2:465-75.

[17] It is less likely that the L.C. scribe would copy from the Isabelle calendar itself, unless it had not yet been bound with the rest of the manuscript. Though the hands for the Isabelle and L.C. calendars are very similar, they are not the same. The tironian "et" and the ligated R, which has a tail in the Isabelle calendar, show the difference; compare the entries for Ste. Honorine, virgin and martyr, on February 27, and those for the word "cathedra" on February 22 (figs. 1.1-1.2). While the overall folio size differs among all three manuscripts because of trimming, the size of the writing space (apart from the calendars) is remarkably close: ca. 123 x 85 mm. for the psalters and ca. 122 x 80 mm. for the breviary.

[18] The head of Blaise was included in the first group of relics received from the Near East in 1241 and was among those subsequently kept in the Grande Châsse, the focal point of the altar end of the Sainte-Chapelle's upper chapel. Auguste Vidier printed a number of medieval and Renaissance inventories of the Sainte-Chapelle relics in "Le Trésor de la Sainte-Chapelle," *Mémoires de la Société de l'Histoire de Paris* 34 (1907): 199-324, and 35 (1908): 189-339, and the continuation in vol. 36 (1909): 245 ff., includes other documents relative to the history of the relics. For an unusual thirteenth-century perspective on the relics, see Karen Gould, "The Sequences *De Sanctis Reliquiis* as Sainte-Chapelle Inventories," *Mediaeval Studies* 43 (1981): 315-41. The rhymed office for the feast of the Reception of the Relics at the Sainte-Chapelle is transcribed in Judy Louise May Taylor, "Rhymed Offices at the Sainte-Chapelle in the Thirteenth Century: Historical, Political, and Liturgical Contexts" (Ph.D. diss., University of Texas at Austin, 1994).

of Christ, for it was through their witness that the message of redemption became known.[19] As a result, each of the twelve apostles, the least as well as the greatest, was given the special commemoration of duplex rank on his feast day.[20] Once the iconography of the building became known and understood, it left this distinctive imprint on a number of royal books thereafter, until Boniface VIII at the end of the thirteenth century decreed that all apostles, evangelists, and doctors of the church should have duplex rank.[21]

Because L.C. 15 contains both the feast for the Dedication of the Sainte-Chapelle (in the calendar) and the feast of the Reception of the Relics at Notre-Dame (present in the Sanctorale on December 4), it is what Robert Branner would call a manuscript of the royal *capella*, or household, rather than of the Sainte-Chapelle *per se*, the point being that a Sainte-Chapelle book would have its own feast on September 30 for the reception of its relics and would give no notice to the December 4 occasion at the cathedral.[22] This breviary was meant to be an individual's book, and its size, beautiful script, and lack of musical notation give support to this intent.

In its present state, the Library of Congress breviary contains fifteen illuminated initials. They are not historiated, but consist instead of vines, leaves, and dragons in a variety of combinations. Besides these fifteen initials, there were originally at least four more on the missing folios of the psalter; and had the calendar been preserved complete, the succeeding eight months would have included another eight KL initials in addition to the four that remain.

Parisian psalters customarily have an eight-fold division of the psalms in which each of the eight sections is marked off by a special initial or miniature, and that was clearly the intent in the psalter section of this breviary.[23] It contains six-line illuminated initials for Psalms 1, 38, 68, and 80 of this traditional division, but the leaves with initials for Psalms 26, 52, 97, and 109 have been removed, obviously for the sake of the initials. There seems to have been some intent to include a larger number of illuminations in the psalter, however, for after the *Beatus* initial for Psalm 1, two two-line initials occur on succeeding pages for Psalms 3 and 5, but the scheme was abandoned after that point (see table 1.3).

---

[19] The statues' very placement in the chapel, each one positioned against a buttressing wall between the stained-glass windows, makes them appear as if they are sustaining the edifice, a point made in J.-M. Leniaud and Françoise Perrot, *La Sainte Chapelle* (Paris: Éditions Nathan/C.N.M.H.S., 1991), 94. I would add, however, that in thirteenth-century Paris this is an idea with strong Victorine associations. To the Victorines the apostles were, in Margot Fassler's words, "the foundation of the temple, the living stones, the cement holding the building together," and through them, as companions of Christ and preachers of the Gospel, "the mystery and meaning of the cross is transmitted." All this and more is symbolized by the figures of the apostles in the Sainte-Chapelle. See Fassler, *Gothic Song: Victorine Sequences and Augustinian Reform in Twelfth-Century Paris* (Cambridge: Cambridge University Press, 1993), 302-07.

[20] Matthias the Apostle is the only one which appears in the extant four months of the L.C. 15 calendar, but the other feasts of apostles all have duplex rank in the calendars of the St. Louis and Isabelle Psalters. This was simply not done at the cathedral, where the feasts of Matthias, Philip and James, Barnabas, Bartholomew, Matthew, Simon and Jude, and Thomas all had a rank of only nine lessons in the thirteenth century.

[21] The papal decree came in Boniface's *Liber sextus* of 1298, after first being promulgated for the Dominicans in 1295. See *Regesta pontificum romanorum inde ab a. post Christum natum MCXCVIII ad a. MCCCIV*, ed. August Potthast (Berlin: Rudolf de Decker, 1874-75; reprint, Graz: Akademische Druck- und Verlagsanstalt, 1957), 2:1937-38, item 24188, and William R. Bonniwell, *A History of the Dominican Liturgy, 1215-1245*, 2nd ed. (New York: Joseph F. Wagner, 1945), 219. In calendars, the feast of Ambrose (one of the four doctors) on April 4 and Mark the Evangelist on April 25 are the first ones to check in this connection; prior to Boniface's decree, neither had duplex rank in Paris.

[22] Robert Branner, "The Sainte-Chapelle and the 'Capella regis' in the 13th Century," *Gesta* 10 (1971): 19-22. According to Svato Schutzner (see n. 7 above), the L.C. calendar scribe probably did not include the December 4 feast in the calendar.

[23] On this structuring of Paris psalters see Günther Haseloff, *Die Psalterillustration im 13. Jahrhundert* ([Kiel]: n.p., 1938), 21-27.

Table 1.3

Illuminated Initials in Library of Congress, Ms. 75*

ff. 2-3v	Four *KL*'s in the calendar (January-April)
f. 18	*B* for Psalm 1, *Beatus vir*
f. 18v	*D* for Psalm 3, *Domine, quid*
f. 19	*V* for Psalm 5, *Verba mea*
[between 27v-28]	[missing *D* for Psalm 26, *Dominus illuminatio*]
f. 34v	*D* for Psalm 38, *Dixi custodiam*
[between 40v-41]	[missing *D* for Psalm 52, *Dixit insipiens*]
f. 46	*S* for Psalm 68, *Salvum me fac*
f. 54	*E* for Psalm 80, *Exultate deo*
[between 60v-61]	[missing *C* for Psalm 97, *Cantate domino*]
[between 68v-69]	[missing *D* for Psalm 109, *Dixit dominus*]
f. 88	*E* beginning the Chapter at Vespers for the first Sunday in Advent (start of the Temporale)
f. 380v	*D* beginning the prayer at First Vespers for St. Germain of Paris (May 28 in the Sanctorale)
f. 381	*B* beginning the first lesson of Matins for St. Germain of Paris
f. 476	*L* beginning the first lesson of Matins for All Saints, November 1
f. 503v	Small *D* beginning a prayer at a feast of Ste. Geneviève, November 26

* There are also three large red and blue penwork initials: on f. 233v, a *C* beginning the first lesson of Matins for Trinity Sunday; on f. 306, a *B* beginning the Common of Apostles; and, by a later hand, a *G* for the first lesson of Matins for Saint Louis (August 25).

The remaining five illuminated initials show less logic in their placement in the Temporale and Sanctorale, for they do not consistently emphasize either the most important feasts or the large sectional divisions of the manuscript. While the four-line initial on folio 88 begins the Temporale section, there is none for such important occasions as Christmas and Easter; in fact there are no more in the entire Temporale. The Common of Saints, beginning on folio 306, has a four-line red and blue penwork initial rather than an illuminated one. No prominent initial of either sort starts the Sanctorale on folio 328 with St. Andrew (November 30); but suddenly there are two for St. Germain of Paris (May 28),[24] who simply begins the summer section of the church year (which is here undivided). Then there are no more initials until All Saints' Day (November 1) and a feast of Ste. Geneviève (November 26).[25] As a result, the most important saint's day in the Paris use, that of the Assumption of the Virgin, is passed over without artistic distinction. Lastly, two four-line penwork initials appear, one for Trinity Sunday in the Temporale and the second in a later hand for the added feast of Saint Louis.

On the basis of artistic style, Robert Branner in his massive study of Parisian illumination included five manuscripts in what he called the Royal Psalter Group within the larger Sainte-Chapelle atelier: the Saint Louis Psalter and the Isabelle Psalter/Hours; a martyrology for Saint-Germain-des-Prés (Bibliothèque Nationale, Ms. lat. 12834); a book of saints' lives (Ms. lat. 12614); and fascicles 1 and 7 of the Montpellier

---

[24] See color plate 8 in Schutzner, vol. 1.

[25] The illuminated initial for the latter (see fig. 1.13 below) begins a memorial prayer for St. Saturninus, the last saint in the church year (November 29). Probably the initial was intended for the beginning of the feast of Ste. Geneviève des Ardens on November 26 (an occasion celebrated only in Paris), but the rubric introducing the lessons of Matins and the lessons themselves were misplaced, as if newly inserted incorrectly in some exemplar. They should come in the left column of text, to be followed by more rubrics and memorials, including the one for Saturninus on the vigil of St. Andrew. (The very same misplacement of the nine lessons for Ste. Geneviève occurs in at least two other Paris breviaries, Bibliothèque Nationale, Ms. lat. 748 and Charleville, Bibliothèque Municipale, Ms. 86, both from the first half of the thirteenth century.) In L.C. 15 the illuminated initial does ornament the first text in larger script, but because the lessons for Ste. Geneviève were inserted at a later point than they should have been, the highlighted text is a memorial prayer for Saturninus rather than something for Geneviève.

motet manuscript (Montpellier, Bibl. Interuniversitaire, Section Médecine, H 196). He labeled three more manuscripts as related: two Bibles (Bibl. Ste.-Geneviève 15 and Bibliothèque Nationale, Ms. lat. 15185) and Raymond of Peñaforte's *Summa de casibus poenitentialibus* (Vienna, ÖNB 1371).[26]

Some two decades after Branner's study, the seminal role of the Isabelle Psalter in the decoration of later Parisian manuscripts seems increasingly clear; its "ordinary" pages (without miniatures, but including illuminated initials and line endings) are significantly more influential than those in the companion volume made for Saint Louis.[27] The initials in the L.C. breviary are among the Isabelle Psalter's many descendants. They show the closest relation to those by the artist Cockerell designated as hand 1 of the Isabelle Psalter,[28] which are slightly older than L.C. 15; to the Saint-Germain martyrology (lat. 12834); and to the book of saints' lives (lat. 12614), both of which are a few years younger than L.C. 15. In each of these sources we must focus primarily upon the nonhistoriated and the flourished red and blue penwork initials for the most direct connections. The same kinds of initials in the related Bible, lat. 15185, also bear a demonstrable relation to those in L.C. 15. And because of their direct relationship to the style of initials in the Library of Congress breviary, we may add to this group all the illuminated initials in Arsenal 203, a Paris missal of the late 1270s;[29] several in Ms. lat. 830, another Paris missal of the late 1260s or early 1270s;[30] and two calendar pages from a Paris breviary of probably the 1280s, destroyed in World War II: Metz, Bibliothèque Municipale, Ms. 1244.[31]

Of the eleven non-calendar illuminated initials in L.C. 15, four have fairly widespread connections with other manuscripts and feature little dragons with red or white heads amid the coils of vines, buds, and leaves. Two of the four dragons—those on folios 46 and 54 (fig. 1.3)—are footless, and their gnawing heads are frequent in both line-endings and initials by Cockerell's hand 1 in the Isabelle Psalter, as can be seen on folios 10 and 43v (fig. 1.5). Although one of these footless dragons in L.C. looks to the right rather than the left, the design elements are the same, with a single leaf below and neat geometric tendrils above. L.C. folio 46 is closely matched by Arsenal 203, section D, folio 1. Likewise, L.C. folio 54 (fig. 1.3) is virtually identical to the initial E at the bottom of folio 7 of lat. 830 (fig. 1.6), as well as being a close ancestor to Arsenal 203, section D, folio 31 (fig. 1.4).[32] Typical of most L.C. initials are the gold frame around the initial and the three white dots in the corners, whether the background is rose or blue.

---

[26] Branner, *Manuscript Painting*, catalog pp. 238-39.

[27] Because scholarly attention has been focused almost entirely on the full-page and smaller miniatures, these "ordinary" but influential pages in the Isabelle Psalter are amost never reproduced. The only published example I can cite is f. 11r, included as fig. 14 in *Les Heures de Nuremberg: Reproduction intégrale du calendrier et des images du manuscrit Solger 4.4° de la Stadtbibliothek de Nuremberg*, introduction et commentaire par Eleanor Simmons, traduction de l'américain par Charles Scheel (Paris: Éditions du Cerf, 1994), 60.

[28] Cockerell, 24-25. Hand 1 did the two-line psalm initials and line endings on ff. 1-70, 77-79, 81, 94-117, and 209v-10r.

[29] Victor Leroquais, *Les Sacramentaires et les missels manuscrits des bibliothèques publiques de France*, 3 vols. and plates (Paris: Protat Frères, 1924), 2:184, in his notice of this manuscript assigned it to the beginning of the fourteenth century, one of the very few cases in which he erred. Quite apart from the style of the script and decoration, one indication of an earlier date is the fact that on September 19 in the calendar, a later hand has added an obit for a churchman who died in 1287; the manuscript was certainly completed before that date.

[30] Described in Leroquais, *Les Sacramentaires*, 2:137.

[31] Described in Leroquais, *Les Bréviaires manuscrits*, 2:257-60; in plate 11, the caption mistakenly labels the manuscript a breviary of Metz use.

[32] Arsenal 203 has a very restricted repertory of designs in its illuminated initials. Although their extenders show some modernization, the initials' interiors merely repeat four types found among those of L.C. 15; one type has nine variations on the same theme. The missal Bibliothèque Nationale, Ms. lat. 830, incidentally, shows how different Parisian workshops could collaborate. Branner, *Manuscript Painting*, 229, assigns the miniatures and historiated initials in this manuscript to the Bari atelier, but the non-historiated illuminated initials are direct relatives of those in L.C. 15.

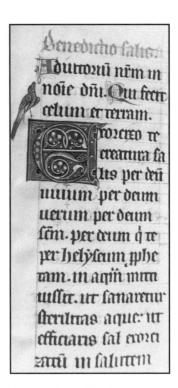

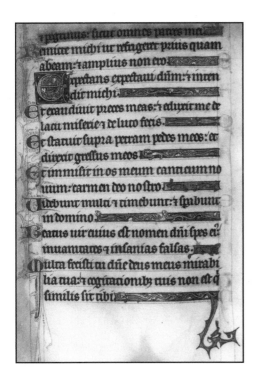

Fig. 1.3. Library of Congress, Ms. 15, f. 54:
Psalm 80

Photo by author

Fig. 1.4. Paris, Arsenal Ms. 203, section D, f. 31

Photo by author

Fig. 1.5. Cambridge, Fitzwilliam Museum,
Ms. 300, f. 43v

Photo by Fitzwilliam Museum

Fig. 1.6. Paris, Bibliothèque Nationale, Ms. lat. 830, f. 7:
Beginning of Advent

Photo by Bibliothèque Nationale

The other two L.C. initials with prominent dragons also contain the single leaf encoiled in vines below, but in these—on folios 34v (fig. 1.7) and 381—the dragons are footed and have a distinctive loop in the neck. A disposition somewhat similar to that on folio 34v of L.C. but with the head and neck loop reversed can be seen on folios 34 (fig. 1.8) and 38 of the Isabelle Psalter, where the leaves are more sharply pointed (see also fig. 1.15 below). The most extravagant dragon in L.C. (on f. 381; see Schutzner's color plate 8) is almost a mirror image of one on folio 49 of the Isabelle Psalter.

Fig. 1.7. Library of Congress, Ms. 15, f. 34v: Psalm 38

Photo by author

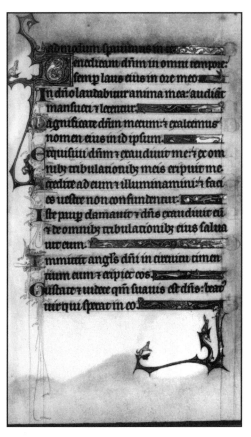

Fig. 1.8. Cambridge, Fitzwilliam Museum, Ms. 300, f. 34

Photo by Fitzwilliam Museum

Of several geometric designs in the breviary initials, the most eye-catching is that on folio 88 (fig. 1.9). There are numerous precedents for the design of its lower half; two examples are on a couple of the added folios at the end of the first Evangeliary of the Sainte-Chapelle, Bibliothèque Nationale, Ms. lat. 8892.[33] Successors of the L.C. design can be seen in the Saint-Germain martyrology, folio 106v (fig. 1.10), and particularly in the missal Arsenal 203, section B, folio 95 (fig. 1.11).

Because of their small size, the three two-line initials in the L.C. breviary have correspondingly less elaborate designs. That of Psalm 5 on folio 49 is enhanced by a dog chasing a rabbit across the extenders—animals that abound in the Isabelle Psalter and other manuscripts of the shop—and the

---

[33] See, for instance, the top of plate 21 in Branner's *Manuscript Painting*, which shows part of f. 30; the whole initial is reproduced again as fig. 379.

Fig. 1.10. Paris, Bibliothèque Nationale,
Ms. lat. 12834, f. 106v

Photo by Bibliothèque Nationale

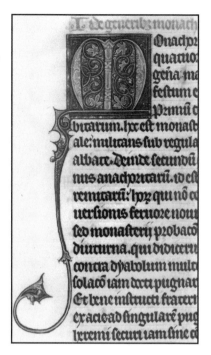

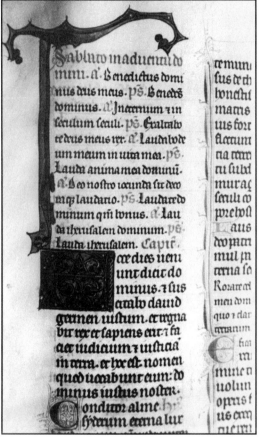

Fig. 1.9. Library of Congress, Ms. 15, f. 88:
Beginning of Advent

Photo by author

Fig. 1.11. Paris, Arsenal Ms. 203, section B, f. 95:
Pentecost

Photo by author

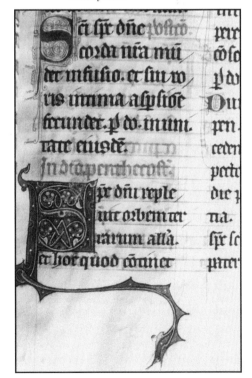

interior of the initial includes a footed dragon with red head looking to his rear. Birds are perched on the extenders of the initials of Psalm 3 on folio 18v and the *D* on folio 503v (fig. 1.12), and these extenders are more slender and graceful, tending to split into double cusps at the end of the shafts. This type of extender becomes increasingly popular in later manuscripts, but there are also precedents in the Isabelle Psalter (fig. 1.13; the animal heads inside each initial are virtually identical).

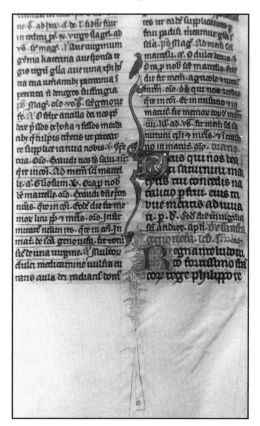

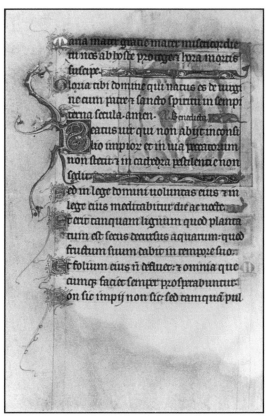

Fig. 1.12. Library of Congress, Ms. 15, f. 503v

Photo by author

Fig. 1.13. Cambridge, Fitzwilliam Museum, Ms. 300, f. 209v

Photo by Fitzwilliam Museum

Similarities to the infilling of the KL initials in the calendar of the breviary can be seen in the later KL initials of the Saint-Germain martyrology (lat. 12834, fig. 1.14 below) and the destroyed breviary that was Metz 1244. In fact the calendar miniatures of the Metz manuscript seem to be less elegant but direct copies of miniatures in the Saint-Germain martyrology.[34] The descent of Metz 1244 from the Royal Psalter Group, its French rubrics, and its concluding section of feasts added later to update the Sanctorale suggest that it too may have been intended for royalty or nobility.[35]

---

[34] Plate 11 in Leroquais's *Les Bréviaires manuscrits* shows the calendar pages for the beginning of January and the beginning of May in Metz 1244, apparently the only illustrations from this manuscript to survive. Compare the two miniatures for May with the same subjects in the Saint-Germain martyrology, f. 49, plate 2 in Georg Vitzthum's *Die Pariser Miniaturmalerei von der Zeit des hl. Ludwig bis zu Philipp von Valois und ihr Verhältnis zur Malerei in Nordwesteuropa* (Leipzig: Quelle & Meyer, 1907).

[35] It is perhaps worth noting that the heraldry on the shield held by the twins in both calendars seems to match that of Marie de Brabant, who was the reigning queen of France from her marriage to Philippe III le Hardi in 1274 until his death in 1285 (when her stepson Philippe le Bel assumed the throne). Both manuscripts are appropriate to the decade of Marie's queenship.

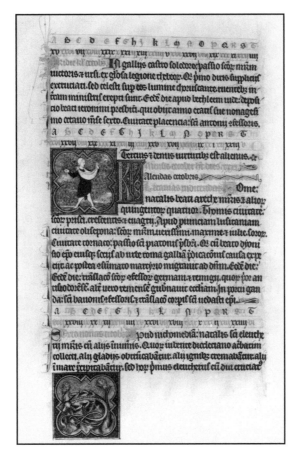

Fig. 1.14. Paris, Bibliothèque Nationale, Ms. lat. 12834, f. 74v

Photo by Bibliothèque Nationale

Finally, the numerous red-blue penwork initials and their extenders in L.C. 15 bear a demonstrable relation to those of one flourisher in the Isabelle Psalter as well as other manuscripts of the shop that follow in the 1270s, such as the Saint-Germain martyrology (fig. 1.14) and the lat. 15185 Bible (fig. 1.15).[36] The beautiful penwork *R* on folio 503v of L.C. 15 (fig. 1.12) has bi-colored filigree (both red and blue together, rather than one or the other), as do several initials on the immediately following folios. This type appears repeatedly in the Paris gradual Arsenal 110 from the later 1280s, whose historiated initials also form a link between late works of the Royal Psalter artists (such as Metz 1244 and the lat. 15185 Bible) and the work of Honoré and others in the 1290s.[37] The penwork initials in the section of added feasts at the end of the L.C. manuscript are not at all far from ones in the breviary of Philip the Fair, lat. 1023, from the end of the thirteenth century.

---

[36] Compare the Isabelle Psalter's penwork initials and extenders in Cockerell, especially the plates for ff. 26, 57, 70v, 89v, 107, and 125v.

[37] One very prominent decorative motif in the Isabelle Psalter (see the miniature borders on f. 26 in Cockerell's plates) is a three-branch sprig design; it appears elsewhere pressed into the gold grounds of miniatures in the Saint-Germain martyrology (fig. 1.14) and the *Somme le Roy* in the British Library (Add. Ms. 54180), in the lower border of the January KL initial in Metz 1244, and in the corners of historiated initials in the Arsenal 110 gradual, the Bible that is Bibliothèque Ste.-Geneviève Ms. 15, the breviary of Philip the Fair, and the Nuremberg Hours (cf. f. 22, plate 28 in Simmons).

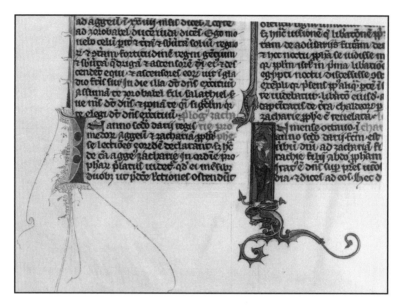

Fig. 1.15. Paris, Bibliothèque Nationale, Ms. lat. 15185, f. 320v

Photo by Bibliothèque Nationale

It remains to be suggested what member of the French royal family might have owned the Library of Congress breviary in the thirteenth century. As was noted earlier, the manuscript is too late to have been Saint Louis's own breviary, which he already possessed in the 1240s. The only clue to ownership is a cryptic obit added to the calendar in the fourteenth century. In the gutter of the page on February 17 is written "Obiit do[minus] J., comes vindocinen[sis]" (fig.1.1). This, as it turns out, is Jean of Vendôme, the sixth count of that name and the nineteenth to hold the title. There is a more precise obit for him added in the fourteenth century to the calendar of a Paris breviary from the 1290s, Bibliothèque Nationale, Ms. lat. 10482, which gives his death date as 17 February 1362—in the new-style calendar, 1363.[38]

It was probably Jean of Vendôme's daughter Catherine who had her father's obit entered in L.C. 15; she became countess of Vendôme after the death of her older brother Bouchard VII in 1371. But how might a book with royal connections have belonged to the house of Vendôme? Although the counts of Vendôme had served the French crown at least since the reign of Saint Louis, it is most likely that L.C. 15 came into the hands of Catherine of Vendôme when she married Jean I of Bourbon in September 1364, for her new husband was the great-grandson of Robert of Clermont, the youngest son of Saint Louis.[39] My hypothesis is, then, that the royal breviary was originally owned by Robert

---

[38] In lat. 10482, the entry on February 17 reads "Obiit nobilis ac sancte memorie dominus Johannes Comes Vindocinensis, Anno domini m.ccc.lxii." For more on Jean VI of Vendôme, see Pierre Anselme de Sainte-Marie, *Histoire généalogique et chronologique de la Maison royale de France, des pairs et grands officiers de la couronne, de la Maison du Roy et des barons du royaume . . .*, 3rd ed., 9 vols. (Paris: La Compagnie des Libraires, 1726-33; partly revised by Potier de Courcy, Paris, 1868-90; reprint, New York: Johnson Reprint, 1967), 8:727. Anselme dates Jean's death in February 1368, but Raoul Comte de Saint-Venant's *Dictionnaire topographique, historique, biographique, généalogique et héraldique du Vendômois et de l'arondissement de Vendôme*, 4 vols. (Blois: C. Migault et Cie, 1912-15), 2:231, places Jean's death "at the latest, in February 1365 (n.s., 1366)."

[39] Robert, Count of Clermont and Sire of Bourbon (1256-1318), married Béatrix of Burgundy (d. 1310); their son Louis I of Clermont (1279-1341) married Marie of Hainault (d. 1354); their son Jacques I of Bourbon (d. 1361) married Jeanne de Châtillon St. Paul (d. 1370); their son Jean I of Bourbon (d. 1393) married Catherine, Countess of Vendôme (d. 1412). This genealogy comes from Jean-Dominique Joannis and R. de Saint-Jouan, *Les Seize Quartiers généalogiques des Capétiens*, 4 vols. (Lyon: Sauvegarde Historique, 1958-65).

of Clermont, born in 1256, perhaps a decade before the production of the manuscript, and that it passed in succession through the family to his great-grandson. When Catherine of Vendôme came into this household some eighteen months after her father's death, she had the notice of his passing neatly added to her husband's breviary.

Within four years of Catherine's marriage to Jean of Bourbon, her brother Bouchard VII married Jean's widowed sister, Isabelle of Bourbon, thus doubling the marital ties between the houses of Bourbon and Vendôme.[40] Given the fact that the counts of Vendôme had connections to the royal house for a century prior to this time, it is of course possible to postulate other lines of descent for this manuscript, but the one proposed here seems to me the most likely. My presumption is that Saint Louis furnished his last son Robert with the breviary sometime between 1265 and 1270. The king's interest in the observance of the liturgy and in the education of his children, who were expected to be able to read and were made to recite the Hours, is well documented by Joinville and later writers. Though no specific occasion for a gift to Robert is evident, Louis and his three oldest sons took the cross for his fatal crusade in March 1267, and thereafter the king set about putting his affairs in final order.

Beautifully copied and carefully corrected though it be, this breviary can serve to remind us again that not all royal manuscripts are splendid luxury books, sumptuously decorated to feast the eye as well as the mind.[41] Yet at the same time L.C. 15 provides a clear link between those luxury books and plainer manuscripts from the shop of the same artists, broadening our insight into the different levels of quality in the diverse production of a single major Parisian atelier. And though this manuscript could not claim the miraculous attributes reported about Saint Louis's own breviary, it nonetheless did one thing the king's book apparently failed to do: it survived.

APPENDIX 1

The Calendar in Library of Congress, Ms. 15

JANUARY [42]

Iam[43] prima dies et septima fine timetur.
Januarius habet dies .xxxi. luna .xxx.
Januarii.

1. Circoncisio[44] domini duplum.   Dies
2. Octave sancti stephani .iii. lectiones. Si dominica fuerit .ix. lc.
3. Genovefe virginis .ix. l. Oct. sci. iohannis .memoria.
4. Oct. sanctorum innocentium .iii. lc. Si dominica fuerit .ix. lc.

---

[40] Saint-Venant, 1:183, dates this second wedding "vers 1368."

[41] A point well made by Robert Branner in his "Saint Louis et l'enluminure parisienne au XIIIᵉ siècle," *Septième centenaire de la mort de Saint Louis, Actes des colloques de Royaumont et de Paris (21-27 mai 1970)* (Paris: Société d'Edition "Les Belles Lettres," 1976), 69-84.

[42] Except for the "modern" numbering of the days of the month and the omission of golden numbers and dominical letters, I have tried to give as literal a transcription of the calendar as possible. When it has seemed useful to expand abbreviations, however, I have underlined the expanded portions.

[43] So for *Iani.*

[44] So for *Circumcisio.*

5. Oct. sci. thome episcopi et martyris .iii. l. Symeonis conf. mem missa de
6. Epyphanie domini. Annuum festum.   vigilia
7.   Hic ponitur clavis .lxxᵉ.
8. Luciani et maximiani[45] et iuliani mr. mem.
9.
10. Guillermi bituricensis archiepi. semiduplum.
11.
12.
13. Oct. epyphanie. duplum. hylarii et remigii episcoporum .mem.
14. [xix Kl.] Februarii felicis. In pincis .iii. lc.
15. Mauri abbatis .iii. lc. Boniti epi. et conf. mem.
16. Marcelli pape et martyris .iii. lc. fursci[46] conf. mem.   ¶antonii abb.
17. Pseusippi. eleusippi. meseulippi[47] mr .iii. lc. sulpicii epi.
18. Prisce virginis .iii. l. sol in aquario. Inicium .lxxᵉ.
19. Launomari abbatis.[48]
20. Fabiani et sebastiani .ix. lc.
21. Agnetis virginis .ix. lc.
22. Vincentii martyris. Semiduplum.
23. Emerentiane virginis .iii. lc.
24. Babile sociorumque eius martyrum .iii. lc.
25. Conversio sci. pauli. Duplum. preiecti mr .mem.   Dies
26. Policarpi epi. et mr .iii. lc.
27. Iuliani epi. et conf .ix. lc. Johannis epi. et conf .mem.
28. Agnetis secundo .iii. lc.
29. Paule matrone .iii. lc.
30. Batildis regine .iii. lc. si dominica fuerit .ix. lc.
31. Metranni martyris .mem.

FEBRUARY

Quarta subit mortem. prosternit tercia fortem.
At februi quarta est precedit[49] tercia finem.   ditur unus.[50]
februarius habet dies .xxviii. luna .xxix. et si sextus fuerit feria ad-

1. [Kl.] febr. Ignatii epi .iii. lc. Brigide virginis .mem.
2. Purificatio beate marie annuum festum.
3. Blasii epi. et martyris. Duplum.
4.   .Dies.
5. Agathe virginis et martyis .ix. lc.
6. Vedasti et amandi episcoporum .iii. lc.
7.

---

[45] So for *Maximiniani.*

[46] So for *Fursei.*

[47] So for *Speusippi* and *Meleusippi*

[48] L.C. 15 is correct here, while the Saint Louis and Isabelle Psalters have *Lannomari.*

[49] So for *procedit.*

[50] In the Isabelle Psalter calendar this line following the number of lunar days reads "et si bissextus fuerit additur unus" but is obscured by the KL initial for January (and hence overlooked by Cockerell).

8. Obitus roberti comitis attrenbat<u>ensis</u>.[51] Initium .xl^e.

9.

10. Scolastice virginis .iii. lc.

11.

12. Eulalie virginis et m<u>artyris</u> .iii. lc.

13.

14. [xvi Kl.] Marci.[52] Valentini mr .iii. lc.

15.

16.

17. Sol in piscis.[53] ultim<u>us</u> terminus .lxx^e.   Obiit do. J.

18. Adam hic peccavit.   Comes vin

19.   docinen.

20.

21.

22. Cathedra sci. petri .ix. lc. Initi<u>um</u> neris.[54]

23.   ¶et co<u>n</u>currens.

24. Mathie a<u>post</u>oli. Dup. loc<u>us</u> bisexti quota fer<u>ia</u>

25.

26.   D<u>ies</u>.

27. Honorine virginis et mr.

28.

MARCH

Primus mandentem disrumpit. quarta bibentem.
Marcis primat[55] necat cuius sub cuspide quarta est.
Marcius h<u>abet</u> dies .xxxi. luna .xxx.

1. [Kl.] Marcii albini epi et c<u>onf</u>. m<u>em</u>.   hic mutant<u>ur</u> co<u>n</u>currentes. D<u>ies</u>.

2.

3.

4.

5.

6. vltima incensio lune.

7. prima incensio lune

8.

9.

10.

11. Clavis pasche.

12. Georgii[56] pape .ix. lc.

13.

14.

---

[51] So for *attrebatensis.*

[52] So for *Marcii* in all three calendars.

[53] So for *sol in pisces.*

[54] So for *initium veris.*

[55] So for *prima.*

[56] So for *Gregorii.*

15.

16. [57]

17. Gertrudis virginis mem. sol in ariete.

18. Primus seculi. hic mutantur anni ab origine mundi.

19.

20. Equinoctium.

21. Benedictus[58] abbatis.

22. primum pascha sedes epactarum. hic incipit cidus[59] decenno-

23.   ¶venalis

24. locus concurrentium.

25. Annunciatio dominica. [in red]

26.

27. Resurrectio domini. Annuale festum.

28. Dies eger.

29.

30.

31.

APRIL

Denus et undenus est mortis vulnere plenus.

Aprilis decima est undena a fine salutat.

Aprilis habet dies .xxx. luna. xxix.

1.

2.

3.

4. Ambrosii epi. et conf .iii. lc.[60]

5.

6.

7.

8.

9.

10.   Dies.

11. Leonis pape et conf .mem.

12.

13. Eufemie virginis .iii. lc.

14. [xviii Kl.] Maii. Tyburtii. valeriani et maximiani[61] mr. iii. lc.

15. Claves rogationum.

16.

17. Sol in tauro.

18.

---

[57] *Aprilis* (for 17 Kalends of April) is missing in L.C. 15, the Isabelle Psalter, and the Saint Louis Psalter.

[58] So for *Benedicti*. The rank of nine lessons is omitted in all three calendars.

[59] So for *ciclus*.

[60] Cockerell in his transcription of the Isabelle Psalter calendar erroneously placed Ambrose on April 5; in the manuscript Ambrose is on April 4.

[61] So for *Maxiani*.

19.
20.   Dies.
21.   ¶tune v. mem.
22. Inventio corporum. dyonisii sociorumque eius. dupl. Opor-
23. Georgii mr. quasi .ix. lc. Reguli epi: mem.
24.   ¶mum pascha.
25. Marci evangeliste quasi .ix. lc. letania maior. Ulti-
26. Dedicatio sancte capelle par. Annuum festum.
27.
28. Vitalis mr .iii. lc.
29. Petri martyris .quasi .ix. lc.
30.

APPENDIX 2

The Office for Saint Louis in Library of Congress, Ms. 15

Several unusual features distinguish the office for Saint Louis added in L.C. 15 (ff. 554-59) from the usual version of *Ludovicus decus regnantium*. The standard version is attributed to the Dominican Arnaut du Prat and was issued between 1301 and 1306, though the nine lessons of Matins were not published until the Dominican General Chapter of 1306.[62] The earliest extant manuscript source of the complete office (including the Mass) is thought to be Bibliothèque Nationale, Ms. lat. 911 from the early fourteenth century, and this is the copy that has been edited by Alban Heysse.[63] The lat. 911 version of *Ludovicus decus regnantium* is the one found in most liturgical books of Paris use, despite the fact that the lessons of Matins, taken from the life of Saint Louis written in 1302-03 by the Franciscan Guillaume de Saint-Pathus, tend to dwell on Louis's good relations with the friars—a matter of some irritation to the Church of Paris.

In contrast, the Library of Congress breviary includes a completely different set of nine lessons for Matins in its version of *Ludovicus decus regnantium*. Rather than beginning *Beatus Ludovicus*, these lessons begin with the words *Gloriosissimi regis Ludovici* and are largely drawn from the earlier life of Saint Louis by his confessor, the Dominican Geoffroy de Beaulieu (d. ca. 1275). Much more appropriately, they emphasize the saintly king's piety and spiritual qualities, but I know of no other Parisian liturgical book that includes this set of lessons as part of *Ludovicus decus regnantium*.[64]

The Mass for Saint Louis in L.C. 15 also has its quirks. First among these is the Introit, which is a different composition from the standard *Gaudeamus omnes* with verse *Domine in virtute tua* that is widely used for more than a dozen saints in the Paris liturgy. The L.C. Introit reads:

---

[62] Leonard E. Boyle, "Dominican Lectionaries and Leo of Ostia's *Translatio s. Clementis*," *Archivum fratrum praedicatorum* 28 (1958): 366 and 385-87. See also Marcy J. Epstein, "*Ludovicus decus regnantium*: Perspectives on the Rhymed Office," *Speculum* 53 (1978): 283-334.

[63] Alban Heysse, "Antiquissimum officium liturgicum S. Ludovici regis," *Archivum franciscanum historicum* 10 (1917): 559-75.

[64] For Geoffroy de Beaulieu's life of Saint Louis, see *Recueil des historiens des Gaules et de la France*, ed. Daunou and Naudet (Paris: Imprimerie Royale, 1840), 20:4ff. Elizabeth A. R. Brown found the first eight lessons of the set *Gloriosissimi regis Ludovici* in the office for Saint Louis included in a fifteenth-century Roman breviary with Franciscan hallmarks, Mazarine 351; the ninth lesson there is the standard one as found in Bibliothèque Nationale, Ms. lat. 911. I am indebted to Professor Brown for this information and for the identification of Geoffroy de Beaulieu as the source for most of the lessons of the set *Gloriosissimi regis Ludovici*.

Magnificatus est rex pacificus super omnes reges
terre divitiis et sapientia: et universa terra desi-
derabat videre vultum eius.
(V.) Et nunc, reges, intelligite: erudimini, qui
judicatis terram.

The choice of the text *Magnificatus est* seems to have been prompted by the second of two sermons preached upon the canonization of Louis IX by Boniface VIII on 11 August 1297. This sermon took as its text that of an antiphon used at Christmas Vespers, *Rex pacificus magnificatus est, cuius vultum desiderat universa terra*, and expounded the meaning of both *rex pacificus* and *magnificatus est* with particular reference to Saint Louis.[65] The L.C. Introit combines text from *Rex pacificus* with that of another Christmas Vespers antiphon, *Magnificatus est rex pacificus super omnes reges universe terre*, to produce the complete Introit antiphon given above. The verse of the Introit, *Et nunc, reges*, comes from Psalm 2:10, a psalm that is also part of the Christmas liturgy.

Following this Introit, L.C. 15 gives only an incipit for the Gradual *Domine prevenisti* with verse *Vitam petiit* that appears in lat. 911 and is taken from the Common of Confessors. The breviary then adds a completely different Gradual with Verse, which reads:

(R.) Domine, in virtute tua letabitur rex,
et super salutare tuum exultabit vehementer.
(V.) Desiderium cordis eius tribuisti ei,
et voluntate labiorum eius non fraudasti eum.

These texts are the first two verses of Psalm 20. With slightly altered wording (*In virtute tua, Domine* and *Desiderium anime eius*), they are both used in the Common of Martyrs in other chants. Whereas lat. 911 includes four Alleluias, all of which mention Louis by name, L.C. 15 includes only the first of these, *Felix corona Francie*; and it similarly includes only the first of two proses or sequences, *Regem regum veneremur*, leaving out *Letabunda* as found in lat. 911.[66] The rest of the Mass is the same.

The only other source known to me that contains L.C. 15's version of this Mass is Paris, Bibliothèque Nationale, Ms. lat. 1123. This early fourteenth-century manuscript, only 43 folios long, is mostly occupied by a processional that belonged to the College of Navarre in Paris. Folios 38-40v, originally separate and only bound later with the processional, contain a musically notated copy of the Mass for Saint Louis as it is found in L.C. 15, beginning with an historiated initial *M* for *Magnificatus est*. In artistic style it appears to date from the first decade of the fourteenth century.

Three other fourteenth-century Paris missals include the Introit *Magnificatus est* as the Introit for a daily Mass of Saint Louis, labeled a *missa cotidiana*. In each case this single item precedes the Mass beginning *Gaudeamus* intended for the August 25 feast day. The manuscripts are Bibliothèque Nationale, nouv. acq. Ms. lat. 2649, a noted missal copied after 1317 (beginning on f. 265v); Arsenal 607, a missal without music copied after 1323 (f. 209v); and the noted missal Brussels, Bibliothèque Royale Albert Ier, Ms. 9125 (f. 404v), copied after 1317 with a calendar that shows royal hallmarks. In this latter manuscript, the Mass *Guadeamus* includes only two Alleluias—*Felix corona Francie* and *Pater sancte Ludovice*—along with both proses.[67] Lastly, on preliminary folio B of Bibliothèque Nationale, Ms. lat. 15615, a mid thirteenth-century noted missal, a fourteenth-century hand has included both Introits, *Gaudeamus* and *Magnificatus est*, as options in the standard Mass. The singular Gradual does not appear.

---

[65] The sermon is in the *Recueil des historiens des Gaules et de la France*, 23:152-53.

[66] The sequence *Letabunda* is an adaptation of the verse form and melody of the sequence *Letabundus*, used in the Paris liturgy for Christmas, the Assumption of the Virgin, and the feast of the Reception of the Relics at Notre-Dame.

[67] In an early fourteenth-century noted missal, British Library Add. Ms. 16905, which has Saint Louis as the most recent feast in both the calendar and the Sanctorale, the text of the Introit *Magnificatus est* is written under blank musical staves after the rubric *De sancto Ludovico rege*; then follows the Mass *Gaudeamus* with the rubric *Ad magnam missam*.

Leonard Boyle, in noting the distinction to be made in the Dominican Order between the date a feast was first proposed, was ultimately approved, and was provided with lessons, remarked that "generally lessons for a new feast were not issued" until the feast had received full approval, which required a minimum of three years.[68] The feast of Saint Louis was first proposed in the Dominican General Chapter of 1298 (the year after canonization), approved in 1300, and confirmed in 1301, but the lessons were not published in the acts of the General Chapter until 1306. Thus eight years elapsed before the Dominican office for Saint Louis—Arnaut du Prat's *Ludovicus decus regnantium*—was complete and officially available for celebration. We cannot believe that either Notre-Dame or the royal chapel waited eight years to begin regular commemoration of a saint so important to both the cathedral and the king.

In fact, the royal accounts from the year 1299 show that the king's *magister capelle* paid seven pounds "pro pluribus historiis et legendis de sancto Ludovico pro capella scribendis," plus another 48 sous "pro libris religandis, historiis et legendis de sancto Ludovico in libris capelle situandis."[69] Thus multiple copies of "historias and legends of Saint Louis" were made and bound in with the capella's books, and evidently by May 1299 the royal chapel was prepared with a liturgy for Saint Louis.

The royal accounts also show that over a period from June to August of 1298 Philip the Fair paid the sum of 100 pounds to several men to produce chants and an *historia* for Saint Louis, presumably to be used at the first celebration of the day on 25 August 1298, at Saint-Denis. The first payment of 10 pounds did not name the recipients; it went "for the expenses of certain ones learned in music for making chant for the historia of Saint Louis, King."[70] Beginning three days later, the remaining 90 pounds were paid to three men—Geoffroi, who was a chaplain of Jacques de Saint Pol; Maître Geoffroi Duplessis; and the musician Pierre de la Croix d'Amiens— "pro expensis compilando hystoriam beati Ludovici," as it was usually put.[71] This historia, together with "legends" (implying undivided lessons for the octave), may well be what was copied into books of the royal chapel by May of the following year. Could it also have been the version included in L.C. 15?

At the moment we cannot say definitively which version of *Ludovicus decus regnantium*, the one with L.C.'s lessons *Gloriosissimi regis Ludovici* or the other with Arnaut du Prat's lessons *Beatus Ludovicus*, came first. It is likely, however, that the lessons *Gloriosissimi* in L.C. 15 came before the lessons *Beatus Ludovicus*, if only because the source for the *Beatus Ludovicus* set, Guillaume de Saint-Pathus's life of Louis, was not begun until 1302, whereas Geoffroy de Beaulieu's life, which furnished the material for the set *Gloriosissimi*, had been extant for more than twenty years at the time of Louis's canonization. It is also worth bearing in mind that both the added section of L.C. 15 containing this office and the portion of Bibliothèque Nationale, Ms. lat. 1123 that includes the notated Mass for Saint Louis appear to be slightly earlier than lat. 911, which contains the approved Dominican version.

Nonetheless, the version of *Ludovicus decus regnantium* with lessons *Beatus Ludovicus*, as found in lat. 911, is the one which ultimately prevailed in both the royal and the Paris liturgy. Its success may well have been sealed by 1309, when, in keeping with a custom initiated on other feast days by his grandfather, Philip the Fair accorded the annual celebration of the feast of Saint Louis at the Sainte-Chapelle to the Dominicans and Franciscans.[72]

---

[68] Boyle, 385.

[69] Auguste Vidier, "Notes et documents sur le personnel, les biens et l'administration de la Sainte-Chapelle du XIIIe au XVe siècle," *Mémoires de la Société de l'Histoire de Paris* 28 (1901): 331. The word "historia," implying a biographical orientation, can refer just to the lessons of Matins or to the complete office for a given feast; DuCange also listed a usage that refers to the responsories sung after the lessons of Matins.

[70] Jules Viard, ed., *Les Journaux du Trésor de Philippe IV le Bel* (Paris: Imprimerie Nationale, 1940; first published in 1917), xxxiv and entry number 698. This material is also printed in Auguste Vidier, "Le Trésor de la Sainte-Chapelle," *Mémoires de la Société de l'Histoire de Paris* 36 (1909): 271.

[71] Viard, nos. 727, 799, 902, 928, 941, and 1008. Viard observed that 60 pounds of the total sum went to Pierre de la Croix, who evidently did the lion's share of the work. As reported by Robert Folz, Michel Huglo offered the suggestion that the king's payments to Pierre de la Croix might have been for composing an office to be used during the octave of the feast of Saint Louis. See Folz, "La Sainteté de Louis IX d'après les textes liturgiques de sa fête," *Revue d'histoire de l'église de France* 57 (1971): 32, n. 4. Folz, on the other hand, regarded all the contributors as engaging in a competition.

[72] Vidier, "Le Trésor de la Sainte-Chapelle," 287.

CHAPTER 2

Double Offices at the Lateran
in the Mid-Twelfth Century

Joseph Dyer

As the Frankish bishop Amalar (ca. 775-ca. 850) examined a Roman Antiphoner of the early ninth century, he noticed several liturgical customs not practiced in his homeland, or at least not at Metz, whose liturgy he was then revising. One of these customs was the celebration of two night offices ("duo officia nocturnalia"), each of three Nocturns, for the feast of Christmas.[1] Amalar, who had been sent to Rome about the year 830 on an official mission for Emperor Louis the Pious, had access to the highest ranks of the Roman clergy, and he sought an explanation for the Christmas offices from a cleric who had been educated "from the cradle in the holy Roman church." (This might have been the archdeacon Theodore, mentioned in the prologue to *De ordine antiphonarii*.) His source told him that the two offices he had seen in the Roman antiphoner should be celebrated in the reverse order, just as they were entered in the antiphoner used by the papal court. The second office, whose first nocturn included the antiphons "Dominus dixit ad me," "In sole posuit," and "Elevamini portae aeternales," was actually chanted before midnight ("in vigiliis") at the church of S. Maria Maggiore by the pope and his clergy.

What appeared to be the first office in the antiphoner consulted by Amalar, with the antiphons "Dominus dixit ad me," "Tamquam sponsus," and "Diffusa est gratia," was sung in the early morning hours at St. Peter's by the clergy of that church. This office began with the normal Christmas invitatory "Christus natus est," traditionally omitted at Rome from the first office.[2] Amalar incorporated both offices in his (now lost) antiphoner for Metz, but he suggested that one of them could be sung on the octave of the Nativity. Indeed the papal Vigil office at S. Maria Maggiore entered the subsequent liturgical tradition as the office of the octave.[3] Amalar provided little detail on these Roman double offices (more precisely double Nocturns), since *De ordine antiphonarii* was designed merely as the

[1] *Liber de ordine antiphonarii* 15; *Amalarii episcopi opera liturgica omnia*, ed. Jean-Michel Hanssens, 3 vols., Studi e Testi, 138-40 (Vatican City: Biblioteca Apostolica Vaticana, 1948-50), 3:49-51. See also Hanssens's valuable *tabellae* of the offices described by Amalar (3:139-224). Amalar's life and works are surveyed by Hanssens, 1:39-82.

[2] Both Old Roman antiphoners retain the double office for Christmas in the order specified by Amalarius' Roman informant; Archivio di S. Pietro B 79, ff. 25v and 27v, and London, British Library, Add. Ms. 29988, ff. 21v and 24.

[3] See Raymond LeRoux, "Les Antiennes et les psaumes de matines et de laudes pour Noël et le Ier janvier," *Études grégoriennes* 4 (1961): 65-170. Honorius of Autun (d. ca. 1145-52) mentioned the celebration of double offices "more antiquo" in the *Gemma animae* 3.6; Patrologia latina 172:644.

introduction to a complete edition of all the chant texts of the office (Amalar says nothing about the music) in their proper order.

Amalar's account of these Roman double offices is confirmed and complemented in a nearly contemporary source. *Ordo romanus* 12 from the late eighth or early ninth century contains a partial description of an all-night Christmas observance—Vigils and Matins—that parallels the one discovered by Amalar in a Roman antiphoner.[4] *Ordo* 12 lists eight responsories for the (first) Christmas office "ad vigilias, sicut agitur ad sanctam Mariam," while for nocturns it mentions the presence of the invitatory, and the fact that the twelve ferial psalms are combined with nine lessons and eight responsories "de natale domini." When the ninth responsory was omitted, one would expect that the Te Deum took its place, but this was not an invariable Roman practice. Amalar asked Theodore about the nine lessons but only eight responsories on Sunday, and he was told that the Te Deum was sung only "in natalitiis pontificum."[5] (For the remaining offices of the day *Ordo* 12 refers to another book, the *capitulare*.)

Table 2.1 compares *Ordo* 12 with Amalar's *De ordine antiphonarii* and three later Roman sources: 1) the *Liber politicus* (ca. 1140-43) by Canon Benedict of St. Peter's, 2) the Old Roman antiphoner of St. Peter's, and 3) the *ordo* compiled before 1145 by Prior Bernard of the Lateran.[6] The nomenclature of the individual sources has been retained: "Vigil" can be either singular or plural, while "Matins" can mean either Nocturns, called "matutinum" in the sources, or the office that later came to be known as "Lauds." (Comparable offices are aligned horizontally in table 2.1.)

Table 2.1
Christmas Double Offices at Rome

Ordo romanus 12.4 (8-9th century)	*De ordine antiphonarii* 15 (early 9th century)	*Liber politicus* 15-20 (12th century)	*Archivio di S. Pietro,* B 79, f. 25 (12-13th century)	*Ordo lateranensis* 25-28 (12th century)
Vigils at S. Maria Maggiore: [festal psalms?]	Vigils at S. Maria Maggiore (papal): festal psalms	Vigils at S. Maria Maggiore	Vigils at St. Peter's: festal psalms	Vigil
Matins + Mass	[Mass (papal)]	Mass (papal)	Mass (canons)	Mass (canons)
Nocturns: ferial psalms	Nocturns at St. Peter's (clerical): festal psalms	Matins at S. Maria Maggiore Mass (S. Anastasia) Mass (St. Peter's)	Matins: dominical psalms	Matins
Matins	Matins		Lauds	Lauds

---

[4] *Ordo* 12.4; Michel Andrieu, ed., *Les Ordines romani du haut moyen-âge*, 5 vols., Spicilegium sacrum lovaniense, 11, 23-24, 28, 29 (Louvain: Université Catholique de Louvain, 1931-61), 2:460-61. The *ordo* also records double offices for the feasts of saints, "qualiter apud romanos celebrentur" (*Ordo* 12.23; Andrieu, 3:465-66).

[5] *Liber de ordine antiphonarii*, prol. 7; Hanssens, 3:14. The *Ordo lateranensis* (mid-twelfth century) cites "antiquam Romanam consuetudinem" that no more than eight responsories are ever sung. If the Te Deum is omitted, the next office (lauds) begins immediately. See *Bernhardi cardinalis et lateranensis ecclesiae prioris Ordo officiorum ecclesiae lateranensis*, ed. Ludwig Fischer, Historische Forschungen und Quellen, 2-3 (Munich-Freising: Datterer, 1916), no. 16, p. 6.

[6] The *Liber politicus* is included in vol. 2 of Paul Fabre and Louis Duchesne, eds., *Le Liber censuum de l'église romaine*, Bibliothèque des écoles françaises d'Athènes et de Rome, 2 sér., vol. 6, nos. 1-2 (Paris: Boccard, 1889-1952): 145-46. The text of the St. Peter's antiphoner was published in Giuseppe Maria Tommasi, *Responsorialia et antiphonaria romanae ecclesiae*, Opera omnia 4, ed. Antonio Francesco Vezzosi (Rome: Typographia Palladis, 1749); for the feast of Christmas see pp. 37-41. The same volume contains an edition of *Ordo romanus* 12 (pp. 321-27).

The twelfth- and thirteenth-century sources cited in table 2.1 were designed to serve different functions. Although the *Liber politicus* usually describes special papal services, its directions correspond in this instance with the nearly contemporary antiphoner of the basilica. The Vigil office in the St. Peter's antiphoner conforms in turn with the Old Roman antiphoner from an unknown Roman church (British Library, Add. Ms. 29988). The psalms of Vigils and Matins follow a gapped numerical sequence, chosen according to the suitability of their allusions to the festal celebration, the ferial psalms of nocturns in *Ordo* 12 having been superseded by a later custom in which all psalms at both offices are festal.[7] The lack of an invitatory at Vigils is either mentioned explicitly in the sources (*Ordo* 12 and Amalar) or presumed retrospectively if the invitatory is mentioned only in the case of Nocturns/Matins (St. Peter's antiphoner, *Liber politicus*, *Ordo lateranensis*).

Since *Ordo* 12, Amalar, and the *Liber politicus* concern themselves in varying degrees with the papal stational practice, they note the location of the Vigil office and following Mass at the stational church for the feast, S. Maria Maggiore. The *Liber politicus* traces the papal court's movement to the other two stational Masses at S. Anastasia, beneath the western slope of the Palatine, and at St. Peter's across the Tiber. Although the station for the third Mass of Christmas was officially St. Peter's, both the antiphoner of that basilica and the *Liber politicus* record that the Mass actually took place at S. Maria Maggiore in consideration of the "shortness of the day and convenience of travel."[8] At St. Peter's and the Lateran the first Mass of Christmas, which began about midnight, had a less public character. After celebrating Vigils the canons of St. Peter's processed to the oratory of the Holy Veil (*Sudarium*) at the eastern end of the outer south aisle of the basilica for Mass.[9] At the Lateran one of the hebdomadary bishops of the basilica celebrated Mass for the canons and presumably any of the faithful who happened to be present.

Double offices also marked the celebration of important feasts in the Roman sanctoral cycle. In the prologue to the *De ordine antiphonarii* Amalar described the scope of the Roman usage:

> On the greatest festivals of the saints it is the custom of our holy mother, the Roman church, to perform during the night two offices, which offices are entitled "de vigiliis." The first of them, sung at the beginning of the night, is performed without alleluia. The other, indeed, which begins about the middle of the night and ends at daybreak, has alleluia both with the antiphons of the third Nocturn and with the antiphons of Matins.[10]

---

[7] Eugene Leahy, "Archivio di San Pietro, Cod. B 79, and Amalarius: Notes on the Development of the Medieval Office," *Manuscripta* 28, no. 2 (1984): 79-91.

[8] *Liber politicus* 17 (Fabre-Duchesne, 145): "propter parvitatem diei et facultatem vie." See also Archivio di San Pietro, B 79, f. 25v: "Statio in basilica beati Petri principis apostolorum, sed propter brevitatem diei celebratur apud sanctam Mariam maiorem" (Tommasi-Vezzosi, 4:39).

[9] No. 115 on the sixteenth-century plan of Old St. Peter's published by Tiberio Alfarano: *Tiberii Alpharani de Basilica Vaticanae antiquissima et nova structura*, ed. Michele Cerruti, Studi e Testi, 26 (Rome: Tipografia Poliglotta Vaticana, 1914).

[10] "In praeclarissimis festivitatibus sanctorum consuetudo est sanctae matris nostrae Romanae ecclesiae duo officia peragere in nocte, quorum officia praetitulantur de vigiliis. Primum eorum, quod canitur in initio noctis, sine alleluia peragitur; alterum vero, quod habet initium circa medium noctis et finitur in die, habet in tertia nocturna in suis antiphoniis alleluia, et in antiphonis de matutino"—*Liber de ordine antiphonarii* 59.5; Hanssens, 3:96. Here "matins" means the hour that later came to be known as "lauds" (cf. "in laudibus matutinis"). The night office was usually called "vigils" or "nocturns" in the earlier middle ages, but vigils implied only very rarely watchfulness throughout the night. In a canonical miscellany (Vaticanus latinus 1351, f. 78) from the Roman church of S. Lorenzo in Damaso (third quarter of the eleventh century) "vigilie" is simply the name for the night office. The bibliography on the history of nocturnal and matutinal prayer is very large. Various viewpoints are discussed in Anton Baumstark, *Nocturna Laus: Typen frühchristlicher Vigilienfeier und ihre Fortleben vor allem im römischen und monastischen Ritus*, ed. Odilo Heiming, Liturgiewissenschaftliche Quellen und Forschungen, 32 (Münster in Westfalen: Aschendorff, 1957); Paul Bradshaw, *Daily Prayer in the Early Church*, 2nd ed., Alcuin Club Collections, 63 (London: Alcuin

In Amalar's time these double offices were celebrated at Rome—to what extent remains uncertain—to commemorate the feasts of St. Stephen, St. John the Evangelist, Holy Innocents, St. John the Baptist, Sts. Peter and Paul, St. Lawrence, the Assumption of the Virgin, and St. Andrew. Amalar noted that the first Vigil office, celebrated "circa vespertinam horam," was called "proper," while the later office of Matins was either ferial or from the common of the saints.[11] Amalar included in his Messine antiphoner a double office on the Roman model to honor Sts. Peter and Paul,[12] but this Roman idiosyncrasy was not accepted north of the Alps.

The first of the double offices for Peter and Paul was sung privately by the pope and his clergy. The laity and *clerus*—presumably the canons of St. Peter's—attended only the second office. This double office for the two sainted patrons of Rome dated back at least a century. A homiliary from the Roman church of Sts. Philip and James, known as the homiliary of Agimond, has separate readings for two vigil offices for St. Peter and separate double Vigils for St. Paul.[13] The rubric in the homiliary for the first office reads "de prima vigilia"/"in vigilias" and for the second "in secunda vigilia." By the time of Canon Benedict's mid-twelfth century *ordo* the canons of St. Peter's were collaborating with the clergy of the papal court by reading the lessons of the first nocturn.[14] Benedict cites only the first antiphon of each of the two offices ("In omnem terram" and "Si diligis me," respectively), pieces that correspond to the St. Peter's antiphoner. In that source the antiphons and psalms of the first office are drawn from the common of several apostles. While the antiphons of the second office are proper to St. Peter, the psalms (1-4, 8, 10, 14-15, 19) are selected from the ordinary dominical psalms.

Liturgical commemorations of the martyrs were at first limited to the places of their burial: an all-night vigil at the tomb culminated with the offering of Mass in the saint's honor.[15] A wider observance of their cults was ratified at Rome when Pope Gregory III (731-41) founded an oratory at St. Peter's in honor of Christ and the Blessed Virgin, in which he placed relics of apostles, martyrs, and confessors that had been brought into the city. According to the *Liber pontificalis*, "he decreed that in the oratory dedicated to their name . . . Vigils should be celebrated daily according to the

---

Club, 1983); Camillus Callewaert, *Liturgicae institutiones tractatus secundus: De breviarii romani liturgia*, 2nd ed. (Bruges: Beyaert, 1939), esp. 58-59, 235-36; Herbert Goltzen, "Nocturna Laus: Aus Arbeiten zur Geschichte der Vigil," *Jahrbuch für Liturgik und Hymnologie* 5 (1960): 79-88; Jean-Michel Hanssens, *Nature et genèse de l'office des matines*, Analecta Gregoriana, 57 (Rome: Gregorian University, 1952); Josef Jungmann, "The Origin of Matins," in *Pastoral Liturgy* (New York: Herder and Herder, 1962), 105-22; Carlo Marcora, *La vigilia nella liturgia: Ricerche sulle origini e sui primi sviluppi (sec. I-VI)*, 2nd ed., Archivio Ambrosiano, 6 (Milan: Ambrosius, 1954); Robert Taft, *The Liturgy of the Hours in East and West: The Origins of the Divine Office and Its Meaning for Today* (Collegeville, Minn.: Liturgical Press, 1986), esp. 165-90; Paul Tirot, "Vigiles et matines: Liturgie monastique et liturgie cathédrale," *Études grégoriennes* 22 (1988): 24-30.

[11] *Liber de ordine antiphonarii* 17; Hanssens, 3:53.

[12] *Liber de ordine antiphonarii* 59-63; Hanssens, 3:96-98.

[13] These were cited by Michel Huglo, "Le Chant 'vieux-romain': Liste des manuscrits et témoins indirects," *Sacris erudiri* 6 (1954): 115. See also Réginald Grégoire, *Homéliaires liturgiques médiévaux: Analyse de manuscrits*, Biblioteca degli "Studi Medievali," 12 (Spoleto: Centro italiano di studi sull'alto medioevo, 1980): 362-70 (Biblioteca Apostolica Vaticana, lat. 3835-3836); Antonie Chavasse, "Le Sermonnaire d'Agimond: Ses Sources immediates," *Kyriakon: Festschrift Johannes Quasten*, ed. Patrick Granfield and Josef Jungmann, 2 vols. (Münster in Westfalen: Aschendorff, 1970), 2:800-10; Chavasse, "Le Sermonnaire des Saints Philippe-et-Jacques et le sermonnaire de Saint-Pierre," *Ephemerides liturgicae* 69, no. 1 (1955): 17-24.

[14] *Liber de ordine antiphonarii* 60; Hanssens, 3:97. *Liber politicus* 67; Fabre-Duchesne, 157-58.

[15] On the development of festal offices see Camillus Callewaert, "Les Offices festifs à Rome avant la Règle de Saint Benoît," in his book *Sacris erudiri* (Steenbrugghe: In Abbatia S. Petri, 1940), 149-68; Callewaert, *Liturgicae institutiones*, 58-60; LeRoux, "Les Antiennes, 66-170; Pierre Jounel, "Le Sanctoral romain du 8e au 12e siècles," *La Maison-Dieu* 52 (1957): 59-88.

existing order by the monks of the three monasteries serving the basilica and that Masses for their feast days be celebrated in the same place."[16] According to *Ordo* 12, readings "de ipso natalicio pertinentes" had been introduced to the Vatican basilica by Pope Hadrian I (772-95).[17]

The abandonment of strict adherence to the weekly recitation of all 150 psalms, the *psalterium per hebdomadam*, was accelerated by the emphasis given to the sanctoral cycle over the temporal cycle. The practice described in *Ordo* 12 reflects an intermediary phase, that of the "double" office, in which the memory of a saint was recalled without disrupting the weekly recitation of the Psalter.[18] Something like a remnant of that phase, long since an archaism in the Roman liturgy, was preserved as a relic in the Old Roman antiphoner from St. Peter's in the choice of dominical psalms at Nocturns on the patronal feast of the basilica.[19]   In addition to Christmas and the feast of St. Peter, two further double offices—the third Sunday of Advent (Dominica de Gaudete) and the Assumption—were mentioned by Canon Benedict as still being celebrated by the canons of the basilica.[20]   The Vigil portion of the Advent office[21] consisted of the first three psalms of the Psalter sung to the three antiphons of the first nocturn of the following office of Nocturns. (At Nocturns each of these antiphons had four psalms.) A rubric in the St. Peter's antiphoner for the feast of the Assumption directs that the first nocturn of the feast be sung as the Vigil office.[22]

The liturgical practices of the Lateran basilica in the mid-twelfth century can be reconstructed on the basis of an *ordo* that describes the ceremonies for Mass and Office as well as other devotional and disciplinary observances of the canons.[23]   Known as the *Ordo officiorum lateranensis ecclesiae* (OL), this document represents a unique source of information about the liturgy of Rome during the Middle Ages. (Unfortunately, a relatively small number of liturgical texts are cited, usually only by incipits.) Although the original *ordo* no longer exists, its text has been preserved in a nearly complete copy with a few adaptations made by an Augustinian canon of Salzburg cathedral about the year 1220. The principal contents of this manuscript (Österreichische Nationalbibliothek, Ms. 1482) are, in addition to the *ordo*, Hugh of St. Victor's commentary on the rule of Augustine, *consuetudines* of

---

[16] "Hic fecit oratorium intro eandem basilicam, iuxta arcum principalem, parte virorum, in quo recondivit in honore Salvatoris sanctaeque eius genetricis reliquias sanctorum apostolorum vel omnium sanctorum martyrum ac confessorum, perfectorum iustorum, toto in orbe terrarum requiescentium. Quorum festa vigiliarum a monachis trium monasteriorum illic servientium cotidie per ordinem existentia atque nataliciorum missas in eodem loco celebrare." Louis Duchesne, ed., *Le Liber pontificalis: Texte, introduction et commentaire*, 2 vols. (Paris: Thorin, 1886-92), complemented by Cyrille Vogel, *Additions et corrections* (Paris: Boccard, 1957), 1:417. The oratory, chosen by Gregory III as his burial site, is no. 38 on the plan of Alfarano: *Tiberii Alpharani de Basilicae Vaticanae*, 59 and 186.

[17] *Ordo* 12:24-25; Andrieu, 2:466.

[18] Until the reform of the Roman Missal under Pope John XXIII in 1960, feasts were still ranked as "double of the first class," "double of the second class," "double major," "double," or "semidouble."

[19] Archivio de San Pietro, B 79, f. 131v.

[20] *Liber politicus* 7-9 (Dominica de Gaudete), 15 (Christmas), 67 (St. Peter), 72 (Assumption); ed. Fabre-Duchesne, 143, 145, 157, and 158. The texts of the chants are edited in Tommasi-Vezzosi, 4:25, 37, 121, and 133. See also Leahy, 88.

[21] Archivio di San Pietro, B 79, f. 11.

[22] "In vigilia assumptionis beate Marie cantatur ad matutinum totum primum nocturnum cum ii responsoriis eiusdem festivitatis"—ibid., f. 148. Although the wording is confused, this rubric could not mean that the nocturnal office of the Vigil (i.e., the day preceding) of the Assumption consisted of only a single nocturn of three psalms.

[23] The sanctoral cycle of this manuscript has been studied by Edward B. Garrison, "Three Manuscripts for the Lucchese Canons of S. Frediano in Rome," *Journal of the Warburg and Courtauld Institutes* 38 (1975), esp. 4-12.

the Augustinian canons, and a "breviarium per circulum anni."[24] The modern editor of the *Ordo lateranensis*, Ludwig Fischer, proposed 1145 as the *terminus ante quem* for the composition of the original, since its author, who identifies himself as "Bernhardus Lateranensis ecclesie humilis prior," was named by Pope Eugene III (1145-53) cardinal-priest of San Clemente in that year, and later rose to the rank of cardinal-bishop of Porto.[25] He is probably to be identified with the cardinal of the same name mentioned in a nearly contemporary source: the revision of the *Descriptio lateranensis ecclesie* prepared by a certain John, deacon of the Lateran congregation, during the pontificate of Alexander III (1159-81).[26] Bernard must have held the office of prior of the Lateran canons until the beginning of 1145, because Pope Lucius II (1144-45) addressed a letter to him (January 31), in which the pope granted the Lateran canons the church of S. Giovanni a Porta Latina and a *hospitale* near the basilica itself.[27] Since Bernard, "humilis prior," must have written his liturgical and disciplinary *ordo* before his elevation to the cardinalate, it can be concluded that it dates from no later than 1145 or probably a few years earlier.

The *Ordo lateranensis* borrows quite heavily from a non-Roman *ordo* that the Lucchese canons brought with them from Tuscany. About half of the text of Prior Bernard's *ordo* is found in an *ordo* (Lucca, Biblioteca Capitolare, Ms. 608) that reflects the practice of the canons of the cathedral of St. Martin in Lucca.[28] Bernard adapted this model to the Roman traditions of the Lateran, not least of all to the configuration of the church itself and its important baptistery, as well as to the practices of the curia whenever the pope celebrated a station at the church. On some of these occasions the Lateran canons collaborated with the curia; at other times they were little more than spectators. One of the most striking characteristics shared by the two *ordines* is the provision for double offices. In the Lucca source Vigils on important feasts are called "major Vespers" (*vesperae maiores*). At Lucca these tended to be celebrated on feasts of local significance (Sts. Jason and Maur, St. Agnellus, etc.),[29] while generally at the Lateran the most important feasts of the universal calendar were so honored. The Lucchese major vespers ended with a short chapter, verse, the Benedictus antiphon, and a closing prayer.[30] Major Vespers of nine lessons were also known at Lucca.

---

[24] I would like to express my thanks to Dr. Ernst Gamillscheg, director of the Manuscript and Incunabula Collection of the Austrian National Library, for facilitating my access to this manuscript.

[25] *Bernhardi cardinalis . . . ordo officiorum*, ed. Fischer, xiv.

[26] John's edition, with readings from earlier versions and later interpolations, is in Roberto Valentini and Giuseppe Zuchetti, eds., *Codice topographico della città di Roma*, 4 vols., Fonti per la Storia d'Italia, 81, 88, 90-91 (Rome: Istituto Storico Italiano per il Medio Evo, 1940-53), 3:319-73; see p. 349.

[27] Julius von Pflugk-Harttung, *Acta pontificum romanorum inedita*, 3 vols. (Stuttgart: Kohlhammer, 1881-86; reprint, Graz: Akademische Druck- und Verlagsanstalt, 1958), 3:64. Previous to becoming a member of the curia, the pope (Gherardo Caccianemici) had been a canon of S. Frediano, the same congregation charged by Paschal II (1099-1118) with reforming the Lateran canons.

[28] Pierre-Marie Gy, "L'Influence des chanoines de Lucques sur la liturgie du Latran," *Revue des sciences religieuses* 58 (1984): 31-41; Martino Giusti, "L'*Ordo officiorum* della cattedrale di Lucca," *Miscellanea Giovanni Mercati*, 6 vols., Studi e Testi, 121-26 (Vatican City: Biblioteca Apostolica Vaticana, 1946), 2:523-66. Gy established 1186 as the *terminus post quem* of the Lucchese *ordo*.

[29] For a listing see Giusti, 534 n. 56.

[30] "Vesperae maiores, sonatis signis, sic celebramus. Unus de schola incipit antiphonam a primo nocturno et cantatur tres psalmi cum tribus antiphonis, deinde versus; leguntur tres lectiones de festivitate; secundum responsorium festivius canitur. Inter lectiones incensantur altaria et datur incensum clero et populo. Post tertiam lectionem non cantatur responsorium, set dicit sacerdos capitulum, sequitur versus; postquam incipitur antiphona ad Benedictus. Finita oratione, dicitur festive 'Benedicamus'" (Giusti, 533). Whereas vigils at the Lateran included the Te Deum, that chant seems to be missing at Lucca, but Giusti believes that its omission from the Lucchese *ordo* was accidental.

An extensive observance of double offices at the Lateran basilica in the middle of the twelfth century is documented in Prior Bernard's *ordo*. The "Vigils" are virtually all created by anticipating the first nocturn of the following Matins. They are not intended, as some earlier double offices were, to observe a sanctoral feast, while at the same time preserving uninterrupted the weekly *cursus* of psalmody. Though the Lateran canons claimed for themselves the role of faithful guardians of the ancient basilical traditions, the Vigils they celebrated were not wholly the continuation of older Roman customs (*Ordo* 12 and Amalar), but rather part of a wider development that had led monastic and canonical communities to embrace numerous special votive offices and pious devotions in addition to their regular liturgical Office.

Table 2.2 lists the double offices observed by the Lateran canons according to Prior Bernard.[31] "Double office," the term employed by the *Ordo lateranensis* (OL 185), describes a commemoration involving: 1) a Vigil office celebrated after Vespers, and 2) Matins at the normal time in the early hours of the morning. With the exception of Christmas, John the Baptist, the Assumption, and the Dedication of the Lateran, all of the first Vigil offices consisted of three psalms, three lessons, and two responsories, the last responsory replaced by the Te Deum (OL 33).[32] The numbers in parenthesis next to the feasts in table 2.2 refer to the numbered sections in Fischer's edition of the *Ordo lateranensis*. Generally, only the passage relating to the Vigil office is quoted in the second column.

Table 2.2

Double Offices in the *Ordo lateranensis*

Feast	Text of the Ordo lateranensis
Christmas (25, 27)	Responsoria omnia cum "Gloria patri" canantur. In I° nocturno Vs. *Tamquam sponsus*, in II° nocturno *Sponsus foris*, in III° *Ipse invocabit me.* Tres lectiones de Isaia "Primo tempore," "Consolamini," "Consurge." Tres de sermonibus sanctorum patrum. Tres de omeliis trium evangeliorum, prima Gregorii, secunda Ambrosii, tertia Augustini. [Both offices of 9 psalms and lessons.]
Stephen (30, 31)	legimus III lectiones in propriis sermonibus (30)
John the Evangelist (32-34)	vigiliam cum tribus lectionibus de vita eius (32); quotiescumque vigiliam trium lectionum celebramus, duo tantum responsoria cantamus . . . finita tertia lectione hymnum *Te deum laudamus* (33).
[Fer. ii post Pascha, Ascension, Fer. ii et iii post Pent., Peter, Laurence, Decoll. Joh. Bapt., Augustine]	Notandum quod tertia feria post pascha et in die ascensionis, secunda et tertia feria post pentecosten, in festo sancti Petri, sancti Laurentii, in decollatione sancti Iohannis, in festo sancti Augustini, licet duplex facimus officium, tamen in hora sua cantamus nonam.
Andrew (249)	post collationem vigilias celebramus in quibus III lectiones legimus in passione eius.
Nicholas (249)	quia altare eius nomine in porticu maioris ecclesiae habemus . . . post collationem vigiliam legentes in vita ipsius et de confessore cantamus.

Continued

---

[31] This list is considerably longer than that given by Dom Pierre Salmon in his study *L'Office divin au Moyen Age: Histoire de la formation du bréviaire du IXᵉ au XVIᵉ*, Lex orandi, 43 (Paris: Editions du Cerf, 1967), 99, n. 1.

[32] Bernard apologizes for the choice of lessons on the feast of St. Thomas (OL 250; ed. Fischer, 124), since they derived from an apocryphal source, probably the Acts of Thomas. See Klaus Zelzer, *Die alten lateinischen Thomasakten*, Texte und Untersuchungen zur Geschichte der altchristlichen Literatur, 122 (Berlin: Akademie Verlag, 1977), and *Bibliotheca hagiographica latina antiquae et mediae aetatis*, 2 vols., Subsidia hagiographica, 6 (Brussels: Socii Bollandiani, 1898-1901), no. 8136. The text is found in two eleventh-century lectionaries from the Lateran: Archivio Lateranense, A 80, ff. 335v-346v, and A 81, ff. 282-287v. See Alfred Poncelet, *Catalogus codicum hagiographicorum latinorum bibliothecarum romanarum praeter quam Vaticanae* (Brussels, 1909), 68 and 78.

Table 2.2–*Continued*

Double Offices in the *Ordo lateranensis*

Feast	*Text of the* Ordo lateranensis
Thomas (250)	vigilias in quibus III lectiones in passione eius pro antiquo usu populo recitamus, licet inter apocryphas deputetur
Silvester (250)	vigilias in communi choro dicimus
Finding of the Holy Cross (268)	lectiones legimus in his vigiliis in tractatu de inventione dominice crucis in quadragesima
John before the Latin Gate	vigilias in quibus legimus III lectiones de vita eius a principio: "Secundam post Neronem Domitianus persecutionem exercuit" usque ad id: "ad Ephesum cum honore remearet."
Pancratius, Nereus, and Achilleus (271)	quia de beato Pancratio ecclesiam nomini eius consecratam iuxta maiorem basilicam et de eiusdem martyris inibi in altari habere meruimus, festum eius apud nos devote colitur. Ideoque post vesperam processionem ad eandem ecclesiam cantando resp. *Beatus vir* et post collationem vigilias facimus, in quibus III lectiones legimus in passione eius.
Venantius and Companions (271)	quia ecclesiam miro opere constructam iuxta fontes et eorum nominibus consecratam habemus . . . vigilias secundum consuetudinem facimus.
John the Baptist (273)	[Both offices of 9 psalms and 9 lessons with a vigil of three lessons for the octave (280); see the discussion below.]
Peter and Paul (279)	facimus vigilias in communi choro in quibus III lectiones legimus in gestis beati Petri editis a beato Lino, que sic incipiunt: "Licet plurima de apostolicis signis, . . ." Responsoria propria.
Sts. Rufina and Secunda (281)	post collationem celebramus etiam vigilias, in quibus passio earum legitur et de virginibus cantamus.
Mary Magdalene (283)	vigiliam in choro canimus et de propriis sermonibus lectiones legimus. I. Resp. *Vidi speciosam.* II. Resp. *Regnum mundi.*
Laurence (289)	vigiliam cum tribus lectionibus de passione eius
Assumption (291)	in maiori ecclesia vigiliam sollempniter decantamus . . . in quibus sex lectiones leguntur in tractatu beati Hieronymi de assumptione beate Marie ad Paulam et Eustochium, qui sic incipit: "Cogitis me, o Paula." III ultime in omelia Augustini de evangelio "Intravit Iesus in quodam castellum." [Both offices of 9 psalms and lessons.]
Augustine (295)	festive sonantibus omnibus signis, cantamus vigilias in choro.
Beheading of John the Baptist (296)	celebramus vigilias cum tribus lectionibus, in quibus antiphone et Vss. erunt de uno martyre. Lectiones vero et responsoria dicantur de eius proprietate.
Anthony, martyr (296)	In vigilia post vesperas diei facimus processionem ad cappellam eiusdem martyris que sistit in porticu maioris ecclesie cantando Resp. *Domine, prevenisti eum*; ibique post collationem cantamus etiam vigiliam legentes in passione eius.
Nativitas BMV (297)	vigilias . . . in quibus cantatur et legitur in sermonali de proprietate eiusdem sollempnitatis.
Exaltation of the Holy Cross (298)	Ibi [in the oratory of the Holy Cross] etiam post collationem, festive pulsantibus omnibus signis, cantamus vigilias cum tribus lectionibus, in quibus prima antiphona dicitur *Propter lignum servi facti sumus.* Ps. Cantate I. II. ant. *Adoramus te, Christe.* Ps. Dominus regnavit, exultet. III. ant. *Salvator mundi, salva nos.* Ps. Cantate domino II. Vs. *Per signum crucis.* Legitur tractatus de exaltatione sancte crucis.
Chrysanthus and Daria (299)	post vesperas imus cum processione in ecclesiam sancti Pancratii, ubi post collationem vigiliam facimus III lectionum et cantatur omnia de martyribus.
All Saints (300)	vigilias in choro facimus, in quibus leguntur III lectiones omnium sanctorum de sermone qui sic incipit: "Hodie, dilectissimi," et cantatur responsoria hec: *Absterget deus* et *Hec est vera fraternitas.*

Table 2.2–*Continued*
Double Offices in the *Ordo lateranensis*

Feast	Text of the Ordo lateranensis
Dedication of the Lateran (301)	Antiphone et resposoria et psalmi ut habentur in antiphonario. In I° nocturno Vs. *Hec est domus domini*, in II° nocturno Vs. *Domus mea*, in III° nocturno Vs. *Bene fundata est domus domini*. VI lectiones leguntur de sermonibus beati Augustini, quorum primus apud nos sic incipit: "Quotiescumque, fratres karissimi, altaris," item "Recte festa ecclesie colunt," item alius "Beatos apostolos sermo divinus," item idem "Celebritas huius congregationis," unde supra "Dominus noster Iesus Christus virtute patris." Tres vero ultime de omelia sancti Augustini de evangelio: "Ingressus Iesus perambulabat Iericho." Nonam lectionem legat episcopus, si adest. Responsoria reiterantur a capite. Ad singulas lectiones altare incensatur ab episcopo, et incensum canonicis ab eodem episcopo datur. Post hec dicitur *Te deum laudamus*, deinde dicit episcopus orationem. Sonatis vero signis, episcopus incipit matutinas: "Domine, labia mea aperies et os meum" "Deus in adiutorium." Invitatorium IIII cantent: *Sanctificantem dominum tabernaculum suum*. Lectiones, responsoria, versus, antiphone, psalmi, sicut supra denotavimus ad vigilias, ita dicantur omnia ad matutinas. [Both offices of 9 psalms and lessons.]

Several feasts listed in table 2.2 were accorded the distinction of a double office because the Lateran possessed relics of the saint or an altar dedicated to the saint's memory, to which the canons would process for the singing of Vigils. The location of these altars and chapels in or near the basilica is generally known from other sources, principally the *Descriptio lateranensis ecclesiae*, a guide to the church and its treasures that originated in the late eleventh century and underwent subsequent revisions. The evidence of the *Ordo lateranensis*, however, does not agree in all respects with that found in the *Descriptio*. For example, the *ordo* locates the altars of St. Nicholas and the martyr St. Antonius in the portico in front of the basilica ("in porticu maioris ecclesie," OL 249 and 296). The first edition of the *Descriptio* places these altars on the north side of the nave and in the north aisle, respectively (fig. 2.1, nos. 15 and 13).[33] By the third edition of the *Descriptio* Nicholas is no longer mentioned, and the dedication of the other altar had changed to St. Antoninus, but it was still located in the same place "a sinistro vero latere basilice" near the tomb of Anastasius IV (see fig. 2.1, no. 9).[34] The relics of Sts. Crysanthus and Daria reposed in an altar at the rear of the ambulatory that encircled the apse of the medieval basilica (see fig. 2.1, no. 10).[35] By the time John revised the *Descriptio*, the relics had been transferred to the safety of St. Pancratius, an oratory that stood outside the walls of the basilica proper. This oratory, presumably part of the canonry itself, contained many relics; it was located south of the medieval apse and ambulatory

---

[33] "In alia vero parte, id est in sinistro latere ecclesie, est altare sancti laurentii, deinde altare sancti nicolai. Postea vero in medio ecclesie est altare sancti antonii, in eadem parte inter duas columpnas sicut est in alia parte altare sanctorum XL martyrum." *Descriptio* 10; Valentini-Zuchetti, 3:346-47.

[34] *Descriptio* 10; Valentini-Zucchetti, 3:351.

[35] The apse can be seen in old photographs and in an anonymous view from the second half of the sixteenth century in the Ashby Collection; see Raymond Keaveney, ed., *Views of Rome from the Thomas Ashby Collection in the Vatican Library* (London: Scala, 1988), no. 37. The original apse was rebuilt by Nicholas IV (1288-92), then demolished and constructed anew between 1875 and 1886.

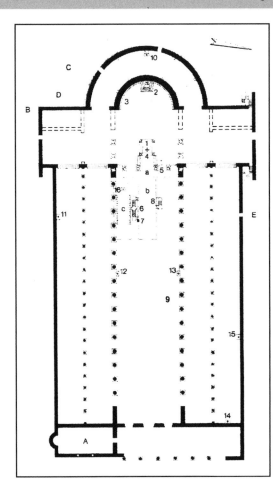

Fig. 2.1. St. John Lateran in the Late Twelfth Century
(after *Descriptio lateranensis ecclesiae* and
de Blaauw, *Cultus et decor*)

1. Main altar
2. Cathedra
3. Subsellia
4. Confession/crypt
5. Bronze columns/chancel barrier
6. Ambo for the Gospel
7. Paschal candlestick
8. Ambo for the Epistle
9. Tomb of Anastasius IV
10. Altar of Sts. Crysanthus and Daria
11. Altar of Sts. Vincent and Anastasius
12. Altar of the Forty Martyrs
13. Altar of St. Antoninus
14. Altar of St. Lawrence
15. Altar of St. Nicholas
16. Altar of the Canons

A. Main Sacristy
B. Cloister
C. Chapel of St. Pancratius
D. Sacristy of the Canons
E. Lateran Palace

a. Vestibulum altaris
b. Main Choir
c. Canons' Choir

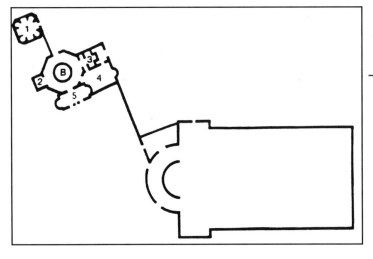

Fig. 2.2. St. John Lateran and the Lateran
Baptistery in the Twelfth Century
(after de Blaauw, *Cultus et Decor*)

1. Chapel of the Holy Cross
2. Chapel of St. John the Baptist
3. Chapel of St. John the Evangelist
4. Chapel of St. Venantius
5. Narthex

B. Baptistery

(see fig. 2.1, C).[36] The Dalmatian martyrs St. Venantius and Companions had been honored with a large chapel (see fig. 2.2, no. 4), most probably adapted from an already existing room or chapel, on the east side of the baptistery.[37] Begun by Pope John IV (640-42) as a votive offering, it was completed under his successor Theodore (642-49). Both popes are depicted in the apse mosaic of the chapel, reached at present by means of a narrow corridor from the baptistery. During the pontificate of Sixtus III (432-40), if not before, a twin-apsed narthex or portico was added on the south side of the baptistery. The chapel dedicated to Sts. Rufina and Secunda occupies the western apse of the narthex (see fig. 2.2, no. 5).[38]

Two of the double offices at the Lateran were marked by special solemnities, the anniversary of its dedication, observed on November 9 (OL 301), and the Nativity of John the Baptist, patronal feast of the basilica on June 24 (OL 273-77).[39] On the first of these occasions the papal court participated in the celebration of Vespers on the evening preceding the feast. The *Ordo lateranensis* directs the prior of the canons to pre-intone the first antiphon of Vespers ("Domum tuam decet") and the Magnificat antiphon ("Fundamenta templi huius") for the pope. One of the cardinal bishops presided at the following Vigil office, Matins and Lauds, and second Vespers. The court returned only for the celebration of Mass.

The patronal feast of the basilica was observed with even greater solemnity in the sumptuously adorned church. As Prior Bernard reminded the canons,

> If, on account of his merit, the blessed John is devoutly venerated by all, how much
> more does it behoove us to do everything possible, so that on his Nativity we might
> be able reverently to manifest whatever praise, whatever honor, whatever solemn
> magnificence of ornamentation or illumination we can, just as we do on feasts of
> the Lord.[40]

The veneration of the Baptist at the Lateran complex went back at least to the pontificate of Pope Hilarus (461-68). In thanksgiving for his deliverance from danger at the "robber council" of Ephesus before becoming pope, he had built onto the Lateran baptistery two chapels, one dedicated

[36] *Descriptio* 10; Valentini-Zucchetti, 3:346-47. John attributed the transfer to an outrage committed by certain "schismatics." Adinolfi believed that it might have been connected with the disputed papal election of 1130; see Pasquale Adinolfi, *Laterano e Via maggiore: Saggio della topografia di Roma nell'età di mezzo* (Rome: Tipografia Tiberina, 1857), 16.

[37] Pope John IV was a native of Dalmatia and his own father's name was Venantius. On the history of the baptistery and annexed structures see Giovanni Giovenale, *Il Battistero Lateranense nelle recenti indagini della Pontificia Commissione di Archeologia Sacra*, Studi di Antichità Cristiana, 1 (Rome: Pontificio Istituto di Archeologia Sacra, 1929). Some of his conclusions were questioned by G. Pellicioni, "Le nuove scoperte sulle origini del battistero Lateranense," *Atti della Pontificia Accademia Romana di Archeologia: Memorie*, 12, no. 1 (1973), and defended in turn by Margherita Cecchelli, "Laterano," in *San Giovanni in Laterano*, ed. Carlo Pietrangeli (Florence: Nardini, 1990), 39-60.

[38] John notes that the bodies of the two saints were "discovered" by Anastasius IV (1153-54), and that the pope dedicated an altar to them, "astantibus nobis omnibus." *Descriptio* 11; Valentini-Zucchetti, 3:353.

[39] In both cases the Vigils, like the usual night office of Matins, had nine psalms and nine lessons. The list of churches appended to the guide-book entitled "De locis sanctis martyrum" (after 755) calls the Lateran "basilica Constantiniana quae et Salvatoris; ipsa quoque et sancti Iohannes dicitur" (170-71). See *Itineraria et alia geographica*, ed. Frater Glorie, Corpus christianorum: Series latina, 175 (Turnhout: Brepols, 1965), 321. On the observance of the feasts of the Dedication and St. John the Baptist, see Pierre Jounel, *Le Culte des saints dans les basiliques du Latran et du Vatican au douzième siècle*, Collection de l'École Française de Rome, 26 (Rome: École Française de Rome, 1977), 305-07 and 377-79, respectively.

[40] "Et si pro sui eccelentia beatus Iohannes ab omnibus sollempniter veneratur, multo magis nobis convenit, ut quidquid laudis, quidquid honoris, quidquid etiam sollepmnis apparatus tam in ornamentis quam in luminaribus ecclesie possumus, sicut in sollempnitatibus domini, reverenter eiusdem nativitati exhibeamus." OL 273; ed. Fischer, 138.

to John the Evangelist (see fig. 2.2, no. 3) and the other to John the Baptist (see fig. 2.2, no. 2).[41] The dedication (John) of these two chapels was soon applied to the Lateran basilica itself, and the basilical monastery of St. Pancratius received an additional dedication to the two saints. John the Baptist eventually took precedence because of the Constantinian baptistery attached to the church and the basilica's ownership of reputed Johannine relics. It has been pointed out that the titles affixed to the sermons delivered by Gregory the Great (590-604) indicate that he preached early in his pontificate "in basilica beati Iohannis" and "in basilica sancti Iohannis Baptistae."[42] The *Liber pontificalis*, however, avoided the Johannine title until the tenth century, preferring the more ancient epithets "Constantiniana" and "Salvatoris."

A Roman liturgical observance of the Nativity of John the Baptist is first attested in a collection of fifth- and sixth-century Mass booklets (*libelli*) from the Lateran archives known as the Sacramentary of Verona. This sacramentary contains five formularies for John the Baptist, one of them marked "ad fontes," presumably for a Mass celebrated within the baptistery itself or in one of the contiguous chapels.[43] Despite the fact that the commemoration of the Baptist's birth had a history of many centuries at the pope's cathedral, one cannot assume that Prior Bernard's *ordo* represents the faithful preservation of ancient custom. The description of the feast typifies the kind of information customarily furnished by the *Ordo lateranensis*, but the quantity of detail is far greater than usual. The course of the ceremony, the various locales in which it was carried out, and the roles of the participants can be followed exceptionally well, even though very few of the chant pieces are mentioned by name.

As the hour for Vespers approached, the pope, cardinals, and members of the curia, already vested in copes (in the case of bishops and deacons) or chasubles (for priests), descended from the Lateran palace on the north side of the basilica. They entered directly through the door connecting the palace with the north aisle of the basilica (see fig. 2.1, E). The pope and his entourage proceeded to the bronze chancel barrier that screened the altar end of the main choir and, surrounded by his deacons, the pope stood on a carpet placed to the right of the main altar (see fig. 2.1, no. 1).[44] (The right/left nomenclature of the *ordo* will be retained, but the reader must reverse these directions

[41] *Liber pontificalis*, ed. Duchesne, 1:242-48; Raymond Davis, transl., *The Book of the Popes (Liber pontificalis)*, Translated Texts for Historians: Latin Series, 5 (Liverpool: Liverpool University Press, 1989), 38-41. On Hilary's building campaigns see Hartmann Grisar, *The History of Rome and the Popes in the Middle Ages*, transl. Luigi Cappadelta, 3 vols. (St. Louis and London: Herder-Kegan Paul, 1911-12), 2:79-83. When Constantine founded the baptistery at the Lateran, he included in his lavish donations a nearly life-size silver statue of the Baptist weighing 125 pounds (*Liber pontificalis*, ed. Duchesne, 1:174). On the various feasts of the precursor see Karl Adam Heinrich Kellner, *Heortologie oder die geschichtliche Entwicklung des Kirchenjahres und der Heiligenfeste von den ältesten Zeiten bis zur Gegenwart*, 3rd ed. (Freiburg im Breisgau: Herder, 1911), 165-69. The Lateran observance is discussed in Jounel, 247-48.

[42] Herman Geertman, *More Veterum: Il liber pontificalis e gli edifici ecclesiastici di Roma nella tarda antichità e nell'alto medio evo*, Archeologica Traiectina, 10 (Groningen: Tjeenk Willink, 1975), 135. Sermons 16, 22, 25-26, 39; Patrologia latina 76:1134, 1174, 1188, 1197, 1294. Not all manuscripts of the sermons include reference to the Johannine dedication of the church.

[43] Cunibert Mohlberg, Leo Eizenhöfer, Peter Siffrin, eds., *Sacramentarium veronense (Cod. Bibl. Capit. Veron. LXXXV [80])*, Rerum Ecclesiasticarum Documenta, series maior: fontes 1 (Rome: Herder, 1956), nos. 232-56. The Gregorian Sacramentary contains a vesper prayer "ad fontes" for the feast of John the Evangelist (no. 71) and a prayer with the same rubric, followed by "aliae orationes" (nos. 578-82) for John the Baptist. See Jean Deshusses, ed., *Le Sacramentaire grégorien: Ses Principales formes d'après les plus anciens manuscrits*, 3 vols., Spicilegium Friburgense, 16, 24, 28 (Freiburg: Éditions Universitaires Fribourg Suisse, 1988-92), 1:109, 240-42.

[44] "Domnus papa venit ad cancellum ereum quod in capite maioris chori est, a dextra scilicet maioris alta<ris> et ibi stat super tapetium, diaconis ei circumstantibus"—OL 273; ed. Fischer, 139. More than a century later, a Syrian visitor witnessed a similar scene; see Anton Baumstark, "Die österliche Papstliturgie des Jahres 1288 nach dem Bericht eines syrischen Augenzeuges," *Ephemerides liturgicae* 62 (1948): 185-86.

when looking at fig. 2.1: "left" is north and "right" is south.) The cardinal bishops, wearing miters and carrying pastoral staffs, passed through another bronze gate and stood to the left (i.e., the onlooker's right) of the altar.

Prior Bernard does not mention in his description the four monumental columns of bronze that stood in the nave at the triumphal arch just before the transept (see fig. 2.1, no. 5). These "grete pileres of brasse" (as they were called by a medieval English pilgrim) were all that remained of a lavish Constantinian donation: an impressive fastigium, once crowned by a triangular, silver-plated attic storey adorned with statues of Christ and the twelve apostles.[45] Plundered by the soldiers of Alaric (410) but replaced by the emperor Valentinian III (425-55), it probably fell prey to the Vandals in 455. In the twelfth century, surmounted by an architrave upon which stood an image of Christ, the columns formed part of the chancel barrier. Even in the late sixteenth century Andrea Palladio called them the "four pillars of the bronze railing."[46] For Vespers the cardinal priests occupied places on the left side of the main choir in the center of the nave (see fig. 2.1, b) along with the Lateran canons. Although Prior Bernard does not mention it, one can assume from a later passage about Vigils in the baptistery that the other members of the Curia and the Schola Cantorum sat on the right side of the choir.

When all had taken their places the pope, turning towards the altar, began Vespers with the usual versicles. He then turned to face the choir, and the prior pre-intoned for him the first antiphon ("Ipse preibit"). One of the Lateran cantors pre-intoned the next antiphon, either for one of the bishops at the altar or for one of the cardinal priests in the choir. The other antiphons and psalms were treated in like manner. As on all solemn feasts at the Lateran, the antiphons were sung in their entirety both before and after the psalm.[47] Prior Bernard noted that to enhance the solemnity of the occasion the antiphons (and presumably the psalms as well) were sung "tractim et spatiose," a phrase used elsewhere in the *ordo* to describe the "Gloria in excelsis" of the Easter Vigil (OL 163), singing during the processions on Easter day (OL 175), chants on the feast of the Purification (OL 259), and the Dedication of the Lateran (OL 301).

Bernard lists all the antiphons and psalms of Vespers, noting that the verse "Fuit homo missus a deo," was sung by "duo ex fratribus in medium [*sic*] chori." The prior pre-intoned the Magnificat antiphon ("Ingresso Zacharia") for the pope, who incensed the altar during the singing of the gospel canticle. Afterwards, one of the Lateran bishops incensed the cardinals and clergy in attendance. The hebdomadary bishop (i.e., the bishop assigned to preside over the liturgy at the Lateran for the

---

[45] The quotation is from John Capgrave, *Ye Solace of Pilgrims: A Description of Rome, circa A.D. 1450*, ed. C. A. Mills (London: Frowde, 1911), 73. See Sible de Blaauw, *Cultus et decor: Liturgia e architettura nella Roma tardoantica e medievale*, 2 vols., Studi e Testi, 355-56 (Vatican City: Biblioteca Apostolica Vaticana, 1994), 1:117-27, 249-52, and his proposed reconstruction of the fastigium (fig. 3). For another hypothetical reconstruction see Ursula Nilgen, "Das Fastigium in der Basilica Constantiniana und vier Bronzesäulen des Laterans," *Römische Quartalschrift für christliche Altertumskunde und Kirchengeschichte* 72 (1977): 1-77. It is believed that the columns still exist, incorporated in the altar of the Sacrament erected in the left transept of the basilica by Clement VIII (1592-1605).

[46] Andrea Palladio, *The Churches of Rome*, transl. and ed. Eunice D. Baker, Medieval and Renaissance Texts and Studies, 72 (Binghamton: State University of New York, 1991), 77. The same John, the deacon who revised the *Descriptio lateranensis ecclesiae*, wrote to Vitellio, cardinal deacon of SS. Sergio e Bacco, about a vision in which a dove perched on the head of the statue of the Savior, "que est in supremo supra columnas ereas," as quoted in André Wilmart, "Nouvelles de Rome au temps d'Alexandre III (1170)," *Revue bénédictine* 45 (1933): 78.

[47] By the twelfth century it had become customary to abbreviate the antiphon before the psalm to merely the incipit. On the richer traditions of the Vatican, as attested by the antiphoner, Archivio di San Pietro, B 79, see Edward Nowacki, "The Performance of Office Antiphons in Twelfth-Century Rome," *Cantus Planus: Papers Read at the Third Meeting—Tihany, Hungary, 19-24 September 1988* (Budapest: Hungarian Academy of Sciences, Institute for Musicology, 1990), 79-91.

week) presented the sacramentary to the pope for the prayer of the day.[48] After the pope had imparted his blessing, the Lateran community went in procession to the baptistery ("ad fontes") singing the responsory "Precursor domini." In the baptistery the canons celebrated Vespers for a second time ("breviter," according to Bernard) with the same antiphons and psalms, except for the Magnificat antiphon, "Pro eo quod non credidisti." After this Vespers had been concluded, all of the cardinals who would remain to celebrate the night office retired with the Greek monks to the old chapter house in the cloister (see fig. 2.1, B) to enjoy some wine from the bishops' cellar ("de parte episcoporum potum").[49] Meanwhile, the canons partook of a collation, read in chapter, and sang compline in their private oratory of San Pancrazio (see fig. 2.1, C). During this time, the sacristans prepared candles, service books, and seating arrangements in the baptistery for Vigils.

Prior Bernard now interrupts his description of the course of events to mention a special circumstance: certain singers ("strenuos V vel VI cantores") from outside the Lateran community had to be hired for the offices of Vigils and Matins, though they were apparently needed neither for Vespers nor for Mass. Bernard's justification for this exceptional procedure, that the Lateran canons "Romanorum more cantare nesciunt," has been construed as an indication that the canons, who came from outside Rome, did not know Old Roman chant, still presumably the repertory of the Schola Cantorum and the papal court. Indeed, this could be true, but I have argued elsewhere that the problem in this instance might have had less to do with different chant repertories and more to do with different versions of the Psalter.[50] The native Romans in the curia would have memorized the "Roman" Psalter while the non-Roman canons of the Lateran ("ex diversis terrarum partibus," as Bernard proudly noted) might have been familiar with the more common "Gallican" Psalter version.

No assistance would have been necessary at Vespers in the basilica, for the canons were joined on their side of the choir by the Roman cardinal priests, for whom the Roman Psalter was the familiar text. Since not all of the cardinals remained for Vigils and Matins, the canons had to hire a few local Roman singers to respond to the Curia and Schola Cantorum for the alternation of psalm verses during the night offices. Bernard mentions that two canons (if this is what "duo ex nostris" implies) joined members of the Schola in chanting the verses of the invitatory psalm. This text would have presented no problem, since it was the sole survival of the Roman Psalter preserved in the medieval liturgy, and known even to clerics who chanted the "Gallican" Psalter. It is highly significant that on the first Sunday of Lent and on Palm Sunday the Lateran canons alternated with singers of the Schola Cantorum in singing verses of the tracts—a circumstance difficult to explain if they did not share the same chant repertory. If the Lateran canons intended to lay claim to the basilica that prided itself in being the repository of ancient traditions as "mater et caput" of all the churches of Christendom,

---

[48] According to the custom of the Lateran, only the pope himself or one of the Lateran bishops could say the proper prayer of the day. If neither was present, the "Pater noster" was substituted. OL 3; ed. Fischer, 1-2. This practice is also noted in the *Descriptio lateranensis ecclesiae* 8; Valentini-Zucchetti, 3:343.

[49] The *Descriptio lateranensis ecclesiae* provides for "et vinum ad potum ante vigiliam omnibus clericis, et grecis et latinis." *Descriptio* 19; Valentini-Zucchetti, 3:372. On the no longer extant cloister structures of this period consult Sible de Blaauw, "A Medieval Portico at San Giovanni in Laterano: The Basilica and Its Ancient Conventual Building," *Papers of the British School at Rome* 58 (1990): 299-316. Bernard explains the presence of the Greek monks by reference to "reverentiam et dignitatem huius sancte Lateranensis ecclesie que patriarchium et prima sedes apostolici est et omnium ecclesiarum caput et magistra" (OL 275; ed. Fischer, 140). The "caput et magistra" title was jealously defended for centuries by the Lateran clergy, though it had little practical meaning.

[50] OL 274; ed. Fischer, 140. See my "Roman Singers of the Later Middle Ages," *Cantus Planus: Papers Read at the Sixth Meeting—Eger, Hungary, September 1993*, 2 vols. (Budapest: Hungarian Academy of Sciences, Institute for Musicology, 1995), 1:45-64.

they would need to "romanize" themselves thoroughly, a process that involved learning the local version of the Psalter. A manuscript containing a Roman Psalter, canticles in an Old Latin version, litanies, a *computus*, and calendar has been identified as in use at the Lateran about the beginning of the thirteenth century.[51] Unfortunately, nothing in the text of the *Ordo lateranensis* provides incontrovertible proof on this matter.

The observance of the feast continued with Vigils. The Latin clergy proceeded to the baptistery (see fig. 2.2, B) by the light of candles and torches. Meanwhile, the Greek monks entered the basilica, probably through one of the doors in the ambulatory that encircled the medieval apse until its demolition in the late nineteenth century. They celebrated Vigils in the canons' choir on the south side of the nave (see fig. 2.1, c), for which candles and incense were provided by the chapter. The Lateran canons, members of the Curia, and the Schola Cantorum entered the baptistery through the narthex (see fig. 2.2, no. 5) and took up their places in front of the small chapel of St. John the Baptist (see fig. 2.2, no. 2). The cardinal priests, Lateran canons, and the singers hired by the canons sat to the left of the door leading to the chapel, while the deacons and subdeacons of the Curia stood with the Schola on the right side.

As usual at Roman Vigils, there was no invitatory, nor does the *Ordo lateranensis* mention any hymns. Whenever the court participated in a festal office at one of the principal basilicas, the canons of the church (or monks in the case of St. Paul's) had responsibility for the first three lessons and responsories of Vigils and Matins. The prior himself, or a designated priest, read the first lesson; the second was read by one of the canons with the rank or deacon; the third was assigned to a canon sub-deacon. The *Ordo lateranensis* indicates that either the canons or the hired singers performed the responsories: an indication that the latter were not needed because of any problems with the chant repertory.[52] The remaining six lessons of Vigils (and the following Matins) were read by members of the Curia, and the [five] responsories associated with them were sung by the Schola Cantorum. The first eight lessons were drawn from patristic sermons about John the Baptist, while the ninth was a reading from Ambrose's homily on the gospel text "Elisabeth impletum est tempus pariendi." Unfortunately, Bernard does not list the antiphons, psalms, and responsories proper to the Vigil, as he had done for Vespers. He states only that "the antiphons and responsories are repeated," probably an indication that the responds were repeated in the Roman fashion, *a capite* after the verse or the "Gloria patri."

During each lesson (or more likely between, as in the Lucca *ordo*) the altar was incensed by the bishops and cardinals, who then honored the clergy present with incense. The singers of the responsories received a stipend (18 *papienses denarios*) from the senior cardinal deacon. After Vigils had been completed, the bells were rung while all proceeded to the main choir of the basilica (see fig. 2.1, b) for Matins (Nocturns). The Greek monks then retired to the baptistry for their own Matins, sung "sollempniter secundum morem suum."

At Matins all of the Latin participants took the same places in choir as they had for Vespers: the cardinal priests and Lateran canons on the left, the curia with the Schola Cantorum on the right. Matins began in the usual way with the invitatory, but again without a hymn. As at Vespers, the antiphons were sung in their entirety before and after the psalm. Other than mentioning the invitatory antiphon and the verses that precede the readings in each of the nocturns (1. "Fuit homo," 2. "Inter natos mulierum," 3. "Elisabeth Zacharie"), Bernard offers no details about this office. The reading of the lessons was subject to the same assignment as at Vigils.

---

[51] Vaticanus latinus 4406, from Lucca. See Garrison, 12-32.

[52] "Responsoria cantantur vel ab eisdem canonicis vel a cantoribus, si eis iniunctum fuerit." OL 274; ed. Fischer, 140.

Lauds receives merely a summary treatment. Bernard prescribes the antiphon series beginning with "Elisabeth [Zacharie]." He also specifies the verse preceding the Benedictus ("Iste puer") and the antiphon for this canticle ("Apertum est os Zacharie"). The conventual Mass with the introit "Iustus ut palma" was sung in the baptistery, but the principal Mass of the day was celebrated in the basilica by the pope with the bishops, cardinals, Schola Cantorum, and the entire Curia in attendance.[53] Although the Lateran canons were present in their own choir, they took no part in the ceremonies, but said Terce and Sext quietly to themselves ("privatim inter nos"). For the little hours of Terce, Sext, and None, Bernard lists: 1) the brief chapter reading with alternatives for Sext and None, 2) the first words of the short responsory, and 3) the versicle. On the feast itself the canons again sang two Vespers, one in the main choir of the basilica, the other in the baptistery, both with the same antiphons, the "Ipse preibit" series with the Magnificat antiphon "Puer qui natus est nobis." Mass and Vespers were celebrated in the baptistery every day during the octave.

Even from the fragmentary description of this office in *Ordo lateranensis*, it is clear that the order of the chant incipits does not correspond with that found in either of the two extant Old Roman antiphoners. The largest block of antiphons cited by Prior Bernard, the proper antiphons for Vespers, are lacking in both the Old Roman antiphoners.[54] *Ordo lateranensis* lists "Elisabeth et cetere" for lauds, but the antiphon series for this office in the Old Roman antiphoners begins with the antiphon "Innuebant patri eius." (The antiphon "Elisabeth Zacharie" occupies second place.) While the Old Roman antiphoners prescribe the antiphon "Ipse precedet" for the gospel canticle at lauds, Bernard calls for "Apertum est os Zacherie." The conclusion is inevitable that the canons did not sing from an antiphoner containing chants of the Old Roman repertory. Mostly non-Romans, they were familiar with Gregorian chant.

Since the canons collaborated musically with the Curia on other occasions, even acting as cantors by ceremonially pre-intoning chants for the pope and higher clergy, one might presume that the papal court, whose members were not by any means exclusively Roman, had also by the mid-twelfth century adopted the Gregorian repertory. Beginning in the late eleventh century, the papal court traveled frequently outside Rome to avoid the turbulence caused in the city by the emperor, the nobility, or the native population.[55] Antipopes contested the rights of canonically-elected popes within the city. For the papal court to have preserved Old Roman chant—still an oral tradition for most of the eleventh century—under such circumstances would have been exceedingly difficult. Wherever new singers were recruited for the papal chapel outside of Rome, they would have been familiar only with Gregorian chant.

Certain aspects of the canonical reform at the Lateran may shed further light on this question. Prior Bernard's *ordo* attested to the success of a long campaign to renew canonical life at the Lateran basilica. At the Lateran synod of 1059, Hildebrand, then archdeacon of the Roman church, denounced in harsh, sarcastic, and in some respects unfair, terms the mode of life followed by most of the clergy who lived according to the then-prevailing norms of the canonical life, based on the disciplinary

---

[53] This Mass was distinguished by a large decorated initial (now removed) in the papal sacramentary, Vaticanus latinus 12989, f. 106v (ca. 1200). The manuscript also contains a prayer "Ad vesperas" (f. 107).

[54] Both the *Ordo lateranensis* and the B 79 antiphoner of St. Peter's call for the Magnificat antiphon "Ingresso Zacharia." *Ordo lateranensis* does not mention the responsory "Hic [est] precursor." The absence or presence of "est" would serve as an indicator of the Old Roman ("Hic precursor") or Gregorian ("Hic est precursor") repertories. Louis Brou, "Un Passage de Tertullien conservé dans un répons pour la fête de St. Jean-Baptiste," *Ephemerides liturgicae* 52 (1938): 237-57.

[55] Pope Lucius II, mentioned earlier in reference to the authorship of the *Ordo lateranensis*, died from wounds received as he was leading papal troops in an attack against the stronghold of the Roman commune on the Capitoline hill.

legislation confirmed by the Council of Aix-la-Chapelle (816).[56] This fiery and inflexible prophet of reform, the future Pope Gregory VII, demanded that canons embrace the *vita communis et apostolica* that entailed the complete renunciation of private property, strict observance of chastity, and a modest, even ascetic, way of community life.[57] Neither the undivided support of Pope Nicholas II (1058-61), nor the fact that Hildebrand soon held the papal office himself (1073-85), nor the election of the reform-minded Urban II (1088-99) as his successor, was successful in imposing on the canons who served the cathedral of the bishop of Rome the reform principles that had begun to make headway in other parts of Italy, as well as in Germany and France.

The earliest documented attempts to reform canonical life at the Lateran date from the pontificate of Alexander II (1061-73), previously bishop of Lucca, who summoned the canons of San Frediano from his former episcopal see.[58] He assigned to them the church of Santa Maria Nova on the Roman forum. This church passed to the Lateran canons in 1119, an indication of the progress of the reform process there.[59] The details of the reform that transformed the Lateran monastery of San Pancrazio at the southwest corner of the basilica into a canonry remain obscure. It is known that Pope Paschal II (1099-1118), a protégé of Gregory VII, renewed efforts to reform canonical life at the Lateran. He championed the clerical common life there by confirming the presence of the canons of San Frediano at the cathedral of Rome. Not until the pontificate of Gelasius II (1118-19), however, were the reform canons definitively installed.

Why it required more than a half century for strong-minded popes to reform the canons at their own cathedral remains a mystery. It would not be unreasonable to surmise, however, that the canons of so eminent a Roman church were chosen from the aristocratic families of the city and that their selection was not exclusively in the hands of the bishop. Members of Rome's powerful families did not join the ranks of the clergy to live like monks, to renounce their rights to wealth and property, or

---

[56] Evidence of these norms at Rome is the canonical miscellany (Vaticanus latinus 1351), copied between 1059 and 1063, containing the Carolinigian canonical legislation. Hildebrand proposed, however, a Roman profession formula "qua usque nunc in hac Romana urbe clerici, instar primitivae ecclesiae, communiter victuri, se ipsos obligare sunt soliti," as quoted in Ferminio Poggiaspalla, *Le vita commune del clero dalle origini alla riforma gregoriana*, Uomini e dottrine, 14 (Rome: Edizioni di Storia e Letteratura, 1963), 161.

[57] On Gregory's initiative and subsequent developments, see Germain Morin, "Règlements inédits du pape Saint Grégoire VII pour les chanoines réguliers," *Revue bénédictine* 18 (1901): 177-83; Georg Denzler, "Die Kanonikerbewegung und die Gregorianische Reform im 11. Jahrhundert," *Studi gregoriani* 9 (1972): 225-37; Michele Maccarrone, "I papi del secolo XII e la vita comune e regolare del clero," *Romana ecclesia cathedra Petri*, 2 vols., Italia Sacra, 47-48 (Rome: Herder, 1991), 2:757-819, reprinted from *La vita commune del clero nei secoli XI e XII*, Atti della Settimana di studio: Mendola, settembre 1959, 2 vols. (Milan: Società Editrice Vita e Pensiero, 1962). For a survey of the situation in Rome see the chapter "The Religious Life of Canons in Medieval Rome" in Joan Barclay Lloyd, *The Medieval Church and Canonry of S. Clemente in Rome*, San Clemente Miscellany, 3 (Rome: San Clemente, 1989), 203-25.

[58] According to John the deacon's revision of *Descriptio lateranensis ecclesiae*, Alexander II "renovavit communem regularium canonicorum vitam in ipsa." *Descriptio* 10; Valentini-Zucchetti, 3:349. The original document is lost, but Anastasius IV referred to it in two letters (30 December 1153 and 19 May 1154), confirming and enlarging the possession of the Lateran canons. See also Tilman Schmidt, "Die Kanonikerreform in Rom und Papst Alexander II (1061-1073)," *Studi gregoriani* 9 (1972): 199-221; Carl Egger, "Canonici regolari della Congregazione del SS. Salvatore Lateranense," *Dizionario degli istituti di perfezione*, 2:101-07. Many of the important documents are cited in Sible de Blaauw, *Cultus et decor*, 1:203ff.

[59] Licia Marti, "Santa Francesca Romana (Santa Maria Nuova)," in *Rome sacra: Guida alle chiese della città eterna, terzo itinerario* (Rome: Elio de Rosa, 1995), 41. When he restored the monastery, Gregory III (731-41) assigned the monks the task of observing "cotidie sacra officia laudis divine," according to the model of St. Peter's. *Liber pontificalis*, ed. Duchesne, 1:419. (This was probably not an entirely new assignment for a monastery that dated back at least to the late sixth century.) On San Pancrazio see Guy Ferrari, *Early Roman Monasteries: Notes for the History of the Monasteries and Convents at Rome from the V through the X Century*, Studi di Antichità Cristiana, 23 (Vatican City: Pontificio Istituto di Archeologia Sacra, 1957), 243-53, and Sible de Blaauw, "A Medieval Portico at San Giovanni in Laterano."

to surrender their personal freedom.[60] Even the determination of a series of reforming popes in the latter part of the eleventh century could not eject them. By the time Prior Bernard composed his *ordo* the situation had changed.[61] The reformed Lateran canons were no longer exclusively Romans, but had come "ex diversis terrarum partibus . . . ad serviendum deo." The *Ordo officiorum lateranensis* provided the blueprint for an ascetic life devoted to prayer and silence, to the chanting of the canonical office, to the observance of supplementary devotions, and to care for the poor.

A visitor who came to Rome twice in the 1120s, Gerhoch of Reichersberg (1093-1169), commented approvingly on the fervor of the reformed Lateran canons. Gerhoch stood at the beginning of a career which was to make him one of the most fearless critics of abuses in the Church. The halfway measures of the recently concluded Concordat of Worms (1122), that attempted to resolve the investiture crisis, were to him completely insufficient, and he regarded clerical reform—particularly the imposition of the common life as the norm for the secular clergy—the most urgent challenge facing the pope and bishops. He presented his unyielding views on both topics in *Opusculum de edificio dei*. Gerhoch held up the reformed Lateran canons as exemplary models in the observance of the common life, and he contrasted their demeanor with the disorderly behavior of their worldly predecessors.[62] Elaborating on the gospel's reference to Jesus as a "faber" (craftsman), Gerhoch adopted a prophetic pose:

Faber iste fabricat Romae in Lateranensi patriarchio, ubi per gratiam ipsius iam reflorescit vita canonica, tanto citius omnem scoriam depositura, quanto illi tanquam in medio Babylonis positae fornax tribulationis a quibusdam palatinis, non Petri discipulis, sed regis Nabuchodonosor ministris, iugiter accendetur. In qua tamen ipse dominus apostolicus, velut quidam angelus, consolabitur tribulatos; ut, dum in medio tribulationis ipsum habeant suas angustias revelantem, videantur sentire in medio fornacis quasi ventum roris flantem. De ipsis vero illius fornacis incensoribus erit aliquis ita concremandus, ut autem cum Saulo conversus ecclesiam defendat, aut cum Saulo irrevocabiliter perversus in infernum descendat. Pueros autem Christi, veros videlicet canonicos, omnino non tanget ignis, neque contristabit, nec quidquam molestiae inferet; imo tantum utilitatis conferet, ut per hunc ignem vinculis peccatorum consumptis libere incedant, et quasi ex uno ore in medio fornacis deum benedicant.

Fuit enim ante aliquot annos ecclesia illa talibus clericis exposita, qui non canerent quasi ex uno ore, sed quasi ex ore diverso ac multum dissono; tum propter vocis incon- cinnos organismos theatralibus quibusdam modulis variatos;

This craftsman labored at Rome in the Lateran patriarchium where, through his grace, the canonical life now flourishes, having as quickly thrown off its slag as did those in the midst of the Babylonian furnace of suffering [Daniel 3], kindled constantly by some palace retainers, not disciples of Peter but ministers of King Nebuchadnezzar. Indeed, in this furnace the apostolic lord himself, like an angel, will console those in distress, so that, even in the midst of tribulation they might have him revealing his narrow pathways, [and] they might seem to feel something like a dewy breeze in the midst of the furnace. Truly, of those lighting that furnace there will be someone so blistered that, either having repented with Saul, he will defend the church or in his malice will with Saul descend into hell. The fire will not touch the servants of Christ, that is, true canons, at all, nor sadden them, nor bring them any harm, but rather confer such benefit that, the chains of sins having been consumed by this fire, they might move freely and bless God with one voice in the midst of the furnace.

A few years ago that church was abandoned to the sort of clerics who did not sing with one voice, but with a conflicting and dissonant voice, in part due to uncouth singing em- bellished with theatrical flourishes, in part due to disordered

---

[60] Ironically, in 1299 Boniface VIII supplanted the canons of San Frediano with secular Roman canons who had ties to urban aristocratic families, because it was thought that these canons would be more capable of defending the property rights of the basilica.

[61] Bernard forges links with the liturgical reforms of Gregory VII by quoting three times a passage from Gregory's decretal on the office, *In die resurrectionis* (OL 171, 221, 225; ed. Fischer, 77, 109, 114). See also Morin, "Règlements inédits du pape Saint Grégoire VII."

[62] *Opusculum de aedificio dei*; Patrologia latina 194:1187-1336. Peter Classen, *Gerhoch von Reichersberg: Eine Biographie* (Wiesbaden: Steiner, 1960). The first edition dates from 1128/29, but the work is preserved only in its second edition of 1238 (Classen, 407). Gerhoch knew Cardinal Guido of Castello, dedicatee of *Liber politicus*, and accompanied him on a reform trip to Bohemia in 1141. See Erich Meuthen, *Kirche und Heilsgeschichte bei Gerhoh von Reichersberg*, Studien und Texte zur Geistesgeschichte des Mittelalters, 6 (Leiden and Cologne: E. J. Brill, 1959), 49.

variatos; tum propter mores incompositos et magna discre-
pantia contra invicem divisos. Nunc autem, deo gratias,
psallitur et canitur in ecclesia illa quasi ex uno ore, tam in
vocis matura et consona modulatione, quam in morum sancta
iuxta claustralem disciplinam compositione, in qua (si quid
adhuc addi opportet) qui coepit, ipse perficiet. Gaudeat ergo
ecclesia Sancti Fridiani Lucensis, quae velut hortus irriguus,
Romanas mensas de suis locupletat fructibus; dum inde
quantuluscunque canonicorum numerus, quasi parvum
sinapis granum in Romanam ecclesiam quasi in mortario
conterendum mittitur, ut odor notitiae Christi per hoc longe
lateque spargatur, quando in ipso mundi capite reflorescit
Ordo communis vitae.

behavior and the great discord that divided them from one
another. Now, however, thanks be to God, in that church
they chant the psalms and sing with one voice, as much in
mature and harmonious melody, as in a holy blending of
virtues according to claustral discipline, which (if anything
needs be added), he will perfect what he has initiated. Therefore let the church of S. Frediano of Lucca rejoice; like a
fertile garden it enriched Roman tables with its produce,
for from thence was sent to the Roman church a tiny number
of canons, like a small mustard seed to be ground in the
mortar, so that the fragrance of the knowledge of Christ
might thus be disseminated far and wide, when in this "caput
mundi" the order of the common life flourishes once again.

Gerhoch's passion suggests that he had some knowledge of the situation on which he reported, though the unruly canons might have been already ejected before his first visit to Rome in 1126. While a few allusions to individuals may be tentatively identified (the "craftsman" Honorius II and perhaps the emperor Henry V), others (the "concremandus," and "Saul") are not so clear. The pope destined to assume the role of the angel in the fiery furnace might be the reform pope Innocent II (1130-43), former cardinal deacon of the Roman church of S. Angelo in Pescheria. (This reference would thus be an addition to the second edition of the *Opusculum*.) All of the allusions symbolize in some way the conflicts that plagued the reform of canonical life at the Lateran.

Gerhoch's observations about disunity in the singing can, of course, be interpreted in more than one way—and such was possibly their author's intent. His complaints about discord and theatrical singing join a long line of similar criticisms leveled by church reformers at clerics or monks whose disedifying behavior drew their condemnation. One plausible reason for the existence of singing "quasi ex ore diverso ac multum dissono" might have been the introduction of a new and different chant repertory. The unreformed Lateran canons of the early part of the century, Romans reluctant to give up their privileges, would have attempted to remain entrenched as long as possible. As native Romans, they sang—even if badly—Old Roman chant. The canons summoned from Lucca and elsewhere would have known only Gregorian chant. Until the transition could be completed and the reform party strengthened with the arrival of more "foreign" canons, discord in singing the Office—a symbol of deeper spiritual problems in the Lateran community—would have been inevitable.

Bernard, for his part, does not mention any modification of the chant repertory; the replacement of the Old Roman repertory by Gregorian chant may have taken place before he arrived at the basilica. Nevertheless, he was very interested in claiming that his own *ordo* preserved traditional practices "secundum antiquorum patrum statuta et secundum prefate ecclesie consuetudinem" (OL 1), and occasionally he contrasted uniquely Roman or Lateran customs with those observed else-where. Bernard's claim to earlier Roman authority would not stand close examination, to be sure, though some scholars have seen support for it in a nearly contemporary remark of Peter Abelard. He asserted that "not even the city [Rome] itself adheres to the ancient custom of the Roman see, but only the Lateran church, which is the mother [of all the churches], retains the ancient Office. None of her daughters follow her in this respect, not even the church of the Roman *palatium*."[63] Abelard was

---

[63] "Antiquam certe Romanae sedis consuetudinem nec ipsa civitas tenet, sed sola ecclesia Lateranensis, quae est mater omnium, antiquum tenet officium, nulla filiarum suarum in hoc eam sequente, nec ipsa etiam Romani palatii basilica." Epistola 10 (Patrologia latina 178:340), as quoted in Bruno Stäblein, *Die Gesänge des altrömischen Graduale Vat. lat. 5319*, Monumenta monodica medii aevi, 2 (Kassel: Bärenreiter, 1970), 142. Abelard's statement is placed in the context of "la grande époque du mythe de l'Église du Latran 'mater omnium'" in Pierre-Marie Gy, "L'Unification liturgique de l'occident et la liturgie de la curie romaine," *Revue des sciences philosophiques et théologiques* 59 (1975): 601-12.

trying to prove to an unfriendly Bernard of Clairvaux that liturgical diversity should be tolerated within the unity of faith, and he asserted that the liturgical customs of the mother church of Christendom were not observed in the pope's own chapel. Abelard seems to have accepted uncritically the perspective of the Lateran canons basking in the glory of an ancient Constantinian foundation. The Vatican basilica had been, in fact, more faithful to the ancient urban liturgy than the Lateran.[64]

The last witness to Roman double offices was a northerner, Ralph of Tongres (de Rivo), whose *De canonum observantia* dates from about 1397. He admired what he knew of older Roman liturgical practices, a devotion that won for him the title of "der letzte Vertreter der altrömischen Liturgie" from the modern editor of his treatise.[65] Ralph cited the practice of clerics he called "Romani," who celebrated a *vigilia* of 3 psalms with antiphons, 3 lessons and responsories, the usual versicles, and the "Pater noster." He also mentioned that certain "antiqua antiphonaria Romana" had Vigil offices of nine lessons for the feast of Sts. Peter and Paul and for Christmas.[66] While these double offices were indeed a venerable Roman tradition, the Lateran canons stood only on the periphery of that tradition. Instead of following authentic Roman custom, they reinterpreted the "major Vespers" of Lucca in a Roman context as "Vigils," now deprived of their original function of protecting the integrity of the *psalterium per hebdomadam*, and they thus created extra opportunities for commemorating the most important feasts of the Kalendar.

As the surviving Old Roman graduals and antiphoners attest, some Roman churches zealously guarded their ancient musical and liturgical traditions, even as others went over to the nearly universal musical language of the medieval western church, Gregorian chant. The Lateran double offices, particularly that for John the Baptist in which the papal court collaborated, maintained a tradition that antedated even Amalar's time, but the twelfth-century canons clothed it with new music and a contemporary spirituality. Little attention has heretofore been focused on the gradual replacement of the Old Roman chant repertory by Gregorian chant at Rome, but a close examination of the double offices in Prior Bernard's *Ordo lateranensis* confirms its presence at the Lateran by the first half of the twelfth century. The final stages of this development are represented by the papal court's adoption of the Franciscan liturgical books,[67] but the gradual internationalization of the papal curia and the canonical reform movement had prepared the ground more than a half century earlier. The canons' use of the Gregorian repertory also added a new dimension to the perennial rivalry between the Lateran basilica, priding itself on its Constantinian foundation, and St. Peter's, which had adhered more steadfastly to the ancient musical traditions of the city, Old Roman chant.

---

[64] Stephen J. P. van Dijk and Joan Hazelden Walker, "The Twelfth-Century Offices of the Lateran," in *The Origins of the Modern Roman Liturgy: The Liturgy of the Papal Court and the Franciscan Order in the Thirteenth Century* (Westminster, Md., and London: Newman-Darton, Longman & Todd, 1960), 67-87.

[65] *Radulph de Rivo, der letzte Vertreter der altrömischen Liturgie*, ed. Cunibert Mohlberg, 2 vols. (Louvain: Université de Louvain, 1911).

[66] *De canonum observantia*, propositio 21, ed. Mohlberg, 2:123.

[67] See the study of Stephen van Dijk (n. 64, above) and the valuable overview in Morné Bezuidenhout, "The Old and New Historical Views of Gregorian Chant: Papal and Franciscan Plainchant in Thirteenth-Century Rome," *Actas del XV Congreso de la Sociedad Internacional de Musicología*, Revista de Musicología, 16, nos. 1-2 (1993), 2:883-900. Old Roman chant books were permeable to outside influences, as studies by Michel Huglo and others have shown. The tradition had weakened to such an extent that, when the Old Roman antiphoner, British Library, Add. Ms. 29988 (ff. 128v-130) took over a series of Gregorian responsories for the feast of St. Michael, the scribe did not even bother to adapt the responsory verses to the traditional Old Roman tones. He retained only the Old Roman version of the first responsory "Factum est silentium" with its traditional verse tone.

CHAPTER 3

Jacob Obrecht's Mysterious
Missa Græcorum

Dean D. Bouzianis

Among those Renaissance cyclical masses with unidentified cantus firmi is included Jacob Obrecht's *Missa Græcorum*, published along with *Missa Je ne demande*, *Missa Fortuna desperata*, *Missa Malheur me bat*, and *Missa Salve diva parens* by Ottaviano Petrucci in Venice in 1503,[1] two years before the composer's peripatetic and restless life was ended by the plague in Ferrara. In most sources, the terms "unidentified" or "enigmatic" appear in reference to the cantus firmus of the *Missa Græcorum*, but more than the cantus firmus of this mass remains unidentified or unexplained. The curious title generates considerable speculation relative to the possibility of a connection with the cantus firmus; could it be that the music of the cantus firmus is actually the melody of some hymn from the Greek church—from Byzantine chant, perhaps? The expectation of such a connection is not extraordinary. Was it not often the case that the title of a mass identified the source of the tune on which it was composed? However, it is a rather extraordinary possibility that a Roman Catholic priest-composer would devote his attention and talent to the composition of a mass on a subject borrowed from the literature of a church from which his had been separated for some four centuries and with which the Church of Rome had co-existed on less than cordial terms, shall we say, since 1054. Why would Obrecht have composed such a work in the first place, and what elements make it a *Mass of the Greeks*?

Earlier research and speculation, though sometimes negative and conflicting, has yielded information sufficient in quantity and quality to suggest that additional inquiry proceed in a particular direction. Valuable information, together with some apparently erroneous speculation and conclusions, are provided by Otto Ursprung, who states that it would be unthinkable for Obrecht to have used material from a schismatic and inimical church as the basis for his *Misssa Græcorum*.[2] Setting aside the question of which is the schismatic church, we may conclude that the religious and political animosity flowing from West to East had little reason to be so great as to preclude such a possibility. However, Ursprung does offer some valuable factual information—that in Bruges, where Obrecht served on more than one occasion, there was a church, "Jerusalem," on whose grounds a replica of the Holy Sepulchre was being built. Mayor Anslem Adornes traveled twice to Jerusalem to inspect the original and thereby assure the accuracy of the replica. Ursprung speculates that perhaps in

---

[1] *Die Musik in Geschichte und Gegenwart* (1961), s.v. "Obrecht, Jacob" by Ludwig Finscher.

[2] "Alte griechische Einflusse und neuer grazistischer Einschlag in der mittelalterlichen Musik," *Zeitschrift für Musikwissenschaft* 12 (1930): 218.

Jerusalem there was a *Missa Græca* in practice and that Obrecht might have designed the cantus firmus and composed his mass for the Jerusalem church in imitation of some of the elements of that mass. Presumably that would have been accomplished with reliance on musical information he received from Anselm Adornes, who may have heard such a mass in Jerusalem.[3]

Though André Pirro agreed that the title of Obrecht's mass is enigmatic, he speculated that since the Epistle and the Gospel were read in Greek in the Pontifical chapel during the Mass of the Resurrection, perhaps Obrecht's cantus firmus is somehow derived from those chants. He made the very significant observation that in the "Hosanna," Obrecht introduced the "Victimae paschali laudes" melody against the cantus firmus.[4]

Berhard Meier notices that Obrecht identified the "Et incarnatus" as the central movement of the *Missa Græcorum* by presenting the Gregorian Credo I melody in the superius of that movement. He points out that Obrecht uses the Credo I melody for the same purpose in his *Missa de Sancto Martino*.[5]

Today, it is a simple enough task to determine whether or not Obrecht's cantus firmus could belong to the body of music known as Byzantine chant. Ample transcriptions of Byzantine melodies have been written from most decipherable notational periods to permit comparison of characteristic and definitive features. It might be helpful to explain here that transcription of those melodies is made necessary by the fact that, for many centuries and even in the present, those melodies have been and are being written using a diastematic notation that identifies intervals separating successive pitches in the melody rather than the pitches themselves. Each hymn is composed in one particular mode (ἦχος—*echos*) of the eight fundamental modes (hence, ὀκτώηχος—*octoechos*), and each mode has its own signature (μαρτυρία—*martyria*). At the outset of each hymn the μαρτυρία of the mode, together with the initial pitch reference point, are given; often, this is the fundamental of the mode. From that point on, each symbol which governs pitch indicates the quantitative interval to be taken to the next pitch. Additional symbols governing rhythm, articulation, and expression are also employed, and over the centuries these multiplied as the music grew in complexity, or as cantors needed reminders of elements implicit in earlier signs. If, by comparison to transcriptions of Byzantine melodies, it can be shown that Obrecht's cantus firmus is Byzantine in origin, we shall certainly enjoy the added benefit of possessing a fifteenth-century example of Byzantine chant in Western notation, transcribed in effect and on the spot, by Jacob Obrecht himself. To some degree, this will help assess the accuracy of modern transcriptions.

As the cantus firmus stands in the *Missa Græcorum* in terms of tonal organization, it can be described as G-Dorian without conclusive ending on the fundamental (see ex. 3.1). For purposes of

Example 3.1. *Missa Græcorum*, cantus firmus. Music references and excerpts from the *Missa Græcorum* are after Albert Smijers, ed., *Jacobus Obrecht: Opera omnia*, vol. 1, fasc. 11 (Amsterdam: G. Alsbach and Co., 1954).

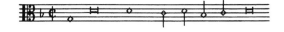

---

[3] Ibid. Though Ursprung provides no documentation, his information, exclusive of speculation, is generally correct.

[4] Pirro, *Histoire de la musique de la fin du XIVe siècle à la fin du XVIe* (Paris: H. Laurens, 1940), 204.

[5] Meier, "Zyklische Gesamtstructure und Tonalität in den Messen Jacob Obrechts," *Archive für Musikwissenschaft* 9 (1953): 296.

Example 3.1.—*Continued*

comparison to transcriptions of Byzantine melodies, which are generally untransposed, we present it below (see ex. 3.2) a perfect fourth lower, in D-Dorian, and note that the melody divides into three segments: the "a" and the "b" segments are separated by rests, and the third section, the "a´," begins with the return of the opening melody after a measure of rest.

Example 3.2. The cantus firmus transposed to D-Dorian.

   The formal structure is that of a b a´, an abbreviated simple ternary, which because it is uncharacteristic of Byzantine melodies, can be addressed as a negative item later if there are enough positive items to make discussion worthwhile. Making all the notes in segments "a" and "b" of equal duration, it is obvious that the two are nearly identical in all important tonal details (see ex. 3.3). (Segment "a´" has been excluded here since it is melodically redundant.)

Example 3.3. Comparison of segments "a" and "b" of the transposed cantus firmus.

Segment a.

Segment b.

On the basis of the tonal organization of these segments—initial is *d* or *a*, dominants (reciting tones and those on which cadences are made) are *d*, *a*, *g*, and the fundamental is *d*—both modern and fifteenth-century Byzantine music theory could assign them to the first authentic mode. In Byzantine chant of antiquity as well as in the modern system—however, there is enough duplication and sharing of characteristics between the first and first plagal modes that it is often impossible to assign an excerpt exclusively to either one mode or to the other.[6] These segments consist of several short figures or formulas which are connected by the tenor or by brief transitional passages (see ex. 3.4).

Example 3.4. Melodic formulas of segments "a" and "b."

These formulas compare favorably with those appearing in the lists of formulas scholars have compiled for that mode.[7]

Leaving further conjecture and speculation for the moment, we may draw appropriate conclusions relative to the nature and source of the cantus firmus by comparing it to transcriptions of a portion of the repertory of the Greek Orthodox church—that of the Middle Byzantine musical period or "round" system, a reference to the notational style current from about the thirteenth to the fifteenth century and to the literature with which Obrecht might have been familiar. At this point we have a firm enough basis from which to approach such a comparison with known Byzantine melodies.

In the example below (see ex. 3.5), segments "a" and "b" from the cantus firmus are compared to opening segments from three hymns from the Byzantine repertory. Segment "c" is the opening of a hymn to Sts. Peter and Paul from Codex Athens Ms. 883, f. 169, in the National Library at Athens.[8] Segment "d" is taken from the opening of a hymn to several martyrs of the Greek Orthodox church that appears in Codex Theologicus Græcus 181 from the year 1221 in the National Library of Vienna.[9] Segment "e" is the opening setting of two verses of Psalm 134 by Kornelios the Monk (Athens Ms. 2458, f. 89v, in the National Library in Athens, copied in 1336).[10] To facilitate comparison of essential features, segments "c," "d," and "e" are treated as were segments "a" and "b"; all notes have been assigned equal durations.

---

[6] The interested reader may wish to review a study devoted exclusively to those two modes by Melpo Merlier, *Études de musique byzantine: Le Premier Mode et son pagal* (Paris: Librairie Orientaliste Paul Geuthner, 1935).

[7] See H. J. W. Tillyard, *Monumenta musicae byzantinae: Subsidia*, vol. 1, fasc. 1, ed. Carsten Hoeg, H. J. W. Tillyard, and Egon Wellesz, Handbook of Middle Byzantine Notation (Copenhagen: Levin and Munksgaard, 1935), 32, and Egon Wellesz, *A History of Byzantine Music and Hymnography* (Oxford: Clarendon Press, 1949), 272-73 and 328-29.

[8] From a transcription in Tillyard, *Byzantine Music and Hymnography* (Charing Cross: Faith Press, 1923), 53.

[9] From a transcription in Wellesz, 266-67.

[10] From a transcription by Edward V. Williams, "The Kalophonic Polyeleos Psalm 134," in *Studies in Eastern Chant*, vol. 4, ed. Milos Velimirovic (Crestwood, N.Y.: St. Vladimir's Seminary Press, 1979), 240.

Example 3.5. Comparison of segments "a" and "b" to the beginning of three hymns from the Byzantine repertory.

There remains little reason to doubt that the general source of Obrecht's cantus firmus is Byzantine chant. Each of the five segments is crafted from the melodic formulas, initial, dominants, and finalis of the first mode and, with one exception, each ends with the same cadential formula. The exception is segment "b," and we shall consider that matter subsequently. The very close relationship between the melodic characteristics of the cantus firmus and the segments from the actual literature of the Byzantine church would indicate that, at the very least, Obrecht had the Byzantine musical idiom in mind when he composed the tenor for the *Missa Græcorum.*

Two items require further discussion here. First, in our examination of the lists of melodic formulas as well as the literature of the first mode, we find that the segment earlier labeled "a‴" with the ascending fifth at the outset is often found at the beginning of a hymn or phrase but not as part of a terminal cadence. Second, segment "b," as noted earlier, is different from each of the other segments in one important aspect: it concludes on *g* rather than on *d*. In the first-mode pieces of both the Middle Byzantine period as well as in the modern, cadences may be made on *g*, but they cannot be terminal cadences. Melodically, those cadences are to Byzantine chant that which a half-cadence is harmonically to Western music. Each closes a phrase, offers a moment of repose, and leads the listener to expect that more will follow immediately. Even to Western ears, the ending on *g* in the contextual equivalent of the Dorian mode lacks finality. This would seem to confirm our view that the ending of the cantus firmus with segment "a‴" represents Obrecht's manipulation of the material, a restatement of the beginning of segment "a," rather than an actual occurrence in Byzantine music. This arrangement was probably devised to provide a satisfactory conclusion of the cantus firmus after the "b" segment, and there may be other reasons, perhaps equally as practical and related to length. The fact that this creates a form inconsistent with Byzantine musical structure may be of some limited interest, but is of little significance; the cantus firmus often assumes attitudes and versions that make it formally nondescript and aurally unrecognizable.

Let us make another comparison of segment "a" to segment "b." The former is a rather gracefully contoured melody which, after a single ascent to the highest peak above the initial and fundamental of the mode, makes its way to the fundamental through a series of gradually descending arches. It spans the interval of a seventh and concludes with the typical cadential formula. On the other hand, the latter segment spans the interval of a fifth, and after the initial statement of one of the melodic formulas for this mode involving the ascent of a third, the melody hovers around the notes *a*, *g*, and *f*. The general musical topography is rather flat, and in fact out of a total of twenty-three notes in all, twenty are either *a*, *g*, or *f*. The segment ends inconclusively on *g*. In terms of grace and general contour, "b" does not compare favorably with "a," but it is typical—typical of a melody designed to move rather rapidly, an expeditious rather than ingenious melody. On the basis of these important compositional differences, it is the view of this writer that the two segments "a" and "b" are taken from different pieces in the Byzantine repertory and that the texts with which they are associated must have a liturgical significance which justifies their presence in this mass. Surely, there can be very little other basis for Obrecht's having chosen to include the "b" segment.

Eliminating all speculative items from earlier research, three emerge sharing a common denominator, so to speak: 1) "Jerusalem," 2) the Holy Sepulchre, and 3) "Victimae paschali laudes"—all associated with Easter. Jerusalem is geographically significant, of course—the Holy Sepulchre is central to the Easter theme, and the "Victimae paschali laudes" sequence is part of the Easter mass in the Roman Catholic church. If Obrecht were to choose music from the Greek church on which to build his cantus firmus, is it not probable that that music would also be related to Easter? Could the *Missa Græcorum* itself be associated somehow with the Easter season? The absence of immediately negative responses to those questions is encouraging.

In the Byzantine church, and in others as well, "Jerusalem" has more than a mundane geographic significance. "New Jerusalem" is the celestial residence of the redeemed (Revelations 21:2) and is addressed in the opening of the 9th ode of St. John of Damascus's (d. ca. 780) canon for Easter, the Resurrection Canon:

Φωτίζου, φωτίζου, ἡ νέα Ιερουσαλήμ ἡ γὰρ   Shine, shine, O New Jerusalem, for the glory of
δόξα Κυρίου ἐπὶ σε ἀνέτειλε . . .   to the Lord is risen upon thee . . .

This is chanted during *orthros* (ὄρθρος), the morning service immediately preceding the Divine Liturgy, on Easter Sunday in the Eastern Orthodox church, and that same portion of the text with its music is included in the Easter Sunday liturgy. The first segment of the cantus firmus accommodates the text perfectly well, both in terms of accentuation and stylistic propriety if we omit the repetition of "φωτίζου" and the words "ἡ νέα," a total of six syllables:

Example 3.6. Segment "a" of the cantus firmus with addition of the Φωτίζου text.

In many respects—the opening ascending fifth, the melodic formula *a c′ b a g a*, the dominant or tenor *a*—the above version compares favorably with transcriptions of two other versions from the literature of the Orthodox church which are offered below (see ex. 3.7).

Example 3.7. Opening segments of two versions of the Resurrection Day Canon, 9th Ode, from the Byzantine repertory.[11]

---

[11] Both transcriptions are by Egon Wellesz. The first is from Codex E. γ. II, Grottaferrata, and completed in 1281. It appears in Wellesz's *The Music of the Byzantine Church*, Anthology of Music, 13 (Cologne: Arno Verlag, 1959), 22. The second is from Codex Iviron 470 from the eleventh or twelfth century in the library of Iviron Monastery on Mount Athos, and appears in his *History of Byzantine Music and Hymnography*, 192.

Relying on even the brief examination of the modal characteristics which lie within the limitations of this study, as well as on whatever additional information is yielded by the two versions from the literature, we are able to provide that which appears to be a reasonably accurate reconstruction of the Greek hymn (see ex. 3.8). Accurate as this may be, it does not explain why the omission was made in the first place. We shall return to that question.

Example 3.8. Segment "a" with Φωτίζου text and missing portion reconstructed.

Perhaps we may set aside musical considerations temporarily to examine the *Missa Græcorum* from another direction and through the matter of relations between the Byzantine church and that of Rome in the fifteenth century. Initially, interest in this approach was generated by Ursprung's theory that the poor relations between the two churches precluded the possibility of Obrecht having employed any Greek elements in this mass—presumably, so deep was the animosity between the two churches. It is quite correct that relations between East and West were poor even before the separation of 1054, and among the issues which contributed to that separation was the unilateral addition of "filioque," the so-called "filioque" clause, to the Nicene Creed by the Church of Rome: "et [credo] in Spiritum Sanctum Dominum et vivificantem: qui ex Patre *filioque* procedit" ("and [I believe] in the Holy Spirit and giver of life; who proceedeth from the Father *and the son*"). Not only was that alteration of the Creed a major contributor to the schism in the eleventh century, but it has remained an important obstacle to all reconciliatory efforts ever since. The apparent success of one such effort not far removed from Obrecht's day occurred in Ferrara in 1438-39, in the very city where Obrecht was to serve Hercules I some thirty-three years later, and it was just that—only an apparent and illusory success.

In view of the title of this mass and the very high probability that the cantus firmus originates in the Byzantine repertory, it is of no little significance that "filioque," a fixed item in the fifteenth-century Roman ritual and one still supremely offensive to the Eastern church after five centuries or more by Obrecht's time, has been omitted from the Credo in this mass. Though, as Martin Luther demonstrated only twelve years after Obrecht's death, the Roman church was not absolutely secure in the West, and papal authority could be challenged, there is nothing in Obrecht's life to indicate that the peculiar and identifying features of this mass represent either a challenge or an act of defiance which Ursprung mentions as unlikely together with the unthinkable possibility of a Greek cantus firmus. Keeping in mind the profound economic and cultural influence, which for centuries Byzantine civilization exerted on the Western world, Ursprung's view notwithstanding, there is ample support for the position that, in some respects and at certain levels in the West, the schism was both incidental as well as unpopular. Some of those enigmatic features including the omission of "filioque," not only from this mass but from others of the same period, very probably were conciliatory gestures directed toward the East[12] and tolerated, if not actually encouraged, in the West. This may even be coupled with elements of remorse for Rome having failed to provide military assistance to the Eastern Empire and to the "Mother Church," besieged and ultimately overrun by the Ottoman Turks in 1453. Unlike other such gestures which may be interpreted as conciliatory, however, Obrecht's gesture is

---

[12] See Ruth Hannas, "Concerning Deletions in the Polyphonic Mass Credo," *Journal of the American Musicological Society* 5 (1952): 155-85.

not a solitary item buried deep in the Credo; it is a broad, probably multifaceted gesture involving title, at least one segment of the cantus firmus as well as the absent "folioque." That gesture, in order to be effective and to serve any useful purpose, must have been obvious in its day, especially to those toward whom the gesture was directed. The music could not have been that from some obscure source whose very obscurity would defeat the purpose of gesture. More likely to be chosen is the music from a hymn that was well known, unmistakable and easily recognizable. At this point and for the sake of consistency, it would also seem likely that the hymn would be included in the Easter repertory of the Eastern church. For that portion of the cantus firmus still unidentified, the "b" segment here so-called, one such possibility comes to mind immediately: the Χριστὸς ἀνέστη (*Christos anesti*—Christ is risen), undoubtedly the best known of all Easter hymns in the Orthodox church. "Χριστὸς ἀνέστη!" is also the greeting exchanged by Orthodox Christians throughout Pentecost. Among those Christians today, the words can hardly be uttered or contemplated without the accompanying music ringing in the ears—so frequently is the hymn heard and sung—and practice was not radically different in the fifteenth century. That hymn is sung several times by the priests, the choir, and cantors, and by the congregation at every service throughout that joyous season. Each time it is sung there is one statement and two immediate repetitions of the entire hymn. The initial statement and first repetition would end with an incomplete cadence, since, in each case, a repetition follows. Segment "b" of the cantus firmus also ends with an incomplete cadence (as in ex. 3.9 from the modern literature).

Example 3.9. Χριστὸς ἀνέστη with incomplete cadence from the modern literature of the Greek Orthodox Church.[13]

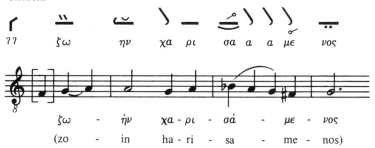

Another aspect of this hymn concerns its two versions which exist in present-day practice of the Greek Orthodox Church and which undoubtedly existed in the fifteenth century. A moderately slow, stately version occurs early in the Easter services, and at least one other version is often employed for occurrences later in the service. The latter has neither the melodic grace nor the stateliness of the former; it moves much more quickly and is designed to consume little time and thus to avoid prolonging the service unduly. It is sung by the cantor in a syllabic, almost *recitativo* style, and the characteristics of this latter version seem to relate positively to those of segment "b" of the cantus firmus.

Perhaps at this point, it would be profitable to determine how well the text of the Χριστὸς ἀνέστη is accommodated by segment "b" of the cantus firmus. Using the transposed version, adhering to the stylistic limitations of a primarily syllabic chant and matching metrical accentuation of the music to the grammatical accentuation of the text results in a very comfortable union between the music and most of the text. Once again, however, we are confronted by the problem of either too much text or too little music (see ex. 3.10):

---

[13] The excerpt is taken from Μουσικός Πανδέκτης, τόμος ὄγδοος, Πεντηκοοτάριον (*Musical Pandect* 8, Pentecostarion) (Athens: Zoe Brotherhood, 1938), 6. Transcription is mine.

Example 3.10. Segment "b" of the cantus firmus with the text of Χριστὸς ἀνέστη.

Nothing that we have encountered thus far provides a better explanation for the disparity in length between music and text than the theory that Obrecht has abbreviated the music of the Greek hymns for reasons not yet discerned by us. We may, therefore, proceed to reconstruct the missing portion of segment "b" in a manner consistent with the reconstruction of the missing portion of segment "a" (see ex. 3.11).

Example 3.11. Segment "b" with Χριστὸς ἀνέστη text and missing portions reconstructed.

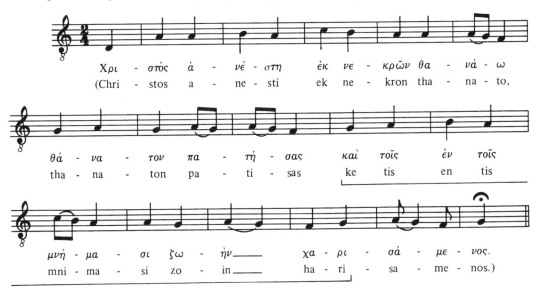

Again, the reconstructive process yields a hymn that appears to be authentic in every respect, but it is also important to notice, just as was the case with the music of the Φωτίζου hymn, the absence of the reconstructed portion does not disfigure the melody to a point beyond recognition; one who knew the melody would certainly recognize it even in its abbreviated form. However, we are still confronted by the need to explain why the abridgments apparently made by the composer were necessary to begin with. The answer to that and to other related questions lies in the "Hosanna," where we find some of the music of the "Victimae paschali laudes" presented simultaneously with the cantus firmus.

At the outset of the movement, a portion of segment "a" of the cantus firmus in double aug-mentation appears in the tenor against the familiar music of versicle 1 of the "Victimae paschali laudes" in the superius. These and all other sections to which reference is made here have been extracted from the movement and are presented together with the chant version of "Victimae paschali laudes" in modern notation,[14] in equal note-values, and transposed to G-Dorian to facilitate whatever comparisons may be useful (see ex. 3.12).

Example 3.12. Superius and tenor of the Hosanna with chant version of "Victimae paschali laudes," versicle 1.

In addition to the symbolic significance which the presence of the Greek Resurrection Canon music could have in the *Missa Græcorum*, it should not escape notice that, liturgically speaking, the ninth ode of that Canon bears a functional relationship to the "Victimae paschali laudes." The two are liturgical counterparts; both belong to that body of chants known as Graduals for which the Greek term καταβασία (*katavasia*) derives from the verb to descend, καταβαίνω (*kataveno*). This describes the physical activity of the cantors at one point during ὄρθρος in earlier times as they descended from their seats to chant that hymn from a position in front of the choir, and this corresponds to the

_____

[14] Transcribed from *Chants of the Church*, ed. and compiled by the Monks of Solesmes (Toledo, Ohio: Gregorian Institute of America, 1953), 162-63.

very similar practice in the Roman church. Though undoubtedly the Greek hymn would have been chosen as a source of music primarily because of its text, Obrecht was probably not unaware of the liturgical relationship between the Greek and Latin hymns, and this could only have enhanced what appears to be his already ingenious choice.

     Segment "a" of the cantus firmus continues, and Obrecht next introduces the music of "Victimae paschali laudes," versicle 4 or 6—the music is the same for both—against the remaining portion of segment "a" (see ex. 3.13):

Example 3.13. Superius and tenor of the Hosanna with chant version of "Victimae paschali laudes," versicle 4 (6).

(begins segment "b" of c.f.)

The superius is generally faithful to the chant version of the "Victimae paschali laudes" music except at points where extended melodic cadential formulas occur.

     The succeeding portion of the Hosanna is devoted to presenting the untransposed music of versicle 8 of "Victimae paschali laudes" in conjunction with segment "b" of the cantus firmus. With the exception of some minor departures, marked here by arrows, the superius is faithful to this portion of the chant version as well. It is clear that Obrecht made the effort to preserve at least the melodic contour of the original in those instances where tonal divergence became necessary for one reason or another (see ex. 3.14).

Example 3.14. Superius and tenor of the Hosanna with chant version of "Victimae paschali laudes," versicle 8.

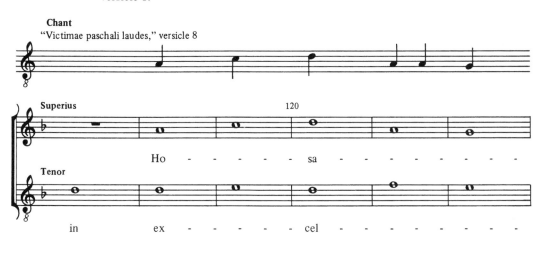

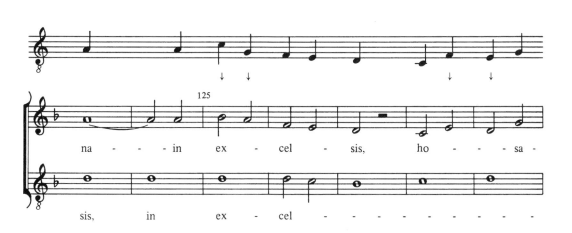

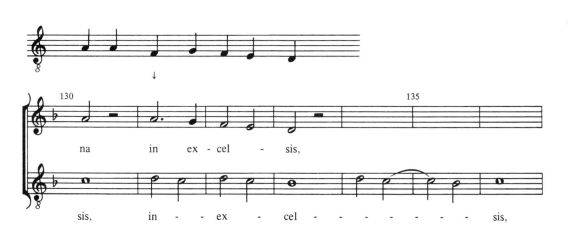

Returning to our deliberatons relative to the source of the melodies of the cantus firmus, we may take a moment to review the information which has directed us toward specific hymns in the Byzantine repertory. This involved matters in addition to the manner in which the music accommodates the texts of the Greek hymns, although that is not an insignificant consideration. The probable source of the melody for segment "a" of the cantus firmus was identified on the basis that its text refers to the New Jerusalem, apparently employed in this mass as a reference to the Jerusalem Church in Bruges. It is also an Easter hymn in the Eastern Orthodox Church, and serves as a Gradual. Therefore, a close functional relationship is established with the "Victimae paschali laudes" music with which it appears. As for the probable identity of segment "b," Χριστὸς ἀνέστη is proposed. It is also an Easter hymn in the Orthodox church, and it is the best-known and most frequently sung of all Easter hymns in that church. In each instance of its liturgical appearance, the first two of the required three statements end with an incomplete cadence, as does this segment of the cantus firmus. These have provided a reason-able and promising basis from which further inquiry may proceed, and that inquiry is now directed toward the possible significance and relevance of the texts of those hymns whose melodies Obrecht employed.

At the outset of the Hosanna, the superius is given the opening melody, the music of versicle 1 of "Victimae paschali laudes" in which Christians are exhorted to offer praise and sacrifice to the Paschal Victim ("Victimae paschali laudes, immolent Christiani"). The Easter theme could not have been established more quickly or more effectively. The next music of the Easter sequence Obrecht presents is that of versicles 4 and 6; the same melody serves both. In versicle 4, Mary is asked to tell what she saw on the way ("Dic nobis Maria, quid vidisti in via?"), and versicle 6 contains the second part of her response, which makes reference to garments within the tomb ("Angelicos testes, sudarium et vestes"). Versicles 4 and 6 (whether Obrecht intended reference to either one exclusively or to both is impossible to know) provide indirect reference to Christ's tomb. Versicle 4 (6), together with versicle 1 and the text of the Greek hymn "Shine, shine, O New Jerusalem," with whose melody their melodies are sounding, constitute the symbolic triptych: the reference to Easter, to the Jerusalem Church, and to its reproduction of the Holy Sepulchre. This conclusion has an apparent weakness, however, related to a much more direct reference to the Tomb available in versicle 5, the first part of Mary's" response: "sepulchrum Christi viventis, et gloriam vidi resurgentis." If it were Obrecht's purpose to make symbolic reference to the Holy Sepulchre through musical means, one might ask, why would he not have chosen to do so through the music of versicle 5? The music itself answers that question. We might examine the result of combining the music of versicle 5 with the remainder of segment "a," that portion not already engaged by the music of versicle 1, in the manner established by the composer himself (see ex. 3.15):

Example 3.15. Music of "Victimae paschali laudes," versicle 5 with the cantus firmus.

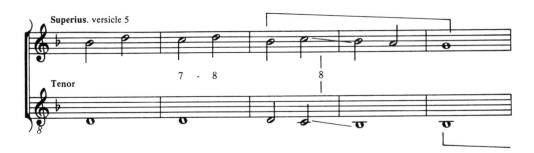

Example 3.15.—*Continued*

It is obvious that the music of versicle 5 and the portion of segment "a" are so much alike that the simultaneous appearance of those two melodies would have sounded like imitative counterpoint between tenor and superius based on a single subject rather than the skillful and effective union of two different melodies. On a more practical level, however, certain unacceptable contrapuntal weaknesses would also have been present. Attempts to combine those two melodies differently would have been just as unsuccessful without radical and disruptive changes in texture and strained contrivance. Obrecht then chose to make reference to versicle 4 with or without 6 (or vice versa), and may even have intended to include versicle 5 by implication, perhaps, since direct quotation was impossible. All of this provides encouraging support for the theory of derivation of the cantus firmus segments proposed and pursued here. But it remains for a comparison of the texts of the two melodies that follow—the identity of the Latin chant certain, and of the other still conjectural—to provide compelling evidence of the validity of that theory.

Χριστὸς ἀνέστη ἐκ νεκρῶν
θανάτω θάνατον πατήσας
καὶ τοῖς ἐν τοῖς μνήμασι
ζωὴν χαρισάμενος

Scimus Christum surrexis
a mortuis vere: tu nobis,
victor Rex, miserere.

Christ is risen from the dead
by death has trampled on death
giving life to those in the tombs.

We know that truly Christ
is risen from the dead:
Thou victorious King,
have mercy on us.

These are parallel texts. Each refers to the Resurrection of Christ, each refers to his victory over death, each addresses mercy—one in the form of a supplication, and the other as a gift of life to those in the tombs. There is more here than can be explained away as simple coincidence. It now appears that in this movement, the "Hosanna," we find the seed for the entire musical flower of the *Missa Græcorum.* We conclude that the compositional process must have begun here, not with music but rather with the search for and selection of appropriate texts from Greek and Latin sources. Musical considerations were secondary, and those select melodies of "Victimae paschali laudes" came to serve as a reasonably fixed reference point and standard of measurement. It was against that standard that the appropriate dimensions of the cantus firmus were determined. In Obrecht's brilliant scheme of things, it was absolutely imperative that those specific Byzantine melodies be employed in the mass, less for their musical characteristics and more for their extra musical significance, due to the texts with which they were associated. In their original source and state, those melodies were substantially longer than were the "Victimae paschali laudes" melodies with which they were to appear. It was essential that the

Byzantine melodies be sufficiently condensed to occupy only the available musical space and to function in a contrapuntally acceptable manner with the "Victimae paschali laudes" melodies. Obrecht accomplished this in admirable fashion, and in the shortened form the salient and characteristic features of the original are preserved to such an extent that we are able to assign texts to the fragments without difficulty once the identities of the melodies are surmised. To reiterate, one who knew the originals would have had no difficulty in identifying the source of the condensed version and in making the association between music and texts for which the composer had hoped.

It is of some interest that while Obrecht recognized and took advantage of the close textual relationship between the eighth versicle of "Victimae paschali laudes" and Χριστὸς ἀνέστη, he was also probably well aware of the inherent musical relationship between the "Victimae paschali laudes" music and another hymn whose title, "Christ ist erstanden," is the German equivalent of the Greek Χριστὸς ἀνέστη. Its melody derives from "Victimae paschali laudes,"[15] it is known to have been in existence since the twelfth century,[16] and German polyphonic versions were being composed in Obrecht's day. Further, Obrecht's treatment of the liturgical and borrowed melodies in the Hosanna is not dissimilar to a technique employed by his German contemporary Heinrich Isaac. In the "Resurrexi" of the *Choralis Constantinus*, the liturgical melody, which in this instance is the cantus firmus, is above the "Christ ist erstanden" melody,[17] just as the liturgical melody of the Hosanna, "Victimae paschali laudes," is in the superius above the Greek Χριστὸς ἀνέστη.

Reflection on the circumstances under which Obrecht might have composed the *Missa Græcorum* redirects our attention to that medieval city of numerous canals and some fifty bridges from which its name, "Bruges," derives, and to Longfellow's city of

> Lombard and Venetian merchants, with deep-laden argosies;
> Ministers of twenty nations; more than royal pomp and ease.
> —*The Belfry at Bruges*

It is also the city of the Jerusalem Church to which Ursprung's reference was noted earlier and from which church and its owners Obrecht must have received either pure inspiration or a commission.

The history of the Jerusalem church is closely associated with that of the Adornes family in Bruges. Though the information offered by sources differs somewhat in terms of personnel and chronology, there is concordance on a number of items. Two Adornes brothers, one of whom was named Jacques, founded the Hotel d'Adornes in 1428.[18] The Jerusalem Church was built by the same two brothers, and it was intended to be the private chapel of the hotel. Construction of the church began not long after the hotel was built and continued in a rather sporadic manner for several decades. The final stages of construction began in 1482 with the installation of stained-glass windows

---

[15] Gustave Reese, *Music in the Middle Ages* (New York: Norton, 1940), 201.

[16] Philipp Spitta, *Johann Sebastian Bach*, transl. Clara Bell and J. A. Fuller Maitland, 2 vols. (London: Novello, 1889; reprint, New York: Dover, 1951), 2:393.

[17] Discussed in Gustave Reese, *Music in the Renaissance*, rev. ed. (New York: Norton, 1959), 648-49.

[18] W. H. J. Weale identifies the Adornes brothers as Pierre and Jacques. Together with their wives, Elizabeth Broadericx and Anne Masins, they founded the Jerusalem Church in 1428. The church was still incomplete in 1465. The replica of the Holy Sepulchre was founded before June 1435. The Hotel d'Adornes became the convent of Les Soeurs Apostolines who came to Bruges in 1717. See Weale, *Bruges et ses environs*, 4th ed. (Bruges: Desclée, de Brouwer et Cie., 1884), 171-72. Ernest Gilliat-Smith identifies the two Adornes brothers as Anselm and John. In his version the hotel was built in 1428, the Jerusalem Church begun in 1465 and completed in 1482. Also, he refers to a trip to Palestine by one of the founders of the hotel and church, as well as to a trip to the same area by the founder's son, Anselm. See Gilliat-Smith, *The Story of Bruges* (London: J. M. Dent and Co., 1905), 306 and 320-23.

depicting members of the Adornes family and their patron saints, executed "horriblement" according to Weale. By 1560, six of the eight windows of the church had been installed.

The replica of the Holy Sepulchre which this appropriately designed oriental, Middle-Eastern style little church includes is entered through a passageway so low and narrow that only one person at a time, practically on hands and knees, may pass. The room at the end of the passage is lighted by a single candle or oil lamp shining on an effigy of Jesus realistically executed and with "ghastly" effect.[19] The events in the history of the Jerusalem church coinciding with Obrecht's known presence in Bruges are related to the occasional installation of stained-glass windows in that church. Obrecht was in Bruges from October 1486 to August 1487, from August 1488 to January 1491, and for some time between the years 1498 and 1500.[20] The *Missa Græcorum* was probably composed at some point during those years and most likely without the influential or helpful contribution from Anselm Adornes that Ursprung suggested. The life of Anselm Adornes, son of one of the founders, ended in Scotland in 1483,[21] two or three years prior to Obrecht's arrival in Bruges. Anselm was a refined gentleman of distinguished ancestry and with an internationally prominent reputation in diplomacy and commerce. For a time, he was in the service of James III of Scotland.[22] It might very well be that it was for the dedicatory ceremony of a stained-glass window in honor of Anselm himself and of his deceased wife that the *Missa Græcorum* was written. In any case, the view that the mass was composed for that event or for a similar event related to the dedication of stained-glass windows in the Jerusalem Church is provided some circumstantial support and credibility by information which indicates that Obrecht probably composed music for such a purpose in another religious establishment in Bruges. During the time that the windows were being installed in the Jerusalem Church, beginning in 1483, an identical project was begun, perhaps by the same artisans (and hopefully with better results), in Bruges' twelfth-century romanesque Chapel of Saint Basil.[23] That "O beate Basili" must have been written for a ceremony in connection with that chapel is a reasonable assumption. Why else would Obrecht have composed a motet dedicated to the father of Eastern monasticism, a Greek, neither highly revered nor even well-known in the West beyond the vicinity of Bruges during the fifteenth century? The occasion could very well have been related to the dedication of one, in particular, or more stained-glass windows in that chapel.

As noted earlier, the Credo I melody has a purely architectural function in the "Et incarnatus" (see ex. 3.16):

Example 3.16. The Credo I melody in the "Et incarnatus."

---

[19] In accounts by George W. T. Ormond, *Belgium* (London: A. and C. Black, 1908), 26, and George W. Edwards, *Belgium Old and New* (Philadelphia: Penn Publishing Co., 1920), 159.

[20] *The New Grove Dictionary of Music and Musicians* (1980), s.v. "Obrecht, Jacob," by Edgar H. Sparks. Reinhard Strohm gives the first date exactly one year earlier; see his *Music in Medieval Bruges* (Oxford: Clarendon Press, 1985), 38.

[21] Weale, 171.

[22] Strohm, 65.

[23] Gilliat-Smith, 100.

Exclusive of that, ample reference to Easter exists in the conception and execution of both *Missa Græcorum* and the Jerusalem Church to justify a close association between the two. With such an emphasis, one might wonder if it were not intended that the mass be performed on an Easter Sunday at some point during Obrecht's stay in Bruges. Such an event would have been entirely appropriate, not only because of the references themselves, but also because that would have been such fitting complement to another major event in the history of the Jerusalem Church, the consecration of that church on Palm Sunday many years earlier.[24] We can only wonder about the effect that the emotionally overwhelming experience must have had on those knowledgeable witnesses and participants who were aware of the source and dual significance of the borrowed melodies and of the mass itself. In the Jerusalem Church on that day there was probably no mystery concerning either the unusual title of the mass or Obrecht's kind gesture toward the Eastern church. It may be somewhat presumptuous to believe that the only mystery that remains concerns the exact location of the Byzantine melody repository for Obrecht's version of the Greek Resurrection Canon melody. The Χριστὸς ἀνέστη may never be found; it may not have been written down. Valuable space in manuscripts was not usually given to hymns unlikely to be forgotten.

---

[24] Weale, 171.

CHAPTER 4

Extant Sixteenth-Century Prints as Performance Practice Sources

Eugene Casjen Cramer

Performance practice studies often rely on the writings of a theorist to legitimize an idea of how a particular passage should be interpreted or how the problem being discussed should be resolved. If a treatise that can be called on and used as an authority is not to be found, investigators sometimes rely on the memoirs of a contemporary observer to support their point of view. Analysis of the evidence in a piece or a source is also a favored method of supporting position on a particular point. This study, however, will eschew all of these more traditional approaches. Instead, this difficult and occasionally contentious subject is approached through an examination of extant practical sources—specifically, the surviving copies of the original sixteenth-century prints of the music of Tomás Luis de Victoria.

Although not often discussed, it is generally well-known by researchers working with the music of the sixteenth century that many, if not most, of the extant prints from this period prints contain emendations, that is, handwritten changes that have been made over the years. The extant prints of Victoria's works are no exception. Clearly, it is impossible to identify exactly who made a particular emendation or when it was made, and this makes it difficult to use these emendations to establish either a definitive text or to postulate on practices of a particular period. Still, the emendations in a particular source should not be dismissed or even overlooked. In actuality, the accumulation of emendations is a very useful record of what was done with a particular work in a particular source during its history by the chapelmasters and singers who used it. As such, they can serve as an informative guide for modern performers and conductors. For the purpose of this study, ninety-nine original printed sources of Victoria's works were consulted: fifty in Italy, twenty-eight in Spain, seven in Portugal, and fourteen in Germany.

The first kind of emendation does not concern a performance practice matter as such. It is, however, related and instructive in its own way. This kind of emendation is a correction, usually of a pitch. These corrections are often accomplished by scratching out the original and pasting a piece of paper with the correct note drawn in its place. Since sixteenth-century printers were far from infallible, emendations of this sort are common. Quite apart from correcting mistakes, the presence of such corrections in a print is important because they indicate that the particular source has been

The author wishes to acknowledge the assistance of the Social Sciences and Humanities Research Council of Canada for providing the funds that made it possible to visit many of the music libraries and archives in Spain, Portugal, Italy, and Germany with significant collections of Victoria's prints.

used at one point in its history and was not just another volume in a collector's library. They serve, in fact, as validation that that particular source was once a living thing. In this regard, it is interesting to observe that several of the extant copies of Victoria's works have no markings at all, not even corrections such as those mentioned above. In all likelihood, these particular copies, such as the Tarazona copy of the 1581 *Hymni totius anni*, were never used in performance. Fortunately, such apparently unused sources of Victoria's music are few.

Turning now to matters more directly concerned with performance practice, it is disappointing to note that the original prints of Victoria's works provide almost no insight into and certainly no solution to the problem of *musica ficta*—one of the most controversial matters to surface in early music in the recent past. The number of notes to which accidentals have been added in the sources consulted is exceedingly small—five in all—and quite localized: four in Spanish sources and one in a Portugese source. As might be expected, the notes altered are F, C, and E—the first two by a sharp sign and the last by a flat. Not included in the above statistics is the addition of accidentals to the chant for the hymn "Sanctorum meritis" found in the Coimbra copy of the 1581 *Hymni* (see ex. 4.1). (It bears noting in this regard that Spanish chant sources generally contain a more liberal use of accidentals than is common elsewhere, and therefore emendations of this sort should not be viewed as unusual.)

Example 4.1. Tomas Luis de Victoria, hymn "Sanctorum meritis" from his *Hymni totius anni* (Rome, 1581), 124, end of the second phrase of the chant. (From copy in the Biblioteca Geral da Universidade, Coimbra, Portugal.)

ge - sta - que   for - ti - a:

More disappointing still is the information in these sources regarding the practice of ornamentation. While it can be documented that sacred music by Victoria was ornamented,[1] there is no evidence for this practice in the sources consulted.

By contrast, a newly composed addition to the original musical text is one of the most common and significant emendations found in the extant copies of Victoria's printed music. Six kinds of musical additions have been identified.

First, in the Loreto copy of the 1585 *Officium hebdomadae sanctae* a fourth voice (cantus) is added to the *a 3* setting of "Sine videamus" that Victoria included in his setting of the St. Matthew Passion. As well, this source adds a third voice (tenor) to the verse "Bonum erat" in the responsory "Amicus meus." Further, in the Loreto copy of the 1592 *Missae, quattuor, quinque, sex, & octo vocibus concinendæ, una cum antiphonis, aspergis, & Vidi aquam totius anni, liber secundus* a fourth voice (tenor) is added to the "Christe" of the *Missa quarti toni*. Since all of the examples of this kind of addition are found in sources in Loreto, it may be concluded that adding a voice to an existing composition was a penchant of this locale, or possibly of a particular chapelmaster in the Loreto Basilica.

Second, new endings have been provided for the "Gloria" verse of the hymn "Ad coenam agni" and for all three of the verses of the hymn "Vexilla regis" in the Santa Maria Maggiore copy of the 1581 *Hymni*. As can be seen in the excerpt in ex. 4.2a-b, the general style of the original, including rhythm and voice-leading, is maintained. The only difference is the cadence, now on F instead of D. Indeed, this is the exact type of change made in three of the four instances cited above.

---

[1] Giovanni Battista Bovicelli, *Regole, passagi di musica*, facsimile, ed. Nanie Bridgman (Kassel: Bärenreiter, 1958), 53-63.

Example 4.2a. Victoria, hymn "Vexilla regis" (Roman melody) from his *Hymni totius anni* (Rome, 1581), 38-39, "O crux ave" verse, meas. 49-51. *Opera omnia*, ed. Filipe Pedrell, vol. 5 (Leipzig: Breitkopf & Härtel, 1908), 26.

b. The same, from a handwritten addition to the Archivio Capitolare de Santa Maria Maggiore copy, now housed in the Biblioteca Apostolica Vatican.

The new ending for the third verse, "Arbor decora" of "Vexilla regis," is a special case, for although it also changes the cadence from D to F, the nature of the change is much more thoroughgoing (see ex. 4.3a-b). It begins by revising the cantus in meas. 31 (the other two voices remain unchanged). It then proceeds to the ending which is new not only in pitch level, but also in voice-leading, rhythm, general style, and length. The reduction in length is achieved primarily by dropping the plagal extension of the original version (the plagal extension was also dropped in the "Gloria" verse of "Ad coenam agni") and by compressing the cadential motion into three measures instead of four.[2]

Because in each case both the original and new cadences are perfect, the changes cannot have been made to update the work—that is, to make it more tonal. While those for "Vexilla regis" do effectively change the mode from D to F, the other one merely changes the cadential point for the end of the hymn from the tonic of the mode to the dominant. Perhaps these changes made these works more compatible with other music being performed in conjunction with them, but we shall never know for certain. Since this practice seems to be limited not only to this one source, but also to these two works, it probably represents the needs of a particular occasion or the ideas of a particular chapelmaster.[3]

---

[2] The Santa Maria Maggiore emendation of the "Arbor decora" verse presents a problem because there is a sharp sign below the penultimate note in the cantus. Inasmuch as this sharp sign produces a *f♯′* that clashes noticeably with the F's in the other two voices, I can only believe that it is a mistake and have not, therefore, indicated its presence in ex. 4.3b.

[3] A variant of this practice is found in a manuscript copy of Victoria's *Lamentations* found in the Lisbon Cathedral archive, where Victoria's music for each lesson is maintained for only a few measures. The remainder of the text of the lesson is given a completely new musical setting—probably by Emmanuelle Soares. Additions as extensive as this one are really no longer emendations as such, but amount to new compositions. They are really parodies in the manner of the parody masses of the sixteenth century.

Example 4.3a. Victoria, hymn "Vexilla regis" (Roman melody) from his *Hymni totius anni* (Rome, 1581), 36-37, "Arbor decora" verse, meas. 31-42. *Omni opera*, 5:24. (Only the voices rewritten in ex. 4.3b are included.)

     b. The same, from a handwritten addition to the Archivio Capitolare de Santa Maria Maggiore copy, now housed in the Biblioteca Apostolica Vaticana.

Third, one finds in the Loreto copy of the 1581 *Cantica B. Virginis vulgo magnificat quatuor vocibus* an alternate setting of the "Et misericordia" verse of the *Magnificat primi toni*. The practice of using alternate settings is corroborated by Cappella Giulia Ms. XVI.25, a manuscript of Victoria's *Missa pro defunctis* with an alternate setting for "Vidi aquam."

Fourth, one of the Spanish printed sources consulted, the Badajoz copy of the 1592 *Missae*, reveals the practice of adding complete pieces of music to various works. In this source one finds a four-voice "Nec recordaris" and a "Requiescat in pace" *a 4* inserted into the *Missa pro defunctis*. That this practice was relatively common is confirmed by the presence of two four-voice graduals and two *a 4* offertories in the copies of the *Missa quarti toni* found in the manuscripts Cappella Giulia IV.158.1 and 2. It may be noted that these particular additions serve to make these particular sources of the *Missa quarti toni* proper to the feasts of either St. Egidio or St. Thomas, depending on which gradual/offertory set is sung.

Fifth, the Valladolid copy of the 1572 *Motecta que partim quarternis, partim quinis, alia senis, alis octonis vocibus concinuntur* contains a line of new music at the end of the motet "Senex puerum." Unfortunately, the relationship of this music to the motet, if any, cannot be determined at this time. New music is also found throughout the Avila partbooks for the 1572 *Motecta*. These additions appear to be parts of new compositions, but music in the treble clef appears in the bassus partbook, therefore the exact reason for the new music is unclear.

Finally, it should be noted that Victoria's sixteenth-century prints now often have completely new works added to them or bound into them. For example, at the end of the Bologna copy of the 1581 *Hymni* one finds *a 4* settings for seven hymns, all of which are without composer attributions. Likewise, the Chigi copy of the 1581 *Hymni* contains four unattributed *a 4* hymns, and the Teruel copy of this print has three unattributed hymns. Further, in the Valencia copy of the 1585 *Motecta festorum totius anni cum communí sanctorum* an incomplete two-voice work and six complete pieces (one by Miguel de Canal) as well as some chants are now present. The Avila copy of the 1572 *Motecta* and the Cappella Giulia and Cappella Sistina copies of the 1581 *Hymni* now also include chant pieces.

Let us move on to some of the other kinds of emendations to be found in these sources. First, although it has no aural significance, in two copies of the 1585 *Motecta*, in Valencia and Toledo, one finds that the mode of some pieces is indicated either in the index or in the margin. In the Valencia copy the mode (*tono*) is given for eighteen works, and in the Toledo copy it is given for four works, three by Victoria and one by Francesco Suriano.

Second, examination of Victoria's prints shows that rhythmic emendations are relatively rare. In fact, they are limited to the addition of barlines and the writing in of Arabic numbers over certain notes and ligatures. In regard to the former, four Spanish sources and three in Italy (one of the 1572 *Motecta quae partim quarternis, partim quinis, alia senis, alia octonis, alia duodenis vocibus concinuntur quæ quidem nunc vero melius excussa & alia quam plurima adiuncta*, one of the 1583 *Motecta*, two of the 1585 *Motecta*, one of the 1576 *Liber primus qui missas, psalmos, magnificat ad virginem dei matrem salutationes*, and two of the 1592 *Missae*) have barlines added to some of the works. In none, however, is the addition of barlines systematic either in every work or in all parts, or even in all of a single part in a given piece. Barlines are also found scattered throughout the Regensburg copy of the 1581 *Cantica* and the Munich copy of the 1581 *Hymni*.

In the cantus and altus parts of the copy of the 1589 Milan *Motecta* in the Cappella Sistina archive one finds several notes and ligatures with Arabic numbers over them. The numbers seem to indicate the number of beats in that particular note. This type of addition is also found in the Munich copy of the 1581 *Hymni*. Interestingly enough, both of these kinds of emendation indicate an unfamiliarity with the notation of the source on the part of the user, and this probably means that they were added some time after publication, possibly as late as the eighteenth century.

Another change indicating post-sixteenth century use is the addition of dynamic markings. Such markings, however, are found in only one source—the Cappella Giulia copy of the 1585 *Officium hebdomadae sanctae* and are, therefore, the exception rather than the rule. In addition to *piano* and its abbreviation "p:o" and the abbreviation for *forte*, "fe," one also finds *cresc.* The last of these, especially, indicates that they are very late additions, maybe even nineteenth-century ones.

Before moving on to emendations affecting the text, one more example of post-sixteenth century use is worthy of being quoted. In the Valladolid copy of the 1576 *Liber primus* the tenor of the antiphon "Ave regina coelorum" has been emended by crossing out the *d* in an under-third cadence on F one passage (see ex. 4.4a). No other note is changed and one must presume that the preceding *e* was lengthened in compensation, although no indication of this is present in the source (see ex. 4.4b). The impetus for such a change was probably a desire to make the work more acceptable stylistically to contemporary performers and listeners.

Example 4.4. Victoria, antiphon "Ave regina coeli *a 5*," tenor voice (in the melisma on the middle syllable of "coelorum"), meas. 8-9, from his *Liber primus qui missas, psalmos, magnificat, ad virginem dei matrem salutationes* (Venice, 1576), f. [c^v], from the Archivo Musical de la Catedral de Valladolid copy.

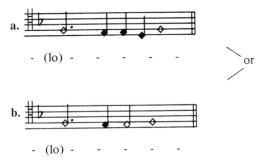

Post-sixteenth century use of these sources is also confirmed by the presence of dates entered into eleven of the original prints consulted. Interestingly enough, three of these are, in fact, sixteenth-century dates, and significantly all three of these are in German sources. The Munich copy of the 1581 *Hymni* has the date 1591. The notation in this source also indicates the donor and the new owner: "Collegii Societatis Jesu Monachi es haerdi^ae [R.D.] Mgr. Adam Cesarim." The binding of the Augsburg copy of the 1589 Dillingen *Cantiones sacræ Thomæ Ludovici A Victoria Abulensis musici suavissimi, quatuor, quinque, sex, octo, et duodecim vocum, nunquam antehac in Germania excussæ* is dated 1593, and the second copy of this print in Munich, bound with two volumes of madrigals, is dated 1594.

Seventeenth-century dates include the notation of 1608 in the Valencia copy of the 1585 *Motecta*, 1618 in copy 1 of the 1589 Dillingen *Cantiones sacræ* in Munich (which also has the rubric "Utriusque Bavariae Ducum"), 1641 in the Valencia copy of the 1572 *Motecta* partbooks along with the name Don Diego Vigue, 1653 in the Cappella Giulia copy of the 1581 *Hymni*, and 1677 in the cover of the cantus partbook of the Valladolid copy of the 1572 *Motecta*.

The sextus of the Cappella Sistina copy of the 1589 Milan *Motecta quae partim quaternis, partim quinis, alia senis, alia duodenis vocibus concinuntur* has the date 1728, and all parts have "Ioyalij cantaris ad usum Capp^ae Pontificiae," which would confirm its use in the papal chapel in the eighteenth century. In the Regensburg copy of the 1585 *Officium hebdomadae sanctae* one finds the date 1767 and the notation "Del Monasterio di San Piero di Gubbio." This notation probably indicates that this print came from Gubbio, Italy, to Regensburg in 1767. Finally, the Tudela copy of the 1576 *Liber primus . . .* contains a series of eighteenth-century dates—1759, 1708 (or 1728), and 1709—on different and widely spaced folios.

On the basis of the data used for this study, text underlay is one of the aspects of sixteenth-century music which seems to have been most often changed by performers and/or chapelmasters. A total of ten sources (two Italian, two Portugese, five Spanish, and one German) contain changes in text underlay. The works affected include settings of "Gaude Maria," "Regina coeli," "Lauda Sion," as well as the Magnificat and the Mass. One of the more interesting of these is found in the Coimbra, Casanatense, and Tarazona copies of the 1581 *Cantica* in the tenor of the setting of the *Magnificat tertii toni* (see ex. 4.5). In all three of these copies of this one print the underlay for this passage has been changed from the standard rules as codified by Zarlino to one that does not—that is, it now has a melisma on the final syllable of the word "eum," whereas formerly the final syllable and the final note coincided. That this emendation occurs in three of the extant copies of this print but not in the others may indicate that at one point in their history these now widely separated volumes had something in common and that Zarlino's rules were sometimes disregarded.[4]

Example 4.5. Victoria, *Magnificat tertii toni* ("Anima mea"), "Et misericordiae" verse, tenor voice, meas. 19-20, from his *Cantica B. Virginis vulgo magnificat quotour vocibus* (Rome, 1581), 36-37, from copies in the Biblioteca Geral de Universidade (Coimbra, Portugal), Biblioteca Casanatense (Rome), and Archivo Capitular (Tarazona, Spain).

e - - - - um

One finds examples in the printed sources examined for this study where lines of text have been crossed out. Emendations of this kind are found in the Granada copy of the 1583 *Missarum libro duo*: in the bassus of the Agnus dei of the *Missa Surge propera* and the tenor of the Kyrie of the *Missa de beata Maria*. Interestingly, in the Coimbra copy of this print these same portions of the text have been crossed out. However, in the first of the passages identified above, the original text, "peccata mun-," has been written back in! This particular change would appear to be at least a second-generation emendation, but, of course, when it was actually done cannot be determined.

Among the textual emendations found in the original printed sources one also finds that short passages of text have been altered, and occasionally that an entire text has been changed. An example of the former practice is found in the Santa Maria Maggiore and Cappella Giulia copies of the 1581 *Hymni*, where the text "et referans paradisum" is changed to "et paradisum referans," and "hoc passionis tempore" is changed to "hac triumphi gloria." A slightly more substantive change is found in the Cappella Sistina copy of the 1589 Milan *Motecta*, where the text "Paradisis voluptatis" is changed to "consolatrix afflictus."

---

[4] When Pedrell edited this work for Victoria's *Opera omnia*, vol. 3 (Leipzig: Breitkopf & Härtel, 1904), 23-24, he ignored the original placement of the text in this passage—one of the many places in his edition of Victoria's works that differs from the printed source indicating that he may have used one of these three sources as his source or that there is another source in which this change has been made.

More interesting and significant are instances where a totally new text is substituted for the original. Several examples of this practice are found, three of which involve hymns. In the Teruel copy of the 1581 *Hymni*, Victoria's "Sanctorum meritus" is copied out in a manuscript addition with the next text "Al mocum tumidam." In this same manuscript addition, his hymn "Lucis creator optime" appears as "Jesus spes poenitentibus." The Santa Maria Maggiore copy of the 1581 *Hymni* changes the text of "Christe redemptor" to one beginning "Cos prima Christi."

The practice of changing texts, however, is not confined to hymns. The Valladolid copy of the 1572 *Motecta* gives the text "Felix Tomas Doctor" to Victoria's Palm Sunday motet "Pueri hebraeorum." And, although it is not a printed source and therefore outside the general terms of reference for this study, it may be noted that Cappella Sistina Ms. 298 and Mus. Hs. 16.698 [A.N. 38.B.18] in the Österreichesche Nationalbibliothek in Vienna preserve Victoria's *a 6* motet "Vidi speciosam" with the text "Petrus apostolus."

Equally interesting in this context is the interpolation of the name "Basilio" between the two syllables of the word "sancto" in the altus at the end of the Gloria of the *Missa quarti toni* in the Tudela copy of the 1576 *Liber primus*. It is not known if Saint Basil had a special connection with the Tudela Cathedral, but at the very least it may be surmised that this change was probably made for an occasion on which Basil was honored.

Other types of emendation do occur, but rather infrequently and often in only one source. While they confirm that the source was used, generally they do not have the import of the emendations discussed above, and therefore they will receive only brief mention here. Changes of this kind include, first, the indication in the Valladolid copy of the 1600 *Missae, magnificat, motecta, psalmi, & alia quam plurima* that the *altus secundus* of the *Magnificat primi toni* is really a *tenor secundus*; second, the addition of a fermata on the last note of the Gloria in the *bassus* of the *Missa Simile est regnum* in the Orfeo Catala copy of the 1576 *Liber primus*; third, the assignment of the two settings of the hymn "Christe redemptor" to "In nativitas Domine" and "In festo omnium Sanctorum," respectively, in the Cappella Giulia copy of the 1581 *Hymni* as well as other hymns to Santa Teresa, S. Venantii, and San Giuseppe. The notations in the Tarazona copy of the 1585 *Motecta* that the *a 5* motet "Domine Jesu Christe" is a "Motete para la Dominica de Pasion y para la Virgen de los Dolores," that "Ecce dominus veniet" is "para la Domenica la adviento y para da 2a y 4a de adviento," and "Ardens est cor meum" is "en 3° die Resurectionis et Domenica" are further examples of this type of emendation.

The final emendations on which comment will be made are the notation "tace" in front of the two *si placet* duos in Victoria's setting of the St. Matthew Passion in the Cappella Giulia copy of the 1585 *Officium hebdomadae sanctae*, and the crossing out of these two sections in the Santa Cecilia conservatory copy of this print. From these two emendations we can conclude that in spite of the latitude given by the composer in the original source it probably was not common to sing these sections when performing this Passion, and modern performances might well take this fact into account.

In summary, on the basis of the evidence accumulated over the years in the emendations found in the extant prints of Victoria's works, we can conclude that if a modern conductor or performer wishes to change the ending of a work, or add a voice, or even substitute an entirely new composition, or change the text underlay, or even to change the text entirely, there is justification in the sources for doing so. If, however, one wishes to change the performing resources, or add an accidental, or introduce dynamic markings, or even add an occasional fermata, the justification in the sources is not so unequivocal, and therefore should be undertaken hesitatingly and with the utmost discretion if some semblance of "authenticity," even in its most general sense, is to be achieved.

CHAPTER 5

Melody-Bass Lines and the Early Italian Trio Sonata

L. Jonathan Saylor

The inception of the Italian trio sonata during the first two decades of the seventeenth century offers us a wide array of fascinating issues: origins, function, genre types, and terminology, to name a few.[1] Perhaps one of the most interesting topics arising from this repertory, however, revolves around the concept of texture. As in most incipient periods of a genre, experimentation abounds in this music, and textural variety remains a constant point of interest. The most common texture, is of course, the paired treble lines accompanied by continuo (SS/bc). During these early years, however, some subtle variants occur. The key element in these variants is the added bass line, or melody-bass (SS<u>B</u>/bc), a line which in many ways attempts to bridge the treble/bass polarity established by the standard texture.

Before examining the role of the melody-bass line, however, let us examine possible ties between texture and genre. The primary terms associated with trio textures are canzona, sonata, sinfonia, and numerous dance-types (branle, gagliarda, etc.). The more improvisatory, experimental elements usually occur in the sonata, with the canzona being more conservative. The sinfonia and dances are short (often no more than fifteen measures) and, at least in the case of the former, were probably functional in nature. Aside from these general statements, however, it is difficult to align a specific formal/structural expectation with the genres.[2]

From Salomone Rossi's famous, pioneering 1607 collection (the first SS/bc publication) to Biagio Marini's landmark *Affetti musicali* of 1617, there are approximately 117 works for SS/bc or SSB/bc textures (see list on following page). These include 67 sinfonie, 30 dances, 12 sonatas, 5 canzonas, and 3 arias. It would seem clear that in the early history of the trio sonata, the shorter sinfonia was the prevalent genre, with the sonata appearing more often than the canzona.[3]

---

[1] See Saylor, "Italian Instrumental Trio-Texture, 1600-1621," 2 vols. (M.A. thesis, Boston University, 1985). Volume 2 contains an edition of most of the works discussed in this study.

[2] See Thomas D. Dunn, "The Sonatas of Biagio Marini: Structure and Style," *Music Review* 36 (1975): 161-79; see also Eleanor Selfridge-Field, "Canzona and Sonata: Some Differences in Social Identity," *International Review of the Aesthetics and Sociology of Music* 9 (1978): 111-19.

[3] One should be wary of overly stringent distinctions, however; Stefano Bernardi's *Madrigaletti* (1621) announces "alcune sonate" on the title page, then lists seven "canzoni" in the table of contents.

ITALIAN INSTRUMENTAL TRIO-TEXTURED WORKS, 1600-21

Based on Claudio Sartori, *Bibliografia della musica strumentale italiana stampata in Italia fino al 1700* (Florence: Olschki, 1952; supplement, 1958)

The two numbers after the publisher refer to the total number of instrumental compositions in the collection, followed by the number of SS/bc and SSB/bc works.

> Salamone Rossi, *Il primo libro delle sinfonie et gagliarde* (Venice: Amadino, 1607) – 27/20
> Salamone Rossi, *Il secondo libro delle sinfonie* (Venice: Amadino, 1608) – 35/32
> Gian Paolo Cima, *Concerti ecclesiastici* (Milan: Tini & Lomazzo, 1610) – 6/1
> Marco Antonio Negri, *Affetti amorosi* (Venice: Amadino, 1611) – 3/3
> Giovanni Battista Riccio, *Il primo libro delle divine lodi* (Venice: Amadino, 1612) – 2/1
> Salamone Rossi, *Il terzo libro de varie sonate* (Venice: Vincenti, 1613) – 33/33
> Giulio Belli, *Concerti ecclesiastici* (Venice: Gardano/Magni, 1613) – 2/1
> Giovanni Battista Riccio, *Il secondo libro delle divine lodi* (Venice: Amadino, 1614) – 7/2
> Antonio Brunelli, *Varii esercitii* (Florence: Zenobi Pignoni, 1614) – 1/1
> Francesco Usper, *Messa e salmi* (Venice: Vincenti, 1614)
> Marco da Gagliano, *Musiche* (Venice: Amadino, 1615) – 1/1
> Antonio Brunelli, *Scherzi, arie, canzonette* (Venice: Vincenti, 1616) – 4/2
> Biagio Marini, *Affetti musicali* (Venice: Gardano/Magni, 1617) – 27/19
> Francesco Usper, *Compositioni armoniche* (Venice: Gardano/Magni, 1619) – 10/1
> Herole Porta, *Sacro convito musicale* (Venice: Vincenti, 1620) – 4/1
> Biano Marini, *Arie, madrigali, et corenti* (Venice: Gardano/Magni, 1620) – 6/5
> Adriano Banchieri, *Primo libro delle messe e motetti* (Venice: Vincenti, 1620) – 1/1
> Giulio Mussi da Lodi, *Il primo libro delle canzoni* (Venice: Vincenti, 1620) – 16/3
> Giovanni Battista Riccio, *Il terzo libro delle divine lodi musicali* (Venice: Gardano/Magni, 1620) – 12/3
> Giovanni Martino Cesare, *Musicali melodie* (Munich: Hanrico, 1621) – 14/5
> Francesco Turini, *Madrigali a una, due, tre voci* (Venice: Gardano/Magni, 1621) – 4/4
> Steffano Bernardi, *Madrigaletti a due et a tre voci* (Venice: Vincenti, 1621) – 7/7
> Dario Castello, *Sonate concertate* (Venice: Gardano/Magni, 1621) – 12/7

Five collections deserve special mention at this point. Rossi's 1608 publication includes 21 sinfonie (SS/bc) and also advertises "alcune canzoni per sonar a quattro"; the presence of these three canzonas (the only ones ever composed by Rossi) marks a clear distinction between the traditional, conservative 4-part texture, and the newer, innovative trio-texture. This collection is also interesting since it includes six 5-part works (five sinfonie and one gagliarda), and five 4-part works (four sinfonie and one gagliarda), all marked "a 3 si placet," displaying the flexibility of performance we know must have existed, but which can be difficult to document. Gian Paolo Cima's *Concerti ecclesiastici* (1610) is a largely vocal collection, but typically includes some instrumental works at the end. Textural variety is evidenced within the vocal works by the inclusion of solos, duets, trios, and quartets. Cima then includes a sonata for violin, a sonata for trombone, and the first documented sonata using the SSB/bc texture (violino, cornetto, and violone/bc). Of added interest is his *Sonata a 4* (SATB), using a texture generally reserved for the canzona. Giovanni Battista Riccio's *Secondo libro* (1613) also features a canzona and sonata, both showing 4-part texture. Finally, Antonio Brunelli's *Scherzi* (1616) is significant, as it provides a fascinating link between vocal and instrumental performance. In one instance, it has the simpler, vocal version of a "balletto" (also called a "gagliarda" here) on the left ("Dell bell'ar"), and on the facing page a more complex instrumental version (S/bc). Following this comes a trio-textured piece specifically meant to be played, not sung: "[un] altro ballo per sonare solo senza cantare A3" (SS/bc). Of greatest interest, however, is the "Scherzo, a 2. soprani, a tenore fatto per sonare senza cantare." While having the direct specification to be played, not sung, the succeeding music is texted ("Gia di Paglia," SS/bc). The collection clearly underscores the close relationship between dance-songs and instrumental dance-types, particularly through the presence of texted and untexted versions of dances such as the "balletto."[4]

While ties between texture and genre might prove elusive, at least during these early years the role of the melody-bass line, while subtle, is more concrete. This role can be related not only to the Italian *basso seguente* but also to the apparent single-line bass accompaniment option specified in sources such as Dowland's lute songs. His *First Book of Songes or Ayres* (1597) specifies that the works may be sung "to the lute, orpherian, *or* viol de gamba" (emphasis mine). The option of solo viol accompaniment seems to be contradicted, however, by the full title of Dowland's *Second Book* (1600), which states: ". . . with tablature for the lute, or orpherian, *with* the viol de gamba" (emphasis mine). At any rate, the added bass line, probably in conjunction with the lute, provides an intriguing counterpart to the melody-bass role in contemporary Italy. Another example of the melody-bass line taking on the role of solo accompanist comes in Stefano Bernardi's *Madrigaletti* (1621), which on the title page announces "con alune sonate a tre per due violini overo, cornetti, & un chitarrone, trombone, overo fagotto." Even more explicit is the basso continuo's table of contents: "a Tre. doi Violini, o cornetti, & una tiorba, o fagotto o trombone." Like the Dowland, this would seem to allow for a solo melody-bass accompaniment. Echoes of this practice will surface at the end of the century with Corelli's publications.

*   *   *   *

Italian instrumental music within the first two decades of the seventeenth century, then, presents us with a great variety of textures. Even a cursory examination of early seventeenth-century Italian instrumental publications, however, reveals a remarkable consistency of texture designation. Texture was reckoned by number of melody parts (disregarding range), and never included the basso continuo; the latter would appear later in the title, usually as "col suo basso continuo per l'organo" or some similar indication. Texture was often a means of classifying the compositions of a given publication. This underlines what might be termed "textural awareness" on the part of composers. An excellent example of this is Girolamo Frescobaldi's *Primo libro delle canzoni* (1628), where he not only categorizes by texture, but also by range (i.e., "canto solo," "basso solo," "a due canti," "due canti, e basso," with the continuo added to all textures). The collection uses only the canzona genre but is completely democratic in textural types, favoring none: S/bc, B/bc, SS/bc, BB/bc, SB/bc, SBB/bc, SSB/bc, SSBB/bc, SATB. Thus, while the principle of texture designation remained consistent, the compositions themselves reflect a great variety of textures.[5]

Few-voiced instrumental music textures encompass the following settings: SS/bc, SB/bc, BB/bc, SSS/bc, and SSB/bc.[6] Scholars have usually regarded the standard trio sonata as involving the SS/bc and SSB/bc textures. This view naturally hinges on the fundamental principle of the inner

---

[4] Adding even more weight to this connection is the fact that we find so many of the few-voiced instrumental works at the end of vocal collections.

[5] On the pragmatic side, it must be admitted that increased variety in texture also increased marketability.

[6] Significantly, within few-voiced instrumental textures one rarely finds parts for alto and tenor, ranges which are frequently found in few-voiced vocal works.

workings (dynamics) available through the polarity of paired melody voices supported by a harmonic bass line. Furthermore, it is commonly assumed that the two voices above the continuo will be of equal importance, and will lie within the treble range. Thus, while "melody line" would not necessarily imply a treble range, such a case is assumed within the concept of the trio sonata. The reasoning behind this becomes readily apparent: as the range of a melody line nears that of the basso continuo, it runs a proportionally higher risk of losing independence. Thus, by virtue of range, a treble voice is assured at least some degree of prominence. If a composition features a solo instrument of the bass range (e.g., B/bc), although its range approximates that of the basso continuo, the instrument will naturally emerge as the principal line by virtue of its carrying the melody. The addition of a treble line to this texture, however, might relegate the "melody-bass" line to a position similar to that of the basso continuo.

At this point, let us formally define the term "melody bass": it is a specified bass-range, monophonic part, separate from that of the basso continuo. At times this "basso" part can be quite independent, but the above specification uses "melodic" primarily as the designation of a single-line instrument. The precise function of the melody-bass line is complex. The main focus of this article is to examine the types and roles of this line within the confines of the early trio sonata.

As mentioned above, the presence of one or two treble lines, together carrying the melodic weight, almost always relegates the melody-bass line to a close alignment with the continuo. Thus, it is virtually impossible to find a completely independent melody-bass line in the SSB/bc configuration. More likely, the melody-bass line will serve as an "ornamented, melodic" version of the continuo line, often representing simple divisions on the latter, but seldom straying far from the actual line itself.[7] The independence of these melody-bass lines varies, however, making their classification at times difficult and involved.

A useful classification of the melody-bass line's role could be structured as follows: 1) a melody-bass line strictly doubling the continuo throughout the work; 2) a melody-bass line functioning as an ornamental extension of the continuo, where it might occasionally enter into imitative dialogue with the upper lines; 3) an independent melody-bass line, which functions as a true melodic voice in the bass range, and contains soloistic, unique material.[8] Admittedly, the second and third categories might at times be difficult to distinguish; the distinction would mostly depend on the frequency of continuo doubling and the presence of truly independent material. It should be stressed that while one can find works that feature entirely one type of category, more often what is found is a mixture of category types, with one usually dominating. Even the third category will most often be aligned with the continuo to some degree.

An examination of the seventeen SSB/bc-textured works from 1607 and 1617 reveals the following break-down of melody-bass types: 8 (category 1), 8 (category 2),[9] 1 (category 3). The same study of 20 works extant in 1618-21 reveals the following results: 12 (category 1), 4 (category 2), 4 (category 3).

---

[7] A significant characteristic which is not common in Italy but rather frequently found in England, is role-reversal between the melody-bass and continuo; that is, alternating which of the two voices plays the ornamented line.

[8] John Daverio, in discussing a Dario Castello SB/bc setting, proposes a similar tri-partite function within one work: treble/bass two-part counterpoint (melody-bass line doubling the continuo), melodic bass line supporting the continuo, and an alternation between two and three real parts. See Daverio, "Formal Design and Terminology in the Pre-Corellian 'Sonata' and Related Instrumental Forms" (Ph.D. diss., Boston University, 1983). It should be mentioned that the SB/bc texture allows the melody-bass line greater freedom, since in an SSB/bc setting, the second treble part can usurp much of the independence potentially available to the melody-bass line. It is all the more interesting, then, to find most melodic bass lines in SB/bc textures closely aligned to the basso continuo.

[9] Five of these are what might be called "weak" examples, meaning that the embellishment is minor and not frequent.

These findings suggest that doubling remained the most common function, while an active melody-bass line is seen more often by the 1620s. Of particular interest is the large increase in works within such a short period of time; the period 1600-17 yields essentially the same number of works as the succeeding three years (1618-21). This certainly displays the growing interest in trio-textured works.

As the list above makes clear, the majority of melody-bass lines double the basso continuo. Thus, while an SSB/bc texture consists of four voices, it really only features three distinct lines. In many instances, however, the continuo plays throughout, while the melody-bass line has occasional rests. This is usually to provide the effect and added color of a bass line participating in imitative entries while still maintaining a harmonic foundation undergirding the whole. Bernardi's "Canzon Terza" (*Madrigaletti*, 1621) affords just such an example; he usually omits the melody-bass at regular intervals, using its entrances to highlight a motive. The melody-bass line at times seems to be an option, as in Francesco Turini's "Sinfonia a 3" (*Madrigali*, 1621), which includes the inscription "Istromento, che si puo tralasciare volendo." One other variant is almost impossible to document: the probable on-the-spot improvising that players would engage in, even when given a line doubling the continuo.

At this point it would seem worthwhile to exemplify the role of the melody-bass line, especially within categories 2 and 3, by examining some key sources of the period. The earliest SSB/bc texture known is found in Cima's *Concerti ecclesiastici* (1610). The one SSB/bc composition in this collection is also the first trio-textured work to be called a sonata: "Sonata per il violino, cornetto & violone." The sonata features strict doubling between the melody-bass and continuo lines.[10] A point of some interest, however, is the active role taken by the bass line. This line becomes actively engaged in imitative exchanges, at times imitating them; there are even two instances where the bass line has extended soloistic sixteenth-note passages, although never lasting for more than two measures. The role of the bass, while doubled, is clearly beyond innocuous background support.

A similar collection is Turini's *Madrigali* (1621). Like Cima's, Turini's publication is primarily a vocal one, with some instrumental works at the end. Its sonata *a 3*, "Il Corisino," is one of the best SSB/bc works of the period. Again, like Cima's sonata, Turini's work displays mostly identical bass lines. While the melody-bass's primary notes clearly coincide with those of the continuo, the former are undeniably linked melodically or thematically to the motivic exchanges of the upper lines.[11] This work is also interesting for its economy of means; the entire 202-measure composition is based on two motives. Turini thus weaves an interesting permutative complex, with the same motives being constantly exchanged between all three lines. The traditional triple-meter dance section features the main motive in augmentation.

Bernardi's *Madrigaletti* (1621), another vocal collection with added instrumental works, contains seven "canzoni," all featuring the SSB/bc texture. Of these, all but the third and fourth show a melody-bass line clearly doubling the continuo (category 1). In all seven, Bernardi typically interrupts the melody-bass line to feature its participation in an imitative entry (while the continuo plays throughout). In "Canzona Terza" and "Canzona Quarta," however, the melody-bass line acquires some independence. In the former work there are two specific instances showing this freedom: measures 33-36 feature the melody-bass line ornamenting or making "divisions" on the continuo, which is involved in stepwise descent. The second instance, while also following the contour of the continuo line, features greater

---

[10] In three instances, the melody-bass line drops out briefly to provide a bass "imitative entry" while allowing the continuo to support the upper lines throughout.

[11] Measures 39-55 feature a particularly good example of the melody-bass line's independence and contrapuntal participation with the upper lines.

independence, and significantly there is not a motive that has been exchanged between the upper lines. Rather, this passage (meas. 57-62) seems to form a bridge to the conclusion of the canzona (meas. 63-76). "Canzona Quarta" is most significant because of its construction and inscriptions. The canzona opens with the typical half and two quarter notes stated by all voices. At measure 9, however, the second treble line is marked "solo" and indeed is accompanied only by the continuo. This passage lasts until measure 18, at which point the melody bass line is marked "Fagoto," and this passage, while not marked "solo," is accompanied only by the continuo playing the same bass line. This is followed by an entrance marked "solo" in the top treble line at measure 27. What is especially noteworthy is the fact that the material played by the upper lines is identical (one step apart), while that played by the bassoon is unique. A similar, more extended passage for the bassoon is found in measures 55-67, but in a slightly different context. This second passage, moreover, features an independent melody-bass line, rather than one doubling the continuo, as in the first scenario. The rest of the work features doubling between the two bass lines.

Castello's first book of *Sonate concertate* (1621) contains unique compositions, featuring an overall scope and complexity previously unknown within instrumental trio-texture.[12] Castello's sonatas contain some of the most active and independent melody-bass lines extant. "Sonata Nona" (SSB/bc) features a wealth of melody-bass functions. Throughout the composition the bassoon takes an active part in motivic exchanges; while these clearly distinguish the line from the continuo, the two are most often related, at least in fundamental note progression (e.g., meas. 1-17). The piece also contains exact duplication between bass lines (meas. 18-21, 25-32), and sections where the bassoon is clearly embellishing, or making divisions on the continuo (meas. 40-49). In many instances, however, it is also clear that the bassoon is regarded as a separate entity from the continuo; this is evident from its motivic and contrapuntal activity (meas. 1-20, 35-39, 60-63), and most dramatically, by the solo "cadenza" (meas. 98-113). "Sonata undecima" likewise features a highly active bassoon part. After resting for the first ten measures, the bassoon enters alone, following the harmonic contour of the continuo line but with considerable embellishment (meas. 11-18). Imitative repartée occurs between all three "melodic" voices (especially at meas. 49-54 and 72-77) and, like the ninth sonata, the eleventh also features one extended bassoon solo (meas. 103-17). Of particular interest is the highly virtuosic final "cadenza" (meas. 158-59) for solo bassoon. The two most significant features which lend the melody-bass line independence seem to be contrapuntal activity and pitch distinction. The first of these can be explained as "division-making," and still relates the two lines. Pitch distinction would seem to offer the strongest support for melodic-bass independence, yet it is all too rare, and when it does occur it seldom lasts for long. Moreover, the discrepancy often is due to a motivic gesture's shape, or a desire to avoid open octaves. While the Castello works might feature the earliest extended examples of an independent melody-bass line, the set would seem to be an innovative exception rather than a standard model.

Marini's *Affetti musicali* (1617) is perhaps the most significant collection from the first two decades, in six main contributions: 1) a wide variety of genres: sinfonia, canzona, sonata, and numerous dances; 2) a variety of textures: SB/bc, SS/bc, SSB/bc, BBS/bc, S (solo); 3) it specifies the instrumentation for all the works; 4) it is the earliest completely instrumental collection to feature all of the above traits; 5) it contains the earliest SSB/bc texture to specify a bassoon as the melody-bass instrument;

---

[12] The earliest extant printing of this *Libro primo* is 1629, but Eitner's *Quellen-Lexicon* mentions the existence of a 1621 edition in the Berlin Staatsbiblithek; unfortunately, the print has since been lost. See *Dario Castello: Selected Ensemble Sonatas, Part I*, ed. Eleanor Selfridge-Field, Recent Researches in the Music of the Baroque Era, 23 (Madison: A-R Editions, 1977), which includes Sonata nos. 3, 5, 9, 12 of the 1621 collection; Sonata no. 11 is in my thesis (see fn. 1).

6) it features the earliest trio-textured sonata to call for the use of "tremolo" (in "La Foscarina," a sonata set for SSB/bc). Of the twenty-seven works in this collection, fourteen feature the SSB/bc texture: two balletti, five symphonie, two sonatas, two arias, one brando, and two corenti. The specified instruments typically include violins or cornetti for the upper lines and bassoons, trombones or simply "basso" for the melody-bass line.

The two sonatas will be discussed shortly; of the other twelve works, one balletto, "Il Vendramino" features exact doubling of bass lines, while the other, "Il Zontino," displays some independence.[13] In the latter we find staggered entrances and typical embellishments. Thus, rather than playing a quarter note, the melody-bass has octave eighths (beat 3).

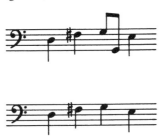

Even bolder departures are seen (see ex. 5.1):

Example 5.1. Biagio Marini, balletto "Il Zontino," from *Affetti musicali* (1617), bass lines, meas. 15-17.

The above figurations are typical of the category 2, "ornamental" melody-bass line. The ornamented line seldom strays from the structural contour of the continuo, whose harmonic rhythm establishes the limits of the ornamentation. Notice the sequential pattern in both lines. Interestingly, Marini adds the following annotation after the title: "Ad imitation de viole grosse." All five symphonie feature what might be called mild, or weak category-2 melody-bass lines; that is, one finds some, but not elaborate embellishments of the continuo line by the melodic bass instrument. The most active of the five is clearly "La Zoppa," which, as one might expect, features highly dotted and rhythmic-intensive melodic lines. Perhaps to establish the agogic foundation that will underscore the syncopations, the continuo line consists of almost constant quarter notes. In general, if a contrasting triple-meter dance section occurs in these works, the melody-bass seems to be less active here than elsewhere. The two arias and the brando are short, simple works, and feature almost exact duplication of bass lines (category 1).[14]

---

[13] All twenty-seven works are typically given character titles, as above; the title usually relates to a family, printer, or even location being honored (e.g., in the aria "La Soranza," all parts have a brief text underlay near the end: "Viva Viva Ca[sa] Soranzo").

[14] Unfortunately, the two corenti could not be checked since the *basso principale* (continuo; fascicle D) did not include these two works (the last page), even though listing them in the Tavola. The basso, melody-bass part, fascicle C however, does not seem to feature much ornamentation.

By far the two most interesting SSB/bc works of the collection are the sonatas, "La Foscarina" and "La Aguzzona." The former is multi-sectional, and features a clear category 2 melody-bass line; while at times embellishing the continuo line, it never really establishes complete independence. It is clear, however, that the melody-bass participates in the imitative repartée of the upper lines (e.g., meas. 1-10). To summarize, of the total 104 measures of the work, the melody bass line has 26 measures of rest (mostly to allow for a bass "entrance," although during meas. 21-32 the line was simply omitted for textural variety), 30 measures of exact duplication, and 48 measures of some (however slight) embellishment of the continuo line. The melody-bass role, then, roughly breaks down into 25% resting, 25% doubling, and 50% ornamenting of the continuo and participating in imitative repartée with the upper lines. Regarding instrumentation, "La Foscarina" specifies "doi violini o cornetti e trombone o fagotto." If a trombone were used, its presence would certainly be felt throughout the passages where the bass lines are doubled, even if the continuo line were to be played on the organ (even more so if a chitarrone or spinet played the continuo line).

"La Aguzzona," unlike "La Foscarina," has a single specified instrumentation: "doi violini e fagotto," thus becoming the first trio sonata to specify the use of the bassoon. Interestingly, it has exactly the same number of measures (104) as "La Foscarina." Of these, the melody-bass rests during 7, duplicates the continuo throughout 52, and embellishes or plays independently in 45 measures. Surprisingly, while exact duplication is at 50%, the melody bass rests only 7%, thus leaving around 43% as an independent line. Upon further examination, moreover, it becomes clear that the melody-bass in the work establishes itself as an independent line. Its independence is based on two factors: 1) constant interchange with the upper lines, usually in exact rhythmic duplication (which the continuo approximates but does not equal—e.g., meas. 11, 16), and most significantly, 2) its "solo" status (meas. 34-39). The bassoon has an elaborate solo in these six measures, accompanied by whole notes in the continuo, clearly establishing the former's independence. Moreover, measures 53-63 involve a repartée section between the upper treble line and the bassoon line; while the continuo undergirds with half-notes, it is the melody-bass line alone that enters into the repartée with the upper voice. Even more interesting is the repartée at measures 73-80, where both treble lines are paired in a lively exchange with the melody-bass, while the continuo has whole notes. In the above cases, the materials providing the melody-bass line's independence are the actual repartée gestures of the entire texture. Thus, "La Aguzzona" is not only the first trio sonata to specify the bassoon, but also the first to feature an independent melody bass line (category 3).

*   *   *   *

The question that naturally arises is whether a pattern in the melody-bass/basso continuo relationship can be observed upon chronological survey. The earliest SSB/bc texture known is the Cima Sonata (1610), which displays strict duplication of bass lines. Belli's Canzona from his *Concerti ecclesiastici* (1613) shows equivalence of bass lines, but not strict duplication. By 1617, with Marini's *Affetti musicali*, the melody-bass line has attained considerable autonomy and displays examples of all three categories of melodic-bass line function. This can especially be seen in his "Sonata La Aguzzona," where the bassoon enters fully into motivic exchanges and even a solo statement. This independence is also clearly seen in Castello's 1621 collection. Before Marini's 1617 publication, however, the melody-bass line seems to have been limited most of the time to continuo duplication. As we proceed throughout the seventeenth century, the independent melody-bass line remains an option until the end of the century. Thus, in Marini's *Sonate da chiesa e da camera*, op. 22 (1655) we find a "Balletto Primo" (SSB/bc) with a highly soloistic variation for the melody-bass line. Likewise, in the same collection's

"Sonata prima a due violini e basso," the melody-bass line doubles the continuo for most of the piece, but does have some soloistic ornamentation. Giovanni Legrenzi's *Sonate a due a tre*, op. 2 (1655) features eight SSB/bc works. Of these, two include exact duplication of bass lines, and six exemplify category 2, with some embellishment of the melody-bass line. By the time we reach Corelli's landmark trio sonatas, however, the independent melody-bass line has all but vanished, with bass line doubling throughout.[15] We find here, however, a performance option reminiscent of Rossi's suggestion at the beginning of the century: leaving the continuo out altogether.[16] This option, of course, would give full weight to the melody-bass instrument, and render the doubling question irrelevant.[17]

The issue of continuo instrumentation is a complex one, remaining controversial and elusive. It is possible that a separate melody-bass instrument was present, even if not specified. Moreover, the presence of a specified bass instrument part, even when duplicating the continuo, could both prove that this was simply a concrete example of an existing practice, or that the melody-bass instrument should be used only when there was a separate part-book for it. In such a context, it can be seen that the melody-bass is the direct influence on what eventually became the assumed doubling of the continuo line by a bass instrument. It would appear that the first melody-bass lines were, in fact, duplicates of the continuo, then gradually became "contrapuntal extensions" of the continuo—perhaps reflecting performance-practice trends—while the latter remained a harmonic support. By the second decade of the seventeenth century, experimentation involved increasingly independent melody-bass lines, which at times were given solo status. By the late seventeenth century, both bass lines, with few exceptions, had merged into one (two performers), but often retained the contrapuntal activity hitherto usually associated with the melody-bass line. Marini's *Affetti* of 1617 is especially interesting in that it is the first to feature all three types of melody-bass roles. It also underscores the ultimate reliance of the melody-bass on the continuo line, since even a completely independent melody-bass line at some point associates itself with the continuo. Another imponderable lies in the possibility of melody-bass players spontaneously improvising embellishments on a line that duplicates the continuo. While proof of this can be difficult to document, what one does find for certain is interest in texture, and the desire to experiment with textural possibilities. In fact, within most of the works mentioned, textural variety and imitative repartée seem to have been a higher priority than a clearly identifiable melody. Most gestures are, if not formulaic, at least closely related to each other, with rhythmic vitality and imitative exchange of paramount importance.

In closing, one should emphasize that early seventeenth-century Italian instrumental music features instability of terms and conditions; it is dangerous to formulate rules and inflexible categories within such a richly experimental era. It is precisely this experimentation, however, that remains so compelling. As the new century gave birth to the trio sonata, so that latter's grappling with textural variety gave birth to a rich field of investigation.

---

[15] This does not mean that a solo melodic bass line is never used at this time. One of the most active of all melodic bass lines in a trio-texture setting can be seen in the six sonatas for two oboes, bassoon, and continuo by Jan Zelenka (1715).

[16] Corelli specifies this option for his *Sonate da camera*, op. 2 (1685), and op. 4 (1694).

[17] Purcell's *Twelve Sonatas of Three Parts* (1683) features the SSB/bc texture with the melody bass part ornamenting the continuo lines. In the preface to this collection, however, Purcell blames the delay of publication in part to a last-minute decision: "There has been neither care, nor industry wanting, as well in contriving, as revising the whole work; which had been abroad in the world much sooner, but that he [Purcell] has now thought fit to cause the whole Thorough Bass to be engraved, which was a thing quite besides his first resolutions." Could this imply an original non-continuo conception? It would lie in the tradition of numerous non-continuo English instrumental works of the seventeenth century. Moreover, Purcell is clearly "introducing" Italian concepts and terminology to his English audience. Another possible placement for the melody bass part was in substituting a treble part (with corresponding octave displacement); such is the case in Telemann's Quartet in D minor from *Tafelmusik*, part 2 (Hamburg, 1733), which specifies SSSB/bc, and also allows the substitution of a bassoon or cello for the recorder part.

CHAPTER 6

The Cantor/Capellmeister Issue in Bach Scholarship: Blume's "Outlines" Revisited

John Ogasapian

Joseph Kerman calls the mid-century tidal wave of Bach research occasioned by the preparation of the *Neue Bach Ausgabe* "perhaps the most brilliant achievement of positivistic musicology after the war."[1] Whether or not one considers Kerman's assessment extravagant, he cannot be gainsaid in at least one particular. Beyond cavil, no project involved so many scholars working simultaneously over such distances as did the work done on Bach in the wake of Alfred Dürr's destabilization of the Leipzig cantata chronology. From Georg von Dadelson's watermark studies at Tübingen to Arthur Mendel's Princeton seminars, an international phalanx of the discipline bent to the task, and a whole generation of scholars emerged from the incubator of Bach studies at major universities in Europe and America.

Their work has brought to the fore several questions relative to Bach, many of which are simply not susceptible to positive answers given the known extant documentary evidence, among them the subject of this paper. The issue is one that would in all likelihood not have been raised before mid-century, but which has engendered a good bit of scholarly crosstalk since then. Essentially, it is this: what can be inferred about Bach's musical vocation from the personal and professional contexts of his life, insofar as they can be known? Did Bach see himself primarily as church cantor, a court capellmeister, or as a combination?

In one sense, the enigma of Bach's *métier* has been with us since the beginning of Bach scholarship. During the course of just over a century, his best-known biographers drew different images of him. In 1802, Johann Nikolaus Forkel, scientific musicologist, Göttingen *magister*, man of the Enlightenment, and a patriotic German, cast Bach—accurately or not—as a performer, composer, working professional, and a sort of social and cultural icon:

> His virtues . . . he showed . . . by his conscientious performance of his social and civil duties. His acquaintance was agreeable to everybody. . . . These social virtues, united with the great reputation of his art, caused his house to be very seldom without visitors.

This paper grew out of a talk I was invited to give during the 1994 Bach Aria Group Institute at SUNY-Stony Brook on "The Enigma of Bach's Religious Thought." My discussions there with Dr. Joyce Irwin, whose expertise in seventeenth- and eighteenth-century German theology and religious history and their relationship to music is formidable, clarified a number of points, and caused me to rethink several positions I had taken. Needless to say, I am most grateful to her.

[1] Joseph Kerman, *Contemplating Music* (Cambridge: Harvard University Press, 1985), 49.

Forkel closes his work with a ringing commendation of Bach as a paragon of Germanness: "a great composer, great soul and German. Let his country be proud of him . . . but at the same time worthy of him."[2]

The Prussian finance minister Carl Bitter's 1865 biography opposes Forkel with a picture of Bach as the pious cantor and servant of his faith. Even if necessity prevented him from time to time, Bitter's Bach, in his unpietistic orthodox piety, sought only to provide music for the enhancement of worship and the honor and glory of God.[3]

If Forkel and Bitter pose the bases of the dialectic, Bach's definitive biographer, Philipp Spitta, is ambiguous in the matter of his piety relative to his music. Indeed, Spitta adduces material enough to buttress special pleadings on both sides. As is well known, Spitta, like Forkel, was a "scientific" musicologist. But he was also a student of theology and the son of a clergyman, hymnodist, and theologian. Accordingly, his view of Bach in the context of the cantor/capellmeister question is often interpreted critically as consistent with the Lutheran neo-Pietism and the romantic religious revival of Spitta's era.

Yet passages like "All his actions were based on a genuine piety which was not the outcome of any mental struggle, but inborn and natural . . ."[4] are, in the end, problematic. In fact, although his 1873-80 study placed Bach in the sequence of Lutheran cantors, even on casual reading, Spitta may also be seen to portray the man himself as an almost Pateresque sort of romantic, living a "quiet, modest and reserved life absorbed in the contemplation of the ideal of his art," and for whom "instrumental music—that is to say, music for music's sake—was the aim and essence of his being."[5]

By the end of the nineteenth century, Bitter's image of Bach had become the norm: that of the pious if sometimes irascible Lutheran cantor—"not conscious of the extraordinary greatness of his work," as Albert Schweitzer put it in his 1905 biography—whose art was consecrated to the praise of his God.[6] And such remained the general view of Bach through the first half of the twentieth century. In the words of the 1954 *Grove's Dictionary* entry: "Music, to Bach, was the apparatus of worship."[7]

The discoveries made in the 1950s seemed to shift the balance back toward Forkel's view. Briefly, it then seemed clear that Bach had composed increasingly less for his Leipzig churches after 1729. Instead, he repeated whole pieces, re-used movements from earlier works, and borrowed from other composers, devoting most of his creative energies to such civic, secular, and independent musical activities as directing his instrumental Collegium Musicum, publishing his music, and composing as his artistic interests led him.

By 1962, no less a personage than Friedrich Blume reversed field.[8] Fifteen years earlier, he had faulted Carl Friedrich Zelter for failing to recognize Bach's style as representing "the full and adequate expression of his orthodox belief." As for Johann Friedrich Rochlitz, he had not grasped Bach's

---

    [2] Johann Nikolaus Forkel, *On Johann Sebastian Bach's Life, Genius and Works* (1802), transl. A. C. F. Kollman [?] (1820), in *The Bach Reader*, ed. Hans T. David and Arthur Mendel, rev. ed. (New York: Norton, 1966), 333, 353. In context, Friedrich Blume's redaction of Forkel—"a religious element at the heart of Bach's character . . . rootedness in the Holy Scripture and Christian dogma [and] stubborn orthodoxy"—is puzzling. See Blume, *Two Centuries of Bach: An Account of Changing Tastes* (London: Oxford University Press, 1950), 40.

    [3] Carl H. Bitter, *Johann Sebastian Bach* (Berlin, 1865); an enlarged edition appeared in 1881. See also Blume, *Two Centuries*, 62-63.

    [4] Philipp Spitta, *Johann Sebastian Bach*, transl. Clara Bell and J. A. Fuller-Maitland, 3 vols. (London: Novello, 1883-85; reprint, New York: Dover, 1951), 3:265.

    [5] Ibid., 2:6.

    [6] Albert Schweitzer, *J. S. Bach, le musicien-poète* (Paris, 1905), transl. Ernest Newman, 2 vols. (Leipzig: Breitkopf & Härtel, 1911; reprint, New York: Dover, 1966), 1:166.

    [7] *Grove's Dictionary of Music and Musicians*, 5th ed. (1954), s.v. "Bach," by Charles Sanford Terry, 1:304.

    [8] Blume, "Outlines of a New Picture of Bach," *Music and Letters* 44, no. 3 (July 1963): 214-27. The paper was originally a lecture delivered at the International Bach Society Festival on 1 June 1962.

"uncompromising directness of an openly professed faith . . .the awful certitude of original sin, the humble reality of death and judgment and the radiant vision of grace and mercy." Arnold Schering had "completely failed to touch on the vital problem of the bases of the essential Bach spirit, of Bach's relation to God and man." Blume asserted that the most fruitful and promising field for future Bach research would be the theological thought of the period.

> . . . to understand [Bach's music] a whole training in the subtleties and sophistications of the old Lutheran scholasticism is required. This interpretation seems to open a door on the whole world of Bach's innermost conceptions and ideas. To open it still further must now be one of the most urgent concerns of future Bach research.[9]

André Pirro, Philipp Wolfrum, and Hubert Parry, influenced by "snobbish æsthetes," had

> . . . removed Bach from both the national and the ecclesiastical soil which after all had fostered his development. . . . Under the influence of a mistaken liberalistic outlook they believed that Bach had mostly followed his own genius in his work, and that his church and home locality, his faith and belief in dogma, his family and his craft were simply unavoidable restrictions on the artistic freedom of a great personality.[10]

But in 1962 Blume staked out a new position close to, if not precisely at, the very one he had condemned in Wolfrum, Pirro, and Parry fifteen years before. In fact, Blume could now assert that Bach had less interest in "well-regulated church music," as he himself put it, than in advancing his career, and that he "resolutely turned his back on the service of the church" when he moved to the Duke of Weimar's court in 1708 after only a year as organist in Mühlhausen.[11]

Perhaps Blume's polar revision of his earlier views should be viewed in the context of post-World War II German cultural disillusionment and quasi-Marxist secularism.[12] After all, Forkel, empirical and scientific though he tried to be in his musical writings, breathed the air of the *Aufklärung* in Göttingen, and Spitta combed carefully and tirelessly through documents against a background of German neo-Pietism (although, as we have seen, he seems to have resisted absolute capitulation to it in his view of Bach).

Predictably, Friedrich Smend, the conservative Bach scholar of Blume's generation and stature who held out against the New Chronology and its implications, evidence and scholarly consensus notwithstanding, fought what seemed like a rear-guard action against the decentering of church music in Bach's vocation. This time, however, Smend was not alone. Blume's conclusions were based on a radical extrapolation from the chronological data, in and of themselves unassailable but certainly not warranting so drastic a set of conclusions. Even Alfred Dürr, a scholar whose work is most closely associated with the New Chronology, took issue with Blume.[13]

---

[9] Blume, *Two Centuries*, 42, 46, 83-84.

[10] Ibid., 68-69.

[11] Blume, "Outlines," 218.

[12] Gerhard Herz, "Toward a New Image of Bach," *Bach* 1, no. 4 (October 1970): 26, implies that Blume's new position was gratifying to the East German "nomenclatura," although he does not follow the string to its logical end: that adopting the government's secular proletarian-tinged view enhanced the chances of access to Bach documents in Eastern libraries and archives during the Cold War years. In any event, the issue would probably not have loomed as large, musically or politically, had not Bach become the archetype of the Christian church composer.

[13] Alfred Dürr, "Zum Wandel des Bach-Bildes," *Musik und Kirche* 32 (1962): 151; Friedrich Smend, "Was bleibt?," *Der Kirchenmusiker* 13 (1962). Smend was by no means alone. See, for instance, Willibald Gurlitt, *Johann Sebastian Bach—Der Meister und sein Werke* (Kassel: Bärenreiter, 1959).

Gerhard Herz made a thorough and reasoned analysis of the evidence and state of research in 1970-71;[14] in a 1985 article I reviewed the elements of the controversy, but stopped short of drawing any conclusions;[15] and shortly thereafter historian Jaroslav Pelikan discussed the issue in some depth in his book *Bach Among the Theologians*.[16]

In general, the recent literature on the issue of Bach the cantor and Bach the capellmeister seems to have moderated, but by no means abandoned, Blume's "outline." Bach is now the thoroughgoing professional musician, maintaining his professionalism in the context of the general piety of his era, preferring court to choirloft, but working within the constraints of whatever position he occupied at any given time.

Hans Heinrich Eggebrecht has argued for a reconciliation between the cantor and capellmeister. He reminds us that Bach's original and primary medium of performance was the keyboard, both in church (organ) and chamber (harpsichord); that his position in Leipzig, Thomasschule cantor and city music director (*director musices*), was civic rather than ecclesiastical; and, most important, that Bach and his contemporaries considered all music as belonging to God, so to speak, and would thus have drawn no bright line between sacred and secular music.[17] Eggebrecht's position is well taken: there can be no question that on a metaphysical level Bach and his contemporaries viewed secular music as a "recreation" for the spirit, thereby serving God's purpose. It is by no means clear, however, that such a view informed Bach's creative life or professional self-identity at a practical level.

Ultimately, of course, we cannot come to a conclusion through any clear preponderance of factual data. But we *can* review the matter dialectically; i.e., as a question that is probably not subject to definite resolution, but that can, at some level, be brought closer to an answer by cross-examining the available data for alternate interpretations. My intent here is to revisit one aspect of the issue in just such a manner, by way of example. I shall engage what I take to be one of Blume's salient contentions: that Bach "resolutely turned his back" on church work in departing Mühlhausen for Weimar in 1708.[18]

Now there can be no doubt that Bach's move to Weimar marks a major watershed in his musical development. His exposure at Weimar to the Italian melodic and rhythmic traits that came to dominate his style signals the beginning of Bach's magisterial maturity. But even if we accept the idea—and I think we must—that Weimar represents the defining phase in determining Bach's subsequent musical language—and even if we stipulate that he somehow knew it would—it does not necessarily follow that his move to Weimar represents a correspondingly defining long-term career decision.

Let us also stipulate without hesitation that career advancement was a major factor, possibly even the main factor, in Bach's decision to depart for Weimar after but a year at Mühlhausen. He would certainly have been attracted by a financial incentive that represented almost twice the salary he had been earning, to say nothing of the advantage and prestige of being associated with a court musical establishment, and possibly even the prospect of satisfying a single, highly cultured patron rather than the conflicting whims of an Arnstadt consistory or Mühlhausen city council. Yet such

---

[14] Herz, "Toward a New Image of Bach," *Bach* 1, no. 4 (October 1970): 9-27; 2, no. 1 (January 1971): 7-28.

[15] Ogasapian, "Bach, the Fifth Evangelist," *Journal of Church Music* 27, no. 3 (March 1985): 13-20.

[16] (Philadelphia: Fortress Press, 1985). Professor Pelikan was generous enough to refer to my work, and too generous to make a point of my having overcautiously avoided committing myself to a position either substantively on the question or critically on the bibliography.

[17] Hans Heinrich Eggebrecht, "Thomaskantor Bach," *Musik und Kirche* 61 (1991): 63-72. A similar position was elucidated in some detail over a quarter century ago by Jan Chiapusso in his *Bach's World* (Bloomington: Indiana University Press, 1968), 123-38.

[18] Blume, "Outlines," 218.

considerations, whatever their weight in his decision, do not in the end mitigate against the credibility of his resignation letter to the Mühlhausen authorities: that in striving to attain his ideal of "well-regulated church music" he had encountered "hindrance" and "vexations," and that a call from the Weimar court offered him a chance to realize that ideal.

Had there been no basis for truth in his statement—if instead Bach's interest in church music had flagged and he now "turned his back" on it—there would seem to be no reason for him to go out of his way to rehearse his frustrations at Mühlhausen by firing what could certainly be viewed as a gratuitous parting shot at the city that had treated him well in general, and that would continue to hold him in high regard. He could simply have attributed his request for dismission from the city to the summons of the imperiously paternalistic Duke Wilhelm Ernst, and left it at that. In the custom of the time, one can scarcely imagine the councilors denying him. No young musician like Bach could afford to decline the honor of a ducal summons to service; nor would the authorities have presumed to thwart the formidable ducal will by delaying his release. Instead, Bach chose to highlight his ambition for good church music, the opposition he encountered at Mühlhausen, and the more promising prospects for realizing that ambition at Weimar as the reasons for his departure. Accordingly, we must examine those reasons closely and in context.

Subsequent writers have almost uniformly taken Spitta's lead and blamed Bach's frustration on resistance from his Pietist congregation and pastor, J. H. Frohne, to any music beyond the simple arias with instrumental *ritornelli* favored by his predecessors, Johann Rudolph Ahle and his son, Johann Georg. Bach, or so the reasoning goes, had come to maturity in orthodox surroundings and was thus unprepared for the Pietist opposition to his ideal of "well-regulated" church music from his own parish.

Yet the evidence is not necessarily consistent with that view. First, Bach was by no means unaware of the tenets of Pietism as a young man in Mühlhausen. Indeed, as Leo Schrade noted nearly a half century ago, Bach's first experience with Pietism probably occurred during his student years in Ohrdruf, when he would have been most impressionable. The town had a vocal and active contingent of Pietists, as well as "zealots, seceders from other religions [that had] found shelter there." It is thus no wonder that the authorities required not only teachers at the school but town officials as well to affirm their orthodoxy by signing the *Formula concordiae*.[19]

But Schrade goes even further: "Pietism began to affect his religious thought fundamentally; later he possessed in his own library all the important literature of the Pietistic theologians. . . . A religious experience appears side by side with his artistic beginnings."[20] Although a critical look at Bach's library of theological works as inventoried after his death is outside the scope of this paper, it should be borne in mind that in addition to Pietist writings he also owned eighteen volumes of Luther's works and the three-volume translation of the Bible by Luther with commentary by the orthodox stalwart Abraham Calov.[21] All by way of pointing out that even though Bach's background and education were certainly orthodox, his Lutheranism, like that of most Germans of the time, was

---

[19] Leo Schrade, *Bach: The Conflict between the Sacred and the Secular* (New York: Merlin Press, 1947), 18-20. Schrade cites letters from the school's rector, Johann Christoph Kiesewetter (whom Bach was later to encounter at Weimar), as well as an article I have been unable to locate a copy of, as of this writing: Theodor Wotschke, "Der Pietismus in Thüringen," *Thüringische-Sächsische Zeitschrift für Geschichte und Kunst* 18 (Halle, 1929). On the strict orthodoxy of the school, see also Spitta, 1:188.

[20] Schrade, 26.

[21] Indeed, the collection has come in for a good bit of study and comment. See among numerous publications, Robin Leaver, "Bach and Luther," *Bach* 9, no. 3 (July 1978): 9-15, 26-30, and especially his *Bachs theologische Bibliothek: Ein kritische Bibliographie* (Neuhausen-Stuttgart: Hänssler, 1983).

no more rigidly orthodox than it was ardently Pietist. In fact, Pietistic thought and rhetoric had infused orthodoxy to a large extent, and it therefore need not surprise us that the Salomo Franck texts Bach set at Weimar, to say nothing of the polemically orthodox Erdmann Neumeister's cantata librettos, are couched in Pietism's deeply personal terms.

Granting for a moment the juxtaposition with which the Schrade quotation ends, how do we reconcile a religious experience related somehow to Pietism (as distinct from "piety") and the beginnings of Bach's artistic awareness? Joyce Irwin has refined our grasp of the relationship between church music and Pietism against which Bach worked.[22] Irwin has shown that the Pietists' objection was to theatrical and even recreational music, which they viewed as inimical to Christian morality.[23] As far as "well-ordered" church music was concerned, and notwithstanding individual Pietists' antipathy, Pietism was essentially indifferent.[24]

In fact, the "vexations" that drove Bach to leave Mühlhausen seem to have had little if anything to do with Pietism. A quarter-century ago, Howard Serwer revisited the question of opposition to Bach's musical ideals at Mühlhausen, by looking critically at Ernst Ludwig Gerber's account of his father's student days in Mühlhausen.[25] Heinrich Nikolaus Gerber, later a student of Bach, had begun attending what he recalled as being the best Gymnasium in Thuringia in 1717. But so bad was the music in Mühlhausen's churches—the orthodox Marienkirche as well as the (relatively moderate) Pietist Divii Blasii—that by 1721 the elder Gerber convinced his father to send him to Sonderhausen instead.[26]

Nor had things changed by the time Johann Lorenz Albrecht was in Mühlhausen. In Friedrich Wilhelm Marpurg's *Historische-kritische Beyträge zur Aufnahme der Musik* (1762), he described how on festal days the few performers the city had were split between the two larger churches; on most Sundays the full group alternated. The net result was that on low Sundays better music could be heard in one of the churches than could be heard in either church on major feasts. Moreover, no concerted service music was permitted by longstanding custom and order of the City Council on the last three Sundays in Advent and all the Sundays of Lent. Indeed, during the latter season, the organ was not allowed to accompany congregational singing of the chorales, an archaic practice that had prevailed generally during the previous century, but had largely disappeared by Bach's time, let alone the later years of Albrecht's account. Good Friday Passion music was restricted, again by custom and municipal policy, to *stilo antico* settings, like those of Schütz. And finally, on no Sunday could the texts be other than those from the Bible or the chorales.[27]

Clearly, Bach was obstructed in his ideal of "well-regulated church music" by these archaic musical customs of Mühlhausen that had nothing to do with his Pietist pastor and congregation, but

---

[22] Joyce Irwin, "German Pietists and Church Music in the Baroque Age," *Church History* 54, no. 1 (March 1985): 29-40, and *Neither Voice nor Heart Alone: German Lutheran Theology of Music in the Age of the Baroque* (New York: Peter Lang, 1993).

[23] See ibid., passim, but especially 117-26.

[24] Or *adiophora*, as it was termed. See ibid., 118-26. In passing, this is an interesting but totally reasonable inversion of the English Puritan position that allowed for recreational music but rigorously limited its use in worship. For the Calvinist Puritans, Sunday "meeting" was "God's schoolhouse," so to speak; for the Lutheran Pietists, it was still *Gottesdienst*.

[25] Howard Serwer, "'Wiedrigkeit' and 'Verdriesslichkeit' in Mühlhausen," *Musical Quarterly* 55, no. 1 (January 1969): 20-28; *Bach Reader*, 264.

[26] Evidently, the assessment of Mühlhausen's "high musical traditions, from which it had somewhat degenerated before Bach's arrival" in Charles Sanford Terry, *Bach: A Biography*, rev. ed. (London: Oxford, 1933), 76, was somewhat optimistically wide of the mark.

[27] Serwer, 26-29.

rather applied with equal force to the orthodox parish in the city. One can only imagine his vexation at being able to utilize so limited an amount of the sacred repertory he had studied, beginning with the vast historical treasure of *antico* music stretching back some two centuries, with which he had become acquainted during his years in Lüneburg. The *Abendmusik* arias of Buxtehude that Bach had listened to in Lübeck were proscribed, to say nothing of settings, his own or others', of texts in the revolutionary Neumeister cantata style he had doubtless first encountered on his trips to Hamburg years before, with or without the affective devices and quasi-operatic manner their author intended. It must especially have galled Bach that with his assistance churches in surrounding "smaller townships" had music that was "often better than the harmony" he was allowed in his own city church.[28]

At such a juncture, the opportunity to become organist to the firmly orthodox (albeit not doctrinaire) Duke of Weimar, a strictly religious man who had studied theology at the University of Jena and whose musical interest centered on his court chapel, could well have seemed to Bach like a relatively unfettered opportunity to pursue anew the ideal that was clearly beyond his grasp at Mühlhausen. Moreover, the chapel music as a whole was under the direction of the court capellmeister Johann Samuel Drese, sixty-four years old and in poor health. An ambitious Bach would certainly have measured favorably his chances to take over Drese's responsibilities—and eventually his post—and sooner rather than later.

My point here is that Bach knew perfectly well that his duties at Weimar were to be primarily those of chapel organist to the deeply religious duke, and he cannot have considered himself to be abandoning church music—or at least worship music—by accepting the call, especially with management of all chapel music in reasonable prospect. On the contrary, the Weimar court offered Bach the chance to realize his ideal of concerted church music. He so informed his Mühlhausen employers, and there is simply no reason to doubt his candor.

In this context, Bach's candidacy for Friedrich Wilhelm Zachow's post at the Liebfrauenkirche in Halle, only five years after he had "resolutely turned his back" on church music, seems at once consistent with his move to Weimar and inconsistent with Blume's contention. Put simply, Bach gave serious consideration to leaving his court appointment to take another church position. It does not seem unreasonable to suggest that he felt he had exhausted the professional possibilities at Weimar, especially since his duties had not changed in the manner he might have hoped when he first took the position.

Doubtless he was attracted not only by the prospect of a new field for his mission of "well-regulated church music," but also by Halle's intellectual atmosphere, the professional prestige of succeeding Handel's own teacher, Zachow, and the large new organ being built for the church. Moreover, although Halle's university was the fountainhead of Pietism, the Liebfrauenkirche services included cantatas on special feast days, and were thus well beyond the typical Pietist simplicity. As part of his application, Bach evidently performed Cantata 21 (*Ich hatte viel Bekümmernis*): in passing, a piece that deftly utilized the sort of Italianate devices against which some Pietists inveighed in a secular context, to highlight the affective aspects of the text's Pietistic overtones.

But all this is beside the point. The situation at Halle reinforces my primary contention: that Bach had not turned his back on church music at all in 1708, but rather had turned his face to the Weimar court not only because it offered him far more money, but also, and maybe even primarily, because it gave him the opportunity to realize his ideal of church music, precisely as he had maintained in his letter of resignation from Mühlhausen.

In the end, Bach remained at Weimar because the Halle authorities could not or would not match his salary. Moreover, Wilhelm Ernst created a new position of concertmaster especially for Bach—a position

---

[28] The resignation letter, in translation, may be found in *Bach Reader*, 60-61.

(subsequently eliminated from the ducal establishment upon Bach's departure for Cöthen in 1717) that gave him the special duty of composing a new cantata for the ducal chapel each month—and raised his salary again.

Since Wihelm Ernst must certainly have known that he was countering an offer that was already lower than what he was paying Bach, we may reasonably infer an awareness on his part, or at least suspicion, that Bach had heretofore found Weimar less adequate for the pursuit of his ideal of "well-regulated church music" than he had anticipated in 1708, and was therefore seeking a more hospitable field. In that context, Bach's new duties assume a significance greater than his new title, and the raise in salary, on its face a reward for loyalty, looks far more like a pre-emptive counter-offer against future bids, calculated to price Bach out of the "church market," as it were.

Moreover, the Duke's anger at Bach's acceptance of the post of capellmeister at the reformed court of Cöthen four years later emerges as something more than the arrogance of a petty eighteenth-century aristocrat at the disloyalty and stubborn *lèse majesté* of a disappointed and resentful servant. Wilhelm Ernst had accommodated what he interpreted as Bach's "ideal" of "well-regulated" church music. He had raised Bach's salary, and continued to do so year after year, in effect subsidizing the development of his skill in cantata composition. And now, as if to spite Wilhelm Ernst's strict Lutheran sensibilities, Bach was cynically intent on taking a position in a non-Lutheran court with no chapel duties, but yet another considerable increase in salary.[29]

As it turned out, Bach stayed at the Cöthen court until 1723. Though he would later characterize himself as having been content enough to remain there for the rest of his life, in 1720 Bach again seems to have been drawn professionally back toward the church. He at least allowed his name to be considered for the position of organist of the Jakobikirche in Hamburg. The city was, of course, a center of Italianate opera in Germany, and the pastor of the church was the great cantata poet and orthodox stalwart Erdmann Neumeister, who in 1700 had introduced cantata librettos tailored to the musical style and affective devices of opera, such as Bach had set in Weimar.

As a city, Hamburg offered more artistic and intellectual attractions than had Halle seven years earlier. It was a cosmopolitan cultural and musical center that had drawn Bach like a magnet during his student years in nearby Lüneburg. Moreover, he would have certainly given serious consideration to Hamburg because of his family situation. The death and burial of his wife during a lengthy absence must have made the associations at Cöthen painful at the least. In addition, his two eldest sons, Wilhelm Friedemann and Carl Philipp Emanuel, were both of an age such that their education was a consideration. Hamburg had no university at the time, but it had a superb Gymnasium that the two boys were the right age to take advantage of. In short, Hamburg was an intellectual center and a scintillating city, and Bach had good reason, apart from any pull back to the employment of the church, to seek an opportunity to live and work there.

It is, of course, impossible to factor with any certainty how much weight the foregoing had relative to the advantages of working in the Jakobikirche, a prominent church with a magnificent Arp Schnitger organ (still extant). Even though the post in question was not that of cantor, officially charged with setting Neumeister's texts and performing the pieces in the Jakobikirche and elsewhere in the city,

---

[29] Although the subject is, strictly speaking, beyond the scope of this paper, it still seems appropriate to observe in passing that the court was *German* Reformed, rather than the more ascetic Genevan strain that informed Calvinism in Western Europe: Dutch, French, and Scottish, for instance. That is, although the chapel admitted no ornate figural music, it is less than accurate to say, as does Terry (116), that its music was exclusively Calvinist metrical psalmody. In fact, Lutheran and Reformed music overlapped in the use of a common body of chorales. See Walter Blankenburg, "Church Music in Reformed Europe," in Blume, *Protestant Church Music* (New York: Norton, 1976), 23-24.

Bach must certainly have anticipated composing cantatas in some sort of partnership with the pastor, and performing them with the professional musical forces of the Jakobikirche, seven singers and about sixteen instrumentalists. Indeed, he may well have been measuring his chances to succeed to the post of cantor and director of all church and municipal music that fell to Telemann a year later.

But, as at Halle, financial considerations intervened. What could in all likelihood have been a fruitful and historic partnership of pastor and musician, poet and composer, evidently foundered on the so-called gratuity expected of the successful candidate. Bach withdrew and another, more affluent if less talented, was appointed. But all this is beside the fact that Bach, once again, far from having "resolutely turned his back" on church music, had at least passively sought the Hamburg post and a change from his Cöthen activities—a far more profound change, in fact, than Halle would have represented seven years before. Put plainly, Bach was evidently quite ready to return to Lutheran church music after only three years as a court Capellmeister, doing little or no sacred music.

In passing, it is also worth noting that (however much he was impelled by family considerations and personal grief) Bach entertained the possibility of moving to Hamburg during the "high noon" of his years at Cöthen. The Prince's unsympathetic bride, the economies that would force reductions and the eventual dissolution of the musical establishment after Leopold's premature death—all these lay in the yet unseen future.

Bach left Cöthen for Leipzig in 1723. By October 1730 he had become permanently disillusioned with his situation and wrote his childhood schoolmate Georg Erdmann of his intention "with God's help to seek my fortune elsewhere." He recalled fondly his Cöthen years and described his initial reluctance to accept the Leizpig cantorship, suggesting to Erdmann that he had considered it a step downward, professionally and socially.[30] But this letter must be seen in the context of its timing. Unlike his 1708 letter to the authorities in Mühlhausen, Bach's letter to Erdmann was disingenuous; for whatever his level of resentment with the city and university authorities by 1730, there is no evidence that Bach thought himself to be making a poor career decision when he accepted the Leipzig cantorship seven years earlier. On the contrary, there had been many good reasons for him to seek the appointment in 1723, even if he had forgotten or chosen to ignore them in 1730.

Nor could the Leipzig cantorate, with its celebrated succession of Lutheran musicians back to Georg Rhau and including Johann Hermann Schein, Seth Calvisius, and most recently Bach's immediate predecessor Johann Kuhnau, and the varied musical opportunities offered by that great commercial and university city, be seen as anything but an improvement over the post of capellmeister at the small Cöthen court, whose musical establishment had begun being cut back for economic reasons even during Bach's last two years there, and now, under Leopold's successor, was all but defunct.[31]

Indeed, far from having "turned his back" on church music as early as 1708, Bach climaxed his career at its halfway point by attaining one of the most prominent and prestigious positions in Lutheran church music. Then, in the signal reversal of that success, disillusioned with his work, frustrated in his ideal of "well-regulated" church music, facing a series of "vexations" and "hinderances" from university, school, and municipal authorities, unable to move and with a two-decade denouement stretching before him—then and only then did Bach in fact "resolutely turn his back" on church music, not in Mühlhausen in 1708, but in Leipzig sometime after 1729. Unable to gain refuge for his mature artistry in another post, he eventually turned inward, to seek and find it in his own genius.

---

[30] Letter dated 28 October 1730. For the text, see *Bach Reader*, 125-26.

[31] On the relative merits of Cöthen and Leipzig, see Christoph Wolff, "New Perspectives on Bach Biography," in his *Bach: Essays on His Life and Music* (Cambridge: Harvard University Press, 1991), 7-8.

CHAPTER 7

The Emergence of Conducting, as Seen in Some of Its Illustrious Protagonists

Daniel J. Koury

The métier of conductor, as we know it, appears to have been an outgrowth of the nineteenth century. A gesticulating interpreter, standing on a podium, back to the audience, seems to have been unknown in the eighteenth century. True, in churches or places where performers were numerous and/or widespread, a time-beater might have been employed, wielding a roll of paper, or perhaps even a stick, but such a personage would have been just that: a time-beater and probably not in any sense an interpreter.

Practice in France was exceptional. Remember Lully and his lethal injury, caused by striking his foot with the long stick he used for evidently audible time-beating. Even at the Opéra at Paris the so-called *baton de mesure* held sway.[1] Rousseau was bitterly critical of the resulting noise—*bruit insupportable*.[2] A similar situation prevailed at the Concert spirituel, even in the 1760s. But the wielder of this instrument was a time-beater and not an interpreter. There is even the possibility that he may have beaten time in the air, at least at times. So it will not be surprising if later baton-conducting will be at first referred to as the "French style."

Double Direction

Eighteenth-century orchestras, in general, were controlled by the keyboard player and/or leading violinist. Primacy in this double-direction varied by genre and even by locale. Musicians differed, even philosophically, on this point. J. J. Quantz favored violin leadership,[3] while C. P. E. Bach believed the keyboard player to be in the best position to control the performance.[4] It therefore seems contradictory

---

[1] See Jean-Jacques Rousseau, *Dictionnaire de musique* (Paris: La Veuve Duchesne, 1768), s.v. "*Bâton de Mesure*," 50.

[2] Ibid., "Orchestre," 355.

[3] Johann Joachim Quantz, *Versuch einer Anweisung die Flöte traversiere zu spielen*, facs. of 3rd ed. (Breslau, 1789), ed. H. P. Schmitz (Kassel: Bärenreiter, 1953), 178-79; or transl. Edward R. Reilly as *On Playing the Flute* (New York: Free Press, 1966; 2nd ed., New York: Schirmer Books, 1985), 207-08.

[4] Carl Philipp Emmanuel Bach, *Versuch über die wahre Art das Clavier zu spielen*, 2 vols., facs. of 1st ed. (Berlin, 1753 and 1762), ed. Lothar Hoffmann-Erbrecht (Leipzig: Breitkopf & Härtel, 1969), 1:16; transl. William J. Mitchell as *Essay on the True Art of Playing Keyboard Instruments* (New York: Norton, 1949), 33.

that C. P. E. maintained that his father worked best conducting from the position of first violin,[5] though other sources suggest he conducted, at least in church, from the keyboard.[6]

In actual practice, the composer at the keyboard was the paramount director at the opera, at least for the first three performances. After that and in most other situations, the violin leader was in full control (hence the term *Konzertmeister*—"concertmaster"). Thus Mozart rushed to the keyboard to resume conductorship of *Die Entführung*,[7] but would have "grabbed" the violin to take control of a symphony in Paris.[8] At Esterháza, Haydn led from the position of first violin.[9] And in the 1790s when Haydn "presided" at the piano during the famed London concerts, Salomon probably really controlled the orchestra. Even as late as 1835, the concertmaster at the Gewandhaus in Leipzig led all purely orchestral works until the advent of Mendelssohn as conductor there.[10]

Double-direction, however, was not always silent. Striking chords on the harpsichord was considered noisy by some listeners. Foot-stamping and bow-tapping were not uncommon. Even Mozart stamped his foot while leading at the Gewandhaus in an attempt to control the tempo.[11] So while leadership came from someone who was simultaneously engaged in playing an instrument, as time went on, more and more of his time was probably devoted to trying to keep ensemble by indicating tempo with bow, hand, or foot.

Double-direction persisted well into the nineteenth century. It seems especially evident at the Philharmonic Society concerts in London. In 1823, Moscheles was astonished at the continued presence of a piano there; in 1831, he remarked that a "conductor" was still at the piano without a baton.[12] The leading violinist controlled the performance; the "conductor" at the piano watched the full score, ready to correct mistakes or straying parts. This deduction is reinforced by remarks by George Hogarth, an honorary secretary of the Society,[13] and by that keen observer William T. Parke:[14] the leading violinist, acted as what we now term the conductor—he was truly the master of the concert

---

[5] Could he have here meant in chamber music or other than church? See *Johann Sebastian Bach: Leben und Werk in Dokumenten*, ed. H.-J. Schulze (Kassel: Bärenreiter, 1975), 196; or *The Bach Reader*, ed. Hans T. David and Arthur Mendel, rev. ed. (New York: Norton, 1966), 277.

[6] See the description by Johann Mathias Gesner of Bach leading from the organ in *Bach, Dokumenten*, 172-76; or *Bach Reader*, 231.

[7] He was in Vienna in 1782 in order to appear as composer before the visiting Russian royalty. Wolfgang Amadeus Mozart, *Briefe und Aufzeichnungen, Gesamtausgabe*, ed. W. A. Bauer and O. E. Deutsch, 7 vols. (Kassel: Bärenreiter, 1962-75), 2:239; or *The Letters of Mozart and His Family*, transl. and ed. Emily Anderson, 2nd ed. by A. H. King and M. Carolan, 2 vols. (New York: St. Martin's Press, 1966), 2:828.

[8] In 1778, Mozart, *Briefe*, 2:388; or *Letters*, 2:557-58.

[9] Forkel's list for this orchestra in 1783 shows Haydn as "Direktor und Capellmeister," adding "Also plays first violin." Johann Nikolaus Forkel, *Musikalischer Almanach für Deutschland auf das Jahr 1783* (Leipzig: Schwickert, 1783), 100-01.

[10] See Eberhard Creuzburg, *Die Gewandhaus-Konzerte zu Leipzig, 1781-1931* (Leipzig: Breitkopf & Härtel, 1931), 56-57.

[11] This occurred in 1789; he stamped so energetically that the buckle flew off his shoe. Whether this occurred during the concert or rehearsal is unclear—one certainly hopes the latter. See Creuzburg, 35-36.

[12] *Aus Moscheles' Leben, nach Briefen und Tagebüchern*, edited by his wife, 2 vols. (Leipzig: Duncker & Humbolt, 1872-73), 1:74, 228; or transl. A. D. Coleridge as *Recent Music and Musicians, as Described in the Diaries and Correspondence* (1873; reprint, New York: Da Capo, 1970), 51, 166.

[13] Quoted in Robert Elkin, *Royal Philharmonic: The Annals of the Royal Philharmonic Society* (London: Rider, 1946), 15.

[14] See, for example, Parke, *Musical Memoirs, Comprising an Account of the General State of Music in England from the First Commemoration of Händel in 1784 to the Year 1830*, 2 vols. (London: H. Colburn & Bentley, 1830), 2:150-51.

or *Konzertmeister*. So when Parke discussed oratorios given at the Theatre-Royal in Haymarket, for instance, he noted that "Mr. Salomon led the band."[15]

Bow Conducting

As the century progressed, the concertmaster played less and conducted more, using his bow as a baton. François-Antoine Habeneck (1781-1849) was perhaps the best known of these violinist-conductors. He was chief conductor at the famous Paris Conservatory concerts as well as at the Opéra for almost two decades. His career spanned the transition from violin-leader to time-beating *chef d'orchestre*. Even Wagner was amazed in 1839 at the precision and understanding with which the Conservatory Orchestra under Habeneck performed the Beethoven symphonies.[16] This echoed observations made by the Englishman Henry F. Chorley on a visit to Paris in the 1830s: "Nothing can exceed his perfect sway over his forces. Though he directs with his violin-bow, I have never seen him use it . . . ," probably meaning on his instrument,

> and by the exquisite neatness and precision of the least important or most unmanageable instruments (the *piccoli*, for example), as they enter, not *scramble*, into their parts when the composition demands them, it may be seen that his presence is everywhere— that his method and meaning have pervaded the whole hundred he commands ere they are paraded before the public.[17]

This high praise was embellished by A. A. Elwart in 1845. "Habeneck, at the Conservatory, has all his world under his hand; thus he obtains an ensemble unknown here."[18] Elwart also intimates that Habeneck had earlier used a baton. He claims that at the first performance of *Comte Ory* Habeneck put the baton aside to conduct with the bow. Could he have meant the noisy baton of Lully and others— for he added "The shadow of J. J. Rousseau, who had so ridiculed the wood-cutter of French opera, must have leaped for joy."[19]

It was the noise, however, that really enraged Rousseau, and even Habeneck could be forced into noisy moments, if one believes Berlioz, who claimed that Habeneck realized that people on the opera stage paid scant attention to his gestures and consequently missed cues.

> Since he could not speak to their eyes, he conceived the idea of warning their ears, by rapping with the end of the bow he uses to conduct, thus: *tack!*—a smart rap of wood on wood, which can be heard through all the more or less harmonious emissions of the other instruments. This beat preceding the beat that opens the phrase has today become the one necessity of all performers at the Opera.[20]

---

[15] Ibid., 1:290.

[16] See Richard Wagner, "*Über das Dirigiren*," in his *Gesammelten Schriften und Dichtungen* (1869; 2nd ed., Leipzig: C. W. Fritzsch, 1873), 8:338; or *On Conducting (Ueber das Dirigieren): A Treatise on Style in the Execution of Classical Music*, transl. Edward Dannreuther, 3rd ed. (London: W. Reeves, 1919), 15.

[17] Chorley, *Music and Manners in France and Germany: A Series of Travelling Sketches of Art and Society*, 3 vols. (London: Longman, Brown, Green & Longmans, 1844), 1:20.

[18] "Here" meant at the Beethoven celebrations at Bonn. Antoine Aimable Elie Elwart, *Histoire de la Société des Concerts du Conservatoire Impérial de Musique*, 2nd ed. (1860; 2nd ed., Paris: Castel, 1864), 360-61.

[19] Ibid., 325-26, n. 1.

[20] Hector Berlioz, *Les Soirées de l'orchestre*, ed. Léon Guichard (1852; 2nd ed., Paris: Gründ, 1968), 2:166-70; or transl. Jacques Barzun as *Evenings with the Orchestra* (Chicago: University of Chicago Press, 1973), 127-31.

Berlioz may have been enticed to exaggerate, owing to the grudge he had against Habeneck, who "laid down his baton and, calmly producing his snuff-box, proceeded to take a pinch of snuff" at a hazardous moment during the "Tuba mirum" of Berlioz's Requiem.[21] This incident has been credited with being one of the forces impelling Berlioz to a conducting career. By the way, the story has been both refuted and corroborated.[22] And did Berlioz really mean "baton" or was it perhaps a slip of the pen?

Giacomo Meyerbeer also sounds like a violin-conductor, at least according to Berlioz, who wrote to Habeneck from Germany in 1841. He described the Berlin Opera with chorus and orchestra at full strength, including 120 voices, 28 violins, and double winds, with "Meyerbeer in command at the first desk." Berlioz was especially eager to see Meyerbeer conduct his own work. "He does it as a man would a job he has been doing for twenty years; he holds the orchestra in the hollow of his hand and does with it as he pleases."[23] One senses a growing concept of a conductor in control, whether he wields bow or baton.

Nor did violin-conducting die out as the use of the baton increased. The great Johann Strauss, Jr., conducted with his bow even in 1872 when he led concerts in Boston, Mass., during the Second Peace Jubilee. "His brother Éduard . . . conducted in the same way."[24] His style and technique were perhaps typical of the violin leader:

> His manner of conducting was very animating. He led off with the violin bow to give the *tempo*, but when the right swing was obtained and the melody was singing out from the orchestra, he joined in with his fiddle as if he must take part in the intoxication of the waltz. While playing or conducting he commonly kept his body in motion, rising and falling on his toes in a really graceful manner.[25]

Many others continued to lead in the old style: for example, Jules Pasdeloup, when he founded the Société des Jeunes Artistes du Conservatoire in 1851. One description of Paganini suggests him leading the orchestra as he played:

> For a few moments he stood before his breathless audience, as if thinking of what he should play; then he slowly placed the violin under his chin, as deliberately raised his bow and let it rest on the strings, as if meditating how to proceed. Having apparently made up his mind, he turned to the orchestra, and, with a gentle inclination of his head, gave the signal to commence.[26]

Nor was there lacking critical or theoretical support for the violinist and his bow as leader of the orchestra.[27]

---

[21] Berlioz, *Mémoires*, ed. Pierre Citron, 2 vols. (1870; 2nd ed., Paris: Garnier-Flammarion, 1969), 2:10; or transl. and ed. E. Cairns as *The Memoirs of Hector Berlioz, Member of the French Institute, Including His Travels in Italy, Germany, Russia and England, 1803-65* (New York: Norton, 1975), 231.

[22] See, for example, Michael Kennedy, *The Hallé Tradition: A Century of Music* (Manchester: Manchester University Press, 1960), 14; Berlioz, *Mémoires*, 2:10, 15, 40; or *Memoirs*, 231, 235, 254, 594-95.

[23] Berlioz, *Mémoires*, 2:128; or *Memoirs*, 324.

[24] Thomas Ryan, *Recollections of an Old Musician* (New York: E. P. Dutton, 1899), 36-37.

[25] Ibid., 201.

[26] Henry Phillips, *Musical and Personal Recollections during Half a Century*, 2 vols. (London: C. J. Skeet, 1864), 1:153-54.

[27] See, for example, Édouard Marie Ernest Deldevez, *L'Art du chef d'orchestre* (Paris: Firmin-Didot, 1878), passim.

The Baton

Meanwhile the silent baton was steadily supplanting the bow as a means of controlling the orchestra. As early as the 1780s Johann Friedrich Reichardt, *Kapellmeister* at Berlin, had discarded both keyboard and violin for conducting, using "silent implements to mark time, control the ensemble, and guide the interpretation."[28]

His successor, Anselm Weber, is said to have used a leather baton stuffed with hair. A report of the French opera at Hamburg in 1799 describes the conducting by Guillaume Alexis Paris "as is quite the general custom in France, by means of a small foot-long stick, mostly through signs," with a comment that he was heard only when there was some serious error. The commentator seemed surprised that, although the orchestra consisted mostly of local Germans, and Paris spoke no German, he was able to make himself quickly intelligible "through the precision and steady equality of his signs."[29] And one suspects that the performance of *The Creation* on 27 March 1809, at which Haydn made his last public appearance, was led by a baton-wielding conductor. Antonio Salieri is credited with being the director. And with Fritz Clement as violin leader and Conradin Kreutzer at the piano, Salieri must have been at some sort of podium, conducting with a silent implement.[30]

Beethoven

Ignaz von Seyfried felt that "As a conductor our Master [Beethoven] could in no wise be called a model." For he thought only of the notes and the music,

> ceaselessly engaged in calling attention to their authentic expression by means of the most manifold gesticulations. Thus he often struck *down* with his baton at a strong dynamic point, though it might occur on the weak beat of the measure. He was accustomed to indicate a *diminuendo* by trying to make himself smaller and smaller, and at the *pianissimo* slipped under the conductor's desk, so to say. As the tonal masses increased in volume, he too seemed to swell, as though out of a contraction, and with the entrance of the entire body of instrumental tone he rose on the tips of his toes, grew to well-nigh giant size, and swaying in the air with his arms, seemed to be trying to float up into the clouds. He was all active movement, no organic part of himself was idle, and the whole man might be compared to a *perpetuum mobile*.[31]

Yes, time seems eclipsed; this could be taken for a description of some twentieth-century personage. In fact, Harold Schonberg considered Beethoven "a fascinating figure: a solid, even prophetic, link

---

[28] Adam Carse, *The Orchestra in the XVIIIth Century* (1940; reprint, New York: Broude Bros., 1969), 102.

[29] *Allgemeine musikalische Zeitung* (henceforth, *AmZ*), 70 vols. (Leipzig: Breitkopf & Härtel, 1798-1882), 1:728.

[30] *AmZ* 10 (1807-08):479, mentions only that the concert was "unter der Direction des Hrn. Kapellm.ˢ Salieri," but H. C. Robbins Landon, in *Haydn: Chronicle and Works*, 5 vols. (Bloomington: Indiana University Press, 1976-77), 5:479, has Salieri conducting and Kreutzer at the piano. A reminiscent correspondent to an English periodical, meaning to correct past errors concerning this performance, got the year wrong (making it 1809), but stated that "the signal to begin was given by Salieri, who directed the orchestra. At the piano was Kreutzer, Clementi [Clement] was first violin. . . ." *The Harmonicon: A Journal of Music*, 11 vols. (London: W. Pinnock et al., 1823-33), 3 (1825): 129. Karl Geiringer, *Haydn: A Creative Life in Music* (New York: Norton, 1946), 170, mentions Salieri as conductor and Clement as violin leader. Landon, 4:318 (for example) confirms the alternate spellings of "Clement" and the Italianate "Clementi" for Franz; this performance was in Carpani's Italian translation, possibly the source of the above spelling.

[31] Friedrich Kerst, ed., *Die Erinnerungen an Beethoven*, 2 vols. (Stuttgart: J. Hoffmann, 1913), 2:83-84; or Albert Leitzmann, ed., *Beethovens Persönlichkeit*, 2 vols. (Leipzig: Insel, 1914-27), 1:43; or Oscar George Sonneck, *Beethoven: Impressions by His Contemporaries* (1926; reprint, New York: Dover, 1967), 39-40.

between divided leadership and the tyrannical, choreographic, virtuoso conductors who were to follow not much later." However, he continues: "During his lifetime the baton came into use, but there is no real evidence Beethoven ever used one."[32] Now, such a conclusion does not take into account the description by Seyfried and others who have linked Beethoven with the use of the baton. Robert Haas seems to have thought that Beethoven conducted first with a roll of paper, then later with a baton.[33] Wilhelmine Schröder-Devrient, who sang Leonore in *Fidelio* in 1822 at Vienna's Kärntnerthor Theater, remembered that although rehearsals had been directed by the conductor Umlauf, "Beethoven had requested the honor of conducting his work himself on the ceremonial day"—that is to say, the dress rehearsal. "But Beethoven sat in the orchestra and waved his baton above the heads of us all, and I had never seen the man before!"[34]

Moscheles confirmed the foregoing descriptions of Beethoven the conductor when, at a rehearsal of a Beethoven symphony with the London Philharmonic Society in 1845, he told the orchestra how he had heard this and other great works of the master when they had first appeared, and that he had preserved the tempo-traditions established by Beethoven himself. And he demonstrated, amusing them by imitating Beethoven's conducting style, stooping at soft passages and almost disappearing, then rising up gradually with a crescendo, standing on his toes and bounding up at the loudest place. But he did not forget to add: "Inasmuch, however, as I cannot emulate the great man in his works, I abstain from copying him in his attitudes; with him it was all originality, with me it would be caricature."[35]

Further corroboration is perhaps unnecessary, but it is difficult to omit a somewhat comic description of Beethoven conducting *Wellingtons Sieg in der Schlacht bey Vittoria* in 1813-14, a performance in which Salieri, Hummel, Spohr, Schuppanzigh, Mayseder, and Meyerbeer took part.

> In the middle of the whole academy stood a dumpy man, who so balanced himself with all his limbs, and waved about with his hands, that I thought I was at a Sabbath service in a Synagogue; now is he tall, now short, now one hardly saw him (for there he is hidden under his desk), now he is again risen—and there quite struck me the idea of holy Father Abraham, how he once preached on the Gospel, "a little while so you will not see me, and a little while so you will again see me," and he always at that place disappeared under the pulpit, and again came in sight.[36]

A review of perhaps the same performance of *Wellingtons Sieg* in December 1813 suggests how effective Beethoven's conducting could be prior to his deafness. "A numerous orchestra, manned throughout with the first and most pre-eminent musicians of the area . . . afforded, under the direction of the composer, through its precise collaboration, a universal pleasure, which amounted to enthusiasm."[37] According to Anton Schindler, Beethoven's thoughts ordinarily could only be divined "in his radiant eyes and face, for he never gesticulated, either with his head or with his hands, save when he stood before the orchestra."[38]

---

[32] Harold C. Schonberg, *The Great Conductors* (New York: Simon & Schuster, 1967), 58.

[33] "Beethoven benütze anfangs wohl eine Papierrole, später den Taktstock," in his *Aufführungspraxis der Musik* (Wildpark-Potsdam: Athenaion, 1931), 253.

[34] Kerst, 2:40-41; or Sonneck, 130-31.

[35] *Aus Moscheles' Leben*, 2:139; or *Recent Music*, 314.

[36] "Eipeldauerbriefe," quoted in Haas, 253.

[37] AmZ 16 (1814): 70.

[38] Kerst, 2:20; or Sonneck, 165.

Bettina Brentano's letter to Goethe of May 1810 also tends to confirm Beethoven as a time-beating, interpreting conductor:

> There I saw then this enormous intellect lead his regiment. O Goethe! No emperor and no king has thus the consciousness of his might and that all strength emanates from him, as this Beethoven. . . . There he stood so firmly resolved, his motions, his spirit expressed the perfection of his creation, he anticipated each error, each misunderstanding, no breath was arbitrary, all was through the well-behaved presence of his spirit prompted in the most discreet activity. . . .[39]

Even though seemingly carried away by emotion and hero-worship, this account suggests a conductor with first-rate expressive qualities.

Spohr's account of his first experience with Beethoven's conducting at the concert of 8 December 1813, featuring *Wellingtons Sieg*, corroborates the others:

> Although I had heard a great deal about it, the actuality still came as a shock. Beethoven had adopted the habit of communicating his expressive desires to the orchestra by all sorts of odd movements of the body. For a *sforzando* he would throw apart his arms, hitherto held crossed on his heart. For a *piano* he would bend down, the more *piano*, the lower. Then at a *crescendo* he would rise up gradually, and at the onset of the *forte*, literally spring into the air. He often shouted, too, in order to contribute to the *forte*, although probably unconsciously.[40]

And if more evidence were needed, one could read a similar description of the same concert by the tenor Franz Wild.[41]

However, Beethoven's deafness had begun to take its toll. Even Seyfried admits it:

> With increasing deafness, it is true, a rude disagreement often took place when the *maestro* was beating in arsis and the orchestra was accompanying him in thesis; then the conductor who had strayed from the path found his way back most easily in the soft movements, while the most powerful *forte* meant nothing to him. In these cases his eye also came to his assistance; he could observe the bow-stroke of the string instruments, guess from it the figure they were playing, and soon find his place again.[42]

Discussing the 1822 *Fidelio*, Mme. Schröder-Devrient goes further than Seyfried:

> At that time the Master's physical ear already was deaf to all tone. With confusion written on his face, with a more than earthly enthusiasm in his eye, swinging his baton to and fro with violent motions, he stood in the midst of the playing musicians and did not hear a single note! When he thought they should play *piano*, he almost crept under the conductor's desk, and when he wanted a *forte*, he leaped high into the air with the strangest gestures, uttering the weirdest sounds.

The poor master must have remained utterly unconscious of the resulting confusion, for "with the utmost difficulty we concluded a rehearsal with which he seemed altogether content, for he laid down

---

[39] Quoted in Konrad Huschke, *Beethoven als Pianist und Dirigent* (Berlin: Schuster & Loeffler, 1919), 86.

[40] Louis Spohr, *Lebenserinnerungen*, ed. Folker Göthel, 2 vols. (1840; Tutzing: H. Schneider, 1968), 1:178; or transl. and ed. Henry Pleasants as *The Musical Journeys of Louis Spohr* (Norman: University of Oklahoma Press, 1961), 103.

[41] Quoted in Huschke, 93-94, although the date is given as 2 January 1814.

[42] Kerst, 1:83-84; or Leitzmann, 1:43; or Sonneck, 39-40.

his baton with a happy smile." Needless to say, the following performance could not be allowed to be more of the same; poor Umlauf "had to charge himself with the heart-rending business" of making Beethoven realize this. The master had to content himself with sitting behind Umlauf in the orchestra, "lost in profound meditation."[43] Sir George Smart remembered a performance of a Beethoven string quartet in Vienna in 1825 during which Beethoven directed the performers. "A staccato passage not being expressed to the satisfaction of his eye, for alas, he could not hear, he seized Holz's violin and played the passage a quarter of a tone too flat."[44]

One Friedrich Treitschke was critical of Beethoven's conducting. Concerning a performance of *Fidelio* in May 1814, he claimed that "Beethoven conducted, but his enthusiasm often made him miss the beat, and it was Umlauf who stood behind him and succeeded by look and gesture in keeping everyone together."[45] Schindler, however, refuted this

> This must be denied. The truth is that, despite his poor hearing, Beethoven frequently conducted large orchestral and choral groups in 1813 and 1814, and with complete competence. If he had been unable to do so, he would have put another on the podium.[46]

Perhaps Herr Schindler "doth protest too much." He later returned to Treitschke's assertion, stating that:

> The performances that Beethoven conducted on 8 and 12 December 1813 in the auditorium of the University and the performances in January, February, November, and December 1814 in the Great Redoutensaal, where the podium was pushed forward for him and no helper stood at his side, are proof enough that he was well able to hear masses of instruments and voices as well as soloists and small ensembles. Anyone acquainted with the difficulties of rehearsing and directing the *Battle* symphony could perhaps wonder about the precise entrances of instruments that were at times in separate parts of the auditorium. As one of the performers I can affirm that nothing was lacking, and truly, the difficulties of conducting *Fidelio* are nothing compared to the *Battle* symphony.[47]

But the situation at the dedication of the Josephstadt Theater in 1822 for which Beethoven composed the overture *Zur Weihe des Hauses* seems like a regression of at least 30 years. Again, Schindler tells us:

> Beethoven had stipulated that he should conduct at the ceremonial opening of the theatre. Accordingly he took his place *at the piano* in a position in which he was facing most of the orchestra and where his left ear, which was still of some service to him, was turned toward the stage. The Kapellmeister Franz Gläser . . . placed himself on Beethoven's right where he could oversee the whole performance, while I *led the orchestra* from my place at the head of the first violins.[48]

---

[43] Kerst, 2:40-41; or Sonneck, 130-31.

[44] Smart, *Leaves from the Journals of Sir Georg Smart*, ed. H. Bertram Cox and C. L. E. Cox (London: Longmans, Green, 1907), 109; or Sonneck, 192.

[45] Quoted in Anton Felix Schindler, *Biographie von Ludwig van Beethoven*, 2 vols. (Münster: Aschendorff, 1871), 1:124; or *Beethoven as I Knew Him: A Biography*, ed. Donald W. MacArdle, transl. Constance S. Jolly (1960; New York: Norton, 1972), 126.

[46] Schindler, *Biographie*, 1:124 n.; or *Beethoven as I Knew Him*, 126 n.

[47] Schindler, *Biographie*, 1:200; or *Beethoven as I Knew Him*, 172-73.

[48] Schindler, *Biographie*, 2:8; or *Beethoven as I Knew Him*, 235.

This smacks of conditions when Haydn and Mozart were active, or even contemporaneously at the London Philharmonic Society, but not like Beethoven the conductor described above. Evidently it was the only way the master could be allowed the honor of taking part in the performance, given the state of his hearing.

Spohr

Ludwig Spohr began his conducting career using his violin bow, switched to a roll of paper, and by 1817 was wielding a baton.[49] When he was offered a position at the Theater an der Wien in 1813 it was as "Kapellmeister und Orchesterdirektor," suggesting that the conductor did not then direct strictly orchestral pieces:

> I was committed as orchestra director to play as first violinist in all large operas, to undertake the violin solos in operas and ballets, and to direct as conductor from the full score, if the other conductor should be prevented from doing so through illness or other impediment.[50]

At Frankenhausen in 1810, Spohr conducted a festival which brought together more than 100 singers and more than 100 instrumentalists.[51] A critic wrote glowingly of

> Herr Spohr's direction with the paper-roll, without any noise and without the slightest grimace. One might call it a *graceful direction*; if this word, besides pleasing demeanor, also expresses the precision and efficacy of his motions on the whole multitude, unfamiliar to him and to each other. To this fortunate talent of Herr Spohr do I attribute the greatest part of the excellence and precision—of the stirring power as well as the smooth adapting of this numerous orchestra to the singers in the performance of the *Creation*.[52]

Spohr startled London and made orchestral history in England in 1819 when he appeared at the Philharmonic Society:

> It was still the custom in London that, in the playing of overtures and symphonies, the pianist sat at the piano with the score before him. He did not conduct, but rather read along and joined in when it suited him, which made a very bad effect. The actual conductor was the first violinist, who gave the tempo and, when things went wrong, beat time with his bow. An orchestra as large as the Philharmonic, with the musicians standing so far apart, could not achieve real precision under such a system. Despite the excellence of the individual musicians, the ensemble was much worse than that to which one was accustomed in Germany.

Spohr decided to improve the situation when his turn to conduct arrived:

> I took my place, with the score before me, at a desk especially set up in front of the orchestra, drew my baton from my pocket and gave the signal to begin. Shocked at such an innovation, some of the directors wished to protest. However, when I asked

---

[49] Schonberg, 83-85.

[50] Spohr, *Lebenserinnerungen*, 1:162.

[51] Ernst Ludwig Gerber, "Nachricht von einem in Thüringen seltenen Musikfest," *AmZ* 12 (1809): 745.

[52] Ibid., 751.

them at least to give it a try, they consented. I had conducted the symphonies and overtures on the program many times in Germany and was abundantly familiar with them.
Then I could not only set the tempi with authority but also signal the entrances to the
woodwinds and brass, giving them a degree of security they had never previously enjoyed.

He gained great success and the effect was decisive:

Surprised and delighted by this success, the orchestra expressed its approval immediately
after the first movement of the symphony, and there was no further opposition from
the directors. . . . The victory of the baton was complete and never again was a pianist
to be seen during the playing of overtures and symphonies.[53]

But despite his claims to have forever displaced the system of dual-control there once and for all,
the old system persevered.[54] In fact, when Michael Costa was appointed conductor in 1846, he found
it necessary to stipulate that the violin leader be suppressed and that he, Costa, be in sole control of
the orchestra.[55]

In Cassel in 1825, Spohr seemed to conduct only vocal pieces at a ball. He "beat time in front
with a short stick."[56] In an opera performance there, "Spohr beat time, he did not use his violin when
conducting."[57] If Spohr can be reproached because of his inability to play the piano, necessitating
his conducting first opera rehearsals with a string quartet,[58] he has been credited with introducing the
system of using letters of the alphabet in corresponding places in score and parts to facilitate rehearsal
techniques and to save rehearsal time.[59]

Weber

If one can believe his exuberant son, Carl Maria von Weber came to the baton early in his career. His
first conductorship was in Breslau in 1804. According to Max,

The boy-conductor seized his baton with all the fire of his eighteen summers, perhaps
also with an overweening sense of his new independence, evidenced by his resolve to
lead his army to the musical fray wholly according to his own young will and fancy.[60]

Not only is the style and language highly colored with romantic fancy and perhaps exaggerated in
the translation, but Max Weber cannot possibly have remembered any of this first-hand and may have

---

[53] Spohr, *Lebenserinnerungen*, 2:73-74; or *Journeys*, 205-06.

[54] See, for example, Robert Elkin, *The Old Concert Rooms of London* (London: E. Arnold, 1955), 120; or Elkin, *Royal Philharmonic*, 23, including n. 3; or Reginald Nettel, *The Orchestra in England: A Social History* (London: J. Cape, 1956), 98-99.

[55] Percy Alfred Scholes, *The Mirror of Music, 1844-1944: A Century of Musical Life in Britain as Reflected in the Pages of the Musical Times*, 2 vols. (1947; 2nd ed., Freeport, N.Y.: Books for Libraries, 1970), 1:377.

[56] Smart, 212.

[57] Ibid., 216.

[58] Haas, 256.

[59] Ferdinand Simon Gassner, *Dirigent und Ripienist, für angehende Musikdirigenten, Musiker und Musikfreunde* (Karlsruhe: C. T. Groos, 1844), 46-47.

[60] Max Maria von Weber, *Carl Maria von Weber: Ein Lebensbild*, 3 vols. (Leipzig: E. Keil, 1864-66), 1:96; or *Carl Maria von Weber: The Life of an Artist*, transl. J. Palgrave Simpson, 2 vols. (London, 1865; reprint, New York: Greenwood Press, 1969), 1:58, which is the quite-free translation presented above exceeding young Weber in zeal and "fancy."

only assumed that a baton was used that early. After all, Carl Maria did not marry until 1817, and Max was not born until 1822.

Weber conducted seated, at least in the theater. If a reference such as he "turned round on his conductor's seat" might be a translator's license for "*Dirigentenpulte*,"[61] a description of a rehearsal of Méhul's *Joseph and His Brethren* in Dresden in 1817, containing "He entered the orchestra a few minutes before the appointed hour, seated himself on his conductor's stool . . ." would confirm the seated position.[62] But he was confidently in command, as, for example, in a performance of his own *Sylvana* in Berlin: "All went well, however, and the admirable self-possession and precision of the executants was openly ascribed to the quiet, firm, intelligent conductorship of the composer."[63]

But the baton was not accepted everywhere with equanimity. Weber brought the usage with him to Dresden in 1817. Previously the conductors there had led "after the Italian manner," sitting at the keyboard, marking the beat only in "difficult passages by a wave of the hand" or by "chiming in." The orchestra thus had to follow the first violinist, and nuance and support from the conductor was thus rendered "more difficult." If this was "practical" with the Italian opera, the German demanded a "greater spiritual influence through the director." Therefore Weber began using his "trustworthy" baton from the first day there. Even though the members of the orchestra mastered the difficulty of dividing their attention between the baton and their parts, it "stimulated considerable grumbling."[64] One can assume, inferentially, that Weber's colleague for the Italian opera at Dresden, Francesco Morlacchi, conducted at the piano as described—actually a German "manner" as well as any other at the time.

But dispensing with the score altogether in the twentieth-century fashion and conducting from memory was still a long way off. This does not mean, however, that Weber lacked the ability, as evidenced by the following anecdote. He was to conduct Mozart's *Magic Flute* at Dresden in 1820, but when he reached his desk the score was missing. Weber, however, "laughed to the surprise of the musicians" and "quietly sent for the score," looking towards the boxes and smiling to his wife, whose face had paled out of concern. When the court entered, the "desk was still empty." Weber

> raised his baton, and conducted the whole first act of the opera—with his usual fire
> and without a fault—out of his head, amusing himself, at the same time, by pretending
> to turn over the pages of the score in pantomimic action, at the due places.[65]

So Weber had the mental equipment of the virtuoso conductor and could do without the score, but he evidently did not see the need of making it a matter of habit.

Strangely, from a modern standpoint, when Weber first appeared at the "Oratorio Concerts" at London's Convent Garden in 1826 he did not use a baton but a roll of paper "in German fashion."[66] If this seems like a step backwards as far as progress is concerned, the effect on the public was electric. "When Weber retired, the applause and cheering was general from all parts of the theatre."[67] At the introduction of *Oberon* at Covent Garden in April of that same year, Weber "directed the performance

---

[61] Weber, *Lebensbild*, 1:434; or *Life*, 1:323.

[62] Weber, *Lebensbild*, 2:59; or *Life*, 2:42.

[63] Weber, *Lebensbild*, 1:354; or *Life*, 1:266.

[64] Weber, *Lebensbild*, 2:82-83; or *Life*, 2:60, which is shorter, less clear, not overly accurate, and highly flavored.

[65] Weber, *Lebensbild*, 2:272; or *Life*, 2:195.

[66] Weber, *Lebensbild*, 2:665-66; or *Life*, 2:439-40.

[67] Parke, 2:223.

at the pianoforte."[68] While this may seem like a step back to the older tradition in deference to the English, perhaps, he could well have beaten time from there. One reason may have been Weber's weakened health at the time. His son had described him as "pale" at this appearance.

Spontini

Gasparo Spontini also utilized a baton when conducting. In Dresden in 1844 to conduct one of his own works which had been previously prepared by Wagner, he asked Wagner what sort of baton he used:

> With my hands I indicated the approximate length and thickness of a medium-sized wooden rod, such as our choir-attendant was in the habit of supplying, freshly covered with white paper. He sighed, and asked if I thought it possible to procure him by tomorrow a baton of black ebony, whose very respectable length and thickness he indicated by a gesture, and on each end of which a fairly large knob of ivory was to be affixed.[69]

However, Spontini maintained that he conducted only with his eyes:

> "My left eye is the first violin, my right eye the second, and if the eye is to have power, one must not wear glasses (as so many bad conductors do), even if one is short-sighted. I," he admitted confidentially, "cannot see twelve inches in front of me, but all the same I can make them play as I want merely by fixing them with my eye."[70]

It has also been alleged that he stamped on the floor with his foot.[71] But one critic, perhaps prejudiced, called Spontini's reign in Berlin

> altogether a period of false splendour, ruinous to the spirit of German music, of which Spontini had not an idea. The violent contrasts in which he sought his effects, the startling shocks of his *sforzati*, in fact all his effects, calculated to tell only on the nerves and senses of the listeners, could not but demoralize his orchestra. To this was added, that the perfect precision and control for which his conducting was famous, ceased when he no longer held the *bâton* . . . (for he conducted only what he was pleased to call the *grandes ouvrages*, namely, his own operas). . . .[72]

Berlioz

Hector Berlioz seems to have been impelled to a conducting career through suffering bad performances of his works at the hands of conductors he considered inept, or ill-willed, or both. (The incident of Habeneck and the snuff-box has already been cited.) Berlioz expressed perhaps the first modern-sounding description of the art of conducting, that it was much more than merely beating time:

---

[68] Ibid., 2:228.

[69] Wagner, *Mein Leben* (1865-80; Munich: List, 1963), 331; or *My Life*, 2 vols. (New York: Dodd, Mead, 1911), 2:338.

[70] Wagner, *Mein Leben*, 335; or *My Life*, 2:342.

[71] Hans Hoffmann, "La prattica dell'esecuzione musicale," *L'orchestra* (Firenze: G. Barbera, 1954), 102.

[72] Eduard Devrient, *Meine Erinnerungen an Felix Mendelssohn-Bartholdy und seine Briefe an Mich* (Leipzig: J. J. Weber, 1869), 211; transl. Natalia MacFarren as *My Recollections of Felix Mendelssohn-Bartholdy and His Letters to Me* (London: R. Bentley, 1869), 216-17.

> In a symphony the conductor's conception alone must rule. The quality of the performance depends on his conception and on the art of realizing it; the feelings of the individual players must never make themselves manifest.[73]

The very fact that he appended a tract on conducting to his *Traité d'instrumentation* shows the importance he attached to the métier.[74] He wrote to Liszt:

> the composer-conductor lives on a plane of existence unknown to the virtuoso. With what ecstasy he abandons himself to the delight of "playing" the orchestra! How he hugs and claps and sways this immense and fiery instrument.[75]

This sounds very modern indeed!

That he considered conducting a craft to be learned and not just a mechanical act of time-beating is further attested to by his great joy and satisfaction in a performance of his *Roméo et Juliette* in St. Petersburg in 1847. "I remember it as one of the great pleasures of my life. And I was in such good form that I had the luck to conduct without a mistake, which at that time did not often happen to me."[76] Not every conductor would make such an admission! And, of course, he believed in the baton.

> The orchestral conductor generally uses a small light stick, about 20 inches long (better white than of dark color, for the sake of visibility). . . . Some concertmasters use the violin bow for conducting, but it is less suitable than the baton. The bow is somewhat flexible; this lack of rigidity and the greater resistance it offers to the air because of the hair make its movements less precise.[77]

There were, of course, contrasting views in support of the bow.[78] Berlioz also believed in conducting standing, except perhaps in theaters, where

> it is rather difficult for the conductor to endure the fatique caused by standing the entire evening. On the other hand, it is obvious that the conductor loses part of his power by being seated, and that he cannot give free course to his temperament (if he has any).[79]

Berlioz endorsed the full score for conducting, although many conductors at the time utilized a first-violin part.

> Conducting from a single part containing only the principal instrumental cues, the melody and the bass, requires a needless effort of memory on the part of the conductor.

---

[73] Hector Berlioz, *Grande Traité d'instrumentation et d'orchestration modernes*, nouvelles ed., suivie de *L'Art du chef d'orchestre* (Paris: H. Lemoine, 188-), 303; or *Treatise on Instrumentation*, enl. & rev. Richard Strauss (1904), including *Essay on Conducting*, transl. Theodore Front (New York: E. F. Kalmus, 1948), 413; or see *The Orchestral Conductor: Theory of His Art* (New York: Carl Fischer, 19–), 6.

[74] See Berlioz, *Traité*, 299-312; or *Treatise*, 410-20.

[75] Berlioz, *Mémoires*, 2:78; or *Memoirs*, 285.

[76] Berlioz, *Mémoires*, 2:272; or *Memoirs*, 434.

[77] Berlioz, *Traité*, 300; or *Treatise*, 411; or *Orchestral Conductor*, 4.

[78] See, for example, Deldevez, 2-29, or Édouard E. Blitz, *Quelques considérations sur l'art du chef d'orchestre* (Leipzig: Breitkopf & Härtel, 1887), 47-48.

[79] Berlioz, *Traité*, 310; or *Treatise*, 418; or *Orchestral Conductor*, 16. However, there were other opinions on this subject, too; see, for example, Deldevez, 135-38.

> Moreover, if he tells one of the performers whose part he doesn't have before him
> that he has made a mistake, he exposes himself to the risk of being answered: "What
> do you know about this?"[80]

Berlioz does not seem to have been taken with the idea of conducting from memory.

His diligence, his attitude, his reverence for great masterworks—all would lead one to expect great things from Berlioz the conductor. Yet all were not in agreement as to his excellence. Wagner heard him in London in 1855 with the New Philharmonic Society:

> I thus heard him conduct some classical works, such as a Mozart symphony, and was
> amazed to find a conductor, who was so energetic in the interpretation of his own
> compositions, sink into the commonest rut of the vulgar time-beater.[81]

But this view was not general. One writer claims that "London was thrilled with Berlioz's masterly control of the orchestra," and he quotes a critic to the effect that "Berlioz as a conductor must be placed in the first rank of orchestral generals."[82]

Berlioz on Conducting

Berlioz's ideas on what constituted real conducting can perhaps be surmised from his appraisal of Otto Nicolai as well as from his treatise:

> Nicolai has his enemies in Vienna. So much the worse for the Viennese. I regard him
> as one of the finest orchestral conductors I have ever encountered, and one of those
> men whose presence in a town can give it a position of unchallengeable musical
> ascendancy when they enjoy conditions which provide full scope for their powers.
> Nicolai has to my mind the three indispensable qualities of a good conductor: He is a
> skilled, experienced and at times inspired composer; he has a thorough sense of rhythm
> and its complexities, and an impeccable clear and precise technique; and he is a shrewd
> and tireless organizer who grudges neither time nor trouble spent on rehearsal and
> knows exactly what he is doing because he does only what he knows what to do. Hence
> the excellent moral and physical health of the Kärntnerthor orchestra, its confidence,
> discipline and stamina, and its marvelous sureness and unanimity.[83]

Elsewhere Berlioz gives a rounded picture of the conducting situation in Germany in the early 1840s. He states that

> almost everywhere I went in Germany I found discipline and alertness combined with
> a genuine respect for the maestro. I should say, "maestros," for there are several: the
> composer, who nearly always directs both rehearsals and performances of his work,
> without the conductor's pride being in the least offended; the kapellmeister, generally
> a competent composer who is in charge of the large operas in the repertoire—all the

---

[80] Berlioz, *Traité*, 310; or *Treatise*, 418; or *Orchestral Conductor*, 16. For a description of a violin-conductor's score with its system of cues, see James J. Fuld, "Nineteenth-Century Operatic Violin Conductors' Scores," *Notes* 31 (1974): 278-80.

[81] Wagner *Mein Leben*, 604; or *Life*, 2:628.

[82] Nettel, 152.

[83] Berlioz, *Mémoires*, 2:194; or *Memoirs*, 374.

important works of composers who are dead or elsewhere; and the leader, who looks after the smaller operas and the ballets and, when not conducting, plays the first violin part and in his capacity as leader conveys the kapellmeister's instructions and comments to the back desks of the orchestra, keeps an eye on all the material side of the orchestra's work, sees that nothing is missing with regard to instruments or music, and sometimes demonstrates the bowing or the correct way of phrasing a passage— which the kapellmeister cannot do, as he always conducts with a baton.[84]

It would seem that only a composer had the competence to unravel a score. Also, the leader would not seem to be playing when he conducted. And further, the baton appears to have conquered the bow as implement in Germany even though it was earlier considered as "French" in style or origin.

Mendelssohn

Felix Mendelssohn conducted for the first time in Berlin in 1829; it was the famous performance of Bach's *St. Matthew Passion*. Old niceties of etiquette still remained. In rehearsals before the orchestra was available,

> Felix had both to accompany and conduct, a difficult matter with the rapid alternations of chorus and solos in ever-changing rhythms; here he used to play the accompaniment with the left hand, and conduct with the right.

But later:

> When we had an orchestra, the piano was placed across the platform, between the two choirs; it was then not yet customary for the conductor to turn his back to the audience, except at the opera. By this means, though the first choir was behind Felix, he faced the second and the orchestra. This latter consisted mainly of amateurs, only the leaders of the string and principal wind instruments belonged to the royal chapel. The wind instruments were placed at the back, above the semicircular platform, and extended towards the small concert-room through three open doors. The task of keeping steady this waving mass devolved upon Eduard Rietz.

So Mendelssohn found it necessary to utilize a sub-conductor. As for his technique, it cannot be called that of the iron hand:

> The quiet and simple way in which he by a look, a movement of the head or hand, reminded us of the inflections agreed upon, and thus ruled every phrase; the confidence with which he would drop his *bâton* during the longer movements, when he knew that they were safe, with a little nod as much as to say, "This will go very well without me,"—listen with radiant countenance, occasionally glancing towards me—in all he was as great as lovable.

Whether or not one agrees with such a method of lax control, one has to be impressed with such assurance on a first venture. But Eduard Devrient, baritone and Mendelssohn's biographer, evidently saw eye-to-eye with him on the philosophy of conducting:

---

[84] Berlioz, *Mémoires*, 2:52; or *Memoirs*, 264.

> We had many discussions about the best way of conducting. The continued beating throughout a movement, that must necessarily become mechanical, vexed me, and does so still. Compositions are really whipped through sometimes by this process. It always appeared to me that the conductor ought to beat time only when the difficulty of certain passages, or unsteadiness of the performers, renders it necessary. Surely the aim of every conductor should be to influence without obtruding himself. Felix determined on this occasion to show me how far this could be done, and he succeeded to perfection.

This remained Mendelssohn's style—indeed, would leave him open to later criticism, but not from Devrient:

> I recall these circumstances with peculiar satisfaction, as of late years the extraordinary gesticulations of conductors have been made a feature of in musical performances.[85]

In London, in May 1829, Mendelssohn conducted with a baton at the Argyll Rooms. At the rehearsal of his symphony,

> I mounted the orchestra and pulled out my white stick, which I have had made on purpose (the maker took me for an alderman, and would insist on decorating it with a crown). The first violin, François Cramer, showed me how the orchestra was placed— furthest rows had to get up so that I could see them—and introduced me to them all, and we bowed to each other; some perhaps laughed a little, that this small fellow with the stick should now take the place of their regular powdered and bewigged conductor.

But strangely the concert itself "began with the symphony; old François Cramer led me to the piano like a young lady, and I was received with immense applause."[86] It seems the tradition of the conductor at the piano maintained in London, even though Mendelssohn used a stick!

At Munich, in October 1831, Mendelssohn pursued his style of conducting. In a letter to his father he wrote, "I took up my little English *bâton*, and conducted my symphony."[87] And in Düsseldorf, for the Cologne Musical Festival in April 1835, he again wrote to his father:

> I shall not be able to play the organ for "Solomon," as it must stand in the background of the orchestra and accompany almost every piece, the choruses and other performers here being accustomed to constant beating of time. I must therefore transcribe the whole of the organ part in the manner in which I think it ought to be played, and the cathedral organist there, Weber, will play it. . . .[88]

So the custom of reliance on conducting was proceeding apace.

Until Mendelssohn came to Leipzig in 1835, the old ways persisted at the Gewandhaus. Indeed, Wagner reminisced:

---

[85] Devrient, *Erinnerungen*, 63-65; or *Recollections*, 59-61.

[86] Sebastian Hensel, *Die Familie Mendelssohn, 1729-1847, nach Briefen und Tagebüchern*, 6th ed., 2 vols. (Berlin; B. [E.] Behr, 1888), 209-10; or *The Mendelssohn Family (1729-1847), from Letters and Journals*, transl. Carl Klingemann and an American collaborator, 2nd rev. ed., 2 vols. (New York: Harper & Bros., 1882), 184-85.

[87] Felix Mendelssohn-Bartholdy, *Briefe aus den Jahren 1830 bis 1847*, ed. Paul & Carl Mendelssohn-Bartholdy, 2 vols. (Leipzig: H. Mendelssohn, 1875 and 1882), 1:298; or *Letters of Felix Mendelssohn-Bartholdy from Italy and Switzerland*, transl. Grace Wallace (New York: Leypoldt & Holt, 1866), 302.

[88] Mendelssohn, *Briefe*, 2:83; or *Letters of Felix Mendelssohn-Bartholdy from 1833 to 1847*, ed. Paul & Carl Mendelssohn-Bartholdy, transl. Grace Wallace (Philadelphia: F. Leypoldt, 1864), 74.

> In the days of my youth, orchestral pieces at the celebrated Leipzig Gewandhaus
> Concerts were not conducted at all; they were simply played through under the
> leadership of Conzertmeister Mathai, like overtures and entr'actes at a theatre. At
> least there was no "disturbing individuality," in the shape of a conductor!"[89]

There is similar evidence from another commentator:

> The manner of playing of an orchestra was determined at that time by the Concertmaster
> or *Vorspieler*. While only the conducting of choral performances and furthermore the
> program-construction of the concert was incumbent on the *Musikdirektor* at that time,
> the *Vorspieler* of the first violins directed the symphonies from his desk through motions
> with the violin-neck or violin-bow. These are hardly to be understood as true time-
> beating, they amount more to a beat- or tempo-change and the adjustment of changes,
> "so that the orchestra [could] without visible or audible indications of the director, even
> in symphonies or other pieces or passages for full orchestra, where the expression obtains
> through appropriate retarding or accelerating of the tempo, (ritardando or accelerando),
> perform this wholly exact, without wavering of the whole and blamelessly."[90]

Even in theater works, the burdens of orchestral responsibility remained the same. "The *Musikdirektor*
sits directly in front of the stage, in order to lead the vocal ensemble; the *Konzertmeister* remains
responsible for the orchestral part and unity with the stage."[91]

When Mendelssohn came to the Gewandhaus in 1835, one writer considered his "most important
innovation" to consist in "that he no longer left the leading of instrumental works to the concertmaster,
as had been the custom until now, but that he took them in hand himself and correspondingly also
held all rehearsals for the performances himself."[92] Another opinion goes further:

> We are today much too used to the phenomenon of the modern conductor to be able to
> fully appreciate what really took place then, what inner-personal and outer-social effects
> this radical change was able to and must have produced, finally how questionable the
> power of the baton is. For the precise rendering of the early romantic score the director
> is still no absolute requisite. We read even in 1836 in the *Neue Zeitschrift für Musik*
> in an article on the fashion of conducting the concise sentence: "The less an orchestra
> is conducted, the higher it stands," and we know concerning Mendelssohn's conducting
> that it was confined to wholly sparse, only the most necessary hinting sign-giving.
> Robert Schumann perceives even these as burdensome and is of the opinion, "an orchestra
> must stand forth like a republic, over which no higher being is to be recognized."[93]

Yet Mendelssohn's influence was not slight. One writer commented on the effects of "brilliant
performance" and "precision until now unheard in Leipzig."[94] This praise is echoed elsewhere. "He

---

[89] Wagner, "Dirigiren," *Gesammelten Schriften*, 8:337; or *On Conducting*, 14.

[90] Hans-Joachim Nösselt, *Das Gewandhausorchester: Entstehung und Entwicklung eines Orchesters* (Leipzig: Koehler
& Amelang, 1943), 108, crediting *AmZ* (1803) with the quoted portions.

[91] Ibid., 121.

[92] Alfred Dörffel, *Geschichte der Gewandhausconcerte zu Leipzig vom 25. November 1781 bis 25. November 1881*,
Festschrift zur hundertjährigen Jubelfeier der Einweihung des Concertsaales im Gewandhause zu Leipzig (Leipzig: Concert-
Direction, 1884), 84.

[93] Nosselt, 129.

[94] Creuzburg, 56-57.

had brought the Gewandhaus concerts to a pitch of perfection which placed them at the head of all symphonic performances in Germany, and made them looked up to as the highest standard of excellence."[95] The pianist Richard Hoffman remembered Mendelssohn as

> one of the best conductors, but he would seldom beat more than the first sixteen or twenty-four bars of an overture or movement from a symphony; he would then lay down his baton and listen, often applauding with the audience. He would take it up again when he wished a crescendo or rallentando or any other effect not noted in the parts.[96]

This reminds one of Berlioz's peeve against Habeneck. Dörffel goes into somewhat more detail:

> He rehearsed the works in so painstaking a manner in reference to technique, in so stimulating a manner in reference to spirit of the performance, that the few members of the orchestra who initially perhaps had inclination to opposition very soon were converted and followed his genial leading as willingly as the other members, so that they together set their artistic honor therein, the whole satisfaction of the excelling director to gain.[97]

Nösselt seems less positive—even negative—about the change and Mendelssohn's influence. After bemoaning the loss of "self-forming will, the individually artistic, constantly *chamber-musical* responsibility of the orchestra-musician, his participation wholly from within out," he goes on:

> Mendelssohn himself designates the orchestra as his "Instrument"; it has thus ceased, in the profound sense of the word "body," to be filled with life and spirit. It makes music no more, driven by its own pulse-beat, no more from itself out, but "*under him*"; and the concertmaster will at best play only a middle roll between conductor and orchestra.[98]

Were his views possibly colored by the fact that he was writing in the 1940s at the height of the Nazi regime, and Mendelssohn was Jewish?

Although Mendelssohn possessed a prodigious musical memory, he did not believe in conducting without a score.

> Hallé was impressed by Mendelssohn's memory and has recounted the story that when Mendelssohn revived the *St. Matthew Passion* the wrong score had been placed on the conductor's desk at the first performance. He conducted by heart, but turned the pages so as not to unsettle the performers. "Mendelssohn, and certainly Berlioz, would have been amazed," Hallé wrote, "if they had witnessed the modern craze for conducting without a score; they never did so, even with their own works. There can be no possible advantage in dispensing with the score. . . . No conductor could write by heart 20 pages of the full score of a symphony, or other work, exactly with the instrumentation of the composer, he must therefore remain ignorant . . . of what the minor instruments . . . have to do—a serious disadvantage."[99]

---

[95] Devrient, *Erinnerungen*, 209; or *Recollections*, 214.

[96] Richard Hoffman, *Some Musical Recollections of Fifty Years* (New York: C. Scribner's Sons, 1910), 70-71.

[97] Dörffel, 84-85.

[98] Nösselt, 131.

[99] Michael Kennedy, *The Hallé Tradition: A Century of Music* (Manchester: Manchester University Press, 1960), 15. However, the last sentence can be challenged; see, for example, Howard Taubman, *The Maestro: The Life of Arturo Toscanini* (New York: Simon & Schuster, 1951), 261-62, on Toscanini's feats of memory.

Michael Costa

Dual leadership was still the norm when Michael Costa became active in London around 1833. In March of 1846 he was appointed conductor of the Philharmonic Society. He immediately "stipulated that the still too-assertive 'Leader' should be suppressed and that he should be in sole control as he was at the opera."[100] One writer called him "the first disciplinarian conductor of the kind familiar today. He knew how to control an orchestra. . . . He insisted on a free hand with the orchestra and at once raised standards of performance."[101]

According to Sir George Grove, Costa was "a splendid drill-sergeant, he brought the London orchestras to an order unknown before."[102] Conditions prevailing in at least English orchestras at the time—low salaries, the deputy system, small chance of betterment, older and incompetent players preventing rewards for talent and industry—"tended to drag orchestral playing down to mediocrity. Not even Mendelssohn, with his personality and reputation, could entirely bend the players to his will or secure order. One had to compromise with them. Costa put an end to that. In him the men recognized their master: a stern one, but a just one."[103] In the words of a contemporary,

> From the first evening when Signor Costa took up the baton, a young man from a country then despised by every musical pedant, a youth who came to England without flourish, announcement, or protection, as a singer without much voice, to do what was never done in England before, it was to be felt that in him were combined the materials of a great conductor—nerve to enforce discipline, readiness to the second, and that certain influence which only a vigorous man could exercise over the disconnected folk who made up an orchestra in those days.[104]

Another voice claimed that he was noisy, that he loved the winds.[105]

Costa came to England in 1829 as a singer. He became *maestro al cembalo* at the King's Theatre in 1830, and conductor in 1833. "By the end of the decade he had taken a ragtag group of indifferent musicians and made them a well-drilled group of seventy-seven players."[106] One would expect an iron will and a tough backbone to be behind such control. "Part of this control came from a good stick technique, and part came from pure psychic domination."[107]

Liszt

Franz Liszt expressed himself as against mechanical, measured time-beating. He wanted only periodic delivery with special accents prominent, and melodic and rhythmic nuance. In his own conducting he indicated phrases and periods, rather than measures. He felt that the conductor should make himself superfluous and not carry on the function of a windmill.[108] However, Smart described Liszt's conducting

---

[100] Scholes, 1:377; see also Elkin, 43.

[101] Kennedy, 23-24.

[102] Quoted in Nettel, 142.

[103] Ibid., 144.

[104] Henry F. Chorley, *Thirty Years' Musical Recollections*, ed. Ernest Newman (New York: A. A. Knopf, 1926), 84.

[105] Joseph Bennett, *Forty Years of Music, 1865-1905* (London: Methuen, 1908), 335.

[106] Schonberg, 144.

[107] Ibid., 145.

[108] Haas, 277.

of his own cantata at Bonn in 1845 as "with plenty of twisting of the person."[109] Divided rehearsals seem to have been used by Liszt in preparing *Lohengrin* at Weimar in 1840, for he wrote to Wagner: "I undertake all the rehearsals with pianoforte, chorus, strings, and orchestra."[110] In another letter he states: "Tomorrow and afterwards I shall separately rehearse the wind, which will be complete, in accordance with the demands of your score."[111]

Brahms

In direct contrast, Johannes Brahms avoided all "egocentric subjectivity. . . . He directed as a rule in firm, serious bearing with large, quiet motions. All superfluous 'brandishings' with the baton were repugnant to him." And yet he could be forceful. Conducting his Fourth Symphony at the Gewandhaus in Leipzig, evidently feeling the orchestra was not putting forth enough, he used such lively motions that a cellist fell backwards to avoid being struck with the stick and took another with him.[112] A description by a relative of Theodor Billroth makes him sound similar to Beethoven:

> If he wants a pianissimo, he stoops very low, while in fortissimo he becomes erect and tall, always, however, in wholly natural movement without any theatrical claptrap. One sees in his facial expression, in all his motions, how he really lives through tone for tone. The passion, which goes out from him, carries over entirely by itself to the chorus and orchestra-members.[113]

His biographer notes, however, that Brahms lacked the grotesque, providing a picture of Brahms conducting, perhaps rather well-known, which would suggest an almost unconcerned, lackadaisical leader.[114] In contrast, Hermine Spies opined that "to sing under Brahms is glorious." One made entrances forced by the nobility of the moment, and he was like a "pillar" at the desk. "He works so calmly."[115] So calmly, yet he could hold "summer lightening" in his eyes, and hold his clenched fist over his heart during emotional moments, as if to keep it from "springing forth" from his body.[116]

Louis Antoine Jullien

The famous conductor of the London Promenade Concerts, Louis Antoine Jullien, conducted facing the audience, standing in the midst of his players, not in front of them. Jullien was a great showman.

> He had a dais built in the centre of the orchestra, the floor of which was covered with white cloth having a gold-lace border. On the dais he had a splendid arm-chair of white and gold. When he directed, he stood up and faced the audience.[117]

---

[109] Smart, 301.

[110] *Briefwechsel zwischen Wagner und Liszt*, ed. Erich Kloss, 3rd ed., 2 vols. (Leipzig: Breitkopf & Härtel, 1910), 1:55; or *Correspondence of Wagner and Liszt*, transl. Francis Hueffer, new rev. ed., ed. William A. Ellis, 2 vols. (London, 1897; reprint, New York: Greenwood, 1969), 1:70.

[111] *Briefwechsel*, 1:63; or *Correspondence*, 1:79.

[112] Konrad Huschke, *Johannes Brahms als Pianist, Dirigent und Lehrer* (Karlsruhe: Friedrich Gutsch, 1935), 42-44.

[113] Quoted in Huschke, 44.

[114] Huschke, 44, with facing picture.

[115] Ibid., 43.

[116] Max Kalbech, quoted in ibid., 44.

[117] Ryan, 69-70.

Showman or not, he must have been a musician of considerable abilities, foreshadowing many a modern virtuoso conductor.

> In conducting dance music or anything of a distinctly rhythmical character, he would mark the rhythm so graphically with his baton that people actually saw it at the end of his stick. They could not mistake that, if they had eyes. No one was allowed to go to sleep. When the various soli obligati were forthcoming, he would turn to the players thereof; and the audience then saw him conduct that little or big phrase, give emphasis and expression to it, and coax it out with his baton—his wizard baton—in such a way that seeing and hearing were simply one fact. Jullien did it all.[118]

But Jullien did have respect for great music; yet even his way of showing it smacked of the charlatan. When he conducted Beethoven, he used a special jeweled baton and wore spotlessly white kid gloves. They would be brought to him on a silver salver.[119]

Wagner

Richard Wagner was not a mere time-beater:

> His faith was pinned to the use of a flexible tempo, varying according to the emotional character of the melody. In Wagner's conducting, as Seidl said, it was not the time-beat that ruled; it was the phrase, the melody or the expression. That was the key to Wagner's method of conducting, and also the cause of much trouble and misunderstanding when he stood before orchestras that were not accustomed to his method.[120]

After Wagner's first appearance with the Philharmonic Society in London, 12 March 1855, Ferdinand Praeger wrote that a Haydn symphony

> opened the eyes of the audience to a state of things hitherto unknown, as regards conducting. Wagner does not beat in the old-fashioned automato-metronomic manner. He leaves off beating at times—then resumes again—to lead the orchestra up to a climax, or to let them soften down to a *pianissimo*, as if a thousand invisible threads tied them to his bâton. His is the beau ideal of conducting. He treats the orchestra like the instrument on which he pours forth his soul-inspired strains.[121]

Actually, this sounds not unlike descriptions of Mendelssohn, whom Wagner so disparaged. After playing under Wagner in 1872, Artur Nikisch wrote that

> Wagner was certainly not what one might describe as a "routine conductor"—his very gestures were music in themselves. I have said before that the conductor's baton-technique—if he is not just an uninspired time-beater—is a language whose mastery enables the listener to penetrate the feelings of the artist, and helps his understanding of the work being played. This was Wagner through and through.[122]

---

[118] Ibid., 70.

[119] Nettel, 135.

[120] Adam Carse, *The Orchestra from Beethoven to Berlioz* (Cambridge: W. Heffer & Sons; reprint, New York: Broude Bros., 1949), 353.

[121] Ferdinand Praeger, *Wagner as I Knew Him* (New York: Longmans, Green, 1892), 235.

[122] Quoted in David Wooldridge, *Conductor's World* (New York: Praeger, 1970), 102.

Wagner himself evidently placed great emphasis on the force of the conductor's art. In preparing to mount *Das Liebesverbot* in 1836, with all the concomitant problems involved, he "reckoned further on my own acquired skill as conductor to achieve the final miracle of success." Yet "Unfortunately, we did not consider that in front of the public all these drastic methods of moving the dramatic and musical machinery would be restricted to the movements of my baton and my facial expression."[123]

But all did not always go well for him. In Paris for concerts of his music in 1860, he had problems with the orchestra. "My 6/8 time, which I took as 4/4 time, particularly incensed them, and with tumultuous protestations they declared it should be taken *alla-breva*."[124] On the face of it, one would be tempted to side with the players. However, if the rhythmic movement were quarter-eighth-quarter-eighth notes, then it could be a very clear subdivision, similar to 4/4, with the first two subdivisions (or quarter) corresponding to the downbeat, the third subdivision (or eighth) to the second beat of the 4/4, the fourth and fifth subdivisions (or quarter) corresponding to the third 4/4 beat, and so on. This could be effective.

Perhaps some of his rehearsal techniques are still valid today. In preparing the *Ring* cycle in 1875,

> Wagner's idea in these rehearsals was not to proceed from the single point to the whole, but just the reverse. First the whole, and then the working out of details, so that as a result of this method something relatively perfect was accomplished, and the rehearsals, so far as orchestral and voice parts were concerned, differed but little from the eventual public performances.[125]

If this seems unclear or contradictory, perhaps the following is more articulate:

> For six weeks these rehearsals continued; first the instrumental groups and vocalist were taken separately, next came the single acts, to each of which an entire day was devoted, and finally the complete drama was gone over.[126]

Odds and Ends

In a letter to Wagner from Munich dated 21 June 1869, and referring to a performance of *Tristan und Isolde*, Hans von Bülow claimed to have conducted better because of practice with the baton.[127] David Wooldridge considers this the first reference to baton technique as something more than beating time clearly.[128] Late in the century Felix Weingartner evidently took baton practice even further. "His con-ducting was unostentatious and precise, and his elegant gestures were a household word. . . . Weingartner was the first conductor who was said to practice his gestures in front of a mirror."[129] Sir

[123] Wagner, *Mein Leben*, 137; or *Life*, 1:139.

[124] Wagner, *Mein Leben*, 699; or *Life*, 2:726.

[125] *The Story of Bayreuth as Told in the Bayreuth Letters of Richard Wagner*, transl. and ed. Caroline V. Kerr (New York: Vienna House, 1972), 226-27.

[126] Ibid., 246.

[127] Hans von Bülow, *Neue Briefe*, ed. Richard Count du Moulin Eckart (München: Drei Masken, 1927), 470; or *Letters to Richard Wagner, Cosima Wagner, His Daughter Daniela, Luise von Bülow, Karl Klindworth, Carl Bechstein*, ed. R. du Moulin Eckart, transl. Hannah Waller, ed. Scott Goddard (New York: A. A. Knopf, 1931), 237.

[128] Wooldridge, 92.

[129] Marcel Prawy, *The Vienna Opera* (New York: Praeger, 1970), 86.

Henry Wood was said to have told his players that he put in a half hour of practice with the baton every morning.[130] Hermann Zopff, writing in 1881, suggested that one practice before a mirror and carefully mark the beat and parts of the beat while holding the body quiet. He allowed expedient tapping on the desk for attention before beginning, but the first beat must be "only in the air."[131] In 1887 Richard Strauss, in a letter to Bülow, credited divided rehearsals for the success of concerts in Milan, for which there were only six rehearsals. The program included the *Meistersinger* Prelude.[132]

By the end of the century, conducting was taken for granted as an art and a craft. According to Maurice Kufferath, Brussels had had symphonic concerts since 1865, with famous composers such as Rubinstein, Tchaikovsky, Rimsky-Korsakov, Cui, and Saint-Saëns as guest conductors. But when Hans Richter appeared there in 1890, he created an extraordinarily impression. Within a few rehearsals he transformed the playing, phrasing, nuances, and expression so completely that works, even the well-known classics, appeared almost new, even though they may have been played twenty times before by the same players. Other great conductors followed there: Hermann, Levi, Felix Mottl, Richard Strauss.[133] Many similar experiences could undoubtedly be reported in every great city. And was it not Strauss who insisted that a conductor should never sweat?

---

[130] Nettel, 213.

[131] Hermann Zopff, *Der angehende Dirigent* (Leipzig: C. Merseburger, 1881), 36.

[132] Hans von Bülow and Richard Strauss, *Correspondence*, ed. Willi Schuh and Franz Trenner, transl. Anthony Gishford (London: Boosey & Hawkes, 1955), 64.

[133] Maurice Kufferath, *L'Art de diriger: Richard Wagner et la "Neuvième Symphonie" de Beethoven, Hans Richter et La Symphonie au "ut" mineur, L'Idylle de Siegfried–Interprétation et tradition*, 3rd ed. (Paris: Fischbacher, 1909), 90-100.

CHAPTER **8**

Illusion and Reality in Schubert's Song Cycles

John C. Duffy

. . . the force of the whole piece, is for the
most part, left to the shutting up, the whole
frame of the Poem is a beating out of a piece
of gold, but the last is as the impression of
the stamp, and that is it that makes it currant [*sic*].

John Donne, *Sermons*

I am the opposite of a stage magician. He
gives you illusion that has the appearance
of truth. I give you truth in the pleasant
guise of illusion.

Tom Wingfield,
in Tennessee Williams,
The Glass Menagerie (1945)

The sweetest sounds I'll ever hear
are still inside my head.

–from *No Strings* (1962),
music and lyrics by Richard Rodgers

Introduction

This paper is an attempt to understand the astonishment I felt on first hearing *Winterreise* in recital. There were different and, it seemed, irreconcilable points of view, several realities, and several truths: the truth of the story, the realities of the lyric conventions of the songs, the poetic conventions of lost love and *Doppelgänger*, and the unarticulated truth of the audience's (and my) dumbstruck response. *Winterreise* leaves to the listener the ultimate task of resolving the dissonances between the story (what is textually stated), the conventions of lyric presentation (song cycle in concert performance), and the independent workings of the music. In *Die schöne Müllerin* such dissonances do not persist— its audience is not left to resolve the cycle after it concludes.

The nut of the argument is this: the songs of *Winterreise* are interior. They have no existence (until the end) outside the mind of the hurdy-gurdy player who imagines himself to be (and at one time may have been) an Orphic lover-singer.

The audience has been able to hear those songs by a subtle subterfuge: it hears them from within the mind of the "observed" *Leiermann*. In the final song, as his emotional energy wanes and he is unable

This is a revised version of a paper presented at the spring 1975 meeting of the New England Chapter of the American Musicological Society. I thank Dr. Lefkowitz for his encouragement and suggestions for that presentation. Similarly, I would like to acknowledge the generous advice and support given by the late Professor Jack Stein of Harvard University and Professor Rufus Hallmark, then at MIT, and the assistance provided by the late Francis Gramenz, colleague and former music librarian at Boston University.

to sustain the lyric fantasy, the singer/*Leiermann* is revealed, not as the singer of these richly felt songs, but as the imaginer of them. His own, "outer" music, the listless, repetitive hurdy-gurdy drone and tune, reveals itself to be as monochromatic and unresponsive as the winter landscape he occupies.

Die schöne Müllerin

Edward Cone makes several observations which begin to explain the radically different responses evoked by performances of *Die schöne Müllerin* and *Winterreise*. He remarks on the naïveté immanent in many of the songs in *Die schöne Müllerin*:

> Some lyrics call for a simple and straightforward musical setting that would simulate natural, unmediated vocal expression. For example the first poem of *Die schöne Müllerin*, "Das Wandern," might be read as the utterance of a young man who is not just enjoying life, but consciously *singing for joy*. Schubert's song could accordingly be heard as a simulation of natural expressive singing. An interpretation of this kind, applied to a number of songs in this cycle, would explain their emphasis on the simple melodies and strophic forms: these songs represent not merely the thought of the protagonist, but songs composed (improvised) by him.[1]

This provocative suggestion can help the singer to realize an appropriate negligence or lack of self-consciousness in performance. It assumes the singer is simply playing a role, that of the youthful apprentice who "composes" these songs as he goes on his way or reflects on recent events. Cone then points out a problem in applying this conclusion to the entire cycle:

> The brook, too, seems to be a composer. Addressed as a friend by the hero in a number of the lyrics, it comes to life dramatically in "Der Müller und der Bach," and the last song, "Des Baches Wiegenlied," is fancifully presented as a lullaby sung by the brook itself.

Further,

> . . . the brook is not singing in its own guise, but is itself simulating a mother who sings her child to sleep—and the brook, as the vocal unity of the cycle attests, is in turn only the projection of the hero's gloomy imagination. What we hear, then, is not a natural lullaby nor the simulation of one, but the dramatic portrayal of the imagined situation of a lullaby. . . . The music stands as a constant reminder that behind the image of the mother, evoked by the singing brook that personifies the despondent mood of the hero, we must infer a consciousness whose thought can evoke and control all the relationships in a song of such complex simplicity. It is, of course, the consciousness implied by the interaction of word, voice, and accompaniment throughout the song cycle: its implicit musical persona.[2]

This "musical persona," controlling the action "behind the scenes," as it were, is more a creator, unifier, and observer of the experience than a participant. Both singer and pianist are asked to play more than one role. Our interpretation of events is guided by the musical expression seemingly chosen by the "lyrical I." This "lyrical I," the vocal protagonist, is, in turn, an agent of the controlling musical

---

[1] Edward T. Cone, *The Composer's Voice* (Berkeley: University of California Press, 1974), 55.

[2] Ibid., 55-56.

persona.[3] Understanding this allows both the performers (singer and pianist) and audience a means to comprehend the conventions, points of view, and effects of the cycle and to establish that the singer of these songs, as we hear them, is *not* the young journeyman.

Typically, *Die schöne Müllerin* is presented as a narrative of (or reflection on) real events as they take place. The miller/narrator appears to be the story's protagonist; his audience is the brook. In such a reading the brook is considered a sympathetic companion to the miller. It is then but a short step to equate the miller-lad with the singer and the sympathetic brook with the piano accompaniment.

This standard reading fails in two respects. First, we are at the mercy of the text. The words tell us what happens and how to respond. No matter how expressive or evocative or picturesque the accompaniment seems, the words make situations specific, give them meaning, and lead us in the ways of the pathetic fallacy by assigning significance where there may be none. Second, the piano accompaniment, whatever its glories and challenges, is never independent of the singer (whether speaking as miller, or brook, or maid). That is, it cannot be identified so simply as "brook." Its musical support for the singer cannot be glibly translated into the natural world's sympathy for and support/reflection of the miller's moods.

The first point is most easily confirmed in the strophic songs, which are musically more static and reflective and partake of a different level of time consciousness than more immediate, through-composed songs. In these songs the singer's text provides the specificity, narrative continuity, and signification, even attributing a point of view to the otherwise generalized accompaniment. Even changes of mode or interludes in various figurations acquire meaning from textual referents rather than from unspecified gestural analogies.

The latter point requires a return to Cone's observations, for the piano accompaniment serves several purposes. It is always imaginary, a projection of an implicit persona, though usually seeming to be a projection of the miller (a representation, not realization, of the brook, whose sympathy the miller so easily assumes). We, as audience, easily associate the accompaniment with the brook. The musical relation of accompaniment to singer, the pictorialisms of that accompaniment, and the assumption (implied by the text, and mostly unquestioned until the final songs) that the miller is actually singing these songs, and singing them to a listening brook, all encourage the equation of piano and brook. Thus, the musical sympathy between singer and accompaniment is (falsely) transferred by analogy to miller and brook-piano. Interestingly, it is not transferred to the audience itself.

The accompaniment, however, cannot be equated with the brook, for the brook has a voice of its own. Nor can it be considered of equal importance with the singer, for the singer of the cycle (as distinct from the miller) is the primary vehicle of the controlling consciousness of the work. Neither the stage singer nor the accompaniment is actually a participant in the melodrama. This point is made in the final two songs when we hear the same singing voice, as Cone points out, presenting both miller and brook and, in the penultimate song, when we hear the entwining of musical ideas (effected by a change in the accompaniment) originally associated independently with the miller and the brook.

If both miller and brook are projections of an implicit persona, actors in a series of imaginary vignettes, then the performance, which we hear "realized" in the concert hall, actually takes place in the imagination of the controlling persona, and is presented by singer and accompanist. Moreover, the artful device and convention of the closing lullaby assures us, comfortingly and comfortably, that

---

[3] Cone returned to the subject of the vocal protagonist in "Poet's Love or Composer's Love?," appearing in *Music and Text: Critical Inquiries*, ed. Steven Paul Scher (Cambridge: Cambridge University Press, 1992), 177-92. His article is a model of eloquence and the most productive type of public reconsideration of an issue: an exposition and examination of the essential questions resulting in greater clarity and more powerful argument.

the songs we have heard are not dramatic, not real: that our adolescent miller has suffered only imaginary wounds. We can sympathize with his naïveté in expecting the universe, or at least his brook, to understand and respond to his tortured passion, and we can smile—sadly perhaps—at the shock of recognition which slowly permeates his receding consciousness.

> Ach, Bächlein, liebes Bächlein,
> Du meinst es so gut:
> Ach Bächlein, aber weisst du,
> Wie Liebe tut?

The universe is impersonal, uncomprehending, indifferent. The brook flows on, unperturbed. We expect no sea change. The lullaby brings closure and timelessness with its metrical, musical, and verbal generalities, as if to say "There now, that's not so bad, is it?"

We applaud, moved by the loveliness of the songs and their plangent sentiment, and go home to sleep. The illusory world of this beautiful artifice does not impinge on our more real world. *Die schöne Müllerin* rather quickly becomes "once upon a time and far away," less than dream. Many of the songs are affecting, picturesque, and expressive. They possess a balance of lyricism and intensity, which enhances both their affect and their effect. But they are not immediate or, more precisely, unmediated. The artificial frame of the work is revealed in the final songs, when the singer is dissociated from the characters of the cycle. We then realize, or confirm, that these songs are of imaginary subjects, that what we have witnessed is an entertainment for our enjoyment, a sequence of imaginary events mediated by the singer and accompanist: illusion in the temporary guise of, in this instance, a lyrical and gentle reality. Never fear, the performers are not the characters. As we applaud their performance, our relief is part of our response.

Winterreise

Winterreise is not pleasant, nor, as we realize at the conclusion, is it framed comfortingly. We are inclined at first, however, to regard both cycles as if their resemblances (and possible narrative continuities) are more important than their fundamental differences.

Like *Die schöne Müllerin*, *Winterreise* presents an apparently narrated fiction that begins in a vague past time. These new songs, however, progress in intensity and concentration—not to a conventional and artful resolution or to a climactic explosion or catharsis, but, by subtraction of all ornament and excess, to the terrifying disorientation and collapse of the final song, "Der Leiermann."

Regarding the two cycles together, however, allows for numerous superficially satisfying interpretations, all of which treat *Die schöne Müllerin* as an adolescent version of, or prolepsis to, *Winterreise*. Musical and textual evidence supporting this argument is easily adduced: the maturation of the apprentice into the more mature wanderer, the variable, quick step and daylit vivid greens of *Müllerin* giving way to the icy and often nighttime cold and steadier (and weightier) tread of the latter cycle, the agonized juvenile infatuation of the miller boy transformed into the demented suffering of the alienated wanderer.

It may even be that Schubert, using Müller's poetry, created a portrait of himself (as a musician and maker of songs, not as a lover), which he immortalized in song. Certainly he, as composer, is the controlling consciousness, the musical persona of these songs. But this biographical speculation does not directly concern the audience. Whatever the composer's undocumented intent, we are faced with two cycles, which elicit different responses because they are fundamentally different.

Simply put, there is no final separation of real and illusory worlds in *Winterreise*. In *Die schöne Müllerin* the illusion of reality is swept aside and the artifice is revealed. In *Winterreise* we are left wondering. The conventional, theatrical ambiguity we so enjoyed in *Die schöne Müllerin* is very much part of the audience's appreciation of *Winterreise*'s first twenty-three songs. But that ambiguity of reality and illusion collapses in "Der Leiermann." Recognizing (or intuiting) the nature of that collapse, as confirmed by musical and textual evidence and by the unique effect of this emotionally devastating song, changes the listener's response to the entire cycle.

The "I" of *Winterreise* sings songs of impotent bitterness, anger, resignation, and—finally—desolation. The same kind of easy identifications made with *Der schöne Müllerin* can be made here: the accompanying piano suggests the tread of the wanderer and the surrounding bleak, hard, sometimes desolate world of wintry nature (a personification of the faithless beloved's wintry heart) the words specify. The singer's progress on his (self-inflicted) physical and spiritual journey leads the audience to assume that the journey is not real, but a somewhat inflated analogy for the wanderer's journey of emotional torment. His is the recognizable "voice" of the cycle. As audience, we fully expect his journey to be completed in an aesthetically satisfying way, which we can validate with conventional applause.

If this were all, the cycle could end with the quickly deflated outburst of bitter bravado (more appropriate to the miller boy) and flourish of defiance concluding the antepenultimate song, "Mut."

> Lustig in die Welt hinein
> Gegen Wind und Wetter!
> Will kein Gott auf Erden sein,
> Sind wir selber Götter.

The chill and darkening hymn of resignation, "Die Nebensonnen," provides a calmer sense of closure. Unlike "Des Baches Wiegenlied," however, this closure would be one of isolation, the wanderer bereft of any living companionship (dog, crow, will o' the wisp), and now losing even the final light of the mock sons:

> Ging' nur die dritt' erst hinterdrein,
> Im Dunkeln wird mir wohler sein.

But even this closure is denied. The delirium of intensified desolation which began with the manic "Täuschung" is broken by the stark intrusion of "Der Leiermann." With its unique musical character, mundane prosody, and vision of a second human sufferer, "Der Leiermann" breaks the "lyric conspiracy" of art song conventions. Its dramatic, concluding burst of direct address destroys any sense of lyric repose and composure.

> Drüben hinterm Dorfe   Keiner mag ihn hören,
> Steht ein Leiermann,   Keiner sieht ihn an,
> Und mit starren Fingern   Und die Hunde knurren
> Dreht er, was er kann.   Um den alten Mann.
>
> Barfuss auf dem Eise   Und er lässt es gehen
> Wankt er hin und her,   Alles, wie es will.
> Und sein kleiner Teller   Dreht, und seine Leier
> Bleibt ihm immer leer.   Steht ihm nimmer still.
>
> Wunderlicher Alter,
> Soll ich mit dir gehn?
> **Willst zu meinen Liedern**
> **Deine Leier drehn?**

The sympathy between the wanderer/singer and the organ-grinder is easy to understand. Both are outcasts, frozen (emotionally or physically), singing songs no one hears (or cares to hear), acknowledged only by a solitary crow or snarling dogs. Yet their relationship is more than resemblance, more than reflection, and this final song takes us to an uncharted and unexpected destination.

It is tempting to explain the effect of this last song (and the entire cycle) as resulting from the unrelievedly intense bitterness, alienation, and mental disintegration of the rejected lover. While that is important, the vision of someone whose physical destitution reflects our wanderer's emotional breakdown does not contain or resolve that disintegration.

In fact, our singer does not find someone to whose accompaniment he might continue to sing his songs, even as that alien music intrudes and shapes his own. There is no sympathetic response in the hurdy-gurdy drone. The organ-grinder does not and cannot accompany the wanderer's song. Quite the opposite: the wanderer's lyricism is metastasized to the tune of the hurdy-gurdy and becomes inert. Response in this frozen world remains beyond possibility, yet the wanderer populates his world with a reflection and attributes response and expression to a drone. Finally, at the collapse of "Der Leiermann," we are left with the question: is the hurdy-gurdy player a projection/reflection of the wanderer, or is the wanderer, the "lyrical I," a projection of the hurdy-gurdy player?[4]

Conclusion

The mood of *Winterreise* is intensified organically (tonal continuities, modal consistency, and shrinking melodic range have much to do with this perception), while the individual songs present discrete aspects of the wanderer's loss of his sense of self. This reading accepts the appearance of the hurdy-gurdy as a pictorial element and does not ask further. Perhaps that is as far as one should go, noting that the movement from past tense to present forcibly inflicts a sense of immediacy, "now," upon the audience.

But it is a compelling irony that the lyrical accompaniments of the twenty-three previous songs have been imaginary. That is, the accompaniments can be heard as projections of the wanderer's emotion onto the natural world or a reflection of his thought and movements (as specified in the texts). They are conventional accompaniments for art-songs performed in intimate settings.

In "Der Leiermann" the hurdy-gurdy is introduced not only as a pictorial element, but its music is incorporated as an accompaniment from the world, here and now, though absolutely neutral and inexpressive. The accompaniment is not now simply a projection of the singer. Its strange monotony has an existence outside the arena of the other songs. The music, despite the text, forces the awareness that this "real" accompaniment is, in fact, no more responsive than the cold, unresponsive world of nature. All sympathy, in this cycle, is not simply illusion, but delusion. Moreover, the magnificent pathetic shapelessness of the other songs, with their balanced phrases and completed vocal lines, devolves

---

[4] Cone, ibid., 181, comes to a quite different and less controversial conclusion. For him, there is no question that the vocal protagonist is addressing the organ-grinder. In *The Composer's Voice*, 30, he had written

> The protagonist of "Der Leiermann" hears a hurdy-gurdy, but he does not hear what the actual singer and the audience hear: a pianist playing a stylized version of what a hurdy-gurdy might sound like . . . the sound as heard or imagined by the protagonist is only raw material; what the singer and the audience hear is the composer's transformation of the sound into an element of the accompaniment.

He recasts this now:

> The sound heard by the musician-protagonist is his raw material; what we hear is his utilization of that sound as an element of his accompaniment.

in this song to repetition and banality; a sense of exhausted desperation that erupts in the startling, insistent declamatory question of the singer: an eruption out of the lyrical and reflective mode of the previous songs into the dramatic immediacy of present nightmare.

Thus, in both rhetorical gesture and the use of music ascribed to a real hurdy-gurdy, "Der Leiermann" is the only "real" song of the cycle. What, then, is the relationship of the singer to the organ-grinder? Even though the last song catapults us to a more immediate sense of time present, there is no change of voice. We hear only one person sing. The music (by the union of material in the vocal line and accompaniment) tells us we have one musical consciousness, while the text tells us we have two characters, one of whom is observed and overheard from a distance and to whom the singer's choked and desperate cry is directed.

The introduction of the second human sufferer in the same plane as the singer is quite jarring. The evidence, particularly the fact that the text is sung to the hurdy-gurdy tune, points to the conclusion that the singer and the organ-grinder are not different people, but *Doppelgänger*. They are different aspects of one persona, the unrelieved, artless and airless music and mean circumstances of the one serving as foil and mirror for the inspired art and lyrical sentiment of the other.

The "singer-wanderer" is easily taken as the more real of these characters. After all, we have assumed we were living in his world for the entire cycle. Why not simply accept the organ-grinder and his plaintive hurdy-gurdy tune as yet another projection of the singer's now fragmenting personality or the incorporation of his immediate environment into his song? But the music of "Der Leiermann," even disguised by the tone of a concert grand piano, musically unites singer and accompaniment and becomes increasingly the music of an actual hurdy-gurdy to which one sings, an abrupt collision and intrusion of the real world into the imagined world of the preceding songs.

Thus, the wanderer/singer and the organ-grinder are one, and it is the organ-grinder who is more immediately real: It is his world of isolation, numbness, derision, snarling dogs, and freezing feet which has formed and inspired the world of the singer, that world in which feeling was once, at least, a memory or possibility and misfortune had an explanation. Singer and organ-grinder merge. As the energy to maintain their separation is exhausted, the once-comfortably distant perspective from which we could view them also collapses, and they confront and engulf us.

Consider the possibility that the twenty-three songs we have heard earlier were never sung (sounded) at all. They are songs of the imagination, delusions, will-o'-the-wisps, imagined to be sung. They are songs the hurdy-gurdy grinder imagines himself singing. They tell his story, but do not explain why he is frozen in place. They bear the images of his present, even as they relate his past. They have narrative and pathetic continuity, but their climax is not self-contained.

They impinge themselves to reality in the final song, where their rich and distended illusion and the chilling irreducible reality of the hurdy-gurdy are juxtaposed. At this aweful moment we realize that no hurdy-gurdy could grind out these songs. Yet, what have we heard? The great paradox of actual performance is that we have cared to listen to these imaginary songs. How long would we endure the trivial hurdy-gurdy tune to which our singer would continue?

As that tune finally becomes silent to the ear, it remains startlingly alive in the consciousness, its keening drone somehow encompassing the densely compacted essence of the entire cycle. Our singer, too, then is imaginary, for he is the projection of the organ-grinder, that persona, almost manifest, who had created a world of his own—a world to which he can no longer escape for ultimate relief, yet from which he cannot return to society.

There is no frame, then, to this cycle, for it leaves us in that twilit zone between illusion and reality. There are no easy performances of *Winterreise*, because both singer and pianist must sustain the energy to maintain that immanent ambiguity. There is no easy response to the final emotional implosion. The audience knows that, for whatever implicit persona the singer and pianist have been projections, the travail is not ended.

The possibility of reading too much meaning into these cycles is always present: the act of performance, in itself, is a mode of "distancing," as are the conventions and "composition" of the songs themselves.[5] But the overwhelming effect of the final song is the collapse of artifice and convention, the urgent breakthrough and immediacy of personal experience. In *Die schöne Müllerin* that immediacy is mitigated by tonal balances and strophic forms within the cycle, by the change of mode and tonal area for the benedictory lullaby, and by the generalized nature and transcendant equanimity of the brook's lullaby. The sense of closure, both musically and textually, is somewhat telescopic as we are led to recognize the presence of a larger world (". . . Himmel . . . so weit"), against which this passing drama has been enacted.

Exactly the opposite occurs in "Der Leiermann." The tremendous sense of loss in the later songs of the cycle is focused into the present tense, leading directly to a desperate cry of a weakening will. Even if we are convinced during performance that the events described took place, we hear them not only as process but, in the context of the final song, as memory. Their expressive desolation is not sufficient to explain why fortune has frowned so severely on our outcast and possibly fictive singer. The Orpheus of legend could charm the gods, and the universe responded to his voice and lyre. Our wavering singer-*Leiermann* cannot sustain the illusion, despite having charmed us for twenty-three songs. As his complete despair and isolation are cast against an unfeeling world, the final song is the confirmation of his emptiness, alienation, and terrible continuing and unremarked mortality.

---

[5] This article does not fully acknowledge the vitality and impact of those conventions. The reader looking for other approaches and responses to these songs is referred to Alan P. Cottrell, *Wilhelm Müller's Lyrical Song-Cycles: Interpretations and Texts* (Chapel Hill: University of North Carolina Press, 1970); Arnold Feil, *Franz Schubert, Die schöne Müllerin, Winterreise*, transl. Ann C. Sherwin (Portland, Ore.: Amadeus Press, 1988); Thrasybulos G. Georgiades, *Schubert: Musik und Lyrik* (Göttingen: Vandenhoeck & Ruprecht, 1967); Richard Kramer, *Distant Cycles: Schubert and the Conceiving of Song* (Chicago: University of Chicago Press, 1994); Susan Youens, *Retracing a Winter's Journey: Schubert's Winterreise* (Ithaca: Cornell University Press, 1991) and her *Schubert: Die schöne Müllerin* (Cambridge: Cambridge University Press, 1992).

CHAPTER 9

E. T. A. Hoffmann's Allegory of Romantic Opera

John Daverio

E. T. A. Hoffmann's dialogue *Der Dichter und der Komponist*, first published in 1813 in the *Allgemeine musikalische Zeitung* and subsequently amplified with connecting narratives for inclusion in the first part of *Die Serapionsbrüder* (1819), has long been acknowledged as a milestone in the aesthetics of opera.[1] Turning decisively from eighteenth-century neo-Aristotelian views of drama in general and of musical drama in particular, Hoffmann envisioned a romantic opera populated with fantastic creatures and centered around numinous happenings, the whole colored by a mysterious synthesis of the real and the unreal, word and tone. Nothing could be more striking than the contrast between Rousseau's staid description of opera in his *Dictionnaire de musique* (1768) as "a dramatic and lyric spectacle in which one endeavors to combine all the graces of the fine arts in the representation of a passionate action, with the intention of arousing interest and creating illusion by means of pleasant sensations"—a gloss on Aristotle's classic definition of tragedy in the *Poetics*[2]—and Hoffmann's exhortations to the operatic poet and composer to summon up the "marvelous apparitions of the spirit realm" whose "mysterious language" is music.[3]

Although there has been no lack of commentary on Hoffmann's colorful account,[4] I would like to suggest that his prose has been more often paraphrased than "read," in the strong sense of the

---

[1] Although conceived in 1809, the dialogue was not completed until 1813. In its original form, it appeared in the *Allgemeine musikalische Zeitung* [AmZ] 15, nos. 49 and 50 (8 and 15 December 1813), cols. 793-806, 809-17. My essay draws on the 1819 version from Hoffmann's *Die Serapionsbrüder* (Munich: Winkler, 1963), 74-99; translations are mine unless noted otherwise. An abridged version of the dialogue appears in translation in Oliver Strunk, *Source Readings in Music History* (New York: Norton, 1950), 782-97. See also David Charlton, ed., and Martyn Clarke, transl., *E. T. A. Hoffmann's Musical Writings: Kreisleriana, The Poet and the Composer, Music Criticism* [MW] (Cambridge: Cambridge University Press, 1969), 188-209.

[2] Rousseau's description–quoted from Ulrich Weisstein's translation in *The Essence of Opera* (New York: Norton, 1964), 82–can be easily mapped onto Aristotle's "Tragedy is a representation of a serious, complete action which has magnitude, in embellished speech, with each of its elements used separately in the various parts of the play; represented by people acting and not by narration; accomplishing by means of pity and terror the catharsis of such emotions." Aristotle, *Poetics*, transl. Richard Janko (Indianapolis: Hackett, 1987), 7.

[3] *Serapionsbrüder*, 83-84. For a discussion of the shift from mimetic to romantic doctrines of opera in late eighteenth-century Germany, see Gloria Flaherty, *Opera in the Development of German Critical Thought* (Princeton: Princeton University Press, 1978), 281-300.

[4] The principal studies include David Charlton, "Introduction to *The Poet and the Composer:* Hoffmann and Opera," in *MW*, 169-87; Carl Dahlhaus, *Klassische und romantische Musikästhetik* (Laaber: Laaber-Verlag, 1988), 111-21; Aubrey S.

word. Indeed, a close look at his text may reveal that the musical drama that he apparently describes with the heady abandon of an early romantic *Schwärmer* is in fact a utopian construct, an amalgamation of early nineteenth-century ideologies that he intends not to endorse but rather to criticize. If one of the most striking tenets of contemporary literary criticism has been its insistence on the interdependence of the content and the form of a text, then a necessary first step in reading Hoffmann will be the identification of the discursive mode in which he presents his ideas. In my view, an understanding of *Der Dichter und der Komponist* hinges on our reading it as an allegory, a literary mode whose importance for the nineteenth century has been too frequently minimized. Even though the allegorical nature of Hoffmann's essay has been noted before, further consequences regarding his theory of opera remain to be drawn from this simple fact.

The verbal parrying of Ferdinand the poet and Ludwig the musician, the interlocutors in the dialogue, represents more than the "creative conflict" of words and music, as one writer puts it;[5] it points to a more serious assertion of their incommensurability, and suggests that in romantic opera the relationship between music and determinate meanings is made intentionally problematic. Hoffmann's dialogue thus occupies a place in a line of earlier aesthetic writings in allegorical form (e.g., Rousseau's *Essai sur l'origine des langues*, posthumous publication, 1781; or Heinrich Kleist's "Über das Marionetten-theater," 1810), and at the same time presages the radical theory of opera developed in the writings of Schopenhauer and even Nietzsche (the latter maintained that in opera, music actually searches for a metaphorical expression of itself in a poetic text—a startling reversal of one of the touchstones of opera aesthetics). Hoffmann, I will argue, recognizes the simultaneous presence of two modes of musico-dramatic activity in opera. On the one hand, the discontinuous relationship between opera's musical and semantic layers defines an *allegorical* mode, parallelled by the relationship between plot and meaning in his dialogue; on the other hand, Hoffmann's panegyric to music as the "mysterious language of a distant spirit realm" points toward an absolute-musical, self-referential, or *symbolic* dimension in opera. Romantic opera, in other words, attempts to fulfill the requirements of both modes—a practically impossible task.

The subsequent discussion falls into four sections: 1) a methodological sketch for approaching Hoffmann's text; 2) an account of the allegorical pattern that informs the text and the relationship of that pattern to similar strategies in earlier texts that Hoffmann may have used as models; 3) a summary of Hoffmann's critique of romantic opera; and 4) my interpretation of his critique as a dualistic—partly allegorical, partly symbolic—theory of romantic opera. If recent discussions have tended to stress the tensions, as opposed to the congruence between the verbal and musical components in opera—to emphasize what James Webster calls the "multivalent" principle[6]—then Hoffmann's theory of opera and my gloss upon it may at least serve to complement this increasing body of critical observations.

Garlington, "E. T. A. Hoffmann's 'Der Dichter und der Komponist' and the Creation of the German Romantic Opera," *Musical Quarterly* 65 (1979): 22-47; Judith Rohr, *E. T. A. Hoffmanns Theorie des musikalischen Dramas: Untersuchungen zum musikalischen Romantikbegriff im Umkreis der Leipziger allgemeinen musikalischen Zeitung* (Baden-Baden: Koemer, 1985), 101-200; Rohr, "Wenn Sprache und Handlung Musik werden: E. T. A. Hoffmanns Begriff der 'romantischen Opera'," in *Festschrift Hans Conradin*, ed. Volker Kalisch (Bern: Haupt, 1983), 61-69; Jurgen Schläder, *Undine auf dem Musiktheater* (Bonn: Verlag für systematische Musikwissenschaft, 1979), 258-61; and Herbert Schulze, *E. T. A. Hoffmann als Musikschriftsteller und Komponist* (Leipzig: VEB Deutscher Verlag für Musik, 1983), 72-73.

[5] Charlton, 170.

[6] James Webster, "To Understand Verdi and Wagner We Must Understand Mozart," *19th-Century Music* 11 (1987): 175-93; Webster, "Cone's 'Personae' and the Analysis of Opera," *College Music Symposium* 29 (1989): 44-65; and Arnold Whittall, "'Forceful Muting' or 'Phatic Dithering'?: Some Recent Writings on Opera," *Music and Letters* 71 (1990): 65-71.

*　·　*　　*　　*

The rhetoric of *Der Dichter und der Komponist* is permeated by figurative references to harmonious union. In the narrative preceding the dialogue proper, for example, the poet Lothar poses the question "Isn't perfect unity of text and music [in opera] only thinkable when poet and composer are one and the same person?"; at the center of the dialogue is Ludwig's enigmatic assertion that "the secret of word and tone is one and the same"; and at its conclusion there is Ferdinand's rhapsodic claim "science and art enkindle in a single beam all the holy striving that unites mankind into a single church."[7] Understandably, many commentators have viewed Hoffmann's text as a series of prescriptions for a romantic opera marked by the fusion of disparate entities. David Charlton, to cite one writer, interprets it as an argument for "a subtle and bold interfusing of the outer and inner worlds."[8] Similarly, Aubrey Garlington describes Hoffmann's operatic ideal as a "cohesive art form" in which language and music "can be considered to be in some kind of union"; in his opinion, Hoffmann demonstrates that "the gulf which separates word and tone is not as pronounced as it may first appear to the uninitiated."[9] And Judith Rohr, in her thorough account of Hoffmann's writings on dramatic music, likewise sees *Der Dichter und der Komponist* as a recipe for the synthesis of absolute music and poetic meaning: "To Hoffmann's way of thinking," she says, "the organic interrelation of the separate arts is a necessary condition for [an opera's] dramatic effect."[10]

But Hoffmann's words, like those of many romantic writers, should not be taken at face value. As Carl Dahlhaus has pointed out, a literal reading of Hoffmann's theory of absolute music would lead to the conclusion that opera, not to mention church music, was in some sense a superfluous genre. If Beethoven's symphonies can "unveil before us the realm of the mighty and the immeasurable," why should the visual representation of this realm be necessary in opera? Yet Dahlhaus argues (and convincingly, I think) that Hoffmann's romanticism was essentially a *Theaterromantik* (a romanticism conditioned by the theater), and that his principal aim was an enrichment of opera with techniques developed in the instrumental music of the Viennese classicists, Haydn, Mozart, and Beethoven.[11] To be sure, this intention emerges in Hoffmann's frequent recourse to the term *Tondichtung* ("poem in tones") in his descriptions of opera, for a word such as this automatically imparts intellectual integrity to a genre that was viewed with some suspicion by philosophers and *literati*.[12]

If Hoffmann's claims for the supremacy of instrumental music must be interpreted with circumspection, no less caution should be exercised in approaching his writings on the nature of opera, especially since the diction of his writings is so poetically charged. The poetic criticism of Hoffmann's review of Beethoven's Fifth Symphony gives way to critical poetry in *Der Dichter und der Komponist*. As a species of figurative discourse, the essay should be read with the same critical acumen we would apply to romantic poetry, a body of writing that, in the words of literary critic Jerome McGann, often "incorporates Romantic ideology as a drama of the contradictions which are inherent to that ideology."[13]

---

[7] *Serapionsbrüder*, 75, 83, 95.

[8] Charlton, 173; see also Schläder, 259.

[9] Garlington, "E. T. A. Hoffmann's 'Der Dichter und der Komponist'," 33-35.

[10] Rohr, *E. T. A. Hoffmanns Theorie*, 198; see also pp. 101-03, 113.

[11] Dahlhaus, *Klassische und romantische Musikästhetik*, 113, 117, and Hoffmann's review of Beethoven's Fifth Symphony (1810), in *MW*, 238.

[12] See, e.g., Hoffmann's "Further Observations on Spontini's Opera *Olimpia*" (1821), in *MW*, 433.

[13] Jerome McGann, *The Romantic Ideology: A Critical Investigation* (Chicago: Chicago University Press, 1983), 2.

A drama of precisely this sort is played out in *Der Dichter und der Komponist*, for the prescriptions most frequently taken as the hallmarks of Hoffmann's aesthetic of opera—the union of poet and composer in the same person, the injunction for the poet to draw his subject matter from the realm of the "marvelous," the call for a synthesis of word and tone—add up to little more than an ideology, a loosely connected group of ideas that had already begun to ring hollow in Hoffmann's day. That an ideal opera might result from the efforts of a single artist acting as librettist and composer was already suggested as early as 1715 by Pier Jacopo Martello, who reportedly told Charles Burney that "no music drama would be perfect or interesting until the poet and musician were one, as in ancient times";[14] and by the early nineteenth century a number of composers had already written their own opera texts, Rousseau, Nicolas Étienne Framery, Johann Friedrich Reichardt, and Johann Nepomuk von Poissl among them.[15] In addition, the suitability of the "marvelous" as a topic in operatic libretti had been a subject for speculation in German aesthetics since the mid-eighteenth century. By 1775, when Christoph Martin Wieland indicated in his *Versuch über das deutsche Singspiel* that operatic subjects should *not* derive exclusively from an other-worldly realm, the issue was a well-worn one indeed.[16] And finally, the notion that opera might provide a vehicle for a synthesis of the arts (especially those of word and tone) had been in circulation for some time when Hoffmann appropriated it. Charles Batteux's assertion that the arts of poetry, music, and dance are "never more effective than when united" is perhaps one of the first contributions to that aesthetically suspect concept, the *Gesamtkunstwerk* or total work of art, that would be developed by a long line of writers from Johann von Herder, August Wilhelm Schlegel, and Carl Maria von Weber, to Richard Wagner.[17] In all probability, the source of most of the prescriptions for a union of the arts in *Der Dichter und der Komponist* was A. W. Schlegel's influential *Vorlesungen über dramatische Kunst und Literatur* (1808), a work Hoffmann had studied, where the author systematically presents ideas culled from the essays and fragments of his brother Friedrich.[18] In other words, the notions that Hoffmann apparently argues for in his dialogue constitute at best a body of received ideas, at worst a bundle of clichés. What is genuinely new in Hoffmann's argument is the critical light he sheds on these notions.

How did Hoffmann formulate his critique of romantic opera? Obviously *Der Dichter und der Komponist* is cast as a dialogue, a genre dearly beloved by the early German Romantics, witness Friedrich Schlegel's dialogic presentation of his theory of literature in the *Gespräch über die Poesie* (1800) and the discussions of literary issues in Ludwig Tieck's *Phantasus* (1811).[19] But more to the

---

[14] See Piero Weiss, "Pier Jacopo Martello on Opera (1715): An Annotated Translation," *Musical Quarterly* 66 (1980): 386: "the verse-weaver ought really to be the composer himself"; and Charles Burney, *An Eighteenth-Century Musical Tour in Central Europe and the Netherlands*, vol. 2 of *Musical Tours in Europe*, ed. Percy A. Scholes (London: Oxford University Press, 1959), 103.

[15] Charlton, 178-79.

[16] See Weisstein, 119-20. On the position of the "marvelous" in eighteenth-century German opera aesthetics, see Flaherty, 130, 151, 155, 175, 182, 289; and Garlington, "The Concept of the Marvelous in French and German Opera, 1770-1840: A Chapter in the History of Opera Esthetics" (Ph.D. diss., University of Illinois, 1965), 215-53.

[17] Charles Batteux, *Les Beaux Arts reduits a un même principe* (Paris: Durand, 1747), 300. For a survey of the evolution of the *Gesamtkunstwerk* idea, see Alfred R. Neumann, "The Concept of the *Gesamtkunstwerk* in German Romanticism" (Ph.D. diss., University of Michigan, 1951).

[18] See August Wilhelm Schlegel, *Sämtliche Werke*, 12 vols., ed. Eduard Böcking (Leipzig: Weidmann'sche Buchhandlung, 1846), 5:67-69. On Hoffmann's study of A. W. Schlegel, see Harvey W. Hewett-Thayer, *Hoffmann: Author of the Tales* (New York: Octagon, 1971), 352-53.

[19] On the importance of the dialogue in early romantic aesthetics, see Theodore Ziolkowski, *German Romanticism and Its Institutions* (Princeton: Princeton University Press, 1990), 363.

point, Hoffmann's dialogue unfolds as an allegory, where the disjunction between signifiers (Ferdinand and Ludwig, poet and composer) and signified (words and music) points to the discontinuity between the signifieds themselves. If the meaning of the dialogue emerges from the interaction of its ideological content and its narrative mode, then Hoffmann does not argue for the synthesis of word and tone. On the contrary, he accentuates the gap between them.

On the whole, criticism since the beginning of the nineteenth century has tended to undervalue allegory—a signifying mode that exhausts itself once a fixed meaning has been decoded—at the expense of the symbol, whose potential for generating meanings is theoretically infinite. Yet the work of critics such as Paul de Man and Tzvetan Todorov (and Walter Benjamin before them) has done much to increase our sense for the power of allegory precisely in those periods, such as the nineteenth century, that were supposedly antithetical to it.[20] The prominence of allegory in Hoffmann's writings, both critical and fictional, leaves little doubt that, unlike his contemporaries Schelling, Ast, Humboldt, and Creuzer, he set much store by its figurative capacity.

*   *   *   *

Ludwig the composer and Ferdinand the poet-turned-soldier comprise the principal allegorical figures of Hoffmann's dialogue. It is difficult to imagine two more sharply contrasted characters. As a battle rages about him, Ludwig sits "in his little back room, completely engrossed in the splendid, many-colored, and fantastic world that unfolded for him at the piano." Ferdinand, on the other hand, first appears before his friend "in a plumed helmet, a mighty, clanking sabre at his side, and even disavowed his own voice by shouting for joy in a harsh, rough tone."[21] That is to say: the art of music, allegorized in the person of Ludwig, is completely divorced from the world of events and determinate meanings; it is self-absorbed, self-referential, absolute. Poetry, in contrast, is very much of the world. It is no accident that Ferdinand has taken up a military career (while at the same time continuing his literary work), for through the figure of the soldier Hoffmann points to the active, worldly, ostentatious essence of literature itself. (Baudelaire would have understood this tactic well, though it is unlikely that he read Hoffmann's dialogue; in "Le Soleil" from *Les Fleurs du mal*, he casts himself as a fencer, "duelling in dark corners for a rhyme."[22]) In the broadest sense, Ferdinand thus personifies determinate meaning in general, regardless of whether it manifests itself as word, visual display, or gesture.

The narrative pattern in which the figures interact is simply but boldly conceived. Ferdinand and Ludwig were united in the past as school chums and artistic collaborators, but have not seen one another for many years. Hence the allegory points to an irretrievably lost Golden Age, a state of naïve, unreflective musico-poetic unity that has suffered a breach and now laments its lost harmony. Poet and composer come together by chance, only to find their youthful feelings renewed "as if through some powerful magic,"[23] an indication of the illusory quality of perfect unities, past and present. Given the enigmatic utterances, contradictory positions, and inconclusive arguments of the interlocutors,

---

[20] See Paul de Man, "The Rhetoric of Temporality," in *Blindness and Insight: Essays in the Theory of Contemporary Criticism*, 2nd ed. (Minneapolis: University of Minnesota Press, 1971), 187-228; and Tzvetan Todorov, *Theories of the Symbol*, transl. Catherine Porter (Ithaca: Cornell University Press, 1982), 221ff.

[21] *Serapionsbrüder*, 76, 79.

[22] Charles Baudelaire, *Les Fleurs du mal*, transl. Richard Howard (Boston: Gadine, 1982), 88.

[23] *Serapionsbrüder*, 79.

the rhetorical course of the ensuing dialogue highlights the disjunction between indeterminate (musical) and determinate (verbal, visual, gestural) meanings in the principal subject under discussion: opera. The gap separating what are fundamentally different modes of signification is pronounced by Ferdinand's sudden departure: the call to arms unceremoniously interrupts a disquisition left purposefully incomplete.[24] Thus Ludwig's invocation—"O Ferdinand! What has become of the Golden Age that was our youth?"[25]—should be taken with a grain of salt. If allegory is the projection of a single moment onto a temporal axis, the lost unity to which Ludwig alludes cannot have existed in the first place. The decline that the narrative charts in historical time is *already* present in the cleft between word and tone (or between determinate and indeterminate meaning) that characterizes each moment of an operatic discourse.

Der Dichter und der Komponist can thus be situated within a line of allegorical critiques extending from the late eighteenth through the nineteenth century. Like Rousseau's *Essai sur l'origine des langues*, which ostensibly traces the decline of language from an originary state where word, feeling, and music were one, and Kleist's *Über das Marionettentheater* (an essay Hoffmann knew well), which tells of the gradual corruption of expressive bodily gestures wrought by self-consciousness, Hoffmann's dialogue re-enacts a Fall: from a Golden Age where poet and composer, word and tone, were one, to a degenerate present in which there seems to be little hope for union. (Hoffmann may have been thinking of operas such as Ferdinando Paër's *Sofonisba* and Adelbert Gyrowetz's *Der Augenarzt*, both of which he treated to less than enthusiastic reviews.[26]) And at the same time, *Der Dichter und der Komponist* prefigures the nineteenth century's most formidable allegory of opera: the polemical tale of musico-dramatic decline that Wagner served up as history in *Oper und Drama* (1851).

All of these allegories aim to unmask the notion of unity as an illusion. In the introduction to *Der Dichter und der Komponist*, Hoffmann juxtaposes the quotidian (the enemy at the gates) and the metaphysical (Ludwig's musings on his recently composed symphony) without attempting to reconcile them, as if to remind us that the real and the unreal will not admit to a synthesis.[27] Furthermore, Hoffmann hints at his skepticism regarding the fusion of word and tone in opera through Ludwig's uneasiness over his reunion with his old friend: "It seemed to him like an oft-recurring dream in which one embraces his loved ones, who are then suddenly and oddly transformed, so that the most beautiful delights quickly dissolve into mocking illusions."[28] The discussion in which the friends subsequently engage, far from providing a set of prescriptions for a unified romantic opera, is rather intended to call the whole idea of operatic synthesis into question.

*   *   *   *

Hoffmann's critique proceeds in three stages: first he considers the subject matter most appropriate for romantic opera; next he turns to questions of genre; last comes a discussion of the requirements for an ideal libretto. The dialogue gets underway with Ferdinand's question: why shouldn't a composer

---

[24] Ibid., 94-96.

[25] Ibid., 95.

[26] *MW*, 262-70, 293-96. See also Hoffmann's account of the operatic world of his day (and its "frictionless disunity") in "Further Observations on Spontini's Opera *Olimpia*" (1821), *MW*, 440-46, and his thoughts on the decline of sacred music in "Old and New Church Music," *MW*, 353-54, 375-76.

[27] *Serapionsbrüder*, 76-77. This is also the message of Hoffmann's "The Complete Machinist" (1814-15), which can be read as a satirical account of the meager abilities of early nineteenth-century theatrical designers and effects-men, or as a prophetic description of the illusion-destroying devices of avant-garde theater. See *MW*, 114-22.

[28] *Serapionsbrüder*, 78-79.

write his own libretto?[29] Instead of responding directly, Ludwig counters with vague and enigmatic replies. "True composers," he says, "have chosen only poetic texts" (for their operas); then "poets and musicians are the most intimately related members of *one* church, for the secret of word and tone is one and the same, ensuring for both the highest solemnities"; and finally, his principal statement: "a genuine opera seems to me to be the one in which the music arises directly from the poetry as its necessary offspring."[30] But after all, Ludwig's enigmas aren't so enigmatic after all; in a sense, they are little more than clichés. That Hoffmann thought as much as indicated by an ironic turn, Ferdinand's inability to grasp the notion that music issues directly from a poetic text. Are we to believe that a poet would not understand an idea that goes back to the creation of opera itself?

In fact, the first stage of the critique tries to dismantle the idea that music *can* arise directly from a poetic text. In the course of Ludwig's two speeches on the nature of romantic opera, it becomes clear that music has the upper hand, for both the artist and an audience. Specifically, Ludwig accords aesthetic primacy to the mysterious and sublime language of instrumental music, which says most by saying nothing at all. Through it, an opera's verbal component is "raised to a higher power" so that "the word resounding in music" ("das in Musik ertönende Wort") is stripped of its semantic value.[31] Moreover, Ludwig's injunction for the poet to draw his material from the other-worldly, thereby bringing before our eyes "the marvelous apparitions of the spirit realm,"[32] implies that the new music of the early nineteenth century had developed such powers that it needed to ground itself in correspondingly powerful verbal and visual counterparts. And finally, the "poetic truth" to which an operatic text should aspire, described negatively in the dialogue as an avoidance of "a merely whimsical series of pointless magical events,"[33] can easily be construed, in positive terms, as the network of verbal connections that such a text requires if it is to serve as a fitting analogue for the rich interrelationships in an absolute musical structure. Although Ludwig claims to have shown how music "should arise directly and inevitably from the poetry," he has actually argued for the reverse; the new instrumental music demands a specific type of poetry, the choice of which should be dictated by musical considerations.

Hoffmann's outlook on the relationship between poetry and music—no less than his reversal of the trajectory leading from poetic inspiration to musical realization—represents a remarkable prefiguration of the philosophical insights of Schopenhauer and Nietzsche. In *Die Welt als Wille und Vorstellung* (1819), Schopenhauer likewise developed at outlook on opera in which primacy of place was given to music, the art form that stimulates our imagination "to give shape to the spiritual world [through action and text] . . . and to clothe it with flesh and bone, thus embodying it in some analogous concept."[34] And Nietzsche, in his fragment "Über Musik und Wort"—probably written around 1871 and originally intended as a part of *Die Geburt der Tragödie*—took a similar position, though he expressed it in more radical terms: "When the composer writes music for a lyrical poem, . . . he, as a musician, is not excited either by the images or by the feelings speaking through this text. A musical excitement that comes from altogether different regions *chooses* the text of this song as a metaphorical expression for itself."[35]

---

[29] Ibid., 80.

[30] Ibid., 82-83.

[31] Ibid., 83-84.

[32] Ibid., 84.

[33] Ibid., 84.

[34] Arthur Schopenhauer, *Sämtliche Werke*, 5 vols., ed. Wolfgang von Lohneysen (Stuttgart: Cotta, 1960), 1:365.

[35] Friedrich Nietzsche, "On Words and Music," transl. Walter Kaufmann, in Carl Dahlhaus, *Between Romanticism and Modernism*, transl. Mary Whittall (Berkeley: University of California Press, 1980), 112. See also Dahlhaus's comments on

We need not search long in Hoffmann's text for intimations of a similar point of view, witness Lothar's allusion to "prefect unity of text from out the music," Ludwig's complaints about not yet having found a libretto to his liking, and his claim that Mozart "chose for his classical operas only poems genuinely suitable for his music."[36] Hence Carlo Gozzi's *Il corvo* (The Raven), the plot of which Ludwig relates in some detail, might serve well as the basis for an operatic libretto not because it was conceived with music in mind, but because it is inherently predisposed to musical treatment, both in terms of its subject matter and the richness of its poetic relationships.

Ferdinand initiates the second stage of the critique by asserting that "only in a genuinely romantic work is the comic so pliably mixed with the tragic that both merge into one overall effect,"[37] another statement of harmonious unity that the allegorical pattern of the dialogue calls into question. The fusion of comedy and tragedy is no less an illusion that the union of poet and composer, or of word and tone. Hoffmann seems rather to be saying that tragic opera—particularly the operas of Gluck, which demonstrate a close affinity with church music—and comic opera, best exemplified through the "splendid irony" of Mozart's style, are distinct and clearly definable genres, each characterized by a specific type of content (the interaction of gods and men for tragedy, the incursion of bizarre events into everyday life for comedy) and a specific musical style.[38] Romantic opera, on the other hand, resists cut-and-dry classification by genre; though it may draw on the "marvelous" for its subject matter, its musical style cannot be so easily delimited. In other words, romantic opera should extend beyond the confining bounds of genre.

Indeed, the late eighteenth and early nineteenth centuries witnessed a critical revolution that gave a decidedly new twist to the theory of poetic genre. In the literary and philosophical fragments of Friedrich Schlegel, we may trace the development of a theory that acknowledged the significance of distinct *genres* for ancient or classical poetry, but envisioned for modern poetry a single, "progressive" *genre* that would draw on the qualities of the canonically fixed types, but ultimately transcend them.[39] This at least is the sense behind aphorisms such as: "All of the classical poetic genres are now ridiculous in their rigid purity," or "the modern types of poetry are either one or infinitely many; every poem makes its own genre."[40] For Schlegel, the modern genre *par excellence* was the *Roman* or novel, an ill-inclusive, practically encyclopedic creation marked by its conflation of dramatic, epic, and lyric qualities. Just as Schlegel maintained that the novel "colored the whole of modern

---

the similarities between Hoffmann's and Nietzsche's aesthetics in "The Twofold Truth in Wagner's Aesthetics: Nietzsche's Fragment 'On Words and Music'," in *Between Romanticism and Modernism*, 31, 37-39.

[36] *Serapionsbrüder*, 75, 79-80, 82. As for Ludwig's difficulty in locating a suitable libretto, many nineteenth-century composers faced the dilemma. See Susan Youens, "Hugo Wolf and the Operatic Grail: The Search for a Libretto," *Cambridge Opera Journal* 1 (1989): 277-80. As Wolf told his librettist Rosa Mayreder in a letter of 7 September 1897, the best criterion for a good text is good music. Consider also Richard Strauss's description of his method of composing lieder: "Musical ideas have prepared themselves in me—God knows why—and when, as it were, the barrel is full, a song appears in the twinkling of an eye as soon as I come across a poem more or less corresponding to the subject of the imaginary song." Quoted in *New Grove* (1980), s.v. "Strauss, Richard," by Michael Kennedy, 18:233.

[37] *Serapionsbrüder*, 88.

[38] Ibid., 89-91.

[39] On this point, see Peter Szondi, "Friedrich Schlegel's Theory of Poetical Genres: A Reconstruction from the Posthumous Fragments," in *On Poetical Understanding and Other Essays*, transl. Harvey Mendelsohn (Minneapolis: University of Minnesota Press, 1986), 75-94.

[40] Friedrich Schlegel, *Kritische Fragmente* (1797), no. 60, in *Kritische Friedrich Schlegel Ausgabe* [*KFSA*], vol. 2, ed. Hans Eichner (Zurich: Thomas-Verlag, 1967), 154; and *Fragmente zur Poesie* (1797), no. 1103, in *KFSA*, vol. 16, ed. Eichner (Munich: Thomas-Verlag, 1981), 176.

poetry,"[41] so too did Hoffmann make a similar claim for the musical status of romantic opera in *Der Dichter und der Komponist*. He gave primacy of place to opera in his hierarchy of genres by implying that it might transcend the concept of genre altogether.

The third and last stage of the critique returns to the issues of text and tone raised in the first. Through Ludwig and Ferdinand, Hoffmann continued to undermine the semantic potential of words in opera. The spectator, according to Ludwig, "must be able to fashion an idea of the plot from what he sees happening, almost without understanding a word."[42] Likewise, the words for a libretto should be selected for their expressive impact, their singability, and their inherently musical quality (Ludwig gives as an example "the little word *addio*"); the imagery-laden language of Metastasio's texts, however, is to be avoided.[43] For, as Ludwig says, "the wonderful mystery of music" is summed up precisely in the fact that only "when our meagre words dry up does it release an inexhaustible stream of expression."[44]

Hoffmann's critique appears to end on a negative note. To be sure, a number of troubling questions remain. Why should opera exist at all if its verbal and visual components are continually overwhelmed by the music? And is there not an unresolved dissonance between the two main topics of the critique, between the issues of text and tone on one hand and the question of genre on the other? For how can romantic opera assume its position at the pinnacle of a musical hierarchy of genres if its scenic and semantic elements have been proven superfluous? Of course, Hoffmann didn't find them superfluous in the least. Far from it, they figure prominently as elements of the dialectical theory of opera that can be read out of his *Der Dichter und der Komponist* and his other writings on musical drama as well.

*   *   *   *

As we have seen, Hoffmann's thinking on the relationship between text and music finds a radical counterpart in the writings of Schopenhauer and Nietzsche. For all of these figures, operatic poetry (in fact, all the bearers of determinate meanings in opera, from text to scenic and gestural display) was aesthetically secondary to music. This does not mean, however, that poetry was aesthetically insignificant or indispensible. Hoffmann and his philosophical heirs were simply trying to fix the relationship between what they recognized as two distinct modes of signification. As Schopenhauer put it, the verbal and visual components in opera "are never combined with music, nor do they correspond to it with absolute necessity; rather they stand to it only in the relationship of an arbitrary example to a universal concept."[45] For Nietzsche, an operatic poem relates to music "much like the Egyptian hieroglyph of courage does to a courageous soldier."[46] And even Wagner, in his essay "Über die Benennung 'Musikdrama'" (1872), noted that in opera, music reveals itself through the "parable on stage."[47] Schopenhauer's differentiation between example and concept, Nietzsche's "hieroglyph," and Wagner's "parable" make explicit what is implicit in Hoffmann's thought—namely, that the relationship between operatic music and dramatic event (whether verbal or visual) belongs to the discontinuous pattern of

---

[41] *Athenäum Fragmente* (1797-98), no. 146, *KFSA*, 2:188.

[42] *Serapionsbrüder*, 92-93.

[43] Ibid., 92-93.

[44] Ibid., 93.

[45] Schopenhauer, *Sämtliche Werke*, 1:366-67.

[46] Nietzsche, "On Words and Music," 112.

[47] Richard Wagner, *Gesammelte Schriften und Dichtungen*, 4th ed., 10 vols. (Leipzig: Siegel, 1907), 9:305.

allegory. This is the pattern to which Hoffmann alludes when he says of Mozart's *Don Giovanni* (in his short story *Don Juan*) that "the music alone, quite apart from the text, seems to . . . reflect the whole conflict between these two opposing natures, Don Juan and Donna Anna."[48]

If the allegorical mode in opera manifests itself through such technical devices as naturalistic declamation, sharply chiselled musical motives, pictorial orchestral writing, and a general tendency to coordinate the music with the stage action—that is, through attention to the moment-by-moment course of events—then Hoffmann must have realized the tremendous potential for musico-dramatic coherence afforded by late eighteenth- and early nineteenth-century advances in the realm of "absolute" instrumental music, whose self-referentiality describes a symbolic mode where the part is continuous with the whole. Hoffmann was thinking of the latter mode when he praised Méhul for fashioning coherent scene-complexes in his *Ariodant* through the use of recurrent orchestral motives and logical tonal planning.[49]

Thus the implication in *Der Dichter und der Komponist* is that romantic opera should attempt to employ both modes—allegorical and symbolic—as best it can. While these modes are kept quite distinct in eighteenth-century opera (where the allegorical dimension was consigned to the recitatives, and the symbolic to the concerted numbers), romantic opera plays on their continual interaction. No doubt the musically self-referential, or symbolic mode claims aesthetic primacy, but at the same time romantic opera derives its peculiar character precisely from the tension between the absolute-musical and the allegorical. Hoffmann was well aware that the two domains will never be perfectly united (his allegory of the poet and the composer tells us this); we might even take him a step further and suggest that romantic opera actually thrives on the tensions between musical allegory and musical symbol. In any event, we may have come a bit closer to accounting for the placement of opera at the top of Hoffmann's hierarchy of genres: its richness as an art form stems largely from the many and varied ways in which it generates meaning.

---

[48] Quoted from R. Murray Schafer, *E. T. A. Hoffmann and Music* (Toronto: University of Toronto Press, 1975), 71-72.

[49] *MW*, 403-06.

CHAPTER 10

Forms Made Miniature: Three Intermezzi of Brahms

Camilla Cai

Ways of hearing music are distinctive to a culture as a whole as well as to each individual member of that culture.[1] For example, in a nineteenth-century audience one listener might let the sounds float by moment to moment, listening only for color. Another might focus on personal reactions, noticing primarily responses and feelings that these sounds brought forth. Still others might follow the melody. A Johann Strauss waltz-tune, for example, would be comfortable and easy to follow, but this simple listening method would have been less successful with some of Brahms's music. More demanding ways of listening that focused on the contrapuntal or harmonic aspects of music were necessary. Those who used these methods usually reveled in Brahms's consummate craftsmanship, while those who could not or did not want to expend the effort labeled Brahms's music academic and difficult. None of these ways of listening, of course, precluded the others from being undertaken simultaneously.

For some listeners, seeking out large-scale organization and the overarching plan was an important goal of their participation, and the retrospective discovering of such plans continues to be a mainstay of music analysis. For a listener seeking this structure, in the first hearing one must remember sections and ideas and observe how the continuing material interacts with the past material. Armed with the combined information, a listener can match it to known pieces or principles in order to discover overarching structural designs that might be unfolding—for example, a sonata-allegro, a fugue, an ABA, a hybrid, or a newly invented form. This kind of active attention provides the listener with the pleasures of fulfillment of expectation as well as surprise at the unexpected. In order to understand and appreciate the ambiguities and complexities of formal principle displayed in Brahms's late piano pieces this active listening process is necessary. The analysis of structure presented here is based on this listening process—in particular, exploring various ways of hearing within a frame that seeks to tease out structural meaning. My thesis is that, for Brahms's piano pieces, his hints and suggestions of form, his partial commitments to formal structures, and even his obfuscation of structure are integral to the process of understanding for the structural listener. Further, I suggest that Brahms's complexity of process demonstrates that there are different ways of hearing a single piece.

---

[1] How listeners hear depends on a variety of factors: gender, class, ethnicity, education, musical skill, interest, setting, time of day, personal mood, number of hearings, and more. Studying these factors to understand different ways of listening is a subject in its own right.

A musically informed listener in the late nineteenth century might rightly expect certain musical forms, familiar formal designs of large-scale organization. These principles had been formed by composers through their compositions and described by theorists in treatises and instruction books.[2] Theoretical descriptions of the eighteenth- and nineteenth-century principles of composition sometimes led to codification; their models of form, at first generally descriptive of the past, became prescriptive in instruction manuals. These principles, regardless of their descriptive or prescriptive origins, became common ways of understanding musical organization.

Brahms was regularly criticized in his own time for using old-fashioned musical organization drawn from the Baroque and Classic eras. Large-scale designs of the more conservative type are found not only in his large pieces (symphonies, the *German Requiem*, and others) but also in some small pieces of opuses 116-119. At first glance the context and venue for these piano pieces might suggest that grand, large-scale formal principles would be inappropriate. These pieces, written late in Brahms's life, during the summers of 1892 and 1893 while he was at Bad Ischl, were first performed there at private gatherings of his friends.[3] Such circumstances of composition suggest that this music emanated from the personal part of his life, and that the intimate atmosphere that pervades these pieces comes from an older man, more relaxed and reflective than before. The pieces do not impress with pomp and grandeur; rather, Brahms seems to hone and refine this music for himself and his connoisseur audience. An unadorned ABA form might have sufficed for a lesser composer.

But Brahms's first audience consisted of his friends, the musically literate members of his inner circle. It is likely that they would have been able to discern sonata structure, ritornello practice, ABA form, and other principles of structure, and that these concepts were familiar enough to them that imaginative manipulation of them would not go unnoticed, even if it were not fully analyzed in every case. Brahms seems to have risen to this challenge by employing some of his most sophisticated skills as a composer: he wrote examples in which large concepts and structures are pared down to their essence. If we accept that many of his immediate circle had the sophistication to recognize these processes, an examination of Brahms's formal experiments acquires a double value. It becomes not only a study of "the object itself," but a study of the communication between composer and listener. The possibilities and ambiguities of structure discussed here are not ones that are hidden in the subtleties of a composer's craft, but rather ones that could be audible to an educated listener.[4] Brahms's skill is that he manipulates such a listener's expectations so successfully.

The most interesting formal experiments among Brahms's opuses 116-119 are those in which he applied principles intended for large structures. By using devices that are familiar from large forms he can suggest that he has compressed the whole form into a small space and time. The process entails leaving out many features of the large model, similar to the process of condensing a novel into a movie.

---

[2] In the eighteenth century Heinrich Christoph Koch (in 1782-93) and Francesco Galeazzi (1796) made important steps in describing sonata form; in the nineteenth century Antoine Reicha (1826), A. B. Marx (1837-47), and Carl Czerny (1848-49) added new elements to their descriptions of the form. *New Grove* (1980), s.v. "Sonata form," by James Webster, 17:505-06.

[3] According to Max Kalbeck some may have been written earlier. See his *Johannes Brahms*, 2nd ed., 4 vols. (Berlin: Deutsche Brahms-Gesellschaft, 1912-21; reprint, Tutzing: Hans Schneider, 1976), 4:277f. On visits to Bad Ischl, Heinrich Barth, Ilona Eibenschütz and Max Kalbeck report hearing Brahms play new piano pieces in the summer of 1892 (opp. 116 and 117), and Eibenschütz and Kalbeck report the same for 1893 (opp. 118 and 119). Kalbeck, *Johannes Brahms* (1912), 3:196, and (1915), 4:169, 309. See also Margit McCorkle, *Thematisch-bibliographisches Werkverzeichnis* (Munich: G. Henle, 1984), 466, 469, 472, 475.

[4] I choose this listener-oriented limitation deliberately to exclude musical structures that can be discovered through Schenkerian analysis, the Fibonacci series, the golden mean, or other systems where the musical understandings are available largely through later analytical reflection.

Brahms must choose features that convey the essence of the original; at the same time he may employ only the minimum number of them.

By choosing to limit length, Brahms has chosen one of the most restricting principles available to a composer. Time does not allow development of disparate themes, excursions to distant harmonic areas, or a significant variety of textures and rhythms. The overall design must be quickly comprehensible, contain enough common elements to foster unity, and yet have space for features of contrast.

Brahms manipulated these features as if they were rhetorical devices—that is, he used them as reminders or remembrances of the commonly understood structure. By suggesting a familiar design (known to him consciously and to his audience perhaps subconsciously or intuitively), he provides the unity and stability of familiarity. Other rhetorical devices of development and change provide novelty, contrast, and excitement. The piece suggests the expansiveness of a large structure, while at the same time it is, in reality, only a small one.

First I will summarize Brahms's handling of formal elements in opuses 116-119 to show how he usually viewed form in a small space.[5] On the broadest level the pieces display a principle of balance. Two contrasting ideas (or bits of material) suffice for most of them. Although the two ideas often contain interrelationships, one or more elements—the texture, rhythm, melody or harmony—differ sufficiently to distinguish the two ideas. Opus 116, no. 4, a work that seems to be an exception by containing more than two ideas, will be discussed below. Opus 119, no. 4, another exception, produces four recognizably different ideas by interlocking small *aba* substructures within a larger ABA. In some pieces motivic congruences further hold the two main ideas accountable to each other. Opuses 119, no. 2 and 119, no. 3 are ABA forms in which a single theme is transformed in the B section, and through this characteristic the pieces display the principles of unity and contrast simultaneously.

The exterior model for most of the pieces is the straightforward ABA song-form. Opus 116, no. 5 even uses a rounded binary with written-in repeat signs to balance contrast and repetition. Other ABA pieces are more lopsided, the irregular size of sections throwing off their center of gravity. In these cases various parameters influence form: in opus 116, no. 2 there are added measures of transition (meas. 51-65), and in opus 116, no. 7 there are added measures recalling the texture and rhythmic drive of the A section (meas. 47-61). While these extending parameters smooth the return of A, they also distort the balance of form. In some pieces the subsections of ABA forms divide into balanced structures. These subsections may be so small as to consist of only two phrases in which the second is a variation of the first; the A section of opus 116, no. 2 is balanced into such an *aa´* substructure (9 + 9 measures). Other ABA pieces have substructures that divide each of the main sections into its own *aba*. Opus 119, no. 4 uses this pattern, while the A section of opus 117, no. 3 has an *ababa´* substructure, and B sections of opuses 116, no. 3, 116, no. 7, 117, no. 3, 118, no. 2, and 119, no. 2 subdivide into rounded binary with repeat signs.

However, to say that these pieces consist of an ABA structure with certain substructures does not adequately describe how Brahms handles formal problems. His overall ABA will usually be immediately apparent based on texture alone as the distinguishing mark, though other elements may also help to define each section. Elements not used in defining form (rhythm or melody, possibly) may act to disturb the structure. As we will see below, these disturbances to structure coupled with the listener's expectations of a familiar design will contribute much of the fascination in these pieces.

---

[5] Elaine R. Sisman shows how Brahms viewed form in slow movements. There are many similarities to his formal procedures for opp. 116-119. See her "Brahms's Slow Movements: Reinventing the 'Closed' Forms," in *Brahms Studies: Analytical and Historical Perspectives*, ed. George S. Bozarth (Oxford: Clarendon Press, 1990), 79-103. Brahms's titles for opp. 116-119 do not indicate his formal structures; rather, they suggest mood, character, and sometimes tempo.

To return to Brahms's compression of a normally large design into a small space: opus 119, no. 3, for example, has a hint of the concerto in a gesture that can be interpreted as a rhetorical reminder of a cadenza (meas. 62-65). More impressive, however, are the pieces in which Brahms abandons ABA form altogether. Pieces built on abbreviated and altered sonata-allegro patterns reveal the depths of his understanding of that form's complexity and possibilities. Such principles govern the structure of two of his smallest pieces: opus 118, no. 1 (71 measures, counting repeats) and opus 117, no. 2 (85 measures).[6] The pieces have just enough elements of sonata-allegro form to suggest a sonata movement, but they do not carry out the implications and actually become full-scale sonata movements.[7] These pieces suggest their derivation through gestures that are sonata-like in their harmonic, melodic and developmental techniques. The apparent expansiveness of these pieces, as well as that of the earlier opus 79, no. 2, also built on sonata principles, derives from the reference to the larger form with these gestures suggesting scope and grandeur by analogy. Some pieces include more than one large scheme. Opus 116, no. 1 combines sonata and rondo ideas into a free sonata-rondo with themes reversed in the recapitulation,[8] and opus 116, no. 4 interlocks ideas from the same two forms into a particularly complex and unusual network to be discussed below.

In a number of these pieces—be they ABA or derived from sonata and rondo principles—there is another formal process in operation. Variation designs, both as subordinate effect and as primary force, may cross over the sections of a form to supply an encompassing unity of their own. In opus 119, no. 2 such a variation scheme coexists with ABA: after it threads its way through A, it links into the B section as if to suggest that that section is only another variation or group of variations on the A material. Opuses 116, no. 2 and 118, no. 5 also combine variation principles with ABA form: opus 116, no. 2 uses a motivic-rhythmic connection between A and B, while opus 118, no. 5 makes the B section a series of its own variations. Thus, even seemingly simple ABA forms contain important elements of formal ambiguity.

Brahms further manipulates formal elements through his ambiguous connections between sections. It is easiest to discover this particular technique in his ABA pieces. His most elaborate deceptions are found at the opening of the A return. Opus 116, no. 2 looks and sounds unlike a true ABA because Brahms gives the putative A return (meas. 51) both a modally altered tonic and a drastically changed melody. In opus 119, no. 4 (meas. 153), Brahms alters almost all elements of the A return. In opus 118,

---

[6] Denis Matthews, *Brahms Piano Music*, BBC Music Guides (London: British Broadcasting Corporation, 1978), 64, calls op. 117, no. 2 a "miniature sonata form with 'monothematic' first and second subjects." He does not mention a form for op. 118, no. 1. Edwin Evans, *Handbook to the Pianoforte Works of Johannes Brahms: Historical, Descriptive and Analytical Account of the Entire Works of Johannes Brahms*, 4 vols. (London: Reeves, n.d.), 4:231-33, 238 calls op. 118, no. 1 a miniature sonata movement, but op. 117, no. 2 simply a lyric form in two parts in which the second serves as a coda. F. E. Kirby, *A Short History of Keyboard Music* (New York: Free Press, 1966), 334, and *Music for Piano: A Short History* (Portland, Ore.: Amadeus Press, 1995), 239, calls op. 118, no. 1 a simple binary with coda. The earlier op. 79, no. 2 also acts as a miniature sonata; Carl Dahlhaus, *Between Romanticism and Modernism: Four Studies in the Music of the Later Nineteenth Century*, transl. Mary Whittall, California Studies in 19th-Century Music (Berkeley: University of California Press, 1980), 71, says the "'rhapsody' is made subject to 'sonata form'." L. Michael Griffel, in "The Sonata Design in Chopin's Ballades," *Current Musicology* 36 (1983): 125-36, shows that free sonata-allegro designs can also be discovered in Chopin's ballades. See also Malcolm MacDonald, *Brahms* (New York: Schirmer Books, 1990), 357-58, and Michael Musgrave, *The Music of Brahms* (Oxford: Clarendon Press, 1985), 260-61.

[7] Anthony Newcomb, "Those Images That Yet Fresh Images Beget," *Journal of Musicology* 2 (1983): 245, discusses this concept of implication as found in Wagner's music; it applies to Brahms as well.

[8] John Daverio describes opus 116, no. 1 as an amplified binary in "From 'Concertante Rondo' to 'Lyric Sonata': A Commentary on Brahms's Reception of Mozart," in *Brahms Studies*, ed. David Brodbeck (Lincoln: University of Nebraska Press, 1994), 116.

no. 2 (meas. 73-76) Brahms weaves into the end of the B section hints of A elements, and more drastically, in opus 118, no. 6 (meas. 52-61) he combines the B section texture with complete A themes. His transitions may use A elements, as in opus 118, no. 3 (meas. 72-76), or B elements, as in opus 119, no. 2 (meas. 67-71). Opus 116, no. 4 supplies an extreme example of the difficulty in pinpointing the place of return. The listener ultimately knows that the A section has returned, but that realization is delayed as long as possible. Where codas bring back B material, the form itself at first seems in doubt. Opuses 116, no. 6; 117, no. 2; 118, no. 3; and 119, no. 2 have endings that suggest an ABA expanded to ABAB, and only other parameters clarify that such an interpretation would be false.

Even in pieces where form seems to be a driving compositional force and core of the discourse— opuses 118, no. 1; 117, no. 2; and 116, no. 4, all discussed below—that element does not operate in isolation. It is in constant interaction with other parameters such as rhythm, melodic-motivic play, and counterpoint. Because these parameters do not align along structural seams, phrase cadences, or down-beats, there is a weakening of structural anchors. The multiple forces create tension through ambiguous suggestions, a tension that in turn propels the piece forward. In each of the pieces discussed below, Brahms chooses a different way of making a traditional form interact with other parameters of music.

An Abbreviated Sonata: Opus 118, No. 1

Opus 118, no. 1 exemplifies one way Brahms exploited elements of the sonata-allegro form.[9] At the opening little would suggest the sonata idea. The first theme barely resembles a theme at all; rather than being a melody, it forms a stretched-out phrase that expands and extends one motivic idea. No specific section acts as a transition and no second theme appears. One might in retrospect divide measures 1-4 into an open-ended first theme, measures 5-7 into a transition continuing the material of the first theme and beginning the harmonic movement, and measures 8-10 into a second theme stabilizing the new harmonic area (see chart 10.1 on following page). However, the first audible sonata clue comes with the cadence of these first ten measures in an A-minor sonata's correct secondary key, C major. The instability of the primary, A-minor key area—caused already in the first measure by the unusually strong B-flat appoggiatura over a very weak first-inversion tonic arpeggio—conceals that the harmonic direction moves according to sonata patterns for pieces in minor.[10] This partially concealed modulation combines with the repeat sign to be the only features suggesting a sonata exposition.

Measures 11-20 suggest a development because they use common developmental techniques: sequences, rapid harmonic motion, and—correctly if fleetingly—the dominant is touched with the half-note, *e* (meas. 20, beat 2). The section employs the motivic material of the first theme, but this does not surprise, because as the only material presented in the ten-measure opening it has barely had

---

[9] At least some sonata-allegro elements must be present in order to label a piece "in sonata-allegro form." The overall harmonic scheme with a strong, prolonged gesture to the dominant is most essential. Other characteristics could include modulation to the dominant (or mediant in minor) for the second of two themes, a subsequent developmental section (often ending with a strong V), and a tonic return of both the first and second themes. It might include a transitional section of different character that modulates between the two expository themes, or an analogous recapitulatory transition that links those themes in the tonic. The themes might have contrasting characters; the exposition and development-recapitulation might each repeat. The listener might find harmonic and thematic stability at the opening and harmonic instability with fragmented, but familiar, melodic material in the development. See also Charles Rosen, *The Classical Style: Haydn, Mozart, Beethoven* (New York: Norton, 1972), 30-42.

[10] Edward T. Cone, "Three Ways of Reading a Detective Story—or a Brahms Intermezzo," *Georgia Review* 31 (1977): 567-70, analyzes the three possibilities of meaning for the opening harmonies of the piece and especially the effect of the B-flat in meas. 1. Do we hear C, F, or A as the tonal center?

Chart 10.1

Brahms, Intermezzo, op. 118, no. 1 as an Abbreviated Sonata

Exposition:	A	trans.	B	:‖:	Development	Recapitulation:	A	trans.	B	:‖	Coda	‖
	a		C				a		a		E A	
	(i)		–III		(V)		(i)		–i		V I	
meas.	1-4	5-7	8-10	‖	11-20		21-24	25-27	28-29	‖	30-41	‖

Uppercase keys are major; lowercase ones are minor.

a chance to make itself known. It stands to reason, even without the expectations of a sonata form, that this motive should provide the source for the further progress of the piece. In measure 21, the opening material returns as it should for a recapitulation, and it correctly brings back the tonic, although, like the exposition opening, the key is only weakly established. Because of both the ambiguity of key and the placement of the melodic material into an ongoing sequential pattern, the exact moment of return slips past the listener. Finally, in a gesture harkening back to the more conservative sonata-allegro designs, the development-recapitulation is repeated; this device serves the important functions of balancing the exposition and of making the formal structure more apparent to the listener.

In many sonata-allegro pieces, a strong V-I motion occurs at the end of the development to resolve it into the recapitulation. But in this piece the recapitulation (meas. 21, analogous to the exposition's meas. 1) had started away from a discernible tonic and thus skirted that expected harmonic resolution. If the recapitulation had ended with an A-minor cadence such as the one in the first ending (meas. 28b), that tonic would have lacked sufficient dominant preparation and resolution to conclude the piece convincingly. The coda, therefore, must take on the task of providing a confirming dominant-tonic resolution for the sonata design. That dominant-tonic completion begins with the coda's dominant pedal on E (meas. 31-34) and concludes with tonic stabilization (meas. 39-41). The coda is thus integrated into the piece as part of its main harmonic structure. The coda also assumes its more usual appendage status, however, with an interrupting passage in the subdominant area (meas. 35-38). This passage reduces the tension and makes the ending sound balanced and final.

Another Abbreviated Sonata: Opus 117, No. 2

Opus 117, no. 2 builds its form from different elements of the sonata-allegro design.[11] The proportions of the exposition are in a more normal balance; the A theme is twenty-two measures, the B theme is sixteen. This opening is in distinct contrast to the headlong plunge of opus 118, no. 1. Opus 117, no. 2's slender A theme—clearly audible though hard to extract visually from the written page—begins to repeat (meas. 9-10) but then moves off into new harmonies, a kind of varied repeat found in many sonata designs (see chart 10.2). One might expect this harmonic motion to turn into an active modulation that would become a transition, but instead the repeat simply concludes its melodic phrase on the minor dominant (meas. 17). Only after this cadence is there more active modulation leading to an E-double-flat-major arpeggiated chord (meas. 21-22), a turning point that could arguably be called an enharmonically-spelled raised III in B-flat minor, or, much better, a correctly-spelled flat II, the Neapolitan

---

[11] For a Schenkerian analysis of opus 117, no. 2, see Allen Cadwallader, "Schenker's Unpublished Graphic Analysis of Brahms's Intermezzo Op. 117, No. 2: Tonal Structure and Concealed Motivic Repetition," *Music Theory Spectrum* 6 (1984): 1-13.

Chart 10.2

Brahms, Intermezzo, op. 117, no. 2 as an Abbreviated Sonata

Exposition:	A	(A)	trans.	B		Development	Recapitulation:	A	(A)	B	
	b♭	f		D♭					F	F/b♭	
	(i)	–(v)		III		(V)		(i)	—V	V/I i	
meas.	1-9	9-17	17-22	22-38		38-51		51-60	60-72	72-85	

of the coming key (D-flat major). Brahms's flexible handling of major and minor keys is nowhere more eloquently demonstrated. This passage of transition between themes A and B exists only in the harmonic sense because the melodic material derives exclusively from A. The transition does not include new motivic material or textural change such as can be found in many sonata-allegro designs. The B theme (meas. 22-38) is built on III (D-flat major), and being both stable and melodious, fits well within sonata-allegro principles.

Ambiguity of statement is characteristic of this piece. A short development (meas. 38-51) correctly includes modulatory A material, but its modulation arrives on only a weak dominant (meas. 48-50). This weak dominant merges into one of Brahms's typically altered A returns (meas. 51-52), and though the shape of A and its ambiguity of harmony are familiar, it is not the same as the original. An ambiguous C-flat (meas. 51) replaces the uncertain C-minor first-inversion chord (upbeat to meas. 1), and a drifting secondary dominant (V of iv, meas. 52) replaces the first measure's weak first-inversion tonic. The C-flat of measure 51 is also reminiscent of opus 118, no. 1's ambiguous opening B-flat (meas. 1 and 21). Such weak and ambiguous statements of the tonic area more readily permit digressions to other key areas than when a tonic area is fully anchored. This practice, however, would contradict sonata-allegro expectations for a recapitulation.

Also similar to opus 118, no. 1, the close of opus 117, no. 2's development lacks the strong dominant-to-tonic transition that many sonata-allegro designs have. This important cadencing structure begins instead near the end of the recapitulation's A theme repeat with a dominant arpeggio (meas. 69-71). The cadence into the tonic (meas. 73, here B-flat major with a dominant pedal) also happens to coincide with the B theme beginning. This return of B serves three important functions simultaneously. First, its thematic material is the tonic recapitulatory statement of a sonata-allegro B theme. Second, the slowing of tempo to *più adagio* suggests that it is the coda. Finally, the tension of the dominant pedal supporting the tonic theme delays, but makes apparent, the coming of the final structural tonic. Thus, the only strong dominant statement in the whole piece occurs well into the recapitulation, and this twists the usual minor-key sonata-allegro design (i-III-V-i) askew. Both opuses 118, no. 1 and 117, no. 2 have this twist, avoiding an expected dominant-tonic closing at the development-recapitulation, and placing it instead late in the piece. Opus 118, no. 1 uses the displacement to strengthen the coda; opus 117, no. 2 uses it to conclude the first recapitulatory theme and to sustain the second.

These two pieces show how Brahms applies principles from sonata-allegro designs. He has modified or omitted some and used others to contradict or telescope the form. By borrowing his rhetoric from the larger structure he recreates that form's expansiveness of thought and character. These two pieces show borrowing from a single form. Opus 116, no. 1, with elements of sonata and rondo designs, offers a more complex example of formal interplay, but opus 116, no. 4, with its interlocked gestures from a number of forms, offers the most striking illustration of how Brahms imaginatively solves a difficult formal problem of his own making.

The Hybrid: Opus 116, No. 4

Opus 116, no. 4 provides an elegant interplay of formal elements that test the priorities of their relationship. Its unfolding of formal principles can surprise and delight the listener, and this quality of the unexpected speaks to the core of the listener's curiosity about the construction of this piece. The listener may get a personal delight from this manipulation of form, yet this play with design also supplies the intellectual and analytical attraction.

No single design explains opus 116, no. 4 or provides a complete overview of the important formal elements.[12] Instead, Brahms furnishes a journey of remembrances of form and formal designs with none of his models ultimately appearing *in toto*. There are various layers of form displaying attendant characteristics; these layers exist simultaneously and each affects other aspects of the piece. Large formal principles are reduced to symbols or landmarks that merely hint at the known design. Each landmark is an incomplete gesture that reminds the listener of the whole. Since Brahms used such techniques of suggestion in defining form for other small pieces, it stands to reason that he might use this organizing principle with opus 116, no. 4. I suggest that the reason for his economy of means is that a miniature lacks the physical time to develop expansive motions or to work through the explicitly stated large-scale designs.

Before exploring the formal possibilities of opus 116, no. 4, we must consider briefly how Brahms handled two surface elements that provide some degree of unity. Motivic development and variation, techniques that so often provide similarity among sections in other pieces, occur here in a limited way only. The right-hand, motivically-built A theme (meas. 1-9) and the descending, arpeggio-like B theme (meas. 10-14) share three elements: a quarter-note pulse, a triplet filling motion, and a descending shape with a sense of stasis. This loose collection of attributes might also be extended to the C-section melody (meas. 37-49), whose descending scale line (meas. 37-44) and falling intervals (meas. 44-48) could derive from the similarly downward-shaped intervals of the opening measures. Because these resemblances define only loose, general contours and rhythms, and because in that aspect they differ greatly from driving motivic similarities found in other pieces, op. 116, no. 4's motivic development and variation seem subordinate to the main organization of the piece.

Brahms derives his most convincing surface unity from the frequent use of chromaticism for local-level chord progressions. To point out one example: already in the first measure the *b*-sharp, pushing away from the tonic pedal on E, implies motion to the submediant and takes a step on the way toward the subdominant area of the second measure. The B-naturals in measures 3-4 then reverse the motion back to the tonic. Additional instances of chromaticism used to make local harmonic connections occur in measures 5, 6, 8, 10, and other places. Such chromatic moments, along with the vague motivic

---

[12] Jonathan Dunsby, "The Multi-Piece in Brahms: *Fantasien* Op. 116," in *Brahms: Biographical, Documentary and Analytical Studies*, ed. Robert Pascall (Cambridge: Cambridge University Press, 1983), 175, calls op. 116, no. 4 a two-section form (meas. 36 for the second part) with developing variation. Thomas Mastroianni, "Elements of Unity in 'Fantasies,' Opus 116 by Brahms" (D.M.A. diss., Indiana University, 1969), 6-7, calls it a kind of ternary but vague form, A A´ (meas. 15) B (meas. 37) A (meas. 53) B (meas. 60). He has difficulty explaining the final B and suggests that the twilight mood of the B theme dictated its return. William David Murdoch, *Brahms: With an Analytical Study of the Complete Pianoforte Works* (London, 1933; reprint, New York: AMS Press, 1978), 263, says, "There is a recapitulation, and everything becomes fuller . . . the end is like the beginning—pervaded by a dreamy nocturnal haze." Byung Hoh Yang, "A Study of Part Forms in the Selected Intermezzi (Opp. 116-119) of Johannes Brahms" (M.M. thesis, North Texas State University, 1979), 77, identifies three main parts, I, II (meas. 37), IIIa (meas. 53) and IIIb (meas. 60), and gives labels to many small bits of material; he does not convincingly explain why Brahms might have strung the music together in this order. He apparently bases his three-theme analysis on Evans, 219. Yang, 77, calls opus 116, no. 4 a "free sectional form" or "sonata-related binary form." Musgrave, 259, concludes that "This complex piece . . . reveals several types of growth and variation within its reflective exterior," and MacDonald, 357, suggests only that it "grows fantasia-like from a peaceful melody."

relationships mentioned above, supply a unity of procedure without addressing the central issues of form and balance.

In seeking a formal structure for opus 116, no. 4, none of the conventional structures—rondo, sonata, ABA song form, concerto, or others—seems entirely relevant. At its largest level the piece does not fit one design, and particularly the ABA form that characterizes so many of the other pieces has no place here. Both sonata and rondo characteristics do emerge, but they are not combined into an organization that could suggest even a loose sonata-rondo structure such as that found in opus 116, no. 1.

Since no one design seems to answer this formal puzzle adequately, I examine opus 116, no. 4 from six different angles—twice as a rondo, twice as a sonata, once as a ritornello design, and once as a three-part scheme with sonata implications. Each recommends itself to clarify a collection of formal attributes that are defined through various elements of the music. Each of these formal attributes is a gesture that produces further expectations for the continuation of that form. Since no single formal scheme finally accounts for all these gestures, I have separated the discussion into six layers, each a way of hearing and understanding the piece. The piece resembles a well-told mystery story filled with clues that lead in various directions and tantalize with their expectations.

A Textural Rondo for Opus 116, no. 4. The formal plan perhaps most easily perceived on first hearing is a free rondo built from strong distinctions of texture and rhythm. Predominant in most of the piece is the triplet rhythm with underlying quarter-note motion and a texture that fills the middle range. Measures 37-49 and 60-66 are different (see chart 10.3). They have a texture of scale-descending octave chords in the right hand. In the left hand sixteenth-note arpeggios provide a new bass pattern with faster rhythmic motion and fuller texture. The expanded range and wide spacing between the hands call particular attention to the newness of this texture. Though the second statement of this material lacks the dominant area passage of the first (meas. 37-40), the two sections belong together because they employ similar melodic shapes, textures, and mood characteristics (*una corda* and *ben legato*). Their common likenesses and their strong contrast to the surrounding material suggest setting off these two sections from the rest of the piece. The description ABABA provides a loose mold for describing these contrasting textures and rhythmic patterns. This ABABA design illustrates the simplest of rondo procedures, one that seems reminiscent of, for example, finales in Haydn string quartets.

Chart 10.3
Brahms, Intermezzo, op. 116, no. 4 as a Textural Rondo

	A		B	A	B	A	
	E		B				
	I–		V^7–	(I)	(I)	I	
meas.	1-36		37-49	49-59	60-66	67-71	

Some measures have textural and rhythmic ambiguities, but these irregularities are not strong enough to disturb this rondo pattern. For example, the presence of triplet rhythm in the B section (meas. 48-49 and 66) suggests a bleeding of A traits into the B-section conclusion to prepare more smoothly for the A-texture return. In one case in the A section (meas. 30-32), the contrapuntal lines of triplets produce a secondary meter, a hemiola ¾ meter, but the basic triplet motion of the A rhythm is undisturbed. Two other places in the A section (meas. 33-36 and 50-52) lose the triplet motion because of harmonic extensions, but the underlying quarter pulse remains.

One of the impediments to accepting the rondo design as the exclusive formal description comes from the great imbalance of section lengths: the first AB occupies 49 measures out of a total of 71, the final ABA only 22. In addition, the importance of the left-hand opening figure that evolves a life of its own remains unaddressed by the rondo design. Finally, the harmonic scheme of the piece as a whole does not align with the textural and rhythmic rondo. In naming a harmonic design for the rondo, we would be forced to call it I-V-I-I-I. Such a lopsidedly tonic-focused scheme is not usual for rondos. In fact, the first tonic area, as it must be designated for the rondo scheme, conceals major excursions away from the tonic. Since these excursions figure prominently in the overall harmonic scheme, the rhythmic and text-ural rondo slights some of the most interesting and important harmonic events. Although these facts suggest that contravening forces are at work, the rondo pattern does exist on the rhythmic and textural level.

A Melodic Rondo for Opus 116, No. 4. The frequent return of melodic material suggests another rondo scheme for this piece. There are three types of melodic material: A, the falling interval in quarters (meas. 1-9), B, the descending triplets (meas. 10-14), and C, a scale descent (meas. 37-49) (see chart 10.4). If we accept these three bits of material as having form-giving potential, but ignore for the moment the opening left-hand figure and its later extensions, we gain an ABABCACB form, an odd rondo form at best. Either this quasi-rondo lacks two A sections near the end, or the last B should have been an A. Yet rondo rhetoric appears strongly because the melody of the three A sections returns, beginning at the same pitch level, $g\#''$ to $c\#''$ (meas. 1-2, 15-16, 52-53). Even though these A statements do not continue in the same way, and particularly the third-entrance opening is altered through left-hand arpeggios, all three are strongly tonic-oriented. The first two begin in the tonic area by establishing it with pedals (meas. 1-2 and 15-16), but then move away to the dominant (meas. 9) and the mediant (meas. 25). The third A starts away from the tonic (meas. 52-53) but returns to it and establishes the tonic with a pedal (meas. 55-56). Thus, the principle of repeatedly bringing back opening material in the same key area, a common expectation for rondo design, receives lip service with this melodic rondo.

Chart 10.4
Brahms, Intermezzo, op. 116, no. 4 as a Melodic Rondo

	A	B	A	B	C	A	C	B
	E	B		$g\#$				
	I–	V	I–	iii	–	(I) I		I
meas.	1-9	10-14	15-25	26-32	37-49	52-56	60-66	67-71

The fact that the A material is a self-contained section with a clear beginning and end further replicates the autonomous nature of an A section in a rondo design. That there are two other types of melodic material (B and C), also autonomous and with clear boundaries, additionally suggests derivation from a large rondo design. But finally, this illusive melodic rondo lacks other aspects that might more fully flesh out the rondo. It is not capable of explaining the opening left-hand five-note figure, the harmonic plan, or the inclusion of extra C and B sections at the end.

A Ritornello Design for Opus 116, No. 4. In order to explain Brahms's handling of the opening five-note figure (upbeat and meas. 1, beats 1-2), the Baroque ritornello principle—used here in the sense of repeatedly returning to a single idea—is a useful image to consider.[13] The five-note figure's repeated occurrence suggests that it acts as such a repeating idea and that it is a miniature reflection of ritornello practice in the Baroque (see chart 10.5). One might also call this idea a prominently recurring thought and attach it to the larger idea of reminiscence motive (thematically transformed or not) as used in nineteenth-century opera. However, the image of ritornello works more smoothly since the figure has both melodic and harmonic congruences worth exploring.

Chart 10.5
Brahms, Intermezzo, op. 116, no. 4 as a Ritornello Design

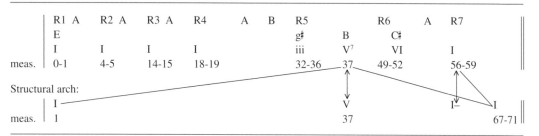

	R1 A	R2 A	R3 A	R4	A	B	R5		B	R6	A	R7	
	E						g#		B	C#			
	I	I	I	I			iii		V^7	VI		I	
meas.	0-1	4-5	14-15	18-19			32-36	37	49-52			56-59	

Structural arch:					
	I			V		I⁻ I
meas.	1			37		67-71

R = ritornello

First we must look at the deceptive role of this five-note figure. It appears so prominently at the beginning that it seems to be the melody, and it lies in the range of a typical Brahms tenor melody. The important clue to its more complex interpretation is that Brahms asks his pianist to play this opening figure and its later occurrences with crossed hands. This unusual instruction suggests a special effect or an unusual balance of sound, because in five of its seven occurrences no technical necessity governs the crossed-hands position. For example, in the Adagio tempo, the right hand could have played the opening figure and then moved from its final *c♯'* up to *g♯''* in perfect control (meas. 1, beats 2 to 3). Rather, the indication suggests that the pianist should give the right-hand note (*E* in meas. 1) special emphasis and relegate the left-hand notes to a more subservient status. The right hand, as the leading hand in piano literature and the one likely to give a more aggressive touch, will make the *E* stand out and establish the tonic with emphasis. The left-hand's apparent melodic figure becomes the weaker sound, more of an internal, almost harmonic, filler.

Understanding the five-note figure as subservient does not lessen its importance. Though it is a more veiled and internal thought than at first understood, it is an important force because it provides unity to the piece. The five-note figure retains the same pitches for its later occurrences, and in this displays a characteristic of many of the returns in a ritornello movement. Brahms alters the notes *b e b b♯ c♯'* only once: in measure 32 the second note of the five-note figure, the expected *e*, becomes *d♯*. The triplet rhythm of this figure is another important characteristic that sets it off as distinct from the rest of the piece. It belongs not only to the five-note figure itself, but provides the accompaniment for the whole A section (meas. 1-9) and the rhythmic pattern for the B section (meas. 10-13). This bleeding of a ritornello characteristic into the continuation material has precedents in Baroque ritornello practice.

Ultimately the five-note figure fails a test of the ritornello when it does not return at the end of the piece to complete an expected arch, and the ritornello loses its claim as the most important organizational principle for the work. Instead, the figure, as a supporting player, takes on different functions

[13] J. A. Fuller Maitland suggested the idea of ritornello already in his *Brahms* (New York: John Lane, 1911), 97.

as it moves through the piece. In two appearances it introduces A material as a mini-introduction (upbeat-meas. 1 and 14-15), and in two others it is simultaneously a cadential harmony and a transition back into the A material (meas. 4-5 and 18-19). In its last three appearances it combines transitional and cadential functions to differing degrees and thus meets larger needs of the piece while retaining its own strength in the fact that it returns frequently.

Its independence further lies in the fact that it is the carrier of a secondary-level harmonic motion, and this harmonic design contains ritornello rhetoric of its own. The five-note figure is supported successively by I, I, I, I, iii, VI, and I. By comparing the submediant chord (meas. 50-52) with the harmony from the source measure (meas. 1), it becomes apparent that the later major submediant is an expanded modal variation of the first-inversion minor submediant chords (meas. 1, beat 2), an excellent example of Brahms's flexible handling of major-minor interchange that here produces a chord substitution.

This possibility of chord substitution has larger ramifications for the harmonic scheme. Since tonic, mediant, and submediant harmonies all support the same fixed-pitch motive in its later occurrences, the harmonies seem to be different hues of a single color rather than separate and new colors. Such a metaphorical image broadens the possibilities for viewing these harmonic relations in ways not commonly given attention today. Using the metaphorical image as the basis, this piece becomes an excellent example for illustrating the principle of *Klangvertretung* (chord representation), an idea advanced by Hugo Riemann in his theoretical system derived from observation of late nineteenth-century harmonic practice.[14] In *Klangvertretung* harmonies a third apart can substitute for a primary harmony; in this case, both the mediant and the submediant would be tonic substitutes. The mediat, as a *Leitton-Wechselklang* (leading-tone exchange chord) of the tonic, can stand in for the tonic because the chord retains the third and fifth of the major tonic and replaces the root with the leading-tone. The submediant is a *Parallel-Klang* (parallel chord), which can stand for the tonic by retaining root and third of the chord and replacing the fifth with the sixth.

In Riemann's system any chord can act in these two roles. The mediant, for example, may not only replace the tonic but can also act as the *Parallel-Klang* of the dominant.[15] In a context that I will discuss below, the mediant will do just that. These secondary triads possess, according to Riemann, the same significance and tonal function as the primary triads for which they substitute. Using his theory, then, all seven occurrences of Brahms's five-note figure are supported by the same functional harmony, the tonic. Calling this harmonic extension part of Baroque ritornello rhetoric seems possible because Baroque ritornello returns are also altered in harmonic ways. Here Brahms adjusts this practice to fit his late nineteenth-century idiom.

The five-note figure with its attendant harmonies—in short, the ritornello—builds a secondary harmonic design that then touches larger aspects of the piece. The first four ritornellos are introductions to the A material, but in the larger sense they are important as structural tonic anchors (refer to chart 10.5). Their four-fold tonic repetition accords them importance beyond a solely introductory function. The remaining three ritornellos (meas. 32-36, 49-52, and 56-59) expand in size and bring the ritornello material into a more prominent position; the fifth ritornello stands out particularly because the expected

---

[14] William Cooper Mickelsen, "Hugo Riemann's History of Harmonic Theory, with a Translation of 'Harmonielehre'" (Ph.D. diss., Indiana University, 1970), 151-52, 155-59, 396, or *Hugo Riemann's Theory of Harmony: A Study by William C. Mickelsen, and History of Music Theory, Book III by Hugo Riemann*, transl. and ed. by William C. Mickelsen (Lincoln: University of Nebraska Press, 1977), 55-58, 64-65, 218-22.

[15] The issue of the mediant and its function within the tonal system is by no means a simple or agreed-upon subject. Statistically, it seems to stand for the dominant more frequently than the tonic; but each example must be examined within its own context.

A material does not follow it. The fifth and the sixth ritornellos carry the harmonic subplot forward and conclude with the piece's only firm, internal cadences.[16] These cadences, each two beats long, stop forward motion and thus contradict the introductory function of the first four ritornellos.

The fifth ritornello is the pivot of the piece. It completes the harmonic motion to the mediant (meas. 36), a process generated, but not completed, in the preceding B material (meas. 26-32). This cadence concludes the most harmonically distant progression of the piece and lies, not coincidentally, at its midpoint (meas. 36 of a total 71). The cadential chord functions not only as this pivot in time but also as the pivot note between tonic and dominant. When the dominant appears (meas. 37), it is gained by an upward third motion. The mediant cadence has now performed two functions; it has been a substitute tonic (up a third, the *Leitton-Wechselklang* in Riemann's system), and now becomes the stepping stone to the dominant (a *Parallel-Klang* to the dominant). The merging of the mediant into the dominant combines the most distant secondary-level digression with the center of the structural tonic-dominant-tonic arch. That this should happen in the central measure of the piece on a hovering two-beat cadence is Brahms's masterfully understated balancing act between two harmonic levels.

The sixth ritornello, by moving to the far side of the tonic with a submediant cadence (meas. 52), counterbalances the mediant and solidifies the tonic. The submediant cadence is a digression within the returning tonic area because the tonic pedal has already been present for nine measures (meas. 41-49). Like the mediant cadence that had strong ties upward to the dominant, this submediant cadence, by being closely related to its surrounding tonic, stands in as a substitute for it, another *Parallel-Klang*.

The seventh and final ritornello (meas. 56-59) reiterates the tonic and completes the secondary-level harmonic arch of thirds away from the home key. Because this final ritornello finishes the secondary arch and helps stabilize the primary harmonic scheme, it completes its purpose as bearer of harmonic motion and does not need to appear again. That the piece continues for twelve more measures suggests that there are other forces still unfinished at the time of the seventh ritornello.

An Abbreviated Sonata for Opus 116, No. 4. Brahms's abbreviated sonata structures in opuses 118, no. 1, and 117, no. 2 suggest that opus 116, no. 4 be examined for similar skeletal aspects, and, indeed, we find them. In opus 116, no. 4 the first and second themes (A, meas. 1-9, and B, meas. 10-14) differ little in character, as in many Haydn sonata-allegro movements, and they lie in tonic-dominant relationship to each other (see chart 10.6). The A theme, built of two four-measure phrases, moves to a strong dominant cadence (meas. 9). That harmony, along with its eighth-note arpeggio and its staccato articulation, delineates the arrival. In the altered repeat of the exposition (meas. 15-36), the B theme with codetta (meas. 26-36) uses the mediant and with that move violates usual harmonic procedure. Because the B theme is fully recognizable melodically and sufficiently stable harmonically this mediant area can be considered a substitute dominant, or dominant by analogy.

When new material begins (meas. 37) it suggests a development has begun, but this material can only stand in for a development because it lacks important developmental procedures, including motivic development and a clear reference to A material. Its two characteristics that suggest a development are sequences (meas. 41-44 equaling meas. 37-40) and a dominant beginning that leads back toward the tonic.

The point of recapitulation remains characteristically ambiguous. We expect the five-note figure (meas. 49-50) to open the recapitulation, and to replicate its opening gesture as a brief stabilizing intro-duction to the A theme. Instead, it expands and delays the A theme's entrance, and its harmonies

---

[16] The rhythmic transitions preceding these two ritornellos (meas. 30-32 and 48-49, the merging points for the textural-rhythmic rondo) now show their importance: their transitional nature directs attention to these two ritornellos and their important cadential areas.

Chart 10.6

Brahms, Intermezzo, op. 116, no. 4 as an Abbreviated Sonata

	Exposition		Altered–Repeat		Development	Recapitulation			trans.	B
	A	B	A	B		A				
	E	B		g♯			C♯			
	I	V	I	iii	V7 (I)	(I) VI	(I)	(I)	I	
meas.	1-9	10-14	15-25	26-36	37-49	50-52	52-59	60-66	67-71	

blatantly avoid tonic stability. Those harmonies move quickly past the tonic (meas. 49) to a strong submediant cadence (meas. 52). At the structural level of sonata-allegro, this submediant can be understood as an area of tonic substitute. It shows a strong parallel to the earlier area of mediant harmony: for the B theme's second occurrence (meas. 26-36), the mediant stood in as a dominant substitute. The recapitulation's ambiguity of return continues because the A-theme material (meas. 52-56) is only half as long as in the exposition, and the five-note figure (meas. 50-52 and 56-59) fills out its length, and this return avoids a clear tonic. Ambiguity such as this is typical of Brahms's recapitulations. Only at the conclusion of the theme and in the repeat of the five-note figure (meas. 55-59) does the tonic area begin to appear in the form of a tonic pedal.

The transition in the recapitulation (meas. 60-66) had no material to draw on from the exposition because there the A and B themes had dovetailed without pause (meas. 9-10). Therefore, this transition on new and expansive material derives from the development stand-in. Though this is an unusual choice, the reuse of the development material in a different part of the form helps to assimilate that material into the prevailing sonata rhetoric. The B theme, slight though it is (meas. 67-71), returns in the tonic as expected in a sonata-allegro design.

Another Abbreviated Sonata for Opus 116, No. 4. In the analyses so far, only some of the features of the piece are accounted for by reference to larger structural designs. In the sonata analysis above, one feature remains particularly problematic: the prominence of the transitional material in the recapitulation. This awkwardness prompts testing yet another design, a sonata-allegro with both halves repeated (see chart 10.7). Consider that measure 37 begins the stand-in development as above, but that the recapitulation is shortened to contain only an A theme (meas. 50-59). Then, measures 60 to 71 would be a varied repetition of the development and recapitulation. This repetition recapitulates only the B theme in the tonic (meas. 67-71) and thus cleverly completes the remaining requirement of a recapitulation.

But even this formal description still contains an awkwardness shared with the first sonata analysis; it does not account well for the use of the mediant area for the B theme repetition in the exposition (meas. 26-36). This point can be fruitfully coupled with another problematic point found only in the second

Chart 10.7

Brahms, Intermezzo, op. 116, no. 4 as an Abbreviated Sonata

	Exposition		Altered–Repeat		Development	Recapitulation		Altered–Dev	Recapitulation
	A	B	A	B		A			B
	I	V	I	iii	V⁷ (I)	(I) VI	(I)	(I)	I
meas.	1-9	10-14	15-25	26-36	37-49	50-52	52-59	60-66	67-71

sonata analysis, the shortened, essentially tonic, development repeat (meas. 60-66). This repeat contains material parallel to measures 41-49 of the development itself (melodic similarities, textural likenesses, and the pedal point), but missing are the four measures of strong dominant harmony (meas. 37-40). These two anomalies share an important point: both avoid the dominant area. The explanation for the omission lies in understanding that this puts less emphasis on the one harmonic area that could truly disturb the tonic and unbalance the structural I-V-I arch. This piece, like all small pieces, needs to be able to return quickly and smoothly to the tonic.

A Three-Part Form with Sonata Suggestions for Opus 116, No. 4. Finally, an irregular three-part form suggests itself: AB with 14 measures (meas. 1-14), ABC with 35 measures (meas. 15-49) and ACB with 22 measures (meas. 50-71) (see chart 10.8). This form seems to grow and expand out of A, which is primarily tonic. The first A theme moves from tonic to dominant for the B theme (meas. 10). For the second A, the harmonic motion expands to tonic-mediant-dominant with a new theme, C, enriching the progression. The third A begins gradually, C and B follow, and all three themes are primarily in the tonic area.

Chart 10.8

Brahms, Intermezzo, op. 116, no. 4 as a Three-Part Form with Sonata Suggestions

	A	B	A	B	C	A		C	B	
	I	V	I	iii	V^7 (I)	(I) VI	(I)	(I)	I	
meas.	1-9	10-14	15-25	26-36	37-49	50-52	52-59	60-66	67-71	
	Exposition		Expanded Repeat			Recapitulation				
	Theme 1	Theme 2	Theme 1	Theme group 2		Theme 1			Reversed Theme group 2	

This expanding form has no particular name, but it does have elements of a sonata-allegro design: a sonata with repeated exposition, no development, and reversed-themes recapitulation. For the exposition, A is the first theme on the tonic, and B the second theme on the dominant. For the repeated exposition, B on the mediant is a link to C on the dominant. The B theme has lost its congruence with its harmonic area, but since it is already known as the second theme, C becomes an extension of it, and B and C act like a second-theme group. Since the form lacks a development, the recapitulation correctly brings all three themes in the tonic. However, the second-group themes are reversed (C, then B), an event well within the realm of sonata-allegro design.

Summary. Ultimately, opus 116, no. 4 belongs to all and none of these forms. Using selected gestures from the various formal schemes, Brahms has built a special form that defines itself differently depending on which parameter of the piece catches the listener's attention. Through these rhetorical gestures that recall well-known structures Brahms encourages his listeners' active participation and anticipation. He uses every parameter of music to present these gestures, but leaves ample room for the imagination to fill in and anticipate the progress of the form. Therein lies the delight and surprise. Brahms's mystery story has carefully and ambiguously parceled out clues.

The flexibility and frequency with which Brahms employs harmonies related by thirds helps to make possible these multiple analyses of opus 116, no. 4. This harmonic device combines as an equal partner with melody, texture, and rhythm to delineate and enhance the multi-level form. Brahms's methods particularly involve the use of harmonic third relationships as substitutions and deceptions for otherwise standard progressions of sonata and rondo designs. Through this practice Brahms shows an affinity to his contemporaries. Within late nineteenth-century harmonic practice, substitutions formed an important part of the style; Hugo Wolf's songs, for example, written at the same time, abound in such third-substitute harmonies,[17] and Hugo Riemann's theories of harmony with *Klangvertretung* were most likely encouraged by his knowledge of such practices.[18] In this respect, then, Brahms does not deserve the label of conservative or retrospective composer. Rather, he stands fully current beside his colleagues in using the harmonic language of his time as progressively and flexibly as they.

His opuses 116-119 display a mature composer's imaginative manipulation of received tradition. While these pieces still retain components of eighteenth- and nineteenth-century formal principles, opus 116, no. 4, in particular, shows how close Brahms had moved to the limits of the formal truths for these structures. This piece could be viewed as a force straining toward a new approach to formal principles, one that might be realized in the next generation of composers. Arnold Schoenberg's reaction to his received legacy of form—disintegrating as it was in the hands of Brahms—was to try to finish off that process of disintegration as he did with tonality. But even his best examples, the wildly experimental *Erwartung* and opus 19, *Sechs kleine Klavierstücke*, though they show new ideas about form-building, still contain reminders and memories of older structures. Schoenberg, like Brahms before him, still found it necessary to pay homage to the tattered legacy of formal design.

---

[17] Deborah Stein, "Hugo Wolf, Heinrich Schenker and Third Relations" (paper given at the American Musicological Society and Society for Music Theory meeting, Ann Arbor, 5 November 1982); also Stein, "Extended Tonal Procedures in the Lieder of Hugo Wolf" (Ph.D. diss., Yale University, 1982), 115-202.

[18] From *New Grove* (1980), s.v. "Riemann, Hugo," by Mark Hoffman, 16:4, come Riemann's words: "It was my greatest wish to co-ordinate the advances in musical composition with the most recent discoveries in acoustics and the physiology of the ear."

CHAPTER 11

Dance, Gypsy, Dance!

Joel Sheveloff

These fugitive notes try to focus on Johannes Brahms's twenty-one so-called *Hungarian Dances*, but with almost no concern for the issues about them raised ever since their initial appearance. One cannot say that these matters have been settled beyond further discussion, but the lack of new evidence keeps such discussions unproductive. It seems necessary to list these old sores anyway, just to get them out of the way.

The claim of Eduard Reményi to have composed much of this music himself, to have it subsequently stolen by Brahms, has largely been discounted in the past, in the light of Reményi's unsavory personality. He has no more claim as "composer" of most of this material than Liszt, Wieniawski, or any of the other figures who "borrowed" it. Max Kalbeck knew this from the outset of Brahms scholarship, and everyone who has followed in his footsteps has largely concurred. That Brahms's arrangements seem most true to the spirit of the originals and most fully captured public acceptance, from 1869 to our own day, makes the issue of who came first moot.

The long argument about the misuse of the word "Hungarian" in the title—not to represent true folk music of Hungary, Magyar music, but to stand for the bistro sonorities of Gypsies—seems tangential and ultimately irrelevant. Gypsies have interacted with numerous European ethnic communities in musical ways for more than a millenium, to create wondrous mixtures, among which the Spanish flamenco may be even more admired than its Central European cousin. Some Magyar contributions must be a part of the sonority that so impressed nineteenth-century musicians, but the ethno-musicological issues here have not even begun to be placed under control, so any evaluation of this matter seems premature. In one case where Brahms used the word "Hungarian" in his title, *Variations on a Hungarian Song*, op. 21, no. 2, the theme sounds Magyar rather than Romany, but this cannot be determined beyond the shadow of a doubt.

The issue of Brahms's actual composition, as opposed to arrangement of pre-existent music, has been guessed at, but we do not know enough to confirm the thesis that the first ten dances of 1869 largely arrange well-known Gypsy band sources, while the eleven others of 1880 tend to create new music in the style of the former. The principal evidence for this, in my view, has remained the far greater popularity of the 1869 pieces than those of 1880, but that sort of circular logic never leads anywhere. Until we have good written sources for all the ideas that went into all twenty-one dances, we cannot answer this question. That the composer eschewed the use of opus numbers for all twenty-one indicates that he felt that they fell in between the realm of arrangement and of composition; it may be fairest to claim that Brahms "organized" this pre-existent material in his own way, each one into a carefully crafted form to bring forth a special character or combination of characteristics representing his view of the Gypsy and his milieu.

The ever-annoying issue of arrangements of these works, both in Brahms's own century, when all sorts of standard media, from piano two-hands, to violin and piano, to most every other chamber group, to wind band, and finally full orchestra (which, in most arrangements, sounds hardly different from a concert band), inspired debates about which medium best served the music. (Our out-of-control age of arrangement, in which these reworkings include every sort of acoustic combination and now have graduated to electronic ones, plays no role here.) After all, the arrangements attempt to retain the musical substance of every measure, and this paper concentrates on dealing with that substance, especially in matters of rhythm and meter, rather than its coloristic manifestations. (I must say, however, that I prefer the piano four-hands version to all others.)

The *Hungarian Dances* served as breakthrough for Brahms to a wide, popular audience, as the *German Requiem* did to the intelligentsia. No longer would he be the unfulfilled Messiah of Schumann's *Neue Bahnen*, the darling of effete musical snobs. The innumerable performances, particularly in bourgeois homes, of all the *Hungarian Dances*, explains why their influence on acceptance of temporal irregularity in Brahms's developing metric-rhythmic techniques as well as those of his contemporaries and immediate successors cannot be overstated. Not only do these pieces appear at a crucial time in Brahms's compositional life, but they coincide with the sort of time-grouping novelties generally associated with eastern European styles, especially those of the newly burgeoning Russian school. Brahms explored such musical parameters at about the same time that they did, but in his own manner, at his own pace, and with results both similar to, and significantly different from them.

Issues of cyclic connection between *Hungarian Dance* movements, tonal plans of either individual dances or of groups of them, possible orders for performance, and other questions of tonality or modality may be meaningful, but tend to fade into the background of this discussion. Meter and rhythm, working together to create special temporal controls over each dance, remain the central focus of this paper. These factors, and the Gypsy connection, do not begin with the *Hungarian Dances*, as everyone knows; the "Rondo alla zingarese" that closes the Quartet for Piano and Strings, op. 25, antedates them, and will be discussed in context below. Before proceeding with an explanation of the nature and extent of their originality in the *Hungarian Dances*, however, an apparent digression on the importance of hypermeter in the nineteenth century seems necessary.

*   *   *   *

To belabor the obvious, the meter in a meter sign, in the eighteenth century, generally represents the true mathematical organization within a measure—in other words, when a meter sign reads $^3/_4$, it means that one feels three quarter beats, of varying strengths, within each measure. This even holds for the few pieces called "Scherzo" by Haydn, like his String Quartet in F major, op. 77, no. 2, in which the speed does exceed that of the usual minuet, but only by a relatively small degree. The hemiolas and other joke-like rhythmic effects would fall flat if the speed of this scherzo reached the breakneck pace of the nineteenth-century model. With the turn of the century and the rise of Beethoven and his many departures from norms of the classic era, appears his scherzo in a meter which reads $^3/_4$, but actually proceeds so precipitously that it must be played as one quick beat per measure, one with a built-in Presto triplet. This creates a situation in which the sense of metric organization at the level of the $^3/_4$ measure becomes compromised, such that the constant downbeats of the conductor grow hypnotic. Humans feel rhythmic groups of two, or three, or four, or more—not of *one-one-one-one-one*, et cetera, the principle of the oriental water torture.

In this musical environment in which the measure actually becomes the beat, the grouping of measures, which we usually read as a secondary hypermeter or middleground meter, suddenly comes to the foreground. In the Scherzo from Beethoven's Piano Sonata in D major, op. 28, we see this emergence in its purest form. The groups of dotted-half notes create an extremely regular four-measure pattern, which we hear and feel as a meter awkward to express in our musical notation, but one truly of $^4/_\downarrow.$, the sort of regularity that Hugo Riemann called *Vierhebigkeit*. In this sonata's scherzo, every one of its 94 measures falls into this grouping except measures 69-70, which function as a deliberate sudden stop, almost certainly intended as a shock. In orchestral pieces employing this technique, the conductor might well be advised to mark the hypermetric downbeats in each part, and conduct in four-measure groupings, to avoid the water-torture effect.

This often seems useful in racing-triple-meter finales as well; a most notable example is that of Robert Schumann's Piano Concerto in A minor, op. 54, in which the Allegro vivace maintains a driving, almost perfect *Vierhebigkeit*. (Because it begins *attacca* from the slow movement, its measure numbers continue those of its predecessor; the first measure of this finale is thus given as 109.) Schumann creates a delicious but deeply disturbing metric anomaly beginning in measure 189, an outer hemiola that tends to negate the four-measure pattern established in the first 80 measures. When the initial pattern returns at measure 230, both soloist and orchestra have great trouble establishing it while keeping the pace of the hemiola section. This becomes so hazardous that I have witnessed great artists in states of deep distress here, as well as at the corresponding place in the recapitulation. If, however, the conductor moved his stick to the *Vierhebigkeit*, and kept the pattern of fours going in throughout the hemiola section, though no sound matched his perverse-seeming beat, everyone could regain the initial pattern with no difficulty. The conductor and performers only need take into account the two parallel exceptions to the pattern, at measures 269-70, and at measures 649-50, as well as the ex-tension in the lyric interlude in measures 403-04, for everything to be kept under safe and sane control.

Some Beethoven scherzos, like that in op. 31, no. 3, behave in a Haydnesque manner, but the majority of them, from op. 36, the Second Symphony, to op. 131, the great C-sharp-minor String Quartet, employ hypermeter at the foreground level; and like op. 28, the regular four-measure grouping seems to dominate this genre. These pieces serve as the models for three subsequent generations, from Mendelssohn to Mahler. The great exception in Beethoven himself occurs in the scherzo in his Third Symphony in E-flat major, op. 55, "Eroica"; everyone knows of the innovations of the other three movements, but few realize how wildly experimental this scherzo turns out to be. It not only largely avoids *Vierhebigkeit*, but even essays beyond the sense of meter altogether in most places. Its irrational, unpredictable rhythms serve as model for a very very few later scherzos, most notoriously the "Queen Mab" scherzo from Berlioz's *Roméo et Juliette* dramatic symphony, and less well-known works of Raff, Borodin, and Sibelius.

Regular patterns of this type dominate other dance forms, fast sonata-allegro movements, even many slow movements. The regularity of hypermeters in nineteenth-century music exceeds that of the eighteenth century! As Romantic-century music grows ever more chromatic, lyric, and rich in harmony and melody, it tends to be increasingly regular in rhythm and meter. This process reaches a zenith (or nadir, depending up one's musical priorities) in the pre-*Ring* operas of Wagner, especially *Lohengrin*, whose regularity extends well past hypermeter to meter and tempo, often tending to produce a numbing effect, one extremely hazardous for a work that takes hours to complete. Then, in the second half of the century, a few composers turned their attention to rhythm as a principal arena of innovation: among the members of this group, Brahms stands very tall, and among his pieces, the *Hungarian Dances* contribute greatly to his sure-footed, ever-increasing sense of mastery of this parameter of his musical language.

*   *   *   *

All the *Hungarian Dances* may be notated in $^2/_4$ meter, but, just like the Beethovenian scherzo, the $^2/_4$ measure serves primarily as the *beat* of a fairly regular foreground hypermeter. Because our notation of whole, half, quarter, and eighth notes bases itself on binary numbers, this $^2/_4$ measure will present a fine basis for hypermetric representation: if, for example, a dance employs absolutely regular *Vierhebigkeit*, we can represent that meter as $^4/_2$—that is, a grouping of four measures in which the half note gets the beat. Meters of $^3/_1$, $^6/_2$, $^4/_1$, etc., may thus be employed with similar clarity. Imagine what sort of reaction a conductor would get from an orchestra, if he placed a $^4/_3$ meter sign at the outset of a scherzo by Beethoven! At least in these dances, we need not have to explain the meter sign's denominator.

The innovations in the *Hungarian Dances* involve internal shifts of hypermeter, as well as subcutaneous employments of odd beats or measures or groups. At no time do any of these pieces enter the never-never land of the "Eroica" or *Queen Mab*, but the structural changes here presage rhythmic-metric achievements of the next generation. The variety of meters employed, the variability of phrase-structures within them, and the power of all this to convey a world of Gypsy moods and character, has tended to be overlooked amidst the myriad of musical wonders produced in Brahms's other work. Like Haydn before him, Brahms made these breakthroughs so quietly that we hardly notice them. Behind the innocuous-looking $^2/_4$ meter lurks a rhythmic organization that reaches to our innermost sense of musical pattern, and unlocks a visceral series of affects that make us sway when we listen in ways unlike most any music in the Western concert tradition of the nineteenth century, but strikingly similar to Eastern European folk and art music, for the latter especially true after about 1870. The music of our century displays these features so commonly that we hardly take note of them, but to nineteenth-century ears these rhythmic gambits seemed very fresh and new.

*   *   *   *

Hungarian Dance no. 1 in G minor begins with a phrase six measures long. Within this phrase, the second measure repeats the first, the fourth does not repeat the third exactly, but intensifies its leading-tone message, and the fifth and sixth bring the whole thing to a cadence. Thus the six may best be grouped into three two-measure groups, so that for each two-measure group the whole-note may be considered the true measure rather than the half-note. All in all, this does result in a three-measure reading of the six measures, or as a meter sign: $^3/_1$. A mere glance reveals that this pattern holds for the first 48 measures, which reveals itself as four large $^3/_1$ measures from measures 1-24, essentially repeating in measures 25-48, with a transfer of register of the melody, from middle to treble. The tonal balance of these four $^3/_1$ hypermeasures could not be more regular: the first establishes and maintains the tonic, the second moves to subdominant, the third to dominant, and the fourth cadences to tonic. A perfect regular subdivided *Dreihebigkeit*.

Without a change of tempo, a modulation, or any other warning, the music in measure 49 suddenly changes to an unmistakable $^4/_2$. Nothing on the page, no notation of any kind, warns us of this change, but it exists and suddenly tightens the reins, from a loose triple to a tight duple. The first clause of this section, in measures 49-60, consists of not four but three four-measure groupings, the tonal logic of which proceeds from I-IV, then V-I, and finally to the reinforcement of the I. A first figural variation of this clause occupies measures 61-72; like the opening material this one essentially repeats, but instead of a register transfer, the intensity comes from motivic development

A third clause occupies measure 73-92: this time its organization is binary with repeats, its hyper-meter $^4/_2$, and the number of groups in each half has been reduced to two. Once again, nothing in the notation warns the player, dancer, or listener about the shifting elements. I can imagine that this would give the duo pianists, or whatever other players of whatever arrangement appears here, cause for a minimum of concern. But once one has felt the shift, it seems relatively easy to adjust to it. I have never hear a performance of this first dance where the shifts of hypermeter gave any well-rehearsed players any trouble. This third clause's binary unit goes from I to V, and then from III back to I. Once more, the clause seems tight, balanced, and complete within itself.

The first clause literally repeats, measures 93-104. The second clause returns in measure 141; its basic statement recurs exactly in measures 141-52, but its variation, after repeating the first two four-measure units, varies the cadence into a great sweep up to a climax in measures 166-67 that ends the dance. The final measure sits under a fermata that probably ought to be interpreted as a literal doubling of the length of the final measures, which would then complete one last $^4/_2$ unit. The resultant form, AB C Ab´, suggests a slightly augmented form of ternary design, in which the AB becomes A and the C becomes B; the C, however, is too short for that—moreover, the most notable borderline in the piece occurs between A and B when the hypermeter changes from triple to duple. Since the tonality never strays from tonic G minor, it plays no role in the large form. Thus the form of the whole seems somewhat truncated and imbalanced.

This first *Hungarian Dance* serves as a good model for most of the others. Its stable tonality, balanced clauses, clearly articulated form parts, and shifts of hypermeter create an effective dramatic whole that leaves a slightly sour aftertaste, because the form of the whole seems to leave a bit of untapped potential energy at the end. Its Gypsy lilt, highlighted by augmented seconds and struck suspensions, seem secondary to these large issues in the æsthetic effectiveness of the whole. While each one presents special motivic questions, anomalies, and hypermeters of its own, the form complex of no. 1 seems representative, most especially of the others that appeared in 1869. The following thematic catalog of the 1869 beginnings, together with my overlay of the hyper-meters expressed at each opening, projects the richness and variety of the metric aspects of these dance complexes (see ex. 11.1).

The true temporal organizations of the dances in this group vary in more than primary, essential grouping. No. 2, in D minor, employs a clear $^4/_1$ meter, both in its main music in D minor, and its contrasting central section in D major. Anomalies do appear in both, but these will be discussed in a separate section, below. One may be tempted to hear no. 3 in $^3/_2$ meter, but I believe the regularity of strong and weak phrases that runs throughout its main sections in F major and the secondary ones in D minor and D major, point rather to $^6/_2$ as metric unit. From the period structure of the very first six-measure grouping, whose antecedent and consequent phrases could not be more square, the compound metric interpretation cannot be denied. No. 4 links tonal and hypermetric contrast: the main sections in F minor drag along in $^4/_1$ meter, while the middle section in F minor offers a marvelous surprise by its $^3/_1$ meter. The famous no. 5 in F-sharp minor seems reminiscent of no. 1 in the way it builds excitement through metric tightening: from $^4/_1$ in measures 1-48, to $^6/_2$ in measures 49-60, to $^2/_2$ in measures 61-76, and then back to $^4/_1$ in measures 77-108, the return of the opening material. The "codettinetta" of measures 109-10 uses one last $^2/_2$ to bring everything to a snappy conclusion. No. 6 in D-flat major keeps its $^4/_2$ going from beginning to end, save for a couple of interesting anomalies and another snappy $^2/_2$ closing tail. Occasional brief, self-indulgent *ritardandi* followed by a quick return

Example 11.1. Brahms, *Hungarian Dances*, nos. 1-10 (1869), beginnings.

Example 11.1.–*Continued*

to the original tempo, mark almost all these dances, but seem particularly favored in the very busy no. 7 in A major, largely in $^4/_2$. The Presto no. 8 in A minor offers several rhythmic complexities within its expansive $^4/_1$. I had trouble making up my mind about whether $^4/_1$ or $^4/_2$ seems most appropriate for no. 9 in E minor before deciding on the latter; its *poco sostenuto* section presents some temporal challenges, as some performers reveal in their uncertain renditions. The several manifestations of unusual grouping within no. 10 in E major have already occurred in previous examples; its main performance issues center around balance and articulation rather than rhythm or meter.

The 1880 group of eleven tend to be shorter, more pungent, somewhat more abstract than their predecessors (see ex. 11.2).

Example 11.2. Brahms, *Hungarian Dances*, nos. 11-21 (1880), beginnings.

Example 11.2.–*Continued*

15.

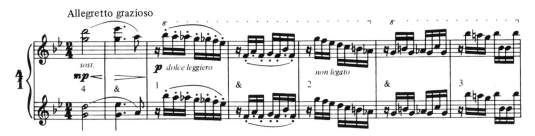

16.

17.

18.

19.

Continued

Example 11.2.–*Continued*

No. 11 looks harmless enough, but turns out to be nothing but trouble. It has engendered tonal arguments for years, less in the literature than in classes or seminars in music theory or history. Some hear it as a Dorian modality on D, some see it as in C major but with the cadences in measures 18 and 58 away from the putative tonic. While I stand among the latter, I regard this issue as tangential to the rhythmic ones here. The piece begins with a thick chordal anacrusis that most pianists, orchestras, and other groups tend to play as though it were a displaced downbeat, over-reacting to the *diminuendo* hairpin Brahms places after it; this results in a grotesque distortion of the basic rhythmic pattern that does not straighten itself out until a measure or two after the melody enters in measure 3. The two-measure length of this opening pattern tends to make the subsequent entrance of the melody sound as though it comes in on the third measure of a hypermetric pattern; this violates all evidence here and in the rest of this dance. The pattern clearly begins on the third measure, with an introductory vamp; the way this usually gets played turns the rhythmic picture on its head. But, once players control the opening properly, the remainder of the $^4/_2$ proceeds with unmarred regularity.

No. 12, now truly and unquestionably in D minor, fails to establish its meter at the outset, but after some explainable anomalies clearly falls into $^4/_2$; the metric ambiguity here seems as Brahmsian as the tonal ambiguities noted throughout his extensive analytical bibliography. No. 13 in D major begins in $^6/_2$, its *grazioso* character strongly reminiscent of no. 3; but the sudden Vivace passage, from measures 19 to 46, not only energizes the beat, but changes its organization to $^4/_2$. On the return to the opening tempo the $^6/_2$ regains its sway, though the accompaniment adds some material from the middle section. The mere 27 measures of no. 14 in D minor may be seen as in $^3/_2$, but I argue that, save for measures 13-15, $^6/_2$ works best; that one three-measure grouping combines factors from measures 1-3 and 4-6 to elide the middle section back to a reiteration of it, and thus keeps the momentum of the middle section from flagging. No. 15 in B-flat begins with a two-measure anacrusis, and thereafter alternates $^4/_1$ with $^4/_2$. No. 16 in F minor, of all the dances in the 1880 group, most resembles the 1869 dances in its length, in the number of differing subsections within it, and its several shifts of both tempo and meter, including $^4/_1$ and $^3/_1$ and a compressed $^2/_2$ at the end. Slow harmonic rhythm marks nos. 16-18, which explains why the notation of $^4/_1$ seems so pervasive in all of them. Fast harmonic-rhythmic change returns in no. 19 in B minor, $^4/_2$. The final two dances follow these patterns.

*   *   *   *

Most of the time, performers of this music seem unaware of these matters, and it does not seem to hurt them, for most of the factors I have spent time and space plotting out reveal themselves clearly to most good musicians who get beyond a first reading. Only no. 11 appears to defeat everyone. Some metric irregularities, on the other hand, occur in about half of these dances, and represent the sort of nuance that performers miss, to their own detriment as well as that of the pieces. That players rely on their musical intuition entirely, without resorting to analytical techniques, has been a complaint of theorists, critics, and scholars for generations. Their stubbornness parallels that of the general who refuses to rely on his intelligence-gatherers, or the doctor who, when his patient complains that it hurts when he raises his arm, advises him not to raise his arm. To give practical assistance to those performers willing to learn, the nature of some of these irregularities need to be reviewed in detail.

No 4 in F minor displays a nearly absolute regularity in both its $^4/_1$ and $^3/_1$ sections, once one realizes that each begins with an anacrusis, a single written measure in $^4/_1$ and two measures in $^3/_1$; in hypermetric terms these two would thus be a half-measure and full-measure. Each phrase makes up for the anacrusis in classic style, so no extra measures are felt, save for the expected change from $^4/_1$ to $^3/_1$ in both cases, a bit of extra time is taken by the composer to prepare the listener for the change (meas. 66-67, 108-09). In one spot, however, one might almost suspect Brahms of carelessness: in the shift of tempo from Poco sostenuto to Vivace at measures 32-33, the musical idea changes from an anacrustic to a powerful downbeat statement. To effect this change, the composer allows measure 32 to play out the end of the preceding material without any sense of upbeat function, and then simply bursts afresh into the new idea at measure 33. So far so good. But when the repeated statement from measures 33-48 returns to the opening material Brahms does not mark it *a tempo*, and in measure 49 immediately offers an upbeat measure to the return. The former action must be an oversight, for it is unthinkable that this material would fail to return to its original tempo. Every performance I have ever heard assumes this position unhesitatingly.

On the question of measure 49, however, the problem touches a nerve, even if a minuscule one. One requires two written measures to get one's bearings in a hypermetric environment in which both meters employ "1" as denominator. The way measure 49 begins seems premature or ill-considered. Performers generally improvise an extra measure of rest between measures 48 and 49, or take measure 49 very very slowly, hiding the extra time in a *rubato* greatcoat. Such a solution violates the spirit of so careful and calculating a musical architect as Brahms usually seems to be. This sort of irregularity might have been calculated by Brahms if he wished to obtain the rhythmic shifting effect we find in some of his fully composed works, in which an idea reiterates itself with all its accents shifted, and thus with an unexpected freshness. I have never been able to tell whether he meant such a shift, or simply failed to calculate the effect. Neither solution sounds just right to me. Perhaps, if performers would attempt to play it as written, I and a consensus of musical scholars could get used to it and finally make up our minds.

*   *   *   *

The irregularity in no. 2, on the other hand, seems carefully planned, both to upset one's expectations and to seem to set them nearly right again a few measures afterwards. The Vivo section from measures 49 to 84 continues the $^4/_1$ pattern established from the outset, merely accelerating it somewhat. Between measures 54 and 55, however, we feel there should have been two more $^2/_4$ measures to complete the pattern, most likely as follows:

Example 11.3. Hypothetical addition to Brahms, *Hungarian Dance* no. 2, between meas. 54-55.

Between measures 68 and 69, the phrase group repeats with the same omission, which further shifts the rhythmic pattern to come out not quite even. The Vivo as a whole works as follows: measures 49-54 is a truncated antecedent phrase, followed in measures 55-62 by a complete consequent phrase; measures 63-68 and 69-76 repeat this pattern up an octave, and then measures 77-84 climax and complete this section by repeating only the consequent. This last iteration brings the section closure, but with some sense of potential energy remaining to be spent—and I feel that Brahms spends it finally at the very end of the return of the opening in the added measures 104-07, where he causes a cadential extension to brake the momentum, not only of this final part but of the unused drive of its predecessor. The performer would be best advised to feel the entire cadential passage from measure 125 to 137 as:

1 & 2 & 3 & 3 & 3 & 4 & 1

Only then would the braking action and the sudden stop reach their full impact. Some performers might feel all this without notating the hypermeasures just above each measure, but Liszt did not think so. In several works in which he felt this to be a problem, he added the numbers himself as a guide; his most famous example, of course, is the *Mephisto Waltz* no. 1 in A major in which he made sure to include these in both the piano original and the orchestral versions. That has not stopped performers of each from grossly violating these markings, taking the opening sonorities as the down-beat of a four-measure phrase rather than the second beat, as clearly specified by the initial measure of rest marked "1" pointedly. Later numerical indications also tend to be ignored. Performers must take these matters much more lightly than questions of notes, tonalities, articulation, and/or dynamics, because they violate them so often, so cruelly, and with impunity from most critics. On matters of rhythm, the easy way out has been the road most travelled. For composers like Liszt, Schumann, Brahms, Musorgsky, Borodin, and Sibelius, this causes distortions that tend to cheapen the whole—and until such music makers learn how to deal with such relatively straightforward examples as these *Hungarian Dances* they can hardly hope to solve the deeply probing devices in complex art music.

No. 7 in A major maintains a *villanella*-like regularity at its Allegretto gait, save for a measure needed between 43 and 44. Brahms elides it away to allow his retransition to overlap into his return. Thus measure 44 functions both as the final measure of the preceding phrase and the first of the succeeding one. Interpreters generally intuit this place correctly. In no. 18, similar elisions take place in measure 14 and in the parallel place in measure 61, compensated for in measures 67-70 just before the final compression of measures 71-73. In this case, little sense of awareness can de detected in most performances. The alighting at the cadences in measure 15 and 62 never seems precipitous enough. At first I felt that the performers' musical intuitions led them to follow a $^4/_2$ meter instead of what seems to me the somewhat more solid $^4/_1$, and that was what caused them to miss the point of the irregularity, but that does not account for it, for one should notice the little bump even in $^4/_2$.

These Gypsy dances contain variant versions of a basic turn figure that seemed to be central to the style. We notice it most clearly in no. 2, measures 2, 6, 9, 12, 16, and often afterwards; in no. 4, measures 36, 40, 44, and 48; in no. 5, measures 36, 40, 44, and often afterwards; in no. 6, measures 2, 6, 10, and parallel places, as well as another type in measures 42, 79, 100, and 121; in no. 7 the turn becomes the primary material from measure 1 to 50; in no. 8 it appears in measures 44, 64, and parallel places; in no. 9 it again becomes the primary idea, manifest in measures 1-2 and much of the time thereafter. Most interesting in this context, the turn becomes the motive for one of Brahms's most dramatic rhythmic irregularities in no. 15, in B-flat major, and a large duple meter, alternating between $^4/_1$ in its outer Allegretto grazioso sections, and $^4/_2$ in the contrasting middle section in B-flat minor. One version of the turn figure appears in measure 19, gets varied in measure 27, and generates main melodic material. A second turn figure appears in measures 22 and 30, and in the usual manner of the Romany fiddlers, merely cadences; in that role, it almost disappears into the line, hardly noticeable amidst all the flashy motivic ideas offered here. At measures 93-97, the very last time we hear both turn figures, the one from measure 19 achieves a headlong plunging effect in measure 93, while the one from measure 22 gets enlarged and delayed in measures 96-97 after an extension in measure 95, of the syncopated figure that sets it up. Players usually play all the notes and rhythms right, and bring out the dramatic effect, heightened by the composer's notation of a *ritenuto* from the second half of measure 95 all the way through measure 101, but they seem to miss the inner qualities of it. It seems to me that this results from not plotting out the hypermeter, which reveals the nature of the several alterations in tempo, grouping, and cadential function most clearly. The return to the main tempo in the closing progression in measures 102-03 never seems to fall quickly enough, like the guillotine stroke it truly is.

*   *   *   *

Elisions, insertions, augmentations, diminuitions, and final compressions mark many of these dances. They seem almost artless here, compared to the way Brahms employs them in works of fluid meter, such as the song "Agnes," op. 59, no. 5, where the $^3/_4$, $^2/_4$ meter adds up to unpredictable shifting combinations of five and seven beats, the pattern of which finally emerges near the end, or the Andante grazioso third movement of the Piano Trio, op. 101, in which two different sets of odd meters keep the flow roiling and uncertain. The groupings become so experimental in late works that they even include five as a primary hypermeter, for almost every measure of op. 117, no. 3, in C-sharp minor, and for the main material of op. 119, no. 4 in E-flat major. I tend to think that what attracted Brahms to the "Chorale St. Antoni" of his op. 56 *Variations on a Theme by Haydn* was its five-measure thematic grouping, alternating with a four-measure groupings in its B section. At both metric and hypermetric levels, Brahms groped for new mechanisms of propulsion, steering, braking, and lift.

These *Hungarian Dances* helped him find his way, though he allowed himself greatest liberties in works with opus numbers. The brilliant "Rondo alla zingarese" from op. 25 seems most relevant to this discussion, being one of his earliest essays in Gypsy rhythms, as well as one of his most complex. Its patterns of organization shift, twist, and achieve ambiguity with far more richness than in any five of the *Hungarian Dances* put together. A table of the movement seems obligatory (see table 11.1). The interaction of the $^6/_2$ with the $^3/_1$ constitutes a hypermetric hemiola, most notably between measures 323 and 334, though dramatically important in the first 172 measures as well. These shifting meters rarely get played intelligently, and the tricky places between measures 256 and 322 tend to sound directionless and, at best ambiguous; at worst, confused. Mixing Gypsy rhythmic patterns with his sense of Teutonic structure, Brahms creates anomalous places that hide behind a simple $^2/_4$ meter, in the finale of op. 25, as well as throughout the *Hungarian Dances*.

Table 11.1

Outline of Brahms, Quartet for Piano and Strings, op. 25, movement 4

Inclusive measures	Total measures	Hypermetric pattern	Number of groups	Irregular places by measures number
1–30	30	6/2	five	——
31–66	36	6/2	five	37–39, 52–54
67–79	13	6/2	two	79
80–91	12	3/1	two repeated	——
92–115	24	3/1	four repeated	*rit.* 102–03
116–84	33	6/2	five	146–48
149–54	6	3/1	one	——
155–72	18	6/2	three repeated	——
173–205	33	4/2	four plus four, at repeated	195
206–09	24	4/2	seven	——
230–37	8	4/1	one	——
238–55	18	6/2	three	——
256–92	37	6/2	five	262–64, 277–79, 292
293	1	free cadenza ——————————————————		
294–322	29	4/2	six	301, 311–12, 321–22
323–38	6	6/2	one	——
329–34	6	3/1	one	——
355–62	28	4/2	seven	——
363–83	21	6/2	three	381–83
384–89	6	3/1	one	——
390–405	16	4/2	four	——

The other movement famous for folding in Gypsy ingredients, the Finale of the Piano Concerto no. 2, op. 83, in B-flat major, marked, as so many of the movements of this type seem to be, Allegretto grazioso, can be botched in performance if one flags in vigilance. In this case, the performer has tested his stamina through three long, difficult movements, each a bit less weighty than its predecessor. This Finale, lightest of all, can sound insipid and unworthy of the whole if one does not articulate all its special features precisely. The theme notable for its Gypsy qualities enters in measure 65, and recurs in the usual ways and places. Unlike the other Gypsy movements, this one maintains a steady, serene *Vierhebigkeit* throughout its 488 measures, save for a few anomalies, mostly two-measure extensions or elisions, with little ability or propensity to deflect the train from its track. The opening pace of ♩ = 104 maintains itself, save for a brief and slight ritard in measures 247-51, changing only in the coda beginning in measure 377 to ♩ = 138, *un poco più presto*. The motivic material changes both often and suddenly, so the pianist and conductor are hard pressed to keep that easy, steady pace throughout the first 376 measures; this, however, differs greatly from the many metric patterns and irregularities of the other Gypsy movements.

In fact, Brahms seemed to take the greatest number of risks in the smallest time frame in op. 25, spread these out somewhat in the *Hungarian Dances*, and dilute them most in the late works, particularly the Gypsy improvisations by the clarinet soloist in the second movement of the Quintet for clarinet and strings, op. 115, in B minor. The many metric-rhythmic problems of that movement stem entirely from Brahms's usual syncopations, hemiolas, overlappings, 2 vs. 3 accompanying figures— in other words, his personal mannerisms irrespective of Gypsy influence factors. He works to make the irregularities as logical as they are expressive, as tightly controlled as his formal mastery will allow.

Joseph Joachim's "Hungarian" Violin Concerto tends to sound wooden to our ears, but it exerted a considerable influence upon young Brahms as he entered into the arena of Gypsy music. For Brahms, the Romany influence added a special spice to much of his work, and seems to have helped him think out many, if not most, of the rhythmic innovations that helped lead concert music out of its rhythmically moribund condition. The dance of the prototypical Gypsy, constantly striving to keep himself free of the constraints and manners of Western society, while falling into those special kinds of ethnic pattern that both enslave and liberate at the same time, fascinated many serious composers since the fad for Gypsy music began, some eight-score years ago. Pablo de Sarasate, Manuel de Falla, Frederick Delius, even Johann Strauss, Jr., all succumbed to its magic. Perhaps the greatest single masterpiece devoted to expressing the simultaneous plight and glory of the Gypsy may be Maurice Ravel's *Tzigane*, but we all find ourselves returning again and again to these *Hungarian Dances* as models for every later attempt to capture that style, as well as for lessons in control of mixed, compound, or complex rhythms and meters.

*   *   *   *

Postscript

Of all the musical scholars I have known, the dedicatee of this volume may be the most accomplished, bold, unbridled dancer. Whenever he danced, he thought of nothing else. Had I attempted so uninhibited a turn on the floor, I would have looked like a prancing pygmy pachyderm. I have never seen him cavort in the Romany mode, but have little doubt that he could do so with his startling grace and elan. Of his lack of shame on the dance floor, I have always been enormously envious. This essay on rhythm was written with a vision of him leaping on the large table in Boston University's Mugar 213 (alas, no longer a classroom), to demonstrate a pavan or galliard in his inimitable manner. What more fitting tribute could I offer than a stylized dance before my computer screen? It may not be Astaire and his mop, but they also serve who only stand and wait.

CHAPTER 12

Stravinsky's "Lyke-Wake Dirge" Revisited: A Possible Source

D. Stephen Cushman

This report is a preliminary result of evidence that the "Lyke-Wake Dirge" of Stravinsky's *Cantata*[1] may have linkage to another work of identical title and text appearing in a late nineteenth-century collection of Scottish song[2] and that the proposed prototype, a "Lyke-Wake Dirge" setting by Sir Harold Edwin Boulton (1859-1935) may indeed support Robert Craft's informally-expressed feeling that Scottish influences existed in Stravinsky's setting of the "Dirge."[3] If such a linkage is defensible, then again a situation comes up that connects a distinct area of musical literature to the composer's own creative process and his personal tendency to draw on prototypes that are in some way suitable to the new context—in Richard Taruskin's words, "aptness to the scenario."[4]

Since much of the present proposals are results of a basically inductive method of melodic study and contextual comparison (a method discussed in Taruskin's article, and which is also discussed extensively in two earlier studies of my own),[5] it is probably desirable only to point out here that main criteria for comparative study of the Stravinsky and Boulton dirges are limited to matters of melodic

---

[1] *Cantata for Soprano, Tenor, Female Chorus, and a Small Instrumental Ensemble* (New York: Boosey and Hawkes, 1952).

[2] A. C. MacLeod and Harold Boulton, eds., *Songs from the North, Gathered Together from the Highlands and Lowlands of Scotland* (London: J. B. Cramer and Co., n.d.). Discussion of several editions of this collection, together with full title and the problem of dating, is treated in the main text of this essay.

[3] Robert Craft, *Stravinsky: Chronicle of a Friendship, 1948-1971* (New York: Knopf, 1972), 43. In this context (originally a dinner conversation), W. H. Auden had been present, giving descriptive definitions of the terms "Whinney-muir" and "Brig o'Dread" to Craft and Stravinsky. Stravinsky had replied that "he had not thought of the 'Lyke Wake Dirge' as Scottish." Craft's opinion: "It seems to me that the accompaniment has a Scottish drone." On the other hand, Ricercar II of the *Cantata* is compared with the "Scotch snap" rhythmic figuration by Henry Cowell in an early review of the work, in *Musical Quarterly* 39, no. 2 (April 1953): 253.

[4] Richard Taruskin, "Russian Folk Melodies in *The Rite of Spring*," *Journal of the American Musicological Society* 33, no. 3 (fall 1980): 509.

[5] David Stephen Cushman, "Joseph Haydn's Melodic Materials: An Exploratory Introduction to the Primary and Secondary Sources, Together with an Analytical Catalogue and Tables of Proposed Melodic Correspondence and/or Variance" (Ph.D. diss., Boston University, 1973). A paper on aspects of the findings was also prepared as a brief presentation for a round table in Washington, 1975, published in *Haydn Studies: Proceedings of the International Haydn Conference*, ed. Jens Peter Larsen, Howard Serwer, and James Webster (New York: Norton, 1981), 377-81.

morphology and relations between rhythm, range, or underlying modal qualities. Secondly, it has been necessary to avoid too-insistent dependence on direct, "literal" resemblance, where Stravinsky's own methods tend toward rhythmic and intervallic reworkings of models. What concerns us instead is evidence of a generic, generalized source—one that comprises a generative stimulus for assimilation, transformation, and development, but where evidence remains of a retained character and context of the original model.

As it turns out, Stravinsky appears to have derived the main material of the "Lyke-Wake Dirge" from a single internal section in Boulton's setting—namely, the refrain "Ev'rie nighte and alle." Here we see utilization of what is essentially a sectional entity, but one which also functions as the second quadrant of a single phrase that divides into halves—and both halves of which are subdivided into a sole statement of text together with a four-part choral response on alternating segments of the refrain. But it is the evidence of longer-range development of pitch and rhythmic materials in Stravinsky that begins to emerge as an evolution of shape-process beyond that of the "Lyke-Wake Dirge" itself, "abstracted," so to speak (in William Austin's words), outward into subsequent *Cantata* segments such as both Ricercar I and II.[6] That subsequently raises the question whether or not we may regard the "Lyke-Wake Dirge" as the generative source for the *Cantata* as a whole. The duet "Westron Wind" is more difficult to assess in this regard, for any degrees of relationship appear to be much more generalized, more dependent on strategic uses of syncopation, ostinato patterns that are only approximately consistent to materials elsewhere. There is some justification in regarding this piece as an element of genuine contrast within the *Cantata*. However, any unifying process in the work as a whole (apart from the Prelude/Interlude/Postlude format of the Dirge itself) again raises the question of the degree to which Stravinsky's assimilations are to be appreciated for their possible metaphorical implications—especially if there is any evidence of "doctrinal or psychological symbol" present in the usage. If anything, a look at the *Cantata* as a whole seems to reaffirm the view that Stravinsky's assimilations serve primarily as musical organizing factors, and that such organization becomes its own commentary, as it were, on the allusions to style and/or content borrowed from without.

Songs of the North came into my hands entirely fortuitously, as part of a larger group of materials (primarily American popular sheet music) that had been donated to Wheaton College, and which required a general sorting-out and evaluation. Full reading of the title-page is as follows:

> Songs of the North, Vol. I, gathered together from the Highlands and Lowlands of Scotland. Edited by A. C. MacLeod and Harold Boulton. The Music arranged by Malcolm Lawson. Twenty-third Edition. London, J. B. Cramer and Co., Ltd.; Simpkin, Marshall, Hamilton, Kent and Co., Ltd. New York, Edward Schuberth and Co., 11 E. 22nd St.[7]

One feature appears within vol. 1 of the 23rd edition: the initials "HB" and "ML" (Boulton, Lawson) are autographed in bluish-black ink on the blank leaf covering the title-page. Since there is no printed numbering or verbal statement to indicate a limited edition, it is likely that this autographed copy was either part of a given number of volumes that had been initialled by the arrangers/editors, or was in the possession of someone who had had personal contact with these individuals. Other features of vol. 1 include the frontispiece engraving of "Proud Maisie" (by Frederic Sandys), depicting the girl

---

[6] William W. Austin, *Music in the Twentieth Century, from Debussy through Stravinsky* (New York: Norton, 1966), 526.

[7] During the co-editorship of MacLeod and Boulton, *Songs of the North* was published as a 3-volume collection, although it is 2 volumes, with continued use of Malcolm Lawson as arranger, in Thomas R. Nardone, ed., *Classical Vocal Music in Print* (Philadelphia: Musicdata, 1976), no. A-875.

in the poem (song no. 9) by Sir Walter Scott.[8] There is also a dedicatory page: "Dedicated by Gracious Permission to Her Majesty The Queen" (most likely Queen Victoria). Measurements of the clothbound volume are 32 x 25 cm, and a title vignette is included. The color of the covering is maroon-brown, while an embossment of a stylized thistle within a rectangle appears in the lower half of the front cover. Absence of dating makes it difficult to place the 23rd edition into a perspective relative to both earlier and late editions of the collection. On the other hand, the paper-quality and type of this edition is believed by William Favata (Special Collections, Wheaton College Library) to have occurred late in the nineteenth century (ca. 1890-95). The dedication seems to support this view, if only because of the categorical nature of the wording—in other words, the implicit fact that the British queens between Victoria and Elizabeth II were not ruling monarchs.

There are two prefaces. The first, to the edition itself, states a basic objective: to "set Scottish [Lowland] and Highland songs . . . not familiar for the most part to the many enthusiastic admirers of the minstrelsy of Scotland." Settings are largely for solo voice with piano accompaniment, and are presented as settings of materials that were earlier intended for harp, pipe, or violin. Thus, the accompaniments are arrangements largely intended for private, parlor usage, with Boulton and Lawson predominating as arrangers of the settings. Two or three melodies of the 46 songs in the volume are newly-composed. In a few other instances the editors have set Highland melodies to texts of Lowland origin, where Lowland tunes were lacking—a practice cited as precedented by Robert Burns. The second preface is a repeat of that to the second edition, and mentions the first edition, with its illustrations and designation "edition deluxe."

The fifteenth song is the main object of our study. The full title reads: "A Lyke Wake Dirge, or chant sung by those watching over a corpse."[9] The title appears alone on page 61, and the music, with shortened/re-ordered text underlay, on the next two pages. The full nine stanzas of the Dirge are printed in order, however, on page 64.[10]

Sir Harold Edwin Boulton (1859-1935) was the Second Baronet of the Boulton Family of Copped Hall, Camberley (Surrey), and was educated at Harrow and at Balliol College, Oxford. By the year of his death *Who's Who* lists a comprehensive review of Boulton's society memberships and appointments: Knight of Justice of the Order of St. John of Jerusalem in England, and Captain of the Queen's Own Cameron Highlanders, Militia.[11] He was in the Rough Riders (1914-17) and held several administrative

---

[8] Cited in *Who's Who* (London: A. and C. Black, 1935), 345.

[9] The Stravinsky setting, obviously, does not include the subtitle.

[10] The anonymous north England source for "A Lyke Wake Dirge" is found in Sir Walter Scott, *Minstrelsy of the Scottish Border* (1802), later edited by T. F. Henderson, 4 vols. (Edinburgh: W. Blackwood, 1902; New York: Thomas Crowell, 1931, 1 vol. in 3 parts), part 2, p. 398, where Scott had originally included the "Dirge" under the heading of "Romantic Ballads." Stravinsky's source for the "Dirge" was *The New Oxford Book of English Verse, 1250-1950*, ed. Helen Louise Gardner (New York: Oxford University Press, 1972), no. 361. On the other hand, sources for the other texts in the *Cantata* (also in ibid.) list for "The Maiden's Came" (originally "The Bridal Morn") British Library, Harley Ms. 7578; for "Westron Wind," British Library, Roy. App. Ms. 58. Of the nine stanzas in the "Lyke Wake Dirge," nos. 1 and 9 are the same, and there is evidence that a stanza originally dealing with imagery and action concerning "Brig o' Dread" is missing between the present stanzas 5 and 6. "Whinny-muir" is the gorse-moor in which the dead were punished by thorns for ungenerous behavior in life (root: "whin/ whyn" for gorse and/or briars in Scottish dialect and in north England border areas). Origins of the imagery "Brig o' Dread" are also discussed in Scott's *Minstrelsy*, 398-400, where the image of a bar of hot iron, suspended over a chasm between Heaven and Hell, is traced to Islamic sources. See also James Orchard Halliwell-Phillips, *A Dictionary of Archaic and Provincial Words* (London: Routledge, 1924), and the *Oxford English Dictionary*. The term "lyke wake" ("late-wake" or "night-watch") is traceable to Chaucer's *Knight's Tale*, line 2100.

[11] *Who's Who*, ibid. See also *Burke's Genealogical and Heraldic History of the Peerage, Baronetage and Knightage*, 105th ed., ed. Peter Townend (London: Burke's Peerage, 1970), 318-19.

positions relative to hospitals, nursing associations, and working-men's social clubs. Boulton's musical contributions seem to have centered primarily on administrative activities and songwriting/editing of materials with strong regional or patriotic allusion. He was president of the Scottish Literature and Song Association, Aberdeen (1929), and was director of the Royal Academy of Music (1931). Virtually all references to Boulton list his "Skye Boat-Song" (song no. 18) and "Glorious Devon," while his other collections included *Twelve Lyrics*, *Our National Songs*, and *Songs of the Four Nations*.

*   *   *   *

Stravinsky's apparent incorporation of Boulton's "Lyke-Wake Dirge" is a process of some complexity—one in which the model shows a basically 3-layered method of reworking. The first layer can be described as the single auxiliary figure *e′ d′ e′* set to "Ev-rie nights," which in Stravinsky really constitutes a genuinely gestural figure, basic to both the rhythmic character of the "Dirge," and also to Ricercar I (exx. 12.1-12.2). In a larger sense, the limited intervallic range both of the Boulton model and the overall ambitus of the soprano line of the Stravinsky "Dirge" is reflected in the

Example 12.1. Boulton, "A Lyke Wake Dirge," soprano, meas. 5-6.

Ev'   rie nighte and   alle.

Example 12.2. Stravinsky, *Cantata*, soprano:

a. Verse 1, meas. 1-7.

b. Verse 1, meas. 8-14.

c. Verse 4, meas. 25-31.

d. Same.

range-limits and stepwise character of the 11-note series in Ricercar II. In the micro sense this correspondence acts as an interlocked assortment of auxiliary-note groupings, with potentials for many options in internal, larger regroupings. Indeed, this possibility is realized as another layer of Stravinsky's structuring of the "Dirge" (ex. 12.3), described below. In the first layer, however, the figure appears primarily either as initial gesture (ex. 12.2a), or as internal (and rhythmically manipulated) phraseological connective-tissue and/or caesura (ex. 12.2b-c). This auxiliary-note layer is motivic to much of the *Cantata*, becoming part of overall rhythmic growth in Ricercar I (ex. 12.4), including incorporation into both long and short-range resolutions from a pivotal *c´* within the wider ambitus of a 3rd and 4th. The ritornello of Ricercar II also begins with this gesture. In a more remote fashion the canonic pitch series also embeds it, as suggested above.

Example 12.3. Stravinsky, *Cantata*, verse 1, soprano:

a. Meas. 8-11.

b. Same.

c. Meas. 11-14.

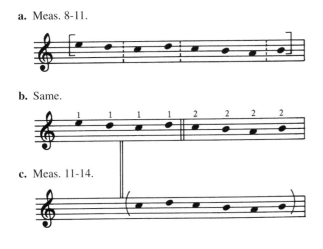

Example 12.4. Stravinsky, *Cantata*, Ricercare I, flute 1:

a. Meas. 1-3.

b. Meas. 2-4.

c. Meas. 50-53.

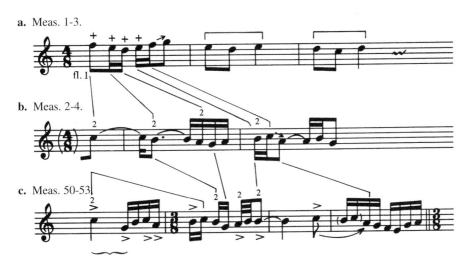

Stravinsky's second layer of incorporation emerges as a process of pitch subgrouping into three interactive units, as they cumulatively unfold within the "Dirge" stanza. Referring to the first verse, the basic process is visible in measures 8-14, where skeletal features of the model appear at measures 8-11; the remaining function as an extension of measures 9-11 (ex. 12.3a). An apparent dual grouping of 4 notes, *e′ d′ c′ d′* and *c′ b a b*, is differentiated in ex. 12.3b by numbers 1 and 2 as groups of equivalent intervallic nature, of separate development. The third unit incorporates elements of both groups 1 and 2 (see parentheses, ex. 12.3c). Although it may be argued that the *d′* found in group 1 also appears in group 2 (and that hence meas. 9-11 are variantly-repeated in meas. 12-14), the corresponding *d′* in measure 9 possesses much more resolutionary force as rhythmic extension of the opening gesture than the upper auxiliary *d′* found in measure 12. (That is to say: in a micro sense the tones *c′ b a b* of measures 10-11 comprise prefiguration of the entire extension of 11-14.) Looked at interactively, all three units tend to add ambiguity—or both "forward and retroactive" manner—to the way the ear assimilates the undulating quality of this line.

Evolution of ex. 12.2b from 12.2a and the near-parallel features of ex. 12.2c, verse 4, postlude are quite apparent. Example 12.2d is a functional reduction of 12.2c to primary linear motion in order to suggest proximity to Boulton's model. Variances in either source are given in reduced note-heads. If there is noteworthy difference, it is the *c′* found in ex. 12.2b (meas. 11), following the dotted quarter. In Boulton, this is actually the tone of cadential resolution, whereas Stravinsky uses it as a rhythmic conjunction (syncopated) for phraseological extension.

The third unit of incorporation is a generalized stretching of the model into the initial four measures of the "Dirge"'s stanzas (and thus indirectly the three-measure extension). Secondly, it is possibly the source of the 11-note series of Ricercar II.

It is particularly interesting that this latter usage appears as it does at the very outset of Ricercar II, entirely in 32nd-note values. Note-against-note action of the three instruments and the dynamic level *forte* suggest a certain impartial, uninflected quality to this series-statement. There is an extra tone: cadential resolution on C (via octave displacement) that becomes correspondent to the original model. The fact that pitches *d′-e′* appear twice tends to enhance the function of *d′* as a directional pivot. Motion both above and below *d′* is equidistant—although rhythmically displaced—and recalls a somewhat analogous usage of *d′* as a pitch in the model. (In the latter, however, it is a tone for auxiliary and accented-passing motion.)

There is another implication, however, inherent in the relative clarity of this introduction to Ricercar II. It is the suggestion that, even as the bracketed auxiliary-figure at measure 1 of Stravinsky's "Lyke-Wake Dirge" is proleptic to extensive development of the same figure along contoural/rhythmic lines in the *Cantata* as a whole, so the "shape aspects" of the "Dirge" model appearing in Stravinsky's setting are (at least aesthetically) proleptic to the essentially unfettered statement commencing Ricercar II. If this is so, it places the "Sacred History" as centerpiece of the *Cantata* by virtue of motivic development/transformation that is also worked out elsewhere. The figural and rhythmic ornamentings that interlace both cantus and canons become a kind of saturative, Franco Flemish-reminiscent *cantus-firmus* treatment that adds specific corroboration to Heinrich Lindlar's early proposal that the songs "are all deeply interrelated" in the sense of having the "same basic style."[12] In brief, I propose that the songs indeed have the same basic source, and that the source's greatest significance lies in the multi-functional way in which it has been abstracted and re-expressed across individual *Cantata* sections.

---

[12] Heinrich Lindlar, "Igor Strawinsky: 'Cantata'," *Tempo* 27 (spring 1953): 29-30.

Example 12.5. Stravinsky, *Cantata*, Ricercare II, flute 1:

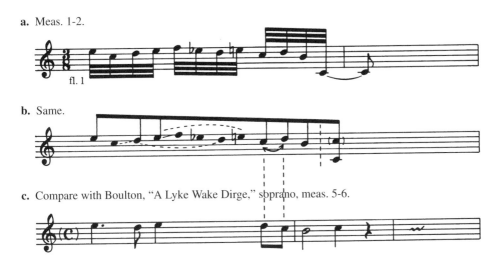

a. Meas. 1-2.

fl. 1

b. Same.

c. Compare with Boulton, "A Lyke Wake Dirge," soprano, meas. 5-6.

Ricercar I, for example, does not present a contextual wholeness of the model. Instead, it separates out the 4-note unit designated 1, 2 (ex. 12.3b) for the instrumental outset (ex. 12.4a), and then displaces it in ornamented augmentation into the internal portion of the soprano's first phrase (ex. 12.4b) and also into the soprano's seemingly-new material at measure 50 (ex. 12.4c). It is a process of abstraction that is ultimately derived from phraseological midpoints or endings in Stravinsky's "Dirge," but by its consistent reworking becomes the unifying base for both "Dirge" and both Ricercars alike.

There are a few questions that remain basically unanswered. Is there, for example, any relation between the final double cadence of the Stravinsky "Dirge," and the rising contour of Boulton's final cadence? (The latter has modal suggestions that emerge, if the accompaniment is temporarily removed.) I feel that such a relation is too remote—or abstracted—to be evaluated with assurance. Still, one might take into account the function of d' as a goal of ascending contour in Stravinsky's vocal cadences to each of the four "Dirge" settings. Settings 1-3 employ the soprano line (given in ex. 12.6b), while the verse 4 cadence alters the contour to include the figural drop of $a'\ b'\ g'$ preceding

Example 12.6. Stravinsky, *Cantata*, verses 1-3:

a. Soprano, meas. 8-10.

And Christe   re-ceive   thy   saule.

b. Soprano, meas. 19-22.

And   Christe re - ceive   thye   saule.

Continued

Example 12.6.—*Continued*

c. Soprano, meas. 19-22 and 36-39.

and   Christe re - ceive thye   saule.   and   Christe re - ceive   thy   saule.

d. Soprano and reduced accompaniment, meas. 19-26.

resolution on *d´´* (ex. 12.6c). As an example, verse 1 uses *d´* both as its own tonic and as a fifth, relative to measures 21-22 pull in the tenor range toward *g* (English horn); but also toward C as the governing tonal center within a trifocal referencing of tones (ex. 12.6d). Are there analogies to a "5th scale-degree resolution," as it is (tonally) expressed in Boulton? At best, this must remain only speculative. As another question: what actual contact might Stravinsky have had with *Songs of the North*? And with what particular edition? Direct response to this pair of questions would best lie in the hands of those who have had working knowledge of Stravinsky's personal library—access which I do not possess. Yet it is a question needing to be posed, and deserving of a qualified response. Again: why is it that Stravinsky, with all of his assimilations or allusions, from Tchaikovsky to Lanner, to Pergolesi, to Bach and Machaut, uses in this instance a source from which he also possesses identical title? As an incorporation (i.e., assuming its defensibility), it is quite unusual in a lifetime practice where "contextual aptness" between model and reworking is seen to be consistently paired by Stravinsky, but where "title-aptness" is much less of an issue. In any event, to have a parallel title is an instance of a "practice of aptness" being carried an extra degree—if only as evidence of a respect on Stravinsky's part for a merger of content and intent, or for a merging of the musical organization with the larger metaphorical surroundings.

CHAPTER 13

"Diabolus triumphans": Stravinsky's Histoire du soldat in Weimar and Nazi Germany

Joan Evans

Stravinsky's *Histoire du soldat* owes its earliest triumphs not to Switzerland, where it was composed and given its first performance, or to France, where Stravinsky was shortly to make his home, but to Germany. As is well known, the outbreak of Spanish influenza following the premiere in Lausanne on 28 September 1918 forced the cancellation of a planned tour; thus the premiere remained for nearly five years the only staged performance.

The German premiere of *Histoire*, which took place on 20 June 1923 in Frankfurt's Schauspielhaus, marks the second production of the work.[1] It was conducted by Hermann Scherchen, who was the driving force behind the earliest German productions. Werner Reinhart, Stravinsky's Swiss patron (and a friend of Scherchen), reported to the composer that the premiere had been a "tremendous success" and that the public was "enthralled." The production had been "meticulously prepared," the music was "beautifully rendered" by Scherchen, the acting "truly good," and the musicians "excellent"—especially the violinist, the young Paul Hindemith.[2] Following the Frankfurt premiere, Scherchen conducted successful performances of *Histoire* in several other German cities. The most notable of these was given by the Frankfurt performers on 19 August 1923 in Weimar, during a festival of modern art at the Bauhaus. Stravinsky attended the performance and was favorably impressed by Scherchen's conducting.[3] He was seated next to Busoni, who was so moved by the work that he and his wife "cried real tears."[4]

Scherchen's performances were definitive for the acceptance of *Histoire* in Germany, as well as in the rest of Europe. By 1930 the work had been staged in theaters in over one hundred European cities,

---

[1] *Histoire* had undergone substantial revisions after its 1918 premiere, however, while further revisions were made following the early German performances. See Robert Craft, "*Histoire du soldat:* The Musical Revisions, the Sketches, and the Evolution of the Libretto," in *Stravinsky: Selected Correspondence*, vol. 3, ed. Craft (New York: Knopf, 1985), 461-74 (Appendix A).

[2] Werner Reinhart to Stravinsky, 26 June 1923; ibid., 148. See also Reinhart's letters of May 25 and June 6; ibid., 145-47. Reinhart was less impressed with the dancer, who, he wrote on August 10, "needs instruction concerning your intentions" (ibid., 149). See also Peter Sulzer, *Zehn Komponisten um Werner Reinhart*, vol. 1 (Winterthur: Stadtbibliothek, 1979), 30-38.

[3] Stravinsky to Ernest Ansermet, 9 September 1923; *Stravinsky: Selected Correspondence*, vol. 1 (1982), 170.

[4] Ibid., 171. Busoni's reaction to *Histoire* may have influenced Stravinsky's verdict on that composer's *Fünf kurze Stücke zur Pflege des polyphonischen Spiels*, performed at the festival by pianist Egon Petrie ("not bad at all"); Hindemith's "interminable" *Marienleben*, on the other hand, "bored me a great deal" (ibid.).

and numerous concert performances had taken place.[5] New productions continued to appear in Germany after 1930, despite the growing opposition to modern music fueled by the increasingly troubled economic and political situation. By 30 January 1933, when Adolph Hitler was named Chancellor, theater audiences in at least thirty-five German cities large and small had been introduced to the work.[6]

In his *Chroniques de ma vie* of 1935, Stravinsky recalled the invigorating atmosphere of the Weimar years. "In contrast with the pre-war custodians of old dogmas," he wrote, "a fresh public joyfully and gratefully accepted the new manifestations of contemporary art."[7] But despite (or because of) this heady atmosphere, many "new manifestations" had to contend with strong opposition. *Histoire*, in particular, was a favorite target of the conservatives. Already in December 1924, following Otto Klemperer's Wiesbaden premiere, local critics decried the work as "a box of tricks" and pronounced it—significantly, in light of future events—"a symptom of cultural decline," while early in the new year a Hamburg Opera production had to be abandoned because of vociferous opposition.[8]

Opposition to modernist art (and to the Weimar "system" that fostered it) became increasingly vocal after the National Socialists achieved their first major victory in the Reichstag elections of September 1930. Stravinsky was a convenient target. Though he himself repeatedly (and heatedly) rejected the modernist label, he was considered by friend and foe alike to be the leading modernist composer. "One says 'Stravinsky' and means modern music," observed a critic in 1932, "or one speaks of cacophony, soul-lessness and anarchy and means Stravinsky."[9] Added to this, the fact that Stravinsky was Russian raised the specter of communism. Furthermore, he had adopted as his second homeland Germany's traditional enemy, France, and he was rumored to be Jewish.[10] Thus Stravinsky provided a lightning rod for the favorite (and largely synonymous) epithets of the anti-modernists: "atonal," "Bolshevist," "international," and "Jewish." In this environment *Histoire du soldat*, more than any other work by Stravinsky, assumed the character of a *bête noire*, a reputation it was to maintain throughout the Nazi period.

*   *   *   *

What was it about *Histoire* that so aroused the ire of the anti-modernists? The answer lies partly in the music (and the plot), but, more importantly, in the theatrical conception that governs the work. Also of crucial significance were ideological issues: the cultural, political, and racial factors that became increasingly important during the final years of the Weimar Republic.

---

[5] Michael Trapp, *Studien zu Strawinskys "Geschichte vom Soldaten" (1918): Zur Idee und Wirkung des Musiktheaters der 1920er Jahre* (Regensburg: Gustav Bosse, 1978), 163-64.

[6] These included Aachen, Baden-Baden, Barmen-Elberfeld, Berlin-Charlottenburg, Bremen, Breslau, Cologne, Danzig, Darmstadt, Dessau, Dresden, Düsseldorf, Essen, Frankfurt am Main, Gera, Hagen, Hamburg, Heidelberg, Karlsruhe, Kassel, Koburg, Königsberg, Lübeck, Magdeburg, Mainz, Munich-Gladbach, Münster, Nuremberg, Osnabrück, Oldenburg, Plauen, Rostock, Stettin, Weimar, and Wiesbaden. This information is taken from Trapp, 163, and from royalty statements received by the composer from B. Schott's Söhne, Mainz (Stravinsky Collection, Paul Sacher Stiftung, Basel).

[7] *Igor Stravinsky: An Autobiography* (New York: Norton, 1962), 138.

[8] Peter Heyworth, *Otto Klemperer: His Life and Times*, vol. 1: *1885-1933* (Cambridge: Cambridge University Press, 1983), 203.

[9] "Sn.," "Strawinsky im Königsberger Sinfoniekonzert," *Ostpreußische Zeitung*, 5 November 1932. Stravinsky's reply to a Spanish interviewer in 1928 provides a typical example of his aversion to the "modernist" label. To the question "Are you pleased to be called 'modern'?" the composer replied, "No, never that!" See *Igor and Vera Stravinsky: A Photograph Album*, ed. Robert Craft (New York: Thames and Hudson, 1982), 18.

[10] After Klemperer's German premiere of *Oedipus Rex* in Berlin in 1928, the stridently nationalist critic Paul Zschorlich referred to the composer as "Isidor—sorry, Igor—Stravinsky"; quoted in Heyworth, 264.

Not surprisingly, Stravinsky's use of jazz rhythms (or, more precisely, ragtime rhythms) drew fire from nationalists long engaged in a bitter struggle against jazz, this "degenerate" and "un-German" music. *Histoire* thus formed an unholy trio with Ernst Krenek's *Jonny spielt auf* and Kurt Weill's *Dreigroschenoper*. Nationalists also launched sallies against Stravinsky's parodistic use, in his "Cubist" chorale, of "Ein' feste Burg," that most beloved of Lutheran hymns: a "shameless travesty," wrote Munich's Wilhelm Zentner, that "should have been forbidden by both artistic taste and human delicacy."[11] The plot of *Histoire* also came under attack. It is, of course, based on the ancient Faust theme, in which man sells his soul to the devil in return for knowledge or wealth. But in the version of the tale that Stravinsky used, there is no redemption for the hapless hero. The resolution of the plot is utterly pessimistic: "man falls with no hope of reprieve; he is trapped and torn to pieces by the evil forces which gather about him."[12] The *Zeitschrift für Musik*, that venerable mouthpiece for conservative and nationalist sentiments, took particular issue with this ending. "The story of the deceived devil and the triumph of good is stood on its head," complained a Dresden critic. "Diabolus triumphans."[13]

To conservative German audiences accustomed to naturalistic theater, *Histoire* provided a visual as well as an aural affront. Stravinsky's conception of theater was diametrically opposed to the Wagnerian ideal, and for many Germans this seemed a provocation designed "to desecrate the old gods."[14] Stravinsky makes no attempt in the stage works of his "Russian" period to fuse the various musical, poetic, and theatrical elements into a unified *Gesamtkunstwerk*. The elements remain distinct, each fulfilling its purpose more or less independently of the other. Although Stravinsky never acknowledged the influence, the impetus for this approach must surely have been the great Russian stage director Vsevolod Meyerhold, whose early experimental productions took place in St. Petersburg during the years of Stravinsky's early adulthood, and whose ideas are reflected in most of Stravinsky's theatrical works before *Oedipus Rex*.[15] The most striking characteristics of *Histoire*, its "mixture of mime, dance and speech, its blend of fun and morality and its device of the Narrator figure who steps into and out of the action: these are purely Meyerholdian conceptions."[16]

In Weimar Germany, Stravinsky's pioneering work of musical theater was considered to have foreshadowed the theatrical innovations of Bertolt Brecht. The musical and dramatic autonomy of *Histoire*, the stark simplicity of its staging, the use of a narrator, the drastically reduced orchestra with

---

[11] Wilhelm Zentner, "Musikfeste und Festspiele. II. Musik-Woche in München," *Zeitschrift für Musik* 97 (1930): 298. The description "Cubist" is from Stephen Walsh, *Stravinsky: Oedipus Rex* (Cambridge: Cambridge University Press, 1993), 1.

[12] Roman Vlad, *Stravinsky*, transl. Frederick Fuller, 3rd ed. (New York: Oxford University Press, 1985), 66. According to Stravinsky's own account, he pieced together the "skeleton of the play" from "Devil-soldier episodes" in Alexander Afanasiev's anthology of folk tales; the libretto of course was provided by C. F. Ramuz. See Stravinsky and Craft, *Expositions and Developments* (Berkeley: University of California Press, 1962), 90. On the possible influence of Russian oral folk theater on the conception of this work, see Simon Karlinsky, "Igor Stravinsky and Russian Preliterate Theater," in *Confronting Stravinsky: Man, Musician, and Modernist*, ed. Jann Pasler (Berkeley: University of California Press, 1986), 3-15 (esp. 12-13).

[13] O. Schmid, "Konzert und Oper. Dresden," *Zeitschrift für Musik* 97 (1930): 57. This periodical had long waged a vicious battle against Stravinsky's music, in particular *Histoire du soldat*. For examples of polemic masquerading as criticism, see the passages quoted in Trapp, 164-71 ("Die negative Kritik: Protest").

[14] Helmut Kirchmeyer, "Strawinsky im Lichte der zeitgenössischen Musikkritik," in *Igor Strawinsky: Eine Sendereihe des Westdeutschen Rundfunks zum 80. Geburtstag*, ed. Otto Tomek (Cologne, 1963), 26; quoted in Trapp, 162.

[15] Walsh, *Stravinsky: Oedipus Rex*, 13-14. Walsh notes elsewhere that Meyerhold was in fact responsible for the Russian premiere of *Le Rossignol* in St. Petersburg in 1918. See Walsh, *The Music of Stravinsky* (London: Routledge, 1988), 68.

[16] Walsh, *Stravinsky: Oedipus Rex*, 14. The composer himself ascribed the "intercession of the narrator in the action of the play" to the influence of Pirandello (*Expositions and Developments*, 91). Walsh, 101-02 n. 6, finds it doubtful, however, that Stravinsky, or any of the other artists involved in the premiere, could have been familiar with Pirandello's ideas as early as 1918.

its "bony instrumentation,"[17] the "distancing" effect produced by having all the participants, including the "orchestra," on stage—in short, the studied absence of "pathos" and "illusion"—led easily, if somewhat anachronistically, to the appellation "Brechtian."[18] The fact that Brecht's experiments in "epic theater" were fueled by his political beliefs added a special *frisson* to the opposition to *Histoire*, for Stravinsky's enemies were only too happy to assume that the Russian composer shared Brecht's communist views. This assumption must have deeply dismayed the Russian Orthodox émigré, who made no secret of his hatred for the regime that had deprived him of his homeland, and whose political beliefs during the interwar period can safely be described as reactionary.[19]

The Brechtian associations of *Histoire du soldat* were further strengthened by the powerful influence of this "folk play with song and dance" on German composers committed to creating stage works that would speak directly to an audience in a language shorn of late-Romantic excess.[20] Kurt Weill, writing in 1926, noted that the mixed-genre approach of *Histoire* might "form the basis of a certain type of new opera."[21] Two years later a "new opera" that owes a great deal to *Histoire* was first performed: *Die Dreigroschenoper*, that fantastically successful collaboration between Weill and Bertolt Brecht. As Stephen Hinton points out, "the economy of forces, the visibility of the instrumentalists, the use of modern dance idioms, the epic structure, the separation of elements, the ironic humour"—all these can be traced back to *Histoire*,[22] while the parodistic use of the Lutheran chorale style at the end of *Die Dreigroschenoper* palpably recalls the earlier work. Nor did the similarities escape the notice of contemporary observers. "Without *Histoire du soldat*," noted the philosopher Ernst Bloch in the midst of the *Dreigroschenfieber* that swept Germany after August 1928, "there could hardly be a *Dreigroschenoper*."[23]

The connections between *Histoire* and *Die Dreigroschenoper* were not lost on the anti-modernists, who regularly castigated Weill and Stravinsky in the same breath. Racial slurs directed primarily at Weill encompassed both composers. Thus Hans Fleischer, writing in the periodical of the Kampfbund für deutsche Kultur (Combat League for German Culture), an organization dedicated to the "purification" of Germany's cultural life, sneeringly referred to Stravinsky and Weill, along with Ernst Toch, as "temple defilers" and "atonal Jews."[24]

In addition to its association with Brecht and Weill, Stravinsky's enemies were quick to point out the support given *Histoire* by other artists of leftist orientation. These included, most notably, Hermann Scherchen, whose socialist views were well known, as well as Otto Klemperer, whose highly publicized "left-wing" productions at Berlin's Kroll Opera, including a staging of *Histoire* in 1928, made him a favorite target of conservative attack.

[17] The quote is from Heyworth, 203.

[18] Further on Brecht and Stravinsky, see Vera Sonja Stegmann, *Das epische Musiktheater bei Strawinsky und Brecht: Studien zur Geschichte und Theorie* (New York: Peter Lang, 1991).

[19] See Craft, "Stravinsky's Politics: Left, Right, Left," in Craft and Vera Stravinsky, *Stravinsky in Pictures and Documents* (New York: Simon and Schuster, 1978), 545-58 (Appendix D).

[20] The description of *Histoire* is Kurt Weill's, in a letter written to Busoni from Frankfurt on 21 June 1923 (the day after the German premiere); quoted in Stephen Hinton, *Kurt Weill: The Threepenny Opera* (Cambridge: Cambridge University Press, 1990), 208 n. 2.

[21] Kurt Weill, "Die neue Oper," *Der neue Weg* 55 (1926): 24; quoted in Hinton, 182.

[22] Ibid.

[23] Ernst Bloch to Theodor Wiesengrund-Adorno, 4 November 1928. Published in *Ernst Bloch: Briefe, 1903-1975*, vol. 2, ed. Karola Bloch et al. (Frankfurt: Suhrkamp, 1985), 412.

[24] Hans Fleischer, *Deutsche Kultur-Wacht* 22 (2 September 1933); reprinted in Joseph Wulf, *Musik im Dritten Reich: Eine Dokumentation* (Hamburg: Rororo, 1966), 78.

A performance of *Histoire* at Hamburg's modern-oriented Schiller Opera during the final days of the Weimar Republic provided the now-powerful Nazi Party with an opportunity to attack in a single blow its most reviled enemies: modernism, communism, and Jews. The occasion was the second of two evenings devoted to stage works of Weill, Hindemith, Krenek, and Stravinsky. A modernist décor was provided for *Histoire* by a Bauhaus designer who was a member of the German Communist Party. Present for the occasion were Nazi storm troopers, who during the performance voiced their objections *en masse*; they had erected by the theater entrance a sign that announced "Jews are employed here."[25]

*   *   *   *

The impact of the Nazi takeover of January 1933 on performances of Stravinsky's music was immediate, as the *völkisch* attitudes of his late-Weimar opponents now became everyday reality. For a period of more than three years, Stravinsky's music all but disappeared from German opera houses and concert halls.[26] By 1936, however, the turbulence of the early Nazi period had given way to a more stable situation, as the regime's efforts towards *Gleichschaltung*, the coordination of all aspects of German life in terms of Nazi policy, bore fruit. At the same time, an improved economic situation brought about a lessening of the xenophobia that had characterized the earlier period. Slowly, foreign music and musicians—subject to political and racial considerations—were heard again in Germany.

Stravinsky's German "rehabilitation," as it was widely described in the German press, was given a crucial impetus in the spring of 1936, when Stravinsky and his son Soulima presented the German premiere of his Concerto for Two Solo Pianos at the inauguration of an annual festival of contemporary music in Baden-Baden.[27] Renewed interest in Stravinsky's music continued during the following season, which, among other performances, saw the German premiere of *Perséphone* in Braunschweig, an event that drew musicians and critics from all over the country. Despite "little excursions into atonal regions,"[28] *Perséphone* was hailed as a "masterpiece."[29] Even *Der Angriff*, the mouthpiece of Joseph Goebbels, commented favorably.[30]

The 1937-38 season saw more performances of Stravinsky's music than any other during the Nazi period. The most significant of these was the European premiere of *Jeu de cartes* at the Dresden State Opera in October 1937, the first staging of the work since the world premiere in New York the previous April. The performance, conducted by Karl Böhm, was the crowning event of the Gaukulturwoche, the regional arts festival supported by the Nazi Party. *Jeu* was enthusiastically received by audience and

---

[25] Bettina Fellinger, "Oper und Theater im NS-Staat Hamburg," in *Zündende Lieder—Verbrannte Musik: Folgen des Nationalsozialismus für Hamburger Musiker und Musikerinnen*, Katalog zur Ausstellung in Hamburg im November und Dezember 1988, ed. Projektgruppe Musik und Nationalsozialismus (Hamburg: VSA-Verlag, 1988), 123-24. The January 1933 performance was reviewed by Max Broesike-Schoen in *Die Musik* 25 (1932/33): 528.

[26] See my "Die Rezeption der Musik Igor Strawinskys in Hitlerdeutschland," *Archiv für Musikwissenschaft* 55 (1998): 91-109.

[27] That Stravinsky was eager to resume his artistically and financially profitable guest appearances in Germany is clear from the excerpts of his correspondence with his German publisher Willy Strecker in *Selected Correspondence*, 3:217-72. Further, see Evans, ibid.

[28] Martin Koegel, "Musikalische Ereignisse bei der Festwoche zeitgenössischer Dichter und Komponisten in Braunschweig: Ein neues Werk von Strawinsky," *Allgemeine Musikzeitung* 64 (1937): 395.

[29] Alfred Burgartz, in *Die Musik-Woche*; quoted (without title or date) in a pamphlet published by the Russischer Musikverlag following the premiere (Stravinsky Collection).

[30] Erika Kupfer, in *Der Angriff* (see previous note).

critics alike. Herbert Gerigk, for example, writing for the Party's official newspaper, noted approvingly the "thoroughly tonal" nature of Stravinsky's recent works. The future co-author of the notorious *Lexikon der Juden in der Musik* also reflected the changed attitude towards the composer when he reminded his readers that at one time Stravinsky's works had been "mistakenly lumped together with corruptive Jewish music."[31]

The premiere of *Jeu* was followed by concert performances in half a dozen cities throughout Germany.[32] The parallels with the early German reception of *Histoire* are striking: the second production of each work took place in Germany, and both works garnered their "greatest success" in that country.[33] But the Germany of 1937 was light-years away from the artistically stimulating atmosphere of the Weimar Republic.

In September 1934 the musicologist Wilhelm Altmann noted that a "certain cleansing" of the operatic repertory had already taken place. Gone were works by Hindemith, Krenek, Milhaud, Schreker, and Weill, as well as *Wozzeck*—and *Histoire du soldat*.[34] In fact, with the exception of a single performance that took place two weeks after the Nazi takeover, *Histoire* disappeared from German stages after January 1933.[35] Nor did Stravinsky's post-1936 "rehabilitation" extend to this work. Although all but the most hard-boiled of the *völkisch* critics eventually withdrew their blanket condemnation of Stravinsky's music, *Histoire* could not shed itself of the taint of "cultural Bolshevism."

The Dresden musicologist Hans Schnoor, for example, who after the successful premiere of *Jeu de cartes* argued strongly in support of Stravinsky, firmly drew the line at *Histoire*, this "Satanic work."[36] In November 1938 Richard Ohlekopf published the most outspoken defense of Stravinsky to appear during the Nazi period.[37] Stravinsky's music deserves a place in Germany's cultural life, Ohlekopf argued. But as with any great composer, certain works constitute "border-line cases." He singled out the "bitonal" pieces for piano, four-hands—and *Histoire du soldat*.

Herbert Gerigk, that pillar of the Nazi musical press, also defended Stravinsky.[38] Though his support was more qualified than that of Schnoor or Ohlekopf, the very fact that Gerigk's comments appeared in an official Party publication is a significant indication of the profound change of attitude towards Stravinsky that had taken place since the early years of the Nazi regime. Not surprisingly, Gerigk stresses the composer's "Aryan" background, as well as his anti-communist and anti-liberal

[31] Herbert Gerigk's review appeared in the *Völkischer Beobachter* on 6 January 1938. *Lexikon der Juden in der Musik*, written in collaboration with Theo Stengel, was published in Berlin in 1940.

[32] These included Hamburg, Berlin, Wiesbaden, Münster, and (in the following season) Leipzig.

[33] The phrase is Stravinsky's, who recalled the German success of *Jeu de cartes* in Stravinsky and Craft, *Themes and Episodes* (New York: Knopf, 1967), 35.

[34] Wilhelm Altmann, "Kritische Opernstatistik," *Die Musik* 26 (1933/34): 903.

[35] The exception was a Bremerhaven performance of 16 February 1933.

[36] Hans Schnoor, "Das tanzende Kartenspiel: Strawinskys neues Ballett im Opernhaus umjubelt," *Dresdner Anzeiger*, 14 October 1937. In his case for the composer, Schnoor drew attention to Stravinsky's anti-communist views as expressed in his *Chroniques de ma vie*, the German translation of which had just been published by Atlantis-Verlag. Ironically, a page from the manuscript of *Histoire* constituted one of the two facsimiles illustrating the German edition. Further on the German reception of this publication, see my "Some Remarks on the Publication and Reception of Stravinsky's *Erinnerungen*," *Mitteilungen der Paul Sacher Stiftung* 9 (1996): 17-23.

[37] Richard Ohlekopf, "Gedanken über ein Fragezeichen hinter Strawinskij," *Signale für die musikalische Welt* 48 (1938): 641-42. This lead article by the editor of *Signale* was prompted by the inclusion of Stravinsky in the now infamous "Entartete Musik" exhibition, to be discussed below.

[38] Herbert Gerigk, "Musikpolitische Umschau," *Nationalsozialistische Monatshefte* 106 (1939): 86-87.

views. He also points out that, as a representative of a foreign "Volkstum," Stravinsky is not "part of our cultural circle." But as long as "false prophets" do not try to make of Stravinsky's music a model for German composers, Gerigk finds no reason to exclude it. Like Ohlekopf and Schnoor, however, Gerigk finds certain works unacceptable, among them *Sacre du printemps*—and *Histoire*.[39]

*   *   *   *

To the surprise of many, including the numerous conductors and directors who had successfully programmed Stravinsky's music during the 1937-38 season, the composer was singled out for attack in the exhibition of "Entartete Musik" (Degenerate Music) that opened at the Kunstpalast in Düsseldorf on 24 May 1938.[40] It was the brainchild of Hans Severus Ziegler, Intendant of the Weimar theater and a long-time enemy of Stravinsky's music, who while in charge of cultural affairs for the province of Thuringia in the early 1930s had successfully banned from state-supported concerts works by "musical Bolsheviks" such as Hindemith and Stravinsky.[41]

Other prominent composers included in the exhibition were Schoenberg, Hindemith, Krenek, and Weill; Alban Berg, Ernst Toch, Josef Hauer, and others were described as "kleinere Bolschewisten-größen."[42] On display were photos or caricatures of the "degenerate" artists, accompanied by "explanatory" placards. Next to Stravinsky's portrait was written: "We respect national art, but we reject the international in art. That is the Stravinsky 'problem'."[43] Books and scores were also displayed, among them the German edition of Stravinsky's autobiography—and *Histoire du soldat*.[44] In a lecture on the "historical and racial fundamentals" of music that was illustrated with recorded examples from *Firebird* and *Sacre*, Jena's Otto zur Nedden accused Stravinsky, along with Hindemith and Weill, of attempting to demolish "musical form" and of stirring up "the basest of instincts."[45]

Recordings were available to patrons in specially constructed booths. That music from *Histoire* was included is suggested by information concerning the further showings of the exhibition that

---

[39] Gerigk's objection to *Histoire* was no doubt strengthened by his implacable objection to jazz. See his attack on Eduard Künnecke's *Tänzerische Suite* in "Was ist mit der Jazzmusik?" *Die Musik* 30 (1937/38): 680; a shortened version is printed in Wulf, 387-88. See also Erik Levi, *Music in the Third Reich* (New York: St. Martin's Press, 1994), 122-23.

[40] For details concerning this exhibition, which was modelled on the infamous "Entartete Kunst" exhibition that had taken place in Munich in 1937, see Albrecht Dümling and Peter Girth, eds., *Entartete Musik: Eine kommentierte Rekonstruktion zur Düsseldorfer Ausstellung von 1938*, rev. ed. [*sic*] (Düsseldorf: Der Kleine Verlag, 1993).

[41] Reinhard Bollmus, *Das Amt Rosenberg und seine Gegner: Studien zum Machtkampf im nationalsozialistischen Herrschaftssystem* (Stuttgart: Deutsche Verlags-Anstalt, 1970), 34. Ziegler's speech opening the Düsseldorf exhibition, which was later published as *Entartete Musik: Eine Abrechnung* (Düsseldorf: Völkischer Verlag, 1938), is reproduced in Dümling and Girth, 174-90.

[42] The phrase, quoted in Wolfgang Steinecke's article "'Entartete Musik': Eröffnung der Düsseldorfer Ausstellung," *Deutsche Allgemeine Zeitung*, 25 May 1938, can be translated as "lesser Bolshevist big shots."

[43] "Wir achten die Kunst der Nationen, aber wir verneinen die Internationale in der Kunst. Das ist das 'Problem' Strawinsky." The organizers suggested a communist connection by printing the word "Internationale" in a contrasting color. The portrait displayed was a reproduction of a well-known one by Jacques-Emile Blanche, whose caption raised yet again the question of Stravinsky's origins: "Who invented the story that Stravinsky comes from the Russian nobility?" ("Wer erfand Strawinskys Herkunft aus einem alten russischen Bojarengeschlecht?"). Also displayed was a quote from the opening measures of *Petrushka* and an article written by "the Jew Alfred Einstein." (Photographs of the exhibit are preserved in the Stravinsky Collection.)

[44] Wolfgang Steinecke, "Was die Ausstellung 'Entartete Musik' zeigt," *Deutsche Allgemeine Zeitung*, 26 May 1938. The article is reproduced in Dümling and Girth, 194.

[45] Quoted in Karl Holl, "Die Reichsmusiktage in Düsseldorf," *Frankfurter Zeitung* [28 May 1938]. Nedden compared Stravinsky's music unfavorably with that of the "Nordic" Sibelius.

took place the following spring and summer within the framework of the travelling "Entartete Kunst" exhibition.[46] At the time of the combined exhibition in Vienna, a local critic listed *Histoire* among the recordings of "degenerate" music available.[47] This report has recently been confirmed by the Austrian composer Paul Kont, who as a young music student attended the Viennese showing many times.[48] Kont recalls that of the music heard there, *Histoire* impressed him the most, "so that it became very important for my own composition"—an effect hardly intended by the organizers of the exhibition.

The "Entartete Musik" exhibition was not restricted to composers, but included other prominent musical figures as well. Weimar's Otto Reuter, noting the inclusion of Hermann Scherchen, recalled pointedly that it was this very conductor who during the Bauhaus period had "treated us to Stravinsky's *Histoire du soldat.*"[49]

*   *   *   *

Given Stravinsky's indifference to the fate of German musicians under Hitler, it is ironic that the only production of *Histoire* to take place in Germany after the early weeks of the Nazi period was given by a group of musicians who since 1933 had been systematically excluded from participation in the country's cultural life.[50] Stravinsky's appearance in Baden-Baden in the spring of 1936, an event so crucial to his "rehabilitation," did not go unnoticed by his admirers in Germany's Jewish community. In July of that year Willy Strecker informed the composer that Berlin's Jüdischer Kulturbund (Jewish Culture League) had requested permission to mount a production of *Histoire*.[51] The dismay with which both Stravinsky and his publisher responded to the Kulturbund's plans is well documented. Strecker feared that a production of *Histoire*, a work that had generated so much opposition in the past, might trigger renewed attacks. Moreover, a performance under Jewish auspices would be sure to animate the old rumor that Stravinsky was Jewish: ". . . if you permit the Jewish Kulturbund to perform it," he wrote to the composer, "your enemies will gleefully term you, as well as your art, 'Jewish,' spoiling

---

[46] See Christoph Zuschlag, "An 'Educational Exhibition': The Precursors of *Entartete Kunst* and Its Individual Venues," in *"Degenerate Art": The Fate of the Avant-Garde in Nazi Germany*, ed. Stephanie Barron (Los Angeles: Los Angeles County Museum of Art, 1991), 83-103. The combined exhibitions were shown in Weimar, Vienna, Frankfurt, and Chemnitz. Albrecht Dümling claims that a further showing of the Entartete Musik exhibition had been planned for Munich. Dümling, "'Entartete Musik': Zur Rezeption der Ausstellung in Düsseldorf, Weimar und Wien 1938-1939," *Beiträge '90: Österreichische Musiker im Exil*, ed. Österreichische Gesellschaft für Musik (Kassel: Bärenreiter, n.d.), 90. If so, it seems not to have taken place.

[47] [Unsigned], "Jüdischer Kunstdilettantismus: Entartete Malerei, Plastik, Lyrik und Musik im Künstlerhaus," *Volks-Zeitung*, 5 May 1939. The writer also noted the inclusion of music from Schoenberg's Serenade, op. 24, and Hindemith's dance pantomime *Der Dämon*. I am indebted to Christoph Zuschlag, Heidelberg, for photocopies of this source, as well as that referred to in n. 49.

[48] Paul Kont to the author, 20 September 1995.

[49] Otto Reuter, "Entartete Musik," *Allgemeine Thüringerische Landeszeitung*, 24 March 1939.

[50] See Craft, "Stravinsky's Politics," 553. Further instances of Stravinsky's indifference are documented in Evans, "Die Rezeption."

[51] Strecker to Stravinsky, 6 July 1936 (see *Selected Correspondence*, 3:243 n. 42). On the background of the Jüdischer Kulturbund, which had been established in June 1933, see Fred K. Prieberg, *Musik im NS-Staat* (Frankfurt: Fischer Taschenbuch Verlag, 1982), 78-106 ("Musik unter dem Davidsstern"), and, especially, *Geschlossene Vorstellung: Der Jüdische Kulturbund in Deutschland, 1933-1941*, ed. Akademie der Künste (Berlin: Akademie der Künste, 1992).

everything we have managed to nurture."[52] Since he considered it unwise to refuse permission outright, Strecker hit upon a way to discourage the Kulturbund's interest. He demanded an inflated fee of 100 marks per performance, one he was "certain they could not pay. . . ."[53] Shortly thereafter, however, Strecker reversed his position and asked Stravinsky to allow the performance, even advising (as "an exception under these circumstances") a "small reduction" of the fee.[54] He had learned that performances of the Kulturbund were restricted to members of the Jewish community, and thus would not attract un-favorable publicity. Moreover, the Kulturbund's plans had since been authorized by the Reichstheaterkammer. To refuse now, Strecker explained, would be interpreted as "an explicit act of unfriendliness towards Jews" that might result in "unfavorable repercussions" for the composer, especially in America.[55] Fearful of "losing all of the ground that we have gained," Stravinsky was initially reluctant to agree.[56] But Strecker's argument was persuasive. Permission was granted, and plans for the production went ahead. *Histoire* was performed in Berlin on 4 November 1936 and 23 January 1937, with a "run-out" to Breslau on January 17.[57]

The composer and critic Jakob Schönberg reviewed the successful premiere for the Jewish press. Given their context, his comments have a resonance that extends well beyond the work itself. *Histoire*, he writes, depicts "an unequal battle" between the good and evil qualities in human nature. Evil wins, Schönberg comments—"a depressing philosophy of life that lets man be destroyed by life's adversities."[58] He noted that it took "raw idealism" and "courage" to present such a controversial work to a general audience and praised the high quality of the production; a certain "nervousness" he ascribed to the "disturbing fact" that the curtain failed to operate.[59]

Histoire du soldat was not the only music of Stravinsky's to be performed under the auspices of Berlin's Kulturbund before it was dissolved in 1941.[60] The *Suite italienne* was played in March 1935 by violinist Andreas Weissgerber and pianist Kurt Sanderling; Franz Osborn included *Petrushka* in a piano recital performed the following month; violinist Wilhelm Graf and pianist Kurt Bieber played the *Duo concertant* in March 1938; and the *Firebird* Suite was included in an orchestral concert given in April

---

[52] Strecker to Stravinsky, 6 July 1936; translation from *Selected Correspondence*, 3:243 n. 42.

[53] Ibid. A comparison of Stravinsky's royalties from German performances of stage works during the Nazi period confirms that 100 marks per performance was indeed an unusually high fee.

[54] Strecker to Stravinsky, 28 July 1936; translation from ibid., 244 n. 44.

[55] Strecker to Stravinsky, 3 August 1936; translation from ibid.

[56] Stravinsky to Strecker, 1 August 1936; translation from ibid., 243.

[57] Schott's royalty statements to Stravinsky, 31 December 1936 and 1 April 1937 (Stravinsky Collection). The production was conducted by Wolfgang Fraenkel and directed by Nikolai Eljaschoff, with stage design by Heinz Condell. The performers were as follows: Bert Baer/Heinz Kahnemann (Soldier), Alexander Lipschitz (Devil), Ilse Vordemberge (Princess), and Herbert Meyerowitz (Narrator); Wilhelm Graf (violin), Werner Düsterwald (contrabass), Josef Neumann (clarinet), Heinz Bramson (bassoon), Heinz Schlesinger (trumpet), Lothar Simenauer (trombone), and Hildegard Lewin (percussion). See *Geschlossene Vorstellung*, 406 (where, however, the date of the performance is given as November 10).

[58] Jakob Schönberg, "Strawinsky: 'Geschichte vom Soldaten.' Aufführung in Berlin," *Jüdische Rundschau*, 6 November 1936. The review includes a photograph of the production (photocopy kindly provided by the Akademie der Künste, Berlin).

[59] Another reviewer stressed the debt that *Histoire* owed to *Pierrot lunaire*. Half of the music derives from Stravinsky's genius and half from Arnold Schoenberg, wrote Arno Nadel. "Without Schoenberg, its arbitrariness, its captivating freedom, would be unthinkable." Nadel, "Die Geschichte vom Soldaten," *Gemeindeblatt der Jüdischen Gemeinde zu Berlin*, 15 November 1936; quoted in Prieberg, 95.

[60] The following details are taken from photocopies of concert announcements, programs, and reviews kindly provided by the Akademie der Künste, Berlin.

1939. Grete Sultan's performance of the Piano Sonata in January 1940 is especially noteworthy, for it may have been the only "public" performance of Stravinsky's music to take place in Germany during World War II.[61]

Epilogue

At the beginning of July 1946 there took place in Munich under the direction of Hans Rosbaud the first production of *Histoire du soldat* in Germany since the Jüdischer Kulturbund's performances nearly ten years earlier, and the first public performance since 1933.[62] Among the listeners was the eminent musicologist and critic Hans Mersmann, who as editor of the periodical *Melos* from 1924 had been a leading supporter of new music, and one of Stravinsky's staunchest supporters, until he was forced out of his journalistic posts by the Nazis.[63] Following the performance, Hans Rosbaud received an appreciative letter from Mersmann, in which the musicologist recalled vividly the impact of Scherchen's and Klemperer's performances on Berlin audiences of the 1920s, as well as the isolation of the years that followed.[64]

Rosbaud's production, wrote Mersmann, provided more than a "reacquaintance" with a pioneering work of art. For along with the performance "unfolded a part of one's own life," a life carried along by an inevitable fate, like that of "the Soldier's march 'between Chur and Wallenstadt'."[65] Mersmann recalled that his introduction to *Histoire* had been at Scherchen's Berlin performance, shortly after the Frankfurt premiere. The impact was such that he and his colleagues "walked out of the theater into a bright, sunny day hardly knowing where we were," but realizing that "something new, something important" had taken place. Whether as a result of the force of "a new musical language that pushed heedlessly forward," or because of the "new form of 'epic drama'," which pointed the way to "a future for opera," modern music had found in Stravinsky a standard for "further artistic developments."[66]

By the time Mersmann heard Klemperer's performance at Berlin's Kroll Opera five years later, the significance of the work, with its "victory over the psychological music drama," its "restoration" of the autonomous role of music, had been fully confirmed by Stravinsky's further development. For in the "oratorical monumentality" of *Oedipus Rex*, "epic drama" had been brought to full fruition.[67] But Mersmann also recalled the flood of protests ("a not entirely insignificant symptom") that had greeted Klemperer's performance. These, however, were not directed so much at the music, "which

---

[61] As a citizen of France, Stravinsky came under the Reichsmusikkammer's general edict of 18 September 1939, banning "performance of composers of enemy lands." Peter Raabe, "Fortführung des Konzertlebens," *Amtliche Mitteilungen der Reichsmusikkammer* 6 (1 October 1939): 57 [*sic*]. The intent of the RMK bulletin of 1 February 1940, a document often misleadingly referred to as the Stravinsky "ban," was to clarify the composer's status at a time when Russian composers, thanks to the Hitler-Stalin Pact of August 1939, were (briefly) popular in Germany. Raabe, "Strawinsky-Aufführungen während des Krieges unzulässig," *Amtliche Mitteilungen der Reichsmusikkammer* 7 (15 February 1940): 8.

[62] See my *Hans Rosbaud: A Bio-Bibliography* (New York: Greenwood Press, 1992), 43.

[63] Mersmann was included among the "Theoretiker der Atonalität" in Düsseldorf, where his *Musik der Gegenwart* (Berlin, 1923) was among the books exhibited. See Steinecke, "Was die Ausstellung 'Entartete Musik' zeigt" (also n. 44).

[64] Hans Mersmann to Hans Rosbaud, 8 July 1946 (Rosbaud Collection, Washington State University, Pullman). A slightly modified version of this letter was published as a review in Munich's *Neue Zeitung*, and reprinted in Mersmann's *Neue Musik in den Strömungen unserer Zeit* (Bayreuth: Verlag Julius Steeger, 1949), 32-35 ("Strawinskys Geschichte vom Soldaten").

[65] Ibid., 32.

[66] Ibid. The Berlin premiere of *Histoire* took place on 13 January 1924.

[67] Ibid., 33.

would have been understandable," as at the scaled-down, everyday aspect of the production. The performance took place on a "roughly built little wooden stage," and the conductor, following Stravinsky's directions, appeared in ordinary dress. This flouting of tradition outraged certain segments of the audience. When one went to the opera, Mersmann noted ironically, one expected to see the conductor in tails, and on stage "a 'beautiful illusion' in which one could slowly lose oneself."[68]

Then came the dark years, he recalled, when the already familiar term "cultural Bolshevism" spread a "filthy veneer" of propaganda over the achievements of decades.[69] But there were still scores that one could read, and there were recordings. In Stravinsky's case these existed in his own authoritative interpretations.[70] At the beginning, close friends would gather together to listen to recordings. Students were introduced to this repertory, especially, as the years went by, younger students who had never heard actual performances of the works. "A group of musicians (among them several well-known names) assembled regularly in my home," Mersmann wrote. "We listened and we talked." The increasing pressure of the times "sharpened our ears."[71]

During those years it became an "important responsibility" to provide such "little oases." Even at the height of the war (that is, even after it was officially banned), Stravinsky's music formed the center of those evenings. *Histoire du soldat*, in particular, played a memorable—and poignant—role. Mersmann owned Stravinsky's recordings of the music, and since he also owned a copy of the score, he was able to piece together a "performance" of the work, combining his own narration with the recordings of the music. This he presented several times before enthusiastic "audiences" of fifty or sixty people in his home. The "performance," he admitted, presented only a "reflection" of the work, but one that by its very deficiencies strikingly demonstrated its "original power." "In my little apartment," Mersmann recalled, "lingered the spirit of a masterpiece that no power could take from us."[72] From this little oasis in the middle of war-torn Berlin, the strains of Stravinsky's music rose, phoenix-like, above the ashes of the Thousand Year Reich.

---

[68] Ibid.

[69] Ibid.

[70] Interestingly enough, the Reichmusikkammer's edict banning the sale of recordings made in enemy countries (or recordings of music written or performed by nationals of enemy countries) was not issued until 9 February 1942. Even then, a grace period of six months existed for recordings of pre-Soviet Russian music or French music. The edict, "Verbot feindländischer Schallplattenmusik," *Amtliche Mitteilungen der Reichsmusikkammer* 9 (15 February 1942), is reproduced in Prieberg, 400.

[71] Mersmann, 33.

[72] Ibid., 34.

Publications of Murray Lefkowitz

"New Facts Concerning William Lawes and the Caroline Masque." *Music and Letters* 40 (1959): 324-33.

William Lawes. London: Routledge and Kegan Paul, 1960.

William Lawes: Select Consort Music, transc. and ed. Murray Lefkowitz. Musica Britannica, 21. London: Stainer and Bell, 1963; revised edition, 1971.

"Matthew Locke at Exeter." *Consort* 22 (1965): 5-16.

"The Longleat Papers of Bulstrode Whitelocke: New Light on Shirley's *Triumph of Peace*." *Journal of the American Musicological Society* 18 (1965): 42-60.

Review of John Jenkins, *Three-Part Fancy and Ayre Divisions for Two Trebles and Bass to the Organ*, ed. Robert Austin Warner, Wellesley Edition, 10 (Wellesley: Wellesley College Music Department, 1966). *Notes* 24 (1968): 788-90.

Review of Dietrich Buxtehude, *Alles was ihr tut*; *Das neugeborne Kindlein*; *In dulci jubilo*, ed. Günter Graulich and Paul Horn (Stuttgart-Hohenheim: Hänssler Verlag, 1969). *Notes* 26 (1970): 601.

Trois Masques à la cour de Charles Ier d'Angleterre: The Triumph of Peace; The Triumphs of the Prince d'Amour; Britannia Triumphans. Livrets de John Shirley et William Davenant, Dessins d'Inigo Jones, Musique de William Lawes. Introductions, commentaires et transcriptions par M. Lefkowitz. Paris: Centre National de la Recherche Scientifique, 1970.

"Shadwell and Locke's *Psyche*: The French Connection." *Proceedings of the Royal Musical Association* 106 (1979/80): 42-55.

The New Grove Dictionary of Music and Musicians, ed. Stanley Sadie. London: Macmillan, 1980. S.v. "Lawes, William" (10:558-66); "Locke, Matthew" (11:107-17); "Masque" (11:756-69).

INDEX

Contributors

Rebecca A. Baltzer is professor of musicology at the University of Texas, Austin. She specializes in the musical culture of France, and especially Paris, from 1150 to 1400. Her most recent book is an edition of the two-voiced clausulae from *Florence Pl. 29.1*, published as volume 5 of Oiseau-Lyre's *Le Magnus Liber Organi*.

Dean D. Bouzianis is associate professor of music theory and composition at the University of Massachusetts, Lowell. He is active both as a composer and performer, and is conductor of the Whittier Chamber Orchestra.

Camilla Cai is professor of music history at Kenyon College. Her publications center on the critical analysis of nineteenth-century piano music, especially that of Fanny Hensel and Johannes Brahms.

Eugene Casjen Cramer is professor emeritus of musicology at the University of Calgary, having retired September 1998. He has published several articles on the music of Victoria and is author of *Tomás Luis de Victoria: A Guide to Research* (Garland, 1998).

D. Stephen Cushman is professor emeritus of music history at Wheaton (Illinois) College Conservatory of Music. His research interests include Haydn and the folksong and religious music.

John Daverio is professor of music and chair of the musicology department at Boston University. He specializes in nineteenth-century music and musical thought. His most recent book is *Robert Schumann: Herald of a "New Poetic Age."*

John C. Duffy is an independent scholar now living in the Boston area. His research interests include music of the late Renaissance and the nineteenth century. He is the author of *The Vocal Works of Alfonso Ferrabosco the Younger*.

Joseph Dyer is associate professor of music at the University of Massachusetts, Boston. His specialties include Old Roman chant, psalmody, medieval theory and performance practice, and most recently the liturgy in Rome during the Middle Ages. He is also co-editor of the journal *Plainsong & Medieval Music*.

Joan Evans teaches music history at Wilfrid Laurier University. She has done research on the music of Michael East and more recently on musical life in Germany during the first half of the twentieth century, including the reception of Stravinsky's music during the Third Reich. Recent publications include "Some Remarks on the Publication and Reception of Stravinsky's *Erinnerungen*," *Mitteilungen der Paul Sacher Stiftung* 9 (1996), and "Die Rezeption der Musik Igor Strawinskys in Hitlerdeutschland," *Archiv für Musikwissenschaft* 55/2 (1998). She is the author of *Hans Rosbaud: A Bio-Bibliography*.

Daniel J. Koury is associate professor emeritus of music at Westfield (Massachusetts) State College. His research centers on the history of conducting. He is the author of *The Orchestra in the Nineteenth Century: Physical Aspects of its Performance Practice*.

John Ogasapian is professor of music history at the University of Massachusetts, Lowell. His primary interests are nineteenth-century American organ building and church music. His most recent book is *English Cathedral Music in New York City: Edward Hodges of Trinity Church*.

L. Jonathan Saylor is associate professor of music and head of the music history and literature department at Wheaton (Illinois) College Conservatory of Music. His research areas include the early Baroque trio sonata and the theorist Antonio Eximeno. More recently, he has published in the area of eighteenth century orchestral literature. He is also active as a bassoonist.

Joel Sheveloff is professor of music at Boston University. His areas of research interest include the keyboard music of Domenico Scarlatti and Russian and eastern European music of the nineteenth century.

SCREWBALL EXPRESS

By Kenneth H. Cass

Bombardier of its Original Flight Crew

**Authentic Biography of a B-17G Flying Fortress
Assigned to 379th Bomb Group (H)
Kimbolton, England, World War II**

**Verified with Mission Reports maintained by
The National Archives
and other reliable sources**

TURNER PUBLISHING COMPANY

Screwball Express on hardstand in 526th Squadron area of 379th Bomb Group at Kimbolton, England. (Photo by 379th BG Photographic Section)

FOREWORD

This book is essentially the story of the author's crew and an airplane. Many excellent books have been written on this subject, but Ken Cassens has expanded his theme far beyond the conventional scope. Readers will find a wealth of material presented in such a way that the larger story of the Eighth Air Force is impressively revealed. Cassens has done a tremendous amount of research, digging through the mass of data that has become available in recent years. Details of what was happening at the Squadron, Group, Wing and Air Division levels are very complete.

During the period of time featured in this book, the Germans were peaking out in flak and fighter strength. The flak was always present, but Eighth Air Force fighter utilization had made a dramatic change – from close support for the bombers to a focus on downing enemy fighters. It was agonizing to watch the German fighter planes maneuver into position for an attack on a formation of bombers, initiate the attack, and then – after what seemed an eternity – see our fighters come roaring in and destroy the enemy after the attack on the bombers was already in progress. In the long run, this probably was the best utilization of the entire force.

Cassens has touched on one of the most complex questions of the war. What made air crews fly into this hornet's nest day after day and never turn back due to enemy action? It was a rare occasion when a crew member or a crew failed to go. The support echelon never failed us, either. Through this book one gets a dramatic picture of The Mighty Eighth Team in which

M/Gen. Lewis E. Lyle, USAF, Ret.

mutual support and respect were powerful incentives to do your best.

Ken has brought together, from every available source and his personal diary, a barrage of facts about the Eighth Air Force and presented them in a deadly accurate and interesting way.

This book will help all of us who were at various combat levels learn more about the war we fought and won. Whether you are interested in the intimate details of a crew's experience or the broader picture of the air war, this book has a lot to offer. The facts will enlighten you and bring back many exciting events. The ageless story of man and his flying machine is still a great love affair.

Lew Lyle

M/Gen. Lewis E. Lyle, USAF, Ret.

During World War II, M/Gen. Lyle was a pilot, Squadron CO, Air Exec. and Commander of the 303rd Bomb Group; Commander of the 379th Bomb Group; and Commander of the 41st Combat Wing in England, during consecutive periods beginning in October, 1942 through June, 1945. Currently, he is President and Chairman of The Eighth Air Force Heritage Center's Board of Directors.

ACKNOWLEDGEMENTS

The eight surviving members of the original flight crew of Screwball Express:

- Howard E. Towers
- James C. Moore
- James R. Keller
- Kenneth H. Cassens

- Frank R. Craig
- Jerold L. Lindsey
- Thomas A. Kiblin
- Ernest Koshuta

These authors, historians, publishers and researchers:

- Cliff T. Bishop – East Anglia Books, Bishop's Stortford, England
- Richard L. Boylan, Howard H. Wehmann and Rick Wayman – also
    Victoria Washington and Sharon Holley of the Research Room,
    and Kathy Jacobs, Archivist – The National Archives,
    Military Archives Div., National Records Center, Suitland, MD
- George Cully, Captain, USAF –Timothy Johnson, Archivist – Master
    Sergeant A. Lawrence, USAF – Headquarters United States
    Air Force Historical Research Center, Maxwell AFB, AL
- Roger A. Freeman – Author & Historian, Colchester, Essex, England
- Alwyn T. Lloyd – Boeing Aircraft Co., Seattle, WA
- Mrs. Thomas P. (Georgette) Scott – Ocala, FL
- H. A. J. Steedman, Group Captain, RAF, retired – Kimbolton, England
- Halbert S. Stevens, Colonel, U.S.Army, retired – Ocala, FL

These members of the 379th Bomb Group World War II Association

- Frank L. Betz, editor/historian, & past president – Lancaster, PA
- Carl D. Carden, lead navigator on June 20, 1944 – Cleveland, TX
- Stanley C. Kircher, secretary, – Phoenixville, PA
- Lewis E. Lyle, M/Gen., USAF, retired – Hot Springs, AR
- Reverend Canon Roy Meadows – Kimbolton, England
- John A. Sanda, Lt. Col., USAF, retired, – San Antonio, TX
- Robert J. Watkins, mission folder custodian – Mont Clare, PA

These members of the flight crew aboard Screwball Express on its last mission

- Sam N. Reaves, ball turret gunner – Memphis, TN
- John D. Roberts, radio operatior – Port Aransas, TX
- Carlos A. Whitehead, togglier/nose gunner – St. Louis, MO

LETTER FROM THE AUTHOR

This book presents an authentic biography of a B-17G Flying Fortress assigned to the 379th Bomb Group at Kimbolton, England, during World War II. Ten young men were privileged to be members of that bomber's original flight crew. It was my good fortune to be one of them.

It has been an exciting experience for me to search through the haystack of memories that have survived for nearly half a century in the minds of my crew members and myself. I have interlaced emerging pieces of those genuine, wartime recollections into this factual account of unique and dramatic events experienced during our associa-

Photo of original diary written by Kenneth H. Cassens at Kimbolton, England, March - July 1944.

tion with this remarkable aircraft and with each other. Ours was a partnership of reciprocal trust between a bomber and its crew.

Quotations attributed to our crew's members are accurate to the point of expression, but are not implied as being verbatim. Accounts of the crew-related incidents are written as precisely as I can recall, and were compared with recollections of other members of our crew for credibility and completeness before being included.

Much of the information in this book resulted from the generous assistance of persons named under Acknowledgements; through the wealth of details found in books listed under Bibliography; and with the excellent cooperation of centers, companies, organizations and publications mentioned under Reference Sources. Accuracy of the multitude of facts contained in this book has been verified through four years of meticulous research.

I still have the diary I kept about our crew's combat missions. All of its entries have been diligently compared with the 379th Bomb Group's Mission Reports maintained by the Military Archives Division of The National Archives. Nevertheless, as in any compilation of historical facts, there may be an inadvertent error or omission in this material. I will appreciate your patience and forgiveness in such event.

Thank you for choosing this book.

Kenneth H. Cassens

LETTER FROM THE PUBLISHER

It is with great pride that I present to you the Screwball Express History Book. It is truly an outstanding literary work representing years of commitment and extensive research by Ken Cassens.

I first met Mr. Cassens at the 8th Air force 50th Anniversary Celebration in Savannah, Georgia, when he approached our military history book display and told me about the book he had just finished writing. Several weeks later, while on a business trip in Florida, I met with Ken and had the opportunity to review his computer printout of the Screwball Express. I was taken aback by the detail and obvious dedication that had gone into his work, and knew it was exactly the type of book that belonged in our already extensive and personal collection of military history books.

I respectfully thank M/Gen. Lew Lyle for his support and endorsement of this long-overdue and historic tribute to the 379th Bomb Group and Screwball Express. We also extend our appreciation to the 379th Bomb Group WWII Association for its permission to promote this book in *Contrails*, the official magazine/newsletter for members of that Association.

Screwball Express details the missions, the men who flew them and their thoughts. Maps, charts and photographs complete this book to give the reader a unique insight into the daily life of a bomber crew. It is our belief that you will get as much enjoyment and education from reading this book as we did in producing it.

Sincerely,

Dave Turner, President
Turner Publishing Company

DEDICATION

To My Wife, GERI
And Our Children, DEBRA and STEVE

and to the 10 Members of the
Original Flight Crew of Screwball Express

"...One Nation..."

IN REMEMBRANCE

JOSEPH MILWORM

Radio Operator - Gunner
Brooklyn, New York

"Always on Center Stage"

Deceased, April 14, 1966

ROBERT G. MATHEWS

Left Waist Gunner
Shively, Kentucky

"The Harlan County Lover"

Deceased, July 3, l977

"...Under God..."

TABLE OF CONTENTS

TABLE OF CONTENTS

Charts

Development of the B-17 Flying Fortress

Following much debate early in 1928 between advocates of naval power and air power, Boeing Aircraft Co. initially designed a series of commercial planes with features that were later used in bombers. Although this concept was promoted by the Army Air Corps, Boeing had the responsibility of designing and financing the entire project. Boeing also drew plans for a Model 214 military bomber that was designated the B-9 by the Air Corps in the spring of 1931.

Engineering was begun in 1933 to determine whether an aircraft capable of carrying a one-ton bomb load several thousand miles could be built. The dream of a "flying battleship" began to materialize when the Air Corps awarded Boeing preliminary contracts in mid-1934. A production model was ordered: a multi-engined aircraft capable of carrying a ton of bombs at more than 200 m.p.h. over a distance of 2,000 miles at 10,000 feet.

The first of the B-17 predecessors – Model No. 299 – took to the air on July 28, 1935, from Boeing's field at Seattle, Washington. The aircraft's dimensions and armament were extraordinary: wingspan 103 feet – fuselage 69 feet – an aluminum body – four Pratt & Whitney Hornet 750 horsepower engines, each with three-bladed propellers – a gun position in the nose, another in the cabin's rear, one under the fuselage and one at each side of the aircraft. The Seattle Daily News published a picture of the new plane with its five machine guns and called it a Flying Fortress.

On August 20 the plane was flown to Wright Field, Ohio, for testing. The flight of more than 2,000 miles from Boeing Field took only nine hours. It was a non-stop flight, much of the way on autopilot at an average altitude of 12,000 feet and an average speed of 232 m.p.h. – breaking all speed records for the distance. The Boeing 299 surpassed all Army specifications for speed, climb, range and load-carrying requirements. Step by step the bomber that would change the face of the coming war, and also the face of Europe, came into being.

The Boeing 299, later designated the XB-17, was grandfather of the Flying Fortress – the bomber that later became trailblazer and pacesetter of all heavy bombardment aircraft in World War II. The B-17 Flying Fortress was a 10-man aerial weapon with great defensive firepower and tremendous aerial bombardment capability. It was no surprise that it became a major factor in winning World War II through effective aerial bombardment in the European Theatre of Operations.

On September 1, 1939, Hitler unleashed his Panzers and Stukas against Poland. Exactly 50 days after World War II began in Europe, the first production versions of the B-17 Flying Fortress were obtained by the Army Air Corps. Boeing built 646 B-17 Flying Fortresses as of September 5, 1941. These included Models YIB-17, YIB-17A, B-17B, B-17C, B17-D and 512 B-17Es.

The remarkable combat record of the Flying Fortress began on December 7, 1941, at Pearl Harbor. During early months of the war in the Pacific, B-17s were blowing up Japanese ships and shooting down Japanese planes. With the help of the B-17, the United States carried the war to the enemy throughout the South Pacific Theatre of Operations. Fortresses also flew at low level through dense fog and bombed the Japanese out of the Aleutian Islands.

The B-17 was destined to become a legend in the flak-torn skies over Adolph Hitler's Third Reich. Beginning on August 17, 1942, Flying Fortresses brought daylight, high altitude, precision bombing to Europe by bombing a strategic target in France. B-17s also flew over deserts to force the Germans out of North Africa and the Mediterranean, and then helped open the way to Rome.

It had become apparent that wartime production needs could not be satisfied by only one aircraft manufacturer. Consequently, the Army Air Corps decided a consortium of B-17 manufacturers should be developed to produce the F and G models. Boeing made the prescribed arrangement with the Douglas plant at Tulsa, Oklahoma, and the Vega-Lockheed facility at Burbank, California.

The B-17G Model was a combination of many major improvements over the 299 Model: mid-wing monoplane of all metal aluminum alloy, with stressed-skin construction, wing span 103 feet 9 inches, length 74 feet 9 inches, height 19 feet one inch, horizontal stabilizer 43 feet, prop diameter 11 feet 7 inches, four 1,200 horsepower Wright Cyclone engines of the nine-cylinder, radial, air-cooled type, with turbo superchargers, maximum speed of 300 m.p.h. at 25,000 feet, cruising speed 160 m.p.h, 3,600 gallons of fuel with bomb bay tanks, 13 .50-caliber machine guns, maximum bomb load of 8,000 pounds, maximum gross weight of 64,500 pounds, and a range of 2,000 miles at 180 m.p.h. at 10,000 feet. The 1944 price tag of a B-17G was about $300,000.

The Chin Turret and 2 nose guns of a B-17G

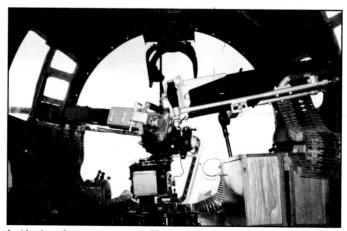

Inside view of nose compartment. The Bombsight is at photo's center. Navigator used guns at left and right.

The consortium of Boeing, Douglas and Vega-Lockheed was so effective that in March of 1944 it produced 578 Flying Fortresses in one month. In April of that same year Boeing produced 16 B-17s every day. Flying Fortresses were penetrating deep into Europe and no corner of it was safe from bombing attacks by the 8th Air Force. The BDV consortium built 3,405 B-17Fs (2,300 by Boeing), and 8,680 B-17Gs (4,035 by Boeing). Of the 12,731 total (which includes the 646 referred to in an earlier paragraph) 6,981 were built by Boeing, 3,000 by Douglas and 2,750 by Vega-Lockheed by the end of the war. Approximately 169 B-17 models C, E, F and G were delivered to England's Royal Air Force where the Cs were referred to as Fortress I, the Es and Fs as Fortress II and the Gs as Fortress III.

Model 299 and the early B-17s up until the E Model were conceived for a specific defensive purpose – the protection of United States coastlines from foreign navies . However, the primary role of the B-17 during World War II was offensive bombing, a function that led to the origin of the name "Flying Fortress." It had at various times also been called "Queen of the Bombers," "The Big Bird," "Glory Wagon," "The Sky Queen," "Mamma Eagle" and "Battleship of the Skies." Flying Fortress is the name that outlasted all the others.

The flight crews used their imagination – and their love and respect for the Flying Fortress – when it came to selecting names for the nose art: Adorable, Battle Wagon, Carolina Queen, Damn Yankee, Eager Eagle, Flak Dancer, Green Hornet, Hitler's Headache, Iron Maiden, Jolly Roger, Kayo, Liberty Run, Man O' War, Nasty Habit, Outhouse Mouse, Pistol Packin Mama, Quitchurbitchin, Reich's Ruin, TS, Unmentionable, Vicious Virgin, Wabash Cannonball, X Virgin, Yankee Raider, Zombie – and of course, Screwball Express.

Such were the names attached to Flying Fortresses by their flight crews ... names which in the bitter years of World War II became almost as celebrated as the honorable men who flew in them.

(**Special Credit**: Please refer to *B-17 Flying Fortress, Part I-Production Versions*; *B-17 Fortress At War*; *B-17 Specifications and General Description*; *Boeing B-17 Flying Fortress, 1935-1985*; *Flying Forts, The B-17 In World War II*; and *Flying Fortress, The Illustrated Biography Of The B-17s and The Men Who Flew Them*; under Bibliography.)

Top Turret. The bomb bay doors are open in this photo.

Twin Tail Guns. Sighting mechanism is at base of vertical stabilizer.

Ball Turret—shown in stowed position for takeoff and landing.

Left Waist Gun — one of two such guns in waist of B-17G. (Armament photos on pp. 12 - 13 courtesy of Collings Foundation of Stow, MA)

379th Bomb Group Photo — December 20, 1943

SCREWBALL EXPRESS

379th Bomb Group Photo — Cologne, Germany - May 28, 1944

THE MIGHTY EIGHTH

Following are some of the major developments and achievements of the United States 8th Air Force during World War II. These events span the period beginning with activation of this important air arm in 1942 to the end of World War II in the European Theater of Operations. These impressive highlights are presented here so readers will have opportunity for fuller appreciation of the significant role filled by the 8th Air Force in the fighting and winning of World War II.

Most certainly, compilation of outstanding accomplishments by other branches of the armed forces in the same and other theaters of operation is also highly appropriate. Because it is widely accepted that the demise of Hitler's Third Reich is primarily credited to the United States 8th Air Force, only achievements of The Mighty Eighth are included in the following recognition:

1942 – "The Takeoff Year" for the 8th Air Force, beginning when it was initially constituted as the VIII Bomber Command on January 19, and its activation in Savannah, Georgia, on January 28. Its first combat mission was August 17, when 12 B-17Es from the 97th Bomb Group attacked the marshalling yards at Rouen, France. Less than two months later, more than 100 B-17s and B-24s attacked airfields in France.

1943 – A Year of Innovation and Growth. Precision bombing by a formation of 8th Air Force bombers from high altitude first occurred in January. Its first mission to Germany was on January 27, when 91 bombers attacked Wilhelmshaven and Emden. Automatic Flight Control Equipment was used with the Norden Bombsight for the first time in March. The first mission involving more than 200 bombers occurred in May, and P-47s began escorting bombers up to 200 miles during that same month. Five new Groups of Fortresses brought the operational total to 12 Groups. One hundred and two B-24s of the 2nd Air Division (on duty in the Mediterranean Theater of Operations) were dispatched to Ploesti oil fields on August 1, with a loss of 30 B-24s. On August 17, 60 bombers were lost in the attack on Schweinfurt and Regensburg, at a cost to the Luftwaffe of 319 fighter planes. The first use of radar to bomb through clouds was September 27, and over 5,000 tons of bombs were dropped during that month. Flying Fortress strength was at 17 Bomb Groups and P-47s flew bomber escort up to 325 miles. On October 14, 60 bombers were lost on the mission to Schweinfurt's ball bearing industry. Over nine percent of all U.S. bombers flying over enemy territory during October were shot down. P-38 fighters become operational in October and escorted bombers up to 520 miles. Five hundred seventy-four bombers attacked Wilhelmshaven on November 3, the first mission with over 500 heavy bombers. At year end, 1,261 four-engine bombers had been lost to the enemy since the war began.

1944 – Year of Dominance and the Invasion. More than 10,000 tons of bombs were dropped during January. P-51s joined fighter escorts in February. Four bombing attacks were made on German aircraft plants and assembly factories February 20-25. The VIII Bomber Command was redesignated the Eighth Air Force on February 22. The first major 8th AF attack on Berlin was on March 6, with 69 U.S. bombers missing in action for the 8th's largest one-day loss. Over 20,000 tons of bombs were dropped during March. The first mission with more than 1,000 bombers was flown on May 7 to Berlin. June 6—D-Day – 40 Bomb Groups were operational; over 2,500 heavy bombers were dispatched in two raids, and nearly 2,100 P-47s, P-51s and P-38s provided escort. Personnel of the 8th Air Force totaled 200,000 by mid-year. U.S. fighters encountered 747 enemy aircraft on November 27, largest number in one day, and destroyed 102 of them. The largest bomber mission to date was flown on December 24, when more than 2,000 heavies attacked the "Ardennes Bulge."

1945 – Year of Ultimate Victory. On January 14, fighter planes of the 8th Air Force downed 161 enemy aircraft for its largest one day claim. An all-time record total of approximately 2,800 heavy bombers and 1,500 fighters were on assignment to the 8th Air Force in January. Six days of highly successful bombing attacks on marshalling yards in Berlin, Dresden and Nurenberg took place during February. The last mission to Berlin, the most heavily bombed U.S. target, was on March 28. March had the largest one-month bombing effort with nearly 74,000 bomb tons – and 92% of the attacking bombers were effective. German jet aircraft destroyed 24 U.S. bombers in March. The last B-17 was produced at Boeing's Seattle plant on April 9. U.S. fighters destroyed 752 enemy aircraft on April 16... 34 of our fighters were shot down. On April 25 the 8th Air Force flew its last bombing mission. The Mighty Eighth destroyed more than 2,000 enemy aircraft during April. VE-Day was May 8, 1945.

Most 8th Air Force combat groups were located north and northeast of London, and extended from Northampton eastward to the coast. The area is generally identified by drawing a line on a map of England from beneath Ipswich, westward beneath and past Bedford, then north between Bedford and Northampton toward Peterborough, and then northeastward to Cromer. Air bases of the 8th's bombers and fighters occupied approximately 40,000 acres of hedge-lined, stone-bordered English farmland. Records indicate approximately 130 airfields were jammed into an area about the size of Vermont. Many of the roads leading to these bases were constructed by early Roman settlers centruies ago. Modern airfields were located in sight of structures considered new if less than several hundred years old. The hands of time had generously and ornately sprinkled the surrounding countryside with churches, cathedrals and castles. It was an area of magical charm, filled with sophisticated instruments of aerial warfare.

The 8th Air Force was comprised of three heavy Bombardment Divisions. The bombers in the 1st Division were all B-17s and the 2nd Division consisted of B-24s. The 3rd Division included bombers of both types, however, records indicate the B-17s and B-24s were never scheduled to fly in the same Groups. In early 1944, the 1st Bomb Division contained 12 Bomb Groups and the 2nd and 3rd Divisions each contained 14, for a total of 40 Bomb Groups. On normal mission days in early 1944, the 8th Air Force could put up approximately 750 bombers at one time by using planes in only three of every four available squadrons. Later, using every squadron on every heavy bomber base as well as all spares, more than 2,000 B-17s and B-24s frequently filled the air over Europe. One historical source lists eight Groups of P-47s, five of P-51s and five of P-38s, a total of 18 U.S. Fighter Groups. That same source lists 24 B-17 Groups and 21 B-24 Groups, for a total of 45 Bomb Groups (H). The numbers in this paragraph apply to 8th Air Force Fighter Groups and Bomb Groups (H) on combat status as of June 6, 1944. The Mighty Eighth could dispatch as many as 1,000 fighter planes on a single mission.

The 8th Air Force was credited with the destruction of 18,787 Luftwaffe planes during World War II. A breakdown of that number is as follows: gunners on B-17s and B-24s received credit for the destruction of 6,236 enemy aircraft in the air; another 3,079 Luftwaffe planes were destroyed on the ground during 8th AF heavy bomber attacks. Fighter planes of the 8th Air Force were credited with the destruction of 5,222 enemy planes in the air and 4,250 on the ground.

Bomb tonnage dropped by all planes of the 8th Air Force during World War II exceeded 725,000 tons – more than 531,000 tons of which were dropped on Germany. During operations in the ETO the 8th Air Force launched 266,565 successful heavy bomber sorties that delivered 686,406 tons of bombs to enemy targets. For these reasons, the 8th Air Force became known as "The Mighty Eighth."

One-half of all USAAF casualties in World War II were suffered by the 8th Air Force – nearly 50,000 casualties, with up to 30,000 killed.

More than 350,000 8th AF personnel served on the many bases in England during World War II. Over one million persons have been associated with The Mighty Eighth since it was activated in 1942.

(**Special Credit:** Please refer to *One Last Look*, under Bibliography.)

THE 379TH BOMB GROUP (H)

The 379th Bomb Group was activated November 26, 1942, at Gowen Field, Boise, Idaho. It consisted of four squadrons of B-17s – the 524th, 525th, 526th and 527th. The Group was formed at Wendover Field, Utah, in December and trained there and at Sioux City AAB, Iowa, until March of 1943.

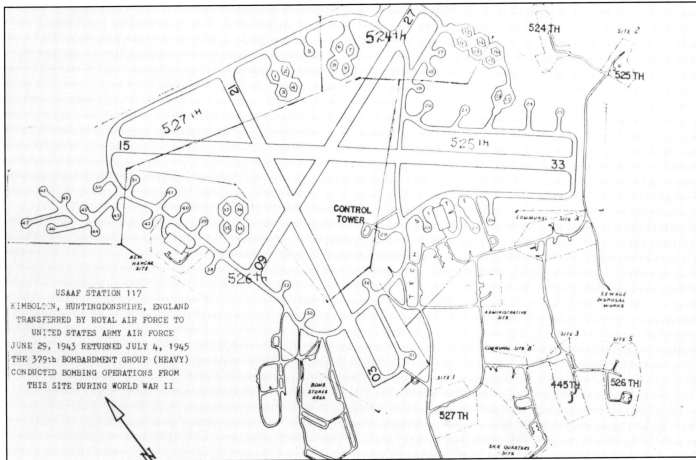

Diagram of 379th Bomb Group's Air Base, showing squadron hardstands near runways, and barracks areas at upper right & lower right quadrants. (Courtesy of 379th BG WWII Association)

526th Bomb Squadron

Overseas movement began in April, and in May the 379th arrived at Kimbolton, England, AAF Station 117. Its first combat mission was the bombing of German U-boat pens at St. Nazaire, France, on May 29, 1943. Col. Maurice A. Preston was the original commanding officer until October 10, 1944, when he became commander of the 41st Combat Wing headquartered at Molesworth. Col. Lewis E. Lyle then assumed command of the 379th Bomb Group until May 5, 1945, when he became commander of the 41st Combat Wing. Lt. Col. Lloyd C. Mason was then named commander of the 379th Bomb Group, and was followed by Lt. Col. Horace E. Frink.

Like many B-17 bases in England, the airfield at Kimbolton was originally a fighter base for the British. When it became evident Germany was not going to invade England, the RAF decided it didn't need many inland fighter bases and was happy to lease most of them to the United States as airfields for heavy bombers. The runways and perimeter ramps were too thin to accommodate the weight of our Flying Fortresses and Liberators, so the United States paid the British to repair and replace the runways to meet necessary specifications.

The 379th Bomb Group was one of 12 heavy Bombardment Groups in the First Bombardment Division of the United States 8th Air Force. The following list shows the conventional makeup of Group and Wing bomber formations which attacked the variety of targets described in following chapters.

All B-17s of every Group within the 1st Bombardment Division had a large triangle painted at the top of the vertical stabilizer. Each Group's assigned code letter was painted in the triangle. The 379th's planes were assigned the letter K, and were known as the Triangle K Group. Code letters of other Groups within the 1st Division were as shown in the left column below.

The 379th Bomb Group flew its first 300 missions in less time than any other heavy Bombardment Group. During all of its 330 bombing missions it dropped 25,553 tons of bombs on enemy targets, shot down 315 enemy aircraft, and lost 149 of its B-17s to enemy action. Eighty of those 149 Fortresses were shot down between May 29, 1943, and March 31, 1944. The other 69 Fortresses were lost between April 1, 1944 and April 25, 1945. One record lists 308 Flying Fortresses assigned to the 379th Bomb Group during World War II. It is very startling that more than 48% of those 308 Fortresses were lost to enemy fighters and antiaircraft guns.

Information in the 8th AF News indicates the 379th Bomb Group lost one B-17 to enemy action for every 70 sorties flown by its Fortresses, for a loss rate of 1 bomber for every 2.2 combat missions. This compares to 1 bomber lost per 30 sorties by the Group with the most bad fortune, and 1 bomber lost per 230 sorties by the Group with the least bad fortune. The average loss rate for 40 Bomb Groups listed was 1 bomber per 88 sorties.

The 379th led the 8th Air Force in bombing accuracy, flew more sorties than any other heavy Bomb Group, and had a lower loss and abortive ratio than any unit in the 8th Air Force for an extended period of time. Some of its other accomplishments include: development of the 12-plane squadron formation and 36-plane integral Group; and use of a straight line approach on the entire bomb run. Both of these techniques considerably increased bombing accuracy.

1st BOMBARDMENT DIVISION
"The Triangle First"

Code	Bomb Group	Combat Wing	Base	Assigned
A	91st	1st	Bassingbourn	14 Oct. 1942
L	381st		Ridgewell	5 Jun. 1943
W	398th		Nuthampsted	1 Apr. 1944
B	92nd	40th	Podington	15 Sept. 1943
G	305th		Chelveston	26 Nov. 1942
H	306th		Thurleigh	7 Sept. 1942
C	303rd	41st	Molesworth	21 Oct. 1942
K	379th		Kimbolton	20 May 1943
P	384th		Grafton Underwood	26 May 1943
J	351st	94th	Polebrook	15 Apr. 1943
S	401st		Deenethorpe	4 Nov. 1943
U	457th		Glatton	22 Jan. 1944

In May, 1944, it was announced that the 379th had made an unprecedented "8th Air Force Operational Grand Slam" during the preceding month. This meant that during April the 379th was first in every phase of bombing in which Bomb Groups of the 8th Air Force were graded. The 379th Bomb Group was the only unit ever awarded the 8th Air Force Grand Slam, a very unique honor that included recognition of the following achievements:

1-Best bombing results (greatest percent of bombs on target)
2-Greatest tonnage of bombs dropped on targets
3-Largest number of aircraft attacking
4-Lowest losses of aircraft
5-Lowest abortive rate of aircraft dispatched

The 379th received two Presidential Unit Citations for its accomplishments in combat. The Group flew its last combat mission on April 25, 1945. The 379th Bomb Group remained active for two years, seven months and 29 days. During this period approximately 6,000 personnel were assigned to the Kimbolton airfield. The Group was deactivated on July 25, 1945, at Casablanca, French Morocco, Africa. Currently called the 379th Wing, it is a unit of the Strategic Air Command, made up of B-52s and based at Wurtsmith AFB, Michigan.

(**Special Credit**: Please refer to *Air Force Combat Units Of WW II*, *Shades Of Kimbolton* and *The Mighty Eighth*, under Bibliography.)

Inscription by Lt. Gen. Doolittle reads: "The 379th conducted more sorties — delivered more bombs with greater accuracy — had lower aborts than any GP — & maintained a lower loss rate than any B-17 GP in the 8th Air Force..." Inscription by Lt. Gen. Eaker reads: "I never observed a better bombardment organization in WWII." (Courtesy of 379th BG WWII Association)

The Memorial Wall at U.S. Air Force Academy, Colorado Springs, Colorado, with 379th Bomb Group's Plaque in center. (Courtesy of 379th BG WWII Association)

SCREWBALL EXPRESS

This very special aircraft – a B-17G Flying Fortress – came off the assembly line of Boeing's Seattle, Washington, plant on January 30, 1944, and was accepted by the U. S. Army Air Corps the following day. Serial number 42-97128 was painted on its vertical stabilizer, stamped in a metal plate on its fuselage and officially identified this metallic-finish aircraft. It was one of a block of 115 B-17Gs manufactured with modifications that were identified by the number 40. The Flying Fortresses in this block of heavy bombers carried serial numbers 42-97058 to 42-97172.

On February 2, 1944, it arrived at Cheyenne, Wyoming, where it was equipped with special armament, starting with 13 .50-caliber machine guns. These included three twin turrets: one in the nose section, one on top of the fuselage behind the cockpit, and one under the fuselage behind the bomb bay, for a total of six guns in turrets; the other seven guns included: a pair in the tail section, one on each side of the waist section, one on each side of the nose compartment and one above the radio room. The machine guns were tested by firing them at tow targets over the Gulf of Mexico while the aircraft was temporarily stationed at Alexandria, Louisiana, between February 15 and March 1. The bomber's armament also included manual and electrical bomb release racks in the bomb bay, and a gyro-stabilized Norden Bombsight connected electrically to the Automatic Flight Control Equipment. The Norden Bombsight was credited with much of the very successful precision formation bombing from high altitude during the air war over Europe.

On March 4 this aircraft arrived at Presque Isle, Maine. It departed the United States on March 5 to begin its service with the 8th Air Force. This Flying Fortress, like thousands of other B-17s before and after, entered the European Theatre of Operations by flying the northern route from the United States to Newfoundland, Iceland, and finally to Prestwick, Scotland. It was delivered to the 379th Bomb Group at Kimbolton, England, on March 23, 1944, and was assigned to the 526th Bomb Squadron. Kimbolton is 11 miles north of Bedford, which is approximately 50 miles north of London.

Screwball Express was the 168th B-17, the 64th B-17G, and the 30th B-17G made by Boeing to be assigned to the 379th Bomb Group. It was code-named Mystic M for Mike and its original flight crew named it Screwball Express. Its nose art included a white cumulus cloud, with the letters in its name appearing thereon in a variety of bright colors. A large baseball was painted at the lower corner of the cloud and in its center was a bright red screw. The design was originated by Frank Craig, the crew's top turret gunner. Screwball Express received its unique name because its baseball-loving flight crew believed that, with the capabilities of this sophisticated, heavily armored aircraft, it could deliver a screwball pitch the enemy would be incapable of hitting, and that it could do so with "express dispatch." A bit corny? Perhaps – but we understood the meaning, and we liked it.

Ours was the original flight crew of Screwball Express, but we flew our first mission in another bomber on March 24, 1944, in an attack on an aircraft engine component plant at Frankfurt, Germany. Screwball Express flew its first combat mission – the second mission for our crew – on March 26 to a fly-bomb site at Wizernes, France. This Flying Fortress was "a home away from home base" for its original flight crew on all but four of our 33 combat missions. On 14 occasions it carried our crew in lead positions, four times as Low Squadron Lead, six times as High Squadron Lead and four times as Group Deputy Lead. Our crew also flew three other Fortresses in Lead positions, once in a High Squadron, once in a Low Squadron and once as Group Deputy, for a total of 17 Lead positions.

Records of the 379th Bomb Group indicate Screwball Express flew its first 107 combat missions over enemy-occupied Europe without an abort, and reveal only two aborts by this aircraft. Its first abort is recorded as taking place on January 3, 1945, on the 260th mission of the 379th Bomb Group and was caused by the pilot's stuck mike button and malfunctioning of the ball turret and chin turret. Its second abort resulted from a runaway prop on April 3, 1945, during the Group's 315th mission. It was on operational status for 376 of its 431 days of existence. During that period the 379th Bomb Group flew 229, nearly 70 percent, of its 330 combat missions. The other 55 days of this airplane's existence were spent being preflighted, armed, ferried to the European Theatre of Operations, being repaired for damage caused by flak or enemy fighters, or "stood down" when not flying a combat mission.

This amazing B-17 flew 12 combat missions in only 16 days during the period beginning July 4, 1944. And then, after only one day on the ground, it flew 10 more consecutive missions in the 15-day period beginning July 21, 1944. These two time periods include 22 combat missions in only 32 days. Additionally, this outstanding aircraft flew another 12 consecutive combat missions during the 24-day period October 9 through November 1, 1944.

Many times it was so riddled with holes caused by enemy machine gun bullets and antiaircraft shell fragments that flight was nearly impossible. It brought its crew back to England on many occasions when hope for a safe return to its home base at Kimbolton seemed very unlikely.

This B-17 — like all B-17s — was a verifiably tremendous aircraft.

The United States 8th Air Force, lst Bombardment Division, 41st Combat Wing, 379th Bomb Group, 526th Bomb Squadron, Lt. Howard E. Towers' flight crew, Screwball Express. The sound of those names generates a feeling of great respect within me. I am especially proud to have been a part of each of them.

The story of Screwball Express and details about its early combat missions would be incomplete without relating numerous incidents involving its original combat flight crew. Some of those incidents were happy – some were sad – a lot of them were funny – too many of them were horrifying. In addition to its engines, fuselage, instruments and armament, its original flight crew was an integral part of this B-17.

(**Special Credit**: Please refer to *Fortresses Of The Big Triangle First*, under Bibliography; and Mission Reports Of The 379th Bomb Group; and the Individual Aircraft Record Card at the National Air And Space Museum, Archival Support Unit Of The Smithsonian Institute, at Suitland, Maryland; under Reference Sources.)

Original Crew of Screwball Express

Assembly of our crew began in October of 1943, at the B-17 Combat Crew Training Station at Ardmore, Oklahoma. The pilot, bombardier, engineer, radio operator and most of the gunners were the first ones assigned. In November, less than five months before our first combat mission, the crew reached its full compliment of 10 members when our co-pilot and navigator became fellow crew members.

The crew represented a somewhat narrow range of ages, from 21 to 25 years, at the time our crew was first formed. Howard was the oldest, having been born May 27, 1918. It was appropriate he should be the oldest crew member. He was the pilot and our crew's commander. When we called him "the old man," it was a literal fact stated in figurative reference. As if by some plan of seniority ranking, co-pilot Jim Moore and our crew's second-in-command was the second oldest. Jim was born September 29, 1919. Bob Keller, our navigator, was born August 20, 1920. To the best of my knowledge, the other crew members were born in 1921 and 1922 and most of us were 21 or 22 years old at the time. Tom Kiblin, our ball turret gunner/engineer, was born on November 10, 1922, making him the youngest in our crew. I was second youngest with a birthdate of May 23, 1922.

Our nationalities, on the other hand, were not so closely related. Our crew's paternal and maternal parentages included the following: Scotch and English/Irish; Dutch/Irish and Dutch/Irish; English and English; German and German; Irish and German; Scotch and Irish; Irish and Dutch/Irish; and two of the crew members' parentages were Polish. I remember Ernie Koshuta's response when I asked him about his parents' nationalities. He winked a little smile, and said, "They were both Roman Catholic."

Our first six training flights were in the area around Ardmore. The flying time on each of these flights ranged from 3 hours and 35 minutes to 5 hours and 15 minutes. These missions consisted of practicing takeoffs and landings, flying out to the bombing range to drop M-38 practice bombs on improvised targets, and generally becoming familiar with every bomber crew's primary objective. That primary objective was to get the aircraft's bomb load into a precise position over a preselected target, and destroy that target.

Our seventh training flight was on November 22, 1943, a few days before our navigator was assigned to our crew. Jim Moore, our co-pilot, was flying as an observer and a Lt.

Back row, left to right: Lindsey, Craig, Milworm, Koshuta, Mathews and Kiblin. Front row, left to right: Keller, Cassens, Towers and Moore. (Photo by 379th BG Photographic Sec. March, 1944)

Original Crew of Screwball Express

Rank	Names	Positions	Home Towns--1943
2nd Lt.	Howard E. Towers	Pilot	San Francisco, CA
2nd Lt.	James C. Moore	Co-pilot	Louisville, TN
2nd Lt.	James R. Keller	Navigator	Knoxville, TN
2nd Lt.	Kenneth H. Cassens	Bombardier	Edwardsville, IL
S/Sgt.	Thomas A. Kiblin	Ball turret gun.	Buffalo, NY
S/Sgt.	Joseph Milworm	Radio Oper./gun.	Brooklyn, NY
Sgt.	Frank R. Craig	Top turret gun.	Mount Holly, NC
Sgt.	Jerold L. Lindsey	Tail gunner	Loveland, OK
Sgt.	Ernest Koshuta	Right waist gun.	Lansford, PA
Sgt.	Robert G. Mathews	Left waist gun.	Shively, KY

Goodekunce was aboard as substitute co-pilot. The flight was listed as a combination formation/night navigation mission from Ardmore, Oklahoma, to Fort Smith, Arkansas, and return. For the night navigation leg of the mission to Ardmore we were to fly a compass heading which was provided via a radio message from the formation's lead plane.

The compass heading given to us was in error, or may have been misunderstood. It should have been about 250 degrees, depending on our exact location when we separated from the lead plane, but for some reason we flew a 350 degree heading. We peered through the dark at land beacons which at night flashed code letters that, unfortunately, were not identifiable as beacons located between Fort Smith and Ardmore. Our estimated time of arrival at Ardmore came and passed, but Ardmore was nowhere in sight. Efforts to establish our position through radio navigational aids showed such a discrepancy in relation to where we thought we should be that the readout was considered unreliable.

Eventually we saw the lights of a fairly large city far in the distance. Lt. Goodekunce again went to work with the radio compass and determined the city was Leavenworth, Kansas. A course was plotted that would take us to Ardmore. We flew a little east of Wichita, Kansas, and near Ponca City, Oklahoma, it was determined we were about 90 miles off course due to a severe wind shift of almost 180 degrees after we had replotted our new heading to Ardmore. There was only a small amount of fuel remaining in the tanks, so the decision was made to go back to Wichita. As we eagerly approached it, we saw the welcoming sight of an airport at the outskirts of the city. Unfortunately, we were not able to make radio contact with the airport's control tower. We buzzed the field to get green-light landing clearance. In a few minutes (it seemed like hours) we were safely on the ground at Wichita. The engines sputtered to a stop just as we reached the parking area. We were out of gas.

Our flight time for that part of the training mission was 6 hours and 45 minutes. We slept at a hotel in Wichita and returned to Ardmore the following morning, in only 2 hours and 10 minutes.

During the latter part of November we made a successful navigation mission to Memphis, Tennessee and back, thanks to Bob Keller, our newly assigned navigator. Flights during December were mostly local and almost all of them involved practice bombing. This routine continued in January, 1944, although we did make another successful cross-country flight to Galveston, Texas. During that flight we were able to participate in air-to-air gunnery practice over the Gulf of Mexico. Firing at a moving target towed by another aircraft

was far from the reality of combat, because the target could not fire back at us. At one point during this flight our aircraft was caught in a downdraft while descending through clouds and dropped nearly 9,000 feet before becoming stabilized.

At the conclusion of one of our practice bombing flights the bomb bay doors failed to close. This was a situation experienced by many flight crews, because it was not unusual for a bomb bay door to malfunction. With the assistance of Frank Craig, I climbed into the bomb bay and discovered a motor-driven screwlift had come loose from one of the doors. Frank took a firm hold of the harness of my parachute and in a few minutes I was able to reconnect the screwlift. We sat on the bomb bay's catwalk and watched proudly as the electric motor closed the bomb bay doors. (Frank remembers that I almost fell out of the plane while in the bomb bay that day.)

Also in January, during a training flight that emphasized formation flying, one of the planes flew too close to ours and one of its propellers chewed off part of our plane's tail section. Fortunately, the damage was relatively minor. Jerry Lindsey, our tail gunner, was understandably very upset by the incident; however, all of us understood accidents were inevitable and to be expected. On another of our formation training flights the plane flying our right wing position got too close and bumped our right wing — once, twice, three times –with its left wing tip. We knew this was not an accident and cringed in fear of the possible outcome. The pilot of that plane told us before takeoff he was going to show us how great he was at flying close formation. He had recently returned from a tour of missions in the ETO and was catching up on his flying time by participating in this training exercise. That turkey!

Our 35th and final training exercise at Ardmore was a combination day and night flight of 5:25 hours on January 22, 1944. As of that date our crew had completed 136:40 hours of flight time in B-17F Flying Fortresses.

On January 31 we were shipped to Grand Island, Nebraska. Our primary purpose there was to preflight a B-17G Flying Fortress, preparatory to our crew ferrying it to Scotland for assignment to the U.S. 8th Air Force. On February 6 our crew performed a 5 hours and 45 minutes final test flight of the aircraft. February 17 we started the trip overseas by flying eight hours from Grand Island to Grenier Field near Manchester, New Hampshire. The next leg of our overseas flight via the Northern Route was to Goose Bay, Labrador, Newfoundland, and lasted 5 hours and 30 minutes on February 20. On February 22 we flew 9 hours and 45 minutes en route to Meek's Field, approximately 40 miles from Reykjavic, Iceland. The following day we flew 7 hours and 30 minutes to Prestwick, Scotland, where the aircraft was taken over by the 8th Air Force. Our total flying time from Grand Island to Prestwick was 30 hours and 45 minutes.

Only three B-17s previously destined for combat duty with the 379th Bomb Group had failed to complete the Northern Route flight. Each of those planes was a B-17F, one of which went down in the Atlantic Ocean in April, 1943. The other two crashed the following month, one at Prestwick, Scotland, and the other at Bunderan, Ireland.

Some of our crew proceeded by ground transportation to Bovingdon, England. Others of the crew were sent to Stone, England, and then to The Wash at the mouth of the Thames river on the east coast. While there they went through two weeks of combat orientation training. On March 17, 1944, our entire crew arrived at Kimbolton, England, a small English village with a population of 750. Upon reaching the U. S. airfield at the edge of town we became Crew AA-96 and were assigned to the 526th Bomb Squadron, 379th Bomb Group (Triangle K), 41st Combat Wing, 1st Bombardment Division, United States 8th Air Force. It was immediately obvious that the number of military personnel assigned to the 379th Bomb Group was much larger than the population of Kimbolton.

Five days later, on March 22, we flew our only fully-crewed training flight while stationed in England. The flight was a combination of day and night flying, and lasted 6:10 hours. Its purpose was to help us gain additional confidence as a crew before our first combat mission over enemy-occupied Europe.

We had flown a total of 179:20 hours since we were first organized as a crew in late 1943. The Air Force had proclaimed we were combat ready. Our first combat bombing mission was only two days away. Not one member of our crew had fired a .50-caliber machine gun since our air gunnery practice over the Gulf of Mexico, two months earlier. We had not practiced dropping bombs or flying in formation since we left Ardmore, Oklahoma.

Nevertheless, we were combat ready – ready or not!

(**Special Credit:** Please refer to *Crew AA-96 And Their Screwball Express*; under Bibliography)

The First 83 Days of 1944

The following information provides a graphic and factual account of the intensity of aerial warfare over Europe during the early part of 1944, before our crew and our plane entered the fighting.

January 1 through March 23, 1944, was a period of heavy activity for the 8th Air Force, the 379th and other heavy Bomb Groups. Long-range fighter support for U. S. bombers had become a reality. Radar bombing techniques were becoming more successful. Production lines back in the States were setting records for the manufacture of planes and armament. The invasion of Europe was in the minds and conversations of everyone in and out of uniform. The large presence of U. S. airmen in England was partly overshadowed by American, Belgian, British, Canadian, French and Polish ground forces. Airborne troops, artillery, engineers, the infantry, armored divisions, the navy, paratroopers and tankers had been united into the largest and most effective invasion force in history.

The Germans were also very aware of the planned invasion. The Luftwaffe's planes made desperate attempts to protect German airfields and aircraft factories from the

The 525th Squadron lost this B-17, serial number 42-29889, due to an accidental fire on Feb. 23, 1944. Photo by 379th BG Photo. Sec.)

increasing number of bombing raids by the 8th AF. Antiaircraft gunners were very skillful at shooting down Allied bombers.

On the January 5 mission of the 379th Bomb Group to Kiel, aircraft number 42-5827 was hit by a rocket but managed to land in Sweden. Plane 42-29747 crashed on takeoff. During assembly the 379th's 42-37887 collided in mid-air with the 303rd Bomb Group's 42-31441 and crashed at Covington, England, killing seven of its crew. The 303rd's aircraft crashed at Catworth, England, killing all of its crew. The loss of 42 B-17s on January 11 during the bombing mission to the aircraft assembly plant at Oschersleben was the Triangle 1st Division's highest loss since the October 1943 mission to Schweinfurt. On January 29, the 1st Division sent a record number of 366 bombers to Frankfurt. On January 30, 349 planes were sent to Brunswick to bomb an aircraft parts plant. The 379th lost four bombers on that mission: 42-31535, 42-31643 and 42-31692; each of which had been assigned to the Group for only six days, and 42-3325. Plane number 42-31021 of the 379th crash landed at Ash, England. In addition, the 379th had to salvage plane 42-39889 as a result of heavy damage from enemy 20 mm cannon fire. The 1st Division lost 85 B-17s to enemy fighters and flak during January and 10 of that number were from the 379th Bomb Group. Another 29 B-17s of the 1st Bombardment Division were lost because of accidents and other causes for a total of 114 during that month. By comparison, the 3rd Division lost 55 aircraft in combat during the same period of time.

Bombing emphasis began to include Noball targets along the French coast of the English Channel. These were the fly-bomb sites, or V-1 and V-2 rocket launching ramps and pads. Bombing penetrations by the 8th Air Force into Germany became deeper and deeper. The number of B-17s and B-24s per mission increased from previous records of 200 and 300 to 500, 600, then 700 and 800. Aircraft 42-38036 became the 379th's first February casualty following a local formation practice flight. Six Combat Wings, with the 41st

Wing in the lead, were assigned to bomb shipbuilding facilities at Wilhelmshaven on February 3. A total of 348 bombers were sent on the mission and 306 bombed the target. An engine component plant at Frankfurt was bombed the next day, and on February 5th four airfields in France were attacked. More airfields in France were bombed on February 6th, Frankfurt again on the 8th, and the marshalling yards at Frankfurt on the 11th.

Then came what was called The Big Week, February 20 to 25, when the 8th and 15th Air Forces had nearly 6,000 bombers pounding Germany's aircraft industry. The Luftwaffe lost over 450 planes trying to stop them. The biggest effort of the month took place on February 20, when 417 planes were dispatched to the Leipzig/Mockau airfield where assembly plants housing Me-109 fighter planes and Junkers bombers were major targets. On February 22, the 1st Division lost 38 bombers during the mission to bomb the aircraft factory at Halberstadt, Germany. Five of that number were from the 379th Bomb Group, aircraft 42-5828, 42-29829, 42-31028, 42-31510 and 42-97520, for a total of eight from the 379th during February. On February 24, 266 bombers were dispatched to hit the ball bearing plant at Schweinfurt, scene of the August 17 and October 14, 1943, losses of 81 Fortresses by the 1st Bomb Division – more than at any other of its targets in the war to date. On the 25th the German aircraft industry was again the target at Regensburg, Furth, Augsburg and Stuttgart for bombers of the 8th AF and 15th AF.

General Hap Arnold said, "The Big Week changed the history of the air war." The Luftwaffe had essentially been converted into a defensive air force. Losses to the United States during The Big Week included 244 bombers and 33 fighter planes.

On February 28, 85 bombers hit enemy defense installations in the Pas de Calais area of the French coast. The 1st Bombardment Division lost 105 B-17s in combat during February; the 3rd Division listed 86 aircraft missing in action.

On March 3, the ball bearing plant at Erkner, 16 miles southeast of the center of Berlin, was the primary target and Berlin was the secondary target. The 94th Combat Wing was leading, followed by the 1st Combat Wing, then a composite Wing, the 40th Wing and finally the 41st Combat Wing. Due to heavy cloud cover, the formation flew north of the intended route and at a higher altitude than assigned at the morning's briefing. It was decided to abandon the mission when clouds reached 28,000 feet. About that time a group of planes from the 3rd Division accidentally flew through the 40th Combat Wing. Planes scattered widely but were able to reform and return to their bases in squadron formations. The lead and second Combat Wings dropped bombs on Wilhelmshaven through overcast skies as they approached the enemy coast on the return trip. Of the 260 bombers that had been dispatched, only 61 dropped their bombs. Three of the planes on the mission were shot down. Erkner was the target again on the next day with the 41st Wing in the lead, followed by the 40th, the 1st, the 94th, and a 40th/41st composite Wing. Weather made assembly very difficult. The clouds got worse and it was again decided to abandon the mission. Targets of opportunity were bombed at Bonn, Dusseldorf and Cologne. A total of 264 bombers were sent on the mission but only 186 were able to do any bombing. Four bombers were lost in action that day by the 1st Division. Three of those four were from the 384th Bomb Group, one of the three Groups that made up the 41st Combat Wing.

On March 6, the ball bearing plant at Erkner was again the primary target, and the industrial center of Berlin was the secondary target. Clouds prevented visual bombing of Erkner, but the suburbs of Berlin were bombed visually. Friendly fighters were greatly outnumbered over the target by more than 200 enemy aircraft that attacked in mass formations. The 8th Air Force lost 69 heavy bombers on its first major raid to Berlin. This was the largest single day's loss by the 8th Air Force during the entire war. Eighteen Fortresses in the 248-plane bombing effort of the 1st Division were shot down. One of those planes, number 42-31555, was from the 379th Bomb Group.

March 8 saw another mission to Erkner, with Berlin as the secondary target. On March 9, the Heinkel aircraft factory at Oranienburg was the primary target and Berlin was again the secondary target. A few minutes before reaching the Initial Point in the bombing run, cloud cover required Pathfinder bombing and the secondary target was hit in Combat Wing formation with the 40th Wing in lead position. Other Wings that followed included the 41st, the 1st and the 94th. On March 18, major attacks were directed by the 1st Bomb Division at Oberpfaffenhofen, Lechfeld and Landsberg, with Munich as the secondary target. Of 290 bombers dispatched, 284 bombed the primary targets. Six bombers were downed on the mission, but four of the six made landings in Switzerland.

On the 19th of March primary targets of the Triangle First were the V-weapons sites at Wizernes and Watten. March 20 the target was Frankfurt, with an engine component plant as primary target and the center of Frankfurt as secondary target. Only 101 bombers dropped their bombs, although 231 planes were on the mission. High cirrus clouds and dense contrails made formation flying very difficult and several Groups abandoned the mission. Berlin has hit again on March 22. Oranienburg was the primary target but was clouded over, so 277 bombers dropped their bomb loads on the German capital. Bombs of the 379th Group hit the German Air Ministry Headquarters as planned. On March 23 the largest mission of the month for the 1st Division took place when 296 of 300 dispatched bombers hit Munster and targets of opportunity. The 41st Wing bombed Beckum, Noubeckum and Ahlen. The 94th Wing bombed Orensteinfurt and the 1st Wing bombed Ahlen. A composite 40th/41st Wing bombed Hamm.

The weather over England and the Continent was very uncooperative with the flying of combat missions by 8th Air Force Bomb Groups. Rain, clouds and overcast skies forced the 379th to scrub nine missions during this period of time and recall two others after its bomber formations were enroute to their targets.

During those first 83 days of 1944 the 1st Bombardment Division lost 259 bombers and 2,590 crewmen to the enemy. Twenty-one of those planes were Flying Fortresses of the 379th Bomb Group, ten in January, eight in February and three in March as of the 23rd day of that month. The 210 airmen flying in Fortresses of the 379th Bomb Group were killed or became prisoners of war during those 83 days.

Screwball Express was assigned to the 379th Bomb Group on the 83rd day of 1944. The 379th's bombing missions flown by our crew during the next three months included similar numbers of aircraft losses and deaths.

The spring and early summer of 1944 was one of the toughest periods for heavy bombers of the 8th Air Force. From the highest echelon of authority at 8th Air Force Headquarters came the decision that the primary objective of U.S. fighter planes was no longer to protect bomber formations. Instead, heavy bombers would become bait with which to lure enemy fighter planes into the air. In theory, U.S. fighters could then more quickly proceed with the Luftwaffe's destruction. This daring decision was the harbinger of many records for U.S. fighter planes.

The existence of this stunning military strategy was known only to top echelon officers at 8th Air Force Head-quarters and commanders of its Combat Wings and Bomb Groups. However, results of this decision were seen almost daily in the number of Luftwaffe planes destroyed by 8th Air Force fighters—and in the number of B-17s and B-24s shot down by enemy planes. Although this decision took a large toll of bomber crews and bombers, many thousands of Allied airmen, paratroopers, ground troops, support ech-elon and naval personnel survived D-Day and the war in Europe because of it. In retrospect, it helped enhance and guarantee an Allied victory in the European Theatre of Operations more quickly than would otherwise have been possible.

It was a decision of historic significance in the winning of a terrible war.

(**Special Credit**: Please refer to *Fortresses Of The Big Triangle First*; and *The World War II Quiz And Fact Book*, under Bibliography.)

Mission to Frankfurt

It was a little before 0245 hours. The operations officer shook me by the shoulder and jerked the army blanket down to the foot of my bunk. "Up and at 'em," he said to me. "You're flyin' a mission today." He quickly took the same action with Howard Towers, Jim Moore and Bob Keller and made identical announcements to them. He went through the same routine with officers from some other crews in our barracks. In another barracks, not far away, someone was giving the same long-awaited news to the other six members of our crew: Frank Craig, Joe Milworm, Jerry Lindsey, Tom Kiblin, Ernie Koshuta and Bob Mathews. A total of 23 flight crews, 230 crew members in three of the four Squadrons of the 379th Bomb Group, were awakened with the same message that morning. It was Friday, March 24, 1944.

We hit the latrine, shaved, dressed quickly and headed for the mess hall. In the few minutes it took to arrive there our minds filled with many questions – Where were we going? Did I mail that letter last night before I hit the sack? Where did some of the guys get those bicycles, and why do I have to walk? How long will this mission be? Wonder if I'll make it back? Is it always this foggy in England? We repeated some of these questions aloud as we went through the chow line and sat down to eat. I hardly noticed that those of us who were served real eggs were the ones assigned to fly the day's mission. I gulped down the eggs, trying my best not to look nervous. Still swallowing the last bite, I chased it down with a final slurp of coffee. We were due in the briefing room in less than 10 minutes.

When we arrived, the briefing room was already beginning to cloud with grey cigarette smoke. It was a room filled with odors of shaving lotion, hair oil and sweat. Special odors came out of every boot, pants and jacket in the room. Crewmen sat on folding chairs, mumbling to each other about getting up so early, and about the bitter taste of the coffee that was so abundantly available to everyone. It was a room that filled from the front to the back, because no

one dared to miss one word of the briefing session. When seated up front one could see and hear what was happening. The huge map on the wall was covered with a white sheet, and the course to the target was laid out with a piece of yarn. Upon entering the room, everyone visually checked the position of the yarn pulley at the left side of the map. If the pulley was near the top and all the yarn used, it was very likely the mission would be a rough one – to a place like Berlin, Munich or Sorau. However, if the pulley was near the bottom it was possible the mission might be to Sottevast or Marquise, maybe an easy "milk-run." The pulley's position indicated something between. The dozens of separate conversations taking place included dozens of predictions on where and what our target would be.

The Top Brass of the 379th sat in the front of the room. They knew where we were going, and some of them were going with us. It was like a room full of hide-and-seek. Why didn't they pull the sheet off the front wall and let us in on the big secret! We waited, shuffled our feet, coughed up phlegm and threw cigarette butts on the floor. Our impatience was answered with a loud, "Tain-hut," as we were called to attention. Colonel Preston entered the room and walked briskly to the front. He looked around the room at us for what seemed an eternity. Finally, he spoke. "Gentlemen, the target for today is Schweinfurt, Germany," he announced. At that precise moment the sheet was pulled off the wall, providing what seemed like a visual exclamation point to the colonel's statement.

The room echoed with gasps of "Oh, no!" "Not Schweinfurt!" "Is this trip really necessary?" There were hoots and catcalls, but each utterance was an attempt to hide fear – a fear that grabbed hold of you and wouldn't let go. Several officers on Preston's staff, each taking his turn, told us how important it was that the ball bearing industry at Schweinfurt be destroyed. Forty-five percent of all German anti-friction bearings were produced there. Maps, charts and diagrams told us what we should expect the weather to be en route to and from the target, where the antiaircraft guns were in relation to our flight plan and how many enemy fighter planes we might encounter during the mission. Everything was so precise.

The single greatest 8th Air Force loss in the European air war to date occurred at Schweinfurt on October 14, 1943— Black Thursday. At the time it was the deepest penetration into Germany by the 8th Air Force. It was there that 60 Fortresses were lost out of 257 that bombed Schweinfurt on that mission – a loss of 23 percent. A loss of more than 44 percent was incurred on the same mission by our 1st Bombardment Division which lost 45 of its 101 planes in the 257-plane armada. The 379th went to Schweinfurt twice in 1943: the mission on August 17 cost the 379th four B-17s and on the October 14 mission the 379th lost six of its planes. (Our Group's October 14 loss matched two previous record one-day losses; six of its Fortresses were lost on the June 11 attack on Wilhelmshaven and another six on the June 25 mission to Hamburg, both in 1943.) The 379th flew 54 combat missions and lost 58 Flying Fortresses in 1943. It was sobering to us that 10 of those 58 losses happened on the two missions to Schweinfurt. The name of the city at which today's target was located had a bad sound to it –very bad.

The general briefing didn't last very long and we were soon dismissed to attend separate briefings, one for the pilots and others for the radio operators, the navigators, the bombardiers, etc. The briefings dealt with the specifics of each crew member's specialty as it applied to this particular mission and target. Meanwhile, the gunners went ahead to the flightline locker room for parachutes, heated flying suits and Mae West life preservers. The rest of us soon did the same thing. Moore was responsible for signing out an escape kit for each member of the crew. An Army truck transported us to the plane we were to fly. The truck went past the hardstand, or cul-de-sac, where a brand new Flying Fortress was parked. Due to the lack of activity around it, we realized it was not going on this mission. Its first combat mission was yet to come. The truck stopped at the next plane. Our flight crew and our gear were unloaded in front of a B-17G produced by Vega and delivered to the 379th Bomb Group on October 19, 1943. The serial number of this aircraft was 42-39789.

We were not aware this particular Fortress barely made it back from the 379th's 50th mission, on December 20, when the Group's target was the FW-190 plant at Bremen. During that mission this aircraft, affectionately named "Skunkface" by someone in the 526th Squadron, lost the top half of its rudder and most of its right horizontal tail section as the result of a flak burst. It had received an excellent "facelift" by its ground crew and looked "almost new," certainly not "almost an MIA." (See photo on page 14)

Everyone in our crew started performing various preflight checks of equipment. Howard and Jim checked the exterior and interior of the plane. Bob Keller checked all his maps and navigation paraphernalia. I checked the bomb bay racks and the bombs they held. Joe checked his radio equipment. Frank, Jerry, Tom, Ernie and Bob Mathews checked their guns to make certain they were ready to use. Everyone was busy checking and rechecking. Then all of us just sat there for 30 to 45 minutes, waiting for the weather to clear. Finally, all 23 planes assigned to the mission were given orders to start engines. The mission was "on." Our pilots checked and rechecked a host of items, revved the engines and taxied our plane into takeoff position.

Fear still had its hold on me. I probably wasn't the only one. As the four Wright Cyclone radial engines roared with the combined thrust of 4,800 horsepower, I started to sing one of my favorite songs – The 23rd Psalm. The following words of that psalm seemed especially proper:

"Yea, though I walk through the valley of the shadow of death I will fear no evil: for Thou art with me; Thy rod and Thy staff, they comfort me."

The roar of the engines drowned out my singing to everyone but me.

We took off at 0606 hours and assembled 2,000 feet above the clouds. Our crew was assigned the number five position in the Low Squadron of our Group. That position was called Coffin Corner because of its vulnerability to attack by enemy fighters. This was "an honor" accorded many new crews. The absence of a bombsight in the plane we were flying contributed to our awkward feeling of unimportance.

The 379th Bomb Group flew Lead Group for the 41st Combat Wing. We picked up the 303rd High Group near Molesworth shortly after 0700 hours at 10,000 feet . The 384th Low Group fell in behind us at Northampton. At 0754 hours we reached the English coast at 17,500 feet, passing over Northforeland on schedule. I saw three of our Fortresses turn back to Kimbolton and wondered what they were doing, not then realizing they were spare aircraft for the mission and were not needed today. At 0813 hours we

crossed the enemy coast at 20,000 feet about five miles north of Dunkirk. My first sight of enemy antiaircraft fire was over Belgium. When it exploded it first looked like little black clouds that quickly mushroomed in size. A direct hit was big trouble. Flak could also cause much danger with the many pieces of jagged shell fragments that flew out of the explosion and cut like sharp knives through the fuselage and its miles of wires, tubing and hoses, and through clothing and flesh. The Germans called it Flieger Abwehr Kanonen, which means antiaircraft cannon. The Americans and British called it flak, for short.

The 20 bombers in our Group were dispatched to bomb the Kuget-Fischer ball bearing plant at Schweinfurt. One of our 20 planes formed up with the 457th Bomb Group, which also had been assigned the Schweinfurt target. When the remaining 19 planes of our Group approached the target area with the 303rd and 384th Bomb Groups, cloud cover described as 10/10 was too dense to permit any attempt at accurate bombing. After our Group leader notified our Combat Wing and our fighter support, our Wing went to Frankfurt, Germany, the secondary target for this mission. Frankfurt (am Main) is approximately 70 miles west of Schweinfurt. We were very relieved by our leader's decision. When we arrived at Frankfurt we found a slightly improved overcast of only 9/10. The heavy cloud cover was not considered bad enough to present a bombing problem. It was a lot better than going to Schweinfurt.

After turning at the Initial Point of the bomb run, over the town of Giessen, I called Joe Milworm on the intercom and told him to "throw out the chaff." Chaff was a batch of aluminum strips packed into cardboard boxes, several of which were stored in the radio room of the plane. The aluminum strips were cut to match the wavelength of German search radar. Upon approaching large numbers of antiaircraft gun installations, procedure called for the boxes to be opened and dumped into the yawning bomb bay. The floating aluminum strips reflected the enemy's radar signals. This gave the impression to enemy sighting mechanisms of a large formation of planes at that point, when actually the formation had already moved ahead. Joe heard my order, but in the excitement he forgot to open the boxes and threw them down through the open bomb bay. The Germans probably had a difficult time figuring out what type of 'bombs' we had dropped, and for what purpose. Joe and all the others on our crew often laughed about this incident in the months that followed.

The actual target at Frankfurt was an aircraft engine component plant within the city. Each of our 19 Fortresses on the 12-minute bomb run carried five 1,000-pound demolition bombs. We did not know at the time that 12 minutes would be the longest bomb run our crew would ever fly. Our Group dropped its 95 bombs from an altitude of 23,500 feet at 0940 hours; the 303rd and 384th did likewise. Like other bombardiers in our Group, I dropped our plane's bombs when I saw our Group leader drop his. Antiaircraft fire en route to and at the target was heavy but inaccurate, although eight of our bombers received minor damage from flak. Our bombing was completed by the Pathfinder method and our results were described as "very good," despite our variance from assigned heading and altitude due to heavy cloud cover and strong wind currents. The 303rd Bomb Group dropped incendiary bombs that adjoined the bomb pattern made by the 379th Group. Bomb strikes made by the 384th Group were not immediately discernable because of heavy clouds and smoke. A total of 162 B-17s bombed

Frankfurt between 0909 hours and 1028 hours that morning. Some of the smoke at the target was presumably a result of a night bombing raid by the British Royal Air Force on the previous evening.

Our Group did not encounter any enemy fighter planes during the mission. Several rockets were fired at us from the ground in the area around Frankfurt, but all of them failed to reach our altitude.

All of our Group's planes returned safely to our home base at Kimbolton. The total flying time for the mission was 7 hours. That brand new B-17G was still sitting on the hardstand where we saw it earlier that day. It was waiting for assignment to some lucky flight crew.

An article in the Stars and Stripes newspaper the next day supplied us with more information about activities of the 8th Air Force on this date. In addition to the bombing our Group had done at Frankfurt, those B-17s that managed to beat the weather to Schweinfurt did a very good job of bombing the ball bearing plant there. B-24 Liberators were able to visually attack enemy fighter plane bases at Nancy and St. Dizier in France. About 200 to 250 Fortresses and a like number of Liberators took part in these attacks. Three 8th Air Force bombers, two of which collided over Germany, and five U.S. fighter planes failed to return to England. Additionally, the newspaper stated that only three enemy aircraft were destroyed, all on the ground. There were two apparent reasons for the Luftwaffe's failure to challenge the American bombers: 1) The Fortresses had run into very cloudy weather, making defensive fighter operations difficult, and 2) the Liberators were operating over French territory that Reichsmarshall Hermann Goering had obviously decided not to defend vigorously until some later time.

At this time in the war, flight crews of 8th Air Force Fortresses were required to fly 25 combat missions in order to complete their operational tour and be sent back to the States.

Our crew had completed its first combat mission. Only 24 more and we'd be heading home.

God heard me singing.

(**Special Credit**: Please refer to *One Last Look*, under Bibliography.)

Bomb damage to Frankfurt, Germany, following daylight attack on March 24, 1944. (Reprint from an 8th AF publication, circa April, 1944)

Mission to Wizernes

March 26, 1944. The lack of fog and drizzling rain made the morning a stimulating experience. The bells of St. Andrew's church in the town of Kimbolton reminded me it was Sunday. The sky was blue in almost every direction with a collection of white, cumulus clouds off to the east at approximately 6,000 feet.

The time was about 0830 hours. We had finished eating breakfast an hour ago. Jim, Bob and I were playing catch with a much used softball in the area near our barracks. Towers had gone directly from the mess hall to our squadron headquarters to see if the 379th Bomb Group was going on a mission today, and whether our crew was assigned to it. We knew the weather was very good for a flight across the English Channel, so the odds heavily favored what we assumed would take place.

Towers came trotting briskly down the path to the improvised ball diamond. Jim caught sight of him just as Bob tossed Jim the softball. Towers' voice was clear and his words were directly to the point. "Fellas," he said, "briefing is at 0900 hours. We're flying." We ran into the barracks for our flight jackets and caps, and dashed away to the briefing room. The softball was left where it had fallen.

During briefing we learned bad weather over part of Germany had caused a mission to Merseburg to be scrubbed. We all cheered. However, we also learned our target was a V-1 launching ramp near the town of Wizernes, France. Officially, the day's target was called a fly-bomb site, or Noball target. The letter V in the weapon's name stood for Vergeltungswaffe, which is German for "revenge weapon." The 8th Air Force code name for bombing raids against Germany's Noball launch sites was Operation Crossbow.

The V-1 was a dagger-shaped flying bomb, technically simple, mass produced, pilotless, jet-powered and ramp-launched. The pulse jet of the V-1 made a guttural drone, hence the nickname "buzz bomb." The V-1 cruised at approximately 350 m.p.h. Its pulse jet would cut out near its target and its one-ton explosive warhead would fall to earth, usually with non-precision results. The first of these weapons would hit London on June 13, 1944. By the end of the war, nearly 2,500 of these "flying bombs" reached London, eluding antiaircraft fire, balloon defenses and most of the RAF's radar-guided fighters. Over 6,000 civilians were killed during this period and an additional 18,000 were seriously wounded. The Hawker Tempest, a British fighter-bomber, was credited with intercepting and destroying more than 600 V-1 flying bombs. Hitler, intent on revenge against the people of England, failed to use the V-1 on military objectives around Southampton and Portsmouth. This was most fortunate, because these cities were vital seaports from which supplies would be sent to our invasion troops in France.

A piloted version of the V-1, known as the "doodlebug," was designed as a suicide aircraft. Although 175 "doodlebugs" were built, they were never used operationally.

The V-2 rocket – or 'Second Revenge Weapon' – was a streamlined, rocket-launched ballistic missile with a very complex design. The liquid-filled V-2 was the more formidable of the two types because it flew at nearly 3,600 m.p.h., its approach could not be detected and it could not be intercepted. It was reasonably accurate because it was radio controlled. It was first launched against London on September 8, 1944, falling at Chiswick where it killed three people. During the next six and one-half months 1,100 V-2 rockets fell on England. Of that total, 516 reached England's capital, killed 2,754 civilians and seriously injured an additional 6,523 persons.

Wizernes is five miles south of St. Omer, which is approximately 22 miles southeast of Calais and 22 miles south of Dunkirk. The 379th Bomb Group flew as a solitary Group, which means our Group was not accompanied on this mission by other Groups of bombers. The mission was to be less than five hours in duration and friendly fighter escort was to provide us with good cover during most of the flight. It sounded like it was going to be an easy mission – a "milk-run" – if only the flak wasn't too intense. We dismissed our thoughts of flak in the same manner as the Colonel dismissed the briefing - quickly, and with expressions of "good luck."

We went through the routine of checking out our flight gear and jumped into the truck waiting to take us to a bomber. After a fast, bouncing ride out to the ramp, the driver of the truck braked it to a sudden stop. We climbed over the truck's tailgate and turned our heads toward the plane assigned to us for this mission.

Before our eyes was that brand new B-17G Flying Fortress we saw the previous day. Its natural metallic finish made it gleam in the morning sunlight like a huge, rare jewel. "What an airplane! And look at that chin turret," I yelled, expressing the pride I felt in its location being under the bombardier's position. At the opposite end of the plane, up on the vertical stabilizer, was painted a big, white letter K in a black triangle. Under it was the serial number 42-97128, and beneath it was painted a big letter M that stood for Mystic M for Mike. On the sides of the fuselage were painted the letters LF, identifying the plane's assignment to the 526th Bomb Squadron. This was the Flying Fortress in which we would fly all but four of our combat missions. We were this bomber's original flight crew. This was the Flying Fortress that our crew named Screwball Express. Every member of our crew quickly climbed aboard this magnificent aircraft. It was our plane – our Flying Fortress – all ours. Well, at least we took tremendous satisfaction in identifying it that way.

L/R— Keller, Cassens, Moore and Towers. (Photo by 379th BG Photographic Section).

Sgt. Joe Starbuck (front row left), Group Crew Chief of Screwball Express, with eight members of his team. (Photo by 379th Photo. Sec.)

Explosions of approximately 20 flak guns, about 750 feet from camera. (Photo from 379th BG Photographic Section, March 26, 1944)

Every member of our flight crew was extremely proud of this aircraft. There were others who shared our pride; they were members of the plane's ground crew, and this aircraft belonged to them as much as it belonged to us. The ground crew's chief was Sgt. Joe Starbuck who hailed from Pennsylvania. None of us remember his exact military rank, but he was held in very high regard by everyone who knew him. After many of our future missions, he and the members of his ground crew would keep Screwball Express flyable when it seemed impossible to do so, either by the magnitude of repairs or by the shortness of time allowed before its next mission. Regular maintenance alone took many hours to accomplish. Damage caused by flak and enemy fighters would have to be repaired after almost every mission, and frequently on an overnight basis. Starbuck was a real star! He and his ground crew never failed to do their job, and they always did it extremely well.

Just before the plane taxied out to the perimeter ramp Starbuck said privately to me, "Lieutenant, here's a little good luck piece I'd like for you to carry when you and your crew fly missions in Screwball Express." He handed me a U.S. five-cent piece. "Call it a loan," he explained, "an interest free nickel loan, as long as you pay it back to me, with the same five-cent piece, when you return from your last bombing mission." I caught the significance of what he was doing, as well as the way in which he did it. He was wishing our flight crew good luck. I put the nickel in my pocket. "Thanks, Sergeant," I said. "It'll be safe with me. And I'll let the other members of the crew know I'm carrying it for all of us." Starbuck turned to walk away. With a proud glint in his eye he said, "Thank you, sir. And you guys take good care of my airplane." Another "owner" of Screwball Express had staked his claim.

Takeoff was at 1145 hours. The 23rd Psalm was again part of the many things that became routine before Screwball Express took to the air and climbed to assembly altitude. Twenty-four of our Group's planes assembled, however, two of the six spares returned to the base as briefed and aircraft 42-31043 was not dispatched and returned early. Our solitary group consisted of 21 bombers. Screwball Express was assigned to fly in the High Squadron. We even had a Norden bombsight aboard, all plugged in and ready to use. What an impressive feeling!

Our hopes for a milk-run were soon shattered by explosions of flak in the front and middle of our formation as we crossed the enemy coast. Rockets were fired at us from the ground at Calais. When we reached the target area one of the B-17s from our 526th Squadron was hit by flak. It was aircraft 42-97485 carrying the crew of 1st Lt. Stanley L. Bielawski. Nine parachutes were believed to come out of that plane before it crashed and exploded. Six of the crewmen in that plane were on their 25th mission. The four officers of that crew had bunked in the same barracks with Howard, Jim, Bob and me. I cannot adequately describe the horror of witnessing such a terrible spectacle for the first time. It was like watching a war movie with an impersonal interest and suddenly realizing you were a member of the cast. Another Fortress had a wing shot off by a direct flak hit and lost its other wing as it plunged helplessly to earth. That plane had the letter "J" in the triangle on its vertical stabilizer and was with the 351st Bomb Group stationed at Polebrook. No parachutes were seen coming out of that plane. It was frightening to watch. Other planes were damaged and several had to leave their formation. The flak was believed to be the most severe experienced so far by the 526th Squadron. In the target area the Germans also fired rockets at us from the ground. An American fighter plane was hit by flak and exploded in the target area.

Each of our planes carried five 1,000-pound general purpose bombs. We dropped them after a visual bomb run from 22,000 feet at 30 seconds past 1500 hours. Our bombs fell directly on the target and results were very good. We crossed the enemy coast exactly nine minutes later on our way out of France.

While returning to England we saw a B-17 from another Group ditch in the Channel. Aircraft 42-37805 from our Group, flown by 1st Lt. Charles L. Brown, circled the downed plane and radioed its location to Air-Sea Rescue. At another place in the Channel we saw a dinghy being picked up by an Allied rescue launch. Statistics at the end of the war would reveal 3,336 B-17 crewmen in the ETO bailed out over or ditched in water, and that Air-Sea Rescue picked up 1,266 of them. During the Battle of Britain, in the fall of 1940, someone in the RAF ordered its pilots to destroy German air-sea rescue seaplanes marked with the Red Cross. This was intended to restrict the rescue of German pilots and lessen their chances of flying again. The order met stiff resistance among RAF pilots.

The 12 Bomb Groups in the Triangle First Division dispatched 243 bombers on this date, and 234 bombed targets at Wizernes, Watten, Le Grismont and Mimoyecques, all in France. Four of the Division's bombers were missing in action, and two others crash landed in England on return.

After we landed we made a damage assessment of Screwball Express. It received only a small baptism of fire on its first combat mission, nine flak holes. Two of the holes were in the Plexiglas nose and several oxygen bottles in the waist section of the plane were hit. Six other B-17s in our Group also had minor damage. One of the flak fragments that came through the Plexiglas nose struck my flak helmet. We did not see any enemy fighter planes on the entire mission. Flying time was 4 hours and 30 minutes.

Screwball Express had completed its first combat mission. Our crew had completed two. Our thoughts were almost audible – only 23 more to go.

After we completed the debriefing process I went to the PX for a couple of candy bars and headed for our barracks. Shortly thereafter the CQ (the sergeant in charge of our barracks) came through the doorway carrying four black barracks bags. He went about collecting the personal belongings of the four officers from our barracks who were shot down on today's mission. Their personal items would be shipped to the States in those black bags. This was a haunting experience. It was bad enough to see their plane go down, but the black bag routine made it too impersonal. When I saw their plane crash I thought of the men. Looking at the black bags made me think of their loved ones back home.

That's probably the reason I never became closely acquainted with any of the fellows in the other flight crews. I did not want to ever see black bags being filled with their personal belongings. The thought of any black bags in behalf of any member of our crew was gruesome.

(**Special Credit**: Please refer to *The Marshall Cavendish Illustrated Encyclopedia Of World War II-1944*; and *The World War II Quiz And Fact Book*, under Bibliography. Also, Imperial War Museum, Cabinet War Rooms, under Reference Sources.)

These photos show typical damage caused to 379th BG Fortresses by small and medium size flak fragments. A direct hit would rip engines from the wings and wings from the fuselage. (Photos courtesy of 379th BG Photographic Section)

Mission to Chartres

The communique was sent from Pinetree just a few minutes after midnight on the morning of Monday, March 27, 1944. Pinetree was the code name for 8th Air Force Headquarters during World War II. Before the war it had been a girl's school at High Wycombe, in Buckinghamshire, England, about 27 miles west-northwest of London. Headquarters of the Royal Air Force was less than five miles away.

The 8th Air Force selected its targets from a priority list that was prepared by the Supreme Allied Headquarters in London. The 8th's headquarter sections then went to work – Intelligence, Planning, Personnel, Ordnance, Armament, Supply, Operations. How many bombs would be needed to wipe out the day's targets? What types of bombs? How many bombers to carry them? Which Bomb Groups would provide the aircraft? Group or Wing bombing formations? Assembly altitude? How many fighter planes to escort the bombers? How far into the mission could the fighters effectively escort the bombers? Where might flak be encountered? Where might enemy fighters be a problem? What about weather? The route in? Best time for attack? Best altitude, air speed and compass heading for the bomb run? The route out? Accurate answers to many details formed a delicately woven pattern essential to a successful mission.

Pinetree's message that morning was relayed to the headquarters of 14 Combat Wings of the 8th Air Force. Within minutes each of them notified their respective Group commanders throughout southeastern England. The records indicate 40 heavy bombardment groups immediately began final preparations for attacks on their assigned targets. Bomb Group commanders decided which three of their four Squadrons would fly the mission. Group operations decided which crews were going. Commanders decided which crews would fly Group Lead, Deputy Lead and Squadron Lead positions. Bombers were loaded with gasoline, bombs and ammunition. Crew members were filled with energy-producing food, a myriad of briefing information and more than a little bit of fear.

Later that morning the 14 Combat Wings of heavy bombers, consisting of 539 B-17s and 168 B-24s, were dispatched by the 8th Air Force to attack nine Luftwaffe airfields and one aircraft factory. Targets of the 1st Bombardment Division included four airfields at Chartres, Tours, St. Jean D'Angely and La Rochelle, plus a Focke-Wulf aircraft repair plant at Tours. The five other airfields were to be attacked by planes of the 2nd and 3rd Bomb Divisions. Of the nine airfields, seven were single-engine fighter advanced training schools. All targets were in western and northwestern France.

Such a massive plan of attack by aerial bombardment was no accident. It didn't just happen. Supreme Allied Headquarters issued the order. The 8th Air Force created the plan. The 40 Bomb Groups made it happen.

Since the beginning of the aerial offensive over Europe, bombing of enemy-occupied territory had been divided between the Americans and the British. The RAF bombed at night using flares dropped by Mosquito bombers to light up the target area for their heavy bombers. The Mosquito was a twin-engine, medium size aircraft called The Wooden Wonder. The RAF did not have an accurate bombsight and depended on radar signals from England to help their navigators determine their position in the air in relation to the target area. This radar technique of the RAF's Bomber Command Pathfinder Force was known as Oboe. Their aircraft were sent over the Channel, each of them having been spaced as to altitude, lateral position and time of passage over specific points. In this manner RAF navigators set up a bomb release point theoretically accurate to one tenth of a mile. The RAF bombers then individually made their bomb runs and literally saturated the entire flare-lighted target area with tons of explosives. Large areas were bombed in order to make certain specific military targets were destroyed. Pinpoint accuracy was not a prerequisite of this technique.

The U.S. 8th Air Force heavy bombardment plan in Europe mandated a campaign of sustained daylight bombing with a high degree of precision and destruction of strategically selected targets. In early 1943, the 8th Air Force adopted the concept of "dropping on the leader" as the most effective technique for placing the maximum number of bombs on the target. This technique was greatly benefited through use of the gyro-stabilized Norden bombsight that was linked electronically to the Automatic Flight Control Equipment (AFCE). This provided lead bombardiers the capability of controlling the flight path of the leading bombers during the bomb run so the bombsight data and settings could be coordinated for an exact time and place of bomb release. The technique was further perfected by pilots flying the Fortresses in well-planned, tightly positioned formations made up of Bombardment Squadrons, Groups, Wings and Divisions.

Formations were modified over time to allow for maximum defensive firepower of the 13 .50-caliber machine guns in each of the Flying Fortresses. Experimentation improved the bomb pattern by having an "immediate drop on signal" by bombardiers watching for the bomb release of the Group's lead plane and dropping their bombs at the same instant. Assuming every plane's bombs were released at the same moment, the bomb pattern on the ground would be a very close facsimile of the formation pattern flown by the planes from which the bombs were dropped.

Understandably, the British thought their method of aerial bombardment was better than the American method. The RAF claimed the .50 cal. armament of the B-17 was overrated and not sufficiently capable of providing adequate defense against the Luftwaffe. RAF heavy bombers like the Short Stirlings and Lancasters carried larger bomb loads than the B-17s. The British ridiculed the awkward positions in which tail gunners like our Jerry Lindsey and ball turret gunners like our Tom Kiblin remained cramped hour after hour. They also maintained the highly praised Norden bombsight, even though a precision instrument, would produce unsatisfactory results because of the continuous evasive action necessary on the bomb run. The British also contended the combined defensive power of German planes and antiaircraft fire would completely annihilate daylight formations of Flying Fortresses. Nevertheless, the 8th Air Force was not dissuaded from believing it had developed the best concept of strategic aerial bombardment. The 8th Air Force was aware of the RAF's depressing report in September of 1941. That report, based on photographs taken by British Spitfires after 100 recent bomber raids and subsequently included in the official history of the Royal Air Force, disclosed the following startling analysis:

… only one in every three RAF aircraft claiming to have attacked had arrived within five miles of its target.

… over the Ruhr, the number of aircraft arriving within five miles of their target was one in ten.

Unsatisfactory bombing results may have been understandable early in the war, but they certainly were not acceptable. The RAF made dramatic advancements in bombing equipment and procedures, and subsequent accomplishments were rewarding proof of its ability to attack and destroy many important targets.

On March 27, the 379th Bomb Group furnished 23 planes, three of which were spares, for the Low Group of the 41st Combat Wing. The 303rd Bomb Group flew Lead Group position for the Wing. The 379th also provided seven Fortresses for the Low Squadron of a composite High Group. That Group consisted of a Squadron of B-17s from each of the 379th, 303rd and 384th Bomb Groups. Screwball Express was assigned to the Low Squadron of the composite High Group. All planes in the 41st Wing were assigned to attack the airfield at Chartres, France, about 48 miles southwest of Paris.

The overall size of a Combat Wing was very impressive. Each of three Bomb Groups in a Wing had a vertical height of about 750 feet, measuring from the top plane in the High Squadron to the bottom plane in the Low Squadron. Allowing for about three hundred vertical feet between the High/

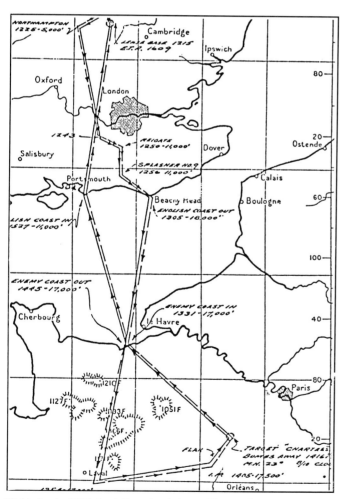

Flight plan for 379th Bomb Group's mission to Chartres, France on March 27, 1944. Our route to targets in France frequently went up and/or down the west side of London. (Photostated from original copy in 379th BG Mission Folder, National Archives Military Records Facility)

Lead Groups and also the Lead/Low Groups, the vertical wedge of a Combat Wing stretched almost 3,000 feet from top to bottom.

Our crew had no way of knowing we were in the second of four consecutive days of bombing missions. Extremely heavy cloud cover over Kimbolton delayed our Group's takeoff until 1120 hours, and I began singing "our takeoff song." All of the planes accomplished assembly without difficulty, and the three spares in the 379th Low Group returned early as planned.

We encountered no flak or enemy fighters on our way to the airfield at Chartres. The barrage of antiaircraft fire directed at our Group just before we reached the target was light to moderate, but managed to put a large hole in each of Screwball Express' wings. Weather conditions over every one of the 10 targets were CAVU (ceiling and visibility unrestricted), with the singular exception of the Chartres target where we encountered 8/10 cloud cover. However, we were able to make our bomb run from 17,500 feet despite spotty visibility. Parts of the target became recognizable through breaks in the clouds, and the crosshairs in the bombsight of our Group's lead plane remained synchronized on the aiming point. The bombsight's release mechanism was triggered and our bombs were away at precisely 30 seconds past 1416 hours.

Each of the planes in our composite Group carried 12-500 pound general purpose bombs, most of them with delayed action fuse settings. This was frequently done by 8th Air Force Groups in order to interrupt the starting of runway repairs immediately after we bombed it. The delay fusing technique enabled us to 'keep 'em guessing' for as long as 72 hours after our bombs hit the airfield.

The visual sighting of bombing by our composite Group revealed very good results. Aerial photography of the target just before the bombs were dropped did not occur due to a batch of clouds. It was difficult to determine from later reconnaissance the amount of damage that could be attributed to bombs dropped during this specific attack. However, it was obvious we had caused considerable damage to a large hangar and some of the runways, and delayed use of the airfield for at least three days. Bombing results at the 1st Division's other four targets were described as "good to excellent" at the Tours and La Rochelle airdromes, "excellent" at the St. Jean D'Angely airdrome, and "fair to good" at the Tours aircraft repair factory.

The 14 Combat Wings in the day's operation were provided escort by 23 Groups of U.S. fighter planes: 10 Groups of P-47s, three of P-38s and three of P-51s from the 8th Air Force; and six Groups of P-47s and one Group of P-51s from the 9th Air Force. Our fighter pilots later reported most of the enemy aircraft they saw during the mission were on the ground. Unfortunately, five P-47s, three P-51s and two P-38s were reported missing in action. Our fighter pilots, whom we respectfully called "our little friends" and "our little brothers," destroyed 38 enemy planes, most of them on the ground.

Flying time for our mission to Chartres totaled five hours and 45 minutes. Records indicate there were no injuries to any of the crewmen from the 379th Bomb Group on this mission, and all planes from the 379th returned to the base at Kimbolton.

Three done – 22 to go!

(Special Credit: Please refer to *Flying Forts, The B-17 In World War II*; under Bibliography.)

Mission to Dijon

How naive can a guy be? After flying only three combat missions, I started the notes in my diary for Tuesday, March 28, 1944, with the words, "Beginning to know France like a book."

That whimsical thought had its genesis in our crew's assignment to fly Screwball Express in the Low Squadron of the 379th's High Group on a mission to another of the many airfields in France. My knowledge of France was by no means of significant depth. Flying over it on two previous days, and a third time on this mission, did little more than impress on me that France is between the English Channel and Germany, and full of enemy flak towers and airfields. I also had strong expectation the Luftwaffe fighter planes on those airfields we were bombing were some day going to come up and start shooting at us.

Following the highly successful attack on Luftwaffe installations in France the previous day, the 8th Air Force issued Field Order #314 calling for six Combat Wings of B-17s to bomb airdromes at Dijon, Reims, Chartres and Chateaudon. An air armada of 373 Fortresses, escorted by 453 fighters, was involved in the operation. The 1st Bomb Division provided 176 bombers for the raids on the Dijon/ Longvic and Reims/Champagne airfields. The 40th and 41st Combat Wings were to attack the former, and the 1st Combat Wing the latter. In addition, 77 B-24s were dispatched to attack a target in Holland, but were recalled because of bad weather just before reaching the enemy coast.

We took off at 1114 hours, using the conventional 30-second takeoff interval between each plane. I sang the song in about the amount of time required for the wheels of Screwball Express and the following B-17 to clear the runway.

There was, as usual, the persistent English fog through which Screwball Express had to climb. Our Wing assembly was completed in the vicinity of Cambridge with the assistance of "Gee" equipment. "Gee" was the first of several navigational and bombing aids developed by the British. It utilized signals received from two ground stations to provide an aircraft with its exact position. The British also developed the H2S equipment, an airborne radar scanner that imaged a crude impression of the terrain below onto a cathode ray tube in the aircraft.

Twenty B-17s from Kimbolton made up the High Group in the 41st Wing and headed for the Dijon/Longvic airfield. Two of our spares returned early as planned, and a third spare filled in with the 91st Bomb Group.

Weather over the English coast was also overcast, a condition that promptly brought radio beacons into use. The beacons were very important navigational tools for our navigators, and were switched on and off intermittently. None of them used the same call sign or stayed on the same frequency for more than a few minutes at a time. Pertinent information concerning this very methodical system was printed on rice paper saturated with sugar. This permitted the navigator and radio operator a less-than-tasty method of chewing and swallowing this secret information in the event of bail-out or crash. Most of these precautions were not followed after early or mid-1944.

There were two primary types of radio beacons, about 30 "Bunchers" and four "Splashers". The "Buncher" was a single frequency beacon over which the majority of Bomb Groups would assemble. It was very common for five or six Bomb Groups within a ten mile radius of each other to use

the signal of the same "Buncher" for assembly. The "Buncher" procedure was very costly in time and fuel, and in planes and men. The more powerful "Splashers" were used by Combat Wings and Divisions as rendezvous points and consequently became Control Point No. 1 for a mission's flight plan. The "Splashers" were Braintree, Brampton, Mundesley and Scole. Since they cut across all frequencies, "Splashers" were also used to warn of barrage balloons and were helpful to pilots attempting to land aircraft during conditions of poor visibility.

The weather over the Channel cleared up in about the time it takes to write what little I know about radio beacons. That was the way it was with the weather over there. First you couldn't see where you were going and then you were in a clear, blue sky. For the moment, we could easily see the French coast straight ahead. Navigators were able to rely on a less complicated method of navigation – pilotage (the use of landmarks) – for the balance of this mission.

Our target, an operational base for twin-engine fighters, was located approximately 155 miles southeast of Paris. The attack plan called for the 40th Wing to drop general purpose bombs on the airfield. The 41st Wing was to follow the 40th and drop M-47 incendiary bombs. Each of the planes in our entire Wing carried 42 incendiary bombs in its bomb bay.

We approached the target in a clear sky at 19,000 feet. We had not seen any flak since entering France and experienced no flak at the initial point of the bomb run or over the target. Our bomb run was about 18 miles long and took about six minutes to cover. Our Bomb Group flew straight and level during the entire bomb run and dropped our incendiaries at 1444 hours. Moments later, eight or nine rockets were fired at our Bomb Group from the ground. All of the rockets traveled short of our position and completely missed the Fortresses in our formation.

The bombs dropped by 61 Fortresses in our Wing were directly on target. The massive flashing of more than 2,000 fires started by our incendiaries was an awesome spectacle. Bombs dropped by the 379th set fire to numerous buildings and barracks. Our Squadron's bombs destroyed three HE-111 Heinkel bombers and started fires on three other planes. Fires were also started in two large, double-bay hangars. Two square-type hangars received direct hits and burned fiercely. A large workshop was hit and the entire administration area was covered with incendiaries. A three-bay hangar received direct hits and was severely damaged. Four workshops received direct hits and two of them were completely demolished. Blast damage from near misses was apparent on four medium size workshops. The 379th Group dropped 882 incendiaries that day – 840 on the Dijon airfield and 42 on the airfield at Reims. Our spare aircraft, number 42-38183, was the plane that filled in earlier with the 91st Bomb Group in its attack on the Reims airport.

The only enemy aircraft we saw on this mission were the 25 on the ground at the Dijon airfield. Some of them attempted takeoff in a desperate effort to avoid the bombing, but none of them got off the ground.

The 8th AF usually did not drop propaganda leaflets while on missions over France and we dropped none today. Hundreds of thousands, possibly hundreds of millions, of propaganda leaflets were dropped by Allied bombers during World War II, most of them over Germany, but some were occasionally dropped over France, Belgium and Holland.

Between October 1, 1943, and March 31, 1944, the 8th Air Force flew a total of 73 "leaflet missions" during which 372 bombers dropped printed propaganda messages. Records of the total tonnage of leaflets used in this manner have not been found, but it is known that 43 tons of leaflets were carried over enemy-occupied territory by the 379th Bomb Group during these six months. The majority of leaflets on one mission was carried by one bomber in a Group of bombers. The leaflets measured about 9 x 12 inches and contained photographs and messages primarily designed to break the morale of Germany's military and civilian population. The two leaflets pictured below raised questions about the aircraft and capability of the Luftwaffe.

On our return flight to England we saw a little flak near Chateau-Thierry and about 25 additional bursts at Troyes and Le Treport, but most of it was meager and inaccurate. A large, camouflaged area was visible about one mile south of Sezanne, approximately 65 miles east of Paris. It covered an area about one mile square and appeared to be a massive amount of netting strung on poles. The Germans were experts at camouflaging entire cities, as we learned later.

When we crossed the Channel into England the sky was still overcast, but it presented no significant problem to our descent and landing. Keller and Milworm, our navigator and radio operator, did not find it necessary to eat the coded radio information. There was no secret treat for either of them today.

This was our third mission in as many days.

All of the planes in our Group returned to home base. Two of the 379th's B-17s received minor battle damage from flak. Our flying time on Mission No. 4 was exactly seven hours.

Twenty-one more missions to go!

(**Special Credit:** Please refer to *The Mighty Eighth* under Bibliography.)

Headline asks, "Where are all the German war planes? Here in the west." Article says 75% of Germany's fighter planes are in the west, protecting transportation and production installations. Therefore, the 25% still defending the eastern, northern, southeastern and southern fronts is no longer sufficient. Upper photo shows what once were German reinforcements. Photos also show bombing of munitions plant at Hasselt, Belgium, and what used to be the freight yard at Amiens, France. (Photos circa March 25, 1944, provided to the author by Dr. Frank R. Craig)

Headline ridicules, "Fighter plane factories without fighter planes," adding that the 75% of German fighter planes in the west, including Germany, are insufficient to defend their own factories. Two upper photos show a Messerschmitt factory in Brunswick, before and after an 8th Air Force Bomber attack. Photos at side show 21 of 48 manufacturing shops at Gnome-Rhone Aircraft Engine Plant were destroyed and the rest greatly damaged; and total destruction of the Erla Machine Works at Leipzig-Heiterblick.

Mission to Brunswick

Wednesday, March 29, 1944. Before the day ended our crew was listed in a 379th Bomb Group report with the heading, "Missing in Action."

At our 0400 briefing we were informed all four Combat Wings of the 1st Bombardment Division were going to attack the Luftwaffe's vital aircraft production center at Brunswick, Germany. The 379th Group was to fly Lead position for the 41st Wing, and the 41st Wing was to lead the 1st Bomb Division. Brunswick is about 95 miles south-southeast of Hamburg and approximately 125 miles west-southwest of Berlin. The attack on Brunswick was programmed to include 236 B-17s. Seventy-two B-24s in the 20th Combat Wing of the 2nd Bomb Division and five Pathfinders were assigned to an attack in the Pas de Calais area of France.

This was our crew's fourth combat mission in four consecutive days. It was the second time the 379th Bomb Group had flown four attacks in as many days, the previous occasion being February 3, 4, 5 and 6 of this year. On those dates the 379th bombed shipbuilding facilities, an engine component plant and two airdromes. The first two of those targets were at Wilhelmshaven and Frankfurt, in Germany; the two airdromes were at Orleans and Chateaudun, in France.

The weather over most of England was heavily overcast. There were two layers of clouds, one extending from about ground level to 4,000 feet and another from 5,000 to 7,500 feet. Takeoff and assembly were delayed and difficult for nearly every Bomb Group. My private vocal recital was presented through the ground-hugging fog when we took off at 1000 hours. Heat from fires in smudge drums lining the runway's edge was barely able to push the fog upward.

We broke through the clouds at 7,500 feet and headed for our Group's assembly point in the vicinity of Splasher #6. We then went to Molesworth for our Wing's assembly at 1103 hours and 9,000 feet. The assembly route took us to Northampton, Buckingham and Sudbury. We then proceeded to Great Yarmouth, a town on the English coast, over which our Wing was to fly at 1200 hours and at 19,000 feet. Finally, we went out over the North Sea where our Combat Wing completed its assembly before crossing the enemy coast at 1231 hours and at 26,000 feet.

We had a problem. It was a big one. We had not seen any planes from our Bomb Group since we were at the end of the runway back at Kimbolton, waiting to take off. Our Division's assembly had not been accomplished according to plan and the 1st Combat Wing had positioned itself ahead of our 41st Wing. This occurred because two of the Wings did not receive our Division commander's radio message at 1030 hours. It was intended to direct them to fly at 9,000 feet for assembly at Molesworth; instead, they were flying at 14,000 feet and 16,000 feet respectively.

Screwball Express flew across the Belgian coast – alone. We then saw a Wing of B-17s in the cloud-filled sky ahead. Towers and Moore managed to get us close enough to determine with our binoculars that the formation did not include the 379th Bomb Group. Planes in one of the Groups had the letter "L" on their tail sections. It was the 381st Bomb Group from Ridgewell – one of the three Groups in the 1st Combat Wing. Apparently, we had flown ahead of our Group after leaving Kimbolton. Our best alternative, instead of dropping back to our Group, was to join the 381st. Evidently, some of its planes also experienced difficulty during assembly, because we were instructed to fly Lead position for its incomplete High Squadron.

The cloud cover at Brunswick was 8/10 to 9/10 and bombing was done with PFF equipment. PFF was the abbreviation for a radar bombing technique employed by the 8th Air Force beginning in September, 1943. The hardstands of the U.S. air base at Alconbury, England, were filled with B-17s and B-24s of the 482nd Bomb Group – part of the "Pathfinder Force" attached to the 8th Air Force. A Pathfinder plane was almost always in the lead position of every bomber formation assigned to bomb targets obscured by clouds. The Pathfinder method was very successful in overcoming the cloudy conditions that frequently concealed 8th Air Force targets.

The 381st Bomb Group's target, like that of the 379th, was an aircraft parts plant near the center of Brunswick. Flak en route to the target was minimal, but at the target it increased in quantity and remained inaccurate. We saw about two dozen FW-190s and Me-109s under our formation as we neared Brunswick. They did not try to attack our Group. Twelve rockets were fired at us from the ground. Our bombs were away from 26,000 feet at 1324 hours, two minutes before the 379th dropped its payload. The bomb load of Screwball Express consisted of 35-100 pound incendiary bombs and 10-100 pound demolition bombs.

Bombing results of the planes that attacked Brunswick were good. All 56 of the 1st Combat Wing's planes, including Screwball Express, bombed the primary target. The same was true for all except one of the 40th Wing's 57 planes. Fifty-three of 55 planes in the 94th Wing bombed successfully. The numbers that day were far from good for the 41st Wing - only 21 of its 61 attacking Fortresses dropped their bombs on Brunswick. Clouds, flak and enemy fighters were the apparent causes for scattering some of that Wing's formations. Thirty-eight of the 41st Wing's planes bombed various targets of opportunity. The 72 B-24s that bombed in the Pas de Calais area also had an unsuccessful day. According to a mission report, only 28 of their 72 aircraft were effective at primary targets. Failure of PFF equipment resulted in no bombs being dropped by 43 B-24s.

Vapor trails from B-17s ahead of our position on March 29, 1944 enroute to Brunswick, Germany. (Photo from 379th BG Photo. Sec.)

Flak became very thick and very accurate after we passed the target. Two Fortresses, believed to have been in the 91st Bomb Group, were hit by flak and exploded. The flak let up and a few enemy aircraft came out of the clouds, straight for our Group. A Focke-Wulf made a pass at our left wingman. Gunners in a Fortress behind us shot down the enemy plane. The Luftwaffe bandits were not observed to have attacked the 379th Group behind us. Fortresses in the 40th Wing were not as lucky and were attacked by approximately 65 Me-109s and FW-190s. Their typical maneuver was to attack in groups of three, so arranged that attacks on the entire Wing were simultaneous. The enemy aircraft would then reform, queue up in a line astern of the Wing and attack the Lead Group head-on. Fortunately, the 381st Group was benefited by a strong tailwind and we were able to leave the area at a ground speed in excess of 320 m.p.h. In the distance we could see as many as 40 enemy planes attacking one of our other Wing formations. Records indicate it was the 94th Combat Wing.

On the way back to England we were confronted by moderate, inaccurate anti-aircraft fire at Hanover and Osnabruck in Germany, and again at Ijmuiden, Holland. Just south of Quackenbruck, Germany, we observed a large excavation which appeared to be about three times the width of a highway and about five miles long. We had no idea what it was, but reported it to Intelligence during our debriefing. There was meager, inaccurate flak at Vechta, Peine, and Walstode, all in Germany, and at Amsterdam, Holland. In the area between Steinhuder and Dummer lakes northwest of Hanover, a black Me-109 was seen trailing an object at the end of a long cable. We were aware the Germans were experimenting with this type of aerial tactic against our bombers. Its purpose was to 'drag' bombs through U.S. bomber formations. A resulting explosion could blow an entire Fortress, perhaps two or more, out of the sky. Imagine the havoc if this tactic ever became successful.

Another problem developed. Weather conditions over England were still heavily overcast at 1630 hours when we

DAMAGE TO IMPORTANT INDUSTRIAL CONCERNS AT BRUNSWICK This area, which has been attacked in daylight on several occasions since February by aircraft of the U.S. 8th. Air Force, is here seen after their most recent attack. The conflagration is amongst the work-buildings of M.I.A.G. aircraft components factory (A) and the adjoining works of Wilhewerke A.G. constructional Engineers (B), in addition an unidentified works is on fire and a number of hits are visible in the railway yards. (Reprint from an 8th AF publication, circa April, 1944.)

crossed the English coast. We left the 381st Group and turned toward Kimbolton where we found the weather much worse than when we left that morning. We were flying at 18,000 feet, having let down only 8,000 feet since we were over Brunswick. The German antiaircraft guns made high altitude a good place to fly. Bob Keller heard on the radio that the ceiling was "not too bad" at Framlingham, England, so Howard Towers decided he would try to land Screwball Express at that airfield.

When we arrived over Framlingham we found a solid mass of clouds at our altitude and almost all the way down to the runway. Bob assured us that he could navigate us down through the mess with his radio navigational equipment. Howard asked some of us what we thought about trying to set down at Framlingham. All of us thought it was the only sensible thing to do. We knew the Kimbolton field was closed. We didn't have enough fuel to fly much longer and the weather was certainly not improving. "Take 'er down."

After what seemed like an eternity of clouds and time, the nose of Screwball Express poked through the bottom of the last cloud layer. Directly in front of us was the runway the Framlingham control tower instructed us to use for our landing. Bob had successfully navigated us down through a mass of clouds 18,000 feet thick, making it possible for Howard and Jim to fly Screwball Express through the mess to a perfect landing. It was an absolutely outstanding feat. The wheels of Screwball Express touched down at 1845 hours, two hours and 15 minutes after crossing the English coast.

When the props quit turning, we jumped out of the plane and kissed the muddy ramp in an emotional display of gratitude for getting back to earth alive. The only battle damage to Screwball Express during the entire mission was one flak hole in the left wing. We completed a partial report on the Brunswick mission. Telephone contact was made with Kimbolton so our base headquarters would know where we were. Hopefully, the other crews from the 379th were safely back at Kimbolton.

Our crew had completed our fifth combat mission. Flying time was 8:45 hours. It was wonderful to know we were 20 percent of the way through our operational tour. After a very good meal, the excitement of the day yielded to our exhaustion and we hit the sack around 2300 hours.

The cloud cover lifted very little after breakfast the next morning. Clouds were hanging about 600 feet above the ground, but we were able to fly the short trip to the Kimbolton airfield. We undoubtedly made a very loud roar flying so low over the houses and farms beneath us, like a buzz job. Immediately after landing we went to headquarters and completed our report on the previous day's mission and our related experiences. We learned seven of the 379th's 21 planes on this mission were not able to land at Kimbolton when they returned from Brunswick the day before. Fog and clouds were the culprits. In addition to Screwball Express landing at Framlingham, one of our planes landed at Wratting Common, one at Mildenhall, two at Sudbury and two at Molesworth. Six of the 379th's "Brunswick overnighters" made it back to Kimbolton on Thursday morning. The one that went to Mildenhall required major repairs and returned to Kimbolton the following month.

It was also learned that 28 other planes of the 1st Bomb Division, a grand total of 35, were forced to land away from their home bases after returning from Brunswick on Wednesday. Seven of the 28 planes were from the 92nd Bomb Group at Podington and another seven were part of the 306th Bomb Group at Thurleigh. Six were from the 401st Group at Deenethorpe. Two planes were from the 457th Group at Glatton and one plane was from the 381st Group at Ridgewell.

Five of the 35 planes that landed away from their home bases were from the 303rd Group located at Molesworth. Ironically, one of those five aircraft, number 42-31405, was able to land at Kimbolton.

We went back to our barracks. It was misting. By 1100 hours it was raining again. Being in a Nissen hut on a rainy day in England did absolutely nothing to make you feel you were winning the war.

Several of us put our raincoats on and walked out to the hardstand where Screwball Express was parked at the north end of the airfield. We wanted to see how the ground crew was coming along with the patching of the flak hole in the left wing. The last thing our ground crew needed was a couple of fly-boys asking questions about something the ground crew was far more knowledgeable of than we were. When we arrived at our plane we heard voices of the ground crew coming from one of their tents. That was very understandable. It was raining, and nobody should have to work in the rain. We entered the tent and found them playing cards. That was also very understandable. The left wing of Screwball Express had already been repaired. Our ground crew was a super bunch of guys. Other ground crews had almost completed repairs to minor flak damage on four other B-17s at the Kimbolton airfield.

There was no chance of a mission in this kind of weather. We headed back to the 526th Squadron's operation hut, sloshing our way through the rain and muddy puddles.

Soon after arriving there we learned the 1st Bomb Division lost nine Fortresses on the previous day's mission. Seven of these were lost to enemy aircraft and two were lost to flak. Later, records showed the 305th and the 306th Bomb Groups, both in the 40th Combat Wing, each lost three bombers. Their serial numbers were: 42-38106, 42-38108 and 42-97466 from the 305th at Chelveston; and 42-37953, 42-39950 and 42-39965 from the 306th at Thurleigh. The 1st Wing lost two B-17s from the 91st Bomb Group at Bassingbourn: 42-3506 and 42-97246. The 457th Bomb Group at Glatton, in the 94th Wing, lost aircraft number 42-31531.

The 8th Air Force lost 11 fighters during the mission, seven of which were P-51s in the target area. Two P-51s collided over the Channel. One P-38 and a P-47 also failed to return. Our "little friends" claimed 44 enemy planes destroyed in the air and 13 on the ground. In addition, our fighter planes destroyed 17 locomotives, 3 trains and an oil dump. They also damaged 18 locomotives, 17 barracks, 8 barges, 6 trains, 6 factories, 2 signal towers and many freight cars, trucks, and buildings during strafing attacks.

A terrible thing almost happened. A Missing in Action report had been prepared with our crew members' names on it, even though we notified our home base on the previous evening of our landing at Framlingham. The error was corrected in time, the MIA report was not sent to the States and family notifications were not initiated. Thank Goodness!

As we looked outside the operations hut it was very apparent that rain had come to stay for a while. We put our raincoats on and ran for the mess hall, chowed down, and then dashed for the hut we called "home."

We spent a lot of time writing letters – and being thankful – during the remainder of that day.

(**Special Credit**: Please refer to *Fortresses Of The Big Triangle First*, under Bibliography.)

Grounded for Ten — London for Three

The clouds, rain and chilly dampness of Thursday, March 30, 1944, continued into the early morning hours of March 31. Around 0500 hours the ceiling appeared to be lifting and the airbase was put on alert for a mission to Oberpfaffenhofen; the mission was soon scrubbed because of weather conditions in that sector of Germany. About 1000 hours another alert involved a possible mission to Ludwigshafen, opposite Mannheim on the Rhine river, in southwestern Germany. At 1130 hours that mission was also scrubbed. Bad weather was everywhere.

During March the 379th Bomb Group flew 18 combat missions. Our crew flew on five of those missions during the eight days we had been operational. The 379th had 59 B-17s – 18 Model Fs and 41 Gs – assigned and on hand at Kimbolton AFB on March 31, 1944; however, only 25 combat crews were assigned to the 379th as of that date. This was the lowest number of combat crews in the Group since October, 1943. At the end of 1943, 47 crews were on assignment to the 379th. Twenty-two of the 379th's flight crews were lost in action during the first three months of 1944.

New crews arrived almost daily at the Kimbolton airfield. They tried hard to hide their inexperience. They didn't see the fear we "old timers" had hidden behind our bragging about how fast we were winning the war.

During the first week of April weather conditions showed no significant improvement. Everyone was becoming very jittery. Sitting around and not flying any missions was not the way to complete our operational tour of combat duty and head Stateside.

On Tuesday, April 4, Howard came splashing through the rain and into our barracks at approximately 1600 hours. His eyes gleamed as he told us our entire crew and some other crews on our airfield were issued three-day passes beginning on Wednesday, April 5, at 1000 hours. Howard had already shared the good news with the other six members of our crew. We didn't have to return to base until 2000 hours on Friday, April 7. I was reminded of the words, "All good things come to him who waits," (to which I added the provision of waiting long enough – and indeed we had.)

Perhaps headquarters issued the passes because of the difficulties many of us experienced on the Brunswick mission a week earlier. Maybe it was obvious we were "climbing the walls" of those Nissen huts because of being grounded by weather for so many days. Whatever the real reason, we were overjoyed at the opportunity for a brief absence from the airbase.

Our crew decided to spend the three days in London. After breakfast the next morning we each packed a few things, like an extra pair of socks, undershirts, shorts, an extra shirt, a razor, a comb and a toothbrush, and headed through the fog and drizzle for the main gate. We climbed into an army truck that had been sent over from the motor pool. The bumpy road was hardly noticed as we bounced our way into Kimbolton and then to the train station in Bedford. Some of the enlisted members of our crew were in a truck ahead of the one in which Howard, Jim, Bob Keller and I were riding. The driver of our truck must have had fog-proof vision because he maintained one constant speed during the entire trip. The slipstream from the truck made the mid-morning fog swirl upward, producing a rolling motion as it settled to the ground.

We were at the Bedford station long before the train arrived. Six or seven cigarettes later it finally pulled in and our group made a wild rush to get aboard. Frank, Jerry and

Author's "Short Snorter", (British One Pound Note) with signature of a captured Me-109 pilot at the bottom (upside down). Glenn Miller's signature is on the reverse side.

others were quick to find seats in one of those compartmentalized passenger cars used in England at the time. Our foursome had trouble finding a compartment with four empty seats, but managed to do so just as the train started to pull out of the station.

The train ride to London seemed to last forever, although the distance traveled was approximately only 50 miles. The train made frequent stops, some of them for ten or more minutes, and I'm certain we never moved more than 30 miles an hour. We were in ground fog most of the way and had little opportunity to see the famed English countryside. The fog was selfishly unkind and hid much of the passing scenery from our view. We managed to see only a few farm houses, some people and what looked like a small representation of what might have been separate flocks of sheep.

Instead of peering through the fog outside the window of our compartment, we talked about the famous places we planned to see while in London. In our pockets were several bunches of candy bars each of us had purchased at the base PX. We heard candy was hard to find in London. Lunch time came and passed. There was no dining car on this train. The more we tried not to think about those candy bars the more quickly we ate them.

The fog lifted as the train moved through the outlying areas of London and pulled into Victoria Station around 1500 hours—nearly two hours late. At first glance Victoria Station looked like any large city's wartime train station. Trains were either coming in or going out on almost every set of tracks. Hundreds of people were hurrying to departing trains, or rushing from incoming ones through the main part of the station and out onto the streets. Uniforms of dozens of military branches, many from foreign countries, were scurrying everywhere.

My eyes turned toward the station's ceiling where for the first time I saw a small part of the bomb damage the Germans were inflicting upon London. It was ironic—we came to London to forget the war for a few days and the very first building we enter has a bomb hole in its roof. A bomb had dropped through it and exploded on a set of tracks at the station's far side. We walked into that area and found repairs were already completed. A Bobby with London's police force told me the bomb crater measured about ten feet across and was almost four feet deep. With pride in his voice, he also said, "...only took three hours to level the hole and lay new rails." In an effort to express my amazement at the incident and it's fast repair I exclaimed, "Wow, that's fantastic." The Bobby replied in an unemotional tone and in typical British style, "And a bit messy y' know." Those Britons were a stalwart lot.

I pondered briefly over some numbers at the back of my mind. We had already dropped more than 100 bombs from Screwball Express. Multiply 100 by the average number of planes on a 379th Bomb Group mission, and multiply that by the number of missions flown by the average Bomb Group, and multiply that by..... the Germans had a lot of holes in the roofs of their buildings, too.

Howard, Jim, Bob and I took a hack (taxi) to the Princess Garden Club, a Red Cross Club on Exhibition Road, where we were able to rent two rooms for our stay in London. We made certain that other members of our crew also found accommodations. While in London we wanted to do as the Londoners did, so we enjoyed "hawving tay n'crumpets" at the customary hour of 4 p.m. (1600 hours military time).

The weather appeared to be drying out a little, so we went sight-seeing. We took a hack to St. James's Park where we were approached by a gentleman—a civilian Londoner—who appeared a bit unsteady on his feet. We assumed he had been drinking and our conversation with him proved we were correct. He offered to be our guide for a while, at a cost of four pounds. As I recall, one English pound was then worth about $4.00, so four pounds was equal to 16 American dollars. That seemed a little expensive, but what the heck – only four bucks for each of us. Besides, who knew when we would get back to London, or if we would. The English gentleman did a very good job of showing us the sights. He was also very good at convincing us we should pay for his drinking while he guided us "aroun' th' town."

He took us first to Buckingham Palace. While we were staring at the marble home of the King and Queen through the iron fence surrounding it, we noticed the Bobbies had stopped all vehicular traffic in the area. The King and the Queen had been to Trafalgar Square and were being chauffeured along The Mall in the royal car. We came to attention and saluted. The King returned our salute and the Queen honored us with a smile and a wave of her hand. The car went slowly past us, through the heavily guarded gate and into the stately grounds of the palace.

On the list of places we visited next were Big Ben, Houses of Parliament and Westminster Abbey. We were filled with awe by the magnificence of their 200-years-old architectural style. We then went by the Cabinet War Rooms and No. 10 Downing Street on our way to Trafalgar Square and the iron statue of Lord Nelson. Our guide took time out for a visit to a pub and we were polite about it. We had a brew with him. Other places we visited included St. Paul's Cathedral and a statue of Abraham Lincoln. We then traveled by bus to the Temple Bar. Unlike the name implies, it is an old gateway to the city of London and the point at which the Lord Mayor used to ceremoniously challenge the King's entry into the city.

Our next stop was on Fleet Street at the Cheshire Cheese Tavern, founded nearly 300 years earlier. The marble step into the tavern showed extreme wear by past imbibers, but was now protected by a metal grill. In the traditional manner of tourists, we touched the step as we entered the tavern in which Charles Dickens and Dr. Samuel Johnson once spent much of their time. In our minds we were taken back in time as we sat in the same seats in which Dickens and Johnson once sat, or so it said on brass plaques nailed to the backs of the seats. At our guide's suggestion we each drank an ale. Our tour included a heavily bombed area along the River Thames. We also had a quick look at the Bank of England, Lloyds of London, the Stock Exchange, the Royal Mint, St. Clemen's Church, Blackfriar's Bridge, London Bridge, and the Tower of London.

Much of our sight-seeing was done from a hack and from the open upper deck of a double-decker bus. The pace set by our guide and the excitement of seeing so much so fast was very tiring. It was getting late, so we invited our guide to have "one for the road." At the Tiger Tavern we officially ended his services to us by drinking one toast to his long life and another one to his financial success. He didn't need the second toast, not in his condition, and not as long as strangers in London were agreeable to his price for guide service.

We took the Underground to Piccadilly Circus. In the States we knew this type of transportation as the Subway. Our guide had told us no decent woman dared be seen around Piccadilly during the evening hours and into the night. He also said any women found around Piccadilly during those hours were prostitutes, and a sure way to attract a veritable horde of whores was with a loud whistle. When we emerged from the Underground onto street level, without any prior warning of any kind, our prankster-navigator literally rent the London twilight with an acutely piercing whistle. Bob was transfixed with icy stares of condemnation from Howard, Jim and me. A goodly number of virtuous passersby also seemed unfavorably impressed. We hurriedly caught a double-decker bus headed in the direction of our hotel.

After freshening up in our rooms, we walked a few blocks looking for a nice restaurant at which to have dinner. We located what appeared to be such a place, went in, and impressed ourselves by ordering the most expensive item on the menu – a T-bone steak for each of us. The waiter informed us such a delicacy was difficult to find, "… what with the war, y' know." His whispered announcement told us some very delicious pork chops were available and we were indeed lucky there were four of them. We ordered very promptly, before other customers learned about the presence of pork chops in the kitchen. The vegetables served to us were tasty. The potatoes were tiny. The chops were tough.

After a night of deep sleep, we left our hotel early on the morning of Thursday, April 6, and headed for Buckingham Palace to watch the changing of the guard. We wanted to see firsthand some of the places and things we had driven by or heard of the day before. After standing around for about half an hour we learned this sightseer's delight happened every other day, like yesterday and tomorrow. We headed for the Tower of London by way of the Billingsgate Fish Market. Our escort through the Tower was an elderly gentleman wearing a high black and red hat, a clergy-like collar, black pants with a red stripe on the side and a black cape. His attire commanded our attention and added authority to the things he told us about this historic site. It contained a lot of towers. The Crown Jewels were kept in Windsor Tower. I was impressed by the various types of weapons and suits of armor in White Tower. There were also at least two chapels on the site, St. John's Chapel and St. Peter's Chapel.

During lunch we drank a happy birthday toast to our top turret gunner, Frank Craig. We hoped Frank would enjoy his birthday more than we enjoyed the strong coffee with which we toasted him. We did not know where he and the other crew members were today, but we knew they were having a good time. One thing none of us had any way of knowing was that a mission by the 379th to Oberpfaffenhofen was scrubbed this morning because of bad weather.

Rainbow Corner Red Cross Club, London, England (Photo courtesy of Gordon & Connie Richards, Bedford, England. Circa 1943-1944)

After lunch we spent considerable time visiting Westminster Abbey. We were astonished by the architectural beauty. It was so ancient and so uniquely beautiful. There was one area we could not enter because of repairs being made to some recent bomb damage. We were fascinated by the splendor of the stained glass windows which depicted Christ, his apostles, various saints, bishops and Old Testament figures.

Our next stops included the zoo in Regent's Park, a stroll in St. James's Park and a close-up view of the barrage balloons in Hyde Park. These balloons were filed with helium and floated above selected sections of London at the ends of heavy cables. Each cable's length was controlled by a winch anchored in the ground and permitted the balloons to frequently be hidden in the clouds. Luftwaffe pilots tried to stay clear of these areas for fear of flying into the cables and crashing to earth.

Our walk back to the hotel was long and tiresome. We fell on our beds and caught a short nap. In what seemed too little time, Jim knocked at the door of the room I shared with Bob and announced it was time to eat supper, and we had better hurry if we wanted "the company of two of the best pilots in England." Bob and I assumed Jim was referring to himself and Howard. Our appetites told us to hurry, but our previous evening's dining experience slowed our expectations. The driver of a hack helped us find a little place that boasted of good food at a good price. We were very pleased to learn "good" meant delicious. It also meant expensive.

Leaving the restaurant, we overheard a group of servicemen talking about Rainbow Corner, a Red Cross Club at Piccadilly Circus. Glenn Miller's band was playing for a dance there that evening, and Miller was everyone's favorite World War II bandleader. Getting inside the Rainbow Corner was like going through a combat zone, but somehow I managed to get in. As I stood near the bar, listening to that wonderful Major Miller Music, I saw one of the fellows from the 379th Bomb Group in the crowd. I was able to get his attention and motioned for him to join me. The instant he did, I asked to see his Short Snorter. A Short Shorter was an English one-pound note, carried in one's wallet and signed by persons for whom the bearer had at one time or another purchased a drink. The "rules of the game" stipulated that if my friend did not have his Short Snorter with him, and bearing my signature, he had to buy a drink for me. He had never heard of a Short Snorter and said something about it being a crazy idea. My reminding him that he was an "officer and a gentleman" prompted him to pay for the round. I then signed his brand-new Short Snorter, thereby releasing him from having to buy a drink for me on some future occasion, in the event I was to again ask to see his Short Snorter. Obviously, it was a good idea to carry it with you everywhere. It was also a bit of fun.

Major Miller announced an intermission, and on the spur of the moment I decided to approach him for his autograph. I grabbed an unusually cold bottle of Coca-Cola from the bartender's hand and replaced it with a ten-shilling note. That was the first time I ever paid $2.00 for a Coke, but it was worth it. As I offered it to the Major I asked, "Sir, would you autograph my Short Snorter in exchange for this ice-cold bottle of Coke?" "Lieutenant," he said, "you've got a deal."

About eight months later, on December 15, Major Glenn Miller left the RAF's Twinwood airbase near Bedford in a Norseman D-64. He intended to join members of his band in Paris, France, where they were scheduled to play at a dance in that allied-occupied city. The plane carrying Major Miller disappeared and has never been located. My priceless Short Snorter, with his signature on it, is still in the mission diary I have kept for nearly half a century.

On Friday, April 7, Jim, Bob, Howard and I planned to visit the London Wax Works and Chamber of Horrors. It was not yet open when we arrived early that morning. There was some activity in front of a little shop along one of the busy streets where someone at a sidewalk stand was selling the pin-on ribbons which signified various military decorations. That seemed out of step with military protocol. I also saw an apothecary—an English pharmacy—and went inside. I was careful to keep my purchase of a small bottle of peroxide secret from the other guys. After paying the proprietor I hurriedly stuck the bottle into a pocket of my trench coat. It was my understanding that daily applications of peroxide would bleach one's hair, and applying it to my temples would make those areas of my hair look gray. Gray hair made people look distinguished—at least in my opinion.

A table model radio was on display in the window of one of the shops. "We definitely need a radio in our barracks back at Kimbolton," I said in a tone that brought quick, affirmative response from the other three members of our foursome. We entered the shop and inquired about the price. It was surprising to discover it was a secondhand radio—the finish on the wood case made it look like new. We were startled by the price of 15 pounds, or about $60.00. The clerk insisted he could not come down on the price, so we left. Before we reached the end of the next block, the shop's owner caught up with us and announced that he would let us have the radio for only ten pounds. His generosity was prompted, so he said, because we were members of the 8th Air Force. We returned to his shop and listened briefly to some music on a BBC station. Each of us chipped in two and one-half pounds and started arguing about who should have the honor of carrying "our" radio.

The time we spent in London was very rewarding. We visited many famous places, experienced some of the tradition and customs of the English people and were fortunate to obtain our own radio for our barracks. It would be a delightful treat to listen to music in our Nissen hut and perhaps tune in one of Axis Sally's broadcasts.

The time of day, and especially the lean condition of our wallets, convinced us we should head for Victoria Station and catch the noon train for Bedford. We had very little trouble getting a compartment all to ourselves. Evidently, most of the fellows on three-day passes were going to leave London on the latest train possible. Weather during the trip to Bedford was still normal for England – mostly fog and rain. The clickity-clack of the train's wheels on the rails made us sleepy, but the train's frequent starts and stops jarred us from napping and filled most of the time on the return to Bedford.

One of our Group's trucks, but no driver, was waiting at the Bedford station. We searched a few pubs and found him engaged in a game of darts. Waiting for him to finish the game presented no problem – there was plenty of time in which to get back to the base before 2000 hours. When we arrived at the base, we learned an afternoon mission scheduled for the 379th to Oldenburg/Vechta had been cancelled because of unfavorable weather conditions over the Continent. So what was new?

Upon reaching our barracks we eagerly plugged in our newly acquired, secondhand, table model radio. It lit up the moment we turned it on. We heard a lot of static, but nothing else. We turned the tuning dial back and forth so much it started to feel warm. Still nothing but static. No music, no

An English 10 Shilling Note

talking – nothing but static. An odor of something burning caught our attention. The sight of black smoke curling up from the back of the radio almost brought tears to our eyes. There was a crackling sound, and then another. Our cherished radio made a final sputter and went completely silent.

We hit the sack. Before I fell asleep Bob quietly said to me, "Ken, it sure would be awful if those darned Germans hit this Nissen hut with one of those buzzard bombs." My response was emphatic, but barely audible.

The following day was Saturday. The weather had been relentless in keeping 8th Air Force bombers on the ground. Mid-morning witnessed a few holes in some of the clouds and a mission alert was sounded. In the briefing room we learned the target was Oldenburg/Diepholz, but before leaving we were told the mission had been scrubbed. The weather played a very dominant role in the air war over Europe. U.S. and RAF airfields all over England had been closed down for ten consecutive days and disruption of Allied bombing objectives reached enormous proportions. Much of the damage caused by the recent bombing of Nazi targets had probably been repaired during the past ten days. Undoubtedly, many of the targets would have to be hit again.

April 9, 1944. It was Easter Sunday. The sun tried to push through the overcast. Clouds dispersed and cleared the way for the sun's warming rays as weather over this part of England finally took a turn for the good. Our crew was assigned to fly in Screwball Express on the 379th Group's mission to an aircraft factory at Marienburg, Germany. We were assigned only as a spare, however, and soon after takeoff it became evident we were not needed on the mission. We returned to Kimbolton, according to plan. We learned our crew was scheduled for a training flight, with an estimated time for return at 1330 hours. This was another indication the weather was improving over this part of England. After we completed our training flight we walked over to the control tower and waited for the Group to return from Marienburg.

The weather's jinx on the 379th was finally broken. We hoped tomorrow would be a good day. With luck, the weather, and Group headquarters, would allow our crew to get back to work.

I wonder if the shop owner in London turned on another radio and fooled us into believing the music we heard came from the junker we purchased. Surely not!

April 11, 1944. Bob Keller wrote a letter to his parents, telling them about our crew's visit to London. (In 1989 Bob provided me with a photocopy of that letter, and it was very helpful to me in retracing our steps during our three-day pass.)

Mission to Brussels

We were awakened at 0330 hours. The early morning ground fog was so thick it almost hid our shoes as we walked to the mess hall. Real eggs and lean bacon were on the menu for us on the morning of Monday, April 10, 1944.

Field Order No. 322 from the 8th Air Force directed the 1st Bomb Division to attack Luftwaffe airdromes and aircraft production/repair centers near Brussels, Belgium. The 2nd and 3rd Bomb Divisions were assigned to bomb airdromes and military installations in France. The overall assignment involved 486 B-17s and 243 B-24s. Escort for these operations was provided by 295 P-47s, 150 P-51s and 51 P-38s. Two groups of P-38 fighter-bombers were assigned to attack two French airfields using a new method of high-level precision bombing – a leading P-38 with a bombardier lying horizontal in the forward section with a bombsight, and two external bombs under the wings. Pilots of other P-38s in the formation salvoed their bombs when the lead plane's bombs were released.

The 379th Bomb Group began its takeoff at 0645 hours. I started singing the 23rd Psalm. After assembling over the Kimbolton air base at 3,000 feet the Group climbed to 15,000 feet, and at 0836 hours we left the English coast at Clacton flying 3,000 feet higher. Nineteen minutes later we crossed the enemy's Belgian coast at an altitude of 22,000 feet. We saw a small amount of inaccurate flak at the coastal city of Ostend, Belgium.

Our Group's target was an airdrome and aircraft factory at Brussels' northeastern suburb of Evere. Screwball Express flew in our Lead Group's Low Squadron. The bombing plan of our 41st Combat Wing was intriguing. The 379th Bomb Group, flying lead position for the Wing, was assigned to drop 500-pound demolition bombs. The 384th Bomb Group from Grafton Underwood was to follow us across the target and drop M-47 incendiary bombs. The 303rd Bomb Group from Molesworth was to finish the job with 1,000-pound general purpose bombs.

Bombs dropped by the heavy bombers of the 8th Air Force came in a variety of shapes and weights, each designed for different purposes. The more common varieties were the general purpose high explosive types and the incendiary types. The general purpose bombs we used were of the 100, 250, 300, 500, 1,000 and 2,000-pound weight classes. Screwball Express usually carried the 500 and 1,000-pound types. Incendiary bombs were almost always of the 100-pound class but occasionally included 500 pounders. Fuses in the nose and tail of each bomb determined whether the explosion would be triggered on impact or at delayed settings. Other types of bombs, but types not generally used by our heavy bombers, included the antipersonnel and fragmentary bombs, and armor-piercing bombs.

Bomb loads were dropped by either the salvo method or by the intervalometer method. As the words imply, the salvo method was the simultaneous release of all bombs by pushing the salvo lever; the intervalometer method allowed the bombardier to manually preselect the desired distance between bombs when they hit the target. The selected intervals were usually 50, 100 or 250 feet, although other selections were available. The intervalometer setting caused the electrically timed release of the bombs from racks in the bomb bay. Bombs could also be toggled out by the bombardier pressing a toggle switch, but this method was seldom employed by heavy bombers in the ETO.

Several bursts of antiaircraft fire were seen over Brussels. Our Group reached the Initial Point of our bomb run at 0912 hours. The IP was the point at which the entire formation turned toward the target and began the bomb run. Initially, we had been trained to use evasive action from the IP to the target in an attempt to evade flak and fighter attacks. It had been contended that evasive action would allow maximum numbers of planes and bombs to successfully reach the target. In actual practice, the use of evasive action by a formation of bombers proved ineffective. Despite the precision of the Norden bombsight, even a small amount of evasive action impaired bombing accuracy. Planes in the formations often became so scattered that many bombs fell short, over or wide of the target area.

Cloud cover at the IP made it necessary for us to change course and fly a compass heading different from the one given us at the briefing. This enabled us to see the target very clearly. We encountered no enemy fighters or flak during the 40 seconds of the bomb run. This permitted lead bombardiers and pilots to devote full attention to the sighting, aiming and bombing operation. The bomb run was the major event of the mission. It was the stage from which all the bombers succeeded or failed in their bombing performance. Flak bursts and enemy fighters encountered on the bomb run had to be ignored. The 379th Bomb Group fostered the concept of flying the bomb run without evasive action, and the Group's enviable record of bombing accuracy was testimony to the concept's success.

The 20 B-17s in our Group each dropped 12-500 pound bombs on prescribed intervalometer settings at 0919 hours from 22,000 feet. Four rockets were fired at us from the ground. All bombs of the 379th Group fell within the confines of the airfield, and most of the bombs fell on the landing area. A large hangar immediately north of the runway was the aiming point and received direct hits. Three smaller hangars and two auxiliary buildings were also destroyed. Two of six aircraft on the field were blown up and three of them set afire. Three blast shelters were hit. The bomb strikes were clearly shown in pictures taken by 16mm movie cameras in the bomb bays of lead planes. These cameras were mounted so they were automatically driven to tilt fore to aft in synchronization with the bombsight and its view of the target as seen by the lead bombardier.

The incendiaries dropped by the 384th Group were spread over a wide area. The pattern reached from the large hangar hit by the 379th over to a group of workshops and hangars, then to other hangars and into a marshalling yard northwest of the airfield. Fires were visible as railway cars burned in the yards. Some fires were also set in the nearby suburb of Helmet. A smaller pattern of incendiaries fell in a cemetery and on the grounds of the Chateau Royal in the northern part of Brussels. Bombs dropped by the 303rd Group struck immediately northwest of the airfield in an area containing workshops and hangars, and adjacent to the marshalling yards.

The bomb pattern of the 303rd measured 2,600 feet by 1,600 feet. The 384th's bomb pattern was 10,000 feet by 3,000 feet. The 379th had excellent bombing results – its pattern was 2,300 feet by 1,600 feet and its center was only 300 feet from the lead bombardier's aiming point. Sixty-one of the 62 B-17s in the 41st Combat Wing attacked the target. They dropped a total of 120 tons of general purpose bombs and 41 tons of incendiary bombs.

After the target, meager flak was observed at Louvain and again at Antwerp, in Belgium. A very heavy cloud formation was encountered when we crossed the Belgian coast on the way back to England, causing us to lose visual contact with our Group. Screwball Express and other B-17s in the Low Squadron flew over the Belgian coast twice before relocating our Group. We observed some more flak on the French coast at Dunkirk. As we were about to cross the coast of England our number two engine started acting up and its props had to be feathered, making it necessary to fly the rest of the way to Kimbolton on three engines. We made three landing approaches before Howard and Jim were satisfied that Screwball Express was in sufficiently proper attitude for a safe landing.

A few of our buddies accused us of intentionally giving Kimbolton a buzz job. The last time we could remember coming so close to tree tops at the end of a runway was the time we clipped off the tips of some tree limbs during a takeoff at Ardmore, Oklahoma.

Starbuck and his ground crew quickly discovered the trouble with number two engine – a spark plug loosened by vibration. He assured us it would never happen again. There was no battle damage to Screwball Express, and all Fortresses of our Group returned safely to base. None of our flight crews saw any enemy aircraft aloft during the mission, although about 60 airborne bandits were seen by crews of the 2nd and 3rd Bomb Divisions. Our flying time today was 4:35 hours. It was our sixth combat mission, and we had 19 left.

The April 10, 1944, mission report by the 8th Air Force included the following data: Twenty B-17s of the 1st Combat Wing were unable to bomb their primary targets and instead attacked targets of opportunity. This happened to only one other B-17 in the entire 1st Bomb Division. Sixty-five of the 2nd Bomb Division's 243 B-24s on this mission bombed targets of opportunity and 185 of the 248 bombers in the 3rd Bomb Division had to do likewise. The combined number of planes that bombed targets of opportunity on this mission totaled 271. Cloud cover over four primary targets in France took a heavy toll on today's bombing objectives of the 8th Air Force. A total of 729 B-17s and B-24s were dispatched, but only 382 hit their primary targets. The 1st Bomb Division accounted for 213 of the 382 planes that bombed primaries – a proud 56%.

Three 8th Air Force bombers were lost in action. One B-24 was shot down by an enemy aircraft. One B-17 was downed by flak and another by unknown cause. Four of our fighter planes were lost: a P-51 and a P-47 from the fighter force escorting the bombers and two P-38 fighter-bombers. Our "little friends" destroyed 46 enemy planes on the ground and eight in the air. In addition, our fighter planes damaged numerous gas and oil storage tanks, hangars, flak towers and water towers in strafing attacks.

Mission to Sorau

Tuesday, April 11, 1944. The 298th operation of the 8th Air Force occurred on this date under Field Order No. 323. An air armada consisting of 643 B-17 Flying Fortresses and 241 B-24 Liberators was dispatched to attack six FW-190 and Junkers assembly and components plants deep in central and eastern Germany. The 1st Bomb Division was assigned targets at Sorau, Gottbus, Stettin and Arnimswalde. The 2nd Bomb Division's targets were at Oschersleben and Bernberg, and the 3rd Division's were at Politz, Stettin, Rostock and Arnimswalde.

The 379th Bomb Group furnished 37 aircraft for the 41st Wing. Of that total, 19 aircraft were assigned to the Lead Group and 18 to the Low Group of the Wing. Screwball Express was assigned to the Low Squadron of the Low Group. The 41st Wing's target was the Focke-Wulf assembly plant at Sorau, Germany, approximately 95 miles southeast of Berlin and about 70 miles northeast of Dresden. The town contained many buildings and facilities used in construction of FW-190 aircraft. (In 1944 Sorau was in southeastern Germany but in 1945 it was assigned to Poland by the Potsdam Conference. The name of the city is now Zary.)

Takeoff for the Group began at 0715 hours. While still over Downham Market west of Norwich, England, our Low Group was forced to climb through an overcast. During this maneuver a 379th aircraft from our 525th Squadron and bearing number 42-31083 exploded for reasons unknown. One of our Group's planes, serial number 42-31228, returned to Kimbolton undispatched. Our Low Group had been quickly reduced in size from 18 to 16 planes, and we were still over friendly territory.

Bombers of the 1st and 2nd Divisions were assigned to make their pentration across Holland. Fortresses of the 3rd Division were assigned to fly a northerly route across the Danish peninsula. The penetration route used by one Division in the morning became the return route of the other Division that afternoon.

Weather over Germany was very cloudy. We observed flak at Ijmuiden, Dummer Lake, Steinhuder Lake, Hanover, Celle and Brunswick. A huge smoke screen was at work near Fallersleben in an attempt to confuse us into believing the location was the city of Brunswick. Some crews reported a barracks area may have been under the smoke. Single engine enemy fighters engaged Fortresses in other Groups in the area between Hanover and Oschersleben. Losses among those B-17s appeared to be heavy. None of the bandits attacked either of our two Groups.

Vast amounts of flak were seen around Magdeburg. Flak bursts had tracked us across most of Germany. The flak was terribly heavy and generally accurate, and caused various degrees of damage to 18 of the 35 Fortresses in the two 379th Groups. A factory was burning at Waggum. At 1100 hours a large, partly camouflaged factory was observed about 3 miles northeast of Burg, and near that city we saw approximately 45 planes sitting at an airfield. Barrage balloons were reported by one bomber crew as we flew past Wittenberg on the Elbe River about 56 miles south-southwest of Berlin. Wittenberg is the birthplace of my paternal grandparents, and I had often wondered what the town looked like. It was difficult to see clearly from several miles above the city and five miles abreast of it.

Wittenberg was the starting place of the Reformation, more than four hundred years earlier, and was also the birthplace of Martin Luther. Historic buildings in Wittenberg include the Augustinian Monastery where Luther lived much of his adult life, the Melanchthon University where he taught, the Stadtkirche where he preached and the Schlosskirche where he nailed his 95 Theses to its doors and started the Reformation in 1517. In 1944 Wittenberg was a wartime industrial city because of its railroad junctions and the manufacture of chemicals, cellulose, rubber and machinery.

A Fortress in one of the other Groups was hit by flak and eight 'chutes came out of it. The plane went into a spin and crashed in a river near a small town. It then exploded with a violent eruption of flames, and smoke mushroomed into the sky.

About that time we saw a FW-190 get shot down by a P-51. It happened right in front of us and at almost the exact altitude at which we were flying. In the vicinity of Rogatz another B-17 was shot down by flak at 1126 hours. Six parachutes emerged from the plane and some of them landed in a lake.

Part of the song repeated itself in my mind. "Yea, though I walk through the valley of the shadow of death …"

The three Groups in our Combat Wing arrived at their respective Initial Points and turned onto their individual bomb runs. The attack by our Wing was the first to be made at Sorau by the 8th Air Force. Our Low Group planned for a bombing altitude of only 11,000 feet because of heavy clouds in the target area. This was the lowest altitude from which our crew bombed on any of our missions. The Lead Group encountered 10/10 cloud cover and was not able to locate the target. That Group's bomb loads dropped at 1212 hours from 14,000 feet, but fell short of the target and may have hit a small town south of Sorau. The bombs were released almost one minute early.

Our Low Group avoided solid cloud cover by flying slightly north of the intended course where we found 7/10 cover that provided our Group a reasonably clear run at the target. We did not see any flak or enemy fighters on the entire bomb run. Bombing conditions were in our favor and our bombs were released at exactly 1217 hours. The bomb strikes of our entire Low Group were directly on the target.

Planes in our Low Group each carried 15-100 pound demolition bombs and 8-500 pound incendiary bombs. The latter type held 100 incendiaries weighing about five pounds each. Six concentrations of general purpose bombs fell into the target area. A textile type building at the western edge of town received a direct hit. A heavy engineering building adjacent to the textile building received two direct hits. At least four direct hits were made on a large building believed to house a small engineering works at the eastern edge of the railway choke point. That choke point was our aiming point. Each of two small textile mill buildings near the center of town received direct hits and incendiary bombs exploded in the same area. A medium sized building on the southwestern edge of the town received two or more direct hits and was additionally blanketed with incendiaries. Two direct hits were seen on a large textile building at the extreme eastern edge of Sorau. The building exploded and fire blew out of the building's side walls. More than a dozen general purpose bombs fell in the marshalling yard. In addition to the destruction caused by general purpose bombs, incendiary bombs incinerated the eastern portion of the railroad yards. Demolition bombs also fell into groups of small buildings on the town's eastern edge.

Our Low Group dropped 36 tons of general purpose demolition bombs and 94 tons of incendiary bombs on Sorau. The damage to almost all of the town was very severe. The incendiary bombs burned up what had been blown up by the demolition bombs. It was a scene of destruction and chaos.

We turned away from the target and headed north along the border of Poland. Shortly thereafter we saw a B-17 get hit by flak and drop out of a Group flying to our left and ahead of us. In the vicinity of Stettin, Germany, a large number of twin engine fighters attacked several Groups of B-17s. A large flak barrage greeted us as we passed Stettin, and another barrage filled the sky over the area around Berlin on our left. The enemy coast out was crossed at 1520 hours and at 14,000 feet, an altitude from which we could vaguely see part of Denmark through the clouds and haze.

During that part of the mission we saw no enemy fight-ers. Flak bursts were in the distance and allowed us to relax a little. My thoughts went back to the devastation at Sorau. It was difficult to justify. Only a few buildings in the entire town escaped fire and/or damage. The loss of lives had to be very high. Regardless of these sentiments, nations were at war with each other. Headquarters of the 8th Air Force was not concerned with saving the lives of the enemy's military personnel and it could not become dedicated to saving the lives of the enemy's civilians. It had to hold its focus on keeping its own losses at a minimum and still do the job assigned to it. In every war the innocent have suffered with the "guilty." There is no absolute distinction between civilians and members of the military. Civilians are instrumental in supplying the military with the means to wage war. Similarly, there are no degrees of death. The victim might be in the military or a civilian – a man, a woman or a child. The victim's skin might be white, black, brown, red or yellow. A small bullet can be as merciless as a bomb blast. The victim is just as dead. I reminded myself that the attack on Sorau, as well as the bombing of other Nazi targets, would not have been necessary if the unconscionable attack on Pearl Harbor had not been committed.

It wasn't a bed of rose petals for U.S. bomber crews and fighter pilots, either. The "wild blue yonder" was not entirely glamorous. We flew miles above the earth, but death still came searching for us in the form of enemy aircraft, machine gun shells, rockets, cannon shells, antiaircraft shells and falling shrapnel. When things really got rough there was no place for us or our plane to hide. There was always the possibility our flight path would intersect with the trajectory of an enemy missile. It could all end at any time. We were being shot at and many of us were killed. Thousands of our airmen were not permitted to live beyond the fatal moment when death entered their aircraft.

The enemy never made the 8th Air Force turn away from a target. We believed in getting to the target on the first attempt so we wouldn't have to go back. There was no such thing as not bombing a target because you might do too much damage. We destroyed our targets as completely as we could.

At 1613 hours a Flying Fortress from one of the other Groups reported it was ditching in the North Sea. Our formation crossed England's coast at 1727 hours flying 2,000 feet above Cromer.

All planes from the 379th returned to Kimbolton, except the one that exploded. Slightly more than half of them were damaged by flak and Screwball Express returned from the mission with only four small flak holes. The 1st Bomb Division lost 19 bombers, 12 of which were from the 40th Combat Wing. No bombers in our Wing were lost to enemy action. The day's losses for the 8th Air Force totalled 52 B-17s and 12 B-24s. Bomber losses would have been greater had it not been for the splendid defensive escort of 13 fighter groups from the 8th Air Force and four from the 9th Air Force. Sixteen of our little friends were shot down on this mission: 12 from the 8th Air Force and four from the 9th. Our fighters claimed 115 enemy planes downed: 51 in the air, 63 on the ground and one on water. They additionally claimed 11 probables and damage to 88 others.

We learned later that nine of the crew members in 42-31083 were killed in its explosion but its navigator parachuted safely to earth with minor injury. That B-17 was not recorded as Missing in Action because its loss was not a result of enemy action. Instead, it was recorded as having "exploded during assembly and crashed." This was part of the practiced method of keeping count of the bombers after a mission. Aircraft status reports included such words as "returned (damaged/undamaged)," "MIA," "on hand," "crashed (enemy territory/England)," "ditched," "salvaged," or "landed in neutral country." The words were descriptive statements for expressing the status of an aircraft and numerically recording its condition. It was all so cut and dried.

The 2nd Bomb Division had generally good bombing results on today's mission. Bombing by the 3rd Bomb Division was adversely affected by bad weather conditions which made formation flying very difficult. The weather also prevented that Division from bombing its long-range targets; it consequently used visual and PFF means to bomb secondary and last resort targets along the coastal area of the Baltic Sea. The Swedish Home Service later reported nine B-17s landed in Sweden with everyone aboard uninjured, except for one crew member who was killed in combat.

Our crew completed combat mission number seven today. We logged 11 hours and 20 minutes of flying time between takeoff and landing – the longest period of time we would spend on one combat mission. That night at the bar, our Group's lead navigator for this mission told me the day's flight plan covered 1,678 miles. A lot of miles, especially over enemy territory.

I was reminded of an old saying that states, "If you don't have a hernia, you're not carrying your share of the load."

The following day's newspaper article in The Stars and Stripes gave a lot of space to the RAF's 4,000 ton assault on Nazi targets during the previous night. It also commented on General Eisenhower's statement to a group of American pilots that they soon would be flying from dawn to dusk in a great land-sea-air invasion of Western Europe that would crush the Germans and "crush them properly." Several paragraphs discussed the role of our medium bombers against targets in France and Belgium. Other paragraphs mentioned the German radio broadcasts that claimed more than 100 American aircraft destroyed on April 11. The broadcasts included an account of fierce engagements between American and German planes in the area between Hanover and Brunswick, and along the Baltic coast. It also told of Fortresses and Liberators bombing Oschersleben and Bernberg.

Not one word about the mission to Sorau.

Wednesday, April 12, 1944	379th Mission to Schweinfurt recalled
Thursday, April 13, 1944	379th Mission to Schweinfurt-bomb ball bearing plant. Our crew "stood down"
Friday, April 14, 1944	Our crew on 1:30 hr. training flight
Saturday, April 15, 1944	Our crew on 3:30 hr. training flight
Sunday, April 16, 1944	Rained all day
Monday, April 17, 1944	379th Mission to Laon/Athie scrubbed

(**Special Credit**: Please refer to *Flying Fortress, The Illustrated Biography of the B-17s And The Men Who Flew Them*, under Bibliography.)

Mission to Perleberg

Tuesday, April 18, 1944, was another cloudy day – but it turned out to be "sufficiently flyable" in the opinion of our weather officer. Howard, Jim, Bob and I were awakened by the CQ. We dressed hurriedly and noticed that Bob had not yet crawled out of his bunk. Yelling at him did not awaken him, and Bob continued snoring loudly. Howard went to Bob's bunk, shook him and yelled in his ear. Bob stirred a little and mumbled something which we assumed meant he was ready to "rise and shine." It was time for us to go, so we left for the mess hall without Bob.

We didn't see our navigator during morning chow. This didn't alarm us because we assumed Bob decided to skip a full breakfast, and instead have some doughnuts and a cup of coffee. We erroneously assumed he was waiting for us at the briefing room.

Orders from 8th Air Force headquarters specified the lst Bombardment Division was to attack Oranienburg, Wittenberg and Perleberg. The 2nd Division was assigned targets at Brandenburg, Rathenow and targets of opportunity in the Pas de Calais area. The 3rd Division was assigned an airdrome at Luneburg and targets of opportunity. Targets for the majority of 501 B-17s and 275 B-24s included aircraft, aircraft engine and electrical manufacturing plants in the Berlin area. An additional 12 B-24s were to attack a military installation in the Pas de Calais area.

None of us saw Bob at the briefing. Maybe he was at the separate briefing for navigators.

The 379th Bomb Group furnished 18 aircraft for the Lead Group and 20 aircraft for the Low Group in the 41st "B" Wing. Each of our Groups included two spares. Records indicate the 305th Bomb Group from Chelveston flew High Group position in our Wing. Our primary target was an aircraft assembly plant at Oranienburg, about 20 miles north of Berlin. Screwball Express was scheduled with the High Squadron in Lead Group "B". Each plane in our Lead Group carried 38-100 pound demolition bombs and a few of the planes also carried M-47 incendiaries.

We counted only nine noses when our crew gathered at the side of Screwball Express. No navigator! We became concerned. Bob was still missing after our preflight routines were completed. It was time to start engines and still no navigator. We were very worried! What had happened to Bob? It was 0945 hours – time to taxi Screwball Express out to the runway. No navigator!

Suddenly a jeep came racing across the field. We didn't recognize the driver, but the half-dressed passenger was our navigator. Bob jumped from the jeep before it skidded to a stop, leaped through the open waist door of Screwball Express, sat on the plane's floor and started pulling on his insulated pants and boots. He giggled a little. He giggled some more. Bob made his way into the radio room where he stayed until after takeoff at 1000 hours. He then squeezed through the bomb bay and past the top turret position. He finally slid down into the nose compartment of the plane. I was already at my station and turned to question him. "Howdy," he said to me, still giggling. "Fancy meeting you here."

His antics prior to takeoff tested my memory of a few of the words in the 23rd Psalm. I'm certain there is nothing wrong in prayer being accompanied by clean humor.

Bob looked almost huge as he sat at the little table on which there was barely enough room to chart a course or figure ground speed. We all looked monstrous in our flight clothing. Crew members on Flying Fortresses wore cumbersome, electrically heated, leather flight jackets and pants, both lined with heavy fleece on the inside. The heated boots and gloves were made in the same way. Flight suits of less bulkiness were made of a lighter weight, dark green material, the "summer" version. We all wore flak helmets, flak vests and parachutes. Some of us wore seatpack 'chutes, some wore the chestpack type and others wore the backpack type. There were many leads to connect, including the tube to the oxygen mask, the electrical leads to the jacket, pants, gloves and boots, and leads to radio and intercom systems. All these were leads to life itself. With temperatures of 40 to 50 degrees below zero, it was not safe to touch the plane with one's bare skin. At such low temperatures, placing your bare skin against the plane's metal usually resulted in leaving a patch of skin and pulling away a bloody finger or a raw palm.

The assembly of our Wing was accomplished in accordance with the briefing plan. Weather conditions soon caused a mix-up in the formation but we were able to regroup. The 1st Bomb Division assembled as briefed, and all Combat Wings left the English coast in about the proper order. Approximately fifteen minutes later a B-17 in a Group ahead of ours blew up over the North Sea. Nine parachutes emerged from the explosion and floated toward the cold water below. Air-Sea Rescue was notified before the 'chutes hit the water. Without a quick rescue, those unfortunate airmen would freeze to death in a matter of minutes.

Flying a previously unused route for attacks in the Berlin area, our bombers proceeded over the North Sea to a point north of Wilhelmshaven and then headed southeast toward the German capital. Our fighter escort was provided by 16 groups from the 8th Air Force and three from the 9th Air Force. Only moderate flak was encountered on our way to the target. It resembled the "Swarm of Bees" type of barrage, named for its visual likeness to a swarming horde of deadly fragments.

Our Lead Group was prevented from bombing the Heinkel assembly plant at Oranienburg because of very heavy clouds immediately over the primary target. The situation was made even worse when a Group of bombers cut across our flight path near the end of the bomb run. The turbulence caused by the prop wash of their planes made it impossible for our PFF plane to hold its course. A radio message from the Lead plane signaled our Lead Group to fly in a northwesterly direction toward Wittstock. We later changed course and flew a compass heading of 261 degrees for an attack at our secondary target, an airfield immediately southwest of Perleberg.

In spite of the confusion, we were able to determine that the 20 planes in the Low Group had successfully bombed the Heinkle plant at Oranienburg with M-47 incendiaries after a visual bomb run lasting almost ten minutes. Our Low Group also dropped several tons of propaganda leaflets.

The airfield at Perleberg was approximately 75 miles west-northwest of Berlin. Flak from 56 antiaircraft guns at the target was moderate in its intensity but fairly accurate. One piece of shrapnel hit our right wing and another fragment went through the window behind Howard. A B-17 in another Group was hit by flak and went down at the IP. Another Group's B-17 was downed by flak over the target. Four parachutes were seen coming out of the first of those planes and 10 parachutes from the second one. A fighter plane, believed to be one of ours, was hit by flak and went down in the target area. Its pilot managed to parachute

safely. Several rockets were fired at us from the ground, leaving long trails of smoke as they ascended toward our position, but none of the rockets reached us. Seconds before we dropped our bombs, two FW-190s attacked our Squadron head-on from beneath our position. They passed under our formation, and moments later both of them were shot down by gunners in a Group behind us .

We had a reasonably clear bomb run at an altitude of 23,500 feet on a magnetic heading of 261 degrees. We dropped our bombs on visual sighting of the target at 1504 hours. The bursts of our bombs formed two patterns, the larger of the two extending across the main hangar and administration building area. Two and possibly three large hangars and one medium hangar received direct hits. Bombs also exploded on four other buildings. The other bomb pattern appeared to include another large hangar and at least several of the 39 enemy aircraft on the field at the time of attack. Smoke from the bomb blasts prevented us from clearly seeing the number of planes destroyed on the ground. Our bombing results were described as "excellent."

We left the target area and headed home along a route parallel to our entry course. Columns of smoke off to our left and behind us indicated another Combat Wing had bombed its target at Wittenberge, a small port on the Elbe river, about 80 miles southeast of Hamburg. Its name is spelled almost like Wittenberg. Only one week earlier we had flown past Wittenberg on our way to bomb Sorau. Wittenberg looked so peaceful that day, even with its barrage balloons floating overhead. On that occasion I liked what I saw. Today a large part of Wittenberge was on fire. I did not like looking at it and turned my eyes away.

A smoke screen was seen as we flew near Hamburg. Antiaircraft fire was observed at various points during the mission, specifically at Cuxhaven, Neureppen, Lubeck, Schweint, Bruenfenfield, Fichbeck and Stade. The anti-aircraft fire at Cuxhaven on the way out was heavy and accurate, but moderate at other points. Flak boats were seen at Helgoland. I fired about 100 rounds of .50-caliber machine gun shells at one of the flak boats, but was not certain I hit it. Conditions and distance were a lot different from those at a skeet range. Four B-17s from the High Group were unable to bomb at Perleberg and selected a dock area at Cuxhaven as a good place to drop their loads.

Dinghies were observed in the North Sea and were reported to Air-Sea Rescue. A convoy of approximately 20 ships was seen between Helgoland and the enemy coast on a heading of 300 degrees. Two small convoys of eight to ten ships each were also seen heading toward Heligoland.

The Swedish Home Service radio announced that one B-17 made a forced landing on Swedish territory, and the undamaged aircraft and its crew of ten were taken into custody. All planes in our two Groups returned safely to Kimbolton and none of the crew members from the 379th were injured. Flying time for our eighth mission was nine hours.

After we landed and parked Screwball Express, Howard and Bob walked to an isolated area and engaged in very serious discussion. It was no secret that Bob did not like noisy chatter in the barracks when he tried to sleep. We did not know he purchased earplugs while we were in London. He overslept this morning because his newly acquired earplugs made it difficult for him to hear the several wake-up calls. That's what Bob told Howard. We never knew what Howard told Bob.

It was learned later the 41st "A" Wing had attacked the

Heinkel factory at Germendorf near Oranienburg with M-47 incendiaries. On this mission that Wing consisted of two Groups from the 303rd and one Group from the 384th. The 384th High Group hit immediately west-northwest of the target with the center of its bomb pattern approximately 3,000 feet from the Mean Point of Impact. A portion of the 384th's pattern appeared to extend into the edge of the target area. Bomb bursts of the 303rd Low Group were not shown by photo reconnaissance.

Formations of the 3rd Division were broken up by a solid mass of clouds west of Berlin that rose 30,000 feet and prevented attacks on their primary targets. The HE-177 assembly plant at Brandenburg was bombed through the overcast with unknown results. All other primary targets and many targets of opportunity were attacked with good results.

Although the 1st and 2nd Bomb Divisions saw only light fighter opposition, the 3rd Division encountered heavy attacks from 60-100 enemy aircraft in the Barnewitz area north of Brandenburg and lost 10 bombers. The 8th Air Force lost a total of 17 B-17s, two B-24s and five fighter planes on this mission. Our "little friends" destroyed 20 enemy aircraft, 16 of which were on the ground.

The Stars and Stripes reported the next day that "some air divisions" on this mission "came home to tell of three-hour battles with as many as 200 Nazi fighters." This was apparently someone's overstatement.

I have often wondered how Bob was able to obtain maps and navigation data for this mission. Frankly, I'm not real sure he had any. But he must have had something. Otherwise, how could he …?

Only 17 more combat missions left.

Mission to Kassel

The total number of Luftwaffe airfields and plants producing German aircraft and component parts was probably never known, not even by the enemy. Airfields were located everywhere in Germany and in all occupied countries in Europe. Aircraft production facilities also seemed to be every place – in large cities, adjacent to large cities, in small towns, next to airfields, next to railroad marshalling yards, in rural areas – everywhere.

On Wednesday, April 19, 1944, like many days before and after, the 8th Air Force went after the Germany aircraft industry. The 308th operation order of the 8th Air Force included the following target assignments:

1st Bomb Division   **Airdromes/Aircraft Assembly Plants at Kassel/Waldau, Kassel/Bettenhausen, Kassel/Altenbauna and Eschwege**

2nd Bomb Division   **Airdromes/Aircraft Assembly Plants at Paderborn and Gutersloh "Crossbow" in Pas de Calais**

3rd Bomb Division   **Airdromes/Aircraft Assembly Plants at Werl and Lippstadt**

The attacks were assigned to six forces made up of 14 Combat Wings. One force of three Wings of B-17s was to bomb FW-190 components and assembly plants at Kassel; four forces of two B-17 Wings each and one force of two B-24 Wings were to bomb five airfields in western-central Germany; one Wing of B-24's was to bomb a military installation in the Pas de Calais area. Escort was provided by 16 groups of 8th Air Force fighter planes and three groups from the 9th Air Force.

The 379th Bomb Group furnished 22 aircraft for the High Group of the 41st Wing in the attack at Kassel/Waldau. Screwball Express flew in the High Squadron of that Group. The 379th also provided 20 aircraft for the High Group of the 40th "B" Wing which attacked Eschwege. We had two spare planes in each of these Groups. The wheels of Screwball Express left the runway at 0630 hours. The two spares in the Group going to Kassel returned early as planned. The other two spares filled in and completed the mission to Eschwege with the 40th "B" Wing.

We crossed the enemy coast at a point north of the Amsterdam, Holland, area at 0909 hours, flying at 22,000 feet. Northwest of Osnabruck, Germany, we headed southeast to a point near Gottingen and northeast of Kassel, which is about 70 miles south of Hanover. We saw many flak bursts all along our route, but none of them were close enough for us to hear them. When an antiaircraft shell exploded close to our position it made a noise like an explosive POOM. The bursts usually came in groups of four, (occasionally five) because there were normally four antiaircraft guns in the majority of German gun batteries, and they were all fired in rapid succession. Whatever the reason, most of the bursts were always in foursomes, a quartet that lacked all harmony of sound, just a very frightening and deadly POOM—POOM—POOM—POOM. When flak bursts were close to Screwball Express we were forever thankful to hear them. If you didn't hear a close one, it was very likely you were dead. The intelligence officer told us during the briefing there were 165 flak guns at Kassel. We prayed we would be able to hear each and every one of them while we were in "the valley of the shadow of death."

Bomb bays of the Fortresses in our High Group were each loaded with 42-100 pound incendiary bombs. The Focke-Wulf assembly plant and airfield assigned to our Wing were a few miles southeast of Kassel. Our plan was to fly past the eastern side of the city, and then make a sharp turn to our right and attack from an altitude of 23,000 feet on a magnetic heading of 270 degrees. This called for a very short bomb run. Cloud cover in the area ranged from 5/10 to 8/10, but we were confident of a visual bombing approach to the target. A ground haze did not seriously impair our view. Flak throughout the bomb run was intense. It was very accurate as to the altitude at which it exploded, but its deflection was off and caused the bursts to be a little to either side of our formation. Our bombs were away at 1038 hours. Four rockets were fired at us from the ground as we turned away from the target. I couldn't tell where, or if, they exploded. Perhaps they fell back to earth, still intact.

The main assembly plant was severely damaged and all of its surrounding installations received direct hits from our Group. The barracks area was completely covered by our incendiaries. At least one separate assembly building was set afire. In a period of seven minutes the 59 Fortresses in our Wing dropped 382-500 pound demolition bombs and 771-100 pound incendiary bombs on the target. The official description of our bombing called the results "very good."

Bombing results at the Kassel/Altenbauna aircraft engine factory were "excellent." The airfield at Werl was bombed with "good" results. The FW-190 components factory at Kassel/Bettenhausen was hit with "very good" results. Results of bombing airfields at Lippstadt and Paderborn were described as "good." The bombing results at Gutersloh's airfield were "fair to good." The results at Eschwege airfield were described as "poor," since only a medium sized hangar and some minor installations were damaged.

After leaving the target, our flight plan back to England took us a little north of Frankfurt, Germany. One of our fighter planes dived toward the ground west of Frankfurt. Its pilot made a strafing run and shot up a concentration of flak towers. Our cheers were muffled by our oxygen masks. We then flew south of Brussels and out of Belgium at Ostend. Our fighter support left us a few minutes later as we decreased our altitude to about 12,000 feet. We crossed the English coast at 1236 hours, north of Ipswich. Our flying time on this mission was seven hours and 30 minutes.

After landing, and before going into the debriefing hut, crews returning from the mission headed for the Red Cross van parked in the headquarters area. Coffee and doughnuts were always available there. If you wanted a shot of scotch, or bourbon, or gin, it was also available – one shot to a crewman. In our case, the ten shots were divided among only the four of us who enjoyed having our blood warmed after breathing oxygen for hours at sub-zero temperatures. Occasionally, it was obvious the debriefing reports of some of the crews were embellished a bit by the booze.

Records of the 8th Air Force show that 799 Fortresses and Liberators participated in the day's operation. Primary targets were attacked by 660 of that number, and 111 planes hit targets of opportunity. The 8th Air Force lost eight planes. Five B-17s were lost to enemy aircraft, one B-24 to flak in the Pas de Calais area, one P-51 to enemy action and another P-51 to unknown reasons. Bombers incurring light battle damage numbered 149 – another 28 had major damage. The 8th Air Force casualty report for the day listed 1 crew member killed, 143 wounded, 54 missing and three rescued.

We did not see any enemy aircraft in the air on the entire mission; however, two Me-109s were reported to have braved the flak over Kassel and attacked another Group of B-17s. Only a modest portion of the Luftwaffe was in the air today, but our fighters claimed 16 enemy aircraft destroyed in aerial action.

The 8th Air Force made the following report about the fighter escort provided to the 1st Bombardment Division during the day's operation: "The 361st (fighter) Group rendezvoused with the 1st Division Fortresses at Egmond at 0902 hours, continued escort uneventfully to Brausche at 0948 hours when the 357th (fighter) Group took over. This Group escorted the bombers for about two hours, arriving south of Brussels at 1150 hours. East of Kassel, 20 single engine enemy aircraft attacked a straggling combat box of 15 B-17s. Our fighters engaged them immediately, shooting down five. The 352nd (fighter) Group had made rendezvous at 1011 hours over Northeim. The Group left the bombers in the vicinity of Cochem at 1110 hours. Southwest of Kassel, however, seven FW-190s and one Me-109 were engaged, and three were destroyed. The 4th Group made rendezvous northeast of Eschwege at 1022 hours. In the target area, 25 to 50 single engine enemy aircraft attacked rear boxes of the 1st Combat Wing, while

about 50 additional enemy aircraft covered the attacking aircraft. Five enemy aircraft were destroyed. The Group broke escort over the Rhine River north of Coblenz at 1103 hours. The 355th (fighter) Group, while on area patrol, at 1015 hours engaged 50 plus single engine enemy aircraft approaching from the direction of Magdeburg, and destroyed three. At 1045 hours, friendly fighters picked up eight to 10 combat boxes of B-17s over Kassel, and escorted them to the enemy coast. Rendezvousing over Fiessen at 1108 hours, the 364th (fighter) Group escorted 10 to 12 stragglers to the English coast uneventfully. The 356th (fighter) Group escorted without incident from 1103 hours to 1235 hours at mid-channel. Fighter escort for this Division was considered excellent."

Flak was in various stages of intensity and was fired at us in many areas along the routes flown by our heavy bombers on this date. An 8th Air Force summary report of flak information obtained during the debriefing of flight crews is as follows: "Intense to moderate and fairly accurate at Kassel/Waldau; intense and accurate at Kassel/Bettenhausen; meager and inaccurate in the Dummer Lake area and at Ostend; meager, inaccurate tracking fire was reported at Werl, Lorbecke, Lippstadt, Le Culot, Meppel, Charleroi, Liege, Brussels, Bruges, Ostend, Hamm, Ghent and Hesepe; meager and inaccurate at Ijmuiden, Lille and Douai; meager and accurate from Bielefeld; moderate and inaccurate from Gutersholm, Hamm and Dunkirk; moderate, accurate fire from Charleroi, Paderborn and Coblenz."

The following information was also reported during the debriefing of crews that flew on the day's operation: "Barrage balloons were observed as follows: 10 to 15 balloons at Cologne, 30 to 50 balloons south of Minden, several balloons at Meppel, Ijmuiden, Amsterdam and Harlem, 30 plus at Coblenz, 12 to 15 at Osnabruck, 25 at Bad Oeynhausen, 13 at 5103N-0738E, 20 at Neuwiede, 20 just north of Vogelsand, and others at Hanover, Detwold, Lemgo, Brussels and Ludensherd."

The summary information continued: "Smoke screens were reported at Bonn, Kassel, Wiesbaden, Bielefeld, Osnabruck, Liege, Cologne, Waldeck, Munster, Hamm, Essen, Gunne, Wallstein, Eschede, Furstenan, Bramsche, at 5136N-0855E (airfield and dam), 5125N-0805E (dam or bridge), and at 5035N-0715E (bridge). Numerous freight trains were sighted at Namur. A large number of barges were seen in the Main River about 20 miles north of Frankfurt. Numerous freight trains were seen at Oeynhausen. Near Ostend, Belgium, large numbers of motorized artillery guns, tanks and vehicles were observed on the sand. Attempts had been made to camouflage them."

Screwball Express was not damaged on this mission, even though the 165 flak guns at our target fired hundreds of antiaircraft shells at our formation. All planes in our two Groups returned safely. Records indicate no injuries were incurred by any of the crew members from our base.

The Stars and Stripes reported between 750 and 1,000 bombers took part in the day's operation, escorted all the way by an equally large number of P-38s, P-47s and P-51s. The publication stated, "The Forts and Libs made round trips of 350 to 550 miles to strike their targets – fighter aircraft factories in the vicinity of Kassel, airdromes at Eschwege, Paderborn, Gutersloh, Lippstadt and Werl, all in the vicinity of Hamm and Kassel. Hangars and barracks were covered with bomb strikes, photos showed. Targets attacked at Eschwege, Paderborn, Gutersloh, Lippstadt and Werl were fighter fields used as parking places for new planes ready for combat."

After a very full day of successful attacks against the German aircraft industry, it was frustrating to read the following summary of observations made by returning crewmen during the debriefing sessions: "The following observations were made of airdromes: several large aircraft, larger than the B-17, and about 30 single engine enemy aircraft were seen at Gottingen airdrome … 20 aircraft on an airdrome at 5215N-0837E ... 10 aircraft on an airfield at Chievres ... many aircraft on an airfield at Ghent ... 50 seaplanes on the Zuider Zee ... 5 aircraft on an airfield at Vogelsand ... 5 single engine and 25 twin engine aircraft on an airfield at Quackenbruck … 2 single engine enemy aircraft on an airfield at Valenciennes. In addition, a camouflaged airdrome, with factory buildings and much activity, was observed at 5038N-0717E; a new air strip apparently under construction at 5212N-0615E; a new airfield under construction at about 5248N-0617E; and an uncharted airfield, where runways seemed to disappear underground, at about 5055N-0325E."

The Germans were very determined to construct and rebuild airfields and aircraft factories almost immediately after bombardment by the 8th Air Force and RAF. Allied visions of immobilizing the Luftwaffe and its facilities were clouded by reports like those in the preceding paragraph. On a brighter side, we had completed nine or our missions. Only 16 more to go.

After dinner some of us drifted from the mess hall to the bar. After 1700 or 1800 hours it was customary for one of three light bulbs above the bar to be turned on. The amber colored light bulb meant "Drink and be merry, but be cautious about it." The green bulb indicated the base was "stood down," meaning no mission was planned for the next day, and the bar would be open as long as it had a customer. The red light meant a mission was tentatively scheduled and the bar would be closed at 2000 hours (approximately). It was good planning that closed the bar early on nights preceding a mission. Since we didn't know which crews would be flying on any particular mission, some of the guys felt the early closing rule was unfair to those who would not fly in combat the next day.

The light was red!

Mission to Sottevast

The excitement of the previous day's mission to Kassel, coupled with advance knowledge of the strong probability of another mission today, caused me to have a night filled with restless sleep. I awakened about 0545 and walked outside of our barracks. The early morning chill took most of the enjoyment out of the cigarette I had lit. I amused myself by blowing big puffs of smoke into the fog, as if to thicken it still more. In spite of the darkness, it was easy to predict that Thursday, April 20, 1944, was going to be another very cloudy day in England. A loon on a nearby pond, probably the pond on Mr. Bigram's farm, was making its familiar early morning call. Everything else was very quiet.

The tranquillity of the moment was interrupted by the roar of a jeep's motor. Its blackout headlights barely penetrated the darkness in front of it, and it came to an abrupt stop only four or five feet from where I was standing. "Is this your barracks?" asked the driver. "Yup," I replied, hoping to make him feel lucky he had not run over me. "All crews in this barracks are flyin' today," he said, and then added, "Save me some time, wake 'em up. Briefing's at 0700." The jeep's engine backfired as it sped toward the next barracks.

The loud "bang" took care of my wake-up job. Regardless, I stuck my head inside the door of our hut and yelled, "Everybody – briefing – 0700."

Scrambled eggs again, real ones, with lean bacon. Combat flying had its perks, and a breakfast made from real eggs was one of them. Powdered eggs did not taste good. They didn't look good, either. The bulky, pale green mass was anything but appetizing in its appearance.

At the briefing we learned Adolph Hitler's Atlantic Wall was going to receive the heaviest pounding of the air war to date. U.S. and Allied bombers and fighters were going to cross the Channel in an afternoon blitz of unprecedented strength. The majority of the day's targets were located along the coast of France and a little inland, between the area around Pas de Calais and the Cherbourg Peninsula. Approximately 750 bombers were involved, escorted by about 700 fighters. Hundreds of other fighter planes were going to attack the Luftwaffe throughout France. It was the first time since January 21 that a major force had targets in the Pas de Calais and adjacent areas. Undoubtedly, the overall operation was a build-up of the air war's prelude to the Allied Invasion. It seemed appropriate that this attack should happen today, on Adolph Hitler's 55th birthday.

The 379th Bomb Group provided a total of 42 Flying Fortresses for the day's mission. Twelve aircraft were in the Lead Group and 12 in the Low Group of the 41st Combat Wing "A." Screwball Express was assigned a position in the Low Squadron of that Wing's Lead Group. Our target was a fly-bomb site at Sottevast, near Valognes, France, on the northern side of the Cherbourg Peninsula. Our target was classified as a key invasion concentration site. Its location was almost due south across the English Channel from Southampton and Portsmouth, England. The 379th also furnished 12 aircraft for the Lead Group of the 41st Combat Wing "C", and six planes in the Low Squadron of the Low Group of that Wing. The "C" Wing was assigned to attack a fly-bomb site at Mesnil au Val.

The truck transporting our crew to the hardstand where Screwball Express was waiting managed to push its way through the fog. When we arrived at our plane, the ordnance crew had just finished hanging three 1,000-pound demolition bombs on each side of the bomb bay's catwalk. I watched as they proceeded to hang another 1,000-pound bomb under each of the wings. "Eight thousand pounds of TNT," I said quietly. "No, sir," said one of the ordnance men, "that's RDX," and proclaimed RDX was "… about 40% more powerful than TNT."

The time was almost 0900 hours, but the fog was still very thick. Our takeoff was scheduled for 1100 hours, so the drums of oil along the runway were not yet burning. "The fog will be almost completely gone by takeoff time," the weather officer predicted at the briefing. He continued with, "You will have a ceiling of about 400 feet, and will then have to climb through 6,000 feet of clouds." Cloud cover over our section of England was mostly 10/10, really solid. He also predicted the cloud cover at our target would be only 2/10 coverage at our scheduled bombing time. "Gosh, only 2/10 cloud cover. Cherbourg Peninsula is having a sunny day," we joked. At 1100 hours the weather still had us socked in, and at noontime it was still 10/10 in our area. I think I remember coffee and doughnuts being brought from the mess hall to the flight crews assigned to this mission. Finally, at approximately 1330 hours, the oil drums along the runway

Author standing next to 1,000 lb. bomb under left wing of Screwball Express. (Photo by 379th BG Photo. Sec., April 20, 1944)

were set afire. The flare gun signalling clearance for takeoff was not fired by the control tower until 1500 hours. Screwball Express was airborne twenty minutes later.

The Group's takeoff was finally accomplished, but 400 feet into the air we lost visual contact with the rest of the world. Singing the 23rd Psalm was comforting in a solid bank of clouds, or in a barrage of flak or while being shot at by enemy planes. At 6,000 feet we were still in the clouds, so our Group leader notified other planes in our Wing that assembly altitude would be 2,000 feet higher than initially planned. At 8,000 feet we broke into a clear sky. The assembly of our Group became normal, but we were more than four hours late in our departure from Kimbolton. It was unknown to us at the time that aircraft #42-38185 in the 41st "C" Wing's Lead Group aborted the mission because of engine trouble. It was also not immediately apparent, but our High and Low Groups were too far behind us to expedite suitable assembly of our Wing's formation.

Winds at our altitude were stronger than predicted. This caused us to be ahead of our new schedule for the entire route. Although our Group was in continuous radio contact with the High and Low Groups of our Wing, we did not make visual contact with them until we reached Splasher #13. Our Lead Group made a 360 degree turn, hoping those Groups would catch up with us. The High Group was in proper Wing position when we approached Portland Bill. Our Lead Group crossed Portland Bill four minutes early, so we throttled back to allow the Low Group to also get into attack position.

The strong wind at our altitude of 20,000 feet carried us close to one of the Guernsey Islands, so our Group turned northward to avoid flying over it. We skirted the island and proceeded to set course for the Initial Point of our bomb run, from which a heading of 65 degrees took us toward the target. During our attempt to avoid the island the Low Group became separated from the Wing. The High Group turned short at the IP and flew directly at the target. The bombardier of our Lead Group was unable to set a sufficient drift angle into the bombsight because of the high wind, and as a result could not properly synchronize the crosshairs on the target. Things were in chaos.

We turned out over the water and set up for another bomb run from the same IP. Wind information in the bombsight was corrected. Weather was clear and visibility was unlimited. Sighting the railroad running south from Cherbourg was helpful to us in pinpointing the target. The wooded area leading to the fly-bomb site was easily seen. The lead bombardier was able to synchronize perfectly on the fly-bomb site and our Group's bombs dropped directly onto the target. We were not able to see the results of our High Group's earlier release, we couldn't find our Low Group, and our Lead Group headed back to England alone.

Antiaircraft fire on the bomb run was intense and very accurate. Screwball Express received five flak holes in the right wing – a large hole and four small ones. Another hole was in the left side of the nose section, only inches behind Bob Keller's position. A piece of flak, evidently about the size of a baseball, glanced off the right side of the chin turret, leaving a dent about two inches deep and nearly four inches across. Almost half of the right elevator of one of the planes in our Lead Group was shot off by flak, and two of the planes returned with feathered props. Feathering a prop, or turning the blades edge-first into the plane's flight path, helped prevent additional damage to an already troubled engine. In this position, however, the engine was not functional. Eleven of the 12 planes in our Lead Group sustained flak damage on this mission. We were told there were only ten flak guns at our target, but it seemed like a hundred. We were lucky we were not attacked by enemy planes, because we had no fighter escort on the entire mission. Our delayed takeoff, our changing of altitude, the stronger-than-expected winds and our second run at the target had undoubtedly contributed to our fighter support's inability to find us. No wonder!

The weather was much different from what we were told at the briefing. Cloud cover over Kimbolton was 8,000 feet, not 6,000 feet. Over the target it was CAVU (ceiling and visibility unlimited), not 2/10. Wind velocity was much stronger than we had been briefed by the weather officer and wind direction at the target was off by 125 degrees. We complained about this during debriefing, even though we knew some of the problems were results of our delayed takeoff. The intelligence officer promised he would ask the chaplain to consider our complaint.

All of the 379th's planes returned to the Kimbolton base. One member of another crew from our field was wounded by flak over the target. Flying time for our mission was 4:30 hours and tied with our mission to Wizernes (Mission No. 2) for the shortest amount of flying time. It was exciting to realize we had completed 40% of our missions. Ten down, and only 15 more to fly.

That evening at the mess hall we visited with some of the

crew members in the Low Group that was unable to keep up during our attempt to skirt one of the Guernsey Islands. When the High Group turned short at the IP, the Low Group did likewise. It followed the High Group's attack on the target and bombed from 18,000 feet. Some of the crewmen in the Low Group thought their bombs hit slightly to the right of the target. Reconnaissance photos later proved part of the Low Group's bomb pattern was centered on the target.

The Stars and Stripes' account of the day's operation stated, "The attack was another tactical switch of the sort which has stretched German air defenses through the winter. It followed two days in a row of solid heavy-bomber blows at targets within the Reich itself, which presumably would have drawn Luftwaffe defenses closer to Germany. There was no announcement last evening of specific targets in the day's attacks, but it was obvious that the planned, relentless breaching by air bombardment of the enemy's Atlantic Wall defenses was being stepped up to pre-invasion intensity."

"In Washington, Secretary of War Henry L. Stimson added yet another estimate of damage done to the German aircraft industry by the Eighth and 15th Air Force attacks (during the past several days). After announcing that our aerial invasion of Europe is continuing and is increasing in pressure and enemy resistance on the whole decreasing, Stimson declared that the Nazi's fighter plane production had been cut 20 percent since January."

Perhaps this partly explained why we had encountered so little fighter opposition thus far. Whatever the reason for this, we certainly did not object. However, why had we not seen or been attacked by huge numbers of the planes existing and still being produced? There were thousands of Luftwaffe planes and pilots. Where were they, and why weren't they more aggressive, or more defensive, instead of so absent?

In reality, the Luftwaffe's leadership was in the middle of a serious dilemma. If the Germans dispatched their available fighters to attack Allied bomber formations, fighter planes of the 8th and 9th Air Forces and gunners on the bombers would practically annihilate the German fighter force. Conversely, if the Luftwaffe was not sent up in large numbers, the Allied bombers could attack any target at will. Additionally, this approach to solving its quandary would exhaust Germany's ability to produce fighter aircraft. They would only be capable of sending their fighters after our bombers periodically, and probably only when our escorting fighters were not in the proximity of our bombers. Evidently, the Luftwaffe could not, or chose not to, adequately defend its major industrial plants. Germany was on the road to inevitable and complete destruction.

However, the war was not yet over. The 8th Air Force, and all of the land, air and sea forces of the Allies, had a lot to do before the war would end. Somehow I knew – all of us knew – one of these days we were going to see huge numbers of enemy fighters in the air. It was a sure bet they would eventually come up after us.

Weather over the continent on April 21, 1944, was again cloudy and wet. Weather around Kimbolton was fairly good, however, our crew was "stood down" from combat today. The average crew at our base theoretically was to fly three of every four missions. We had flown ten of our Group's last 12 missions, missing out on only the April 9

Marienburg raid and the April 13 attack on Schweinfurt. About 1030 hours Screwball Express and our crew were assigned to fly a three hour training mission. When we returned to base, some of us went over to headquarters where we learned the 379th Group had earlier dispatched some planes on a mission to Merseburg, Germany. By the time the planes assembled over our airfield they were recalled because of weather conditions in the target area. They had already returned, and the entire base showed no signs of the earlier hectic rush in preparation for a combat mission. If we hadn't known otherwise, it would have been difficult to believe a war was going on.

While walking back to our barracks I decided to visit the PX and purchase some toothpaste. Unfortunately, but not surprisingly, the PX was out of stock. I continued my leisurely stroll and began thinking about the bottle of peroxide I purchased in London. That stuff certainly wasn't graying my temples. Maybe it would work as a substitute for toothpaste.

Mission to Bonn

On Saturday, April 22, 1944, the 8th Air Force dispatched a strike force of 526 B-17s and 277 B-24s to attack the Hamm marshalling yards. The bomber force was escorted by 13 fighter groups, 12 from the 8th Air Force and one from the 9th. The marshalling yards at Hamm was the largest in Germany. Hamm is located 40 miles east of Essen, and is the point where several railways from Germany converge before radiating to Holland, Belgium and France.

The 1st Bomb Division was assigned the Hamm marshalling yards as its primary target, a secondary target at Bonn, and the city of Hamm as a target of opportunity. The 2nd Division was assigned the Hamm marshalling yards, a secondary target of Coblenz and targets of opportunity in Germany. The 3rd Division's targets were the marshalling yards at Hamm and targets of opportunity in Germany. Target assignments left little doubt about the intention of the 311th Operation Order of the 8th Air Force.

It was very unusual for us to have a briefing after the lunch hour. On most of our missions we had either returned or were well on our way home by this time of day. If everything went as scheduled, we would be lucky to be back before dark.

When the white sheet was pulled back during briefing, Colonel Preston said, "Gentlemen, your target for today, the 379th's 100th combat mission, is the marshalling yards at Hamm." He continued, "There's going to be a big party tonight in celebration of our 100th combat mission." Everyone cheered. The Colonel continued, "Those of you who make it back are invited to be present." Not many of the crew members found any humor in those words. Then the Colonel smiled, and the room's atmosphere lightened a little. It was one of the few times I saw him smile. It was the only time he invited me to a party, and I was honored. Someone reminded us of the importance of flying a tight formation, particularly in the target area. There would be "about 800 bombers heading for their targets from various directions and at different altitudes, so things could get a little confusing."

The 379th furnished 24 aircraft for the Lead Group of the

41st Combat Wing "A" and 20 for the Low Group. Screwball Express received assignment to fly in the Lead Squadron of the Low Group. Our bomb load consisted of 12-500 pound general purpose demolition bombs. It was an unusually clear day, and one had to do a lot of searching to find enough clouds to cause any optimism for not flying the mission. Our takeoff song was definitely an all weather song – it sounded the same in good weather as it did in bad.

This was the latest takeoff our crew would experience on a combat mission – 1545 hours. We departed from above our airfield at 1712 hours at an assembly altitude of 12,000 feet. Visibility over England was absolutely unlimited. The sky was actually blue.

We crossed the coast of Belgium at 1835 hours and at 22,000 feet. The skies over Germany were also clear of clouds. Our flight plan took us a few miles west of Munster. The Lead Group's IP was reached at 1905 hours. Only limited enemy aircraft opposition was encountered by planes of the 8th Air Force, and most of it was in the target area. Flak was generally moderate to intense and accurate over Hamm.

From our altitude of 21,000 feet we could easily see railroad cars of various sizes on the many tracks running through the yards. The attack actually began at 1849 hours from 18,500 feet. Early in the attack two Wings ahead of ours started large fires among the rolling stock and adjacent buildings. The two choke points of the marshalling yards, the rail lines running through the yards in all directions and the sorting sidings received severe damage. The Lead Group of our Wing bombed at 1911 hours from 22,000 feet. Thousands of bombs exploded on the primary target and made subsequent damage appraisal very difficult. Our Lead Group's bombs fell directly into the target area. A large locomotive and a wagon repair shop received numerous direct hits. The large engine works of the Vereinigte Stahlwerke was also well covered with bomb strikes. One of the major buildings of this plant was burning fiercely.

Ours was the next Group to make a bomb run, but what we were witnessing made it appear unnecessary for our Low Group to bomb at Hamm. Our momentary indecision was quickly resolved when the Lead plane of our Low Group radioed the formation that its bomb racks would not function properly. Consequently, the Low Group did not bomb the marshalling yards at Hamm. This presented no problem because there was very little additional damage our Group could do to the marshalling yards. It was already a total mess. Our "observation ride" over the marshalling yards provided our crew a first row seat at the total destruction of the Hamm marshalling yards. It was a fantastic thing to watch.

Situations like this made good reason for having secondary targets. We turned away from Hamm and headed south-southwest for Bonn, about 65 miles away. After our Group completed a well-executed turn, we looked back toward Hamm. A Group of 15 B-17s dropped its bombs at 1917 hours into the heavily built-up area of the city east of the marshalling yards. This area had also been damaged by the three waves of bombers that attacked the primary target. Severe damage resulted in adjacent industrial and residential areas and numerous fires were started. The bombing at Hamm was accurately described as "excellent."

I glanced down at my escape kit to make certain it was still in the knee pocket of my flight suit. It contained a lot of items that would come in handy if I had to bail out over enemy occupied territory – several maps, sulfa drugs, concentrated food (candy), chewing gum, foreign currency, a pencil, compass and a knife. I prayed I would never have to use an escape kit.

Perhaps I would never have the occasion to use one. Perhaps Screwball Express would get hit by a direct burst of antiaircraft fire and explode, allowing no chance for any of us to bail out. Maybe an enemy plane's machine guns would find our gas tanks and blow us out of the sky. Aerial combat conditions made crew members face death in a variety of forms. We were confronted by thousands of shrapnel fragments, projectiles fired by cannons and guns, and the ever-present possibility of fire, or oxygen starvation, or a fall from five miles in the air. We had no aerial fox holes, no hedge rows. There was no place for us to run and no place for us to hide. We were consequently forever thankful for the food we ate, the bunks in which we slept, and the roof over our heads. Essentially, we were in the unique situation of being under combat conditions only when we were flying over the enemy's territory. On other occasions, we were almost at peace.

We reached the Bonn area, and flak began to reach up at us when we arrived over the famous Ruhr Valley. It was fired at us in moderate quantity, but was somewhat inaccurate. The large, black puffs from its bursts filled the sky off to our right and a little behind our formation. The bomb racks in our Group's lead plane had been rechecked and were ready to operate electrically. We were still at our assigned bombing altitude of 21,000 feet. Our formation turned onto a magnetic heading of 122 degrees when it reached the IP. The aiming point of our Lead plane was the docks and harbor area along the Rhine river at the city of Bonn.

After a very good visual bomb run, we dropped our bombs at 1933 hours. I leaned over the bombsight, into the

A German Rentenmark and a French 100 Cent Francs Note. Escape kits carried by crew members contained small food rations, maps, foreign money, compass, etc. in event of being shot down in enemy territory.

Plexiglas nose, and watched for about 35 seconds while our bombs fell toward the aiming point. The Lead aircraft's bombs fell across the harbor area and onto the docks. Bombs from Screwball Express and several other B-17s scored hits on three large ships and seven or eight small ones anchored nearby. A concentration of our Group's bombs fell on the west side of the river across from Konigswinter, south of Bonn, and large fires were started in a sparsely built-up area. Although bombs from our Low Group's Lead plane and from several other Fortresses in our Group hit the target, bombing results went into the record book as "fair to good." I have no love for all not being fair in war.

We turned out of the target area, headed west to the Belgium border and flew abreast of Brussels. The enemy coast was crossed at Ostend at 2050 hours while at 20,000 feet. Twenty-eight minutes later we crossed the English coast at 6,000 feet. Our Group continued on our heading to a point south of Ipswich, then to within a few miles south of Cambridge and finally to Kimbolton.

Our Group encountered no serious flak and did not see any enemy fighters during the entire mission. Four of the 24 planes in our Lead Group were spares. Two of the planes returned early as planned. Aircraft number 42-3524 returned undispatched and aircraft number 42-38161 bombed the primary target with the 305th Bomb Group from Chelveston. Propaganda leaflets were not dropped by our either of our two Groups today - the 379th was temporarily out of supply.

All of the 379th's planes made it back safely. Flying time on our 11th combat mission was seven and one-half hours. Fortresses and Liberators were flying over the coast of England twenty minutes after blackout time – the latest hour at which they had returned from a combat mission. The Stars and Stripes headlined the late arrival hour in the following day's newspaper.

We went to debriefing where information collectively unfolded from the crews after they left their planes and the Red Cross hospitality van. Flak was generally moderate and fairly accurate at Hamm; moderate and inaccurate at Bonn, Alkmar and Dulman; meager to moderate and inaccurate at Coblenz, Ijmuiden, Egmond and Ostend. Intense and accurate automatic weapons fire was encountered at the Belgian coast and at Dortmund on the way out. Flak elsewhere along the routes and over other targets was generally moderate and inaccurate. Five of our Fortresses received minor damage today from flak.

Barrage balloons were seen at ten locations en route. Smoke screens were observed over the entire Ruhr Valley and at 11 cities in other areas.

These additional observations were reported: eight white aircraft, believed to be dummies, on an airfield just north of Charleroi; antiaircraft boats off the Belgian coast south-southwest of Ostend; two dammed canals in the vicinity of Bruges, Belgium, causing flooding five miles inland; flooded coastal area near Ostend and Dunkirk; numerous mounds, believed to be anti-invasion defenses, immediately east of the Zuider Zee; a large, suspected ammunition dump of about 100 buildings ten miles south-southwest of Ghent, Belgium. Death is never pleasant to think about, or talk about. Hearing of the following incident sent a very deep chill down our spines later that night.

An unexpected aerial encounter developed when approximately 20 enemy fighter planes attacked all except two

The lead group of our wing bombed at 1911 hours from 22,000 feet. This picture was taken by camera in bomb bay of B-17 in lead group and shows damage to both choke points of Hamm's marshalling yards. (Photo from 379th BG Photo Sec., April 22, 1944)

of the B-24 Groups as they crossed the enemy coast on their way home. Beginning at the French coast, the bandits made attacks on the B-24's singly and in elements of three. When the attacks were believed to have stopped, the U.S. fighter escort left the 2nd Division's B-24s at mid-channel. The bombers crossed the English coast at 2135 hours at Orford Ness. It was dusk. Unnoticed, a group of enemy JU-88s and Me 410s followed the Liberators inland. Surprise attacks occurred over five of the 2nd Division's bases in the Norwich area northeast of London. Most of the attacks took place while the B-24's were in their landing pattern. As a result of this action, at least ten of the B-24s were shot down or crash landed. The daring of the Luftwaffe pilots gave them an opportunity similar to shooting fish in a barrel. Records indicate all of the enemy planes escaped to the continent.

Other Luftwaffe attacks during the day's operation were less dramatic, but just as deadly. A Group of B-24s was attacked by 50 to 60 Me-109s and FW-190s in an area east of Cologne. The enemy fighters blanketed the bomber formation with timed 20 mm shells. Similar attacks were made south of Hamm by 30 to 50 Me-109s with faked scoops and painted to look like our P-51s. These enemy aircraft simulated escort tactics. On at least two occasions they passed up the leading bombing formations, attacking trailing formations from head on. They then repeated the procedure against following Groups.

A Group of B-17s from the 3rd Division was attacked frontally by about 20 single engine enemy planes between the IP and the primary target at Hamm. A Group that bombed Soest was aggressively attacked by approximately 25 single engine enemy aircraft immediately after the bombing run. This Group was again attacked by six to eight single engine planes just north of Coblenz.

The 8th Air Force lost 15 heavy bombers during the entire operation. Eight of these were B-17s and 7 were B-24s. The 8th had 13 Wings in the air, nine of which lost one or more planes. Eighth Air Force records indicate the ten B-24s shot down over their home bases are not included in these numbers. One hundred twenty-six B-17s and 110 B-24s received light battle damage. Forty-two other bombers had major damage. Five of our escorting fighter planes were lost to enemy action, and the bomber escorts claimed 12 enemy planes in the air. Eight other U.S. fighters were lost, six of them from the 9th Air Force and two from the 8th, in fighter sweeps and strafing attacks. The total number of enemy aircraft claimed by our fighter planes for the day was 40.

Personnel casualties of the 8th Air Force during this mission included 34 crew members killed, 45 wounded and 159 missing. Such was the day's human sacrifice for putting 638 bombers over their primary targets, and another 141 bombers over various targets of opportunity. Bomb tonnage dropped today by the 8th Air Force totaled 1,518 tons of general purpose bombs and 455 tons of incendiaries.

The party celebrating the 100th combat mission got started twice. The first time was at about 2130 hours, by some of the ground personnel and crews that did not fly on the mission. The second time was at about 2300 hours, by flight crews and headquarters staff as they finished debriefing and dinner. None of the three lights behind the bar were turned on. Music was provided by the Toggleers. It was good and loud, so good you liked it, and so loud you couldn't hear what anyone was saying. Customers at the bar made a line about twenty feet wide and two or three persons thick.

As proud as I was about the 379th's 100th combat mission, I was even more proud our crew had finished 11 missions. It was comforting, in a strange sort of way, that we only had 14 combat missions left. I was tired. It felt good to crawl into the sack.

The entire 379th base was "stood down" from combat on Sunday, April 23. The local weather didn't look too bad, but thick clouds over the continent made combat flying impractical. At Kimbolton there was a man-made fogginess hanging over all of the fellows who had outmaneuvered themselves during last night's party. What a staggering experience it was for them!

Screwball Express and some of our crew made a three hour and ten minute training flight about midday.

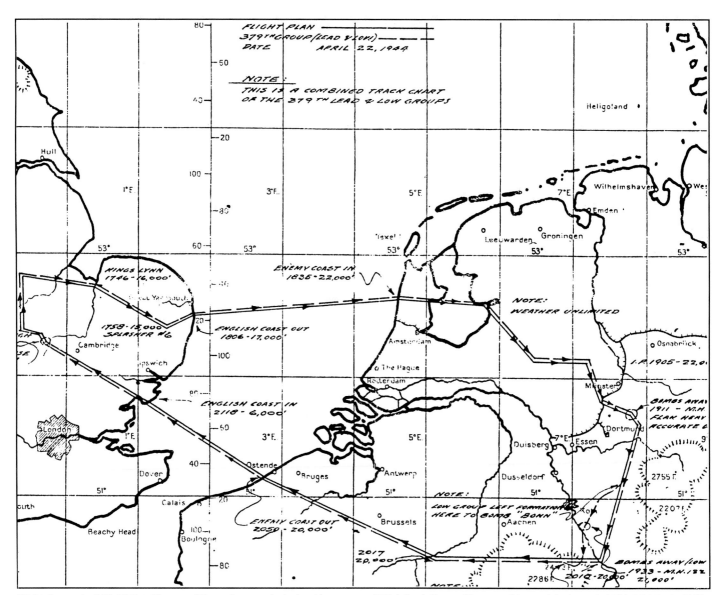

Flight plan on April 22, 1944, to Hamm and Bonn, Germany, by lead and low groups of 379th Bomb Group. (Photostated from original copy in 379th BG Mission Folder at National Archives Military Records Facility.)

Mission to Landsberg

The early morning hours of Monday, April 24, 1944, were filled with excitement on both sides of the English Channel.

At 0100 hours an alert was sounded at Munich, Germany, and the city's residents were ordered into air raid shelters. "Achtung" warnings by selected German-controlled radio stations reported RAF bombers were over Munich. Other German radio stations stopped broadcasting. Frankfurt was also under a night attack. At 0135 the Munich radio announced, "Numerous enemy planes are now over our city area." At 0200 came the news. "Luftwaffe fighters are attacking the raiders over our city." The RAF continued its blanket bombing technique of Munich for more than an hour.

At 0430 hours 42 flight crews of the 379th Bomb Group were awakened for 0530 briefing. Copies of a London newspaper at the mess hall were being scrutinized by everyone. A front page article, under the bold headline "2,000 U.S. Planes Smash Hamm," contained two paragraphs that stood out from the mass of printed praise about the previous day's bombing. Those two paragraphs read as follows, and caused much excitement:

"Meanwhile, a pro-Allied army of millions of saboteurs and guerillas awaits the "attack" signal to hurl itself against the Nazis from the Arctic to the Mediterranean. Slave-workers are secretly striking at Germany's war industries inside the Reich itself; and in the Nazi-held lands the undercover Partisans are telling the peasants and small farmers how to act when the invasion zero hour arrives."

"The Germans are steeling their people against a Channel invasion before May 1. The tides are right this week, the Nazis say, and they gloomily predict "the hardest and bloodiest battles in history.""

I tried to reason things out. If the invasion really was scheduled for "before May 1," perhaps today was the day. On second thought, our briefing is not until 0530, and we won't be in the air until around 0900. I decided it wasn't going to happen today.

By 0530 we had been in our seats in the briefing room for at least 15 minutes. The familiar sheet-covered map was at the front of the room and the yarn pulley was near the top left side. Air in the room was thick with smoke that stirred with the wind that came through the door when crewmen came into the building. Finally, we got the word. We were going to attack an aircraft factory at an airfield just outside of Landsberg, Germany. Landsberg is about 30 miles almost due west of Munich. Flight crews of approximately 1,000 Fortresses and Liberators on U.S. bases throughout southeastern England were making preparations for their part in attacks at targets in Germany and the occupied countries. The areas around Munich and Friedrichshafen were going to receive a lot of attention from the 8th Air Force today.

The mission to the Munich area, deep in southeastern Germany, was not a "milk run." The city and its surrounding area were heavily protected by antiaircraft guns. It was difficult to count the number of Luftwaffe airfields within striking distance of our routes in and out of the area. The RAF's early morning pounding of Munich had undoubtedly put the Luftwaffe and the gun crews on those German flak towers in a lousy mood.

The 379th Bomb Group furnished 42 Fortresses for the mission to Landsberg. Twenty-two of these aircraft were dispatched as the Lead Group of the 41st Combat Wing "A", and that Wing led the 1st Bombardment Division. Four planes in the Lead Group were spares, and three of them returned early by plan. Aircraft number 42-97229 returned early not dispatched. The other 20 planes flew as the Low Group in the same Wing.

On this date we were privileged to have Brigadier General Robert F. Travis, Commanding General of the 41st Combat Wing, fly as pilot in the Lead plane of our Lead Group. Screwball Express flew Lead position in the High Squadron of the Lead Group. Our crew was very proud of this honor, however, eight of us candidly admitted the real reason for this assignment was the superb manner in which Howard and Jim piloted Screwball Express. They were tops in flying tight formation – a basic necessity for precision bombing at high altitude. Bob was an excellent navigator, and I considered myself a very good bombardier, but accolades for our crew's assignment to a lead position belonged to our two pilots. Our egos were humbled a little when we later discovered that, in addition to leading, flying Squadron Lead also involved a lot of following.

Flying in the Lead aircraft of a Squadron was similar to the game of Follow the Leader. The Number One Leader of a bombing formation was in the Group's Lead aircraft, the B-17 at the leading edge of the Lead Squadron. When that B-17 climbed for altitude, you led your Squadron at the same angle and speed of ascent. When it turned left or right, you and your Squadron followed along. It was the "guidepost" for the speed, direction and altitude of every Fortress in the entire formation. When bombs dropped from that plane, bombs dropped from your Fortress and from the Fortresses you were leading – not before, not after, but exactly at the same moment. The Squadron Leaders followed the Group Leader, and planes in each Squadron followed their Squadron Leader. It was this type of copycat, procedural precision that held the Group in close formation and kept its bombs in a tight and destructive pattern.

Our takeoff was at 0850. General Travis has never known that I personally arranged for the 23rd Psalm to be up there with him and the rest of us that day.

Weather over England was overcast and presented some difficulty in forming the various Combat Wings. Assembly was at 4,000 feet over Molesworth at 0956. By 1010 we were at 6,000 feet and headed south on a course that took us a few miles southwest of London. This was our fifth mission on which our flight path out of England took us within a few miles of the western edge of its capital city. After turning to the southeast, we crossed over Splasher #9 at 13,500 feet. Our Wing formation left England at 1100 hours, flying at 16,000 feet over Beachy Head. Ten minutes later we crossed the enemy coast near Dieppe, France, at 17,000 feet.

The famous "Abbeville Kids" of the German Luftwaffe were based only 30 miles left of our route in. The Luftwaffe, under command of Reichsmarshall Hermann Goering, was that branch of the German armed forces known as The Nazi Service, because of the high number of party members who belonged to it. The Abbeville Kids were very skilled German pilots who had destroyed large numbers of Allied planes. Their dreaded Me-109s were easily recognized because their engine cowlings were painted bright yellow. They were referred to as "Goering's Yellow Noses."

Weather became favorable to us. At noontime we were

northwest of Paris, flying at 20,000 feet. At 1245 hours, about 25 miles west of Freiburg at the western foot of the Black Forest on the French-German border, our formation headed eastward for 17 minutes. We flew north of Augsburg, Germany, at 1312 hours and turned to our right at 1325 hours, 1330 hours and again at 1336 hours. This made it appear we were circling Munich on its northern, northeastern, eastern and southeastern outskirts. Our intention was to confuse the Germans into believing we were going to bomb the city of Munich, and evidently that is what they assumed would happen. Flak began to explode in large numbers above the city. In only a few minutes the hundreds of black bursts joined together and formed a huge, deadly cloud. The shrapnel from those bursts looked thick enough to stand on.

Our IP was south of Munich and was reached at 1345 hours. The antiaircraft guns were busy protecting Munich. They let us slip past the city's southwestern outskirts on our bomb run to the airfield at Landsberg. Conditions for bombing were perfect. For the moment, there were no enemy fighters or flak to distract us from our objective. The lead bombardiers of our Lead and Low Groups were able to clearly see the target from several miles away. Our magnetic heading was 304 degrees when Screwball Express dropped its 10-500 pound demolition bombs at 1406 hours from 20,000 feet. Temperature outside Screwball Express was -28 degrees, next to the coldest condition in which our crew would ever attack a target.

Bombs of the Lead Group fell directly on three hangars at the western end of the main line of buildings. Several other buildings were destroyed, as well as many of the 20 aircraft parked in the vicinity of the hangars. The runway received eight direct hits and the tarmacs and taxi strips were damaged severely. Twenty-three twin engine aircraft, believed to be Me-210s or Me-110s, were parked in dispersed positions to the west of the airfield. Twenty-four aircraft of the same type were parked along the southern and eastern perimeter. This accounts for 67 aircraft on or adjacent to the airfield at the time of this attack. The bomb pattern of our Lead Group was approximately 2,000 feet long and 2,200 feet wide. The center of this pattern was only 300 feet short of the MPI, and covered it very effectively.

Our fighter escort was very good during most of the mission, but very thin in the target area. Halfway through its bomb run the Low Group received interference from 50 or more Me-109s and FW-190s. A few Me-110s were also involved. The bandits made several attacks on the Low Group; however, its planes held near-perfect formation and achieved a bomb pattern 1,600 feet long and only 1,300 feet wide. The bomb pattern's center was only 200 feet short of the briefed MPI and covered it totally. Numerous small buildings were hit and other buildings received damage from near misses. The large hangar and some buildings on the east received several hits, as did the railway sidings. The barracks area, store and workshops at the north and west of the hangar line were not damaged.

It was obvious this airfield had been bombed previously. Runway markings indicated that damage by earlier bomb blasts had put the airfield out of commission, but recent repairs returned it to service. Gunners in the Low Group claimed seven enemy fighter planes shot down, and three probables. Crew members of the 379th later reported six or seven B-17s from other Groups were shot down by enemy fighters in the target area. Only three parachutes were seen coming out of those bombers.

The 38 Fortresses in our two Groups dropped 375 500-pound demolition bombs on the target - almost 94 tons of explosives. Major General James H. Doolittle, 8th Air Force Commander at the time, commended the 379th Bomb Group for this attack when he said, "You penetrated unusually severe resistance – and bombed with excellent results."

Considering the tremendous amount of bombing the 8th Air Force and the RAF had inflicted upon Germany's aircraft industry, one particular statistical fact was difficult to understand. Germany's monthly aircraft production rose from 854 in 1940 to 3,300 in 1944. How could it be claimed that Germany's war-making ability was damaged by Allied bombing? The question is answered with another question: What production levels might Germany's war-making ability have attained if there had been no Allied bombings? A large amount of German manpower and production was tied up in detecting and defending against Allied bombers and were neutralized insofar as any offensive use was concerned. According to Germany's own figures, detecting and defending against our heavy bombers required 30% of its gun production, 20% of its ammunition production, 50% of its electronics manufacturing, 33% of its optical industry and two million soldiers and civilians.

It was mentioned in an earlier chapter that some of the Me-109s were painted to resemble our P-51 Mustangs. The Germans also tried to confuse us by painting some of their FW-190s, with their square-shaped wing tips, to look like our P-47 Thunderbolts. The Focke-Wulf was capable of flying about 400 m.p.h., and the Messerschmitt at about the same speed. Fighter planes of the 8th Air Force did not take a second seat to either of these two Luftwaffe types. The P-38 Lightning flew at 415 m.p.h. and the P-47 at 430 m.p.h. The P-51 was a 440 m.p.h. aircraft, but its "H" model could develop an impressive speed of 487 m.p.h. The range of the P-47 and P-51 far exceeded the range of either the Focke-Wulf

Top photo is of a captured German FW-190. Note similarity to U.S. P-47 Thunderbolt. Lower photo is of a captured Me-109, which resembled U.S. P-51 Mustang. These German planes were part of the RAF's Aerial Circus, hence the British insignia of the Me-109. (Photos by 379th BG Photo. Section, Circa 1944)

or the Messerschimtt. The P-47D had a 1,000 mile range, and the P-51D had a range of 2,300 miles. Because of its speed, the range of the P-51's "H" model was reduced to approximately 850 miles.

During this mission flak was seen at approximately seven locations. It was generally described as being off as to distance, and was meager to moderate except over the city of Munich. Use of chaff was very helpful, and only eight of our Fortresses reported any flak damage; however, six crewmen in those B-17s were wounded. Screwball Express was not scratched.

On our return to England the weather began to deteriorate when cirrus cloud formations were encountered at the enemy coast. This made it necessary for our formation to fly across the Channel below the prescribed altitude. All of the planes in our two Groups returned safely to Kimbolton. Our flying time for the mission was 9:30 hours. Our crew had now completed 12 combat missions, and only had 13 more to go.

"Don't mention that unlucky number!" We tried to concentrate only on the number 12.

Ernie Koshuta, our right waist gunner, walked beside me as we went to the truck waiting to transport us to debriefing. "You know," he drawled, "it's sure nice when all my baseball buddies make it back from one of these missions. It's bad enough when the Squadron softball team loses players after they complete their tour and ship home. But, it's darned rough when we lose 'em 'cause they got killed on a mission. I've been lucky. I keep comin' back." His words expressed his heartfelt sentiment.

Crews reported the following at debriefing: A large smoke screen was seen at Stuttgart, and another at Munich. Enemy fighter planes were on the ground at airfields near Stuttgart and Gunsburg. A large ship was seen being towed into the harbor at LeTreport. Considerable activity was observed in the marshalling yards at Kaiserslautem. Intelligence personnel said they would follow up on these reports.

On the following day, April 25, our crew was "stood down." The 379th sent a Group to bomb an airdrome at Metz, France. I spent part of the morning reading newspapers. The Daily Sketch reported the 8th Air Force lost 38 bombers and 17 fighters on the April 24 operation. An article in that publication also stated, "Swiss radio reports that 12 damaged American planes landed in Switzerland. One which refused to land when requested was shot down by Swiss fighters."

The same article also reported Fortresses from Italy hit the Ploesti railway yards in the fifth attack on the oil city. While that raid was in progress, Liberators from Italy attacked the main railway yards at Bucharest, the capital city of Rumania. A third assault was launched during the day from Italy, when Fortresses bombed the Icarus aircraft factory at Belgrade, capital of Yugoslavia.

The newspaper also told about the ban on all travel from Britain, effective on the coming Friday, April 28. Other restrictions were being implemented to prevent leakage about military operations dealing with the invasion. Diplomatic messages and mail also became subject to censorship.

A bold headline above a boxed article on the front page of The Daily Sketch caught my eye. It stated, "And Yet Germany Knew." The article's only sentence was: "In spite of a Censorship ban on the publication of the news on overseas bulletins before 11:30 last night or broadcast in the Midnight Home news, German Overseas Radio from Amsterdam (picked up by "The Daily Sketch" Listening Station) broadcast news of the travel ban at 10:27 last night."

I was eager to tell the gang back at our barracks about all this news. And it was news. We weren't lucky enough to have a radio.

My hot news items quickly simmered down after Howard's announcement that he had managed to get a 24-hour pass for all members of our crew. He had already arranged for a truck to haul us to Bedford that afternoon. It didn't take us long to get ready.

That evening we had dinner in a quaint restaurant near where the truck dropped us off. We held a "planning session" to help us crowd different things into our brief schedule. An unanimous opinion favored seeing a reasonably current movie. I don't remember a thing about the movie, but the vaudeville act we were surprised with was really something great – at least it was for me. Never before had I seen elephants, lions and horses on a theater stage – the stage of the old Wildey theater in Edwardsville, Illinois, would probably have collapsed under the weight. I was amazed to learn the audience could smoke during the entertainment. Not in the Wildey! A magician topped off the night's show. We stopped at the American Red Cross Service Club and topped off the night with a bottle of pop.

The next morning, April 26, we went sight-seeing in the city of Bedford. Much of our time was spent just walking around, because we didn't know which sights to see. We enjoyed lunch at a little sidewalk cafe. The day was bright and the weather was surprisingly pleasant. A lot of the fellows who were also on pass in Bedford were punting on the Ouse. Doing it isn't at all what it might sound like. A punt is a long, narrow, flat-bottomed boat with square ends, and is propelled from place to place by pushing on the river's bottom with a long pole. Bob and I rented a punt and splashed around on the Ouse. Howard and Jim taunted us from the shoreline, hoping we would upset the punt and fall in the Ouse. Limbs of many trees along the shore arched gracefully over the river. The branches met overhead and formed a picturesque network of shade. The charm and beauty of the tranquil scene did not deserve our noisy behavior.

Our 24-hour pass in Bedford wasn't filled with the excitement of our three days in London. We didn't expect it to be. Nevertheless, it overflowed with fun and relaxation, and was very enjoyable. After an early dinner that evening in Bedford, we had a good night's sleep back at the base.

On Thursday, April 27, 1944, for the first time in its history, the 379th Bomb Group flew two separate missions to France on the same day. That morning we heard the engines of 21 of its planes as they took off to attack a fly-bomb site at Mesnil au Val. Screwball Express flew on the morning's mission with Lt. Robert M. Dunn's crew aboard. This was our plane's 12th combat mission and its first without our crew. We breathed sighs of thanks when it approached the Kimbolton airfield completing its morning assignment. Our Fortress was allowed to rest for the balance of the day. During the afternoon we watched 20 of the 379th's Flying Fortresses take off to bomb an airfield at Toul/Croixe de Metz. This was the first of 11 double-mission days the 379th would fly before the war's end. Seven of these were during the period of time in which our crew was operational.

It was exciting to watch a double-mission day unfold. It would have been more exciting to have been part of one of the attacks.

(**Special Credit:** Please refer to *The Air War*, 1939-1945, and *The Rand McNally Encyclopedia of Military Aircraft*, 1914-1980, under Bibliography.)

American Red Cross Sevice Club, Bedford, England: circa 1943-1944. (Courtesy of 379th BG WWII Association)

Mission to Avord

The relentless assault by Allied aircraft on Germany's invasion defenses roared through its 14th straight day on Friday, April 28, 1944.

The 8th Air Force sent its heavy, medium and fighter-bombers against Hitler's West (Atlantic) Wall in almost constant attacks. The day's activities began as the last of a huge fleet of RAF Lancasters returned after bombing Friedrichshafen. Swiss reporters who watched the attack from across Lake Constance described the air raid as the heaviest ever experienced by the German city. In addition to factories that made radar equipment, there were three Dornier aircraft factories and a large Rudolph Diesel plant in Friedrichshafen. Blasts from bombs individually weighing two or more tons shook houses on the Swiss shores 20 miles away.

For the second consecutive day, the U.S. 8th Air Force dispatched two operations in one day. The morning operation primarily included attacks by Fortresses of the 1st Bomb Division on an airfield at Avord, France. The remainder of this operation involved the 3rd Bomb Division and a military installation in the Cherbourg area. In the late afternoon, B-24s of the 2nd Bomb Division attacked a military installation in the Pas de Calais area. Bomber escort for the day was provided by eight Groups of 8th Air Force fighter planes.

The primary morning target was the Luftwaffe airdrome 130 miles south of Paris. Located two miles northwest of Avord, it was formerly an important and well equipped French military airfield. It was now used almost exclusively as a base for Germany's long range Heinkel He-111 bombers.

The 379th Bomb Group furnished 24 Fortresses, including four spares, as the Low Group in the 40th Composite Combat Wing's attack at the Avord airfield. Screwball Express flew in the Low Squadron of the Low Group. Two of the spares returned early as planned. Fortress number 42-31228 filled in with the 92nd Bomb Group from Podington, and B-17 number 42-30298 flew with the 351st Group from Polebrook.

Our Low Group took off at 0840 hours into a relatively clear sky. The drone of our engines tried to blend with the notes for "... I will fear no evil." Our assembly with the 40th Composite Combat Wing took place over Podington at 5,000 feet. We left the southern coast of England at Selsey Bill, a few miles east of Portsmouth, at 1020 hours and 10,000 feet. At 1023 we observed a convoy in that area. Our formation crossed into enemy territory 14,000 feet over Cabourg, France, about 20 miles southwest of Le Havre, at 1048 hours.

Weather over military installations in the Cherbourg area prevented all except 15 aircraft of the 3rd Bomb Division from attacking. The B-24s attacked a military installation in the Pas de Calais area with fair results. Forty-seven B-24s dropped 60-2000 pound general purpose bombs and 246-1,000 pound bombs between 1759 and 1805 hours. The bombs fell in the target area, but only slightly damaged one of five important sections.

In the opinion of many, the B-24 Liberator bomber was a controversial aircraft. It was used by the United States Army and Navy, the RAF and by other Allies. A total of 18,188 B-24s were produced by the Consolidated Aircraft Corporation. It was used more extensively in the Mediterranean area than in Germany.

To men in Flying Fortresses, you flew a B-17 and you drove a B-24. The B-17 was "Queen of the Sky," and the B-24 was "that banana boat." To men in Liberators, the B-17 was "that heavy bombardment training plane." The B-24 was "a real man's ship." Some said the B-24 was designed to be a boat, but leaked so badly they put wings on it and flew it. Others said the B-24s were packing cases in which B-17s were shipped overseas. Some jokers even questioned why B-17s needed fighter escort when B-24s were in the same area. They were referring to the lower altitude at which B-24s frequently flew, supposedly making them easier marks for enemy fighters and flak.

The B-24 Liberator was a very good aircraft. It was flown by very good men. Crewmen in B-24s fought just as valiantly as we did in B-17s. They bled and died in the same way B-17 crewmen bled and died. Bombs from either type of aircraft could miss a target or destroy it. Crew members of B-24s counted their missions in exactly the same way as the men in B-17s counted theirs – one at a time. Crew members of B-24s were very proud of their Liberator bomber. I offer no apology for my partiality to the B-17.

Our Initial Point was reached at 1152 hours. The Wing's lead bombardier was able to recognize the target from eight to ten miles away, even though a severe ground haze was present in the target area. Screwball Express and other planes in the Low Group each carried 20-300 pound general purpose bombs. Our altitude was 14,000 feet. Bombs from planes in a Group ahead of ours hit an ammunition dump at the airfield, causing smoke from the explosions to billow up around 8,000 feet. Moderate, accurate, black flak was present along our bomb run. We were startled by occasional red bursts of flak. Two rockets from the ground barely missed the left wing of a plane in our Lead Group. The rockets then arched downward and exploded with a large flash of flame about 500 feet beneath that formation. Screwball Express was hit by flak in the cowling of number three engine, but without serious results. The actual bomb run lasted 90 seconds. Our Low Group dropped its bombs from 14,000 feet at 1201 hours, on a magnetic heading of 10 degrees. This was next to the lowest altitude from which we had ever bombed in combat.

The 1st Wing and the 40th Composite Wing included six Bomb Groups that attacked the Avord airfield. The 92nd, 379th and 351st Bomb Groups were the day's 40th Composite Wing. The 1st Wing was made up of the 91st, 381st and 306th Bomb Groups. Each of these two Wings had 58 Fortresses in the attack. The 16mm movie cameras in the bomb bays of each leading Fortress provided photographs of the following damage: Two concentrations of demolition bombs fell into the hangar-barracks area located on the southern edge of the airfield. Four large, double-bay hangars received direct hits. The most westerly hangar received one direct hit and lost approximately 20% of its roof. The most easterly hangar was hit near a corner of the building by at least one bomb. The two central hangars were hit by numerous demolition bombs. One of these buildings was 50% destroyed and on fire late in the attack. The other hangar received two direct hits and was also burning.

The barracks area was severely damaged by many direct hits. A concentration of incendiary bombs also fell into the workshops-barracks area. Direct hits were observed on at least 14 barracks and workshops. A concentration of demolition bombs fell directly into the hangar area on the eastern side of the airfield.

Three large hangars received direct hits by demolition bombs. The most southerly hangar received two direct hits and was on fire during the final part of the attack. Two adjacent hangars received five hits and two hits respectively. One of those hangars was demolished, and the other was 50% destroyed. A concentration of fragmentation bombs fell into the dispersal area near the northwestern side of the airfield. Direct hits were made on blast shelters. A concentration of demolition bombs fell into a wooded area immediately adjacent to the dispersal area. Approximately 12 enemy aircraft were parked on the airfield during the attack, and several of them were destroyed by fire.

The 58 Fortresses in the 1st Wing dropped 174 tons of demolition bombs on the airfield. The 40th Composite Wing's 58 planes dropped 65.7 tons of demolition bombs, 37 tons of incendiaries and 34 tons of fragmentation bombs. The 116-plane attack resulted in 310.7 tons of bombs dropped with excellent results on the once-prominent French airfield. The heaviest fighter opposition occurred about ten minutes after our bombs hit the target. A group of Me-109s and FW-190s totaling 35-40 aircraft made attacks that were weak and not persistent. The attacks lasted about three minutes. One mass attack was made from head on. Fortunately, it was not pressed home by all of the enemy planes, many of which failed to come within range of our bombers' machine guns. Eight FW-190s came from beneath our Group and climbed straight up through the bomber formation. It was noted the FW-190s had in-line engines.

Two B-17s were lost in the target area because of antiaircraft fire. A total of 13 parachutes were seen coming from the two Fortresses. These B-17s were from the 1st Combat Wing. The 3rd Division lost two B-17s to flak over Guernsey Island. A P-51 went down in our target area, but its pilot was able to bail out. One of our P-38s and another P-51 were shot down during the day. The 40th Composite Wing with which we flew lost no aircraft. Our fighter planes claimed nine enemy aircraft destroyed on the ground. Eighth Air Force estimates showed 82 B-17s and 19 B-24s received minor damage in the day's operations. Fifteen B-17s received major battle damage. Casualties among 8th Air Force personnel included 41 crewmen missing in action and 12 wounded.

A considerable amount of activity was taking place on the airfield at Romorantin, about 30 miles northwest of Bourges. No opposition was encountered on our way home, although flak bursts were observed in the areas around Orleans and Chateaudun. Cabourg was the point at which we had entered enemy territory on this mission, and it was also the point at which we left it. We were flying at 14,000 feet, the same altitude, on each occasion. My thought of the day: our mission planners should have arranged for us to enter and leave enemy territory at different points, or at least at different altitudes. Doing things the same way on our routes in and out was certainly not a way to confuse the enemy. We saw about 40 vehicles on the beach near Cabourg, and 25 barges in the water. Our Intelligence people were interested in hearing about this, and were delighted our route out was over Cabourg.

Moments later, just off the French coast, a B-17 flying at approximately 18,000 feet turned back to the continent. It may have been one of the B-17s salvaged by the Germans, rebuilt, and now used for scouting purposes. Our formation started letting down and crossed the English coast at 1356 hours over Worthing, near Brighton, at 5,000 feet. A bomb rack in one of our High Squadron's Fortresses evidently malfunctioned during the attack at Avord, and one bomb hung up. That plane's crew managed to release that bomb during our Group's descent over the Channel, and the bomb struck the water near a British convoy. Someone would have to explain the incident as soon as that plane landed at Kimbolton.

All of the 379th's planes returned to our home base, and no injuries were reported by crew members in our Group. Today's flying time was six hours and 30 minutes. Screwball Express and 13 other Fortresses in the 379th Bomb Group sustained minor flak damage while in the target area, on our 13th mission! That sounded very ominous. Only 12 more missions to go! That sounded much better!

Saturday, April 29, 1944. Early this morning we learned the 379th was putting another mission together. Our crew was "stood down" again, so we were unaware of the day's target. We were unable to pry any information out of crew members assigned to the mission. That's the way it was supposed to be. ("Loose lips sink ships.") I assumed it was possible for some clever Nazi spy to infiltrate our airfield and listen to our briefing from the shadows outside the building's thin walls, but I seriously doubt it ever happened. However, secrecy was the order of the day, and rightly so.

After the Group's takeoff, some of us visited with several ground crews and ordnance men. They always seemed to know where the target was, and frequently before some of the personnel at headquarters. "Berlin," one of them whispered softly, and then added, "… a marshalling yards." I yelled, "Berlin? Not again!" My disappointment was prompted by the 379th Group flying a fourth mission to Berlin, without our crew. Howard reminded me this was the 379th's first mission to Germany's capital since our crew became operational.

"We'll have our turn."

(**Special Credit:** Please refer to *B-17 Fortress at War*, under Bibliography.)

Mission to Lyons

Sunday, April 30, 1944. The day was only four hours old when we were awakened for the 14th time in the past 38 days and told we were flying a combat mission. We dressed quickly and ran to the mess hall. Our rush was not because of the culinary skill of our mess sergeant. We didn't dare to be late for briefing, and we certainly wanted to eat before we took off on the day's mission.

I suppose the menus at 8th Air Force mess halls were very much like those of other U.S. military forces in World War II. Following are examples of some memorable taste treats:

Different kinds of meat that came in a can, like Spam
Chipped beef on toast – Something On a Shingle
Mutton – as chops, as stew, you could smell it a mile away —good for airplanes to "home in" on
Brussels sprouts – (ugh)
Powdered eggs – green and sulfurous – buzzard poison
Powdered eggs with catsup – green & red, for Christmas breakfast
Potatoes, almost always mashed, seldom warm – never hot
Swiss steak – horse meat with a yodel
Pancakes– blowout patches
Grape juice - battery acid
Orange marmalade – always orange, never red or blue
Toast, usually cold, sometimes brittle, always burned
Coffee – always in heavy mugs or tin cups – a good hand warmer

United States 8th Air Force Field Order #340, covering its 329th Operation, had the following three-target menu of assignments at the top of its first page:

1st Bombardment Division - Lyons/Bron A/F
2nd Bombardment Division - Military Installation —Pas de Calais
3rd Bombardment Division - Clermont-Ferrand A/F

Two bomber forces totaling 240-B-17s from the 1st and 3rd Bomb Divisions were dispatched to attack the two airfields in southeastern France. One force of 55 B-24s was sent to the target in the Pas de Calais area. Escort was provided by 13 Groups of U.S. fighter planes.

The 41st and 94th Combat Wings received the target assignments of the 1st Division. The 379th Bomb Group flew Lead Group of the 41st Wing and provided 24 aircraft for the mission. Screwball Express was assigned to a position in the Lead Squadron of the Lead Group.

Seven of our 14 targets to date involved airfields. The Lyons/Bron airfield was five miles east-southeast of Lyons, a city on the Rhone river. The target at Dijon, France, our fourth mission a little more than one month earlier, was approximately 80 miles north of Lyons. Today's target was the most southeastern target our crew would bomb in France. Prior to the war, the French used this airfield extensively for civilian and military aircraft. Our Intelligence believed the Luftwaffe was currently using the base for one of their "fighter gruppe," a group of enemy fighter planes.

Only a small amount of ground haze was lingering around Kimbolton when our Lead Group took off at 0655 hours. The windsock wasn't moving. There wasn't even a ripple on the farm ponds around our airfield.

"He leadeth me beside the still waters."

The only movement of air was the prop-wash behind our planes as they climbed into the sky for assembly over Molesworth at 7,000 feet at 0742 hours. Northampton was directly under us at 0750 hours. We then flew due south for about 15 minutes, turned southeast, and at 0812 hours and 13,000 feet our formation was over the southwestern edge of London. Three of our four spares returned early as planned, and aircraft number 42-30720 returned early not dispatched. Splasher #9 was crossed at 0820 hours, and 10 minutes later we crossed the English coast at 15,000 feet over Selsey Bill. We were exactly on schedule for all estimated times of arrival at various points along our route.

We entered enemy territory near Cabourg at 0857 hours flying at 20,000 feet. The weather was very favorable and permitted us to use pilotage navigation during the entire mission. The pilotage method was easy to use. You drew a line on the map, from your starting point to where you wanted to go, and followed it by checking on such things as cities, rivers, railroads and highways so you could determine your position at any given time. That may sound oversimplified, but that's all there was to it.

After crossing the French coast, we flew directly to Lyons. At 0917 hours, between 35 and 40 enemy aircraft were encountered in the area around Champrond. Most of those planes were Me-109s and FW-190s. Attacks on our formation appeared to be half-hearted and gave us the impression the pilots of these enemy planes were inexperienced. The Low Group in our Wing received the majority of the attacks, but none of its planes reported being hit. Some flak bursts blossomed around the city of Chartres, but they were too distant to worry us very much. The strafing of a Luftwaffe airdrome by some of our P-47s was much more exciting to watch, even from so far away. My government-issue M6 binoculars provided an excellent close-up of their activities.

We reached a point southwest of Lyons according to plan, and our target was clearly visible. Turning directly east, we flew toward our IP and arrived there at 1031 hours. A ninety degrees turn to our left put us on our bomb run, a magnetic heading of seven degrees. We encountered no flak or fighters during the relatively short bomb run of 90 seconds. Screwball Express dropped its bomb load, consisting of 5-1,000 pound demolition bombs, from 20,000 feet at 30 seconds past 1041 hours.

The 148.5 tons of demolition bombs dropped on the Lyons airfield by our 41st Combat Wing's 61 Fortresses were extremely effective. Six concentrations of heavy explosives fell into the target area on the western side of the airfield. At least five direct hits were made on the large four-bay hangar located at the southwestern corner of the target area. More than 75% of the hangar was demolished.

A large two-bay hangar immediately adjacent to the northern side of the four-bay hangar received four or more direct hits. Photography during the attack showed this hangar was 60% destroyed. A two-bay hangar near the center of this group of buildings received at least one direct hit, destroying 50% of it.

Three large double-bay hangars at the northwestern corner of the hangar area were damaged by numerous direct hits. The most northerly hangar was severely damaged by at least four bombs. The central hangar was hit by two or more bombs and was on fire late in the attack. The southern hangar in this group received at least four direct hits and was 50% destroyed.

Only one of the ten hangars on the airfield was undamaged in this attack. Eight or nine of the 24 enemy aircraft parked at the airfield received direct hits and were badly damaged or destroyed. Five or more small buildings in the target area were damaged by direct hits and near misses. Our bombing results were excellent.

Our Wing turned to the left and headed for home. The 94th Combat Wing's 53 Fortresses then bombed the airfield and its runways with an additional 129 tons of general purpose bombs.

Seven minutes after our 41st Combat Wing dropped its bombs our High Group was attacked by about 35 enemy fighters in the area around Coullons. The bandits made five attacks, first flying through our formation and then attacking from the rear. Their attacks were directed mainly at our High Group. One of our planes sustained battle damage by a 20mm cannon shell. Our fighter escort was good on the way out, but was outnumbered at this particular point and could not prevent enemy fighters from attacking us. Three enemy aircraft were reported shot down by gunners in two bomber Groups flying behind our Combat Wing.

Our route back to England was exactly the same as our morning route to the target. A B-17 from the 381st Bomb Group went down in flames near Orleans as a result of damage during the fighter attack near Coullons. Four parachutes were seen coming out of the plane. Later we saw flak explosions around Catechumen, but none of them was close to our position. Only a few scattered clouds were in the immediate area, and we continued to navigate using the pilotage method.

At 1252 hours we left the enemy coast at the exact place we entered it that morning, 49 degrees and 18 minutes North, 00 degrees and 07 minutes West. We were flying at 16,000 feet near Cabourg. After thirty-seven minutes of circling and losing altitude over the Channel, we leveled off at 5,000 feet and entered England at Worthing. Our flight plan took us close to the western edge of London as we flew north to Kimbolton.

All of our planes returned safely to our home base. None of our flight crews had any injuries and Screwball Express was undamaged. Our flying time on this mission was exactly 8 hours. We only had 11 more to go!

Flight crews reported the following observations to Intelligence officers at the debriefing: Much activity at the Laigle railway station ... extensive activity in the marshalling yards at Nevers ... a gun emplacement in a forest at 4725N-0230 E ... a factory with 10 smoke stacks 10 miles north of Nevers ... a camouflaged airdrome at Roanne. The Germans were certainly persistent in their war efforts.

The 8th Air Force had 11 B-17s and 19 B-24s with minor damage today, and one B-17 with major damage. Eight B-17s and three B-24s failed to bomb because of a variety of mechanical failures.

At the end of April, 526th Bomb Squadron records show it completed 103 missions in 11 months, making it one of the first B-17 Squadrons to accomplish this feat. The Squadron was included in commendations from Lt. General Doolittle. The records also stated, "S/Sgts Kiblin and Milworm were promoted to T/Sgts," and "Sgts Craig, Koshuta, Lindsey and Mathews were promoted to S/Sgts." The same page states, "Towers to 1st Lt," but says nothing about any promotions for Moore, Keller and Cassens. Oh, well, I suppose accuracy was reserved for bomb dropping.

The Squadron's historical record continues with, "There were dances during the month at the Aeroclub for the enlisted personnel, and the new movie projector was put to good use at the Base Theatre with daily showings of current popular pictures." ("Current" – like maybe 10 years ago.)

"On the athletic field the Squadron has been getting set for the coming league games in softball and volleyball, playing numerous practice games with other units and among themselves. The basketball team finished up their league schedule in last place, with interest falling off considerably."

The 379th Bomb Group flew 15 combat missions in April. That was very good, considering the terrible weather during the first nine days of the month. Our crew flew on nine of the Group's 15 April missions.

On the first day of May the following statement appeared in the Stars and Stripes newspaper:

"Rounding out one of the worst weekends the Germans have gone through, U.S. airmen wrote the following score sheet in widespread operations over France yesterday: B-17s bombed airfields at Lyons and Clermont-Ferrand, in south central France, while B-24s bombed military installations in the Pas de Calais. One bomber and four escorting fighters of the comparatively small forces were lost, and seven German planes were shot down."

Direct hits on airfield at Lyons, France, April 30, 1944. (Photo taken by camera in bomb bay of Lead aircraft; from 379th BG Photo. Sec.)

Mission to Reims

The overall contribution of the 379th Bomb Group was of great importance in support of preparations for the D-Day invasion. High on the list of its many achievements was the record number of 24 combat missions during May of 1944. This was a 33% increase over any previous month in the Group's history. During May the 379th sent 33 Groups of Flying Fortresses into Germany and enemy-occupied Europe.

The first two of those missions were on Monday, May 1, 1944. This was the second time the 379th Group flew two separate combat missions on the same day. The morning's primary target was the airfield at La Longeville, France. Twenty-three of the Group's Fortresses were dispatched, and three spares returned early as planned. The Group was met by 10/10 cloud conditions at the target. It was consequently decided to attack the secondary target, an airfield at Montdidier. Visibility at the secondary target was favorable, but bombing results were only fair. Only 15 of the Group's planes dropped their bombs. The bomb pattern was about midway between the town and the airfield.

During the afternoon, eight Combat Wings made up of 235 B-17s and 151 B-24s were dispatched to attack six marshalling yards in Belgium and northern France. A force of two Combat Wings from the 1st Bomb Division was assigned the Reims and Troyes marshalling yards. Four Combat Wings of the 2nd Division were assigned to attack marshalling yards at Brussels and Liege, in Belgium. Two Wings of the 3rd Division were dispatched to the marshalling yards at Sarreguemines and Metz. The 8th Air Force provided 15 fighter Groups for bomber escort.

The 379th Bomb Group flew as High Group in the 40th Composite Combat Wing on the mission to attack marshalling yards at Reims. Screwball Express flew with the Low Squadron of the High Group. The target was approximately 75 miles east-northeast of Paris. The 379th assigned 24 planes to this mission, four of which were spares that returned early according to plan.

(Reims., France, later became the site of The Supreme Headquarters of the Allied Expeditionary Force. SHAEF's headquarters was known as the Little Red School House. General Dwight D. Eisenhower, future president of the United States, made his VE-Day speech from Reims in May, 1945.)

Our Group took off in the middle of the afternoon at 1455 hours. The sky was splashed with big, white clouds, and the patches of blue added special meaning to the words I sang. Assembly of our Combat Wing at 12,000 feet over Northampton was made without any problems. We departed the English coast at 1645 hours, flying at 19,000 feet over Clacton On Sea, about 15 miles south of Ipswich. A Group of 14 B-17s with the letter "B" in the squares on their tails followed us as our formation flew southeast over the Channel. The enemy coast was crossed at Dunkirk, about midway between Calais, France, and Ostend, Belgium. We were flying at 20,000 feet and the time was 1703 hours. The alto cumulus clouds diminished after we crossed into enemy territory and we were again able to navigate using the pilotage method.

The 40th Composite Combat Wing flew on a southeastward course for 30 minutes. Assisted by a tail wind of almost 50 m.p.h., we arrived exactly on schedule at a preselected point near Charleville, France, at 1733 hours. Our formation

was about 40 miles north-northeast of Reims. We then flew directly south on a path that took us east of Reims and continued on to Suippes. Our course was then due west until we were about 12 miles south of the target. The Group of 14 Square "B" Fortresses was still behind us. It was 1809 hours and we were over the IP. Our flight tactics had been fairly successful, because flak guns were not yet popping away at us. We turned to a magnetic heading of 350 degrees and started our bomb run.

Screwball Express and each of the other 56 B-17s in the 40th Composite Wing carried 6-1,000 pound general purpose bombs. The target was covered with a very dense ground haze. It was evidently very windy on the ground, because we could see the haze blowing away as we approached the point for releasing our bombs. Antiaircraft shells started coming up at us and black puffs filled the air directly in front of our formation. They came closer, exploding in the middle of our Group. The flak bursts were moderate in number, but very accurate. At one point I became unusually frightened by the flak. I pulled my knees tightly to my chest and tried to bury my head and arms between my shoulders. Keller took his oxygen mask off for a moment and yelled at me. "Sit up straight," he said, "otherwise some of that flak might hit me." He quickly replaced his oxygen mask and looked away. Bob pretended he couldn't hear what I yelled back at him.

Weather above the target area cleared and provided our lead bombardier a one-minute bomb run. The Automatic Flight Control Equipment in the Lead plane did not function well, and the bomb run was entirely manual. We released our bombs at 1816 hours from 21,000 feet. The Square "B" Group of 14 planes did not bomb the primary target.

The 57 Fortresses in our Combat Wing dropped 336-1,000 pound demolition bombs with excellent results. The ground below shook as our 168 tons of explosives struck the marshalling yards. Two heavy concentrations of bombs fell into large locomotive sheds and the repair shop area. Two direct hits were made on another locomotive shed. The railway yards around the workshop area received many direct hits. Many freight cars and railroad lines in the area were severely damaged. A concentration of bombs fell on the choke point at the exit end of the sorting siding. Scattered bombs fell among unidentified buildings west of the primary target area.

After enough time had elapsed for the 16mm cameras in bomb bays of lead aircraft to record the bombing results, our Group made a sharp right turn in an effort to get away from the flak bursting around us. After about one minute, the course we were given at briefing was followed for the flight back to England. The course was a straight line.

Flying a straight line meant flying the shortest route. Pros and cons of the straight line concept were always considered by mission planners. It was the quickest way to the target, and the quickest way back to Kimbolton. The shortest route could also result in the use of less fuel and the opportunity to carry more bombs. However, deciding a flight plan without concern for the location of enemy airfields and antiaircraft guns resulted in needless exposure of the bombers and their crews. Longer flight plans usually allowed bomber formations to go around some of the flak barrages and stay away from airfields filled with enemy fighters. Larger fuel requirements and fewer bombs on targets were disadvantages of the longer flight plans.

Flak was seen in the area south of Brussels and around Ostend. Near the French coast a P-47 was hit, apparently by flak, and was seen to crash. A B-17 in another Group was seen going down near Ostend. No parachutes were reported. We crossed the enemy coast at 1917 hours, flying at 18,000 feet.

Our altitude was decreased to 8,000 feet while over the English Channel and we crossed the English coast at Frinton on Sea at 1946 hours. Our Group saw no enemy fighters in the air during this mission.

All of the Fortresses from our base returned safely,

FRC GP18 1541   379th BOMB GP

PAGE 1 OF 2 PAGES
5-2

526TH BOMB. SQ
C UNIT BOMBARDMENT SQUADRON (H)
OFFICE OF THE OPERATIONS OFFICER
Station #117
APO #557

F. O. 342
MISSION # 169
REIMS
379 BOMB GP

1 May 1944.

SUBJECT: LOADING LIST.

TO   : All Concerned.

Ship No. 783-B
P-Lt. Heath, Gilbert C.
CP-Lt. McDaniel, Samuel L.
N-Lt. Tilton, Neel (NMI)
B-Lt. McAloon Jr, William J.
RG-T/Sgt Patton, Malcom W.
TT-T/Sgt Claypool, Warren D.
BT-S/Sgt Green, John H.
RW-Sgt Roundhill, Joseph W.
LW-T/Sgt Hollister, John E.
TG-S/Sgt Roberts, Thomas W.

Ship No. 043-L
P-Lt. Osborne, Joseph (NMI)
CP-Lt. Vogel, Carl G.
N-Lt. Karcich, Mathew F.
B-Lt. Archdeacon, John R.
RG-Sgt Fama, Elmo (NMI)
TT-S/Sgt Jeffcoat, Harry A.
BT-Sgt Dilworth, William L.
RW-Sgt Waite Jr, John (NMI)
LW-Sgt DeSouchet, William O.
TG-Sgt Nelson, William F.

Ship No. 058-C
P-Lt. Dunn Jr, Robert M.
CP-Lt. Churchill Jr, William R.
N-Lt. Krassner, George (NMI)
B-Lt. Jensen, Harry D.
RG-T/Sgt Anderson, Evar W.
TT-T/Sgt Whitelaw, John T.
BT-S/Sgt Fode, John (NMI)
RW-S/Sgt Ayers, Edwin G.
LW-S/Sgt Vukovich, Peter (NMI)
TG-S/Sgt Miller, James T.

Ship No. 128-M
P-Lt. Towers, Howard E.
CP-Lt. Moore, James C.
N-Lt. Keller, James R.
B-Lt. Cassens, Kenneth H.
RG-T/Sgt Milworm, Joseph (NMI)
TT-S/Sgt Craig, Frank R.
BT-T/Sgt Kiblin Jr, Thomas A.
RW-S/Sgt Koshuta, Earnest (NMI)
LW-S/Sgt Mathews, Robert G.
TG-S/Sgt Lindsey, Jerold L.

Ship No. 663-G (524th)
P-Lt. Miller Jr, Walter J.
CP-Lt. Jones, John H.
N-Lt. Horn, Roy R.
B-Lt. Dempsey, Thomas J.
RG-Sgt Guill, Jack R.
TT-Sgt Soper, William R.
BT-Sgt Rizzuto, Charles J.
RW-Pfc Doine, Maurice E.
LW-Sgt White, John R.
TG-Pfc Koska, Edwin (NMI)

Ship No. 800-T
P-Lt. Miller, Milton S.
CP-Lt. Taylor, Fred (NMI)
NG-S/Sgt Wages, Bradley L.
B-Lt. Littlejohn, Robert C.
RG-T/Sgt Neal, Charley E.
TT-T/Sgt Potter, Henry T.
BT-S/Sgt Clement, Jack F.
RW-S/Sgt Wikle, Logan D.
LW-S/Sgt Medlock, George W.
TG-S/Sgt Casella, Charles A.

The May 1, 1944 loading list for the mission to Reims, France, was the last one on which Ernest Koshuta's name appeared as a member of our flight crew. (Photostat of original copy in 379th Bomb Group Mission Report, at National Archives Military Records Facility)

although we had one straggler. A bombardier in one of our planes was wounded. Screwball Express only had two holes, both of which were caused by flak. One of the holes was in a fuel tank in the right wing, and part of the wing had to be removed in order to make repairs. One of our planes received major battle damage on this mission, and 11 others had minor flak damage. Screwball Express had no significant mechanical or electrical problems on any of our missions to date. Flying time on this mission was six hours.

We had completed 15 of our missions. Only 10 more to go. It was difficult to believe, but we had completed 60% of our combat tour.

Counting today's missions, the 379th had attacked seven targets in five days. Two of them were on April 27th, one each on the 28th, 29th and 30th, and two on May 1st. A fly-bomb site, two marshalling yards and four airfields, very good results for a short week's work. These results would be another proud entry in the 379th's record books.

The 8th Air Force lost a total of four B-17s during the day. The 3rd Division lost three Fortresses: one to flak, one to reasons unknown, and another plane was damaged by flak and crashed during landing. The crew of the plane that crashed was uninjured.

The 15 8th Air Force fighter Groups provided 524 aircraft: 259 P-47s, 147 P-51s and 118 P-38s. Five Groups escorted the B-17s that attacked the Reims and Troyes marshalling yards, three Groups escorted the B-24s that attacked the two marshalling yards in Belgium, and four Groups escorted the B-17s that attacked the two marshalling yards in France. Three additional Groups of U.S. fighter planes furnished general withdrawal escort, paying particular attention to stragglers and enemy intruders. The only enemy air opposition was met by those fighters supporting attacks on the marshalling yards at Metz and Sarreguemines. The enemy planes in these areas numbered approximately 125 Me-109s and FW-190s, but they were not very aggressive. Some of our P-51s engaged in combat with about 15 Me-109s north of Luxembourg and shot down four of them. Approximately 75 enemy aircraft in the Geichlingen area fled eastward when another Group of P-51s turned to attack. Our fighters claimed six enemy planes were shot down. Three of ours were lost—a P-51 to an enemy fighter and two P-38s to flak in the Liege area.

Observations reported by flight crews at debriefing were of various types. More than 50 unidentified single-engine enemy aircraft were seen at an airport on the southeast outskirts of Paris. Eight He-111s were observed at the Abbeville-Drucat airfield. Sunken pill boxes were observed east of Furnes at 5105N-0240E. Two gun batteries of four guns each were seen at Guines, (5052N-0152E). More flooding was reported in the Dunkirk area. Nine newly constructed buildings were seen near Alost. Considerable construction and excavation activity had taken place four miles east of Eda. A flak tower was observed between the airfield and the beach southwest of Ostend. Oil tanks were reported at 5105N-0301E. Ten openings, possibly tunnels, were seen at the edge of a woods at 4842N-0520E. A dam was under construction at 5038N-0612E. There was a large camp and training field at 4907N-0450E. Twenty barrage balloons were seen in the vicinity of Cour-trai.

An article in the Stars and Stripes the following morning, Tuesday, May 2, 1944, reported Lt. General Doolittle had announced in a radio broadcast to America that 1,300 German planes were destroyed in the air and on the ground during April. This number was substantially more than

Germany had produced in the entire month. There was also a one-sentence paragraph about the bombing of the Reims marshalling yards during the previous afternoon.

In the mid-morning on May 2nd, Howard walked into our barracks. His face was long enough to stretch the entire length of our Nissen hut. He had been to Squadron Headquarters where he and other plane commanders received a very nasty assignment. He had just returned from the barracks of our other crew members where he told Ernest Koshuta, our right waist gunner, that we would fly with only one waist gunner on future missions. Ernie wasn't the one. Headquarters decided the relatively small number of recent fighter attacks made it unnecessary to have two waist gunners on a B-17. In the future, one waist gunner would alternate between the left and right waist gun positions, depending upon the direction from which the enemy aircraft attacked.

Howard's voice broke as he told us of his conversation with Ernie. I thought I saw a tear start down Howard's cheek. He turned away and walked slowly out of the barracks and into the rain. It was difficult to distinguish the tear from the raindrops.

What a decision! The Luftwaffe would be elated when they heard about this. "Attack from both sides at the same time," they would be saying, "because there's one less machine gun in the middle of those B-17s. The 8th Air Force has reduced its gunners from six to five." Those Nazi pilots would jump with joy when they heard the news.

We really didn't care what the Luftwaffe pilots would say. As for us, we had very little to say, except to curse the decision's unfairness to Ernie, and all the other waist gunners who received the bad news that day.

Ernie kept to himself for several weeks. He didn't want to talk to anyone about what fate's fickle finger did to him. He felt miserable - he really hurt. Our crew had trained together since it was formed at Ardmore, Oklahoma. Ernie had flown 15 combat missions as a valued member of our crew. We had been an extremely efficient and compatible crew of ten.

And now we were nine.

On the 3rd of May we flew a three-hour training flight in Screwball Express. Its waist area looked almost empty. Bob Mathews sat with his back against the left wall of the fuselage, staring at the unoccupied position on the right side of the plane. I called on the intercom for a routine crew check. Inadvertently, I called Ernie's position aloud, "Right waist?" When his voice did not give the customary response, the silence was felt by the nine of us.

On May 4 the 379th Bomb Group went on a mission to Berlin, and again we were "stood down." Instead of flying to the German capital, we went on another training flight for nearly three hours. Extremely adverse weather conditions forced the Group that headed for Berlin to return before reaching the target, an aircraft components plant. Because of the heavy flak encountered en route, some of which struck the 379th's planes, everyone in the planes that were dispatched received credit for a combat mission.

Finally, on May 5th, our crew was alerted for a combat mission to Watten, Germany, but the mission was scrubbed because of bad weather. On May 6 it was again so wet and cloudy we skipped lunch, rather than risk drowning in the downpour or getting lost in a dark cloud on the way to the mess hall.

Mission to Berlin

Sunday, May 7, 1944. Our crew was awakened at 0330 hours. We were going on a combat mission—our first one in almost a week. Somehow, I knew the target for today was Berlin. I had very good reasoning for my assumption. The May 4 early return from the attempt to bomb Berlin, although credited as a mission, caused the Group's envious record of successful attacks to be lacking in absolute continuity. The 379th Bomb Group would go after Berlin again—very soon—probably today.

The briefing room was filled with an atmosphere of anxiety. Everyone was seated long before the briefing was scheduled to begin. More than the usual number of cigarettes filled the room with blue-gray smoke. There was less than the customary amount of conversation, and the silence of the setting reminded me of people holding a wake over a corpse. I studied the yarn pulley at the side of the large sheet that covered the map at the front of the room. I just knew the target today was Berlin.

Colonel Preston entered the room. Someone yelled, "Tain-hut." Before all of us could come to attention the Colonel told us to be seated. He wasn't inclined to wordiness. His eyes scanned the room, and then came the big announcement. "Gentlemen," he said, the target today is Berlin." Everyone cheered. One of the Colonel's staff then mentioned that a mission to Cologne had been scheduled earlier, but was scrubbed because of bad weather over that part of Germany. Screwball Express was on the loading list for that mission, and would have been flown by the crew of Lt. Gilbert C. Heath if the mission had taken place. Instead, the 379th Bomb Group had orders to put up two Groups of B-17s for an attack on Berlin. The two Groups were the High Group in the 41st Combat Wing "A," and the High Group in the 41st Combat Wing "B."

I knew it! Screwball Express and our crew were finally going on a mission to Berlin. Berlin—that's what it was all about. The weather officer said we would bomb using the PFF method, due to anticipated 10/10 cloud cover over Berlin at the time we were scheduled to attack. I wondered to myself—why was the mission to Cologne scrubbed because of bad weather, and the target changed to Berlin where the weather would be just as bad? The logic of the decision escaped me. The significance of the decision was the target. It was Berlin, and our crew was going.

Air space over Berlin was first entered under conditions of war when the RAF dropped leaflets on the German capital on the night of October 1-2, 1939. The city's population at that time was 4.3 million people. Berlin was first bombed on June 7, 1940, by the French Air Force during its brief period of World War II combat service.

On August 24, 1940, 16 German aircraft "accidentally" bombed some non-military targets in London. This event has been referred to as the first London "blitz." On the following night, 81 twin-engine RAF bombers set out to attack Berlin—the first time for the Royal Air Force. Only 29 of those aircraft were able to retaliate by dropping bombs on Berlin, and the RAF lost five bombers on the raid. The attack on Germany's capital city so completely shocked the Nazis that they canceled a victory parade in Paris out of fear the RAF would bomb the parade route. Hitler decided London should receive the same treatment as Warsaw and Rotterdam. On the night of September 6-7, 1940, the Luftwaffe hit London with what was actually the first Blitz Raid on that city.

London was bombed on 57 consecutive nights, during which the Luftwaffe dropped 330 tons of explosives on England's capital city. On August 8, 1941, Russia sent five Ilyushin IL-4 medium bombers to attack Berlin, but the mission failed when only a small section of railroad at the edge of the city was damaged. Two Russian planes were shot down by German antiaircraft guns.

Berlin was the location of many vital war industries. In peacetime its three largest industries included the production of machinery, electrical apparatus and clothing. Its military significance included the manufacture of aircraft and component parts, ball bearing factories, armament plants and large marshalling yards. Berlin was not only a political target—it was also a very significant production center of military hardware.

The first attempt by the 8th Air Force to bomb "Big B" was on March 3, 1944. That mission was recalled due to bad weather which developed as formations of Flying Fortresses headed for the North Sea. On March 4 another attempt was made, but a snowstorm prevented many of the bombers from taking off. That mission was also recalled; however, 29 Fortresses of the 95th and 100th Bomb Groups proceeded to Berlin and were the first 8th Air Force planes to drop bombs on Germany's "sacred city." Crew members of those 29 planes insisted they did not know the mission had been recalled. Unfortunately, cloud cover over Berlin did not allow the bombing to be fully effective. On March 6 the weather improved and 658 heavy bombers made a full scale attack on Germany's capital. The 379th Bomb Group was part of that attack, its first against Berlin. The Luftwaffe was waiting. The 8th Air Force lost 69 Fortresses and 11 fighter planes in that attack. One of the Fortresses shot down on the March 6 attack was from the 379th Group. Eighth Air Force gunners aboard the Fortresses returning from that mission claimed 97 enemy planes. Escorting U.S. fighters shot down 82 Luftwaffe planes that day, as shown on film in their gun-cameras.

The March 6, 1944, mission was the most costly heavy bomber mission for the 8th Air Force during World War II. The six most costly 8th Air Force missions in terms of heavy bombers lost are as follows:

Heaviest Losses of the 8th Air Force during WW II

August	17	1943	60	Schweinfurt/ Regensburg
October	14	1943	60	Schweinfurt
January	11	1944	60	Oschersleben, et al
March	6	1944	69	Berlin
April	11	1944	64	Berlin
April	29	1944	64	Berlin
			377	

Twelve of these 377 bombers were from the 379th Bomb Group; six of the 12 were lost on the October 14, 1943, mission. (There are two other missions on which the 379th Bomb Group lost its record-tying number of six planes per mission, as detailed in Chapter 4.)

Schweinfurt, Regensburg, Oschersleben and Berlin were

terribly rough missions for flight crews of the 8th Air Force. Schweinfurt is remembered by many as the most deadly target in Germany. Based on largest number of bomber losses on a single mission, Berlin was statistically much worse than Schweinfurt or the others, as shown above. On a percentage basis, Schweinfurt was more than twice as bad as Berlin:

October 14, 1943 60 lost out of 257 attacking Schweinfurt = 23.3%
March   6, 1944 69 lost out of 658 attacking Berlin = 10.5%

The 8th Air Force, including the 379th Bomb Group, hit Berlin again on March 9. The 379th was one of the Groups that bombed Berlin on March 22. Its target on that mission was the German Air Ministry Headquarters. Another attack by the 8th Air Force against Berlin was made on April 11. The 379th took part in another Berlin raid on April 29.

Today's mission to Berlin was the second during May for the 379th Bomb Group. It was the 379th's sixth Berlin mission of the war, and the eighth attack on Berlin by the 8th Air Force. On this day the 379th would finish what it started on May 4. The target was the same—an aircraft component plant.

We left the briefing room, picked up our flight gear and rode in customary style to the pad on which Screwball Express was waiting. In accordance with USAF custom, none of us breathed a word about the location of this mission's target. Joe Starbuck, chief of our ground crew, spoke to me very quietly after I completed my initial check of the bomb bay and the bombsight. "Lieutenant," he said, "would you come over to the tent with me for a minute?" There were numerous tents around the pad. The ground crew slept and played cards in the largest tent while we were on a mission. There was a tent in which they stored and cleaned guns, and a tent that contained a large supply of all sorts of things. There was also a makeshift tent to which I had never paid much attention. It measured about eight feet long on each side, and was about the same height. A government-issue padlock and a webbed strap secured the flap that served as the tent's door. Sgt. Joe reached into his pocket and removed a key with which he opened the padlock. Almost ceremoniously, he slowly pulled the door's flap aside and motioned for me to enter.

In the middle of the tent was a platform that measured about five feet square and four feet high. The platform was made of scrap lumber and its sides were fashioned from aluminum salvaged from the fuselage of a crashed B-17. The platform's sides were painted a patriotic red, white and blue. Steps at the front of the platform provided easy access to a wicker chair that was securely bolted to the exact center of the unique structure.

There was an appropriately sized hole in the seat of the wicker chair. Directly under it another hole had been sawed out of the platform. A practice bomb of the M-38 type stood upright on its tail fins, under the hole in the platform. The sand filler, the nose cone and the black powder charge had been removed from the M-38. Then came the dawn! The ingenious contraption was the ground crew's "throne." The M-38 was full of 'you know what.' Signatures of ground crew members who contributed to the weeks of accumulation were scrawled all over the bomb. Printed in big letters were the words, "Poop on Adolph." (The first word is an alternate for the original.)

Joe spoke in a very convincing manner. "You're going to Berlin today," he said, "and the ground crew of Screwball

Express wants her first mission to Berlin to carry very special meaning." Pointing to the blue M-38 "bomb" Joe asked, "Can we put it aboard?"

There was no point in asking Joe how he knew the Group was going to Berlin. He knew! There was no way I could give him permission to load his special "bomb" into the bomb bay of Screwball Express. Leaving Joe standing by the "throne," I walked out of the tent and busied myself with the rest of the flight crew in making preparations for takeoff. I swung myself up and into the escape hatch at the front of the plane and squirmed into the nose section of Screwball Express. I rechecked the bombing data that I would enter in the bombsight after we were over Germany.

Screwball Express was assigned the Lead position in the Low Squadron of High Group "A". Our bomb load weighed 5,500 pounds. The bomb bay of Screwball Express contained 3-1,000 pound demolition bombs and 5-500 pound incendiary bombs. Our High Group "A" took to the air at 0600 hours. Since this was our crew's first mission to Berlin, words of the 23rd Psalm took on special meaning. The 23 planes in our High Group climbed for the assembly altitude. Two of our three spares returned early according to plan, and the remaining spare filled in with another Group.

Before we were high enough to require oxygen masks, I started back to the bomb bay to arm the bombs. This was always done early to make certain there was enough time to do it right. It was also wise to do it when I did not have to carry a portable oxygen bottle. Frank stopped me as I started to crawl past his top turret position. "I've already armed the bombs for you, Lieutenant," he said. I considered it very cooperative of him. He had watched me arm bombs many times, had occasionally assisted me and knew what to do. I gave him a "thank you" salute and crawled back to my position in the nose of the plane.

This was our crew's first mission into Germany since April 24. One aircraft in each of our two Groups carried propaganda leaflets. The brief openings in the clouds made the North Sea look very forbidding. We crossed the enemy coast and climbed to our briefed bombing altitude of 27,000 feet, the highest at which we had flown Screwball Express. Howard and Jim filled the intercom with praise for the way our plane handled at that altitude.

Today the 1st Bombardment Division was assigned to Berlin. Several of its Groups were assigned to various targets of opportunity. The 2nd Division's B-24s were assigned targets at Munster in western Germany, and at Osnabruck in the northwestern part of that country. Fortresses of the 3rd Division were assigned targets in Berlin, targets of opportunity and the Liege marshalling yards in Belgium. German targets were attacked in the morning through 9/10 and 10/10 cloud cover. Bombing of the Liege marshalling yards was in the afternoon. Seventeen Combat Wings were divided into five bomber forces and escorted by 20 Groups of USAF fighter planes and four Squadrons of RAF Mustangs. The number of U.S. planes in the air set a new record for the 8th Air Force—more than 1,000 American heavy bombers, flanked and covered by almost as many U.S. fighter planes.

At 1019 hours Flying Fortress number 42-31927 in the High Group of Wing "B" bombed a target of opportunity, a railroad station, at Witezen. For some reason it was flying at 8,000 feet. Its bombing results were good. Fifteen FW-190s made one weak attack at the lone bomber but failed to shoot it down. Unbelievable!

Our 41st Combat Wing "A" approached the Berlin area from the northwest, and turned to the south so that we flew abreast of the city's west side. When we were southwest of Berlin our formation made a long, sweeping turn to the left and crossed our IP on a magnetic heading of 38 degrees. We imagined we could hear the announcers at Berlin's radio stations interrupting air raid alerts with, "Gustav, Gustav," the code for Berlin's Tempelhof airport located in the south part of Berlin. Without doubt, Germany's Exchange 500 was especially busy. It was the largest telephone and communications center in Germany, and linked Hitler with the German Army High Command and all field commanders in Germany and its occupied countries.

Crew of Lt. Thomas M. Smith, whose B-17 Ser. No. 42-37791 was downed by flak on the crew's first mission, May 7, 1944, at Berlin. (Photo made by 379th BG Photographic Section, April 29, 1944, provided by James C. Moore) See page 68.

The bomb bay doors of our Group's Lead plane began to open. Bombardiers in our other planes acted simultaneously, and doors of all bomb bays in our Group yawned in perfect unison. Our formation was on its bomb run and everything was set for an ideal PFF approach to our release point. Suddenly, hundreds of flak shells exploded at our altitude within seconds of each other. The German gunners in the flak towers below were very good at their specialty. Their shells exploded at exactly 27,000 feet, and about 700 feet diagonally to our right. That was excellent marksmanship—we were a moving target, traveling at a ground speed of nearly 250 m.p.h. and more than five miles in the air. The flak came very close to scoring direct hits on all 20 of our planes! The shiver that went down my spine might have been caused by the -42 degree temperature outside the nose compartment of Screwball Express. I believe it was caused by that abominable flak and the expertise of the German gun crews.

The aiming point for our Lead Fortress was the Friedrichstrasse Railway and Underground Station, several blocks from our target. The aiming point used by the lead bomber was almost always short of the actual target. This compensated for the brief amount of time required for other bombardiers to react after seeing the bombs drop from the lead plane. In the near vicinity of our aiming point were the Gestapo Headquarters, German Presidential Chancellery building, the German Air Ministry Headquarters and four departmental buildings of the German Reich. We were unable to see any part of this particular area of Berlin because of the 10/10 cloud cover. A big barrage of flak filled the air directly in front of our formation. Screwball Express flew in tight formation with our Group to that invisible point in the clouds where the Pathfinder plane automatically signaled for the release of bombs. It was so theoretically simple—providing all the bombing and navigational data were correctly calculated and accurately set into assorted instruments at various locations in the Lead Fortress. The success of the entire theory depended on no more than a few of our planes being shot down, and on our formation not being scattered by enemy opposition. The wall of flak around Berlin measured 20 miles across. It was an extremely frightening experience.

The eyes of 19 bombardiers in our "A" Group were focused on the bomb bay of our Lead plane. We were still at 27,000 feet and on a magnetic heading of 38 degrees. Our air speed was an indicated 150 m.p.h. Air density and temperature at our altitude gave us a true air speed of nearly 215 m.p.h. The tail wind added another 33 m.p.h. At 1115 hours Screwball Express and the 19 other Fortresses in our Group dropped bomb loads of eight bombs each—5,500 pounds of explosives and incendiaries—from each of our bombers. I leaned forward and watched the bombs of Screwball Express fall toward the mass of clouds that blanketed everything between our formation and our target.

Then I saw it. The blue M-38 "bomb" from the ground crew's "throne room" was right in the middle of the bombs I had just released. Everyone from the top turret position back to the tail of the plane knew it was in the bomb bay with the other bombs; Howard, Jim, Bob and I were the only ones "not in the know." I watched with mixed emotions as our bombs disappeared from view. Our formation turned away from the target area and headed for home.

The bombs we had just dropped would strike the target in about 45 seconds. My mind filled with a vision of the coming event. At a temperature of -42 degrees the contents of that "bomb" were frozen solid—hard as a rock. Ingredients in the "bomb" would be fragmented into many bits and pieces upon impact. Chunks of it would fly in every direction. Then the stuff would lie around and thaw. It would really raise a stink.

I remembered the profound advice my father gave me when I was about five years old. My parents and I were visiting my grandmother who lived on a small farm. Dad and I were sitting in the shade of an oak tree in the back yard, admiring the tall, green corn in a nearby field. He explained to me how fertilizer helped make the corn grow. In those days, most fertilizer was the kind dropped in barns and fields by horses and cows. To help me understand the fertilizing capability of animal waste, Dad said, "As you can see, the grass is greener by the outhouse."

Our Group's bombs were hitting the target as I pondered that childhood moment from the past. My thoughts included the present and the future. The grass would be greener in Berlin, too.

Aircraft number 42-37791 from our 526th Squadron was hit by flak over the target, left the formation and disappeared into the clouds. That plane carried the crew of 2nd Lt. Thomas M. Smith of the 526th Squadron. It was his crew's first combat mission. His bunk in our Nissen hut was close to mine. He was from St. Louis, Missouri, on the Mississippi River and only 20 miles from my home town of Edwardsville, Illinois. Flak also hit aircraft 42-38161 from the 525th Squadron of our Group. That aircraft, carrying the crew of lst Lt. Clarence E. Darnell, managed to stay with our formation for several minutes, but then fell behind and was also swallowed by the clouds beneath us. My mind visualized the 18 black bags that would be at four of the Kimbolton barracks before nightfall.

Earlier that morning, German radio broadcasts warned listeners of large U.S. bomber formations heading toward Berlin. They were now also reporting a major U.S. air armada over other parts of Germany. Berlin radioed Stockholm, Sweden, that American raiders were storming against the German capital in three waves for a period of more than one hour. The radio broadcast also said bad weather hampered their air and ground defenses, and described the attack on Berlin as "a terror raid."

Our formation encountered meager flak at seven locations during the mission. We were attacked by moderate flak at six other sites, but most of it was inaccurate. The flak around and over Berlin, however, was heavy and very accurate. Of the 38 Fortresses in our "A" and "B" Groups, two of them were lost because of flak and 20 others received minor to medium flak damage while in the target area. Screwball Express had more than eighty small flak holes in its wings and fuselage.

Our crew had completed our 16th combat mission. Only nine more left. Howard and Jim maneuvered Screwball Express to a perfect landing and taxied to the parking pad. The flying time on this mission was nine hours. Joe and his ground crew looked in the bomb bay the moment the props stopped turning. When they saw the bomb bay was empty they had one question. "Is it in Berlin?" I responded with an affirmative wink. They yelled so loudly they must have been heard down the hill in Kimbolton. Everyone in the ground crew acted as though they had made a personal and major contribution to the winning of the war.

I put my hand on Joe's shoulder and walked him a few yards away from the whooping members of the ground and flight crews. He spoke before I could say anything. "Lieutenant, when I asked you if I could put it aboard, you didn't say I couldn't."

As our flight crew was being trucked over to debriefing I said something sarcastic to Frank about his 'arming the bombs' for me. Howard made a few choice comments for my benefit. Jim and Bob pretended they didn't hear what Howard said. The other fellows in our crew kept looking out the back of the truck—grinning like cats in a room filled with fat mice.

The 8th Air Force lost eight B-17s (two of which were from the 379th Bomb Group) and a B-24 during the day's operation. Six of the B-17's were from the 1st Bomb Division while over Berlin. The B-24 ditched in the English Channel. Minor flak damage was incurred by 247 B-17s and 75 B-24s. Major flak damage was done to 24 B-17s and one B-24.

Four U.S. fighter aircraft were lost—one P-51 and one P-47 to flak, and two P-38s. Both P-38s ditched in the Channel, one of them after it caught on fire. The pilot of that plane was picked up by Air-Sea Rescue.

Personnel casualties resulting from today's 8th Air Force operation included two bomber crew members killed, 20 wounded and 86 missing in action. The day's 86 MIAs included the l8 from the 379th Bomb Group.

Surprisingly, none of the planes in our Group were attacked by enemy fighters during the more than 1,200 miles round trip to Berlin. The 8th Air Force reported weak enemy fighter opposition during the entire day, and no enemy aircraft were claimed by our fighters or bombers.

Our 41st Combat Wing "A" dropped 76.5 tons of demolition bombs and 63.3 tons of incendiaries on Berlin during this attack. Photo reconnaissance the next day showed results of our Group's bombing were very good. The 1st Bomb Division dropped 473 tons of demolition bombs and 310 tons of incendiaries. Total bomb tonnage dropped by the 8th Air Force during this operation included 1,482 tons of demolition bombs and 806 tons of incendiary bombs.

And the war went on.

_____

May 8   379th's 3rd Double Mission day. Aircraft Component plant, Berlin—in a.m. Fly-bomb site, Sottevast, France—in p.m. Lt. Gilbert C. Heath's crew in Screwball Express to Sottevast (Our crew was "stood down"—flew 3:45 hr. training mission)

May 9   Our crew on 3:00 hr. training mission. 379th Group bombed Fly-bomb site at Thionville, Fr. (Our crew was "stood down")

May 11   Mission to Munich scrubbed. 379th Group bombed railroad yards at Ehrang, Germany. Our crew was "stood down"

Sometime in May   We were dispatched early in the A.M. to the 384th airfield at Grafton Underwood; crew to fly Screwball Express with that Group on a mission. After we landed at Grafton Underwood, Howard went to 384th's Headquarters for specific information. The rest of our crew waited at the hardstand where Screwball Express was being refueled and loaded with bombs. While we waited for Howard to return, Frank mentioned to a captain who was "shooting the breeze" with us that we had not yet eaten breakfast. The captain left us with the promise that we would not fly today's mission until we had some food. Howard returned to the hardstand and told us we would not be flying with the 384th Bomb Group that day.

Another flight crew arrived at the hardstand and boarded Screwball Express. While our lower jaws were suspended in speechlessness, that crew taxied our plane to the main runway and took off.

We spent the next six and one-half hours moaning, groaning and eating lunch. Finally, we saw planes of the 384th Group returning to the airfield. Screwball Express had made it back! We jumped to our feet when we saw two red flares fired from it. Wounded aboard! After it landed we rushed to the hardstand to check its condition. The tail section of Screwball Express was filled with flak holes. The waist section was also damaged. We discovered flak had killed the tail gunner and injured two other members of that crew. Our crew was filled with mixed emotions—saddened by the death and injuries aboard our plane, but thankful we had been spared.

In August, 1989, I asked Howard if he knew why our crew had not flown the 384th Bomb Group's mission. His response was typical of a first class B-17 commander. He told me, "The 384th only wanted part of our crew to fly that mission." (Howard said he could not remember which crew members.) Howard added, "I told them our crew had already flown 16 missions together, we intended to fly all our missions together, and I did not want to split up our crew by only part of it flying that mission."

And that's the way it was!

(**Special Credit:** Please refer to *Fortresses of the Big Triangle First; Flying Fortress, The Illustrated Biography of the B-17s and the Men Who Flew Them; Flying Forts - The B-17 in World War II; Simon and Schuster Encyclopedia of World War II; and The World War II Wuiz and Fact Book*; under Bibliography.)

Screwball Express enroute to Merseburg, Germany, May 12, 1944. (Photo from 379th BG Photo. Sec.)

Mission to Merseburg

Friday, May 12, 1944. Today is the 23rd birthday of Jerold Lindsey, our tail gunner.

Our crew was awakened at 0400 for a briefing at 0530. Screwball Express was airborne at 0820. I sang the 23rd Psalm in a very prayerful way. Our safe return would mean we had completed two-thirds of our combat tour.

Screwball Express flew in the company of 17 other B-17's in Lead Group "A" of the 41st Combat Wing. Our assigned position was in the Low Squadron. The 379th Bomb Group also provided 24 Fortresses for the Low Group in this Wing. Four spares in the Low Group returned early, according to plan, and B-17 number 42-31779 in that Group later aborted.

Our target was the I. G. Farbine synthetic oil refinery and chemical plant at Merseburg, Germany. The plant was located approximately 16 miles west of Leipzig. Attacks on twelve of our crew's missions thus far were directed at targets which included Luftwaffe airfields and the German aircraft industry. This was our crew's first mission to bomb an oil refinery.

In late January, 1943, the American and British Combined Chiefs of Staff held the Casablanca Conference. They agreed on a plan that placed an order of priority on the aerial bombardment of targets in the war with Germany. The priority order of the proposed objectives were: 1) German Submarine Construction, 2) German Aircraft Industry, 3) Transportation, 4) Oil Plants, and 5) other targets in enemy war territory. However, the priority of these targets did not reflect the realities of strategic bombing. In fact, the agreement specified the general directive of the Allied strategic air offensive to be 1) destruction of Germany's industrial system and 2) undermining of Germany's morale. (Please refer to chart titled 8th Air Force Aerial Bombing Objectives.)

Following a series of unsuccessful American and British bombing raids on German submarine construction yards, it became obvious that bombing techniques required much improvement, or that other targets be given a higher priority. Fortunately for the Allies, the U-Boat menace was lessened by the end of 1943, because it was given lower priority by the German high command. Admiral Karl Doenitz claimed that to abandon his U-Boat campaign would subject Germany's cities to terrible ordeals because Allied bombing raids were growing in ferocity. He was not mistaken.

The Allies shifted bombing priority to the German aircraft industry during the early months of 1944. This accounts for the large percentage of 379th Bomb Group attacks against airfields and aircraft plants during that time. After the Luftwaffe had been greatly reduced in size, Allied bombing priority shifted to Germany's oil industry. This did not mean the Luftwaffe could be ignored, because it was able to strike back very effectively on many future occasions.

Germany's Achilles heel was petroleum. Its 58 oil refineries and 23 synthetic oil plants were its weakness. Reduction of Germany's oil supply would affect the weakened Luftwaffe and also curtail activities of the German army and navy. Transportation would also suffer. The entire German war machine would fail without an adequate supply of petroleum.

Fifteen Combat Wings, consisting of 886 heavy bombers, proceeded south of Frankfurt and Brunswick to a point south of the Ruhr, and then east and northeast to the target area. Twenty-one USAF fighter Groups provided escort by 576 fighters of the 8th and 9th Air Forces. The 1st Bombardment Division's B-17s had oil refineries at Merseburg (Leuna) and Lutzkendorf for their targets. The 2nd Bomb Division's B-24s went after the refineries at Zeitz and Bohlen. The 3rd Division's B-17s attacked the Brux oil refinery in Czechoslovakia and the aircraft components plant at Zwickau, south of Leipzig. Bombers of the 15th Air Force headed for the refineries at Ploesti, Rumania.

Near Frankfurt, between 150-200 German aircraft attacked the 45th's "A&B" Combat Wing of the 3rd Bomb Division. Most of the attacks were in mass fighter formations, with 30 or more bandits coming in abreast of each other, firing savagely and even ramming the B-17s. The 45th's "A&B" Wing lost 22 of its 66 bombers in fierce attacks and became very disorganized. Escorting P-47s and P-51s came to the rescue and the Wing's 44 remaining bombers continued on the mission. However, 33 of the 45th's bombers had to attack targets of opportunity. Only 11 of the 45th's original 66-plane formation bombed primary targets. Other Bomb Groups also saw strong enemy fighter opposition, while some Groups saw none. Our Group saw only one enemy plane—a lone FW-190—during the entire mission. Luck was on our side. The 23rd Psalm made a lot of good sense.

Fortresses in the three Bomb Groups in our Wing each carried 38-100 pound demolition bombs. Flak en route to and at our target was heavy and very accurate. Other Groups bombed the target area beginning at 1338 hours. We bombed through smoke and haze from 24,000 feet at 1409 hours, on a magnetic heading of 29 degrees. Our bombs fell into the middle of the cloud of smoke that covered installations in the central part of the oil refinery. Photo reconnaissance later showed our bombing results were very good. The principal damage was along the western side of the plant, with scattered hits on the northern three-quarters of the refinery. Fires were visible on the hydrogen contact houses, liquid ammonia tanks, several other chemical installations and on numerous buildings. A total of 459 tons of bombs were dropped on this target by 1420 hours. Smoke from the fires rose to 17,000 feet. The target was completely wiped out.

After we turned away from the target Joe Milworm called me on the intercom from the radio room. "Lieutenant," he said, "we've still got one of your bombs in the bomb bay. Would you please get rid of it PDQ—sir?"

Muttering into my oxygen mask, I disconnected it from the main oxygen line and snapped the hose of my mask onto a portable oxygen bottle. This allowed enough oxygen for me to crawl back to the bomb bay and take a look at the problem. Frank Craig was waiting for me there and was also using a portable oxygen bottle. One of the 100-pound demolition bombs was still hanging from the end of one of the lower bomb shackles. The arming wire was still in place, and the arming vane had not spun off. The bomb was still "safe". The solution to the problem was for me to "kick" the bomb out of the bomb bay.

I removed my chest-pack parachute from its harness to allow for greater mobility. With extreme caution, I positioned my right foot on the underpart of the bomb bay's catwalk. I held tightly to the superstructure of the catwalk with both hands and Frank took hold of my parachute harness. I stomped on the bomb with my left foot.

Frank and I were reminded of the similar experience we shared in an open bomb bay during a training flight while stationed at Ardmore, Oklahoma. In that situation, we were flying at a much lower altitude and did not require use of the oxygen system. Today we were dealing with a real bomb, and at high altitude. We required oxygen in order to survive. Joe handed additional oxygen bottles to Frank and me when we signaled for them. We removed the spent bottles and snapped our masks' hoses onto the fresh bottles. I stomped repeatedly

on that bomb. During the next exchange of oxygen bottles, I failed to properly snap the fresh one onto my mask's hose. After a few seconds I began to feel dizzy. I tightened my grasp on the catwalk's framework and prepared for another kick at the bomb. Before I could deliver the kick, the bomb dropped from its shackle. At the same moment I realized my grasp on the catwalk's structure was loosening. I was passing out from lack of oxygen. Most fortunately, Frank had a very tight hold on my parachute harness, or I would have followed that bomb into Germany. Frank and Tom quickly pulled me onto the catwalk and then into the radio room. They plugged my mask into the main oxygen system. My mind cleared, but I couldn't find words to adequately express my thanks to Frank. His response was, "You sure are heavy."

A bombardier and a waist gunner in planes flying our left and right wing positions were injured by flak over the target. A navigator in another of our Group's planes was killed. He was a member of the 525th Squadron.

The 8th Air Force lost 42 bombers during the day's operation. Most of the losses were caused by enemy fighter planes. Ironically, this happened when the Luftwaffe was believed to have been weakened. Thirty-seven of the 42 MIA Fortresses were from the 3rd Division. Bomber crews claimed 115 enemy aircraft, and another 75 were shot down by 8th Air Force fighter pilots. Stars and Stripes reported later that one of our fighter pilots, 1st Lt. Robert J. Rankin, of Washington, reported shooting down five enemy aircraft during today's mission— the second ETO pilot to make a five-in-one-day score.

Of the 190 enemy planes claimed in the preceding paragraph, only 60 are acknowledged in German records. Those records also state the Luftwaffe shot down 81 of our fighters that day. Records of the 8th AF say it was 10.

Flak was observed at Dunkirk, Koblenz, Fulda, Limburg, Ath, Namur, Erfurt, Weimar, Crammont and Eisenach. Some of the antiaircraft guns looked as if they were underground, or in trenches covered with camouflaged netting. Although chaff was used frequently by our Group, it did not appear to be very effective. Thirty-three of our Group's 37 bombers on this mission received flak damage. Only three pieces hit Screwball Express.

Some of our crews reported seeing rockets in the target area. Heavy traffic was reported in the Namur marshalling yards. A B-17 was seen burning on the ground at 5022-0848E. Seven barges were on the Rhine River at 5010-0742E. Another B-17 was seen in the water at 5113-0200E. One of its dinghies was floating nearby, and this was reported through Air-Sea rescue channels.

Seventeen of our missions were completed. This mission had lasted 9:00 hours and was another rough one.

An article in the next day's Stars and Stripes made the following comment about the May 12, 1944, raids on Germany's oil industry:

"As the heavies switched suddenly to a new kind of objective in the campaign to paralyze the German war machine before the western invasion, American and British medium, light and fighter-bombers kept up the pounding of airfields and rail targets in France and Belgium with a follow-up to the RAF's night blows against rail yards at Boulogne and Louvain, and other targets in the same countries."

(**Special Credit:** Please refer to *The Marshall Cavendish Illustrated Encyclopedia of World War II;* and *Flying Fortress, The Illustared Biography of the B-17s and the Men Who Flew Them;* under Bibliography.)

Mission to Stettin

Saturday, May 13, 1944. The 379th's primary target was an aircraft component plant at Poznan, Poland. The city is located 165 miles west of Warsaw and is also known as Posen. This was one of the longest combat missions ever attempted by any Flying Fortress Bomb Group.

The CQ barged into our Nissen hut at 0400 hours. He awakened Jim, Bob, Howard and me, and other officers of some of the crews in our barracks. He told us we were flying a mission today, and in the process woke everyone in the barracks. There were grunts from those of us who had barely returned from the previous day's attack at Merseburg. Others in the barracks grunted because of being awakened even though they were not part of today's raid. People in all branches of the military grunted when they woke up. It seemed like it was the right thing to do. Waking up with a smile was reserved for eager beavers, optimists, and jerks.

We partly dressed and hit the latrine. Our morning ritual there was performed in an orderly routine. First, the urinal—then shave—brush teeth and comb hair. Completion of the routine was hurriedly done at bunk-side by putting on a pair of trousers, a shirt, a pair of shoes and a jacket. Finishing touches included pulling up the solitary zipper, fastening six buttons and tying two shoelaces. Dress code in the ETO apparently insisted the jacket remain open with the collar turned up. Leaving the barracks for the mess hall on mission days invariably included running through the doorway. Once outside, we always paused to set our caps on the top, right side of the head, sharply angled over the right eye.

After chow, we hurried to the 0530 briefing. We were informed the 379th Bomb Group was to furnish 18 planes for the Lead Group and 24 for the Low Group. Screwball Express was assigned to lead the Low Squadron of the Low Group.

The wheels of Screwball Express lifted from the north/south runway of the Kimbolton air base at 0910 hours. They would not touch the ground at Kimbolton until 2010 hours, after 11 hours of combat flying time. Three spares in the Low Group returned early as planned. Aircraft 42-30720 filled in with the 457th Bomb Group of the 94th Combat Wing.

According to my custom, I prayed by singing the 23rd Psalm. "The Lord is my shepherd; I shall not want." My prayer included all the men in my crew, not only myself. It included everyone in the air on this day's operation—all crew members in the 379th Bomb Group's planes, all the men in all bombers and fighters of the 8th and 9th Air Force, the RAF—everybody!

The weekend offensive against the Reich was carried by 750 heavy bombers of the 8th Air Force. Nearly 1,000 8th and 9th Air Force P-38s, P-51s and P-47s, as well as P-51s of the Second Tactical Air Force (RAF), provided escort to the bombers. Approximately 8,000 American and British airmen flew during this day's operation.

Weather was somewhat favorable during our Wing's assembly, but information provided during the morning's briefing warned us to expect heavy cloud formations throughout much of the mission. We headed north-northeast as we crossed the English coast at 10,000 feet over Cromer. The wind was blowing 25 m.p.h. from the south as our formation went up to 12,000 feet.

An exchange of leadership took place about 10 miles north of Helgoland, one of the North Frisian Islands, in the North Sea. At approximately 1245 hours Major Lloyd C. Mason, the leader of our Low Group in aircraft 42-31394, radioed he was aborting the mission and returning to base because of a mechanical failure in his Fortress. The 379th Bomb Group's consecutive-non-abortive Group Leads ended at 153. The increased strain on our B-17s and ground crews, caused by the stepped-up bombing campaign, brought this enviable record to an end. The Group's High Squadron Lead took over as Group Lead. This responsibility fell upon 1st Lt. Clay W. Hedges and his lead crew which included 2nd Lt. Chester W. Paulson, co-pilot; F/O Walter Mueller, navigator; and 2nd Lt. William J. McAloon, Jr., bombardier. This crew was assigned to the 526th Squadron and was flying in aircraft number 42-38058.

At 1255 hours our Low Group crossed into enemy territory near Mildstadt, Germany, flying at 12,000 feet. Our flight plan took us across the northern neck of Germany to Eckernforde where a smoke screen attempted to hide the city from our view. Twelve medium ships and three large ships were in the harbor at Kiel. We flew over Fehmarn Island to a point south of Ribnitz-Damgarten. Seaplanes were at anchor on the water at Damgarten and near the docks at Rostock. Our altitude was increased to 14,000 feet where we changed course to a southeasterly compass heading. The wind changed to 165 degrees and increased to 38 m.p.h.

The weather was fairly clear until we passed the southeastern part of the Danish peninsula. At that point the cloud cover over the Baltic Sea and inland into northeastern Germany became very heavy. In a matter of minutes we were unable to see the ground because of 10/10 undercast. The decision was made to forget the aircraft components plant at Poznan, Poland, and to attack the secondary target at Stettin, Germany.

Bombing today at either Poznan or Stettin would require using the Pathfinder technique. Stettin was 125 miles closer to Kimbolton than was Poznan. Bombing at Poznan would require flying an additional 250 miles. We agreed with the Group Leader's decision to bomb at Stettin.

Stettin and the area around it contained many military targets. The most notable of these included chemical and rubber plants, metallurgical industries and shipbuilding facilities. Stettin is on the border of German and Poland, approximately 75 miles north-northeast of Berlin, and 10 miles south of the mouth of the Oder river. Its location made it an important seaport with access to the Pomeranian Bay in the southern Baltic Sea. (Nearly one year later, on April 26, 1945, Stettin was overtaken by Soviet troops after a long siege and bitter battle. It was assigned to Poland by the Potsdam Conference in 1945, and the city's name was changed to Szczecin.)

Our Combat Wing climbed to our assigned bombing altitude of 23,000 feet. Cloud cover ahead of us was 10/10 as far as we could see. Long before we reached the target area the decision to bomb by PFF was confirmed.

Southeast of Rostock an enemy fighter attacked and heavily damaged aircraft 42-97502 flown by 1st Lt. Joseph Marinello and his crew. This Fortress was from our 527th Squadron. It went down at 1415 hours with its number four engine and right wing on fire. Eight parachutes came out of the plane as it went into a dive. More enemy fighters joined the attack on our Low Group. At 1420 hours aircraft 42-

31972 from the 527th Squadron dropped its bombs in order to maintain altitude after being heavily damaged by one of the Luftwaffe planes. This Fortress was flown by the crew of 1st Lt. John E. Wilds, Jr., and was also in our Low Group. At 1432 hours, its number one engine feathered and on fire, this aircraft dropped out of our formation and went down under control. No 'chutes were seen coming from this plane.

The flight plan called for our Combat Wing to fly south and east of Stettin and then turn sharply around and make what we hoped would be a surprise attack on a vulcanizing plant and rubber factory. Before we made that turn our Group was attacked by 75 enemy planes for a period of 15 minutes. Most of the attackers were Me-109s and FW-190s, but Me-210s, Me-410s and JU-88s were among them. The majority of the attacks started in front of our formation, between 10 and 2 o'clock, and came from a high position. They swept through our formation, returned from the rear and set up for an additional frontal attack. I saw two B-17s in another formation get shot down by the bandits. Gunners in our Group later claimed six enemy planes destroyed and two damaged.

Our fighter escorts were very good, but were outnumbered in the area around Stettin. They engaged in many dog fights, and we saw five enemy planes shot down by our P-51s and P-47s. At 1500 hours, before we turned on our bomb run, aircraft number 42-107082 in our Low Group was hit by an enemy fighter and the bomber's left wing was set afire. It was flying our left wingman position when it was hit. Two parachutes were seen coming out of the plane before it disappeared into clouds southeast of Stettin. This plane carried the crew of 1st Lt. Robert M. Dunn, Jr. of the 526th Squadron.

(The August 1991 issue of *Contrails*, a publication of the 379th Bomb Group WW II Association, states that all nine members of Lt. Dunn's crew parachuted safely but were captured and spent the duration of the war in a German POW camp. Their aircraft, named Lassie Come Home, stayed airborne on Automatic Pilot until reaching the island of Rugen in the Baltic Sea, and then crashed at Store Heddinge, Denmark.)

Flak along our route across Germany was moderate and fairly accurate, but as we neared the target area the antiaircraft fire became more intense and very accurate. Finally, we reached our IP and turned onto a magnetic heading of 310 degrees. Each of the B-17s in our Low Group had 10-500 pound demolition bombs in its bombbay. Fragments of an exploding antiaircraft shell put our radio equipment out of order. Two pieces of flak hit the armor plate behind the butt of the chin turret's guns, preventing the flak from entering the nose compartment of Screwball Express. Our Group leader dropped his bombs at 1520.5 hours using PFF. Bombs in the 15 remaining B-17s in our Low Group were salvoed at that same time. The cloud cover over the target opened up enough for us to see our bomb strikes and record them on the bomb bay cameras. A rocket was fired at us from the target area. Photos of our bomb strikes showed later that we had effectively bombed the Free Harbor area in which the vulcanizing plant and rubber factory were located. Our bombing results were described as "excellent." Large explosions were everywhere in the immediate target area. Small flak holes were everywhere in Screwball Express.

Leaving the target, we turned to the north and flew to the Baltic coast near Dziwnow, Poland. Our formation then headed northwest until we were far out over the Baltic Sea and away from antiaircraft guns. A group of P-51 fighters joined us and escorted our formation westwardly to Denmark's east coast. Our formation was greeted by a 20 mm rocket, fired at us from the ground, as we flew over Hjelm. We continued across Denmark and left enemy territory as we flew over Romo Island at 1652 hours and at an altitude of 15,000 feet.

Two hours, three minutes and 30 seconds later, we crossed the English coast over The Wash at an altitude of 2,500 feet. The weather had cleared up a bit, and England was a very welcomed sight.

We observed flak on this mission at Flensburg, Romo Island, Kiel, Arnis, Vordinborg, Kaaplen, Thumby, Gartz and Juvre. Most of the flak was moderate, but off in deflection. Flak in the Stettin area was the worst of the entire mission. Despite all the flak we encountered on this mission, the three Fortresses we lost today were shot down by enemy fighter planes.

Five B-17s from the 379th had been shot down on two of our crew's last three missions. In less than a week! Forty-five men! Forty-five black bags!

Our 18th combat mission was our second longest—11 hours. It was a rough one!

Only seven more combat missions for our crew to fly.

We didn't know it at this time, but our crew would have another opportunity to bomb a target in Poland—near Poznan—later this month.

May 14 The German people read in their newspapers "—the almost continuous Allied bombing assault was a prelude to the invasion of Europe."

May 15 A Stars and Stripes article about the previous Saturday's operation reported : "12 heavy bombers and 10 fighter planes from the 8th Air Force failed to return; bomber-gunners downed nine enemy fighters; our fighters shot down 54 enemy planes, 17 of which were destroyed by our "little friends" in one Group of P-51s; that Group of Mustangs was commanded by Colonel Joe L. Mason, who personally bagged three of the 17 Nazi fighters."

The same edition of Stars and Stripes told of the P-51's that escorted the B-17s to Stettin, and that also swept into Poland on the deepest penetration of Europe ever made by fighters. It also reported that "P-47 Thunderbolt fighter-bombers thrust 350 miles into Germany on the longest dive-bombing attack ever flown from Britain to hit Bremen's municipal airfield." The report went on: "The Luftwaffe, following its heavy losses in last Friday's assault by U.S. heavy bombers on five synthetic oil plants, was loath to engage the large forces of Allied fighters shepherding the bombers."

May 15 379th Group on mission to Marquise/ Mimoyecques, France, to attack a fly-bomb site. Screwball Express flew this mission, with the crew of Lt. Merlyn P. Wilson aboard. Our crew was "stood down" for this mission.

May 16   A two-day pass to Edinburgh, Scotland, was issued to our crew this morning. Packed quickly and trucked from our airfield to Bedford where we boarded a train to Edinburgh. The trip took most of Tuesday. We decided the two-day pass included parts of three days because it took almost two days just to make the round trip.

Clean rooms were available in a Red Cross Club...an old hotel that had seen its best days more than one hundred years earlier. We looked for Scotsmen in kilts, but found none. We missed a parade that could have satisfied that curiosity.

May 17   On Wednesday we walked the Royal Mile, climbed all the way up to and through Edinburgh Castle, and went to a dance where four Scots entertained about three hundred Allied servicemen by imitating the Mills Brothers of U. S. fame. We drank gin and orange, without any ice, because ice was as scarce in Scotland as it was in England. Besides, the natives didn't like it. (Probably because they could seldom have it.) The Scottish people were very patient with our many questions about their country and traditions. Meeting them in their beautiful homeland made us doubt the stories we had heard about their being miserly. We found them very generous with their friendliness and time, and appreciative of our presence. One shopkeeper was very enterprising. He offered to trace my ancestry and determine my Scottish Clan. He was not the least bit disturbed when I told him I was of German descent. His sales pitch ended when I was persuaded to purchase a silk scarf painted in authentic colors of "the McCassens household."

May 18   After an early breakfast on Thursday, we left for Bedford on the very next train. We arrived at the Kimbolton airfield in the late afternoon. Things had been rather quiet at the base while our crew was gone. Rain had been tapping unique, syncopated rhythms on the metal roofs of the barracks since before we left for Scotland.

Screwball Express had a rest during our absence. It was scheduled for combat missions on May16th to Siracourt, France, and to Wizernes, France, on the 17th, but bad weather scrubbed both missions. We were away for three days and had not missed anything important. What a war!

Mission to Berlin

Friday, May 19, 1944. Two forces of 11 Combat Wings of Flying Fortresses were dispatched to bomb "Big B"—Berlin—fourth largest city in the world. Seven of the Wings were from the 1st Bombardment Division, and the other four from the 3rd Division. The 1st Division provided 413 planes and 250 others were from the 3rd Division.

In addition to the 663 Fortresses scheduled to attack Berlin, the 2nd Division dispatched 331 B-24s to bomb Brunswick. The 994 heavy bombers were escorted by 19 Groups of USAAF fighters.

Today we were in High Group "A" of the 41st Combat Wing and flying Low Squadron Lead. Our bomb bay was filled with 42-100 pound incendiary bombs. The Wing's target was an aircraft component plant in the northern part of Berlin. A variety of other targets was assigned to the different Wings in today's operation. Our crew had flown 15 missions before we had our first opportunity to bomb Germany's capital city. This was our second mission to Berlin in less than two weeks, and we were filled with a special kind of excitement.

The Group's takeoff began at 0900 hours and included 20 Fortresses. Two of our planes aborted because of mechanical failure, one of two spares filled in with another Group, and one plane returned early. Eighteen other planes from our field flew in the 41st Combat Wing "B". Takeoff and assembly were accomplished with difficulty because of weather at Kimbolton airfield and a change in assembly altitude. New instructions were received from the 1st Division ordering a 30-minute delay in departure from the English coast. This resulted in a conglomeration of Forts and Libs in the sky over the radio beacon at Cromer. Our Group made three 360 degree spiraling circles, beginning at 12,000 feet, in order to lose 30 minutes and comply with the new departure time of 1108 hours. At that exact minute we were at the rescheduled altitude of 17,000 feet. The formation tightened itself as we rendezvoused with our Combat Wing over the North Sea and set a northeasterly course for the Danish peninsula.

At some point over the Channel the leader of the 379th's High Group "B" aborted, and that Group's Deputy Leader took over the Lead position. The next string of non-abortive leads was hard to restart.

Cirrus clouds were very prominent and we increased our altitude to 24,500 feet. Our formation turned southeast when we reached a point west of the island of Pellworm. At 1259 hours we crossed into enemy territory at St. Peter-Ordling, Denmark, flying 3,000 feet higher than briefed. We maintained our course until we were north of Hamburg, Germany. Our compass heading was then altered to take us to our IP near Potsdam, southwest of Berlin.

The best fighting altitude for B-17s was believed to be at 22,000 to 26,000 feet. I compared that theory to the experience I had with my Dad's 1936 Dodge while I was in school. It performed much better at 67 m.p.h. than at any other speed. Its miles per gallon were higher at fast speeds, or so I wanted to believe, but the pump at the service station always contested my math when I filled the gas tank. It always delivered more gallons than I thought I had used.

We encountered no flak all the way to Berlin. At 1330 hours, before reaching our IP, we saw a group of enemy fighter planes. We were temporarily without fighter escort, but fortunately, the Luftwaffe did not attack any of the

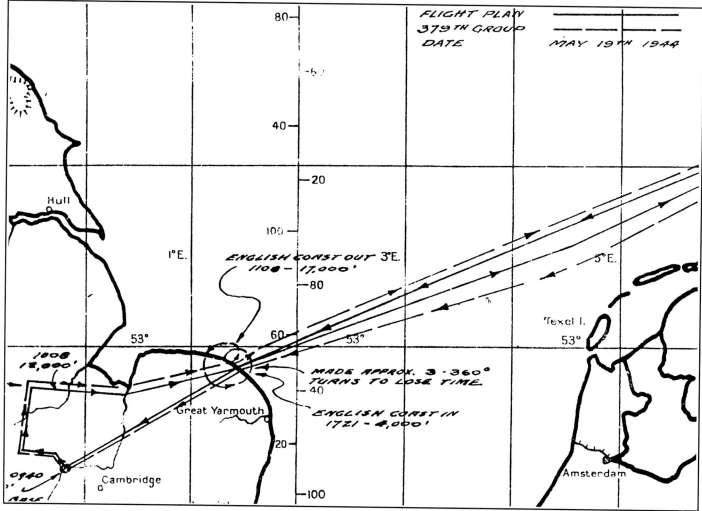

Flight plan of 379th Bomb Group, Kimbolton to Berlin, May 19, 1944.

Fortresses in our Wing. Our "little friends" were undoubtedly looking for us at a lower altitude. Although the enemy later massed two large concentrations of 200 aircraft west of Brunswick and Berlin, effective fighter support diverted most of the attacks from the bomber formations. The heaviest enemy aircraft opposition was encountered by the third force of B-24s, just west of Brunswick. Only one Combat Wing of B-17s attacking Berlin had an encounter with the Luftwaffe. That Wing was in the 1st Division and was attacked by approximately 50 Me-109s and FW-190s a few minutes before it bombed. Another group of 25 bandits made only one head-on attack at that Wing, with only the forward planes doing any firing. Our Wing was lucky, because the attackers flew past our formation without shooting at us.

At the IP our formation turned to the left and flew a magnetic heading of 45 degrees. We were at 27,000 feet, the same altitude from which we had bombed Berlin on May 7th. We were flying almost the same heading as on our crew's first raid on Berlin. Antiaircraft guns began firing at us. Fortunately, our Wing Leader decided to fly a shorter bomb run than briefed. The sky above Berlin became like a crucible filled with deadly, jagged pieces of shrapnel trying to pulverize the metal skin of our B-17s. POOM-POOM——POOM-POOM. Singing the 23rd Psalm during takeoff provided a marvelous comfort zone, but it had become smaller. A large piece of flak came in the left side of Screwball Express, cut through an oxygen line and went out the right side of the aircraft. POOM——POOM-POOM-POOM. Another exploding shell hurled dozens of small pieces of flak into our plane. The entire starboard side of our oxygen system was cut, making it necessary for some of the crew to change to another line. Others of the crew made occasional use of portable oxygen bottles in order to preserve the main oxygen supply. POOM—POOM—POOM——POOM. Flak hit Tom Kiblin, our ball turret gunner, on one of his legs. Luckily, he was only bruised. Antiaircraft shells exploded in every direction and large puffs of black smoke filled the sky around Screwball Express.

Bob Mathews called me on the intercom. "Left waist to bombardier. I'm hit. I'm hit." He stared at the piece of flak sticking out of his pants leg. It was routine for crew members to call their bombardier when making reports and in cases of emergency. Pilots didn't need interruptions, navigators had their thoughts buried in maps, and bombardiers occasionally had time for intercom calls, although certainly not during a bomb run. My face, like my attention, was glued to the bombsight. I didn't have time to respond to the urgency of his call.

Frank asked Mathews. "How bad are you hit?"
Mathews yelled, "I'm hit. I'm hit."
Frank insisted, "How bad is it?" There was no answer.
Frank said, "Pull up your pants leg and see if you're bleeding."

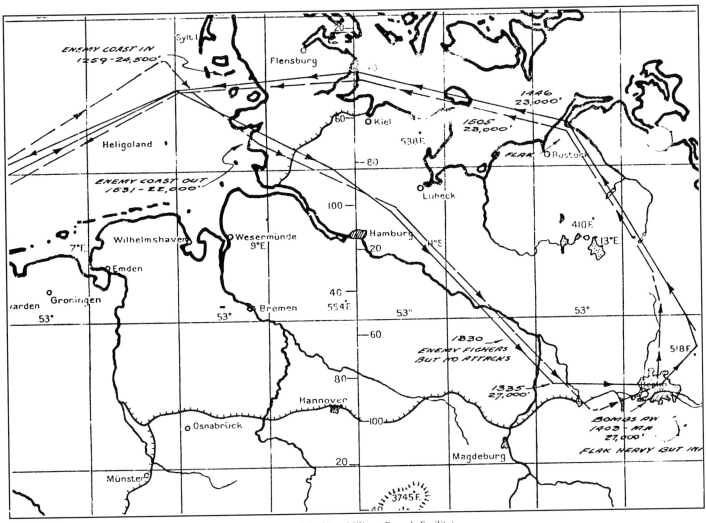

(Photostated from original copy in 379th BG Mission Folder, National Archives Military Records Facility)

Time passed. Mathews responded to Frank, and in a calm voice said,

"I guess I'm o.k."

The bomb run lasted only 30 seconds and was the shortest bomb run our crew ever experienced. Our Wing leader dropped his bombs at 1403 hours. Bombs from Screwball Express and the other 15 planes in our Group followed immediately. Our bombs were released by intervalometer and programmed to strike our target at intervals of 150 feet. Our bomb explosions were visible through breaks in cumulus clouds that extended up to 15,000 feet. The bomb strikes were north of the center of the city, in the Weissensee industrial area.

During the bomb run, aircraft 42-39783 from our Group's 526th Bomb Squadron was severely damaged by what appeared to be a direct hit by antiaircraft fire. That plane carried the crew of 2nd Lt. Merlyn P. Wilson. Just last Monday Lt. Wilson's crew flew Screwball Express on a mission to Marquise/Mimoyecques, France.

Bombing by our Group was done visually, but most Groups used PFF because of 8/10 cloud cover. The bomb pattern of the 51 attacking Fortresses in our Wing was approximately 6,000 feet long and 3,500 feet wide. Our Group's bombing results were recorded as "good." The 18 other Fortresses from Kimbolton, flying in the 41st Combat Wing "B", bombed in the southwest section of Berlin.

Other Combat Wings attacking Berlin on visual bomb runs had generally good bombing results. Heavy damage was done to an area east of the Tiergarten, to the Reichbahn, the Ausbesserungs Werke railway shop, the Schlesischer passenger and freight car repair shop, a bridge over a marshalling yard and a large factory. However, some of the bombs from planes in Groups using PFF fell one to eight miles east and southeast from the center of Berlin into residential and lightly built-up areas and into open fields.

Forty-nine Fortresses in the 94th Division's "B" Combat Wing attacked a secondary target at Kiel with fair results. Fair results were also scored by 272 B-24s at Brunswick. Some of their bombs fell on an industrial plant and two marshalling yards, but the majority hit in the eastern and northeastern parts of the city, causing damage to residential property in lightly built-up areas.

There was always a good feeling among bomber crews about the accurate dropping of bombs on an assigned target. It was a moment of success in the deadly fight with the enemy. It was an action that helped shorten the war. For reasons I cannot justify, there seemed to be very little sensitive thought given to those tragic wartime episodes in which bombs went astray. In retrospect, and most unfortunately, many of those stray bombs greatly magnified the horrors of war.

We saw very little flak or enemy fighters in the immediate vicinity of our formation on the way back to England. Large holes in the clouds allowed us to use pilotage navigation over the German mainland. Our course from the target took us north to Rostock at 1446 hours, generally

P-47s. Seven of our fighters were lost to enemy aircraft and five to antiaircraft fire—the remaining eight to unknown causes. Our fighter planes destroyed 74 Luftwaffe planes in the air, and another 20 planes on the ground.

The 8th Air Force also reported minor battle damage to 269 Fortresses and 164 Liberators. Major damage was done to 65 B-17s and three B-24s. I don't know if the damage to Screwball Express during this mission was listed in the major or minor category. It was probably one of the 65 in the major category, because it had 91 flak holes in its wings, tail and fuselage when it returned to Kimbolton. Two other B-17s in our Group also received major flak damage. We learned at our Group headquarters that another of the 379th's B-17s was missing in action. It is believed this plane was also a victim of flak in the Berlin area.

This was our fourth longest combat mission—nine hours and 35 minutes. Members of our crew now had 19 missions behind us. Only six more to go!

The 379th Bomb Group lost seven Fortresses on three of our crew's four most recent combat missions. Two of those planes were lost to flak on our May 7 raid on Berlin, three others were downed by enemy fighters during the Stettin mission and two more were shot down by flak at Berlin today.

Less than two weeks-63 black bags. All is _not_ fair in war! On May 20 an English newspaper reported the May 19 raid on Berlin. It stated Berlin was bombed by RAF Mosquitoes during the previous Tuesday night, and the attack on May 19 was the tenth air raid by American bombers.

The article continued: "Announcing violent battles over its achtung alarm system, German radio said that "three separate" forces of the USAAF and Luftwaffe were engaged in combat over Berlin at the same time. German radio again gave signs of breaking down under the strain of the raids. At 3:30 PM German News Agency was still sending out the previous day's messages, breaking off each time after a few sentences and starting all over again. Several weeks ago, after a heavy daylight raid, the agency exhibited the same erratic behavior."

May 20   The Group flew a mission to Orly, France, bomb an airdrome. (Our crew was "stood down")

May 20   Our crew flew a training flight of one hour and forty-five minutes.

Today marked the first anniversary of the 379th Bomb Group's arrival at AAF Station 117. Everyone on the base was invited to a party and dance. Highlighted at the event was a birthday cake that was 30 inches high, three feet in diameter and weighed 75 pounds. On top of the cake was the 8th Air Force emblem. The cake was "lovely" and "smashing" to all the residents of Kimbolton who saw it when the committee delivering it to the party stopped at a village pub on the way to the airfield.

Mission to Marquis

Sunday, May 21, 1944. We were awakened at 0500 hours. The fog outside our barracks was so thick it made us uncertain of our footing as we hurried along the slippery path to the latrine. Breakfast included real eggs, the mess sergeant's confirmation that our crew was flying the day's mission.

Briefing started at 0630 hours and lasted until 0740 hours. Target information took up the usual amount of time, but Headquarters spent 15-20 minutes impressing us with the deadly potential of V-1 flying bombs. For several months the German aircraft industry had received top priority on target lists of many heavy bomber Groups. It would continue to be among 8th Air Force objectives; however, "flying bombs" were again being touted by German propaganda. The construction of launching sites on the French coast of the English Channel was steadily increasing, and the Allies feared a bombardment of England was approaching. The fly-bomb sites were small, well camouflaged, near small villages and heavily protected by antiaircraft guns. There were no large buildings to help bombardiers locate fly-bomb sites, and the patchwork of surrounding farmland did not provide adequate check points. Weather had to be almost perfect and precision bombing at its best to obtain good results. These weapons were a serious menace. Knowing so little about plans for their use magnified the threat of their presence.

It was no surprise when our day's target was finally announced...a fly-bomb site at Marquise/Mimoyecques, France. This was our crew's third attack on a fly-bomb site since the beginning of our combat tour, and was the seventh for the 379th Bomb Group in the same period of time.

Someone asked, "Didn't our Group bomb that target on May 15th?"

Someone answered, "Yeah, and we're bombing it again today."

Headquarters attempted some clarifying comments. "Gentlemen, just because we bombed at Marquise/Mimoyecques on May 15 doesn't mean there is only one target to be bombed at that location. Actually, we believe there are several fly-bomb sites there, and we intend to get all of them. As you know, we've bombed many places more than once—Frankfurt, Berlin, Brunswick, Kiel, Schweinfurt."

Someone said, "Yeah, but those are big cities. They've got all kinds of targets."

Someone asked, "Didn't we destroy the target when we bombed at Marquise on May 15?"

The answer to that question, if there was an answer, was lost in the loud voice of an Intelligence officer who interrupted by telling us where to expect flak on the way to the target. Most of our flying time today was going to be over England and the English Channel, so his information about flak was not very newsy. Marquise/Mimoyecques is in the Pas de Calais area, and only a few miles inland from Ambleteuse. Our flight plan over France was scheduled to last four minutes. That part of his information to us was very comforting and greatly appreciated. Intelligence told us to expect antiaircraft fire at the target. The warning was appreciated, but far from comforting.

The weather officer said a lot in a few words. "Gentle-

Striking view from 9,000 feet, looking east across narrow part of English Channel, from South Foreland, England, to Calais, France. (Photo from 379th BG Photo. Sec. circa May, 1944)

men, your flight today will not be much of a sight-seeing trip. Everything is completely socked in. Takeoff is delayed until 1115 hours. You'll be lucky to get off the ground."

On that dismal note, someone suggested we would all be a lot luckier if Headquarters scrubbed the mission. In reality, none of us wanted to see a mission scrubbed—not this one or any other. A scrubbed mission was always a heartbreaker. It didn't matter when it was scrubbed—before takeoff, after the planes were airborne or a few minutes after crawling out of a warm bed. It meant one more day on the growing list of days before members of combat crews would fly their final mission and return to the States. For members of ground crews it meant unloading bombs and gasoline, removing bombsights, guns, ammunition and bomb bay cameras. Every person on the airfield was affected directly or indirectly when a mission was scheduled. Similarly, they were all affected when a mission was scrubbed.

The 41st Wing of B-17s in the 1st Bombardment Division and two Wings of B-24s in the 2nd Division were all assigned targets in the Pas de Calais area. The targets were described as "military installations," but it was evident that all of them were fly-bomb sites.

Screwball Express was assigned to fly with the Lead section of the 379th Bomb Group's formation. Ours was the third Group in the 41st Wing, and consisted of 13 Flying Fortresses, including one spare. We assembled at 14,000 feet over the Kimbolton airfield. The spare B-17 returned to base early, leaving us with 12 attacking aircraft, as planned. Aircraft 42-31189 from the 379th Bomb Group was originally assigned to lead the 384th Bomb Group to one of the other targets in the Pas de Calais area. Because of bad weather conditions, the 379th's plane was unable to locate the 384th Group after its formation left Grafton Underwood. Consequently, aircraft number 42-31189 filled in with our Group and increased our number of attacking aircraft to 13.

The tactic of deploying Squadrons of 12 heavy bombers

(sometimes also referred to as Groups) and 36-plane integral Groups was developed and perfected by the 379th Bomb Group. The 12-plane Group included three four-plane Squadrons. Prior Squadron size usually numbered six or seven planes, with Groups consisting of 18-21 planes. This was not the first attack in which our Group utilized the 12-plane formation. Other Bomb Groups had also become convinced of increased bombing accuracy as a result of minimizing adverse effects of composite formations. This battle tactic of the 379th Bomb Group also provided increased protection against enemy fighters because of the tighter concentration of the bombers' machine guns.

The clouds around us were fluffy and white. We departed from England at 1347 hours over Clacton, flying at 20,700 feet. Our formation then headed almost due south. It could be said that our bomb run started when we left England. The course we were instructed to fly, from our departure at the English coast until we released our bombs on the target, was a straight line between those two points. We entered France at 1406 hours. Our Group Leader used a new type (new to us) of navigation equipment known as GH for this mission. The navigator in the Lead Fortress was very familiar with the equipment and operated it skillfully. It was well he did, because the weather was 10/10 throughout our entire flight. We saw no other bomber formations on the mission.

The altitude of our formation was reduced to 20,400 feet as we neared the target area. Fortresses in our formation each carried six 1,000-pound general purpose bombs in the bomb bay, and one 1,000-pound general purpose bomb under each wing. At 1407.5 hours and on a magnetic compass heading of 187 degrees, the planes in our Group dropped their bomb loads into the clouds that hung like a protective blanket over the fly-bomb site. Our Group's 104 high explosive bombs pierced the thick blanket of white and disappeared into it.

An unusual bit of excitement occurred during our bomb run. The tail fin of the 1,000-bomb under our Group Leader's right wing somehow broke away. When the fin fell, the arming wire was pulled loose and allowed the arming vane to spin off and arm the bomb. We sweated out the possibility of flak hitting the bomb and causing it to explode. That could have destroyed three or four of the B-17s in our Group, and one of them might have been Screwball Express. Thankfully, nothing of that magnitude happened.

Attacking any target in the occupied countries required special consideration. Targets of opportunity were easy to locate in Germany when weather prevented the bombing of primary targets. This was not the case in France, Belgium or Holland. The specific targets had to be found and were usually bombed visually. Otherwise, the bombs were dropped in the English Channel on the return trip, or brought back to base.

There were very good reasons for the "no bombs dropped" entry in Group record books after a mission's debriefing was completed. Many U.S. fliers had parachuted into occupied territory and were being sheltered by friendly individuals and groups. Many of our airmen were thus saved from the experience of life in prisoner of war camps and were able to return to England through the underground. People in the occupied countries were of extreme value to the Allies through Resistance Units. Indiscriminate dropping of bombs while flying over the occupied countries was taboo.

None of these factors had to be considered with regard to the 1,000 pound bomb under the right wing of our Group Leader. It released simultaneously with the 103 other bombs dropped by our Group at Marquise/ Mimoyecques. The

thick cloud cover made it impossible to see the results of our bombing.

Flak bursts over the target were surprisingly meager but, unfortunately, accurate. We made a right turn immediately after bombs away and left the French coast at 1410 hours. We were over France exactly four minutes! I had taken almost the same amount of time to sing the 23rd Psalm during takeoff earlier today.

Screwball Express carried our crew across the English coast at 1416 hours and then followed our Group Leader down through a hole in the clouds about thirty miles from Kimbolton. Our total flying time was four hours and thirty minutes. This was our crew's third mission with that same amount of flying time—mission No. 2 to Wizernes, No. 10 to Sottevast and the attack at Marquise today. All three of these targets were fly-bomb sites.

We did not see any enemy fighters on this mission. Although the 8th Air Force dispatched two Groups of P-47s to provide bomber escort to and from the Pas de Calais area, we likewise did not see any of them. Weather over the continent was usually on the side of the enemy. Clouds could hide targets and clouds could hide enemy fighter planes. The GH equipment found our target for us today. It was fortunate for the bomber crews that the Luftwaffe had not found us. Apparently, the Luftwaffe had the day off.

Although flak over the target was light, its accuracy caused minor damage to eight of our 13 Fortresses. The use of chaff did not lessen the effectiveness of the antiaircraft guns. Some of this damage may have come from an installation of flak guns at the French coast, after we left the target. We were surprised to find only three small flak holes in Screwball Express.

Our crew had successfully flown 20 combat missions. Only five more left. Just imagine! Our combat tour was 80% completed!

May 22 - Aerial reconnaissance confirmed bombs from our Group perfectly bracketed our assigned target. Records indicate only 25 of the 40 Fortresses from the 41st Wing dropped bombs on primary targets at Marquise/ Mimoyecques. Eleven B-24s also failed to bomb. Of the 26 bombers that did not bomb, 12 failed because of electrical and/or mechanical malfunctions, 13 because of weather and one for an unknown reason.

On the good side of the news, there were no personnel casualties or bomber losses in yesterday's operation. We also learned from the newspapers that during this mission 330 P-51s and P-38s of the 8th Air Force engaged in an organized plan of low-level strafing attacks upon enemy transportation systems in northwest Germany, with particular emphasis on the destruction of locomotives. Eighty locomotives were destroyed, 117 were damaged, and 16 trains were set afire. Enemy aircraft and other targets of opportunity were also given special attention. One river steamer was destroyed and three others damaged, 15 high-tension towers were destroyed and considerable damage inflicted on radar signal and radio towers, oil tanks, barges, railroad passenger cars and box cars, railroad stations, switch towers and numerous airfield installations. Our fighter planes destroyed 19 enemy aircraft in the air and 102 on the ground.

Our fighters encountered considerable flak, however, resulting in the loss of 15 aircraft—11 P-51s and four P-38s. We also lost four P-51s and four P-38s to unknown causes. A force of 134 P-47s on glide-bombing assignments lost four of its planes to enemy action.

May 22   379th Bomb Group bombed dock facilities at Kiel, Germany. (Our crew was "stood down," as was Screwball Express.) Early in the evening another Air-Sea Rescue mission was flown over the northern waters of the English Channel. Screwball Express was part of the rescue attempt, was piloted by Lt. Clay W. Hedges and carried a minimum crew. Evidently the rescue efforts failed to locate any airmen, because the Mission Report states the entire search area was scouted twice, but makes no reference to finding them.

Mission to Saarbrucken

Tuesday, May 23, 1944. It was only 0100 hours when the operations officer of the 526th Squadron threw open the door of our barracks and yelled, "Rise and shine, you're flyin'" today." His loud message was intended for everyone in our Nissen hut and he only had to make the announcement one time. The resulting noise and chatter associated with a group of airmen getting up and hurrying to get dressed for a combat briefing was loud enough to wake up the fellows in the barracks adjacent to ours.

Breakfast, briefing, and out to the flight line—it was a very routine order of events on days when we were alerted for combat missions. Equally routine, but far more monotonous, were the fog, drizzle, rain and mud. Most of England's weather included either fog, drizzle or rain. The mud at the Kimbolton airfield seemed everlasting.

I wondered to myself, "With all this precipitation, why isn't more water available in the tanks on the roof of the building housing the showers?" Many crewmen had the same concern, while others evidently had a bad sense of smell. Some of the guys attempted to hide the situation under the disguising aroma of their shaving lotion.

At the briefing we learned the 379th Bomb Group was providing 11 planes for the Lead Group and 18 planes, including 6 spares, for the Low Group in the 41st "B" Combat Wing. Screwball Express was assigned to lead the four planes in the High Squadron of the Lead Group. Our primary target was the Nancy/Essey airfield in France.

We completed preflighting Screwball Express and sat at our takeoff positions, waiting for the control tower to tell our Group if the mission was "on." I remember thinking, "Maybe they'll fire a red flare from the control tower, indicating the mission has been scrubbed." This was my 22nd birthday, and I could think of a lot of things I would like to do, other than fly my 21st combat mission. I had given one of the cooks two British pounds to bake a chocolate birthday cake for me. My plan was to divide it among our crew's members after dinner tonight.

A green flare was fired at 0510 hours, signaling the planes in our Group to start engines and be ready to taxi out for takeoff. The wheels of Screwball Express left the runway at 0530 hours. "Thou preparest a table before me—" I sang, smiling a bit as thoughts of that chocolate cake entered my mind. I prayed we would return safely from this mission— "Let me live through this day, Lord." It crossed my mind that the cooks at the mess hall would eat my birthday cake if we didn't come back today. To make matters worse, I had already paid for it.

Climbing through the overcast had become so common we hardly flinched when wingtips of other bombers poked through the clouds and almost hit Screwball Express. Assembly of our Wing was completed on schedule above Splasher #8 at 18,000 feet. The six spare Fortresses in the Low Group returned early, as planned.

In the early months of World War II, small formations of B-17s and B-24s made diversionary sweeps over the English Channel and the North Sea. These were non-attacking actions, designed to mislead the enemy into pulling its defenses away from the area of the main Allied bombing effort. At the time, most of the heavy bomber targets were not far inland on the continent. Records indicate seven such diversionary sweeps were flown in 1942, but only one in 1943 and none thereafter. In 1942 the number of planes on these missions varied from six to 30. The one diversionary mission in 1943 included 36 aircraft. Presumably, the advantage of these diversions disappeared when bombers began making longer flights into enemy territory and their primary targets became more obvious. The growing number of Luftwaffe planes helped make diversionary sweeps become obsolete. Low-level attacks by fighter-bombers and medium bombers on enemy coastal targets along the Channel also lessened the odds of confusing the enemy about the destination of our heavy bombers.

Our formation turned due south and flew over Beachy Head at 19,000 feet. It climbed to 22,000 feet over the English Channel and entered enemy territory at 0759 hours. We continued a southeasterly heading to St. Denis, a few miles north of Paris, arriving there at 0815 hours. Our compass headings were alternated to 90 degrees, 160 degrees, 145 degrees and then 45 degrees as we attempted what could have been evasive action intended to confuse enemy planes along our route to the target. However, we saw only three enemy fighters along the way. They were a safe distance from us and made no attempt to attack our formation. I felt that pilots of our escorting P-51s and P-47s were very bored with the lack of opposition by the Luftwaffe. Flak along the route to the target area was scarce. This kind of boredom was very infrequent, and the bomber crews welcomed it.

At 0916 hours our Combat Wing reached a point almost due south of our primary target. We turned sharply to our left and flew a compass heading of 352 degrees toward our IP. At 0930 hours we were directly over our IP and could see that the density of clouds ahead of us made it impractical to fly a visual bomb run to the Nancy airfield. It was decided to attack our secondary target at Saarbrucken, Germany, instead. Our formation changed its course to a magnetic heading of 35 degrees. The Wing's leader used the Nancy airfield as the IP for a PFF bomb run to the railroad marshalling yards at Saarbrucken.

The target was an important one, with two steel plants adjacent to the marshalling yards. Saarbrucken is located east of the German border with France, approximately 55 miles northeast of Nancy. The planes in our Group each carried 12-500 pound demolition bombs that would be just as damaging to Saarbrucken's marshalling yards as they would have been to Nancy's airfield.

As we flew along the bomb run I gave the order to throw out the chaff. About 17 rockets were fired from the ground at our formation. They disappeared under and behind us, and fell back to earth. A very heavy but inaccurate barrage of antiaircraft fire exploded behind and below our position. Our Lead Group of 11 aircraft dropped its bombs at 0954 hours from an altitude of 23,000 feet. The Low Group of 12 planes dropped its bombs exactly 30 seconds later from 22,000 feet. Our magnetic heading at bombs away was 35 degrees. We could not see the results of our bombing because of the massive cloud formation which covered the entire target area.

Each of the three Groups in our Combat Wing made a 90 degree to the left and headed for Ostend, Belgium. We saw some flak bursts in the distance near Brussels. Flak gunners at Ostend greeted us, but their hostile gesture was inaccurate. Our Lead Group left enemy territory at 1107 hours, flying at 22,000 feet. We crossed the English coast 26 minutes later at 12,000 feet over Clacton and flew directly to Cambridge. A hole developed in the clouds shortly thereafter and we descended through it. We entered our airfield's landing pattern and flew past the familiar castle at the edge of Kimbolton.

The wheels of Screwball Express touched down seven hours and 15 minutes after takeoff. Mission number 21 was history for our crew. We only had four more combat missions to fly.

The use of chaff during our attack at Saarbrucken was very effective. Only one of our planes received any flak damage, and it was only minor. There were no personnel casualties in any of our Group's Fortresses during this mission.

Four members of our crew had our customary 10 Red Cross treats before we went to the debriefing. We had been up since 0100 hours and were very tired. The hospitality wagon's generosity to four of us added to our sleepiness. Our entire crew skipped dinner and headed for the sack. I even forgot about my birthday cake.

A photo reconnaissance unit reported several days later that our Group had good bombing results at the Saarbrucken marshalling yards. That report states: "Damage was spread throughout the length of the target area. In the western yards two large shops have been severely damaged and a third moderately damaged. A small portion of the passenger station has been destroyed by a direct hit. The center of the yard has been straddled by craters which have severed lines, derailed rolling stock, and damaged the roof of the round-house. Four sticks of bombs have fallen across the eastern yards severing lines of the SW choke point, and damaging one long rectangular and one short rectangular transshipment shed,

The castle at Kimbolton — a welcoming sight and a beautiful landmark. The steeple of historic St. Andrew's Church is visible at photo's upper left. (From photos of 379th BG Photo. Sec. circa 1944)

and severing tracks along the north end. One corner of an industrial building with three tall chimneys has also been destroyed."

That same day other Bomb Groups moderately damaged a marshalling yards at Neunkirchen, and heavily damaged one at Konz-Karthaus and another at Ludwigshaven. An airfield at Brussels and aircraft engine factories at Strasbourg and near Metz were also attacked successfully by 8th Air Force bombers during the day's operation.

The May 24 newspaper carried an article about the U.S. Air Force operation on my 22nd birthday. The headline read, "Heavies, Fighters Sweep Europe Looking for a Scrap, but Nazis Refuse." The lead paragraph of that article stated: "Three thousand American and Allied warplanes stretched an aerial dragnet across the skies of western Europe yesterday, hunting down the German air strength Hitler is saving for invasion day." The following paragraphs told the rest of the story.

"From the edges of the Biscay provinces eastward to the Reich itself, more than 1,000 American fighter craft—greatest fighter force ever sent up on a single mission—escorted some 600 Fortresses and Liberators to six of the Nazis' key air bases, to two rail yards around which central European transport hinges, and to other unspecified targets within western Germany."

"The big air fleet, which pounded out from British bases at dawn's first light, split into task forces across western Europe as it carried into its fourth day the newest phase of the pre-invasion offensive aimed at destroying the German capacity to shift men and material to meet the Allied D-Day."

"Nazi sirens had barely quieted after a night in which the RAF, working on the same plan of widespread attack, had dispatched more than 1,000 heavy bombers to six targets in Germany and the occupied countries. But where the RAF had flown into bitter combats with night fighters, the big fleet of U.S. daylight heavies and their escorts found almost no resistance, and bomber crews and fighter pilots alike came home with stories of Luftwaffe interceptors which refused to give battle and left their bases to be destroyed without interference."

"When it became obvious the Luftwaffe would not fight, Eighth and Ninth Air Force Thunderbolts, Lightnings and long-range Mustangs flying with the bombers went down to earth and strafed locomotives, military trains, airfield hangars and gun emplacements."

"While the heavies were bombing and the fighters were dropping to hedge-tops to strafe transport and communications targets, the RAF sent out light daylight forces in sweeps over the Low Countries and France, and Channel coast observers described late afternoon formations also headed for the Continent."

The article went on to state only one bomber Group reported interception attempts by enemy fighters, and they were beaten off by the escorting fighter planes. One bomber and three fighter planes were reported missing in action during the entire day's operation. The article concluded with, "The Luftwaffe made another series of reconnaissance in force last Monday night against British coastal districts, putting units of swift spy planes over southern England, East Anglia and even the eastern part of Scotland. Authorities reported casualties and damage at localities in southern England, but none in Scotland, and claimed at least four enemy planes destroyed. The German radio version of the night attacks claimed a blow "in considerable strength" at Portsmouth, and said "large fires had been started."

Mission to Berlin

Wednesday, May 24, 1944. Headlines in tomorrow's newspapers would tell today's story: "U.S. Air Fleets Hit Berlin, Paris, Vienna. 'Decisive Eve,' Nazis Warn as 4,000 Craft Strike Three Ways." For those of us in the 8th Air Force, our day began with the issuance of Field Order No. 363. It directed the 379th Bomb Group to provide 18 Flying Fortresses (including one spare) for the Lead Group, and 24 Fortresses (including five spares) for the Low Group in the 41st "A" Combat Wing on the mission to attack Berlin. This was the 22nd combat mission for our crew and the 124th for the 379th Bomb Group.

Every available flight crew of the 379th Group was awakened at 0100 hours for briefing at 0230. At approximately 0130 hours our crew was in line at the mess hall. There were enough scrambled eggs and bacon strips to feed everyone at our airfield, with enough left over to take care of the morning Pub trade in Kimbolton.

The mess sergeant approached me from the other side of a large tray on which at least one hundred slices of toast were getting cold.

"Lieutenant Case-ens?" he inquired.

"Lieutenant Cassens," I answered.

"Thanks for the chocolate cake, sir," he said sheepishly. He quickly disappeared behind two large caldrons of coffee.

As I neared the end of the chow line, the mess sergeant reappeared. In his hand were four Hershey chocolate bars stacked on top of each other and held together by rubber bands. With his other hand he stuck a candle into the top Hershey bar. He carefully placed his "four-layer special" on my food tray.

He didn't sing it. He just said it. "Happy birthday, sir."

At briefing we were told our target for today was an aircraft component plant in the city of Berlin. Fate has a way of catching up. Less that one month ago I complained because the 379th went on a mission to Berlin without our crew. Today's raid on Big B would be the ninth since the war began, and the fifth one this month, for the 379th. Our crew had been assigned to three of those five attacks on Berlin. Catching up was quick—it just wasn't easy. Our first two attacks on Berlin were rough ones. The 379th Bomb Group lost two B-17s during each of those attacks.

The briefing session included the usual comments about weather: "Over Kimbolton it's cloudy. En route to the target it's cloudy. At the target it's very cloudy. On the way home it's mostly cloudy." A lot was said about flak installations. It sounded as though there were at least ten batteries of flak towers for every mile of the entire route. The Luftwaffe was mentioned, but with less seriousness than I felt was warranted. Its recent hide-and-seek tactics had not convinced me it would not be heard from again. Today provided more than enough reason for it to be waiting with all of its guns ready. We were attacking Berlin, capital of Germany. The Luftwaffe would undoubtedly be there to intercept us, whether its pilots wanted to or not.

Our takeoff was at 0610 hours. For some reason I was unusually apprehensive about this mission. Perhaps my uneasiness was caused by this being our third mission to Berlin. Thoughts of a large attack by enemy fighters deep in Germany could make anyone fidgety. In all likelihood, I was frightened by the strong possibility our crew's good fortune might be nearing its end. According to statistics, a bomber crew was living on borrowed time after its 12th or 13th combat mission. This bit of gloom and doom was based on earlier heavy bomber losses of about eight percent. Projecting this logic further predicted a crew would use up about 200% of its chances for survival by the time it completed a 25-mission tour of duty. Hopefully, the same logic did not apply to Flying Fortresses, because Screwball Express was on its 25th combat mission today.

Regardless of the reasons for feeling nervous, I was comforted by words of the 23rd Psalm as I sang them into the roar of our plane's engines.

Screwball Express flew Lead position in the Low "A" Group's High Squadron. At 0746 hours the 41st Combat Wing "A" assembled at 9,000 feet over Molesworth, and twenty-three minutes later we were over Bourne. Our formation then headed due east to the English coast. Since this mission was another of many maximum efforts in which our Bomb Group was recently involved, three of our spares filled in with our own Groups. Our other three spare aircraft filled in as follows: 42-32024 with the 401st Group, 42-1228 with the 351st Group and 42-31085 with the 303rd Group. Finding a Group with which to fly on maximum effort days was very easy. The sky was completely filled with heavy bomber Groups, and it was difficult to stay out of each others way. Medium bombers and fighter planes were also in abundance today.

Of the 42 B-17s dispatched by the 379th Bomb Group, 18 of them flew in the Lead Group and 21 in the Low Group of the 41st "A" Wing. We started across the North Sea at Cromer, at an altitude of 10,000 feet and at 0834 hours. We changed our course to the northeast and flew in that direction for the next one hour and 20 minutes. Our Wing was flying at 20,000 feet at 0954 hours when it turned almost due east and flew north of Helgoland. Four flak boats positioned off the coast of Germany fired eight or ten rounds at us before our formation entered enemy territory at 1013 hours. We then flew at 22,500 feet over Wesselburen on a southeast heading that took us past the northeast suburbs of Hamburg and straight to Berlin.

In addition to the flak at Helgoland, we encountered light, inaccurate antiaircraft attacks near Hamburg, Elmshorn, Waren and Zehoe. We saw no enemy planes in the air while we were on this leg of the mission, but did see 20 Luftwaffe planes parked on an airfield at Neuruppen. We were thankful none of those planes came up to attack us.

It was 1055 hours when we reached our IP. Our Wing's altitude was 26,000 feet, and we stayed on the same heading we had been flying for 42 minutes over Germany. Rockets were fired at the Groups in our Wing and at other Groups of B-17s, but the rockets did not reach sufficient altitude and fell into the clouds beneath us. It seemed as though rockets fired at us during our missions always fell short of our position. We were not concerned with the reason for this, but were certainly happy with the result. I reasoned it was about time for the flak guns at Berlin to start firing at us, so I called Joe on the intercom and told him to throw out the chaff. I notified

Author standing under chin turret of Screwball Express. Ground crew chief Sgt. Starbuck is at right in photo. (Photo by 379th BG Photo. Sec. May 24, 1944)

Howard I was opening the bomb bay doors, because their open position had an affect on the way Screwball Express handled. I pushed a switch on my control panel in order to electrically operate the doors' cranking mechanism.

The amount of flak exploding in and around our Group was somewhat heavy and very accurate. The antiaircraft gunners around Berlin were always "right on target" with their flak shells. Protecting the capital city of Germany undoubtedly was an assignment given only to the very best gun crews. In addition, they probably utilized information from captured B-17s regarding our altitude, heading and speed.

The first B-17 to fall into German hands in flyable condition was part of the 303rd Bomb Group's December 12, 1942 mission to Rouen-Sotteville marshalling yards in northwestern France. Twenty-one B-17Fs were on the 303rd's sixth combat mission. Records show this Group became separated from other bomber formations and was attacked by 30 enemy aircraft all the way from Beauvais to the target. One of the 303rd's bombers (Wulf Hound, serial number 41-24585) was hit and later dropped out of formation. It disappeared into the clouds and then made a wheels down landing in a French field. In 1943, two more intact B-17Fs were captured, one of which landed near Brandenburg, Germany. The first B-17G captured intact was from the 390th Bomb Group. The Luftwaffe used it for dropping supplies to German troops on the French coast during the winter of 1944-45.

Today's attack on Berlin overflowed with excitement. Straight ahead of us a P-38 shot down a FW-190. The enemy

aircraft started into a spin and exploded. One of our P-51s was seen going down, out of control, in the target area.

Each of the 21 Fortresses in our Low Group carried 24 bombs. Eight of these were 500-pound incendiaries and 16 were 100-pound general purpose bombs. Because of 8/10 undercast, it was determined to use PFF equipment on our bomb run. Every bombardier in each of our Groups waited anxiously for the Group's Lead plane to drop its bombs. All of us wanted to get out of the target area and head back to England.

When our Group arrived over the center of Berlin it was caught in the middle of a huge flak barrage that caused our planes to get into a very undesirable bombing formation. POOM-POOM-POOM-POOM. Flak exploded everywhere around us. Black puffs of smoke after each explosion created a breathtaking, frightening sight. Our Group Leader dropped his bombs at 1103 hours and the customary chain reaction occurred as bombardiers in other Fortresses of the Lead, Low and High Squadrons simultaneously emptied their bomb bays. Through holes in the clouds we could see the bombs were dropped over a built-up area near the center of Berlin. Some of our Group's bombs went straight down, but many of them were thrown to the right of their intended path. The entire city of Berlin was at least 80% covered by clouds at the time, and we were not immediately certain where or what the bombs hit. (The Mission Report at The National Archives states the bombs fell into "a well built-up area near the center of the city.")

My earlier prediction became reality as the sky filled with Luftwaffe fighter planes. All of us were easy prey for the enemy fighters, so our scattered formation tried to regroup as we continued flying across Berlin. Immediately after we left the target area, approximately 75 enemy fighters attacked our Lead and Low Groups over Berlin's northeastern suburbs. Most of the Luftwaffe's attackers were FW-190s and some were Me-109s.

The majority of the enemy planes waited for us to get out of the flak barrage over Berlin; however, about fifteen of them braved their own antiaircraft guns and flew straight through our formation, their machine guns blazing away at us.

"Bandits at 12 o'clock, level." (That was Frank's voice.)

"Looks like rockets under their wings." (That was Bob.)

"Bandits at 9 o'clock, low." (Tom's voice was unmistakable.)

Jim's voice warned of six bandits at 2 o'clock, high.

"Three of 'em at 5 o'clock, level." (That was Jerry.)

I grabbed the controls of the chin turret and tried to get a bead on a FW-190. A heavy, pungent odor from the firing of .50-caliber cartridges filled the nose compartment of Screwball Express as my finger squeezed the trigger, sending bullets from my turret's guns at the FW until it went under our squadron. Screwball Express vibrated from nose to tail as all of its .50 caliber guns pounded away at the enemy planes. Howard expressed a very strong dislike for the shattering noise and the pulsating vibration caused by the simultaneous firing of our 13 machine guns.

At 1104 hours, Flying Fortress 42-37784 in our Group was severely damaged by the machine guns of an enemy fighter. The crew of 2nd Lt. Wilton E. Gease was in that bomber. It started down, out of control, and collided with Fortress 42-38082 carrying the crew of Capt. Lytle W. Shumake. Group records indicate the plane of Capt. Shumake may have been damaged by an enemy fighter before the collision. Both of these B-17s were assigned to the 525th Squadron.

The attacking planes also shot down several Fortresses from the 398th Bomb Group. An accurate count of the number of parachutes was not recorded. Two B-17s from the 303rd Bomb Group were hit during fighter attacks while leaving the Berlin area. We saw only seven parachutes emerge from those two aircraft.

Fortress 42-39828 from the 379th's 524th Squadron was hit by an enemy fighter and flak at 1111 hours and exploded. That bomber was flown by the crew of 2nd Lt. Theodore E. C. Kunda. No parachutes were seen coming from that aircraft. The three Fortresses lost on this mission by the 379th Bomb Group were in the Low Group in which Screwball Express was flying.

Our return trip was uneventful. We saw a few bursts of exploding flak at several locations, but none of it was close to us. We could not get out of Germany fast enough. The Luftwaffe came out of hiding today and made a deadly mark on our Low Group. Losing three of our Group's 39 Fortresses during this attack on Berlin brought our loss for this one mission to nearly eight percent! It was more than enough to make us hurry back to England.

At 1232 hours we left Germany over the same point at which we had entered it two hours and 19 minutes earlier, near Wesselburen. Ten black explosions about one thousand feet under our formation let us know the flak boats were still anchored off the coast. Our altitude was 22,000 feet. Our Wing flew to the north of Helgoland and then southwest on a heading that took us to the English coast at 1430 hours. At that point we descended to 3,000 feet, headed north of Cambridge and finally to Kimbolton.

Our flying time on our 22nd combat mission was exactly nine hours.

It was a very rough one. There were now only three more missions left for our crew. Thank Heaven!

The use of chaff at Berlin was not very effective today. Twenty-eight of our 39 Fortresses attacking Berlin received flak damage—71%. Our ground crews had a whale of a job to do, in addition to repairing all the holes made by the enemy fighters' machine guns. Screwball Express received many small flak holes in its wings and fuselage, and one of its Tokyo tanks had to be repaired. Records do not indicate whether it also received damage by enemy planes on this mission.

One of the notations made in my diary that night states, "While we were over Berlin today we couldn't have sold Screwball Express for more than 5 cents, because of the large quantities of flak and enemy fighters."

At this point in our tour of combat duty, 11 Flying Fortresses of the 379th Bomb Group were lost to enemy action during missions flown by our crew. Ten of those 11 aircraft were shot down during only four of our missions, and in only 18 days. Seven of those 11 were shot down during attacks on Berlin. Berlin was bad news.

A total of exactly 100 black bags!

As I crawled into the sack and tried to go to sleep, I kept thinking of the bomb runs our Group flew on our three missions over Berlin:

May 7	Heading 38 degrees	27,000 feet
May 19	Heading 45 degrees	27,000 feet
May 24	Heading 35 degrees	26,000 feet

No wonder I had trouble going to sleep. We certainly made it easy for the Luftwaffe and the antiaircraft gunners to know where to look for us. Our Group flew at about the same altitude and compass heading on all of those bombing attacks. Did our Intelligence people know about this?

With a little luck, maybe our crew would not have to attack Berlin again. I prayed no one would have to fly another mission there—not ever!

Records of the 379th Bomb Group show the Lead aircraft of our Low Group on this mission bombed on a magnetic heading of 80 degrees from 25,000 feet. The same records show the Lead Group's Deputy Leader bombed on a magnetic heading of 95 degrees from 26,000 feet. The magnetic heading and bombing altitude shown on the 379th Bomb Group's map of the flight plan is recorded as 35 degrees and 26,000 feet. All of these records show the same time for bombs away—it was 1104 hours.

The newspapers told the balance of the story on Thursday morning, May 25, 1944, in the following paragraphs:

"From the north, south and west, massed formations of Flying Fortresses and Liberators, covered by American fighter planes, stormed over the Reich and its satellites in what the Nazis themselves officially declared marked "the eve of decisive operations against the Continent."

"While heavies from Britain and Italy were slugging at the capitals of Austria and Germany, as well as France's chief city, American medium and light bombers and deck-level fighters carried on without a pause the timetable pummeling of the Atlantic Wall defenses in the west, and hundreds of RAF and Allied light craft joined in the drumfire of bombs across the English Channel."

"Some 1,000 Fortresses and Liberators, flanked by as many Thunderbolts, Lightnings and Mustangs, sallied out from the ETO in early morning and split into two forces—the majority heading for Germany, the rest knifing straight to Paris. While they split the German defenses west and north, nearly 750 heavy bombers, with their escorts, went up from Italian airfields, slugged it out with Nazi interceptors over the Alps and hammered home new blows on aircraft plants and airfields in the Vienna area."

"The two-way heavy bomber attack on Berlin and Austria was the first pincer mission since Feb. 25, and split the Luftwaffe's fighter defenses based in the center of Germany. Nonetheless, Nazi radio and American bomber crews alike described bitter battles north and south, and the ETO-based formations came home with reported losses of 32 heavies and 13 fighters."

"For battered Berlin, it was the 11th daylight pounding by the United States Strategic and Tactical Air Force, and the fifth this month. It was the 133rd bombing attack—by night and by day—since the war began four years and eight months ago."

The following information about the bombing of Berlin is included here to provide additional dimension to the story of this city's wartime devastation.

The last attack on Berlin by the 379th Bomb Group during 1944 was on June 21. The 8th Air Force lost 44 bombers on that mission. The 379th Bomb Group flew a total of 14 attacks on Berlin during World War II, ten of which were in 1944. Six of those 10 raids were during the time our crew was operational, and our crew flew on three of those six attacks. The 14th and final attack by the 379th Bomb Group against Berlin was on March 28, 1945.

The 379th Bomb Group lost 13 Fortresses on missions flown by our crew. Seven of the 13 were shot down during our crew's three missions to Berlin.

Berlin had the unfortunate distinction of being the "most bombed" city during World War II. It suffered far more bomb damage than did London. The RAF bombed Berlin with nearly 51,000 tons of bombs in 363 attacks. That bomb tonnage is equal to about 11% of the total tonnage dropped on all German industrial towns during the entire war. The area destroyed in Berlin by Allied bombs was ten times larger than the area Germany's Luftwaffe destroyed in London. The destroyed area of Berlin totaled 6,340 acres. Approximately 52,000 people died in the bombing of Berlin—five times more than the number of bombing deaths in London.

On April 14, 1945, Supreme Allied Commander Dwight D. Eisenhower declared the military drive toward Germany's capital would soon stop. The American troops were only 45 miles from the city when he said, "Berlin is no longer a military objective."

The last air raid by Western Allies against Berlin took place on April 21, 1945. The 8th Air Force bombed the city for the last time at 0925 hours that day. Berlin's last air raid siren was sounded a moment earlier.

May 25   379th Bomb Group bombed a railway yards at Sarreguemines, France. Crew of Lt. Clarence E. Jamison flew Screwball Express. (Our crew was "stood down")

May 25   Part of our crew flew a two hour training flight.

May 26   It rained all day and the entire Group was grounded.

(On February 18, 1992, I was glancing through the membership roster of the 379th Bomb Group WW II Association. I saw the name of Ted Kunda. After telephoning the listed address, I found myself speaking to the same Ted Kunda whose B-17 exploded after it was hit by fighters and flak during the May 24, 1944, mission. Ted informed me all of his crew parachuted safely before the explosion. They were prisoners of war until May of 1945.)

(**Special Credit:** Please refer to *B-17 Fortress at War*; under Bibliography.)

Mission to Speyerdorf

Saturday, May 27, 1944. Approximately 2,000 bombers and fighters took part in today's offensive, one of the biggest coordinated assaults ever made in daylight against the southwestern German rail network. The target for two Groups of Fortresses from the 379th Bomb Group was a railroad marshalling yards at Mannheim, Germany. The target was southeast of the city and extended for three miles toward the village of Friedrichsfeld. It had a capacity to handle 7,300 railroad cars every 24 hours and was currently the second largest marshalling yards in Germany.

The 379th provided a High Group of 19 aircraft for the 41st Combat Wing "A" and a High Group of 20 aircraft for Wing "B" on this mission. Our crew and Screwball Express were assigned to the High Squadron of the High Group in "A" Wing. Joe Starbuck, our ground crew chief, and all members of his ground crew had worked feverishly to repair the damage our plane received during the May 24 attack on Berlin. Screwball Express was ready to go today, and so were we.

On our way to the flight line following briefing we sang "Happy Birthday" to Howard. It was "Herky's" 26th birthday. He didn't look that old. Some of us called him "Herky," after the caricature in Air Force training posters that humorously depicted a pilot doing things that resulted in pilot errors. We only used the name in fun, of course, because Howard was undoubtedly one of the finest pilots in the 8th Air Force. Training posters also used navigator and bombardier caricatures to help remind us of unnecessary goof-ups by persons in these crew positions. Radio operators, engineers and gunners were not exempted from this bizarre training technique.

We took off at 0800 hours. The weather was so good it made the sky unbelievably clear and provided visibility of at least two or three miles. I made a mental note to include a comment in my diary about this phenomenon of English weather.

This was combat mission number 23 for our crew. Nothing could have been more fitting than a prayerful rendition of the 23rd Psalm!

After assembly over Molesworth, we flew towards Oxford, turned on a heading that took our formation over southwestern London and then turned toward Beachy Head. We started across the English Channel at 17,000 feet. During the next 21 minutes we climbed in spiraling turns to 21,000 feet and crossed into enemy territory at 1058 hours near Berneval, France. Fourteen minutes later we were met by our fighter escort. Our course and altitude were maintained approximately 55 additional minutes. During this time about 50 enemy fighters were seen in the distance, but the presence of our escorting fighters kept the bandits from attacking our Wing. We then made the first of a planned series of five turns to our left, intending to confuse the enemy regarding our target and the direction of our bombing approach. We watched the 50 Me-109s and FW-190s attack two Wings of Fortresses in front of our Wing. Five of those Fortresses were shot down during fighter attacks in an area southwest of Strasbourg. It was horrifying to see those Me-109s fire their machine guns at 21 or more American crewmen who bailed out and floated helplessly beneath their parachutes. We could not believe our eyes. The horror we witnessed became additionally terrifying when two FW-190s fired their 20 mm cannons at some of the defenseless U.S. Air Force crewmen.

Frank said it was the most horrible thing he remembered seeing during our crew's combat tour. It deeply disturbed all of us.

More of our planned left turns were made to take our Wing north of Freiburg and southeast of Strasbourg. A huge smoke screen was in process over Strasbourg's massive swing bridge that crossed the Rhine river between France and Germany. The bridge was partly visible in my binoculars. Completion of our next turn pointed us almost due north and took us east of Karlsruhe. We reached our IP at 1255 hours, flying at 25,500 feet. Shortly thereafter four Flying Fortresses from another Group were seen going down as a result of a flak barrage. About 18 or 20 crewmen were seen parachuting from those four bombers. One Me-109 was shot down in the target area.

The bomb bay of Screwball Express was filled with 10-500 pound demolition bombs. The High Group in which we were flying in Wing "A" was about to reach the dropping point for the primary target. At the very last moment, just before bombs would have been away, our Group Leader radioed, "High Group A—High Group A—do not drop—do not drop." I looked down through the plexiglas nose of Screwball Express and saw the obvious reason for this very unusual order. The Low Group of our Wing was not in its proper position, but was directly beneath our High Group at the time our bombs would have been away.

A photostat of the flight plan for this mission shows our High Group changed course and headed for our secondary target at Speyerdorf, a short 13 miles to the southwest. We were not disappointed at leaving the Mannheim area. We had received a hot reception there by 148 flak guns in the area around the target. The flak directed at our High Group was moderate to intense, and surprisingly inaccurate. Only four of our Group's planes received damage from this flak attack, and Screwball Express was one of the four. None of the flak damage was serious. Rockets were also fired at us around Mannheim, but took their usual, ineffective course under us.

Our secondary target, an airfield and adjacent barracks area, presented our High Group an opportunity to make a single Group attack, unassisted by other formations of bombers. The mission's flight plan shows we flew a magnetic heading of 249 degrees for the bomb run to our target. The formation of approximately 50 enemy fighters was flying in the distance at our altitude, but gave no indication it would attack our Group. They didn't like flying through flak any more than we did. After a short visual bomb run, we dropped our bombs from 26,000 feet at 1307 hours. One of the B-17s in our High Group did not drop its bombs because of a mechanical malfunction. We flew straight and level for about 50 additional seconds after bombs were away, in order to take pictures of our bomb strikes. Our bombs scored direct hits on the entire hangar area, all of the runways and through all of the barracks area. Our bombing results were very good and the entire target was knocked out of operation. Much to our surprise, the group of enemy fighter planes did not pursue our formation when we turned away from the target. It certainly was a great comfort to have our P-51s, P-47s and P-38s fly escort for us. As always, they were tremendous!

The return trip was uneventful. Our Wing flew straight for Brussels after leaving the target, deviating from our flight plan only once in order to fly around a flak barrage directly ahead of us as we neared that city. Along the way we spotted a new airfield, a large military camp, a water reservoir protected by a balloon barrage, an airfield southwest of Brussels with about 30 aircraft parked on it and many railroad cars in the Brussels marshalling yards. We flew out of enemy territory at 1428 hours over Ostend, Belgium, and 22 minutes later crossed over Clacton on Sea, England, at 9,000 feet.

All Fortresses of the 379th Bomb Group returned safely to Kimbolton. Crew members of the 379th's High Group in Wing "B" reported very good bombing results at the Mannheim marshalling yards. One of the planes in that Group did not bomb the primary target. Other Wings also had very good results in the bombing of marshalling yards and the I. G. Farben Industrie A.G. Works at Ludwigshafen during the day's operation.

Our Intelligence people were interested in various observations reported during the debriefing by crew members who flew on this mission. The new airfield and the large military camp were noted on a list of potential targets. The "eyes" of the 8th Air Force made the hiding of Germany's military installations very difficult, and placed the probability of their continued existence in great danger.

Considering we almost bombed our Low Group, saw nine B-17s get shot down by enemy fighters and flak, and witnessed enemy planes firing machine guns and cannon at American crewmen descending in parachutes, our crew's 23rd combat mission was a rough one. Fortunately, there were no casualties in either of our Groups today. The flying time on this mission was seven hours and 30 minutes.

Only two more combat missions! Only two more!

May 28, 1944 - The morning edition of London's The Sunday Chronicle printed an article which led off with the sentence, "Great waves of Allied bombers and fighters swept over the Channel yesterday." The article continued: "One of their targets was Strasbourg. It was the first time Strasbourg has been bombed since the war began, although an RAF bomber attacked a factory on the fringe of the city in June, 1940. An aero-engine plant and a railway yard were hit at Strasbourg."

The newspaper article included this interesting statement. "According to the Germans, American bomber formations took advantage of the weather conditions, and through unbroken layers of clouds, dropped large quantities of high explosive and incendiary bombs. On account of unfavorable weather, only some of the German fighters were able to establish contact with the enemy."

According to the 379th Bomb Group's Mission Report for May 27, "The Weather was clear throughout most of the route and was clear in the target area and had no adverse effect on the bombing."

Obviously, the German report about weather was incomplete, or in error, or was issued as a face-saver for the Luftwaffe.

Mission to Wustensacken

Sunday, May 28, 1944. Today the 8th Air Force was two years and four months old. Although World War II was far from over, the Mighty Eighth was already a major factor in making an Allied victory not only probable, but clearly foreseeable. It had matured quickly, and its strength was profoundly effective.

This was the fourth double mission day for our Bomb Group, and two successful combat missions were completed today by the 379th Bomb Group. The early morning mission was very unique, and our crew's members were disappointed because we were not assigned to fly on it. Details about the early morning mission are included near the end of this chapter.

The 379th's second mission of the day was originally scheduled to be an attack on an aircraft engine plant at Dessau, Germany, approximately 30 miles north of Leipzig. Our Headquarters assigned 21 Fortresses, including 3 spares, to fly Lead Group in the 41st Combat Wing for an attack on that target. Screwball Express flew that Group's High Squadron Lead.

Screwball Express lifted from the end of the main runway at 1010 hours and began its climb for an assembly altitude of 8,000 feet over Molesworth. Our crew was filled with great excitement at the thought of this being our 24th and next to last combat mission. Singing the 23rd Psalm was very special to me today, as it had been on each of our previous 23 mission days.

Our Wing headed northeast toward The Wash and then flew to Great Yarmouth. At this point one of our spares filled in with another Group, the two other spares returned to base early, according to plan, and one of our Group's B-17s aborted the mission. We left England at 1205 hours and flew due east across the North Sea toward Alkmaar, Holland. It was 1241 hours when we crossed into enemy territory flying at 22,000 feet. At approximately 1300 hours an escorting group of P-47s appeared on each side of our formation. We became a little apprehensive about not changing our compass heading since leaving England. Flying the same heading for a long time frequently attracted enemy fighters. It was also a way to flush the bandits into the open where our "little brothers" could get the enemy planes into combat. Our escort changed to P-51s at 1340 hours when we were about five miles northeast of Hanover. The presence of the P-47s, and now the P-51s, had a relaxing effect on our concern about the Luftwaffe.

We did not see any dangerous flak on this leg of our flight plan. Our formation made two right turns that brought it onto a heading of 170 degrees and toward our IP southwest of Magdeburg. A total of 15 Me-109s and FW-190s made the first of four fighter attacks on our Group but did not shoot down any of our planes. Two of our escorting P-51s were seen to collide near Magdeburg, during combat with the enemy fighters. It appeared that only one of the P-51 pilots was able to parachute from his Mustang. We reached the IP at 1406 hours, flying at an altitude of 25,000 feet, and started a nine minute southeastwardly bomb run at our primary target near the edge of Dessau. The enemy fighters attacked our Group a second time. A FW-190 came head-on at Screwball Express. Howard and Jim made Screwball Express "jump" and the FW's 20 mm cannon shell went under us and fell away. A very thick haze was hanging over the aircraft engine plant and the cloud cover was 4/10. Flak was only moderate, but very accurate. A flak shell hit a Fortress in another Group and the bomber went down. No parachutes were seen coming out of it. The lead bombardier of our Group could not locate the aiming point in the target area and the decision was made to attack our secondary target at Leipzig. The 15 enemy planes attacked us a third time. Fortunately, they were not very good pilots and their shells again missed our B-17s.

Records indicate our secondary target was an airfield, possibly inclusive of a FW-190 plant, at the outskirts of Leipzig. As we neared that city at 1438 hours we found visibility there the same as at Dessau, and the target additionally concealed by a smoke screen. Our Group Leader made the decision to look for a target of opportunity. Our formation flew along the east side of Leipzig to avoid a heavy flak barrage over that city. A Fortress in a Group off to our right exploded and only one parachute emerged from that bomber. The fourth attack by the enemy fighters again resulted in no damage to our Group. The explosions of antiaircraft shells over the outskirts of the city were moderate in number and went off under our formation, causing only light damage to Fortresses in our Group.

It was a miracle! The 15 enemy planes attacked our Group four times, but did not shoot down any of our Fortresses. The pilots of those German planes were very, very lucky, because we didn't shoot down any of them, either.

Our formation continued past Leipzig until it was 10 miles southeast of the city. At 1448 hours our Group's heading was changed to 250 degrees as we flew in search of a target. After about 20 minutes the cloud cover opened up and we saw an airfield three miles west of Wustensacken, Germany. The location of the airfield is shown in the Mission Report as 50 degrees 30 minutes North and 9 degrees 57 minutes East. One reference book identifies this airfield with the city of Fulda. Flak in the target area was moderately heavy and very accurate. We were able to make a visual bomb run

through broken clouds and each of the planes in our formation dropped a load of 10-500 pound demolition bombs from 23,000 feet at 1516 hours. There were 17 Fortresses in our Group at the time of "bombs away." The explosions of our bombs formed a very effective pattern over the airfield. Strike photos also showed a pattern of bombs on several of the large buildings.

After "bombs" away we maintained our compass heading another 44 minutes. Our Group then turned to the northwest and flew toward Ostend, Belgium. We arrived there at 1657 hours flying at 20,000 feet. Except for flak explosions in the distance at numerous points after leaving Wustensacken, our trip home was uneventful. At 1713 hours we crossed the English coast at 9,000 feet over Clacton on Sea.

We did not realize it at the time, but our flight path today took our Group near Buchenwald, reputedly one of the five most notorious concentration camps operated by the Nazis in Germany and the occupied countries. The Buchenwald camp was southwest of Leipzig. The other four notorious camps were: Auschwitz in southern Poland; Belsen, northwest of Celle, Germany; Dachau, northwest of Munich; and Ravensbruck, north of Berlin. On our fifth mission we flew near Belsen when we bombed at Brunswick. We were near Dachau during our 12th mission when we bombed at Landsberg, and close to Ravensbruck during one of our missions to Berlin. The Nazis operated more than 30 concentration camps. These are not inclusive of Prisoner of War camps in which Allied airmen, including a minimum of 560 flight crew members of the 379th Bomb Group, were held prisoners. Records show 28,000 crew members of the 8th Air Force were POWs during World War II. Hopefully, the sight of the 8th Air Force flying overhead provided comfort and encouragement to the unfortunate individuals who were confined in any of the camps. Certainly, the prisoners must have watched the freedom of our flight with great excitement and hope. They knew that, someday, they would again live in freedom.

All of our Group's Fortresses returned safely to Kimbolton, and no injuries were reported by any of the flight crews on this mission. Screwball Express received only light flak damage, as did six other Fortresses in our Group. Our flying time on our 24th combat mission was eight hours. It seemed like a dream ready to become a reality—our crew had completed 24 combat missions and only had one more to fly.

A note in my diary classified this mission as "rough." It was! Screwball Express and the members of our crew were very lucky—and we were very thankful, too.

The Stars and Stripes newspaper of Monday, May 29, 1944, contained an article that made several very interesting statements, causing Allied readers to swell with pride:

"40 Hrs. See Blitz Reach Record Pace. 1,200 U.S. Fighters Escort 1,000 Bombers Over Reich, France." (This was the largest fighter escort force of the war.)

"Bombs Rain on Europe at Rate Of 5 Tons a Minute in Big Blitz"

"Allied air fleets rounded out their biggest day-and-night attacks of the war."

The victories of war are not without sacrifices. Initial reports said the 8th Air Force lost 24 heavy bombers and seven fighters during the day's operation. Later reports were revised to include 34 heavy bombers and 13 fighters lost in action with the enemy. The Ninth Air Force reported five B-26s lost by noon, for a total of 16 of its medium bombers lost to enemy action in 24 hours. Gunners on the bombers and U.S. fighter pilots destroyed 93 enemy aircraft.

The 379th's other mission on May 28 was very extraordinary. Twenty Fortresses from Kimbolton, plus 38 Fortresses from two other Bomb Groups, were loaded with the super-secret Grapefruit bombs for an attack on marshalling yards at Cologne, Germany. The Grapefruit bomb, officially identified as GB-1 for Glide Bomb Model One (also XM-108), was supposedly nicknamed because of its experimentation in Florida beginning in June of 1941. It was a 2,000-pound bomb carried by a high-wing structure with twin booms and a tail assembly at the rear. It looked like a crudely constructed small aircraft.

Many practice missions were flown to perfect the technique of effectively bombing with this new weapon. On several occasions the 379th Bomb Group had scheduled missions and loaded its Fortresses with these new bombs; however, the weather and/or other factors did not cooperate. Today was the first occasion on which American daylight bombers in the European Theater of Operations actually used GB-1s on a combat mission.

The 8th Air Force was not intrigued with the idea of area bombing, but Official Washington's belief that missile attacks launched miles from the targets would save many bombers and crewmen had prevailed, and today's unique mission was finally scheduled. It was a very stunning theory. Bombing formations would have to fly no closer than several miles from their targets, instead of flying directly over them. Long before the Grapefruit hit the target, the bomber formation would be far away and headed for England.

The 379th flew in the Low Group position of the 41st Combat Wing for this unusual type of attack. The 58 Flying Fortresses on this mission each carried two of these bombs, one under each wing. In order to put the bombs into a gliding attitude, they had to be released at an airspeed of nearly 200 m.p.h., much greater than the conventional cruising speed of the B-17. In practice, this was achieved by the bomber formation going into a shallow 2,000 feet/two minute dive as far as 10 miles from the target. One hundred sixteen GB-1s were released when the bomber formation's prescribed dive angle, airspeed and distance from the target were attained. The bombs dropped in a faltering manner for a short time, but started to glide after their fall became partly stabilized. From that moment, the bombs' glide paths were controlled by radio signals from the bombers that released them and were electronically "steered" at the target. The formation then leveled off and turned away from the target. Tail gunners used the intercom to provide lead bombardiers with information regarding the direction of the Grapefruit's glide path. Bombardiers were able to turn the bombs a little to the left or right through radio signals, but they could not change the bombs' angle of descent.

The 379th Bomb Group's report for May, 1944, states that its glide bombs hit and exploded near the center of Cologne. Results of this bombing attack were not good, according to a source that states the 41st Combat Wing's bomb pattern was scattered widely because of air currents, turbulence and a very inadequate guidance system.

Astonished German antiaircraft gunners thought they had achieved an amazing increase in accuracy. They actually believed they saw American mini-bombers plunging from the sky in every direction, crashing and exploding everywhere around Cologne. German war records disclose their flak gunners put in claims for shooting down more than 90 Fortresses at Cologne on this date.

Fortresses from the 526th Bomb Squadron, flying high position in the lead group dropped their bombs in salvo pattern on airfield at Wustensacken, May 28, 1944. (From photos of 379th BG Photo. Sec.)

This new type of bomb provided Axis Sally, Germany's version of Tokyo Rose, with some newsworthy material for her radio propaganda program. She claimed the 8th Air Force had developed miniature bombers, and suicidal pilots were ordered to crash those planes into the target area in kamikaze fashion.

Several months later the unsuccessful GB-1 program was replaced by an inefficient GB-4 with a flare burning on its tail and then by the GB-8 with a transmitter in the bomb's nose, allowing the bombardier to "see" on a small television screen what the missle "saw" as it glided to the target. The latter model was riddled with technical problems that aggravated its users more than it damaged the enemy. All of these programs were canceled.

Axis Sally was irreverently known as The Berlin Bitch by Allied forces in Europe. Born in the United States, she went to Berlin in 1934 to teach English. In 1941 she gained notoriety on German radio. After becoming a traitor to America because of her pro-Nazi radio work, she was brought back to the United States for trial in 1949. She served 12 years in a Federal penitentiary and in 1961 became a kindergarten music teacher. She died in 1988 at the age of 87.

Her cohort in propaganda, Lord Haw Haw, was executed by the British for his traitorous radio broadcasts from Germany during World War II.

(**Special Credit**: Please refer to *Flying Forts, The B-17 in World War II*; under Bibliography.)

Mission to Krzesinki

Monday, May 29, 1944. Tomorrow's newspapers told in the following statements about today's heavy bombardment operation by the 8th Air Force:

"Nearly 4,000 American warplanes carried the weight of a snowballing air offensive to the four corners of Hitler's continental empire and sent Nazi air raid sirens screaming past their 60th nonstop hour throughout France, Belgium, Denmark, Germany, Poland and Austria. More than 1,000 Fortresses and Liberators, escorted for the second day in a row by more than 1,200 fighter planes, flew approximately 750 miles to attack Nazi aircraft plants in Poland. While they were flying another 750 miles on their return trip to England, 600 other Fortresses and Liberators, escorted by as many fighters, flew northward from their Italian bases and dealt the seventh attack of the war to the Messerschmitt manufacturing complex around Vienna. Four hundred Ninth Air Force medium bombers attacked communication centers, transportation and coastal defenses in the occupied countries. As the German achtung system was thrown into chaos by air fleets which flew into the Reich and Austria on coordinated schedule, targets at Posen and Kreising in western Poland and at Cottbus and Sorau in southeastern Germany received destructive blows from the 8th Air Force."

This chapter provides insight into that part of the May 29th operation that relates to mission number 129 of the 379th Bomb Group into western Poland, specifically in the area around Posen. Our crew was awakened at 0300 hours for briefing at 0430 hours. The 379th Bomb Group furnished 21 Fortresses for the High Group in the 41st Combat Wing "A" and 22 Fortresses for the High Group in the 41st Combat Wing "B". Two spares were in each of these Groups. Screwball Express and our crew were assigned to lead the Low Squadron in High "A" Group. We knew the mission was going to be a long one. Looking at the yarn pulley at the corner of the briefing room's big map was confirmation of another deep penetration into enemy-occupied Europe. The two Combat Wings in which the 379th's "A" and "B" Groups flew were assigned to attack the FW-190 engine and assembly plant adjacent to the airdrome at Krzesinki, Poland.

On May 13 our Group was previously scheduled to bomb an aircraft component plant at Posen, Poland, on our 18th mission, but heavy cloud cover forced us to bomb a secondary target at Stettin, Germany. Our crew was anxious to get this one out of the way. God willing, we would return safely from this mission and get back to the States.

Takeoff was at 0800 hours. My singing of the 23rd Psalm had always been a special time for prayer during each of our 24 preceding combat takeoffs, but today the words reached a level of significance not previously attained. This was our crew's 25th takeoff on a combat mission, and our safe return would bring our tour of combat duty in the ETO to an extremely happy conclusion. This was the last time our crew would fly from Kimbolton to attack targets on the other side of the English Channel. Our crew's first mission was flown in the Low Squadron, and our 25th and final mission would also be in the Low Squadron. This seemed like a very good omen. Excited thoughts raced through my mind. Everything had to go perfectly today. Everything! Our Group and Wing assembly had to be on time and flawlessly coordinated. Weather had to be in our favor. Flak had to be light and inaccurate. Enemy fighter planes had to stay on the ground. Only this one mission remained for our crew. Only this one!

One B-17 in each of our two Groups aborted because of mechanical failure. Shortly after our two Groups reached assembly altitude, one spare in our "A" Group filled in and a "B" Group spare joined up with the 384th Bomb Group from Grafton Underwood. One spare in each of the two 379th Groups returned early to Kimbolton, according to plan. The weather was a little hazy until 0900 hours, but then cleared up for the remainder of the mission.

Flak bursts and smoke screens were in great abundance soon after we entered Germany, and all the way to Poland. We were very happy to have our P-47s, P-51s and P-38s escorting us on this mission into a country I never thought I'd see. In the target area enemy aircraft were seen taking off with some type of special assistance. It looked like the aircraft left trails of smoke and flame, similar to a rocket. Our High "A" Group approached the primary target at Krzesinki flying at 23,000 feet. Each of our B-17s carried 10-500 pound general purpose demolition bombs. The airdrome and adjacent FW-190 plant were approximately five miles southeast of Posen, which is approximately 145 miles east of Berlin. Flak in the target area was light and inaccurate. The use of chaff was effective—only Screwball Express and one other Fortress in our "A" Group sustained minor flak damage. We learned later that seven planes in our "B" Group also received minor flak damage.

The nineteen Fortresses in our High Group "A" made a visual bomb run at the target but found the briefed MPI (Mean Point of Impact) hidden by heavy smoke that hung over the target after earlier bombing by the Lead Group of our Wing. Another MPI, located in a newly built up area of the designated factory, was selected by our Group's Lead bombardier and our bombs were away at 1309 hours. Bomb damage included: eight hits on subassembly shops, three hits on medium component workshops and two hits on a small component workshop. A large workshop received four direct hits and three direct hits were made on the main office building. A storage building and the flight hanger were heavily damaged. In one paragraph of the 379th's Mission Report for this date it states the bombs hit the target with fair results; in two other paragraphs of the same Report the bombing results are identified as "good." Two B-17s in another Group went down in the target area with a total of only seven parachutes seen. One of our planes dropped a load of leaflets over Krzesinki.

At 1306 hours approximately 25 enemy fighters made numerous attacks on our High Group "B" flying in the Wing behind ours. A B-17 in that Wing was shot down by enemy fighters. It was sickening to watch a Flying Fortress spin toward earth with flames gushing from two of its engines and the plane falling apart. It was like watching a miracle happen to see 10 parachutes emerge from it. The fighter attacks continued until 1321 hours. Jerry, Tom and Frank were able to see most of these attacks clearly because their positions permitted them to face directly to the rear of our plane. They provided us with blow-by-blow accounts over the intercom.

A P-51 pilot took on four twin-engined Nazi planes and shot down all four of them. A Headquarters check of fighter pilot reports showed it was 2nd Lt. Dale Spenser, of Clymer, New York, who bagged all four ships in a matter of minutes to celebrate his first wedding anniversary. (Frank reported this at the debriefing, and an account of this feat appeared in the May 30, 1944, edition of Stars and Stripes.)

Gunners in the Fortresses of our "B" Group shot down seven of the enemy planes. None of the Fortresses in "B"

Group was lost during these attacks. Unfortunately, by the time "B" Group reached the FW-190 plant at Krzesinki, the target was completely covered with smoke from the explosions of our Group's bombs and it was necessary for "B" Group to look for a target of opportunity. Their bombing opportunity presented itself when they spotted an airfield at Schneidemuhl, Germany. Bombs from 19 of the Group "B" planes were dropped with what was reported as "fair" results.

A few minutes before 1500 hours, 25 enemy planes were observed by our "A" Group in the vicinity of 5430 N-1020 E. Most of the enemy's planes were Me-109s and FW-190s, but they were accompanied by Me-210s and Me-410s. Six of the enemy aircraft attacked our Group head-on and flew through the middle of our formation. They made a lasting impression on Jim who watched through his co-pilot's window as one of the bandits barely missed crashing into our right wing. They impressed Howard, Bob and me, as well, because of our forward positions in Screwball Express. Another of the enemy fighters dived at Screwball Express from two o'clock high with all guns blazing and disappeared under our number four engine. Gunners in Fortresses within our Group destroyed one of the enemy planes. Our fighter escort was excellent during this mission, except for an anxious period of 15 minutes prior to the attack mentioned above.

Flak was observed on the way home at five different locations, but none of it was directed at our "A" Wing. Our return trip provided us with overhead views of an airdrome with a large number of Me-109s parked on it, smoke screens over a number of cities, a large camp in a wooden area, more than 20 seaplanes on the Baltic Sea on ramps and in the water, and a convoy of eight large merchant vessels. At 1646 hours a B-17 was seen ditching in the North Sea and a report was radioed to Air-Sea rescue. Each of these observations were plotted and reported to Intelligence during debriefing.

Screwball Express touched down on the main runway at Kimbolton at 1830 hours, exactly 10 hours and 30 minutes after takeoff and with only one small flak hole in the tail section. Our 25th combat mission was the third longest of our combat tour and covered more than 1,700 miles. Our longest mission, to Sorau, Germany, lasted 11 hours and 20 minutes. Our second longest was to Stettin, Germany, with a flight time of 11 hours.

All of the Fortresses in our "A" Group returned safely to Kimbolton, and none of the planes had any wounded crewmen aboard.

The 8th Air Force lost eight B-17's in the attacks at Posen, Kreising, Cottbus and Sorau—five to enemy aircraft, two to flak and one to unknown reasons. Ninety-seven Fortresses sustained minor battle damage and five others had major damage. Eight crippled bombers on the northerly attack routes managed to reach Sweden where the crews were interned. Total heavy bomber losses for all of the day's targets included 17 B-17s and 20 B-24s. Twenty of these 37 bombers were shot down by enemy aircraft. Twelve of our fighter planes were lost in action with the enemy.

May 30 379th BG bombed aircraft factory at Halberstadt, Germany. Crew of Lt. Edward R. Burke flew Screwball Express.

May 31 379th BG bombed airfield at Gilze Rijen, Netherlands. Some of our crew flew a one hour training flight. Crew of Lt. Charles J. Lamont flew Screwball Express to Gilze Rijen, Netherlands.

May 31 The 379th Bomb Group flew 24 missions during May. Our crew flew on 11 of those missions.

Headquarters informed everyone on the airbase that the 379th Bomb Group received an unprecedented 8th Air Force Operational Grand Slam for April's bombing results:

1- Best bombing results (greatest percentage of hits)
2- Greatest tonnage of bombs dropped on targets
3- Largest number of aircraft attacking
4- Lowest losses of aircraft
5- Lowest abortive rate of aircraft sent out

The 526th Squadron's history for May notes that the officer's softball team was tied at the bottom of its league with one win and four losses...the enlisted men's team in League A was tied for first place...several Squadron members turned out for the Base track team.

The Squadron's history for May also states that Ernie and other spare gunners in the pool were placed on Detached Service with the 1059th Military Police Company to attend Ground Defense School.

June 1 379th BG mission to Hamburg, Germany, scrubbed because of weather. Our crew flew a one hour training flight.

June 2 379th's 5th double mission day. Attacked a four-howitzer medium battery position at Neufchatel, France, in the morning, and a marshalling yards at Juvisy, on the outskirts of Paris, in the afternoon. Crew of Lt. George McHugh flew Screwball Express on mission to Juvisy, France.

June 3 379th BG mission to Mulun scrubbed because of weather.

June 4 379th BG bombed a four-gun field battery at Ambleteuse, France. Crew of Lt. Lewis M. Jolls flew Screwball Express.

June 4 The following bulletin was accidentally transmitted by an Associated Press teletype operator trying to increase his transmitting speed, unaware his practice tape was mixed with the 'live' tape: "Urgent Press Associated NYK Flash Eisenhower's HQ announced Allied landings in France."

379th BG bombed coastal gun emplacements at St. Pierre du Mont, France. Screwball Express was a spare for this mission but returned early to base, according to plan.

Members of our crew made a training flight of three hours and 30 minutes. We were beginning to get angry with the situation—we completed our 25th combat mission a week ago, and we're still making training flights. Someone at our Headquarters is Snafued. We haven't even been officially notified that our tour of combat duty is over. No orders. Nothing! Just disappointment, long days, long nights, lots of waiting, and more disappointment.

Snafu! Situation normal.

June 5 Rome was liberated today!

Above: St. Andrew's Church, Kimbolton, Cambridgeshire, England. (Photo from 379th Bomb Group WWII Association.) Below: Nissen huts.

THE
LAST
MISSIONS

Mission No. 33 for our crew.

Mission No. 118 for Screwball Express.

At Home in the Barracks

Living in a Nissen hut with other officers of B-17 flight crews did nothing to satisfy one's longing for the comforts of home. England's version of the U.S. trademarked Quonset hut was designed by Peter N. Nissen, a British engineer. It was a prefabricated shelter that included a semicircular, arching roof of corrugated iron over a cement floor. A major difference in these nearly identical structures was the wood fiber insulation with which the Quonset hut was blessed—and that most Nissen's lacked.

A group of Nissen huts for flight crew enlisted men and another one for their crews' officers were located in each of the four Squadron areas. Nissen huts were also the living quarters for non-flying personnel on the Kimbolton air base. These buildings came in three sizes, smallest of which was the housing type that was 40 feet long, 16 feet wide and eight feet high at the center. The larger units were used mostly for storage of materials and equipment.

Nissen huts lacked windows in their construction plan and were very dark inside. The only natural light that entered our barracks came through improvised windows and opening of the door when anyone entered or departed the premises. I do not remember seeing even one Nissen hut that was not surrounded by mud. The concrete floor of our Nissen hut was covered with the tracked-in, everlasting reminder of the black, gooey element that constantly encircled our barracks.

Most Nissen huts were filled from end to end with the amalgamated odor of stale cigarette and cigar smoke, woolen blankets that always smelled musty and socks that were without benefit of soap and water for very long periods of time. A blend of perfumed shaving lotion was used in a futile attempt to disguise unwashed armpits. The resulting aroma was very much like that of a poorly maintained pig barn. Heat was inadequately provided by a small, black stove known as The Tortoise, possibly because of its unique shape but more likely because it was so slow in producing even a little warmth. It had an insatiable appetite for coal, a week's ration of the scarce fuel being barely enough to provide one evening of comfort.

The narrow beds, called cots, were constructed of two frames of angle iron each three feet long and held off the floor by angle iron legs. The two frames touched at the middle of the cot and formed an iron ridge that hit most of us at our hips, or in the lower lumbar region, depending on whether one slept on one's side or on one's back. The mattress was actually three separate, biscuit-like, lumpy, cushionless pads stuffed with wood shavings or straw. The middle pad rested on the ridge formed by the meeting of the two frames and constantly shifted position like a seesaw. When either end went up or down it caused cold, damp air to rush in and freeze one's underside.

By any measure, these cots were a thousand-fold improvement on pup tents, foxholes, trenches and hammocks. We were thankful for our cots, for the Nissen huts and for being in an area that was not under constant attack by the enemy.

As thankful as we were, the monotony of a Nissen hut during rain and fog created an atmosphere of uneasiness and boredom for all of us. The members of our crew, and the majority of the fellows in our barracks, had not flown a combat mission for an entire week. On each of those days our crew sloshed over to the 526th Squadron Operations building to inquire about orders sending us back to the States. During that time Howard, Jim, Bob and I flew on three training flights for a total of five and one-half hours, a less than exhilarating way for seasoned combat veterans to spend their precious time. Bad weather caused our Headquarters to scrub two missions. The period from May 30 through June 5 was a time of impatience, dissatisfaction, boredom, moodiness and irritability.

During such a time we had little to do other than sleep, eat, read, write letters and "shoot the bull." The rain made our trips to the mess hall difficult and unenjoyable. Outside recreation was washed out. Splashing through mud puddles between our barracks and Headquarters made the lack of any orders shipping us back to the States additionally disappointing. Rain soaked our clothing and the delay of our orders dampened our enthusiasm. Activity in our barracks on an average morning, afternoon or evening on any of these days was wholesome, serious, funny, provocative, dangerous, entertaining, informative, truthful, untruthful and time-consuming.

A pair of "pinks" hung on a hanger that swayed from a wire over the cot of one of the co-pilots in our barracks. The light-colored trousers worn by Air Force officers were called "pinks" because of the pink tone that livened their basic gray color. These were especially distinctive because on the previous day their owner had dipped them in 100 octane gasoline, a routine cleaning process used by most of us. It was amazing how the trousers kept their crease. The smell of gasoline was barely noticeable after they were hung outside for a few hours. Hanging in the barracks, however, they permeated the entire structure with the odor of a refinery. The odor was too much for the co-pilot, so he went to the base library to write some letters.

Someone placed a hastily scrawled sign at the end of the co-pilot's cot. The sign read, "No smoking. Fumigation in process."

A navigator with about 20 combat missions under his belt was sitting on his cot with his legs crossed Indian-style. At his feet were two sacks of candy he had accumulated by saving it, piece by piece, over several months from food packs issued to him for use during combat missions. The candy was hard, required a lot of chewing before swallowing and usually gave one's stomach an unsettled feeling. Rather than eat his candy during a mission, this sweet-toothed fellow was treating himself to his entire cache in one day.

His pilot said, "If you eat all that candy you're going to gain so much weight we'll never get our plane off the ground again. You're going to be on sick call in the morning."

The navigator: "Saying nice things about me isn't going to get you any of this candy."

The pilot: "I'm expecting a big box of homemade fudge from my girl friend in Arizona, and I'm not going to share any of it with you."

The navigator: "If she cooks like she looks, I don't want any of it."

There was a brief pause in the conversation. Then the navigator added, "Besides, your girl friend in Texas makes better fudge."

The exchange of flying pillows did no one any harm.

A bombardier at the other end of the barracks changed subjects by telling of the threatening prophecy directed to his cadet class one day by a drill sergeant while the cadets were standing at attention.

The drill sergeant: "Eyes right. Eyes left. The men you just looked at are not gonna make it to graduation."

The bombardier: "You know, I felt real sorry for the guys on my left and right—and then it hit me—they had all looked at me, too."

The CQ came through the door, water dripping from his raincoat like a dog trying to shake itself dry. Under the CQ's arm was a box filled with assorted items.

The CQ announced, "Gentlemen, in this box I bring to you some of the lowest priced necessities in all of England. Shaving cream, after shave lotion, shoe laces, toothpaste, two pairs of brand new socks, eight slightly used but freshly washed towels, a bottle of hair tonic, three combs, several decks of cards and three hundred poker chips in those patriotic red, white and blue colors. The items for sale today include only those left behind by men who completed their missions and shipped out. I'll sell these items to you dirt cheap, individually or by the box, either at my rock-bottom prices or to the highest bidders. What's your pleasure?"

At first, no one responded to his merchandising introit. Then a soft voice near me asked, "Do you have any GI shorts in that box?"

"That I do," answered the CQ, "and for only five shillings a pair."

Soft voice: "Give ya four."

CQ: "You drive a hard bargain, sir. I'll meet your price if you buy three pairs. Three pairs for 12 shillings."

Soft voice, a bit loudly, "You've got a deal."

Similar bargaining exchanges took place at most of the cots in the barracks, and in less than ten minutes the CQ emptied his box and pocketed almost 15 English pounds. I didn't buy anything from him, but did ask if he had any peroxide.

I finished writing a letter to Geri, my fiancee. A copy of the newspaper article about the 8th Air Force operation on May 29th was already clipped and ready to be pierced with a pin under the word "Posen." If I was lucky, Geri would save the newspaper articles I sent to her with my letters. A complete collection of them, consisting of one for each of my crew's combat missions, would make a nice album. (The pinholes indicated our target or target vicinity for each mission. I hadn't told her I was going to do this, but I knew she would figure it out. Nothing in any of the news articles was ever blocked out by censors.)

Five of the fellows near the center of the barracks were engaged in a noisy poker game. The tightly-tucked brown blanket on the cot around which they sat was studded with the red, white and blue poker chips one of the players purchased from the CQ a few minutes earlier. A sleeping co-pilot snoring loudly on an adjacent cot gave out a loud snort and one of the poker players told him to be quiet and stop interrupting the game. A nearby bombardier hollered out for "some peace and quiet" in hopes of getting some sack time.

Someone watching the card game broke wind. The area around the wind breaker was quickly vacated, and the poker game moved to the far end of the barracks.

Three brave souls donned raincoats and headed for the Post theater. They returned in several minutes, drenched to the skin and their shoes covered with mud.

"We saw the movie when we were in Preflight School," they explained. "Too soon to see it again. Not very good, anyway."

A voice from near the door: "Leave that mud outside. This isn't a barn—yet."

From a wearer of muddy shoes: "Then what's a cranky jackass like you doing in here?"

Bob Keller stood before a small mirror hanging near his cot and expressed concern over several strands of hair dangling from his comb.

Bob: "At first it's only a few, but before you know it, you're bald."

Howard put down the book he was reading and broke into loud, unrestrained laughter at Bob's worried comment.

A bombardier: "Hey, any of you guys want to go over to the farm pond tomorrow and shoot some loons?"

A navigator: "Not me. Last month a pilot accidentally shot himself in the foot over there while loading his pistol. No more flying for him."

A pilot: "No more flying for the navigator who went over there last week and shot off two of his fingers, either."

Someone else: "Think you could hit one?"

Another person: "A pilot or a navigator?"

The bombardier: "A loon, you nut."

Members of one flight crew were playing indoor catch with the lopsided softball. One of them unintentionally bounced it off the head of one of his crew members. It rolled into a corner in a zigzagging course, made a little spin and wobbled to a stop. No one went after it.

Jim picked up someone's banjo and started picking out a tune. He had told me that he could play a mandolin and a guitar, but I didn't know he could play a banjo. After a few minutes Jim started singing as he played.

"T is for Texas, and T's for Tennessee.
T is for Theresa, who made a fool of me."

A bombardier: "One more time, Jim, and I'll harmonize with you."

The two songsters started out in harmony, but whoever was singing tenor bombed out on several high notes.

Bob was doing pushups on the floor at the side of his cot. The exact source of the blanket with which Bob covered the floor while exercising was never known. During his early youth Bob went through a serious bout with polio. His dedication to a program of muscle-building therapy, together with his strong determination, resulted in his successful recovery. He still exercised frequently and strenuously. Bob had a well-developed body and muscles that had their own muscles.

"Ninety-eight, ninety-nine, one hundred," Bob said, as he rolled over on his back and started a five-minute bicycling routine. I watched in total amazement.

My memory flashed back to the time Bob and I bought a coffee table at the Baker Hotel in Dallas, Texas. We had gone from Ardmore to Dallas on a weekend pass with Howard and Jim. The four of us were registered in one room at the end of a hall. At Bob's suggestion, I was lying on the floor on my back with my knees pulled up above my feet. Bob opened the room's door, walked about thirty feet down the hall and turned around. "Are you ready?" he yelled. "Ready," I yelled back. Bob ran full speed down the hall, through the doorway and dived at me with his arms stretched forward. When his hands caught my knees I grabbed his shoulders and flipped him into a somersault. His feet landed squarely on a wooden coffee table that completely collapsed at the moment of impact. We closed the room's door and stacked the table's kindling in the closet. In a few minutes there was a knock at our door. The house detective entered our room and said, "Some of our guests on the floor below called the front desk and complained about some noise up here. Try to be more quiet, will you?" He started to leave, but noticed the absent coffee table. He looked in the closet. His faced tried hard to smile, but retained its serious expression. "I'll tell the desk clerk there's a coffee table missing from your room. I'm sure he'll allow you gentlemen to pay for it when you check out." I think that table cost the two of us twenty dollars.

Bob completed his exercises and sat at the end of his cot, impatiently drumming his fingers in a staccato beat on the tightly-drawn blanket. His blanket was an inspection sergeant's delight—a half-dollar tossed upon it would bounce about three inches high, turn over in midair and then bounce two more times before quivering to rest.

"I declare," he said, drumming his fingers with rhythmic movement, "if things get any more boring around here I'm going to consider moving to other quarters."

Our barracks was like every barracks in the ETO and other theaters of military operations. Its walls were filled with pictures of girl friends, pinups of swimsuit models, cartoon clips and European maps showing locations of targets bombed by resident flight crews. My favorite pinup was of Geri, wearing a white gardenia in her hair.

The conversation drifted to the time, shortly after our crew arrived at Kimbolton, when Bob, Jim, and Howard came down with something flu-like and were confined to the base hospital for a day.

I asked Howard, "Herky, what in the heck were you, Jim and Bob in the hospital for, anyway?"

Howard: "Beat's me. All I know is, we were mighty sick."

Bob: (Jokingly) "In my case it was probably an extreme example of advance cowardice." We laughed at the absurdity of his comment..

A bombardier: "Our radio operator is always worried about having to relieve himself after we go on oxygen. He hates to untangle himself from all those wires, grab a portable oxygen bottle and go into the bomb bay to use the relief tube." (The relief tube, a hose named for obvious reasons, hung in the bomb bay and had a funnel on the end of it. The funnel benefited a lack of accurate aim. The opposite end of the hose was attached to an L-shaped metal Pitot tube in the belly of the airplane. The metal tube stuck out of the underside of the fuselage and pointed to the rear of the bomber. When the plane was in flight, the fast rush of air past the end of this tube caused a strong suction on the liquid coming down through the hose. This minimized the possibility of an overflowing funnel. More importantly, the liquid was pulled out of the hose and expelled outside the plane before the cold temperatures at high altitude caused it to freeze.)

The bombardier continued: "Well, as I was about to board our B-17 before we taxied out to take off, I saw that tube sticking out and this great idea came to me. I carefully loosened the tube and turned it 180 degrees so it would face directly forward." (The tube conventionally faced forward, but this one had been installed to point to the rear and allow for outward flow of fluid.) "I told all members of the crew, but not our radio operator, why they should not use the relief tube on this mission. As a precaution, these crew members hit the latrine in the special tent set up by our ground crew."

"An hour after takeoff we were flying at 10,000 feet and I reminded the crew by intercom that it was time to use the relief tube before going on oxygen. Our radio operator waited fifteen additional minutes, making certain he would relieve himself at the latest possible moment and not have to use the tube again for a long time. He filled the funnel to capacity, and then to overflowing. The pressure of air rushing in overcame the gravitational pull and contents of the funnel and its tube blew out and covered the clothing worn by the radio operator. It froze into countless little droplets and did not thaw until several hours later when we descended to a lower altitude over the English Channel."

Most of the officers: "You dog!" Their laughter could be heard in the barracks on either side of ours. "What a lousy trick," they chuckled.

Howard: "The other day I was visiting with Tom, our ball turret gunner. He told me about a bombardier who, during a practice bombing mission in Texas last January, dropped a practice bomb right down the middle of a two-holer on a ranch near a bombing range. He hit that darned outhouse dead center. The ranch house, and hopefully the outhouse, were not occupied at the time. The bombardier said the direct hit was accidental and unintentional. Do you believe that, Ken?"

Ken: "Absolutely, Howard! Even if it was intentional, credit for the direct hit on that outhouse belongs equally to the pilot and not only to the bombardier. Remember, the plane's commander helped in setting up the autopilot. That's what's so great about the Air Force, Howard. Teamwork!"

Two pilots, not known for their mechanical cunning but nevertheless attempting to prove their inventiveness, devised a way to keep coal burning in The Tortoise. They rigged a metal tube that ran from inside the stove, up through the barracks' roof, and into a gallon can fastened on the roof's ridge. The can contained a mixture of engine oil and petrol. A small valve in the tube controlled the volume and frequency with which the mixture dripped into the stove.

They carefully built a pyre of wood inside The Tortoise and underlaid it with crumpled paper. With architectural precision they placed selected pieces of coal into a pattern that would have aroused jealousy in an arsonist. They lit the paper with a Zippo lighter and watched the wood catch afire. Minutes later, edges of the pieces of coal started to burn with a red glow. The big moment finally arrived. Slowly, one of the pilots gently opened the valve. The dripping of the mixture was visible through the stove's open door. Minor flashes of flame satisfied the creative novices that the contraption was working. They called it The Automatic Fuel Feeder. What an ingenious idea! The proud pilots beamed with self-esteem. One of them closed the stove's door with a gesture of satisfaction and shook hands with his fellow inventor.

It happen less than three minutes later. An explosion sparked by the accumulation of petrol fumes ripped off The Tortoise's door and spewed out a black cloud of smoke and ashes. The loud bang brought everyone to their feet. Someone instinctively yelled, "Flak," and disappeared under a cot. The smoke and ashes covered everything so completely that it took several hours to sweep things clean and clear the smoke from the barracks. Everyone's clothing had to be brushed several times. Fortunately, the rain stopped and we were able to do the brushing outside the barracks.

Someone dropped in with a prediction the Group would be going on a mission very early in the morning. That was of little concern to Jim, Bob, Howard and me. Our 25-mission tour was done. We hit the sack about 2200 hours.

The Tortoise, without its door, looked like a miniature, yawning oil drum. That co-pilot's "pinks" were covered with black soot and ashes. Unfortunately, they needed another dipping.

Experiences like these are probably very similar to those that occurred in many other barracks throughout England during World War II.

None of us in any branch of military service had enough opportunities for laughter while we were on duty in a combat zone. We leaped at every chance to reminisce and laugh, and enjoyed sharing recollections and humor with each other. Barracks, pup tents, fox holes and trenches throughout the world were not immune to situations in which men were lucky to find one of those rare occasions when something made them laugh.

Laughter helped us endure the frightening and deadly spectaculars of aerial warfare associated with combat missions past and future. It unlocked doors behind which something humorous would otherwise have remained hidden. Laughter was the sound of happiness in a very dangerous yet boring existence.

(**Special Credit:** Please refer to *One Last Look*; under Bibliography.)

Mission to Caen

Tuesday, June 6, 1944. Our crew became part of one of the most spectacular events in military history three hours after we hit the sack last night.

The door of our Nissen hut flew open with a loud bang at 0100 hours. The voice of an officer from Squadron Operations roared an announcement.

"Everybody in this barracks is flying a mission today."

Of course, I knew for a fact he didn't mean Howard, Jim, Bob or me. Our 25-mission tour was behind us. Howard yelled back an appropriate clarification of this fact. Bob, Jim and I echoed Howard's protest.

"Everybody is flying today," blared the Squadron officer. "Everybody!" The emphasis he placed on "everybody" was audible enforcement of his intention to include our crew in his extremely disturbing proclamation.

Howard dressed quickly and headed for the 526th Squadron's Operations hut. He assured us things would be straightened out, but told us to meet him in the mess hall— "just in case."

The message he brought back filled us with total disappointment. "Our tour has been extended to 30 combat missions," Howard said flatly.

"But the 8th AF told us it would be 25," we protested. "We've been planning on that number since before we left the States," we pleaded.

We rationalized the situation among ourselves. Our 25-mission tour of duty was increased to 30 without any warning or even an "excuse me." Such action meant something big was about to happen. The 8th Air Force would not increase the number to 30 without a darned good reason. It must be something big, and our crew was going to be part of it. Howard hurried away to explain the situation to the rest of our crew.

At 0230 hours the briefing officer's opening statement was, "Gentlemen, this is it. Today is D-Day." The briefing room nearly collapsed as wild cheers, whoops and whistles combined in jubilant response to the announcement. Operation Overlord was finally under way.

General Eisenhower's Order of the Day was issued to each individual of the Allied Expeditionary Force. It began, "Soldiers, sailors and airmen of the Allied Expeditionary Force. You are about to embark upon the great crusade, toward which we have striven these many months. The eyes of all the world are upon you. The hopes and prayers of liberty-loving people everywhere march with you." It continued with a comment about destruction of the German war machine and elimination of Nazi tyranny over oppressed

peoples of Europe. It praised the infliction of defeats upon the Germans in open battle, man to man, and reviewed the air offensive's serious reduction of Germany's air strength and its capacity to wage war on the ground. The Order ended with, "Good luck! And let us beseech the blessing of Almighty God upon this great and noble undertaking."

The two messages remembered by most Allied troops on the transport ships came over the ships' loudspeakers. One was a command: "Away all boats." The other was The Lord's Prayer.

The BBC announced the invasion to the French Underground in a two-part message. The first half was, "The long sobs of the violins of autumn." The second half of the message was, "wounds my heart with a monotonous languor." The words are from "Song of Autumn," a 19th century poem by French poet Paul Verlaine.

We were given the following information: More than 1,000 RAF bombers had pounded German batteries along the French coast between 2330 hours last night until sunrise, and would be out in full strength again today. An 8th Air Force armada of 1,365 Fortresses and Liberators would attack more than 100 German targets in the first assault along the French coast in predawn hours. Eighth Air Force fighters would provide blanket-patrol to the entire area. The Ninth Air Force would bomb, strafe and patrol from early morning until dark. Enemy fighters were predicted to be very minimal in number. Flak was expected to be meager, if any at all. Paratroopers and gliders had already dropped on the Cherbourg peninsula. We roared our approval when told of the hundreds of life-size, rubber "paratrooper dolls" dropped to confuse the Germans. The dolls were nicknamed Reuben and covered with firecrackers set to explode upon landing. Navy warships would bombard the beaches. Assault troops would be just a few hundred yards offshore, waiting to land immediately after pre-invasion bombing of coastal defenses stopped. Over 175,000 men would be put ashore by the Allies. Invasion plans formulated in General Eisenhower's Circus Wagon, the trailer he and his staff used in England, were unfolding in dramatic sequence. It was a precisely planned military masterpiece.

Field Order #378 of the 8th Air Force provided us with details pertinent to our crew. The 379th Bomb Group was ordered to dispatch seven squadrons of seven aircraft each and attack the defended locality and the radar and ship watching installations at Arromanches, France. Our target was south across the Channel from Portsmouth, England, and several miles east of Omaha Beach. The 379th's 47 Fortresses formed two Combat Wings, one of three Squadrons (ABC), and another of four Squadrons (DEFG), with each Wing led by a Pathfinder aircraft because of cloud cover at our primary target. The purpose of the seven-plane formations was to keep bomb patterns small and away from thousands of paratroopers in the target area. The precise position of each plane in the squadron, each squadron in the formation and the formation's position in the bomber column were carefully emphasized in a repetitious review.

Our crew was extremely disappointed to learn we were not going to fly this mission in Screwball Express. We had always known "our plane" would be assigned to another crew after our 25th mission. Unlike flight crews, Flying

Fortresses were seldom 'retired' from combat duty and flew until they could fly no more. We believed our tour of duty was completed— our Squadron Operations personnel had the same understanding. The transfer of Screwball Express to another crew was consequently no surprise. However, circumstances had changed and we were flying another mission today—our 26th. In the excitement of D-Day, reassignment of Screwball Express to our crew had somehow been overlooked—at least it had not been done. As a result, our crew was assigned to fly the Arromanches mission in a B-17G delivered to the 379th Bomb Group one week after Screwball Express arrived at Kimbolton. The serial number of our Flying Fortress for today's mission was 42-97170. Our crew had flown 24 of its 25 combat missions in Screwball Express. We were very apprehensive about switching aircraft for the mission today. Some of us felt the situation was unlucky, and one that added deep dimension to the fear that continuously stalked us before and during every combat mission.

The mud at the sides of the taxi strip was thick, slimy and uninviting. It would have been extremely unfortunate to run off the edge and get stuck. As we taxied out to the main runway, I thought back to the time when Howard ran off the edge of a perimeter strip at the Ardmore, Oklahoma, airfield following a heavy rainstorm. In that incident the left wheel of the plane sank almost two feet into a mud hole. To minimize Howard's embarrassment, the fellows in our crew quickly rounded up some shovels and started digging the mud away so he could taxi the plane back onto the perimeter strip. Howard was standing behind us, giving advice. An officer of high rank appeared and asked, "Who's in command of that B-17?" Howard snapped to attention and said, "I am, sir." The other officer snapped back, "Then help dig it out, Lieutenant." Howard never taxied another B-17 into a mud hole.

We heard a loud bang as we taxied for our D-Day takeoff. It sounded very much like an exploding flak shell. Our aircraft stopped in a left-sided lurch when the tire on our left landing gear blew out. A tow truck was dispatched to pull the plane out of the way so others could get by, and another truck transported our crew back to Headquarters. At 0445 hours Squadrons ABC took off on schedule, followed at 0505 hours by Squadrons DEFG. I watched through a pair of tears as Screwball Express, flying in the second formation, disappeared into the clouds above Kimbolton. The crew of 1st Lt. Lloyd L. Burns from the 525th Squadron was on board "our plane." Today was D-Day, and a blowout kept our crew on the ground. It wasn't much to write home about.

Our crew tried hard to accept the treatment Fate heaped upon us on this historic day. Our egos were as deflated as the flat tire that grounded us. Field Order #379 from the 8th Air Force was received at Group Headquarters at approximately 0550 hours. In numeric coincidence, Field Order #379 ordered the 379th Bomb Group to provide a six-plane Low Squadron to fly a mission with a Lead Squadron from the 303rd Bomb Group at Molesworth. Our target was a choke point formed by the intersection of a road and bridge at Caen, about 15 miles southeast of Arromanches and 30 miles south-

"THE ALLIED FORCES HAVE LANDED" In addition to continuous radio broadcasts, hundreds of thousands of these leaflets were dropped by Allied bombers over France and other enemy-occupied countries throughout D-Day. Photos circa June 6, 1944: Provided to me by Dr. Frank R. Craig.

west of LeHavre. The target was in heavy use by German troops and tanks moving to the beaches. During the hastily called briefing, our crew was assigned to fly Fortress #42-31189 in Lead position of the Low Squadron of the 303rd/379th Composite Group. This aircraft was a spare B-17G Lead plane that was assigned to the 525th Squadron of the 379th Bomb Group on November 22, 1943.

At the approximate time our six-plane Squadron was beginning to check equipment and preflight engines before takeoff, the target at Arromanches was bombed by the ABC Squadrons at 0707 hours from 15,000 feet. Squadrons DEFG dropped their bombs on the same target from 14,000 feet at 0711 hours. The early morning bombing by the 379th Group at Arromanches was accomplished by the PFF technique through solid cloud cover and results were unobserved. None of the flight crews on this mission saw any friendly or unfriendly fighter planes, and no flak was encountered by either of these formations. All Fortresses in the 379th Bomb Group's seven Squadrons returned safely from Arromanches, beginning at 0939 hours for ABC Squadrons and at 1010 hours for DEFG Squadrons.

Our takeoff was at 0755 hours. My singing of the 23rd Psalm was done with customary reverence and included a special petition for a successful invasion by the Allied forces. Our six-plane Squadron assembled with the Lead Squadron of the 303rd Bomb Group at 13,000 feet over Molesworth at 0820 hours. The sky over this part of England was still 4/10ths overcast and thickened to 8/10ths over the English Channel and 10/10ths immediately inland from the French coast. Our formation was surrounded by more than 1,000 heavy bombers going to and returning from their targets. We were astounded by the number of naval ships we saw in the Channel as our eyes searched through occasional holes in the clouds. We were witnessing the largest invasion in world history. Almost three million Allied combat and support personnel were involved in the Normandy invasion, and more than half of these were from the United States. (Several weeks later Jim learned a close first cousin of his was killed on one of the beaches.) Records of D-Day disclose 59 convoys were involved in the invasion. Navy records say 5,000 ships were used; British records say it was 4,500 ships. The code name of this mammoth naval movement was Operation Neptune. A worried thought flashed through my mind—what a target all those ships, boats and landing craft would make for the Luftwaffe!

Our 303rd/379th Composite Group was flying at 17,000

Gen. Eisenhower addresses the people of the occupied countries: "To the people of western Europe: the troops of the allied expeditionary forces have landed on the coast of France.." He spoke of the United Nations' plan for liberation of Europe—appealed to everyone, including the underground, to follow instructions already received—urged them to continue to resist, but not to risk their lives needlessly. To citizens of France he spoke of his pride in leading their valiant soldiers—asked all citizens to follow their leaders—cautioned them against premature uprising—reminded them the civil administration of France must be ensured by the French people and promised that traitors to France would be condemned. The French people were guaranteed they would choose their future representatives and government.

feet when it crossed the enemy coast at 0934 hours. In five minutes our bombs would be dropped on our target at Caen. In our bomb bay were 12-500 pound bombs and a 1,000 pounder was carried under each wing. All of the 14 bombs in each of our B-17s were the general purpose type.

On page one of the 379th's Mission Report of our attack at Caen it states, "The 379th Squadron was flying with the 303rd as a Lead and without a PFF ship in its formation." It's D-Day, our Composite Group is supposed to attack a vital choke point at Caen in support of the invasion, the target is completely hidden by clouds and our formation is without a PFF ship. How this unfortunate situation developed was beyond comprehension. The following is quoted from the 6 June 1944 Mission Report of the 303rd Bomb Group concerning the 303rd/379th Composite Group mission to Caen on that date:"We took off with six scheduled aircraft between 0735-0739 hours to fly 1st and 2nd flights of the Composite Group of the 41st Combat Wing. The six ships of the 379th Group joined us over Base at 0820 hours." The Report then details the flight plan to Brighton on the English coast and continues with, "Proceeded straight to the target on course. Undercast, about half way across the Channel, became 10/10ths and completely obscured the target. We flew over the target (at 17,000 feet) and then to the secondary target which was also obscured. We made a run on the last resort target but it was also covered by 10/10ths overcast. We then proceeded to briefed return course to return to Base."

We saw no flak, no enemy planes and very few friendly fighters on this mission. Our six-plane Squadron left the 303rd's Lead Squadron after we crossed the English coast at Portland Bill at 1116 hours. Groups of Flying Fortresses were everywhere around us, waiting their turn to land—the 305th Bomb Group from Chelveston, the 306th from Thurleigh, the 303rd from Molesworth, the 92nd from Podington and the 384th from Grafton Underwood. Our "Fortress for the day" touched down at Kimbolton as gently as a falling feather— Howard and Jim took no chances of jarring the bombs in the bomb bay and under the wings. Our six-plane Squadron's flight time on this mission was 4:50 hours. Our crew now had 26 combat missions behind us. We did not know how many might be ahead of us.

My written report to the Commanding Officer, 379th Bombardment Group, dated 6 June 1944, is included with the Mission Report maintained by The National Archives regarding this mission, and states as follows:

"We ran into solid overcast and could not drop our bombs. We were following the Lead Squadron (from the 303rd BG) and they did not release. We were briefed to drop on the Lead Ship of the Lead Squadron, which did not drop. We returned to base with our bombs on board. All A/C returned their bombs to base."

It was extremely difficult to feel elated over being a part of the D-Day invasion. A blown tire relegates our crew to an aging Flying Fortress, our target becomes hidden by 10/10ths cloud cover and we find ourselves flying in a Composite Group "without a PFF ship in its formation." My report in the preceding paragraph was unquestionably the most difficult I have ever written. Circumstances beyond our control did not permit our crew to be effective in one of the most important military moments of all time. It wasn't much to write home about.

That darned blowout! If only it had not happened. If only we had been on the mission to Arromanches today, instead of this one. If only we had—

If we *had* blindly bombed through the overcast, we could have inadvertently killed hundreds of American and British paratroopers on either side and within one thousand yards of the bridge and road choke point at Caen. It was a blessing— for the safety of those paratroopers and for the peace of mind of every crew member in our attack formation—that we did *not* drop our bombs.

Members of our crew were grateful for the following sentence in an article that appeared in The Stars and Stripes on June 7, 1944: "Most of the bombers in the second raid returned with their loads because the presence of Allied troops made it inadvisable to bomb through overcast." It made the situation a little easier, knowing that some of the crews on other

D-Day missions had also returned with their bombs—and for the same reason.

Field Order #380 from the 8th Air Force was received by our Group's Headquarters shortly after 1200 hours. It ordered the 379th Bomb Group to dispatch 33 Fortresses to form the "B" Group of the 41st Combat Wing for an attack on a road bridge over the river at Conde sur Noireau, France. The target was located about 23 miles south of Caen. Three PFF planes were assigned to lead these Groups. Bombs were successfully dropped by the Lead Group through broken clouds at 2029 hours from 14,000 feet. The High Group used PFF and bombed at 2018 hours from 15,000 feet. The Low Group bombed visually at 2026 hours from 13,000 feet. Two of the planes that were dispatched on this mission failed to accomplish Group assembly because of bad weather conditions.

Flak at the target was meager, but accurate. One of 12 bursts killed the tail gunner in the crew of Lt. Roderick T. French of the 526th Squadron. The serial number of the Fortress flown by Lt. French on this mission was 42-97128— Screwball Express. That crew also flew the morning mission to Arromanches. All of the 379th's Fortresses on this mission returned to Kimbolton, but two other crewmen were injured by flak over the target at Conde sur Noireau.

Another "if" in the sequence of events above could have involved our tail gunner, Jerry Lindsey. If we had flown Screwball Express to Arromanches on the morning mission, we would very likely have flown in Screwball Express to Conde sur Noireau in the afternoon. If we had, Jerry might have been the unfortunate tail gunner from the 379th Bomb Group whose life was snuffed out by flak over France on D-Day.

Officially, June 6, 1944, was the sixth occasion on which the 379th Bomb Group recorded a double-mission day. Actually, the 379th flew three combat missions that day, based on the following factual summary:

Target	Location	Field Order No.	Mission No.
Installations	Arromanches	378	136
Road Bridge	Caen	379	136
River Bridge	Conde sur Noireau	380	137

The mission to Caen was assigned under a separate Field Order and involved a different target, location, flight crews, aircraft and time than the Field Order for the mission to Arromanches. Logically, the mission to Caen should have been given a separate mission number. Our flight crew received credit for the mission, and so did the other five 379th crews that flew with us to Caen, but credit was not given to the 379th Bomb Group. Records indicate the 303rd Bomb Group received credit for the mission to Caen on D-Day.

General Dwight D. Eisenhower, according to one source, was faced with a few more than 400 Luftwaffe planes on D-Day. He had more than 10,500 fighting planes at his disposal, and over 3,200 transport planes and gliders.

It's easy to understand why General Ike was so confident when he said, "If you see fighting aircraft over you, they will be ours."

His forecast about D-Day air cover was almost totally accurate. Only two Luftwaffe pilots attacked Allied troops

THE 379th BOMB GROUP ON D-DAY
JUNE 6, 1944

Mission Data	ARROMANCHES — Squadrons A-B-C (7 B-17s ea. in 1 CBW)	ARROMANCHES — Squadrons D-E-F-G (7 B-17s ea. in 1 CBW)	CAEN — 1 Squadron of 6 B-17s in 303/379 Comp. Grp.	CONDE sur NOIREAU — 3 Groups of 12 B-17s each-- formed 41st Combat Wing "B"
379th Mission No.	136	136	136	137
8th AF Field Order No.	378	378	379	380
379th B-17s on Mission	20 plus 1 PFF	27 plus 1 PFF	6 with no PFF	33 plus 3 PFF
Primary Target	---Radar and Ship Watching Operations---		Bridge/Road Intersection	River Bridge
1st Aircraft Airborne	0445 hrs	0505 hrs	0755 hrs	1745 hrs
Assembly Point & Altitude	14,000' over Base	14,000' over Base	13,000' over Molesworth	18,000' over Molesworth
English Coast Out	0637 hrs at Brighton	0641 hrs at Shoreham	0908 hrs at Brighton	1944 hrs
Enemy Coast In	0708 at Arromanches	0711 at Arromanches	0934 hrs	Ld 2020-Hi 2011-Lo 2025 hrs
Weather at Target	10/10	10/10	No Visibility	Fair Visibility
Bombing Altitude/Heading	15,000' & 227 MH	14,000' & 248 MH	17,000'	14,000' & 190 MH
Bomb Run Type	PFF	PFF	none	PFF
379th B-17s On Attack	21	28	0	34
379th B-17s Not Attack	0	0	6 (10/10 & no PFF)	2 (weather at assembly)
Bomb Load per B-17	6,000 lbs GP	8,500 lbs GP	8,000 lbs GP	6,000 lbs GP
Bombs Away	0707.5 hrs	0711 hrs	no bombs away	Ld 2029-Hi 2018-Lo 2026 hrs
Bombing Results	Unobserved	Unobserved	None	Good
Flak During Mission	None	None	None	12 Bursts at Target
Enemy Aircraft Sighted	None	None	None	None
Fighter Escort	None	None	None	Good
Enemy Coast Out	0730 hrs at Agon	0735 hrs at Agon	None	2052 hrs
English Coast In	0844 at Weymouth	0846 at Weymouth	1116 at Portland Bill	2159 at Portland Bill
English Coast Altitude In	12,000'	12,200'	16,000'	1,500'
1st Aircraft Landed	0939 hrs	1010 hrs	1222 hrs	2310 hrs (dusk)
379th Aircraft MIA	0	0	0	0
379th Personnel KIA	0	0	0	0
				Tail Gunner-Screwball Express
RE: SCREWBALL EXPRESS	Screwball Express Flew Mission in Squadron D		Orig. Crew in 42-31189	Screwball Express flew in Hi Grp

101

during the initial landings at Normandy. Only ten enemy fighters were engaged by 8th Air Force planes that strafed and dive-bombed all day. All other Luftwaffe planes were moved away from the French coast to avoid destruction from Allied bombing.

General Hap Arnold wrote this about the situation: "D-Day should have been a field day for a strong Luftwaffe. Thousands of ships and boats and landing craft were crowded into the Channel. A dominant German air fleet could have created incalculable havoc. The Germans were aware of their opportunity. Their success in the initial phases of the war was largely conditioned on the employment of air power. While the Luftwaffe was now depleted, it had, for months, husbanded its strength in hope of giving violent opposition to our air attacks on vital targets. On D-Day, the Allied Forces—air, sea, ground, service—all struck at the most vital target of all, the overland route to Berlin. Yet the Luftwaffe failed to appear. The USAF and the RAF had made it impossible."

I understand the following saying started making the rounds among older soldiers of the Wehrmacht:

"If you see a white airplane, it's American.
If you see a black airplane, its the RAF.
If you don't see any airplanes, it's the Luftwaffe."

The Ninth Air Force lost two of its Marauders, three fighter-bombers and 15 troop-carrier aircraft in all its operations through noon on D-Day. The 8th Air Force reported four heavy bombers lost in its morning, noon and mid-afternoon missions. A newspaper article the following day said Allied air forces lost 31 aircraft on D-Day. It went on to say enemy aerial activity had picked up slightly, and by 5 pm on June 7 the Allies had lost 70 planes since the first troops landed in Europe. Most of those planes were presumably lost to flak.

High-ranking officers of Supreme Headquarters emphasized, however, that there was no reason to believe the Luftwaffe had been defeated. "Fighting of the greatest severity is in store before the Luftwaffe is wiped out," according to one air officer.

(**Special Credit:** Please refer to *The World War II Quiz and Fact Book*; under Bibliography.

Mission to Flers

Wednesday, June 7, 1944. A wake-up call at 0430 hours reconfirmed our crew's combat tour was still not over. Briefing was at 0600 hours. It quickly became evident the 379th Bomb Group was scheduled for another maximum effort today. Our target was a highway bridge over a railroad marshalling yards at Flers, France, 27 miles south of Caen. The bridge was at the south end of the yards, at a point where two 90 degree railroad lines intersected, and was in heavy use by German troops and tanks moving toward the beaches. Forty-seven Fortresses, including seven planned spares, were furnished by the 379th to form the Lead and Low Groups of the 41st Combat Wing "A". The first aircraft of our Lead Group was airborne at 0925 hours, and the Low Group began its takeoff 15 minutes later.

Our crew knew why Screwball Express was not assigned to us for this mission. Its tail section was badly damaged by flak during its mission to Conde sur Noireau on D-Day, and repairs had not yet been completed. Fortress number 7213-F was ours for this mission. "The Lord is my shepherd; I shall not want," I sang, as this bomber lifted from the runway and carried our crew through 5/10 stratocumulus clouds for Group and Wing assembly at 15,000 feet over Splasher #16. The formation built itself in a very orderly manner, and our Fortress for the day took its assigned position as High Squadron Lead.

During our climb for altitude my battle station in the Plexiglas nose of the aircraft provided me an unhurried opportunity to observe the country-side through the broken clouds. The network of English roads presented a labyrinth of black and gray ribbons upon which cars, lorries and bicycles traveled in lackadaisical fashion. Despite the lethargic progression, everyone seemed to know where they were going and, most importantly, everyone seemed to get there. The roads seldom went directly north, south, east or west, but took off in adventurous angles and curves that knitted the cities, towns and villages into a unique pattern. During the Battle of Britain in 1940, the British had a well-founded fear that German paratroopers would land in England's tranquil countryside and infiltrate its rural areas with hundreds, perhaps thousands, of enemy troops. As a hindrance to such an event, the British had apparently taken down every directional road sign in all of England. The enemy would have been in total confusion about which road went where, and how far anyplace was, and in what direction. The plan was a good one and was still in effect, even though it had been a long time since the Battle of Britain. The lack of road signs created great confusion among us wayfaring Americans, and caused us to make frequent inquiries for directions. It seemed to us that practically everything we asked about was always "a hundred yards down th' road," positioned in front of a very positive and assuring "Y' cawn't missit!"

1940 seemed like a lifetime ago. I graduated from the Edwardsville, Illinois, Senior High School exactly four years ago today--June 7, 1940.

Six of the seven spares filled in and flew the mission--one spare with the 351st Bomb Group from Polebrook, one with the 379th Low Group, one with the 401st from Deenethorpe, one with the 384th from Grafton Underwood, and two with the 303rd from Molesworth. The remaining spare returned to Kimbolton as briefed. Additionally, the 379th sent one Lead GH Fortress to the 457th Bomb Group from Glatton. The 379th was consequently represented in all six Bomb Groups of the 41st and 94th Combat Wings of the 1st Bombardment Division during this mission.

Our Lead Group crossed the English coast out at Shoresham at 1120 hours and an altitude of 20,000 feet. The Low Group was one minute behind us at this point and at 19,500 feet. Records show the High Group informed us their GH equipment was not operating properly, but do not provide additional related information. The thickening cloud cover over the English Channel made visibility difficult, although we were able to catch a glimpse or two of hundreds of naval vessels off the beaches. The French coast was crossed by our Lead Group at 1143 hours, and by the Low Group two minutes later.

Weather over the continent was 10/10ths undercast, with clouds topping out at 12,000 feet. Visibility was unlimited at our altitude. Bombing by our Lead Group was done with GH equipment after a nine minute and 30 seconds bomb run. Each of the B-17s in our Lead Group carried 6-1,000 pound general purpose and RDX bombs, and aircraft in the Low Group each carried 12-500 pounders. Our bombs were dropped at 1158.5 hours from 20,000 feet on a magnetic heading of 268 degrees. We made a right turn after bombs away and headed for home. Our Low Group's leader was apparently not satisfied with its initial bomb run, and led that Group through a 360 degree turn for a second run at the dropping point. Bombs of the Low Group were salvoed at 1235 hours from an altitude of 19,100 feet on a compass heading of 264 degrees. The crew in the Low Group's Lead plane observed through a hole in the clouds that the area around the intersection of the railroad tracks at the south end of the marshalling yards had been damaged by our Lead Group's bombs. Although most of the bomb strikes by both of our Groups were obscured by clouds, photo reconnaissance later confirmed "good" bombing results.

Our Lead Group left the enemy coast at 1217 hours and crossed into England at Portland Bill one hour and seven minutes later at 15,000 feet. Our Low Group was about 35 minutes behind us at both points.

Stratocumulus clouds had a base at 2,000-3,000 feet over southern England and rose to 7,000 feet. The High Group asked permission to return directly to its home base and took advantage of an opening in the clouds for its descent. The cloud cover at Kimbolton was reported as 3/10ths, so our Group felt safe in flying at 8,000 feet for the flight inland. When we arrived at our airfield, however, the cloud cover had increased to 10/10ths. To ensure ourselves a safe letdown, Fortresses in our Lead Group descended individually through the clouds and landed one at a time.

We did not see any flak or enemy fighters on the entire mission. We were further surprised at not seeing any friendly fighters, either. All of the B-17's from the 379th Bomb Group returned safely to Kimbolton. Our attack at Flers today, like our attack at Dijon on March 28th, was very easy and uneventful.

Flying time on our 27th combat mission was 5 hours and 45 minutes.

The June 8, 1944 edition of Stars and Stripes contained a story headlined with the words, "Beaches Clear of Enemy." The article stated, "Eighth Air Force heavy bombers continued their support of ground troops yesterday afternoon by attacking a number of road intersections near towns south of Caen in an effort to block off possible German reinforcements. In addition to escort duty, Eighth fighters strafed and bombed over a 40-50 mile arc in advance of Allied ground forces."

"Up to early afternoon only two formations of 12 enemy aircraft approached the beaches and had no chance to attack Allied troops. A total of 20 German fighters were destroyed at a loss of five Allied aircraft."

"One Me-410 was shot down by a P-47 12 feet above the ground. By late afternoon only 12 fighter-bombers had been lost, all of them to ack-ack fire."

"It was announced yesterday that the Allied air forces, hammering rail centers before D-Day, flew the stupendous total of 21,000 sorties in the first six days of June. So effective was the offensive, SHAEF said, that before the landings 25 railroad bridges and nine highway bridges across the Seine were destroyed."

Mission to Orleans

Thursday, June 8, 1944. Being awakened at 0045 hours was not welcomed with much enthusiasm by crew members of the 379th Bomb Group who were scheduled for today's combat mission. Briefing for 53 flight crews consisting of 477 men was set for 0200 hours. Hundreds of ground crew members, headquarters and support personnel were equally unhappy with such an early morning imposition.

One of the fellows in our barracks complained loudly about having to get up so early. A voice at the front of the barracks spoke for the rest of us when it asked the complainer,

"Would you like for your sentiments to be relayed to the guys on the beaches?"

Today's mission was number 139 for the 379th Bomb Group. The directive, received at our Group Headquarters only minutes before our wakeup call, was issued in Field Order 383 of the 8th Air Force.

During briefing we learned 39 of our Group's aircraft were to form the Lead, High and Low Groups of the 41st Combat Wing "B" on a mission to attack the railroad bridge over the marshalling yards at Orleans, France. Another 14 Fortresses from our airfield were to form the Lead Group of the 41st "D" composite Combat Wing and attack the bridge across the river at Orleans. Destruction of these targets would cause significant disruption to the transportation of German troops and armament being rushed to the invasion area.

Our takeoff was at 0503 hours and the "D" Group left 23 minutes later. My singing of the 23rd Psalm so early in the day was a bit raspy, but my belief in the meaning of its words was as clear as the ringing of a sharply struck bell.

Screwball Express had not been completely repaired and a B-17G with serial number 42-38058 was assigned to our crew for this mission. The landing gear of a B-17 from the 526th Squadron collapsed during take off, preventing other planes from using the main runway. When all of our aircraft were finally airborne our Combat Wing assembled over Kimbolton at 9,000 feet. At 0630 hours a ball turret gunner in the High Group thought he heard the bail out signal. He was in error. Whatever caused the ringing in his ears, it was not the signal to bail out. Fortunately, he jumped out while our Wing was still over England and he parachuted safely down to earth.

We experienced 9/10ths cloud cover from the time we took off until 0703 hours when we flew over Worthing on England's southern coast at 20,000 feet. Four of the eight spare bombers in "B" and "D" Wings returned to base as planned. Three of the eight filled in with "B" Wing and one Fortress from the 525th Squadron filled in with the 351st Bomb Group from Polebrook. Cloud cover half way across the Channel thinned to only 4/10ths, but when we crossed the enemy coast at 0746 hours the clouds had thickened to 7/10ths at 21,000 feet. The direction of metro winds was found to be accurate with the weather information supplied to us at the briefing, but 10 to 15 mph faster than expected. The wind direction at our altitude was checked at 0804 hours and found to be 328 degrees at a speed of 44 m.p.h.

Orleans is approximately 65 miles south of Paris and 70 miles northeast of Tours. During the flight to our target we observed several small formations of German fighter planes, but all of them stayed at considerable distance from our bomber Wing. We saw very little of our fighter escort on this mission. A few small attacks by enemy aircraft were made on other Groups of Fortresses. The significant thing about today's presence of the Luftwaffe, although it was not yet presenting a strong offensive, was that it had started to reassert itself. This was certainly not good news.

Today our crew flew in the Deputy Lead position of the Lead Group in the "B" Wing. Each of the bomb bays in the 36 Fortresses in "B" Wing were loaded with six 1,000 pound demolition bombs. Records indicate the 12 Fortresses in "D" Wing carried the same number and type of bombs. The wind speed at our target had increased to 54 m.p.h. Cloud conditions at Orleans restricted target visibility, causing our lead bombardier to make two bombing approaches. Our Lead Group's second bomb run to the target was a visual run that lasted two minutes on a heading of 330 degrees at 20,000 feet. Bombs of the 12 Fortresses in our Lead Group were dropped at 0852 hours. Bombs of the High Group's 12 Fortresses were away at 0902 hours, followed seven minutes later by bombs of the Low Group's 12 bombers. Thirty-five of our Wing's B-17s successfully attacked the target and excellent bombing results were observed through openings in the clouds. Bombs of one B-17 in the High Group did not release because a control rod became disconnected at station #3 on the bomb rack. Some B-24s apparently attached themselves to the Low Group's formation during its bomb run, and bombs of the Liberators, evidently of a different type then the ones we carried, were seen exploding at the edge of the Low Group's bomb pattern. The "D" Wing successfully bombed the bridge over the river one minute after our Lead Group in Wing "B" destroyed the railroad bridge over the marshalling yards.

A group of 15 FW-190s attacked the High Group of our "B" Wing at 0958 hours, but was driven off by a larger number of British Spitfires. Our route back to England was flown as individual Groups, and our Combat Wing reassembled twenty miles from the French coast. Only meager flak was observed by our crews on this mission, but it was fired at a Combat Wing in front of ours and caused no danger to any Fortresses of the 379th Bomb Group. Our return route was flown substantially as briefed, except for a Combat Wing of two Groups that consistently forced the 379th Bomb Group away from our intended course and through dense clouds. As we approached the French coast, the cloud cover opened and we were able to clearly see hundreds of Allied gliders and huge amounts of military supplies for our invading armies. It was a very impressive sight, and reassured us that "the good guys" were winning this war.

Our formation crossed the French coast at 0952 hours flying at an altitude of 20,000 feet. Forty-one minutes later we crossed the English coast over Selsey Bill at 13,000 feet. The sky was filled with Flying Fortresses, Liberators and clouds. We felt humbled by the challenge of flying unscathed through such a maze of airborne metal and moisture. Our crew was very well trained. We'd make it—like a lot of other B-17 crews, we had done it many times before.

All of the planes from the Kimbolton airfield returned safely, without damage and without any injured crew members. Flying time on our 28th combat mission was 7:15 hours. We learned later the planned spare B-17 that filled in with the 351st Bomb Group, after observing the 351st was not going to bomb, left that formation and individually bombed a railway and highway intersection with excellent results.

Bob and I visited the bar before going to the mess hall that evening. Bob asked, "Ken, do you think we'll ever be told we're through flying combat?" I shrugged my shoulders in an inconclusive response.

It took about 30 minutes for us each to down a mug of stale, warm beer while we discussed the probability of being told tomorrow we had completed all of our combat missions as of today. Neither of us actually believed such an announcement would be part of tomorrow's reality.

Like stale, warm beer, the improbability of such reality was not easy for us to swallow.

Friday, June 9, 1944, was another day that hid under the clouds and overflowed with rain. The 379th's Flying Fortresses looked like a flock of ducks weighted down in acres of muddy water, unable to fly. After breakfast I waded over to the PX to get a copy of the latest Stars and Stripes. One of the headlines stated, "Luftwaffe Beginning to Assert Itself." The following paragraphs told most of the story:

"Sparked by powerful heavy bomber attacks over a wide area south of the Normandy beachheads, the Allied air forces yesterday gave continuous cover to invading troops in the face of increasing Luftwaffe opposition."

"Although the air umbrella was never really challenged as every type of Allied craft cut a wide swathe of destruction behind enemy lines, dogfights above the French beaches yesterday indicated that German fighter reinforcements finally were being drawn towards combat areas."

"To midday yesterday from June 6, Allied aircraft flew approximately 27,000 sorties at a cost of 289 planes, barely more than one percent. In the same period, 176 of the small number of craft the Luftwaffe dared send aloft were destroyed."

"Up to 1,000 Fortresses and Liberators, escorted by almost 500 P-47s, P-38s and P-51s, bombarded bridges, railroad junctions, railroad yards and airfields within 100 to 150 miles south, southeast and southwest of the beachhead."

There was a rumor going around the base about a mission being scheduled for tomorrow. It looked like our crew was going on another one. When Howard, Jim, Bob and I hit the sack on the night of June 9, we had not been told otherwise.

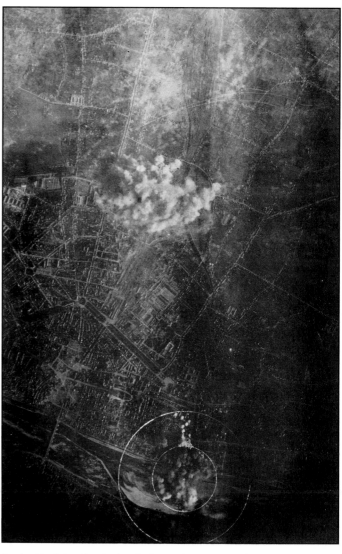

Smoke at top is from bombs of our lead group in "B" Wing on bridge over the railroad marshalling yards, Orleans, France, June 8, 1944. At bottom of photo (taken one minute later) are bomb strikes of 379th "D" wing on bridge over river at edge of the city. This unique photo shows direct hits by two lead groups from the same bomb group, on two primary targets at the same city and on the same day. (Photo taken by camera in bomb bay of "D" wing's lead fortress & obtained from 379th BG Photographic Section)

Mission to Vannes

Saturday, June 10, 1944. Weather conditions today were equally as miserable as yesterday's. Flying conditions were far from desirable, but the urgency to support our invading ground troops with continuous aerial bombardment was adequate reason for the 8th Air Force to issue Field Order No. 385. The Luftwaffe was again becoming a significant threat to our advancing armies. The 379th Bomb Group was ordered to dispatch 45 Fortresses to form the Lead and Low Groups of the 41st Combat Wing "B" on a mission to attack the airdrome at Vannes, France, approximately 55 miles southwest of Rennes.

Briefing was scheduled for 0115 hours. The mass of clouds covering the area around Kimbolton and most of southeastern England extended from near ground level to 19,000 feet. The Lead Group from our airfield was comprised of 23 B-17s, including three spares, that took off beginning at 0450 hours. Takeoff of the 22 Fortresses making up the Low Group (which included two spares) started 13 minutes later, with our crew and Screwball Express flying the Deputy Lead position. It was great to be flying in "our plane" again, even if we were being shafted by having to fly more than the expected number of combat missions. Taking off at exactly 0503 hours on two consecutive missions seemed like something out of Ripley's Believe It Or Not. A 46th Fortress from the 379th Bomb Group, aircraft 42-97229, led the 457th Bomb Group at Glatton on a mission today.

I sang our takeoff song with less raspiness this morning than on our mission to Orleans two days ago. Perhaps my voice was becoming accustomed to early morning recitals. "The Lord is my shepherd; I shall not want." It was such a peaceful song, even with the roar of our plane's engines.

Our Lead Group climbed to 19,000 feet over Molesworth before it rose above the cloud cover. It then proceeded on course at 20,000 feet, but was one minute ahead of schedule. Records indicate the Lead Group made two 360 degree turns waiting for the other two Groups, and left the English coast at 0704 hours over Selsey Bill flying at 22,000 feet. Two spares in the Lead Group returned to base as scheduled, and one spare filled in with the 401st Bomb Group from Deenethorpe.

We were surprised that our Low formation was able to assemble at 9,000 feet over Kimbolton in a clear area under the clouds. We were also surprised to find a hole in the clouds that allowed us to climb safely to 21,000 feet and fly to Newberry, west of London, for our scheduled rendezvous with the Lead Group. Unable to locate our Lead Group, we departed the English coast at 0710 hours and headed for the airdrome at Vannes. The two spares in our Group returned to base according to plan. Our Low Group crossed the enemy coast at 0737, four minutes behind the Lead Group. The assembly of the 41st Combat Wing "B" was never completed, primarily because of extremely poor weather conditions over England. Antiaircraft fire greeted us at 0740 hours about 10 miles west of Caen, but the small number of flak explosions seemed to indicate the enemy was not greatly concerned with our single Group's formation.

Each Fortress in the Lead Group carried 18-250 pound demolition bombs and Fortresses in our Low Group each carried 36-100 pounders. The statement in the Mission Report by the Lead Group's bombardier reads as follows: "We reached the IP at 0813 hours and had from 4/10ths to 5/10ths cloud cover. Bomb bay doors were opened, rack selector switches were turned on, rack selector bar was placed in select position with the knurled knob turned to safe. As I started to turn the knurled knob, the bombs went away. This happened about seven minutes before they should have gone away. Bombs released at 0814 on a magnetic heading of 291 degrees."

Twenty aircraft were in the Lead Group's formation at the time of bomb release. Nineteen of the aircraft dropped their bombs when the malfunction occurred in the lead aircraft. The bombs dropped in open fields about 20 miles short of the target at 4741 N-0222 W. One of the Fortresses returned to base with its bombs still in its bomb bay because of a malfunction of a bomb bay door. Fortress 42-97462 that filled in with the 401st Bomb Group returned with its bombs aboard because that Group did not release.

The flight plan of our Low Group took us almost directly south across France to a point north of Laval at 0751 hours when we changed course to the southwest. At 0820 hours, approximately 15 miles north of St. Nazaire, our Group again changed course and took up a magnetic heading of 300 degrees. Our altitude was 21,000 feet, indicated air speed was 150 m.p.h. and true air speed was 211 m.p.h. Our primary target was formerly known as the Vannes/Meucon airfield, 4 3/4 miles north-northeast of Vannes. Four P-51 Mustangs over the target provided encouragement to our bomber formation. The bomb run was perfect, and not one burst of flak was fired at us in the target area. The statement by the Lead bombardier in the Mission Report's reference to the Low Group reads as follows: "Bombing run was made on AFCE (Automatic Flight Control Equipment), run was about 60 seconds. Slight haze over target. One primary sighting made by Low Group. Bombed by Group formation. Results observed to be excellent. The briefed Aiming Point and MPI were used. Bombs released at 0828 hours on a magnetic heading of 300 degrees. Intervalometer setting was for 100' interval." Only two of our Group's 720 bombs failed to release properly—one in aircraft 42-31720 because of a malfunction of a release arm, and one in aircraft 42-37859 due to an incorrectly installed shackle on the bomb rack.

Bombs of our Low Squadron caught many enemy planes taking off and pitted the runway sufficiently that none of them was able to take to the air. It was possible to identify concentrations of our bombs covering most of the southern portion of the airfield. The northwest/southeast runway was very heavily hit, and the northeast/southwest runway received at least 10 direct hits. One medium sized unidentified building on the northwestern dispersal area received a direct hit.

The four P-51's had witnessed our attack on the airdrome. They flew to the side of our formation and dipped their wings in salute to our bombing accuracy.

We turned right off the target and headed north for Pleubian on the French coast, arriving there at 0856 hours and flying at 22,000 feet. The Luftwaffe, if any part of it was in the air today, was flying somewhere else. This was to the disappointment of our excellent fighter cover throughout this mission. Our formation crossed the English coast at 0939 hours, at an altitude of 14,000 feet over Portland Bill. Our return flight from the English coast to Kimbolton covered about the same route we had flown earlier that morning. The Group's descent was a bit unusual, due to four layers of clouds that persisted in making things uneasy. All Fortresses of the 379th returned safely to Kimbolton. Two of the planes in the Lead Group were damaged by flak, but there were no injured crew members.

Flying time on our crew's 29th combat mission was six hours and 15 minutes.

Maybe, just maybe, Headquarters will give our crew the good news after we complete one more mission. Our 30th mission is next on the list, and 30 is a nice, round number. It would be a good number at which to quit.

On June 11, 1944, we learned that other heavy Bomb Groups of the 8th Air Force bombed enemy airfields at Gael and Nantes on the 10th of June. The bombing results at Gael were described as "good," and as "excellent" at Nantes. The Nantes target was the Chateau Bougon Aerodrome, three miles southwest of Nantes. Seven U. S. heavy bombers and 16 escorting fighter planes were lost in the day's operation.

British newspapers stated it had been officially announced for the first time that targets of two heavy bomber attacks at Pas de Calais yesterday were "German pilotless-plane launching platforms." Approximately 350 Fortresses and Liberators had rocked the French coast in the morning, and another 250 heavies directed attacks against the winged-bomb launching ramps in the afternoon.

It was also announced that P-47 Thunderbolts were now permanently based in France, the first element of any U. S. Air Force to do so. It was revealed previously that U. S. aircraft were landing on airfields in France to refuel and rearm, but this was the first disclosure that American airmen had taken up permanent stations there.

June 11 was a very uninteresting day. In fact, it was extremely dull. It rained again.

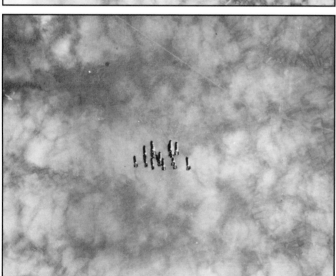

Sequence of photos show target before, during and after bomb release on airfield at Vannes, France. From top to bottom: Airfield at Vannes — Bombs away from 21, 00 feet — Bombs begin to spread out — Rocket fired from ground. Note bombs in circle, also above and right of rocket source — Bomb strikes cover the airfield. Approximately 31 seconds elapsed between first and fifth phot. (Photos from 379th Bomb Group Photographic Section, June 10, 1944)

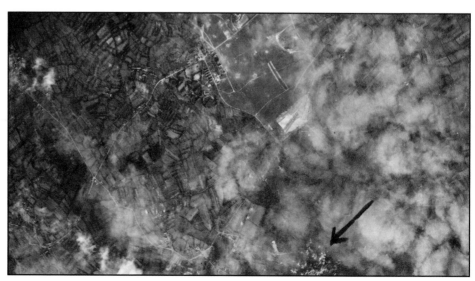

Mission to Pontaubault

Monday, June 12, 1944. The 'morning messenger' from Operations yelled, "Everybody up and at 'em. You're all flyin' a mission today." It was 0045 hours, and much too early for anyone to make such a noisy intrusion.

Briefing started at 0215 hours and lasted about 20-25 minutes. Forty B-17s from the 379th Bomb Group were to form the Lead, Low and High Groups of the 41st Combat Wing "B" formation and attack the railroad bridge over the river at Pontaubault, France. Pontaubault is about five miles south of Avranches and a short distance inland from the Bay of St. Michel. This bridge was in heavy use by the Germans as they transported troops and war materials needed to counteract the Allied invasion.

This would be our crew's 30th combat mission. Our hopes were very high that this would be the last one we would have to fly. Of course, that's what we expected on May 29 after we got back from Krzesinki, Poland, following our 25th mission. However, D-Day had changed the situation and there we were, getting ready for our 30th. Surely, the 8th Air Force would not extend our combat tour past 30 missions. We based our belief on the following facts: American troops were already 18 miles into France; the Luftwaffe, although still in evidence, was badly beaten; more than 1,400 heavy bombers of the 8th Air Force were going to attack six enemy bridges and 16 airfields today. There was no doubt about it! The United States, England and their Allies were

Intelligence photograph for use in target selection. Ink lines indicate pattern of bombing results on this mission. (From 379th Bomb Group Records)

winning the war. There was no conceivable reason why our crew should have to fly more than 30 combat missions.

The first of our 40 Flying Fortresses was airborne at 0545 hours. Our crew's takeoff song was sung as if I would never have an opportunity to sing it again. This was the 30th time in as many takeoffs. Hopefully, no encores would be prompted by additional combat missions.

Our three Groups assembled into Combat Wing formation at 12,000 feet over Kimbolton at 0658 hours. Included in our 40 Fortresses were six spare aircraft, two of which filled in with the Wing and four that returned to base as planned. Weather over Kimbolton included 6/10ths clouds that topped out at 6,000 feet, and visibility of 20 miles. Today's mission was the first on which our bomb load consisted of four 2,000 pound general purpose bombs. One bomb was carried internally on each side of our bomb bay, and one bomb was hung externally under each of the wings. The 36 Fortresses from our airfield carried a total of 138 bombs with a bomb tonnage of equal number. (In reality, 37 Fortresses were in our Wing formation when bombs were dropped, as explained later.)

Our Wing formation crossed the English coast at 0800 hours over Selsey Bill at an altitude of 20,000 feet, and crossed the coast of France exactly 28 minutes later at the same altitude. Some of the elapsed time was used in positioning each Group and Wing for precisely scheduled entry into enemy territory. About 20 bursts of flak exploded under our formation at 0832 hours as we flew south of Bayeux, halfway between the coast and the initial point of our briefed bomb run. Two of our aircraft reported minor flak damage following this attack.

The cloud cover in the target area ranged from 4/10ths to 7/10ths. The Lead Group of our Combat Wing made a visual bomb run of 45 seconds on a magnetic heading of 280 degrees from 20,000 feet. Bombs of this Group were released at 0855 hours. Nine of the 12 Fortresses in this Group each carried four bombs, but the other three B-17s were not equipped with external bomb racks and only carried two bombs apiece in their bomb bays. Forty-one of the Lead Group's 42 bombs released properly at 50 feet intervals. The center of the bomb pattern was slightly left of the target, with several direct hits on the south end of the bridge. That part of the bridge collapsed immediately after the bombs struck.

Our Low Group was unable to make its bomb run on the briefed heading because of clouds. Instead, a visual run of 60 seconds was made on a magnetic heading of 308 degrees at an altitude of 19,000 feet. Screwball Express flew High Squadron Lead in the Low Group. Since the south end of the bridge had been hit and destroyed by the Lead Group, our lead bombardier changed his aiming point from the center of the bridge to its north end. The 13 Fortresses in our Low Group released 50 of its 52 bombs at 0903 hours. (A Fortress from another Bomb Group was leading our High Group, and one of those planes joined our Low Group in order to keep the High Group's number at 12.) Two internal bombs did not release from one of our bombers. Our Group's bombs were also dropped on an intervalometer setting of 50 feet. Our bomb pattern covered the north end of the bridge and knocked down the remainder of its structure.

The High Group's Lead bombardier, who was from the 303rd Bomb Group at Molesworth, made a dry run. The plane (42-31574) in which he was flying was also from Molesworth, but was flown and navigated by officers of the 379th Bomb Group. On the second run clouds obscured the target and the navigator took over and bombed with GH

equipment. The 12 Fortresses in this Group carried a total of 44 bombs: 10 planes each had four bombs, and 2 bombers each had two bombs. Forty-three of this Group's bombs, also set for impact at 50 feet intervals, were dropped from an altitude of 21,000 feet at 0917 hours on a magnetic heading of 245 degrees. Four separate statements in the Mission Report for today's attack state the point of impact for the High Group's bombs was, "approximately one mile left of target," "somewhat to the south of bridge, about 1/2 mile," "somewhat to the left of the bridge," and "a third concentration fell one and 3/4 miles south of the target area in orchards." Stated briefly, the High Group missed.

Our Wing dropped 134 2,000 pound bombs, 91 of which caused severe damage to our primary target. There was no flak fired at us in the target area. The formation turned to the right and headed toward southern England. We crossed the French coast at 20,000 feet and let down to 14,000 feet by the time we flew over Portland Bill at 0959 hours. We did not see any friendly or enemy fighters during the entire mission.

Thirty-three of our Group's 36 Fortresses on this mission returned to Kimbolton safely and on schedule, but three of our B-17s landed away from home base after returning to England. Fuel shortage caused one to land at Grove and another at Brise Norten, but after refueling both planes returned to Kimbolton. The other Fortress landed at the RAF base Worksop with damaged control cables.

The Luftwaffe made some appearances today, but not one enemy aircraft pierced the protective cordon our friendly fighters established around the majority of the record number of Fortresses and Liberators. Nevertheless, seven heavy bombers did not return to England.

Mission number 30 was now part of our crew's combat history. Our flying time today was six hours.

At this point in time our flight crew has been combat operational for 81 days. Twenty-six of our 30 combat missions have been flown in Screwball Express. Our plane has also flown other crews of the 379th Bomb Group on 10 combat missions, and records show it has not yet aborted any mission or required the changing of any of its engines. During our crew's 30 combat missions we have delivered approximately 82 tons of demolition and incendiary bombs on enemy targets, for an average of 2.73 tons per attack.

One of the personnel in the records section at Group Headquarters told me several weeks later that ours was the first flight crew of the 379th Bomb Group to fly 30 combat missions without any replacement because of illness, injury or death. That was real good news, particularly the part about injury and death.

June 13, 1944. The newspaper's report of yesterday's losses of enemy fighter planes stated, "The Luftwaffe, appearing in strength for the first time since the land assault began, lost a sizable part of its precious fighter hoard. Eighth Air Force fighters shot down 25 planes in aerial combat and destroyed one on the ground. Ninth Air Force Thunderbolts took a toll of 22 German fighters while P-51s destroyed 17 on the ground." In addition to their escort duty, U. S. fighters "destroyed or damaged 11 locomotives, 99 railway cars, 117 trucks, one tank, three military buildings, three freight yards, one railway junction and three radio or flak towers."

According to most sources, on this date German V-1 Flying Bombs hit London for the first time.

Today the 379th Bomb Group attacked an airdrome at St. Andre de Leure, France, but our crew was stood down. Maybe our 30th combat mission really was our last one. I prayed it was so.

Mission to Creil

Wednesday, June 14, 1944. Thirty-seven Fortresses of the 379th Bomb Group were assigned as the Lead, High and Low Groups of the 41st Combat Wing "A" and began takeoff at 0435 hours. Screwball Express and our crew were assigned the Deputy Lead position in the High Group. Our Wing's target was the airfield at Creil, France, 25 miles north of Paris. At 0454 hours 24 additional Fortresses of the 379th Group started their takeoff and made up the Lead and Low Groups of the 41st Combat "D" Wing. The target of this Wing was the airfield at Coulommiers, about 30 miles east of Paris.

Four of the Fortresses in our "A" Wing failed to become airborne. One of the B-17s got stuck in the mud at the side of the runway, another developed a gas tank leak during its taxi to the main runway and two others collided with a truck and sustained structural damage sufficient to prevent them from flying the mission. "The Lord is my shepherd—He restoreth my soul—I will fear no evil—thy rod and thy staff they comfort me." Thirty-three of our Group's bombers became airborne in our "A" Wing, including a planned spare. Screwball Express and the other Fortresses in our three Groups climbed to our assigned assembly altitude of 8,000 feet between Molesworth and Eyebrook at 0533 hours.

Two of the planes in our Wing aborted the mission while still over England because their oil pressure transmitters malfunctioned. There were many reasons for an aircraft to abort a mission: rough engines, runaway superchargers, tachometer oscillation, leaking oxygen regulators, sluggish superchargers, weak brakes, generator malfunctions, insufficient oxygen supply, engine oil leaks, engine instrument failure, oil cooler failures, stuck in the mud, creeping flaps, cracked exhaust stacks, cracked air ducts, flat tail wheels, propeller governor failure, overboosted engines, leaking fuel tanks, inoperative fuel pumps, and rotten weather. Group Headquarters did not accept failure of an oil pressure transmitter as sufficient reason for aborting.

We crossed the English coast at Selsey Bill at 0632 hours flying at an altitude of 16,000 feet. A few minutes later, our High Group was forced out of its position in the Wing when a formation of B-24s flew between our High and Lead Groups. The resulting abrupt turn by our High Group caused it to become separated from the rest of our Wing. We were consequently unable to rejoin our Wing's formation and trailed it by four minutes while crossing the Channel and for the remainder of the mission. It was similar to playing catchup with someone who could not, and therefore did not, empathize with our situation. Our High Group caused its own problem when it sacrificed precious minutes by turning out of formation in order to avoid those trespassing B-24s. We felt certain the 8th Air Force would forgive us for acting so selfishly.

The enemy coast in was crossed at 0702 hours by the Lead and Low Groups of our Wing at an altitude of 21,000 feet. Five Me-109s made several passes at Bomb Groups off to our left, but the attacks looked somewhat awkward. The German pilots did not appear to be very aggressive today. Other planes in our Wing, several miles ahead of our position, were not engaged by the Luftwaffe. Antiaircraft guns seemed to be everywhere along the route to our target. Their accuracy and intensity increased as we approached the area around Creil. POOM——POOM—POOM——POOM. Explosions of flak erupted violently as we began our attack on the airfield.

The morning's briefing had directed our Wing to attack the target from an altitude of 21,000 feet while flying a magnetic heading of 265 degrees. The Lead Group followed those directions, and after a visual bomb run of 60 seconds it dropped all of its 452 100-pound demolition bombs at 0818 hours. Exactly four minutes later, from the same altitude but on a magnetic heading of 270 degrees, our High Group released all of its bombs. Our bomb run was 18 miles long and the actual sighting lasted 60 seconds through 4/10 cloud cover. The combined bomb loads of all except one plane in our High Group consisted of 208 clusters of fragmentation bombs. Screwball Express carried 38 100-pound demolition bombs which were released at 200 feet intervals. Our bombs away time of 0822 hours was the earliest release time for any of our crew's combat missions.

Six concentrations of general purpose and fragmentation bombs covered most of the runway areas and the north dispersal area. A heavy concentration of frag bombs fell on most of the hangar area at the southern edge of the airfield and almost completely destroyed those installations. At least 50 direct hits were scored on the northwest-southeast runway. The majority of those direct hits were the bombs from Screwball Express. Forty-seven other direct hits were made on the east-west runway by other Fortresses in our High Group. Two aircraft shelters in the north dispersal area received direct hits and were set on fire. At least four hits were made on fuel storage tanks in that area. The Creil airfield, less than two miles east of that city, had been the base of a Luftwaffe Gruppe of long range bombers engaged in operations against England. Our 41st "A" Combat Wing dropped a total of 1,147 fragmentation clusters and demolition bombs on the airfield. It would be of little use to the Luftwaffe for quite some time.

Immediately after the Lead and Low Groups of our "A" Wing passed over the target, they were joined by an unidentified High Group and Low, Low Group. The enemy coast out was crossed at 0854 hours at 21,000 feet, and the English Coast in was crossed at Beachy Head at 0915 hours and an altitude of 13,000 feet. After our Wing was over England, the two unidentified Groups left our formation and headed for their home bases. The first of our Fortresses to return to Kimbolton landed at 1008 hours.

Our High Group flew through 11 separate zones of attack by antiaircraft guns during this mission. Only one of the Triangle K's 31 Fortresses that attacked the target was lost to flak, and that Fortress limped along until crossing the French coast and then ditched in the Channel. We saw seven other Fortresses from other Groups get hit by flak and go down on this mission. Two parachutes were seen coming out of one of those planes before it ditched in the Channel and exploded. Screwball Express was hit during several of the flak barrages and incurred a major amount of damage. Six other Fortresses from the 379th Bomb Group returned to Kimbolton with flak damage ranging from minor to major.

The flying time on our crew's 31st combat mission was six hours and twenty minutes. It was a rough one. There was no word from Headquarters indicating this was our last mission. The obvious conclusion that our tour of combat duty had not yet come to a happy ending was very disturbing to all of us.

At the mess hall that evening we heard about the attack on the Coulommiers airfield by the 24 B-17s from Kimbolton in "D" Wing. They experienced no flak at their target, had no fighter attacks, but encountered severe problems with cloud cover and intense contrails from a Group of bombers that attacked the airfield a few minutes ahead of them. According to the Mission Report covering this attack, the Lead and Low Groups of "D" Wing each had to make three runs on the target before releasing their bombs. The Mean Point of Impact was obscured by 9/10 cloud cover and contrails hid other aiming points. The Lead Group's bombs were believed to have fallen in dispersal areas with good results, but the Low Group had only fair results.

June 15, 1944. Rain, rain and more rain. The Stars and Stripes lead paragraph in an article about 8th Air Force operations of June 14th stated: "A force of Fortresses and Liberators 1,500 strong, the greatest task force of heavy bombers ever dispatched, yesterday plastered targets in France, Belgium, Holland and Germany as the Allied aerial campaign to knock out Luftwaffe bases and Von Rundstedt's supply lines soared to a new peak." The article listed among the day's targets—an oil refinery at Emmerich in Germany's Ruhr Valley, airfields at Le Bourget, Creil, Bretigny and Chateaudun in France, an airfield at Brussels-Melsbroeck in

Belgium, and another airfield at Eindhoven in Holland. Attacks on these and other targets cost the 8th Air Force 15 heavy bombers and 8 fighter planes.

June 16   379th BG Mission to Avord, France, recalled. 379th BG bombed airfield at Laon/Couvron, France. (Our crew was "stood down") Crew of Lt. Anthony J. Pettrini flew Screwball Express.

June 17   Our crew made a one-hour training flight.

June 18   379th BG bombed dock facilities at Hamburg, Germany. (Our crew was "stood down") Crew of Lt. Willis H. Matter flew Screwball Express— this was its 40th combat mission.

(Special Credit: Please refer to *Flying Forts, the B-17 in World War II*; under Bibliography.)

Intelligence photograph used in selection of Creil target data. June 14, 1944. (From 379th BG photos)

Clockwise from the top: Photo shows our crew after the 38th "Mission Bomb" had been painted on Screwball Express several days after our crew's 31st mission. Crew is wearing Mae West life vests. Standing, left to right: Bob Mathews, Tom Kiblin, Jerry Lindsey, Frank Craig, Joe Milworm. Front Row: Bob Keller, Ken Cassens, Howard Towers and Jim Moore. — Intervalometer release of bombs on airfield at Creil, France, by flying fortress 42-37805, flown by crew of Lt. Roy D. King, 527th Bomb Squadron. — View from bomb bay of bombs dropping in interval. (Photos by 379th Bomb Group Photo. Sec., June 14 - 16, 1944)

Mission to Hamburg

Tuesday, June 20, 1944. A few minutes after midnight the door of our barracks flew open and light bulbs flashed on above our bunks. The immediate brightness kept us from clearly seeing who had invaded our domain. "Up and at 'em," blared the voice of someone who apparently enjoyed exercising his authority. "You're all flyin' today. Climb out of those sacks! Rise and shine!" The intruder was from 526th Squadron Headquarters. He evidently did not hear the question Howard, Jim, Bob and I asked in unison, as if we had rehearsed as a quartet—"Any orders for Towers' crew to head Stateside?" His silent departure was his negative response.

We dressed and hurried to the mess hall. None of us was ever casual about morning chow on days we were assigned to fly a combat mission. Although we always had plenty of time to eat a leisurely breakfast and walk calmly to the briefing room, none of us ever did it that way. It was not the Air Force way of transporting one's self from a sound sleep to the excitement of a combat briefing. Consequently, most of us were usually in the briefing room fifteen or twenty minutes ahead of schedule. Today's briefing was scheduled for 0130 hours; all of our crew, except Howard, were in front row seats at 0110 hours. Howard had stopped off at our Squadron's headquarters to see Lt. Clay Hedges, Operations Officer.

Much of our 20-minute wait was spent making predictions about the location of today's target. The amount of yarn used to plot the flight plan on the map at the front of the room indicated a flight of medium distance. It seemed like hours before those twenty minutes elapsed. Howard joined us in the briefing room. The look on his face told us more than we wanted to know—our crew was still on operational status, and we were flying the mission today. The briefing began and, after a few opening remarks by the commanding officer, the sheet was drawn open and the map was uncovered. Our target was at Hamburg, Germany!

We were told the 8th Air Force campaign to destroy Germany's oil resources was destined to reach a climax today. Over 1,400 Fortresses and Liberators were assigned to smash a dozen refineries and synthetic plants. A First Force of nine Combat Wings, escorted by three fighter groups, was assigned to attack eight oil refineries in the Hamburg area. A Second Force of six Wings, escorted by six fighter groups, was dispatched to attack synthetic oil plants at Politz and an oil refinery at Ostermoor. A Third Force of eight Wings, escorted by seven fighter groups, was dispatched to attack an oil refinery, a wing repair/small engine works, a synthetic oil plant and an army truck ordnance depot in north-central Germany—specifically in the areas around Magdeburg, Fallersleben, Konigsborn and Hanover, respectively. Our Intelligence staff knew the Germans had moved thousands of antiaircraft guns into areas around the oil targets, and some of the refineries were protected by more antiaircraft guns than Berlin itself. We were alerted to expect numerous smoke screens at Hamburg. The Intelligence officer told us that huge labor battalions, with massive quantities of equipment and materials, were stationed near the oil centers so reconstruction might be underway before attacking bombers returned to 8th and 15th Air Force bases in England and Italy. He predicted the Luftwaffe would be conserved until the Germans knew for certain the day's attack was aimed at the oil targets. Unquestionably, the Germans would do everything in their power to protect their refineries and synthetic oil

plants. Oil was the lifeblood of the Nazi war machine, and the Germans had to keep it flowing.

Hamburg is a seaport on the Elbe river in northern Germany, 90 miles from the river's mouth at the North Sea and northeast of Bremen. It was one of many German cities devoted to the production of war materials. The RAF bombed Hamburg many times beginning in 1940. On its fifth and 14th combat missions, June 25 and July 25, 1943, the 379th Bomb Group attacked submarine pens on the river's edge at Hamburg. The heaviest concentration of bombing and greatest destruction resulted from RAF raids in late July of 1943. On each of the nights of July 24, July 27 and July 29 of that year more than 700 British Lancasters, Halifaxes, Stirlings and Wellingtons attacked Hamburg and devastated the city with a total of 2,400 tons of bombs, many of which were incendiaries. At one point in the Battle of Hamburg a massive fire covered an area greater than six square miles. Flames rose three miles above the city and air from the surrounding countryside was sucked inward at 150 miles per hour. What has been called "the first known fire-storm" resulted and civilian casualties were enormous. Somehow, the city managed to rebuild much of its war production capabilities during the following year and again became a prime target of Allied bombing. The 379th Group bombed dock facilities at Hamburg as recently as June 18, 1944, and today's mission was the Group's fourth attack on that city.

The 379th Bomb Group furnished 18 Fortresses, including two spares, for the Lead Group and an additional 24 Fortresses, including six spares, for the Low Group in the 41st "A" Combat Wing to attack an oil refinery at Hamburg. The

Author's A-2 flight jacket, with plane's name & targets bombed by its crew.

High Group of our Wing was provided by the 305th Bomb Group from Chelveston. The pilot of the Lead aircraft in our Lead Group was Brigadier General Robert F. Travis. Screwball Express and our crew were also assigned to the Lead Group and flew the Group Deputy Lead position. The 42 B-17s from Kimbolton started taking off at 0505 hours as part of the first of the three separate Forces assigned to destroy Germany's remaining oil production plants. This was combat mission number 148 for the 379th Bomb Group.

"The Lord is my shepherd; I shall not want. He maketh me to lie down in green pastures. He leadeth me beside the still waters. He restoreth my soul. He leadeth me in the paths of righteousness for His name's sake."

Weather over England duplicated the low ceiling and cloudy skies of the previous day. The overcast at Kimbolton was 9/10 with a base of 500 feet, but was surprisingly only 1,000 feet thick. When Screwball Express emerged from the overcast our visibility was unrestricted for 20 miles. The

clouds beneath us completely closed ranks and wiped out any glimpse of land. After we left the English coast the clouds opened to about 6/10 undercast and we were able to see the cold, unfriendly grayness of the North Sea. At the enemy coast the clouds separated some more and formed only 3/10 cover. Visibility ahead of our formation remained unrestricted.

After we crossed into Germany from the North Sea, we did not observe a flight of six or seven FW-190s and Me-109s that must have been flying in scattered clouds several thousand feet above and ahead of our position. Before we realized what was happening, the enemy planes attacked from 10 o'clock high and dived through our Lead Squadron. No one in our Group had any warning. The attackers disappeared into a large cloud beneath our Wing and vanished without anyone firing a single shot at them. It happened so quickly! Only a few of us in the Lead Squadron caught a brief glimpse of the bandits during the several seconds in which they penetrated our formation. Our crew's members breathed

Above: Refinery is in 5 dock areas in upper left quadrant of photo. Parallel streams of smoke are from 2 rockets fired from ground. — Upper Right: Direct hits on three areas of the refinery. — Lower Right: Smoke from bomb explosions rises high into the sky and casts a shadow on the ground. Groups following us hit other 2 dock areas. (Photos from 379th BG Photo. Sec., June 20, 1944)

prayerful sighs of relief when an intercom check confirmed none of us had been injured by the bandits' machine guns.

In contrast to my account of this incident, the S-2 Mission Teletype Report of the 379th Bomb Group's attack at Hamburg today states, "No E/A (enemy aircraft) were seen by our Groups." However, the 8th Air Force report about today's operation includes these related statements: "The G.A.F. (German Air Force) put up a strong defensive effort against our heavy bomber operations in Germany, marshalling the strongest resistance against those bombers which made the deepest penetration," and, "Sightings of small numbers of FW-190s and Me-109s (2-10 a/c) were seen at Helgoland, Fallersleben, Hamburg and Wesermunde." My account of the attack is based primarily on notations contained in the diary I kept about our crew's combat missions. Inability to reconcile variances in the above accounts is very perplexing.

We did not encounter any flak during our flight into Germany. All of the Fortresses in "A" Wing reached the Initial Point on schedule and turned to a magnetic heading of 266 degrees toward our target. We were flying at our briefed bombing altitude of 25,000 feet. Bomb bay doors opened simultaneously throughout our formation. Each Fortress in our Wing had a bomb load of 12-500 pound demolition bombs. There was no need for any incendiaries—direct hits by demos on an oil refinery would start many fires and cause more explosions, which would then start more fires. All of the bombardiers in our Group were especially alert and concentrated on releasing their bombs precisely upon seeing bombs drop from their lead aircraft.

The antiaircraft gunners around Hamburg were ready for us. Our formation was over halfway on our visual bomb run when the sky around our Lead Group suddenly filled with hundreds of flak explosions. POOM-POOM-POOM——POOM. POOM——POOM-POOM-POOM. The first explosions were in the middle of our formation and caused what Frank still describes as the most frightening of all his combat experiences. Gunners on flak towers nearly five miles below quickly and accurately zeroed in on our formation. Four long minutes remained—with no evasive action—before our bombs would be dropped. POOM——POOM-POOM——POOM.

"Yea, though I walk through the valley of the shadow of death, I will fear no evil, for Thou art with me. Thy rod and Thy staff they comfort me."

The intercom overflowed with, "Flak at mid-formation." "Flak at 12 o'clock level." "Flak at nine o'clock level." "Flak at three and six o'clock—level." A flak shell exploded directly above Screwball Express. Frank's flak helmet was hit by a piece of shrapnel that pierced the plastic dome of his top turret. Howard and Jim stared in disbelief at several shattered gauges on their instrument panel. A flak shell exploded close to the left side of Screwball Express and knocked out one of Joe's radios. Another burst directly in front of our aircraft sent a fragment into my chestpack parachute. Tom's jacket was ripped by a piece that went through the ball turret. Jerry's intercom and his oxygen supply were cut off by pieces of flak that hit the tail section of Screwball Express. Several oxygen bottles behind the pilots' compartment exploded when hit by shell fragments. The control caps of the Automatic Flight Control Equipment were smashed. A window in the waist section and one in the nose compartment were blown out when hit by flak. Mathews was knocked to the floor of our plane's waist section when the concussion from a burst of flak rocked Screwball Express. Ammunition in my chin turret was hit by flak fragments that set off four or five .50 caliber machine gun shells directly under my chair. The plexiglas on front of the chin turret disintegrated. Tom's exposed position under our plane's midsection provided him a very disturbing view of more than 400 flashing flak guns belching up their deadly shells at us. There was no need to pinpoint the clusters of exploding flak by yelling their clock-positions into the intercom. Flak was everywhere. We had never seen so much of it, and had never witnessed such alarming accuracy.

Undaunted by the black puffs of flak-death that hung everywhere around our formation, Bob picked up a K-28 aerial camera, aimed it through the windows of his navigator's position and feverishly took many pictures of the exploding flak. He looked bold and heroic, despite the danger of our situation. "Ken, ol' buddy," he yelled later over the intercom, "I've got some great pictures of that flak."

In spite of the tremendous quantity of antiaircraft fire, our Wing's formation held together. The entire oil refinery, built on five separate dock areas, was clearly visible along the Elbe river. A burst of flak directly under us sent a dozen or more shell fragments through our bomb bay doors. I felt the bombsight's eyepiece vibrate against my right eye when a piece of flak ripped through the plane's nose and glanced off the bombsight's heavy base. The center of the refinery was perfectly centered under the crosshairs in my bombsight. Finally, it was 30 seconds past 0908 hours and our bombs were away at the exact instant of release by our Wing's Lead aircraft.

"Thou preparest a table before me in the presence of mine enemies. Thou anointest my head with oil; my cup runneth over."

Our formation continued flying straight and level so the 16mm camera in each Lead aircraft could get pictures of the bomb strikes. Visual bombing usually achieved much better results than the PFF method; however, bombing through clouds did not require us to fly straight and level after bomb release in order to take photos of the bomb strikes. The visual bombing method was more accurate and shortened the war. The PFF technique attained only fair results, but resulted in many airmen living longer. Notes in my diary show the bombfall lasted 42.17 seconds. The multitude of exploding flak shells in and around our formation made it seem more like 42 minutes. Our indicated airspeed was 150 m.p.h. and our true airspeed was 224 because of the lighter air density at the altitude where we were flying. Our ground speed was 257 m.p.h. because of a tail wind. As fast as that was, it wasn't fast enough. Six B-17s from the Bomb Groups behind our formation were hit by flak and went down at the target and the area around Hamburg.

A total of 144.5 tons of bombs from the attacking Fortresses in our Wing hit directly in the center of the refinery. What a sight! We saw waves of air around the target rush outward as the bombs exploded. It looked like every explosion set off another explosion, or started a fire that touched off an explosion. The main processing plant received many direct hits by our Group. Three oil storage tanks exploded in a flaming eruption. Two storage buildings and three other structures were hit and destroyed. Smoke rose thousands of feet into the sky. It was a fascinating view of total destruction. It was the end of Hamburg's Rhenania-Ossag oil refinery.

Our formation turned away from the target area and headed for England. The doors of our bomb bay were bent out of shape by flak damage and would not close electrically, so they had to be manually cranked into a closed position. A seventh B-17, carrying the crew of 1st Lt. James R. Wheat from the 379th Bomb Group's 527th Squadron, was hit by flak at 0910 hours. Initially, the aircraft was able to stay with the formation. Like the flight into Germany, the flight out was without flak. The intense antiaircraft fire on the bomb run during the attack at Hamburg turned 11 minutes of this mission into a horrible nightmare. Pictures of those 11 minutes of intense flak would provide enough drama for all war stories ever written about B-17 Flying Fortresses. Eventually, the disabled B-17 from the 379th started to fall back. Upon reaching the North Sea that aircraft, serial number 42-97261, radioed it was losing altitude and planning to ditch in the North Sea. The Mission Report indicates it ditched safely shortly after 1133 hours. It was the 13th Flying Fortress of the 379th Bomb Group lost to enemy action on our crew's 33 combat missions. Air-Sea Rescue reported later it had picked up all of that plane's nine occupants.

Crews of badly damaged Allied aircraft were very appreciative of the three emergency landing strips maintained jointly by the 8th Air Force and the RAF. These strips were several miles inland from the English Channel, near Manston, Woodbridge and Carnaby. Runways at these emergency airports were 9,000 feet long and 750 feet wide. The hard-surface runways had 1,500 to 3,000 feet of heavy turf at either end to cushion belly landings. Although Screwball Express was badly damaged, Howard and Jim assured the rest of our crew we would make it back to Kimbolton. Nevertheless, we contemplated dumping some our heavy equipment into the North Sea in an effort to lighten the load and help our pilots' prediction come true.

We were extremely thankful for the very fine landing of Screwball Express at Kimbolton shortly after 1300 hours. I'm certain all of us said a prayer of thanks for being alive. We crawled out of Screwball Express when it came to a stop on its parking pad and began to survey the damage. Our Flying Fortress was a multitude of holes held together by ragged metal. Gasoline was dripping from holes in a Tokyo tank and from two of four damaged wing tanks. Two oil tanks were also damaged. The wings looked like a pair of sieves. The landing lights were missing from the wings. It was apparent the outboard engine in the right wing would have to be replaced. Our crew members, assisted by our ground crew, counted 287 flak holes in Screwball Express. Twenty of the flak holes were within two feet of my position in the nose of the aircraft. Every member of our crew was equally close to injury and death several times during the mission.

"Surely goodness and mercy shall follow me all the days of my life, and I will dwell in the house of the Lord forever."

Flying time on our 33rd combat mission was logged at exactly eight hours. Seven hours and 49 minutes of that time were relatively uneventful. The other eleven minutes were hell. Thirty-six of the 42 planes on this mission from the 379th Bomb Group sustained flak damage. Screwball Express was in much worse condition than any of the other returning Fortresses in our Group. We stared again at the tremendous amount of battle damage it had received, and were then trucked to Headquarters for about thirty minutes of debriefing. Smoke screens were reported at Hamburg, Kiel and

Bremen. Medium sized vessels, possibly oil barges, were seen in the docks at Hamburg. Enemy aircraft were observed on several airfields.

When debriefing was completed, all of us except Howard headed for our barracks. He said something about wanting to finish his earlier conversation with Lt. Hedges.

Jim, Bob and I flopped down on our bunks when we returned to our Nissen hut. We had been reviewing various parts of the mission for about ten minutes, when the door of the barracks snapped open and in flew Howard in a gust of jubilation.

"We're through, fellas," he shouted. "Today was our last mission. Our tour is over. We're done. Hallelujah, we're done." I had never heard him express such overwhelming emotion. "Clay hinted to me before this morning's briefing that today's mission might wind up our combat tour. I didn't want to say anything to you fellas 'til I knew for sure. That's why I waited 'til we landed. I went over to see him as soon as our crew finished with our debriefing. It's official, fellas. Our tour is over." And then he sang, "California, here I come." The notes were a bit shaky, but the words had real meaning.

Bob, Jim and I were equally exuberant about the good news. We all hollered, shook hands with each other, yelled, slapped one another on the back, sang the Air Force song, hugged each other and jumped up and down on the bunks like four jacks-out-of-a-box. The day of our final combat mission had finally arrived—June 20, 1944, mission number 33. It was combat mission number 43 for Screwball Express.

Howard and Jim rushed over to the enlisted men's area to tell the other members of our crew the good news. Frank vividly remembers that he, Jerry and Joe were enjoying some rare minutes of sunshine as they lay on the ground outside the end of their barracks. It was much too cool to be without their shirts, but the unusual opportunity for sunbathing was not to go unused. They were especially happy when they heard the news. The sun's brightness seemed dimmed in the excitement of the moment. They scurried around the area looking for Tom and Mathews. When they found them, more shouts of joy were heard for a great distance.

Bob and I rushed over to the officer's club for a drink. I think I toasted him, then he toasted me, and then we made a joint toast to the rest of our crew. We congratulated each other at least a dozen times. When we finally left the club, we did not take time to notice which of the lights had been turned on—the green light, the amber, or the red.

I ran over to Headquarters to see if I could get someone to send a cablegram to my Mom and Dad. The next day's Edwardsville (Illinois) Intelligencer contained an article which began with the words in the cablegram. "Dear Mom and Dad. My tour completed. Everything fine. Am in best of health. See you soon. Ken."

I commandeered a jeep and drove to the pad where Screwball Express was already being repaired. As I stood there, the sight of that majestic aircraft caused an emotional mixture of pride and relief to swell within me. I felt much pride for having completed 33 combat missions, but was greatly relieved because I had no more missions to fly.

My primary purpose at the flight line that evening concerned some unfinished business with sergeant Starbuck. He was always in, on or around Screwball Express when it needed attention, so it took only a few minutes to find him. He informed me his ground crew would have "our plane" flyable in several weeks. I held my closed hand in front of him, indicating I wanted to give him something. He reached out to receive it. I placed in the palm of his hand the good luck nickel he loaned me on March

26. A very large smile stretched across his face. He said, "Congratulations, Lieutenant. And tell the rest of your crew I said, "Good show." We shook hands in a firm and friendly grasp as we shared a special moment of mutual respect.

Bob was completely dismayed when the photo lab informed him about an hour later that he evidently used all of his film taking pictures of our formation's Fortresses over the North Sea. Fate had completely abandoned him —his photographic efforts with flak were totally unproductive. He did not get a single picture of flak during the bomb run at Hamburg. (In a letter written years later, Bob described this as "the most upsetting" thing that happened to him during his entire combat tour.)

On the following morning, June 21, l944—nearly half a century ago—I stood in front of Screwball Express. Our ground crew was busy with the myriad of repairs that had to be made to "our plane." I considered it a distinct privilege—a special honor—to stand before that severely damaged aircraft. It had provided a tremendous service to those of us who were members of its original flight crew. Screwball Express had continuously stood behind us during 217 hours and 35 minutes of combat flying. We will forever be deeply indebted to, and extremely thankful for, that wonderful flying machine. Our crew flew an additional 24 hours and 50 minutes in four other Flying Fortresses, for a total of 242 hours and 25 minutes of combat flying time.

It seemed notable at the time—our crew flew 33 combat missions in only 89 days. Also noteworthy—our crew flew approximately fifty - four percent of the 379th Bomb Group's 61 combat missions during those 89 days. Screwball Express flew seventy percent of those same 61 missions—a remarkable record.

Inclement weather also caused some kind of a record. In 1944 to date (less than six months) rain and overcast skies forced the 379th Bomb Group to scrub 31 combat missions before takeoff and recall eight others after its bombers were airborne. Twenty-two of those 31 scrubbed missions and six of those eight recalls occurred during the same 89 days in which our crew completed its 33 combat missions—March 24 through June 20.

Screwball Express carried our crew through a memorable kaleidoscope of aerial combat experiences, the majority of which changed continuously—none were identical. Fortunately, one type of experience was always constant. It was repeated at the conclusion of each of the 29 combat missions we flew in "our plane." Screwball Express never failed to bring us safely back to the Kimbolton airfield! The early morning fog was not thick enough to hide the tear that tried to form in the corner of one eye.

"Yank"-The Army Weekly published the following story that humorously illustrates the battle severity of our final combat mission:

The ground crew looked up and saw, coming down for a landing, not a Flying Fortress, but a lone motor. Sitting on the motor was a sergeant with a machine gun across his lap. He brought the motor down to a beautiful no-point landing, and jumped off. "Boy," he said, "were we in a fight."

"The 8th Air Force operation on June 20, 1944," the article continued, "occurred during one of the rare periods of temporary air superiority for the combined German defenses after the Normandy Invasion. Intense concentrations of flak claimed a much greater percentage of bombers shot down than in prior missions. Dogfights were thick over the skies of France and Germany today as the Luftwaffe fought desperately to stave off the huge assault of the heavy bombers. Forty-one enemy aircraft were destroyed in the air and 13 on the ground by escorting fighters of the Eighth and Ninth Air Forces. Twelve additional enemy planes were shot down by bomber crews."

Eighth Air Force statistics for its entire operation of June 20,

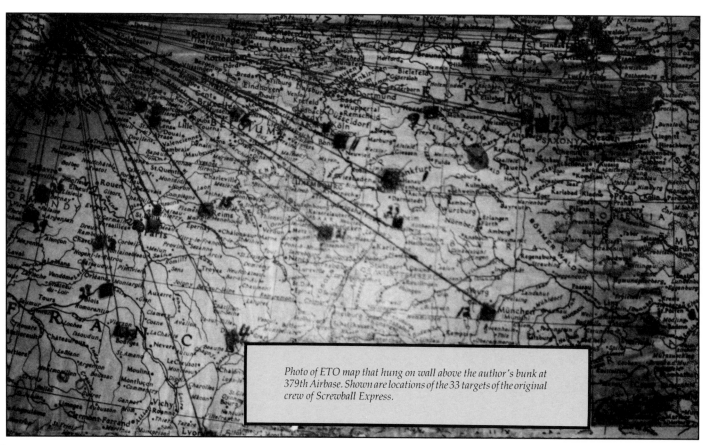

Photo of ETO map that hung on wall above the author's bunk at 379th Airbase. Shown are locations of the 33 targets of the original crew of Screwball Express.

1944, include the data in chart at the right:

The 526th Squadron's Report for June, 1944 states: "Quite a few combat men finished up their tours of operations and left in one large bunch for the Casual Pool, 12th Replacement Control Depot, for return to the States." Names following that sentence include: "Lts. Keller, Moore, Towers; T/Sgts. Kiblin, Milworm; S/Sgts. Craig, Lindsey, Mathews." Thirty-six men were in the "bunch." I remember waving to the departing members of my crew when they were trucked away from the Kimbolton airfield on or about June 26, 1944.

Headquarters somehow failed to include my name in the orders sending other members of my crew stateside. Several weeks passed before my name appeared on a corrected set. What a Snafu!

During the following weeks at the Kimbolton airfield I frequently felt very much alone. All of my crew members except Ernie and me had returned to the United States. I made several attempts to locate Ernie, but was told he was somewhere attending a Ground Defense School. Conversations with new crew members were brief

Bombing Results

	Dispatched	Attacked	Tonnage / Results
First Force	512 B-17s	468	1,370.4 tons / ex-vg-g
		14 t/o *	
Second Force	358 B-24s	328	817.0 tons / vg
		12 t/o *	
Third Force	341 B-17s	456	1,141.4 tons / ex-vg-g
	191 B-24s	3 t/o *	_____
	532 bombers		
Total	1,402 bombers	1,281	3,328.8 tons/very good

* (targets of opportunity)

Aircraft Casualties

	Lost	Damaged
First Force	7 B-17s to flak	81 B-17s major flak damage (4 of these also had fighter damage)
		258 B-17s minor flak damage
		339 B-17s by flak (and fighters)
Second Force	11 B-24s to flak	8 B-24s major damage
	17 B-24s to fighters	197 B-24s minor damage
	2 B-24s collided	
	4 B-24s Sweden	____
	34 to flak & fighters	205 B-24s by flak and fighters
Third Force	1 B-17 to flak	17 B-17s - major damage
	1 B-24 to flak	14 B-24s - major damage
	3 B-17s to fighters	31 bombers - major damage
	1 B-17 assembly/crash	
	1 B-17 take off/crash	99 B-17s - minor damage
	7 to flak, fighters, misc.	75 B-24s - minor damage
		174 bombers - minor damage

Summary of Lost and Damaged Aircraft

20 to flak	120 bombers - major damage
20 to fighters	629 bombers - minor damage
2 crashed	
2 collide	
4 interned	_____
48 bombers Lost	749 bombers - battle damage

and became infrequent. Apparently, they did not understand my reluctance to discuss combat missions with them. My loneliness was accented by a depressed feeling that resulted from the foul-up in my orders. Additionally, when other officers in my barracks were awakened for early morning mission briefings, I was the only one who did not have a lump of fear in my throat. I was also the only person who sat in the back row of the briefing room. It disturbed me to attend combat briefings, knowing I was not going to participate in the mission. Although I was very interested in what was taking place, I felt awkward in expressing that interest. With 33 combat missions to my credit I should have felt important; instead, I felt an agony of loneliness. At a time when I had no more combat missions to fly, and finally felt safe, I was feeling sorry for myself.

Other flight crews were privileged to fly "our plane" on combat missions that followed its return to operational status. The crew of Lt. Anthony J. Pettrini was the first to fly Screwball Express in combat after our June 20 mission to Hamburg. They were preflighting it as I watched on the morning of July 4. It looked like a brand new aircraft, and it

should have, for much of its fuselage had been replaced because of damage it had sustained during our attack at Hamburg. Its engines were revved up, and Screwball Express was taxied out to the perimeter strip. Minutes later it roared down the main runway for takeoff on the mission to Illiers l'Eugene, France. It was a proud moment when "our plane" lifted into the air and climbed gracefully for the assembly with other Fortresses of the 379th Bomb Group. It was the 158th combat mission for the Triangle K Group, and the 44th for Screwball Express.

I still remember the lump in my throat when I gave Screwball Express a farewell salute. The 379th Bomb Group's formation disappeared into the clouds and I walked slowly back to my barracks. I'm confident that Screwball Express will fly forever in my memories of World War II.

(**Special Credit**: Please refer to *Flying Forts : the B-17 in WWII*; under Bibliography.)

The Last Mission of Screwball Express

Thursday, April 5, 1945. The bottom of a 10/10 cloud cover was hanging at 1500 feet over the airfield at Kimbolton, England. The 379th Bomb Group was one of many that held a briefing on this date, with apparent indifference to the moderate amount of rain falling in this part of England.

The briefing by the 379th Group was in preparation for its 317th combat mission under Field Order 678 of the 8th Air Force. Thirty-eight flight crews of the 379th Bomb Group were assigned to attack the ordnance depot at Ingolstadt, Germany, about 42 miles north-northwest of Munich. This depot was very important to the German Army because its primary role was the supply and repair of various types of artillery. Reconnaissance photos showed many artillery pieces at the depot, and it was consequently on the list of targets requiring attention of the 8th Air Force.

The 38 Fortresses, including three spares, comprised the Lead, High and Low Groups of the 41st Combat Wing. Each of these Fortresses was loaded with 34-150 pound demolition bombs and two M-47 incendiaries. Takeoff was scheduled for 0530 hours.

The crew of 2nd Lt. Joseph G. Hourtal, of the 527th Bomb Squadron, was assigned to fly B-17G serial number 43-36507 in the Low Squadron of the Low Group on this mission. Other members of this eight man crew were: 2nd Lt. Martin A. Kane, co-pilot; 2nd Lt. Edwards P. Roberson, navigator; T/Sgt. Richard D. Rowan, top turret/engineer; S/Sgt. Donald S. Millar, tail gunner; S/Sgt. John D. Roberts, radio operator/gunner; S/Sgt. Sam N. Reaves, Jr., ball turret gunner; and S/Sgt. Carlos A. Whitehead, togglier/nose gunner. Bombardiers usually flew only in Lead aircraft near the war's end, and were replaced in other bombers by nose gunners who dropped their bomb loads upon signal from their Group Leader. S/Sgt. Clyde Crouch, waist gunner, flew six combat missions with this crew before the 8th Air Force eliminated the second waist gunner position—the reason this crew currently consisted of only eight members. This was the 19th combat mission for Lt. Hourtal's crew.

Thirty-seven of the 379th Bomb Group's 38 Fortresses scheduled for this mission completed their takeoff, but the aircraft assigned to Lt. Hourtal's crew remained at its hardstand—one of its engines would not start. The airfield's control tower instructed the crew to board a truck that would take them to the 525th Squadron area where they were to transfer to a spare Flying Fortress coded with the letter R.

Lt. Hourtal's crew rushed to complete the exchange of aircraft as the 379th's combat formation disappeared in the thick overcast above Kimbolton. Hurriedly, they climbed aboard an aircraft that was originally assigned to the 526th Squadron more than a year earlier and coded at that time with the letter M. This aircraft, now assigned to the 525th Squadron, was coded with the letter R on or before March 23, 1945. The aircraft had survived much aerial combat and was now used primarily on missions that called for maximum effort. The serial number on the aircraft's fuselage and on its vertical stabilizer was 42-97128. It was Screwball Express.

It is strangely coincidental that Lt. Hourtal's crew flew its first combat mission in an attack on an oil refinery at Hamburg, Germany. Our crew's last combat mission was also to an oil refinery at that same city.

The Gee Box and the radio compass in Screwball Express were not in good working condition, but the control tower instructed Hourtal's crew to get airborne and catch up with the rest of the 379th's attack force headed for Ingolstadt. Screwball Express took off on its 118th combat mission at 0558 hours, climbed for altitude and headed directly for the day's target. A spare Fortress from the Low Group, returning early and according to plan, landed shortly after Screwball Express left the runway.

During the first week of April, 1945, Allied ground forces advanced to positions near Speyer and Landau on the Rhine river south of Mannheim. The southern line of the U.S. 7th Army met at Speyer with the northern line of the 2nd French Corps of the 1st French Army.

The 379th Bomb Group's attack formation crossed the French coast near Le Havre at 0722 hours. At 0759 hours it arrived at the Allied controlled Continental Buncher southeast of Paris and about 20 miles north of Troyes. The formation left the Buncher at 0853 hours, at which time Screwball Express was flying on a direct route to the formation's final time checkpoint before crossing the front lines.

As Screwball Express flew through the layers of clouds, the 379th Group could be heard on the radio but could not be located. Fortress number 43-38979 of the High Squadron in the High Group was also unable to find the formation and turned back at 0914 hours. Its bombs were dropped in the English Channel on the return to England. Fortress number 43-37851, also of the High Squadron/High Group, aborted the mission at 1045 hours for the same reason, but brought its bomb load back to the Kimbolton airfield.

Screwball Express continued flying toward Ingolstadt in its solitary search for Fortresses from the 379th Bomb Group. The Group's coded radio messages could still be heard as its Fortresses crossed into enemy territory. At 1100 hours those Fortresses were guided by their Wing's Lead Group into a wide turn at only 14,000 feet over the initial point. This altitude was chosen so the formation could get under the clouds where visibility was sufficiently clear for a visual bomb run. The 34 Fortresses in the 41st "A" Wing dropped their bombs on the primary target at 1126 hours. Bombing results of the Lead and Low Groups were very good, but a malfunction of Automatic Flight Control Equipment at the moment of bomb release by the High Group caused some of that part of the bomb pattern to fall about 1,400 feet left of the intended point of impact. The "A" Wing turned onto its briefed compass heading for the return flight to England, and at approximately 1200 hours was southeast of Mannheim, Germany, flying at 9,900 feet.

Lt. Hourtal decided to abort the mission when he thought Screwball Express was about 20 minutes from the front line of the American ground forces. Screwball Express was maneuvered down through the clouds so its position could be determined by sighting checkpoints on the map. According to the Mission Report, the 379th Bomb Group's homeward bound "A" formation was in the same general area shortly before Screwball Express came out of the clouds at an altitude of approximately 9,000 feet.

Screwball Express was hit by several antiaircraft shells almost immediately upon emerging from the clouds. One of the shells scored a direct hit on number three engine. Another flak shell exploded near the bomb bay doors and under the radio room. A flak burst under the right wing, between number three and four engines, caused number four to run out of control. The landing gear was knocked down and control cables were severed. The pilots tried desperately to feather the propellers of the damaged engines, both of which had to be shut down because the propellers could not be turned into the wind for minimum resistance.

Screwball Express was severely damaged and extremely difficult to control. It turned itself into the dead engines and began to lose altitude. Bombs were salvoed by S/Sgt. Whitehead in an attempt to lighten the load. They exploded at the edge of a small German town. Lt. Hourtal ordered the crew to prepare for bailout and crew members made certain their parachutes were firmly secured to their harness. The order to bail out came when Screwball Express was at an altitude of only 2,500 feet. Lieutenants Hourtal and Kane left their controls and hurried to the escape hatch. The crippled bomber banked sharply to its right.

In the excitement following the flak hits, Whitehead's intercom became disconnected and he did not hear the order to bail out. The intercom's silence caused him to turn around to see what was happening. He saw an empty navigator's chair, the co-pilot in the forward escape hatch and the pilot waiting to leave the aircraft. These three crewmen quickly exited the plunging Fortress—the co-pilot, then the pilot and finally the togglier/ nose gunner. Screwball Express was only 300 feet from the ground when Whitehead bailed out.

The Mission Report includes a statement by crewmen Roberson and Rowan indicating the sequence in which crew members jumped from the rapidly falling aircraft. The last person to leave was S/Sgt. Whitehead, the togglier/nose gunner, who vividly recalls the crew members parachuting from the aircraft in the following order:

1-tail gunner; 2-ball turret gunner; 3-top turret gunner; 4-navigator; 5-radio operator; 6-co-pilot; 7-pilot; and 8-togglier/ nose gunner.

Shortly before 1200 hours on April 5, 1945, the final flight of Screwball Express ended abruptly when it crashed and burned southeast of Bellheim, Germany. Bellheim is approximately four miles west of the Rhine river, 11 miles north-northwest of Karlsruhe and nine miles east of Landau. At this moment the formation of B-17s from the 379th Bomb Group was descending to 8,000 feet near Mannheim, so it could avoid flying through the thickening layer of clouds.

Tail gunner Millar and ball turret gunner Reaves took longer to reach the ground because they had bailed out first and consequently from a higher altitude. French soldiers shot at them as they floated to the ground, believing they were German paratroopers. When Reaves and Millar landed they were confronted by a group of German civilians wielding pitchforks. Fortunately, the French soldiers arrived at the scene, learned the nationality of the two frightened Americans and chased the hostile civilian group away. The soldiers immediately offered Millar and Reaves a quart of choice wine in a gesture of friendly apology.

The togglier/nose gunner's chest-pack parachute opened almost immediately after his departure from Screwball Express. He floated safely into a swampy area and landed in three feet of water. A thick column of black smoke mushroomed over the spot where Screwball Express crashed. Whitehead removed his parachute, and then saw the silk of another 'chute hanging in a grove of trees. He waded through the water to the grove, where trees stood on hummocks that surfaced like miniature islands from the shallow water surrounding them. Lieutenant Hourtal was dangling from his parachute harness in waist deep water. The opening of his parachute had caused a jerking action that whipped his legs into the tree with great force. Both of his feet were severed from his legs just above the ankles. His shoes were in the water nearby.

S/Sgt. Whitehead removed his pilot from the harness and placed him on the hummock under the tree. Shroud lines of the parachute were used to tie Hourtal's legs and minimize bleeding.

The togglier/nose gunner headed west through the swamp in frantic search for help. About one mile away he found a soldier from the 1st French Army, which included members of the French Underground and some Moroccans, driving a reconnaissance car. Sign language and a friendly smile convinced the Frenchman he should help this stranger who was wearing an American flag armband pinned to the jacket of a heavy flying suit. The twosome drove about one mile to the small town of Bellheim, where a pot factory had been taken over by a graves registration unit from the 142nd Infantry, 36th Division, United States 7th Army.

Other French soldiers had watched the parachutes come out of Screwball Express and followed them to the ground. They found Lt. Hourtal shortly after the togglier/nose gunner left for help. Engineer Rowan, navigator Roberson and radio operator Roberts landed in and around Bellheim. They were joined later in the afternoon by Reaves and Millar who apparently had consumed every drop of their quart of wine. The crew members learned Lt. Hourtal had been moved to a Convent that the French had converted into a hospital at the outskirts of Herxheim, Germany, and immediately traveled the six or seven miles to see him.

Lt. Kane, the co-pilot, was not immediately found because his parachute had not fully opened and was not easily visible in the swamp. He was found laying head first in shallow water. The D-ring handle of his rip cord was missing, indicating he had pulled it. Evidently, the spring-loaded 'chute had been activated but the main 'chute did not open. His body was cared for by an American hospital unit and was later buried in plot C, row 8, grave 31 in the American Military Cemetery at St. Avold, France. The pilot was later transferred to an American hospital at Grunstadt, Germany, about 12 miles northwest of Mannheim.

At 1244 hours the 379th Bomb Group's formation descended to 4,000 feet. The cloud cover had become massive and by 1407 hours the Fortresses from Kimbolton were flying at an altitude of only 1,200 feet. It was as though the thick layer of clouds was a dark curtain, pulled down by the descending formation of B-17s in a futile attempt to hide the fate of Screwball Express from reality.

Screwball Express had been "on stage" for 118 combat performances with a star-studded cast of B-17 Flying Fortresses. This superb performer for the 8th Air Force would never make another curtain call.

On the following morning the five enlisted men in Lt. Hourtal's crew went to the crash scene where small pieces of Screwball Express were scattered over a large area. The vertical stabilizer of its tail section was the only major part of the aircraft that was not destroyed. The picture taken with the radio operator's camera clearly shows the Triangle K insignia on the stabilizer. Under the Group's insignia are the charred, but legible, last three numbers of the aircraft's serial number—128.

The Mission Report indicates other crews on this Ingolstadt mission did not encounter any flak or enemy fighters, and all other Fortresses of the 379th Bomb Group returned safely. On Friday, April 13, eight days after their fateful mission, the uninjured survivors of Lt. Hourtal's crew returned to the 379th base at Kimbolton.

The crash of Screwball Express increased the number of 379th Bomb Group Fortresses lost to enemy action to 147. Those losses occurred in 317 combat missions. Five days later the enemy shot down two more Fortresses of the 379th and enlarged the Group's total MIA number to 149.

The 379th Bomb Group flew its 330th and last combat mission on April 25, 1945, less than three weeks after Screwball Express was lost in action.

Part of one burned up engine of Screwball Express, standing upright several hundred feet from tail section and crash site. (Photos taken April 6, 1945, by S/Sgt. Robert's camera...photos provided by John D. Roberts, Carlos A. Whitehead and Sam N. Reaves, Jr.)

Five members of the last crew to fly in Screwball Express, standing by its tail section in field near Bellheim, Germany. L/R: T/Sgt Richard D. Rowan, S/Sgt Sam N. Reaves, Jr., S/Sgt Carlos A. Whitehead, S/Sgt John D. Roberts, and S/Sgt Donald S. Millar.

Above: Aerial photo by William T. Larkins at Kingman, AZ early in 1947. Left: Dedication of the 379th Bomb Group Memorial at Kimbolton, England.

Building in 524th Squadron area. Currently used as hangar for the Piper Cub of a local resident. The road is an original.

The only remaining hardstand in the 525th Squadron area.

View from 526th Squadron area, from west end of runway 90-270. St. Andrew's Church steeple is at photo's center.

The widest remaining portion of the main runway, looking south from a position opposite the hardstand area of 525th Squadron.

The four photographs on pages 126 and 127 were taken by Robert Beattie, son of Lt. Joseph T. Beattie, 0-820700, of the 525th Squadron, 379th Bomb Group, on August 19, 1989. The crew of Lt. Beattie was listed MIA following its 34th mission, September 8, 1944, to a synthetic oil plant at Ludwigshaven, Germany.

My wife and I had the good fortune of meeting Bob and his wife while in England for the 379th Memorial dedication at the Kimbolton airfield in 1989. Bob made the trip so he could "get to know my Dad a little better."

I sincerely appreciate Bob's permission to publish his photographs on the two preceding pages, and thank him for the privilege of including them in this book.

Lt. Beattie and members of his crew meet the Queen of England and members of her Royal Party during her visit to the Kimbolton Airbase on July 6, 1944. Lt. Beattie is the first Crew Member in the line, holding an oxygen mask. (Photo by 379th BG Photo. Sec.)

The Castle at Kimbolton, England.   August 20, 1989.

Looking up and down the main street of Kimbolton, England. August 20, 1989.

SUMMARY OF THE 33 MISSIONS
FLOWN BY ORIGINAL CREW OF SCREWBALL EXPRESS

No.	1944 Dates	Targets	Locations	Positions Flown	Flak	Fighter Oppos.	Bomb Loads	Bombing Results	Flying Times	Group A/C Hit-MIA	Personnel Casualties	Damage to Our B-17
*1	24-Mar	A/C Engine Component	Frankfurt, Germany	No.5, Low Sqd Lead Grp	Heavy-Inaccurate	None	5-1000 Demos	Very Good	7:00	8 hit	None	None
2	26-Mar	Fly-Bomb Site	Wizernes, France	High Squad. Single Grp	Heavy-Accurate	None	5-1000 Demos	Very Good	4:30	8 hit 1 MIA	10 MIA	Medium
3	27-Mar	Airfield	Chartres, France	Low Squad. High Group	Light-Accurate	None	12-500 Demos	Very Good	5:45	1 hit	None	Light
4	28-Mar	Airfield	Dijon, France	Low Squad. High Group	Light-Inaccurate	None	42-100 Incend.	Very Good	7:00	2 hit	None	None
5	29-Mar	A/C Parts Factory	Brunswick, Germany	High Sqd Lead w/Lead Grp 381 BG	Heavy-Inaccurate	Light	35 -100 Incend. 10-100 Demos	Good	8:45	5 hit	None	Light
6	10-Apr	Airfield & A/C Factory	Brussels, Belgium	Low Squad. Lead Group	Light-Inaccurate	None	12-500 Demos	Excellent	4:35	None	None	None
7	11-Apr	A/C Assembly Plant	Sorau, Germany	Low Squad. Low Group	Heavy-Accurate	None	8-500 Incend. 15-100 Demos	Excellent	11:20	10 hit	None	Light
8	18-Apr	Airfield	Perleberg, Germany	High Squad. Lead Grp "B"	Medium-Inaccurate	2 FW-190	38-100 Demos	Very Good	9:00	1 hit	None	Light
9	19-Apr	A/C Assembly Plant	Kassel, Germany	High Squad. High Group	Heavy-Inaccurate	Light	42-100 Incend.	Excellent	7:30	4 hit	None	None
10	20-Apr	Fly-Bomb Site	Sottevast, France	Low Squad. Lead Grp "A"	Heavy-Accurate	None	8-1000 Demos	Very Good	4:30	11 hit	1 Wounded	Light
11	22-Apr	Docks & Harbor	Bonn. Germany	Lead Squad. Low Group	Heavy-Inaccurate	None	12-500 Demos	Fair to Good	7:30	5 hit	None	None
12	24-Apr	Airfield & A/C Factory	Landsberg, Germany	High Sqd Lead Lead Group	Heavy-Inaccurate	50 Me-109	10-500 Demos	Excellent	9:30	8 hit	6 Wounded	None
13	28-Apr	Airfield	Avord, France	Low Squad. Low Group	Light-Accurate	35-40 Me-109 FW-190	20-300 Demos	Excellent	6:30	14 hit	None	Light
14	30-Apr	Airfield	Lyons, France	Lead Squad. Lead Group	Medium-Inaccurate	35 Me-109.	5-1000 Demos	Excellent	8:00	None	None	None

No.	1944 Dates	Targets	Locations	Positions Flown	Flak	Fighter Oppos.	Bomb Loads	Bombing Results	Flying Times	Group A/C Hit-MIA	Personnel Casualties	Damage to Our B-17
15	1-May	Marshalling Yards	Reims, France	Low Squad. High Group	Medium-Accurate	None	6-1000 Demos	Excellent	6:00	13 hit	1 Wounded	Medium
16	7-May	Aircraft Component	Berlin, Germany	Low Sqd Lead High Grp "A"	Medium-Accurate	None	3-1000 Demos 5-500 Incend.	Very Good	9:00	14 hit 2 MIA	18 KIA	Heavy
17	12-May	Oil Refinery	Merseburg, Germany	Low Squad. Lead Grp "A"	Heavy-Accurate	Light	38-100 Demos	Very Good	9:00	10 hit	1 KIA 2 Wounded	Light
18	13-May	Vulc.Plant & Rubber Fact.	Stettin, Germany	Low Sqd Lead Low Group	Heavy-Accurate	75 Me-109 FW-190	10-500 Demos	Excellent	11:00	8 hit 3 MIA	27 MIA	Medium
19	19-May	Aircraft Component	Berlin. Germany	Low Sqd Lead High Grp "A"	Heavy-Accurate	Light	42-100 Incend.	Good	9:35	5 hit 2 MIA	18-MIA	Heavy
20	21-May	Fly-Bomb Site	Marquis, France	Lead Squad Single Grp	Light-Accurate	None	8-1000 Demos	Excellent	4:30	8 hit	None	Light
21	23-May	Marshalling Yards	Saarbruck-en, Germany	High Sqd Lead Lead Grp "B"	Heavy-Inaccurate	3 Me-109	12-500 Demos	Good	7:15	1 hit	None	None
22	24-May	Aircraft Component	Berlin, Germany	High Sqd Lead Low Grp "A"	Heavy-Accurate	75 FW-190	8-500 Incenc. 16-100 Demos	Fair/Good	9:00	18 hit 3 MIA	27 MIA	Heavy
23	27-May	Airfield & Barracks	Speyerdorf, Germany	High Squad. High Grp "A"	Heavy-Accurate	50 Me-109 FW-190	10-500 Demos	Very Good	7:30	4 hit	None	Light
24	28-May	Airfield	Wusten-sacken, Ger.	High Sqd Lead Lead Group	Heavy-Accurate	15 Me-109 FW-190	10-500 Demos	Very Good	8:00	7 hit	None	Light
25	29-May	A/C Engine Plant & Airfield	Krzesinki, Poland	Low Sqd Lead High Grp "A"	Heavy-Accurate	25 Me-109 FW-190	10-500 Demos	Good	10:30	8 hit	None	Light
*26	6-Jun	RR Bridge Over Hiway	Caen, France	Low Sqd Lead w/ 303 BG Single Grp	None	None	12-500 2-1000 Demos	Grp Ld did not drop	4:50	None	None	None
*27	7-Jun	Hiway Bridge Marshall. Yds	Flers, France	High Sqd Lead Lead Grp "A"	None	None	6-1000 Demos	Good	5:45	None	None	None
*28	8-Jun	RR Bridge & Marshall. Yds	Orleans, France	Grp Dep Lead Lead Grp "B"	None	None	6-1000 Demos	Excellent	7:15	None	None	None

No.	1944 Dates	Targets	Locations	Positions Flown	Flak	Fighter Oppos.	Bomb Loads	Bombing Results	Flying Times	Group A/C Hit-MIA	Personnel Casualties	Damage to Our B-17
29	10-Jun	Airfield	Vannes, France	Grp Dep Lead Low Grp "B"	Light-Inaccurate	None	36-100 Demos	Excellent	6:15	None	None	None
30	12-Jun	RR Bridge over River	Pontau-bault, Fr.	High Sqd Lead Low Grp "B"	Light-Accurate	None	4- 2000 Demos	Very Good	6:00	3 hit	None	None
31	14-Jun	Airfield	Creil, France	Grp Dep Lead High Grp "A"	Heavy-Accurate	5 Me-109	38-100 Demos	Excellent	6:20	8 hit 1 MIA	9 MIA	Heavy
32	19-Jun	Fly-Bomb Site	Zudausques, France	Grp Dep Lead Low Grp "B"	Light-Inaccurate	None	12-500 Demos	Very Good	5:15	None	1 KIA	None
33	20-Jun	Oil Refinery	Hamburg, Germany	Grp Dep Lead Lead Grp "A"	Heavy-Accurate	6 or 7 Me-109 FW-190	12-500 Demos	Excellent	8:00	37 hit 1 MIA	5 Wounded	Heavy
5 in Mar.		9 Airfields	16 Germany	14 Low Squad	18-H	17-None	585 Bombs	13-EX	242 Hours	221 hit	91 MIA	14-None
9 in Apr.		7 A/C Plants	15 France	11 High Squad	8-L	8-H		12-VG	25 Mins.	13 MIA	20 KIA	11- L
11 in May		4 Bridges	1 Belgium	8 Lead Squad	4-M	6-L	403 Demo	5-G			15 Wound.	5-H
8 in June		4 Fly Bomb	1 Poland	13 Lead Grp	3-None	2-M	182 Incen	2-F/G			126 Casualties	3-M
				9 High Grp	18-Accu.		90.35 Tons	1-NBA				
Other B-17s		3 Airfld/Fac		8 Low Grp	12-Inacc.							
*1	789W	2 MM Yards		3 Single Grp								
*26	189X	2 Oil Ref.		12 Squad Lead								
*27	213F	Dock/Harbor		5 Grp Deputy								
*28	058C	Vulcan Plant										

TARGETS AND BOMBING TECHNIQUES

RE: THE 33 MISSIONS OF SCREWBALL EXPRESS' ORIGINAL CREW

Mission	Date	Primary Targets	Secondary Targets	Targets of Opportunity
1	3/24/44	Kuget -Fischer ball bearing plant at Schweinfurt, Ger. 10/10 cloud cover forced us to our Secondary target	Bombed Aircraft Engine Component Plant at Frankfurt, Ger. Used PFF at 0904 hrs. from 23,500 feet; on 165 degrees Magnetic Heading	
2	3/26/44	Bombed Fly-Bomb Site at Wizernes, Fr. visual run, at 1500 hrs. ; 22,000', Mag. Heading of 232 degrees		
3	3/27/44	Bombed Airfield at Chartres, Fr; visual thru 8/10 clouds, from 17,500' at 1416 hrs. 23 degree MH		
4	3/28/44	Bombed Airfield at Dijon, Fr; visual from 19,000' at 1444 hrs. 10 MH		
5	3/29/44	Bombed Aircraft parts/steel at Brunswick, Ger. thru clouds from 26,000' at 1324 hrs. 110 MH		
6	4/10/44	Bombed Airfield & Aircraft Factory at Brusssels, Bel. visually at 0919 hrs. from 22,000'		
7	4/11/44	Bombed Aircraft Assembly plant at Sorau, Ger. at 1217 hrs. visually, from 11,000'		
8	4/18/44	Aircraft Assembly Plant at Orianienburg, Ger. covered by solid overcast	Bombed Airfield at Perleberg, Ger. visually from from 23,500' at 1504 hrs. on 261 MH	
9	4/19/44	Bombed Aircraft Assembly Plant at Kassel, Ger. at 1038 hrs., visually, from 23,000' on 270 MH		
10	4/20/44	Bombed Fly-Bomb Site at Sottevast, Fr. visually from 20,000'		
11	4/22/44	Marshalling Yds at Hamm, Ger. Bomb racks in Low Grp's Lead plane malfunctioned, so went to the secondary target	Bombed Docks and Harbor at Bonn, Ger. visually at 1933 hrs. from 21,000' on 122 MH	
12	4/24/44	Bombed Airfield and A/C Factory at Landsberg, Ger. visually from 20,000' at 1406 hrs. on 334 MH		

TARGETS AND BOMBING TECHNIQUES

RE: THE 33 MISSIONS OF SCREWBALL EXPRESS' ORIGINAL CREW

Mission	Date	Primary Targets	Secondary Targets	Targets of Opportunity
13	4/28/44	Bombed Airfield at Avord, Ft. visually from 14,000' at 1201 hrs. on 10 MH		
14	4/30/44	Bombed Airfield at Lyons, Fr. visually at 1041 hrs. from 20,000' on 7 MH		
15	5/ 1/44	Bombed Marshalling Yds. at Reims, Fr. visually from 21,000' at 1816 hrs. on 350 MH		
16	5/ 7/44	Bombed Aircraft Comp. Plant at Berlin, Ger. Used PFF from 27,000' on 38 MH. Bombs away at 1115 hrs.		
17	5/12/44	Bombed Oil Refinery at Merseburg, Ger. thru haze & smoke from 24,000' at 1409 hrs., 29 MH		
18	5/13/44	Aircraft Comp. Plant at Posen, Poland; had 10/10 cloud cover, so we went to our secondary target	Bombed Vulcanizing Plant/ Rubber Factory at Stettin, Ger. by PFF from 23,000' at 1520 hrs. on 310 MH	
19	5/19/44	Bombed Aircraft Comp. Plant at Berlin, Ger. visually thru clouds from 27,000' at 1403 hrs. on 45 MH		
20	5/21/44	Bombed Fly-Bomb Site at Marquis, Fr. by GH Equipment. Bombs away at 1407 hrs. from 20,400', 187 MH		
21	5/23/44	Airfield at Nancy, Fr. 9/10 overcast forced us to go to our secondary target	Bombed RR Marshalling Yds. at Saarbrucken, Ger. by PFF from 23,000' at 0954 hrs. on 35 MH	
22	5/24/44	Bombed Aircraft Comp. Plant at Berlin, Ger. by PFF from 26,000' at 1104 hrs. on 35 MH		
23	5/27/44	MM Yds. at Mannheim, Ger. Low Grp. under us when our bombs would have been away so went to secondary target	Bombed Airfield/Barracks at Speyerdorf, Ger. visually from 26,000' at 1307 hrs. on 249 MH	
24	5/28/44	Aircraft Engine Plant, Dessau, Ger. Heavy haze covered the target, so we went to our secondary target	Leipzig, Ger. Airfield under smoke & haze, and ID was not possible. We went to a Target of Opportunity	Bombed Airfield at Wustensacken, Ger. visually thru broken clouds, from 23,000' at 1515 hrs. on 260 MH

TARGETS AND BOMBING TECHNIQUES

RE: THE 33 MISSIONS OF SCREWBALL EXPRESS' ORIGINAL CREW

Mission	Date	Primary Targets	Secondary Targets	Targets of Opportunity
25	5/29/44	Bombed Aircraft Assembly Plant Krzesinki, Pol. Bombed thru broken clouds at 1309 hrs. from 23,000'		
26	6/ 6/44	RR Bridge at Caen, FR. Solid overcast forced us to go to the Secondary target, since no PFF plane in our Group	Secondary target (name unknown) also under 10/10 cloud cover, so we went to a target of last resort	Last resort target (name unknown) was also under 10/10 cloud cover, so no bombs were dropped by our formation
27	6/ 7/44	Bombed Highway Bridge over MM Yds at Flers, Fr. Bombed by GH at 1158 hrs. from 20,000' on 268 MH		
28	6/ 8/44	Bombed RR Bridge at Orleans, Fr. Used GH and visual bomb run due to 7/10 cloud cover. Bombed from 20,000' at 0852 hrs. on 330 MH		
29	6/10/44	Bombed Airfield at Vannes, Fr. visually from 21,000' at 0828 hrs. on 300 MH		
30	6/12/44	Bombed RR Bridge at Pontaubault, Fr. visually at 0903 hrs. from 19,000'. 308 MH		
31	6/14/44	Bombed Airfield at Creil, Fr. visually from 21,000' at 0822 hrs. on 270 MH		
32	6/19/44	Bombed Fly-Bomb Site at Zudausques, Fr. by GH from 25,500' at 1039 hrs. and on 263 MH		
33	6/20/44	Bombed Oil Refinery at Hamburg, Ger. visually from 25,000' at 0908 hrs. on 266 MH		
	Totals	Bombed 25 Primary Targets	Bombed 6 Secondary Targets	Bombed 1 Target of Opportunity 1-No bombs dropped
		17-Visual Bomb Runs, Clear 6-Visual Runs, Clouds/Haze 9-PFF and GH Bomb Runs (5) (4)		

LEAD CREWS OF 379th BG FORMATIONS

ON THE 33 MISSIONS FLOWN BY THE ORIGINAL CREW OF SCREWBALL EXPRESS

31 of these missions were flown as part of 41st Combat Wing. Missions 13 & 15 were with 40th Combat Wing.
Apologies to Lead Crew Members whose names were not found in Mission Folders for specific missions.

NO.	DATE	B-17 Ser. No.	FORMATION	PILOT	CO-PILOT	NAVIGATOR	BOMBARDIER
1	3/24/44		Lead Group			Lt. Delmar F. Williams	
2	3/26/44	42-31394	Single Group	Maj. L. C. Mason	Lt J. A. Sanda	Lt. R. E. Holmstrup	Lt. B. J. Shuster
3	3/27/44	42-31394	High Group	Lt. Col. M. M. Elliott	Lt. G. Carpenter	Lt. Delmar F. Williams	Maj. J. A. Brown
4	3/28/44	42-31394	High Group	Capt. R. D. Brown		Capt. J. P. Firestone	Lt. C. M. Olson
5	3/29/44		Lead Group	(from 381st BG)	(from 381st BG)	(from 381st BG)	(from 381st BG)
6	4/10/44	42-31597	Lead Group	Lt.Col L. W. Rohr	Lt. W. A. Elliott	Lt. Delmar F. Williams	Lt. C. M. Olson
7	4/11/44	42-31597	Low Group	Maj. E. D. Carlson	Lt. C. M. Blue	Lt. C. D. Carden	Lt. James Wall
8	4/18/44	42-97533	Lead Group B	Lt. Col. R. S. Kittel		Capt. J. G. Edwards	Capt. J. G. Glaser
9	4/19/44		High Group	Lt. Col. M. M. Elliott		Lt. D. F. Williams	Lt. L. V. Blair
10	4/20/44		Lead Group A	Maj. E. D. Carlson		Lt. C. D. Carden	Maj. J. G. Brown
11	4/22/44	42-107004	Low Group	Maj. L. C. Mason	Lt. J. A. Sanda	Lt. R. E. Holmstrup	Lt. B. C. Shuster
12	4/24/44	801-R	Lead Group	Brig.Gen.R.F. Travis	Maj. W. C. Sipes	Lt. J. L. Rockwell	Maj. J. A. Brown
13	4/28/44	42-30237	Low Group	Lt. Col. R. S. Kittel	Capt. L. A. Gibson	Capt. J. C. Firestone	Capt. J. G. Glaser
14	4/30/44	42-30237	Lead Group	Col. M. A. Preston	Col. W. A. Travis	Maj. A. K. Dutch	Capt. J. G. Glaser
15	5/ 1/44	42-30237	High Group	Lt. Col. L. W. Rohr	Capt. D.H. Buskey	Capt. J. C. Firestone	Lt. C. M. Olson
16	5/ 7/44		High Group A	Maj. L. C. Mason		Lt. R. E. Holmstrup	Lt. B. C. Shuster
17	5/12/44	592	Lead Group A	Lt. Col. M. M. Elliott		Lt. D. F. Williams	Lt. L. V. Blair
18	5/13/44	42-38058	Low Group	Lt. C. W. Hedges	Lt. C. Paulson	F/O W. Mueller	Lt. W. J. McAloon
19	5/19/44		High Group A	Lt. Col. M. M. Elliott		Capt. D. F. Williams	Lt. A. G. Wright
20	5/21/44	42-32000	Single Group	Lt. F. S. Markle	Lt. C. M. Sakryd	Lt. T. W. Peterson	Lt. J. W. Hartman
21	5/23/44		Lead Group B	Lt. Col. R. S. Kittel		Capt. J. L. Rockwell	Capt. J. G. Glaser
22	5/24/44	42-107004	Low Group A	Capt. D. H. Buskey	Lt. A. B. Creo, Jr.	Lts. H. Cain & F. Ford	Lt. A. T. Zaladonis
23	5/27/44	42-31597	High Group A	Lt. Col. M. M. Elliott	Lt. F. S. Markle	Capt. D. F. Williams	Lt. L. V. Blair
24	5/28/44	42-1669V	Lead Group	Lt. Col. R. S. Kittel		Capt.Rockwell/Lt.Sandall	Lt. C. M. Olson
25	5/29/44		High Group A	Lt. Col. M. M. Elliott		Capt. D. F. Williams	Lt. L. V. Blair

LEAD CREWS OF 379th BG FORMATIONS

NO.	DATE	B-17 Ser. No.	FORMATION	PILOT	CO-PILOT (from 303 BG)	NAVIGATOR (from 303 BG)	BOMBARDIER (from 303 BG)
26	6/ 6/44		Single Group	Col. K. D. Stevens	(from 303 BG)	(from 303 BG)	(from 303 BG)
27	6/ 7/44	42-32000	Lead Group A	Maj. J. E. Theiss	Lt. J.F.MacDonald	Lts. C. Davis & H. Strate	Lt. M. R. Martin
28	6/ 8/44	42-97229	Lead Group B	Capt. D. H. Buskey	Lt. E.W.Springer	Lt. J. R. LaBore	Lt. J. E. Wall
29	6/10/44	42-31189	Low Group B	Lt. Col. L. W. Rohr	Capt. R. Williams	Lt. G. E. Sandall	Lt. J. W. Hartman
30	6/12/44	42-32000	Low Group B	Capt. R.S. Williams	Lt. J. L. Swanner	Lts. Heilman & Peterson	Capt. G. E. Beeman
31	6/14/44	42-37888	High Group A	Lt. F. S. Markel	Lt. C. M. Karney	Lt. G. G. Heilman	Lt. J. W. Hartman
32	6/19/44	42-31189	Low Group B	Lt. H. P. McGhee	Lt. R. F. Finch	Lts. G. Sandall & G. Gray	Lt. J. W. Hartman
33	6/20/44		Lead Group A	Brig.Gen. R.F.Travis		Capt. C. D. Carden	Lt. L. V. Blair

SUMMARY — THE TOTALS BY AIRCRAFT, FORMATIONS AND LEAD CREWMEN

B-17 Serial No.
- 3 – 30237
- 3 – 31394
- 3 – 31597
- 3 – 32000
- 2 – 31189
- 2 – 107004
- 1 – 592
- 1 – 801R
- 1 – 1669V
- 1 – 37888
- 1 – 38058
- 1 – 97229
- 1 – 97533
- 10 – unknown

Formation
- 13 Lead Grp
- 9 High Grp
- 8 Low Grp
- 3 Single Grp

Pilot
- 6 Lt. Col. Elliott
- 4 Lt. Col. Kittel
- 3 Lt. Col. Rohr
- 3 Maj. Mason
- 2 Brg.Gen.Travis
- 2 Maj. Carlson
- 2 Capt. Buskey
- 2 Lt. Markle
- 1 Col. Preston
- 1 Maj. Theiss
- 1 Capt. Brown
- 1 Capt. Williams
- 1 Lt. Hedges
- 1 Lt. McGhee
- 1 from 303 BG
- 1 from 381 BG
- unknown

Co-Pilot
- 2 Lt. Sanda
- 1 Col. Travis
- 1 Maj. Sipes
- 1 Capt. Buskey
- 1 Capt. Gibson
- 1 Lt. Blue
- 1 Lt. Carpenter
- 1 Lt. Creo
- 1 Lt. Elliott
- 1 Lt. Finch
- 1 Lt. Karney
- 1 Lt. MacDonald
- 1 Lt. Markle
- 1 Lt. Paulson
- 1 Lt. Sakryd
- 1 Lt. Springer
- 1 Lt. Swanner
- 1 Capt.R.Williams
- 1 from 303 BG
- 1 from 381 BG
- 12 unknown

Navigator
- 8 Capt. D.F. Williams
- 3 Capt. Carden
- 3 Capt. Firestone
- 3 Lt. Holmstrup
- 2 Capt. Rockwell
- 1 Lts. Cain & Ford
- 1 Lts. Davis & Strate
- 1 Maj. Dutch
- 1 Capt. Edwards
- 1 Lt. Heilman
- 1 Lts.Heilman/Peterson
- 1 Lt. LaBore
- 1 F/O Mueller
- 1 Lt. Peterson
- 1 Capt Rockwell/Sandall
- 1 Lt. Sandall
- 1 Lts. Sandall & Gray
- 1 from 303 BG
- 1 from 381 BG

Bombardier
- 5 Lt. Blair
- 4 Capt. Glaser
- 4 Lt. Hartman
- 4 Lt. Olson
- 3 Maj. Brown
- 3 Lt. Shuster
- 2 Lt. Wall
- 1 Capt. Beeman
- 1 Lt. Martin
- 1 Lt. McAloon
- 1 Lt. Wright
- 1 Lt. Zaladonis
- 1 from 303 BG
- 1 from 381 BG
- 1 unknown

SCREWBALL EXPRESS—118 MISSIONS WITH 51 CREWS

NUMBER OF MISSIONS			DATES	CREW OF:	TARGETS	CITIES & COUNTRIES
SCREWBALL EXPRESS	OUR CREW	379th BOMB GRP				
1	2	89	3/26/44	Lt. Howard E. Towers	Fly-Bomb Site	Wizernes, France
2	3	90	3/27/44	Lt. Howard E. Towers	Airfield	Chartres, France
3	4	91	3/28/44	Lt. Howard E. Towers	Airfield	Dijon, France
4	5	92	3/29/44	Lt. Howard E. Towers	Aircraft Parts Factory	Brunswick, Germany
5	6	94	4/10/44	Lt. Howard E. Towers	Airfield/AC Factory	Brussels, Belgium
6	7	95	4/11/44	Lt. Howard E. Towers	Aircraft Assem. Plant	Sorau. Germany
7	8	97	4/18/44	Lt. Howard E. Towers	Airfield	Perleberg. Germany
8	9	98	4/19/44	Lt. Howard E. Towers	Aircraft Assem. Plant	Kassel, Germany
9	10	99	4/20/44	Lt. Howard E. Towers	Fly-Bomb Site	Sottevast, France
10	11	100	4/22/44	Lt. Howard E. Towers	Docks & Harbor	Bonn, Germany
11	12	101	4/24/44	Lt. Howard E. Towers	Airfield/AC Factory	Landsberg, Germany
12		103	4/27/44	Lt. Robert M. Dunn	Fly-Bomb Site	Mesnil au Val, France
13	13	105	4/28/44	Lt. Howard E. Towers	Airfield	Avord, France
14	14	107	4/30/44	Lt. Howard E. Towers	Airfield	Lyons, France
15	15	109	5/ 1/44	Lt. Howard E. Towers	Marshalling Yards	Reims, France
16	16	111	5/ 7/44	Lt. Howard E. Towers	Aircraft Component	Berlin, Germany
17		113	5/ 8/44	Lt. Gilbert C. Heath	Fly-Bomb Site	Sottevast, France
18		---	(approx.)	(384 Crew w/ 384 BG)	(unknown)	(unknown)
19	17	116	5/12/44	Lt. Howard E. Towers	Oil Refinery	Merseburg, Germany
20	18	117	5/13/44	Lt. Howard E. Towers	Rubber/Vulcan. Plant	Stettin, Germany
21		118	5/15/44	Lt. Merlyn P. Wilson	Fly-Bomb Site	Marquis/Mimoy.,France
22	19	119	5/19/44	Lt. Howard E. Towers	Aircraft Component	Berlin, Germany
23	20	121	5/21/44	Lt. Howard E. Towers	Fly-Bomb Site	Marquis, France
24	21	123	5/23/44	Lt. Howard E. Towers	Marshalling Yards	Saarbrucken, Germany
25	22	124	5/24/44	Lt. Howard E. Towers	Aircraft Component	Berlin, Germany
26		125	5/25/44	Lt. Clarence E. Jamison	Railway Yards	Sarreguemines, France
27	23	126	5/27/44	Lt. Howard E. Towers	Airfield/Barracks	Speyerdorf, Gemany
28	24	127	5/28/44	Lt. Howard E. Towers	Airfield	Wustensacken, Germany
29	25	129	5/29/44	Lt. Howard E. Towers	Airfield/AC Factory	Krzesinki, Poland
30		130	5/30/44	Lt. Edward R. Burke	Aircraft Factory	Halberstadt, Germany
31		131	5/31/44	Lt. Charles J. Lamont	Airfield	Gilze Rijen, Netherlands
32		133	6/ 2/44	Lt. George McHugh	Marshalling Yards	Juvisy, France
33		134	6/ 4/44	Lt. Lewis M. Jolls	Gun Positions	Ambleteuse, France
34		136	6/ 6/44	Lt. Lloyd L. Burns	Gun Positions	Arromanches, France
35		137	6/ 6/44	Lt. Roderick T. French	Bridge	Conde sur Noireau, Fr.
36	29	140	6/10/44	Lt. Howard E. Towers	Airfield	Vannes, France
37	30	141	6/12/44	Lt. Howard E. Towers	RR Bridge	Pontaubault, France
38	31	143	6/14/44	Lt. Howard E. Towers	Airfield	Creil, France
39		144	6/16/44	Lt. Anthony J. Pettrini	Airfield	Laon/Couvron, France
40		145	6/18/44	Lt. Willis H. Matter	Dock Facilities	Hamburg, Germany
41	32	146	6/19/44	Lt. Howard E. Towers	Fly-Bomb Site	Zudausques, France
42		147	6/19/44	Lt. Willis H. Matter	Fly-Bomb Sites	Zudausques/Enguine, Fr.
43	33	148	6/20/44	Lt. Howard E. Towers	Oil Refinery	Hamburg, Germany
44		158	7/ 4/44	Lt. Anthony J. Pettrini	Airfield	Illiers l'Eugene, France
45		159	7/ 5/44	Lt. Anthony J. Pettrini	Airfield	Volkel, Netherlands
46		160	7/ 6/44	Lt. Anthony J. Pettrini	Rocket Site	Blanc Pignon Ferme, Fr.
47		161	7/ 7/44	Lt. Anthony J. Pettrini	Aircraft Factory	Leipzig, Germany

SCREWBALL EXPRESS–118 MISSIONS WITH 51 CREWS

NUMBER OF MISSIONS			DATES	CREW OF:	TARGETS	CITIES & COUNTRIES
SCREWBALL EXPRESS	OUR CREW	379th BOMB GRP				
48		162	7/ 9/44	Lt. Anthony J. Pettrini	Bridge	La Possonniere, France
49		163	7/11/44	Lt. Blayne A. Hawthorn	Marshalling Yards	Munich, Germany
50		164	7/12/44	Lt. Edward C. Harris	Marshalling Yards	Munich, Germany
51		165	7/13/44	Lt. Anthony J. Pettrini	Aircraft Factory	Munich, Germany
52		166	7/16/44	Lt. Anthony J. Pettrini	Aircraft Factory	Munich, Germany
53		167	7/17/44	Lt. Fred C. Roberts	Marshalling Yards	Frevent, France
54		168	7/18/44	Lt. Anthony J. Pettrini	Experimental Station	Zinnowitz, Germany
55		169	7/19/44	Lt. Maurice T. Paine	Hydrogen Plant	Hollriegelskreuth, Ger.
56		171	7/21/44	Lt. Harold D. Greiner	Marshalling Yards	Bad Kreuznach, Germany
57		172	7/23/44	Lt. Anthony J. Pettrini	Airfield	Creil, France
58		173	7/24/44	Lt. Anthony J. Pettrini	RR Bridge	Montreul, France
59		174	7/25/44	Lt. Anthony J. Pettrini	RR Bridge	Montreul, France
60		175	7/28/44	Lt. Anthony J. Pettrini	Synthetic Oil	Merseburg, Germany
61		176	7/29/44	Lt. Anthony J. Pettrini	Synthetic Oil	Merseburg, Germany
62		177	7/31/44	Lt. Anthony J. Pettrini	Marshalling Yards	Munich, Germany
63		178	8/ 1/44	Lt. Roland L. Hess	Airfield	Orleans/Bricy, France
64		179	8/ 3/44	Lt. Anthony J. Pettrini	Fly-Bomb Site	Coubronne, France
65		180	8/ 4/44	Lt. Anthony J. Pettrini	Experimental Station	Peenemunde, Germany
66		184	8/ 7/44	Lt. Roderick T. French	Troop Support	Houdan, France
67		185	8/ 8/44	Lt. Howard O. Baron	Troop Support	Caen, France
68		196	8/30/44	Lt. William W. Wiley	Fly-Bomb Site	Fiefs, France
69		197	9/ 1/44	Lt. William R. White	Synthetic Oil	Ludwigshafen, Germany
70		199	9/ 8/44	Lt. Roland L. Hess	Synthetic Oil	Ludwigshafen, Germany
71		200	9/ 9/44	Lt. Robert D. Puckett	Rail Transport	Mannheim, Germany
72		204	9/13/44	Lt. Robert V. Studer	Synthetic Oil	Merseburg, Germany
73		206	9/19/44	Lt. Robert R. Medean	Marshalling Yards	Hamm, Germany
74		208	9/25/44	Lt. Harry L. Arnett	Marshalling Yards	Frankfurt, Germany
75		209	9/26/44	Lt. John B. Moates	Railroad Workshops	Osnabruck, Germany
76		210	9/27/44	Lt. Elmonte R. Miller	Railroad Yards	Cologne, Germany
77		211	9/28/44	Lt. Robert R. Medean	Ordnance Plant	Magdeburg, Germany
78		212	9/30/44	Lt. Hilliard Dozier	Marshalling Yards	Munster, Germany
79		213	10/ 2/44	Lt. Fred A. Lombardi	Marshalling Yards	Cologne, Germany
80		214	10/ 3/44	Lt. Russel B. Meyne	Railway Yards	Cologne, Germany
81		215	10/ 5/44	Lt. Fred C. Lombardi	Railway Yards	Dortmund, Germany
82		218	10/ 9/44	Lt. Thomas E. McCabe	Ball Bearing Plant	Schweinfurt, Germany
83		219	10/11/44	Lt. Robert V. Studer	Synthetic Oil	Wesseling, Germany
84		220	10/14/44	Lt. Robert V. Studer	Marshalling Yards	Saarbrucken, Germany
85		221	10/15/44	Lt. Charles E. May	Marshalling Yards	Cologne, Germany
86		222	10/17/44	Lt. Elwin Hollandsworth	Marshalling Yards	Cologne, Germany
87		223	10/18/44	Lt. Robert V. Studer	Marshalling Yards	Cologne, Germany
88		224	10/19/44	Lt. Robert V. Studer	Ordnance Plant	Mannheim, Germany
89		225	10/22/44	Lt. David E. Galas	Aircraft Factory	Brunswick, Germany
90		226	10/25/44	Lt. Robert V. Studer	Synthetic Oil	Gelsenkirchen, Germany
91		227	10/26/44	Lt. Robert V. Studer	Railway Yards	Munster, Germany
92		228	10/30/44	Lt. Robert M. Leite	Railway Yards	Hamm, Germany
93		229	11/ 1/44	Lt. Robert V. Studer	Synthetic Oil	Gelsenkirchen, Germany
94		231	11/ 4/44	Lt. Charles E. Crutchfield	Synthetic Oil	Bottrop, Germany
95		232	11/ 5/44	Lt. Charles E. Crutchfield	Aircraft Component	Frankfurt, Germany

THE 13 MIA B-17s ON 33 MISSIONS
OF SCREWBALL EXPRESS' ORIGINAL CREW

MISSION	DATE	TARGET LOCATION	AIRCRAFT SERIAL NO.	DOWNED BY	PILOT	SQUADRON
2	3/26/44	Wizernes, France	42-97485	Flak	Lt. Stanley L. Bielawski	526th
16	5/ 7/44	Berlin, Germany	42-37791	Flak	Lt. Thomas M. Smith	526th
16	5/ 7/44	Berlin, Germany	42-38161	Flak	Lt. Clarence E. Darnell	525th
18	5/13/44	Stettin, Germany	42-97502	Fighter	Lt. Joseph Marinello	527th
18	5/13/44	Stettin, Germany	42-31972	Fighter	Lt. John E. Wilds, Jr.	527th
18	5/13/44	Stettin, Germany	42-107082	Fighter	Lt. Robert M. Dunn, Jr.	526th
19	5/19/44	Berlin, Germany	42-39783	Flak	Lt. Merlyn P. Wilson	526th
19	5/19/44	Berlin, Germany	not in Report	Flak	not in Report	not in Report
22	5/24/44	Berlin, Germany	42-37784	Fighter & B-17 Col.	Lt. Wilton E. Gease	525th
22	5/24/44	Berlin, Germany	42-38082	Fighter & B-17 Col.	Capt. Lytle W. Shumake	525th
22	5/24/44	Berlin, Germany	42-39828	Fighter & Flak	Lt. Theodore E. C. Kunda	524th
31	6/14/44	Creil, France	not in Report	Flak	not in Report	not in Report
33	6/20/44	Hamburg, Germany	42-97261	Flak	Lt. James R. Wheat	527th
	1 in March	2-France		7-Flak		4-526th
	10 in May	11-Germany		3-Fighters		3-525th
	2 in June			2-Fighter and		3-527th
				collision w/ B-17		1-524th
				1-Fighter & Flak		

London's Big Ben

Right Wingman at Dusk. (379th Bomb Group Photo)

Crew Reunion in Nashville, TN, April 28-30, 1989. Left to right: Howard and Betty Lou Towers; Ken and Geri Cassens; Jerold and Bettye Lindsey; Doris Craig; Tom Kiblin; Dr. Frank Craig; Jim and Frances Moore.

Photographs

Photographs

Photographs

Bibliography

Air Force Combat Units of WWII—USAF Historical Division, Air University of the Department of the Air Force, Zenger Publishing Co., Inc., Washington, D.C., 1961 and 1980. **Special Credit** is given for data re: Bomb Groups & Combat Wings, shown in "The 379th Bomb Group (H)" section of <u>Chapter 1</u>.

B-17 Flying Fortress, Part I - Production versions—Alwyn T. Lloyd and Terry D. Moore, published by AERO, Division of Tab Books, Inc., 1981. **Special Credit** is given for B-17 specifications, summarized in <u>Development of The B-17 Flying Fortress.</u>

B-17 Fortress at War—Roger A. Freeman, Scribner's Sons, NY, NY. **Special Credit** is given for information about the name 'Flying Fortress,' B-17 armament, B-17G production by BVD Consortium, & production versions of B-17s, mentioned in <u>Development of The B-17 Flying Fortress</u>; for comments about B-17s and B-24s, appearing in <u>Chapter 17</u>; for data re: Germany's use of captured B-17s, in <u>Chapter 26</u>; and for data re: B-17s deployed to Kingman, Arizona, in the <u>Epilogue</u>.

B-17 Specifications and General Description—Museum of Flight, Seattle, WA., 1985. **Special Credit** is given for summarized specifications and for the number of B-17s produced by the BVD Consortium, in <u>Development of The B-17 Flying Fortress.</u>

Boeing B-17 Flying Fortress, 1935-1985—Peter M. Bowers, A Museum of Flight Publication, 1985. **Special Credit** is given for data re: numbers and types of B-17s transferred to England's RAF, mentioned in <u>Development of The B-17 Flying Fortress.</u>

Crew AA-96 and their Screwball Express—Booklet compiled in 1988 by James C. Moore, co-pilot; James R. Keller, navigator; Dr. Frank R. Craig, top turret gunner; and Kenneth H. Cassens, bombardier; distributed in 1988 to members of original flight crew of Screwball Express. **Special Credit** is given re: data relating to our crew's training flights at Ardmore, Oklahoma, and our flight from USA to Scotland, described in <u>Chapter 2</u>

Flying Forts, the B-17 in World War II—Martin Caidin, Ballantine Books, New York, NY, 1968. **Special Credit** is given for information about the origin of the Flying Fortress name, summarized in <u>Development of The B-17 Flying Fortress</u>; for data from RAF's September, 1941 Report, briefed in <u>Chapter 6</u>; for number of bombers lost on Schweinfurt mission, stated in <u>Chapter 20</u>; for GB-1 details and information about attack on Cologne, Germany, related in <u>Chapter 28</u>; for data re: causes of aborts, discussed in <u>Chapter 36</u>; and for background on Battle of Hamburg, reviewed in <u>Chapter 38</u>.

Flying Fortress, the Illustrated Biography of the B-17s and the Men Who Flew Them—Edward Jablonski, Doubleday and Co. Inc., New York, NY, 1965. **Special Credit** is given for data re: Project 299 and early B-17 information, summarized in <u>Development of The B-17 Flying Fortress</u>; for synopsis of combat philosophy of bomber crewmen, contained in <u>Chapter 11</u>; for data re: record numbers of bombers lost on missions to Schweinfurt, Regensburg, Oschersleben and Berlin, listed in <u>Chapter 20</u>; and for data re: Germany's oil industry, reviewed in <u>Chapter 21</u>.

Bibliography

Fortresses of the Big Triangle First—Cliff T. Bishop, East Anglia Books, Bishop's Stortford, England, 1986. **Special Credit** is given for data re: Screwball Express, in the third section of <u>Chapter 1</u>; for statistics and events involving 379th Bomb Group and 8th Air Force, summarized in <u>Chapter 3</u>; for data re: aircraft away from Kimbolton AFB, contained in <u>Chapter 8</u> ; and for data re: the numbers of bombers lost on missions to Schweinfurt, Regensburg, Oschersleben & Berlin, listed in <u>Chapter 20</u>.

One Last Look—Philip Kaplan and Rex Alan Smith, Abbeville Press, New York, New York, 1983. **Special Credit** is given for background information summarized in "The Mighty Eighth" section of <u>Chapter 1</u>; for information about briefing room procedure, atmosphere and related comments in <u>Chapter 4</u>; and for Nissen Hut specifications mentioned in <u>Chapter 30</u>.

Pegasus Bridge—Stephen E. Ambrose, A Touchstone Book, published by Simon & Schuster Inc., NY, NY, 1988.

Pilot Training Manual for the Flying Fortress B-17—Published by Headquarters, AAF, Office of Flying Safety, New Era Litho, NY, NY., 1944.

Screwball Express - The Diary—Kenneth H. Cassens, written at 379th Bomb Group's Airfield, Kimbolton, England, March-July,1944.

Shades of Kimbolton—Derwyn D. Robb, Captain, Air Corps, Newsphoto Publishing Co., San Angelo, TX, Second printing, 1981. **Special Credit** is given for 379th Bomb Group background, summarized in "The 379th Bomb Group (H)" section of <u>Chapter 1</u>.

Simon and Schuster Encypolpedia of World War II—New York, NY, 1978. **Special Credit** is given for data re: record numbers of bombers lost on missions to Schweinfurt, Regensburg and Berlin, listed in <u>Chapter 20</u>.

The Air War, 1939-1945—Dr. R. J. Overy, British Historian, Stein and Day, New York, NY, 1981. **Special Credit** is given for Germany's analysis of the Allied bombing, and the percent of that country's manpower and production required to detect and defend against it, reviewed in <u>Chapter 16</u>.

The Marshall Cavendish Illustrated Encyclopedia of World War II—Volume 6-1944, Marshall Cavendish Publishing, Freeport, NY, 1985. **Special Credit** is given re: data about V-1 & V-2 Fly-Bombs, summarized in <u>Chapter 5</u>; and for information relating to Casablanca Conference and Aerial Bombing Objectives, reviewed in <u>Chapter 21</u>.

The Mighty Eighth—Roger A. Freeman, Doubleday and Co., Inc., NY, NY, 1970; and Macdonald and Company, London, England, 1970. **Special Credit** is given for data re: Bomb Groups and Combat Wings, described in "The 379th Bomb Group (H)" section of <u>Chapter 1</u>; and for information re: types of radio beacons, explained in <u>Chapter 7</u>.

Bibliography

The Rand McNally Encyclopedia of Military Aircraft, 1914-1980, Military Press, New York, NY, 1981. **Special Credit** is given for specifications and performance capabilities of various fighter planes, summarized in <u>Chapter 16</u>.

The World War II Quiz and Fact Book—Timothy B. Benford, Berkley Books, NY, NY, 1986 Edition. **Special Credit** is given re: information about "The Big Week" in <u>Chapter 3</u>; for data about V-1 & V-2 Fly Bombs, summarized in <u>Chapter 5</u>; for data re: specific bombing missions to Berlin, reviewed in <u>Chapter 20</u>; for quotations and incidents related to D-Day, presented in <u>Chapter 31</u>; and for quotations in the first section of <u>Epilogue</u>.

Twelve O'Clock High—Sy Bartlett and Beirne Lay Jr., Book and Screenplay; Ballantine Books, New York, NY, 1948; 20th Century Fox film.

U.S. Army in World War II - ETO - Last Defense—Charles B. MacDonald, Produced by Office of the Chief of Military History, U.S. Army, Washington, D.C., 1973.

Webster's New Geographical Dictionary—G. & C. Merriam Company, Springfield, MA, 1977.

Reference Sources

Boeing Aircraft Company—Seattle, WA.

Central Florida Regional Library—Ocala, FL.

Contrails—Magazine of The 379th Bomb Group WW II Association, published at Lancaster, PA.

Crosshairs—Magazine of Bombardiers, Inc., published at Eagle River, MI and Daphne, AL.

Eighth Air Force Historical Society, Inc., and **8th AF News**, Oldsmar, FL. and St. Paul, MN.

Imperial War Museum, **Cabinet War Rooms** at London, England, and its Air Base/Facilities at Duxford, England. (Data re: V-1 and V-2 Fly-Bombs and Norden Bombsight)

Museum of Flight—Seattle, WA. (Development and Specifications of B-17)

National Archives, Military Field Branch, Military Archives Division—
Washington National Records Center, Suitland, MD.
(8th Air Force and 379th Bomb Group Field Orders)
(8th Air Force Narratives of Operations)
(379th Bomb Group Mission Reports)
(526th Bomb Squadron Mission Data)
(41st Combat Wing's Mission Reports by Bomb Group CO's)

National Air and Space Museum, Archival Support Unit of the Smithsonian Institute, Silver Hill Facility, Suitland, MD. (Data on Individual Aircraft Record Card of Screwball Express)

Royal Air Force Museum—Hendon, England.

Stars and Stripes—WW II Newspaper of the United States Armed Services
(Articles re: 8th Air Force bombing missions, March-June, 1944)

The 379th Bomb Group (H) World War II Association—Lancaster, Phoenixville and Mont Clare, PA.
(379th Bomb Group Mission Reports and Historical Data)

United States Air Force Historical Research Center,
Headquarters, Research Division—Maxwell Air Force Base, AL.
(379th Bomb Group History, March-June,1944)
(526th Bomb Squadron History, March-June, 1944)

Wings Magazine—October 1978 issue, published by Sentry Books, Inc., Grenada Hills, CA.

Index

Index

Index

ABOUT THE AUTHOR

Ken Cassens was born at Edwardsville, Illinois, and attended Shurtleff College in the nearby city of Alton. He enlisted in the Army Air Corps in December 1942, requested bombardier training and graduated with Class 43-12 at Midland, Texas. Ken completed B-17 flight crew training at Ardmore, Oklahoma the following January. In March 1944, his crew was assigned to the 8th Air Force, 379th Bomb Group, at Kimbolton, England, and was the original crew of Screwball Express.

After returning to the States, Ken was an instructor for B-17 crews at Avon Park, FL. He was then transferred to the staff of B/Gen. Leon Johnson, 8th Air Force Personal Affairs Division, Washington, DC. His assignment involved research of USAF records and updating information about flight crew members who were missing or killed in action. Relatives of those airmen made many inquiries requesting confirmation of the MIA and KIA status of their loved ones. Ken prepared detailed letters for the President, General Hap Arnold and others, enabling them to make meaningful responses to the inquiries they received. Ken left active military duty in August, 1945.

In 1947 he joined Country Companies, an insurance/investment services group at Bloomington, IL and served its 11 companies for 38 years as agent, agency manager, training director, assistant sales manager, director/advertising and public relations, vice president/marketing and vice president/administrative services. His business career included more than 1,000 speaking engagements before industry, business and social groups. He was in the USAF Reserve until April 1955, when he was honorably discharged following an automobile accident.

Ken and his wife, Geri, have lived in Florida since his retirement in June 1985. The Cassens have two children. Their daughter, Debra, is an attorney and their son, Steve, is an electrical engineer.

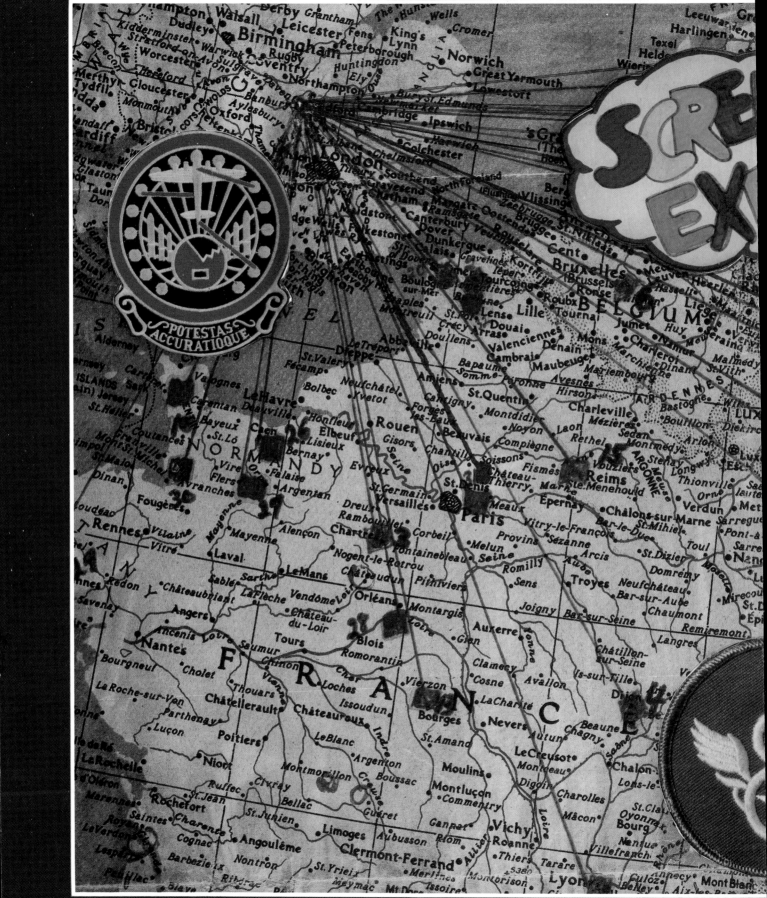